CARLO TRESCA

Portrait of a Rebel

CARLO TRESCA
Portrait of a Rebel

Nunzio Pernicone

AK PRESS
EDINBURGH · OAKLAND · BALTIMORE

Carlo Tresca: Portrait of a Rebel

© 2010 Nunzio Pernicone

This edition © 2010 AK Press (Oakland, Edinburgh, Baltimore)

ISBN-13: 9781849350037

Library of Congress Control Number: 2009933025

AK Press
674-A 23rd Street
Oakland, CA 94612
USA
www.akpress.org
akpress@akpress.org

AK Press
PO Box 12766
Edinburgh EH8 9YE
Scotland
www.akuk.com
ak@akedin.demon.co.uk

The above addresses would be delighted to provide you with the latest AK Press distribution catalog, which features the several thousand books, pamphlets, zines, audio and video products, and stylish apparel published and/or distributed by AK Press. Alternatively, visit our web site for the complete catalog, latest news, and secure ordering.

Visit us at www.akpress.org *and* www.revolutionbythebook.akpress.org.

Printed in Canada on acid free, recycled paper with union labor.
Interior layout and design by Suzanne Shaffer
Cover by John Yates (stealworks.com)

Contents

Acknowledgments

A former colleague once remarked that my work on Carlo Tresca was an act of "filial piety," that is, he believed I had elected to write about this remarkable rebel in order to please my father. Since pleasing my father was an impossible task, it would be more accurate to say that my interest in Tresca and Italian anarchism derived from the stories he related about the days when he directed and acted in an amateur theatrical group (what Italians call a *filodrammatica*) that performed plays to help raise funds for Tresca's *Il Martello* and other Italian radical newspapers. My adolescent awe of Tresca assumed its first academic expression in a graduate seminar paper. Tresca has been part of my professional life ever since. From its inception to its present form—what is left of an original manuscript that exceeded 1,100 pages—my biography of Tresca is the product of a lengthy and arduous undertaking often interrupted for years on end by the vicissitudes of personal and professional life.

If this biography had been of more recent origin, I would never have had the opportunity to benefit from the rich recollections of Tresca related by family members and more than a score of comrades, friends, and acquaintances, the majority of them now deceased. Among the former, I owe a huge debt to Beatrice Tresca Rapport, Peter Martin, Burnham and Claire De Silver, Harrison De Silver, and Andrew Canzanelli, all of whom provided personal knowledge, correspondence, and other vital materials. Among Tresca's many close comrades, political associates, and others who furnished valuable information through interviews and correspondence, I must thank Vincenzo Alvano, Max Ascoli, Roger Baldwin, Michele Cantarella, Egidio Clemente, Alberto Cupelli, Mario De Ciampis, Sam and Esther Dolgoff, Joseph Genco, Joseph Ienuso, Valerio Isca, James T. Farrell, Jack Frager, Eleazar Lipsky, Nancy MacDonald, Vincenzo Massari, Morris Milgram, Vanni Montana, Felix Morrow, Charles Poggi, Giuseppe Popolizio, Hugo Rolland, Raffaele Schiavina, Norman Thomas, and Luigi Quintiliano.

I owe special thanks for their invaluable encouragement, expertise, and sharing of materials to two dear friends and colleagues who are no longer with us: Paul Avrich and Philip V. Cannistraro. Similar thanks and appreciation go also to Spencer Di Scala, Robert Helms, Gary Mormino, Salvatore Salerno, Michael Miller Topp, Mary Anne Trasciatti, Alan Wald, and Dorothy Gallagher, who provided access to the research files she had compiled for her own previously published biography of Tresca. Although I had already accumulated the bulk of this material, I was greatly impressed by Dorothy's willingness to assist my endeavor—rival historians are rarely so generous.

The research for this book could not have been undertaken without the resources made available to me by various archives, libraries, and repositories. I should like to express special thanks to the late Rudolf J. Vecoli, former director, and to Joel

Wurl, former curator, of the Immigration History Research Center, University of Minnesota; to William Le Fevre, Director of Reference Services at the Archives of Labor and Urban Affairs, Wayne State University; to Julie Herrada, Curator of the Labadie Collection at the University of Michigan; to Peter Filardo and Erika Gottfriend at the Tamiment Institute Library, New York University; to Peter Vellon, former acting director of the John D. Calandra Italian American Institute, New York; to the late Rudolf de Jong and the late Maria Hunink at the Internationaal Instituut voor Sociale Geschiedenis, Amsterdam; to Mario Missori and the staff of the Archivio Centrale dello Stato in Rome; and to the staffs of the Biblioteca Nazionale Centrale in Florence; the Istituto Antonio Gramsci in Rome; the Istituto Giangiacomo Feltrinelli in Milan, especially its former librarian Elio Sellino; the Archivio di Stato dell'Aquila; the Boston Public Library; and the National Archives, Washington, D.C., and Suitland, Maryland. Special thanks must also go to Ombretta Missori, who found materials for me in L'Aquila and Sulmona that had escaped my search.

I am appreciative and proud of the fellowships and grants awarded to me in support of my work on Tresca by the American Council of Learned Societies, the American Philosophical Society, the Immigration History Research Center, the Louis M. Rabinowitz Foundation, the Dunning Fund, and Drexel University.

I remain very grateful to Brenden O'Malley, a former editor at Palgrave/Macmillan, for contracting me to publish the original hardback edition of my biography of Carlo Tresca. More recently, my deep appreciation extends also to Zach Blue and AK Press for conceiving the idea to publish a paperback version of the book. Preparing for the paperback enabled me to correct the scores of embarrassing errors that had escaped me and Palgrave's copy editor the first time around. Moreover, AK Press generously allowed me to re-organize a few sections and also to add a new chapter on Tresca and World War Two as well as a brief addendum concerning the controversial statements Tresca made about Sacco and Vanzetti in the early 1940s.

Finally, I cannot sufficiently thank my wife Christine Zervos, who provided love, moral support, and technical expertise throughout the long years I spent immersed in my work. Without her tutelage and periodic rescue missions, I would surely have written this book on a typewriter rather than a computer. And finally, I must acknowledge the warm companionship of the five members of my feline family, who invariably draped themselves on my documents or keyboard rather than less essential areas of my desk.

Introduction

On the evening of January 11, 1943, Carlo Tresca left the office of *Il Martello* (The Hammer), the newspaper he had published in New York for twenty-five years, and started walking toward a nearby restaurant for a late supper. As Tresca crossed the intersection of Fifth Avenue and 15th Street, a Mafia hit-man emerged from the shadows of the wartime dimout and fired two shots that killed him instantly. In homage to his slain friend, the former Marxian intellectual Max Eastman wrote: "For Poetry's sake, for the sake of his name and memory, Carlo had to die a violent death. He had to die at the hand of a tyrant's assassin. He had lived a violent life. He had loved danger. He had loved the fight. His last motion was to swing and confront the long-expected enemy. So let us say farewell to Carlo as we hear him say—as he surely would if the breath came back—'Well, they got me at last!'"[1]

"Carlo Tresca was the last of the line of 'old school' radicals or revolutionaries."[2] So wrote the renowned socialist Norman Thomas after his friend had been gunned down. Thomas's accolade recognized Tresca's place among the most famous subversives who had challenged America's established order during the previous 125 years: Johann Most, Eugene V. Debs, Daniel De Leon, Emma Goldman, Alexander Berkman, Mother Jones, William "Big Bill" Haywood, Elizabeth Gurley Flynn, John Reed, and William Z. Foster. The passage of time has dimmed history's memory of Tresca and so many other radicals and dissenters of his generation. At the pinnacle of his career, however, Tresca was a well-known and much-beloved figure, especially in New York, where he had achieved iconic status as the "Town Anarchist." His murder was front page news in every New York daily and other newspapers elsewhere in America. The investigation of the crime was eagerly followed by the press for many months thereafter, with repeated calls for the intervention of the FBI and other federal agencies.

Media attention of this intensity and duration was not simply a function of the sensational manner of his demise; it reflected the grudging respect and admiration Tresca had acquired in his twilight years, even from former adversaries and critics. For several decades Tresca had been perceived by defenders of the status quo as a dangerous anarchist, an enemy of the state and bourgeois capitalism. And they were correct in this perception. No armchair revolutionary, Tresca meant business, fighting for several decades in the trenches of class warfare, to use one of his favorite images. The fear he inspired in his heyday was aptly described by the eminent labor historian David Montgomery: Tresca was "one man who actually incarnated the conservatives' fantasy of the agitator who could start an uprising with a speech."[3] With his charismatic personality and powerful oratory, Tresca was capable indeed of sparking rebellion among striking workers and political demonstrators with a single speech, and did so numerous times throughout a tempestuous and transnational career spanning more than five decades in Italy and the United States.

Identifying Tresca as a "revolutionary" only begins to define his life and career. Those who knew him intimately—Norman Thomas, Max Eastman, Arturo Giovannitti, John Dos Passos, and a host of others—were unanimous in their portrayal of Tresca as a man who defied categorization, whose uniqueness in terms of his personality, life-style, and political career was such that the only label befitting him comfortably is *sui generis*—one of a kind. Certainly few, if any, 20th century radicals in the United States were as colorful and flamboyant in their persona and lifestyle as Tresca. In his prime, he cut a romantic and dashing figure, sporting a Van Dyke beard, broad-brimmed hat, black cravat, and long-stemmed pipe. His warmth, good nature, and charm were augmented by his inimitable manner of speaking English—Italian with English words, some said. Complementing his colorful physical appearance and larger-than-life personality was a voracious appetite for living, every component of which—spaghetti, wine, tobacco, parties, playing cards, practical jokes, and affairs with women—he indulged in prodigious quantities.

But cohabitating within this epicurean, fun-loving, and eternally-affectionate human being was a formidable adversary who devoted more than fifty years to the struggle against oppression, injustice, and exploitation. At various stages of his career, Tresca called himself a socialist, a revolutionary syndicalist, and an anarchist, but he never truly fit into the conventional categories of radical typology. Arturo Giovannitti, the radical poet who was Tresca's close comrade for nearly forty years, wrote that "he liked to call himself an Anarchist, and if that term connotes a man who is absolutely free, then he was an Anarchist; but from the point of view of pure doctrine he was all things to all men, and in his endless intellectual vagabondage he never really sought any definite anchorage or moorings."[4] Unorthodox and free of dogma, Tresca was a "rebel without uniform," according to his friend Max Nomad, a freelance of revolution for whom personal independence and freedom of action were indispensable.[5] Action always outweighed ideology for Tresca. An instinctive revolutionary, with inexhaustible energy and indomitable courage, Tresca lived for action and the fight. Leading striking workers and mass demonstrations, challenging police, hired detectives, and company thugs, engaging Fascist Blackshirts in pitched battles in the streets of Italian-American communities—such activities suited the requirements of his soul.

Perhaps the most distinctive features of Tresca's career as a revolutionary activist were its transnational focus and multi-dimensionality. After his revolutionary apprenticeship in southern Italy and his emigration to the United States in 1904, Tresca never lost his interest in the political and social developments of his native land, and during the 1920s and 1930s, his main objective was the subversion of Fascism in Italy and its defeat within the Italian American communities of the

United States. Both before and during the Fascist era, however, Tresca was involved in multiple spheres of action, often simultaneously. He distinguished himself as an independent publisher of several radical newspapers, a tribune who led thousands of striking workers and protest demonstrators, an antimilitarist, an advocate for civil liberties, a benefactor of victims of political persecution, the leading Italian anti-Fascist of his era, a staunch anti-Communist, and ultimately a strong defender of democracy.

Born in 1879, Tresca was the *enfant terrible* of his hometown of Sulmona, in the Abruzzo region of Southern Italy, severing ties with the bourgeois class of his birth and conducting class war against local notables by means of his newspaper and leadership of peasant and artisan societies. His slash and burn style of mucking journalism resulted in several convictions for libel. He chose emigration over prison. En route to the United States, Tresca spent a few days in Lausanne, Switzerland, where he chanced to meet his future nemesis, Benito Mussolini, then an aspiring socialist leader in exile. The future Duce of Fascism considered Tresca insufficiently revolutionary; Tresca sized up Mussolini as an opportunist and a poseur.

Once settled in the United States, Tresca quickly emerged as a key figure in the world of Italian immigrant radicals, establishing the pattern to which he adhered for his entire career. Combining his talents as a journalist and direct actionist, Tresca became a one-man guerrilla movement, leading Italian strikers against their American capitalist exploiters and attacking with his muckraking skills the *Camorra Coloniale*—his term for the triumvirate of Italian Consular officials, rich and powerful notables (*prominenti*), and Catholic priests that dominated Italian immigrant communities in their own interests. Although he always remained grounded in the subculture of Italian immigrant radicals, Tresca, as a freelance leader for the Industrial Workers of the World (IWW) in 1912, extended his activities from the insular world of Italian immigrant workers to the broader and more diverse universe of American radicalism, labor, and progressive causes. His critical role in the defense campaign to liberate the imprisoned leaders of the 1912 textile workers strike in Lawrence, Massachusetts; and his activities in the great Paterson silk workers strike of 1913 and the Mesabi Range iron miners strike of 1916, transformed Tresca from an obscure foreign-born radical into a nationally-recognized and feared revolutionary.

Tresca's militant opposition to the First World War resulted inevitably in government suppression of his newspaper, legal proceedings that nearly sent him to prison, and efforts to deport him that continued for many years. Despite his own difficulties following the war, Tresca was able to utilize his connections with prominent Americans on the Left to aid Italian victims of political persecution. In this way, Tresca played an important role in the defense of Sacco and Vanzetti during the initial phase of their tragic odyssey. The postwar atmosphere of fear and repression, however, restricted the scope of Tresca's activities, especially in the labor movement. Henceforth, Tresca would be deemed "too radical" by union officials who feared his participation in a strike would automatically provoke police intervention.

But curtailment of his labor activities provided more time and opportunity to partake in the campaign that became the true hallmark of Tresca's career—resistance to Mussolini and the spread of Fascism within Italian immigrant communities. Tresca in the 1920s had no peer among anti-Fascist leaders, a distinction recognized by Mussolini's political police in Rome who dubbed him the "*deus ex machina* of antifascism," the man upon whom the movement depended more than any other. Fascist efforts to control Italian-American communities through Consular officials, the *prominenti*, and Italian parish priests—the same triumvirate that Tresca had fought before the war—were ignored and indirectly supported by American officialdom, which considered anti-Fascists like Tresca to be "Reds" and far more dangerous than Fascists. Washington and Rome not only saw eye to eye on this issue, they colluded in a scheme to frame Tresca on trumped up charges—sending a two-line advertisement in his newspaper for a book on birth control through the mails—and to deport him back to Italy into the waiting arms of Fascist jailors. But they failed to consider Tresca's legion of American associates and friends, and the backlash to his frame-up resulted in a commutation of his prison sentence by President Coolidge and a wave of bad publicity for Mussolini's regime. By the end of the 1920s, as Norman Thomas observed, "more than any single man in New York or the United States, Carlo Tresca blocked the rise of blackshirted Fascists who terrorized the streets of Italian-American districts. This was a great and too-little appreciated service to American democracy."[6] During the Great Depression, when Italian-American Fascism became more deeply entrenched, and popular support for Mussolini reached its height, Tresca never relented in his battle against Fascism's menace to his fellow immigrants and his adopted country.

By then, Tresca's crusade against the forces of totalitarianism had assumed a second dimension, as he committed himself to all-out resistance against Stalinism and its interventions abroad. Although for practical reasons he had collaborated with Communists during the anti-Fascist resistance campaigns of the 1920s, Tresca had always opposed the Soviet regime as a brutal tyranny, and after the counter-revolutionary campaign Stalinists conducted in Spain during the civil war, he became an implacable foe, combating Stalin's minions in the United States as forcefully as he did the Fascists. Tresca threw down his gauntlet before the Stalinists in 1937, assisting the John Dewey Commission that investigated and rejected the charges leveled against Leon Trotsky during the Moscow purge trials. Thereafter, Tresca specialized in exposés of the crimes committed by the Soviet secret police (OGPU) in Europe, Mexico, and the United States. His most famous public joust with the Communists occurred in 1938, when he charged the OGPU with kidnapping and murdering Juliet Stuart Poyntz, formerly a major figure in the American Communist Party and now a reluctant OGPU operative.

By the early 1940s, in poor health and depressed over the death of his two brothers, Tresca entered the twilight of his career, but he never ceased fighting his enemies, striving above all to prevent Communists and former supporters of Mussolini from gaining admission to wartime anti-Fascist organizations, such as the Mazzini Society and the Italian-American Victory Council formed by the Office of War Information. Tresca waged this battle with his customary militancy and courage until his assassination.

Tresca today is remembered only by the precious few Americans and Italians who are knowledgeable about the history of radicalism, the labor movement, and the anti-totalitarian struggles of leftwing activists in the United States. Historical memory inevitably falls victim to the erosive power of time. Moreover, Tresca was not the kind of individual usually included in history books intended for general consumption. He was a social rebel, a non-conformist, a political subversive, an all-around trouble-maker in the eyes of those who ruled America. He advocated the overthrow of state and church, the abolition of capitalism, and the establishment of a libertarian society—not exactly the beliefs and values embraced by mainstream America today or in the past. What should be recognized, however, is that, in the course of pursuing revolutionary objectives that could never be fulfilled, Tresca excelled as a heroic warrior, battling against Fascism, Communism, and the worst aspects of capitalism. Thus the source of Tresca's greatness and historical importance as a revolutionary lies not in the quest for a societal transformation that he ultimately realized could not be achieved, but in the ceaseless and uncompromising fight for liberty, social justice, and human dignity that became his true mission. The memory of Carlo Tresca is therefore worthy of resurrection and respect, and achieving that end is the purpose of this biography.

1

Revolutionary Apprenticeship

Gently spread across the Valle Peligna and commanded on two sides by Apennine massifs in the Abruzzo region of Italy is the town of Sulmona, birthplace of the Roman poet Ovid. At one end of the Corso Ovidio, Sulmona's main artery, stands a bronze bust of another native son, Carlo Tresca. Sculpted by Minna Harkavy, this statuette bears the inscription, "Carlo Tresca: Socialist Exile, Martyr of Liberty." Until recently, most Sulmonese knew little more about the young firebrand who challenged the town's rich and powerful at the turn of the century and then emigrated to the United States.[1]

Born on March 9, 1879, Carlo Tresca was the sixth of eight children raised by Filippo Tresca and Filomena Fasciani, offspring of very prominent Sulmona families.[1] The Fasciani were professionals and artists, well known for the music school that bore the family name. Don Filippo was one of Sulmona's leading notables at the time of Carlo's birth, having inherited considerable land holdings as well as a carting firm and stationery store. Uninterested in business, he deferred management of his estates to his mother and the stationery store to his wife. A heavy-set, cigar-smoking gentleman, Don Filippo enjoyed the physical pleasures of life, a trait he passed on to Carlo. His principal avocation was politics. Aligned with the Marchese Mazzara against the Barone Sardi De Letto, the heads of the factions that alternated control of Sulmona's municipal government, Don Filippo was Mazzara's political strategist. At home, he was the archetypal southern Italian *paterfamilias*, an autocrat who commanded obedience and respect, while yielding considerable authority to his wife in domestic matters. Austere and distant toward his children, Don Filippo rarely bestowed signs of affection like hugs and kisses, but behind the authoritarian facade was a good-hearted, loving man.

Donna Filomena, in contrast, was emotional and demonstrative, devoted to her children and the Church. Whereas her husband rarely set foot inside a church, Donna Filomena was a paradigm of Catholic conviction in its most superstitious and pagan form. Since religious devotion in southern Italian women was expected and encouraged, lest their minds and bodies seek forbidden outlets, Don Filippo and his sons left her faith unchallenged. Yet Donna Filomena's religious devotion did not prevent her from functioning in the real world.

The Trescas resided in an old palazzo at the Via San Cosimo No. 9: three stories high, stone facade, large central courtyard, and cavernous wine cellar.

Carlo's fondest childhood memories were of harvest time, when peasants from his father's estates gathered in the courtyard to make wine and olive oil, clean grain, sort fruit, and slaughter pigs. He loved to mingle with these peasants, who sang sentimental folk songs, played games with him, sat him on their laps, and told stories. Childhood intimacy with peasants contributed to his lifelong ability to interact comfortably with men and women of the working classes.[2]

Carlo's youth manifested many of the characteristics that defined him as a mature man and radical: rebelliousness against authority, the need to lead and attract attention, enjoyment of action and the fight, and the love of fun and good times. The root of Tresca's rebelliousness, he explained, was the "tyrannical patriarch," Don Filippo: "He sowed the seed of revolt in my heart." As rebellion against Don Filippo was impossible, Carlo turned his "unconscious feeling of revolt against anyone who exercised authority." Carlo was never motivated to apply his intelligence and study in school. He detested homework and resold the text books his parents were required to purchase. His greatest satisfaction derived from challenging the disciplinary powers of his teachers, disrupting the classroom with pranks, and leading other boys in bouts of collective mayhem. Punishment never dissuaded him.

Only by age fourteen or fifteen did Carlo awaken to the need for education, a prospect dimmed by the Tresca family's precarious finances in the 1890s. During the "tariff war" between Italy and France, trade between the two countries was reduced by half, and Italian wine producers—the French imported great quantities of Italian wine, refining and selling it as their own product—were hard hit in the South. Before the "tariff war" ended in 1892, the decline of exports and falling prices (accelerated by the spread of phylloxera) ruined tens of thousands of Italy's wine-producers.

Don Filippo was among the casualties. Difficulties resulting from Italy's economic travails were compounded by his habit of co-signing loans for friends who were forced to borrow during the "tariff war"—loans never repaid. With economic decline now irreversible, Don Filippo accepted defeat and lapsed into depression and inactivity. His wife assumed direction of all business affairs, saving every spare lira for her son Ettore's medical school education. Luisa, the oldest child, married a minor postal official. Her younger sister Anita assisted with household chores, but spent most of her time making shirts surreptitiously, lest neighbors discover the family's true circumstances. The fourth child, Beatrice, a religious ascetic, devoted herself to prayer and fasting; she would die a few years later. Carlo's younger brothers, Lelio and Arnaldo, were still boys when adversity befell. Brother Mario, nearly four years older than Carlo, was handicapped by severe myopia and worked in the stationery wrapping packages. Ettore received his degree in medical surgery from the University of Naples in 1892. Quiet, dignified, and beloved by all who knew him, Ettore was always the "big brother" to whom Carlo could and did turn in times of trouble, especially financial. Ettore became the municipal doctor of the town of Introdaqua, a few miles from Sulomona. The terrible health and wretchedness of the workers and peasants he treated in local hospitals prompted Ettore to join the *Partito Socialista Italiano* (PSI). His work for the movement included giving lectures, writing newspaper articles on science, and organizing a "people's school" (*scuola popolare*) in Introdacqua, where he provided instruction on health and hygiene. Not considered dangerous by the authorities, Ettore was left unmolested to continue his activities. Ettore practiced for nearly a year at the renowned Paolucci clinic in Naples before migrating to the United States in November 1903.[3]

Ettore's meager income could not help finance a good education for Carlo. Donna Filomena, determined to bring "respect and cash" back into the house, decided that Carlo should become a priest. A more unlikely candidate could scarcely be imagined. Carlo already by age fifteen had developed a strong revulsion for religion and the Catholic Church, but he was reluctant to disappoint his mother. Enrolled in a seminary, Carlo quietly rebelled by never attending. This deception continued for a few months, until Donna Filomena learned from a local priest that her son had never been seen at the seminary. The only alternative was to enroll Carlo in an *Istituto Tecnico*, a school that trained the less fortunate sons of the bourgeois for jobs in the bureaucracy, a career prospect almost as dismal as the priesthood. Carlo attended the technical school as a matter of familial duty, eventually completing the required four years but never receiving a diploma.[4]

The bleakness of his predicament inevitably evoked anger, vengefulness, and feelings of "revolt against all, against the world." But his desire for revolt and revenge was as yet unfocused: "Revenge for what? Against whom? I did not know then. It was all subconscious."[5] Lacking a cogent political philosophy, Carlo did not yet perceive his personal dilemma within the larger context of reckless state policies and the cyclical downswings of capitalism. Nevertheless, his undirected and inchoate feelings of revolt were vital ingredients in the process of transforming him into a revolutionary. So, too, was the lure of action and love of a good fight.

Carlo's dreams of battle had been stimulated by "Uncle Paolo" (actually Don Filippo's cousin), who had fought with Giuseppe Garibaldi. When Crete rebelled against Turkish rule in 1897, Carlo wanted to join the volunteer legion of Italians, led by Garibaldi's son Ricciotti, that fought alongside the Greeks. Donna Filomena thwarted this scheme, much to Carlo's frustration. His desire for action and leadership had to be satisfied for now by the rivalry between students of his *Istituto Tecnico* and the Catholic seminary he had ceased attending. Given the reactionary role the Church had played during the Risorgimento, and its continuing opposition to the Italian liberal state, it was hardly surprising that students of a state school were hostile to Catholic seminarians. Envisioning himself a champion of "Free Thought" battling the "Power of Darkness," Tresca frequently organized skirmishes with the "embryo priests."[6]

Carlo's anticlericalism was a basic ingredient in the complex mix of emotional passion and political ideals embodied by all radicals on the Italian Left. Disagree as they might on countless issues, the Italian *sovversivi* were united in their rejection of religion and hatred for the Catholic Church. Having reached, with his anti-clericalism, a critical stage in the metamorphosis transforming adolescent rebel into young revolutionary, Carlo only required exposure to the ideas and role models of a modern revolutionary movement to complete the process.

Italian Socialism and Labor

Tresca's conversion to socialism occurred during a whirlwind of social and economic change that saw workers and peasants agitating and organizing on an unprecedented scale. The 1890s had been a period of intense reaction, with successive governments ruling by authoritarian methods. Thousands of anarchists and socialists were arrested and consigned to *domicilio coatto*—imprisonment on the desolate islands off the southern Italian and Sicilian coasts. The anarchist Gaetano Bresci, a silk worker from Paterson, New Jersey, assassinated King Umberto on July 29, 1900, in revenge for the massacre of workers during the "May Days" of 1898 in Milan. With the ascendance of Prime Minister Giovanni Giolitti in the early-20th century, a new policy of relative toleration toward "the upward movement of the popular classes" was initiated.[7]

In reality, Giolitti hoped to forestall revolution by co-opting the socialist movement and taming its main constituency. The state, in theory, would remain neutral in struggles between workers and industrialists, peasants and landowners— so long as the aims of the masses were economic. Giolittian "toleration" would permit an unprecedented wave of strikes, the growth of the PSI founded in 1892, and the expansion of labor institutions characteristic of Italy: Chambers of Labor, peasant leagues of resistance, and union federations. The growth of PSI and the labor movement took place mainly in northern Italy. In southern Italy—the Mezzogiorno—the vast majority of peasants and workers remained outside the sphere of organized labor and the socialist elements that sought to lead them. The government was far less tolerant of protesting peasants in the South than the striking factory workers in the North, and encounters with troops occasionally resulted in what socialists called "proletarian massacres." Not surprisingly, the great mass of disinherited southerners opted not for political organization or militant strike action but for a more promising and enduring alternative—emigration.[8]

Tresca's native Abruzzo was a predominantly agricultural region of small to medium land owners and their tenants and share-croppers. Labor institutions had scarcely progressed beyond the artisan stage of mutual aid societies, and the PSI was poorly represented, with only 26 sections with 700 members in 1906, although in the Abruzzo as elsewhere, there were more socialists than party members. Lacking industrial workers and a militant peasantry, PSI sections in Abruzzo were composed mainly of intellectuals and professionals, men of the middle and lower middle classes who had become alienated from or ruined by the existing order.[9]

The PSI section in Sulmona differed significantly, however, in that it did possess a modern proletarian element—railroad workers. By the 1890s, Sulmona had become the most important railroad center in the Abruzzo, its location providing a natural hub for the Rome-Pescara (East-West) and L'Aquila-Naples (North-South) lines. But most of Sulmona's railroad workers were not native to the city or even to the Abruzzo, having come from the Emilia, Tuscany, and other regions of north-central and northern Italy. Their presence had only partly to do with operating trains. Railroad men where among the best organized and most radicalized workers in Italy. Until railroad strikes were made illegal in 1905, the government had the option of militarizing the railroads and operating them under martial law, as happened in 1902. A strategy less draconian was to transfer socialist and union militants from urban centers in the North to agricultural regions in the South, thereby minimizing the likelihood of their disrupting service and converting other workers to their cause. In 1898, the PSI section in Sulmona included twenty-seven railroad workers and thirty-eight local and nearby residents, mainly artisans and a handful of professionals and students. Not a single peasant yet belonged.[10] By 1902, the railroad workers in Sulmona had increased to more than 200, nearly all of them socialists and members of *Federazione dei Sindacati e Sodalizi Ferrovieri* (Federation of Railroad Workers Unions and Brotherhoods), the national federation formed in 1900.[11]

The PSI section and the railroad workers league were regarded with intense suspicion by Sulmona's indigenous oligarchy of conservative monarchists. They feared that socialism transmitted by northern railroad workers might rouse local peasants and workers from their traditional apathy and subservience. Sulmona's monarchist organ, *L'Araldo* (The Herald), manifesting both regional and class antagonism, sounded the alarm when five railroad workers of the local PSI section began publishing their own newspaper, *Il Germe* (The Seed), in October 1901. Accusing the northerners of acting like superior beings on a civilizing mission, the monarchist *prominenti* of Sulmona demanded to know "what interest can they have in the good of a city that is not theirs; these subversives come among us to drain their bile and implant class hatred among our workers?"[12] That the editorial staff of *Il Germe* soon comprised mostly natives of Sulmona did nothing to assuage their fear of aliens from the North. For their part, the local editors of *Il Germe* were delighted that the railroad workers represented a "subversive wind from the north" that chilled the oligarchs of Sulmona to their very bones.[13]

Whatever influence brother Ettore might have had on the evolution of Carlo's socialism, the kindly doctor could not have provided the role model craved by the young rebel seeking adventure and heroic deeds. The northern railroad workers, on the other hand, provided an irresistible attraction as veterans of the class struggle and a source of fear to Sulmona's elite. Even before terminating his studies at the *Istituto Tecnico*, Tresca began attending the lectures given regularly at the PSI section. Association with the rough-hewed proletarians—all of them older than he—was a source of excitement and ego gratification. The railroad workers, in turn, eagerly welcomed Tresca into their group; it was not every day that a scion of the landed gentry expressed interest in socialism. Yet, from the outset, the appeal of socialism for Tresca was more visceral than intellectual. His concern with abstract theory and ideological orthodoxy would remain minimal throughout his career. Instead, it was the railroad workers' "talk about the class struggle and the coming revolution [that] awakened my combative spirit," he recalled.[14] Socialism offered a glorious field of action that "suited the requirements of my soul."[15] In his eighteenth or nineteenth year, "comrade Tresca" joined the PSI, a decision that inevitably translated into conflict with the authorities. His first mention in police records was as a member of the Sulmona section, dissolved by decree in May 1898.[16]

Don Filippo vigorously opposed his son's joining the PSI, fearing that "it would prejudice the masters of the political parties of his own class against me."[17] To avoid arousing his father's antagonism, Tresca attended party meetings "on the quiet."

His emergence as the *enfant terrible* of Sulmona had to wait until working-class agitation swept Italy in 1901–1902. Although small-scale in comparison to the unrest in northern Italy or even nearby Puglia, the popular agitation and socialist activity taking place in the Sulmona district contrasted markedly with conditions that had prevailed in the late 1880s, when local Prefects routinely reported that the masses were passive and free from subversive influences.[18] Now, in Sulmona and nearby towns, socialist circles, mutual aid societies, and cooperatives among local artisans and peasants were emerging in appreciable numbers. Most of these popular associations were gravitating into the socialist camp.[19]

The northern intellectuals who dominated the PSI, men like Filippo Turati, had little interest in the predominantly peasant and backward Mezzogiorno. Propagandizing among the southern peasants and artisans became the mission of a small number of southern-born socialists. Tresca's earliest propaganda activity for which there is evidence occurred on April 7, 1902, in the town of Pratola, where he delivered a speech to some fifty artisans. That same month he helped organize a PSI section meeting for some 100 members of Sulmona's *Fratellanza Artigiana*. Although artisans were generally more advanced politically, Tresca's first priority that spring was to bring Sulmona's peasants under the influence of the PSI.[20] Among the poorest in the Abruzzo, Sulmona's peasants, like most in the Mezzogiorno, did not reside in the countryside, where they tilled the soil. They lived in town. Normal conditions of squalor had been exacerbated by the housing shortage that resulted when Sulmona became a burgeoning railroad center. By the spring of 1902, the desperate peasantry was evidencing receptivity to socialism, and a few had formed the *Fratellanza Agricola di Sulmona*.[21]

But the socialist message was just one of several the peasants were hearing. The PSI in Sulmona and its environs competed with the *Partito Repubblicano Italiano*, the small, bourgeois party inspired by Giuseppe Mazzini that advocated abolition of the monarchy and universal suffrage. Declining strength in traditional strongholds like the Romagna had caused the PRI to look south for support. Its local chieftain was Filippo Corsi, a native Abruzzese from Capestrano, who published *La Bandiera* in his hometown and in Sulmona from 1900 to 1902. Corsi had already acquired influence among local artisans, the class from which the republicans traditionally drew support, but had failed to make significant headway among peasants. Tresca discovered that in the smaller towns near Sulmona, Corsi would wait for the peasants to come out of church on Sunday, mount a chair, and launch into a speech. Out of curiosity the peasants would gather around and listen to his message. The same method was ineffective in a larger town like Sulmona, and Corsi's efforts to reach peasants through circulars and placards proved futile because most were illiterate.[22]

Tresca devised a different strategy—seeking peasants at neighborhood taverns where they congregated during their few hours of leisure. Another socialist organizer approaching them in this manner might have encountered the wall of reticence and suspicion that peasants usually erected against outsiders of a different social class. However, as the son of Don Filippo, Tresca automatically commanded respect and attention. When he first entered their taverns, the peasants would stand up and address him deferentially as "Don Carlo," no doubt mystified as to why a scion of the ruling class would want to help them organize against their masters. But the ease and familiarity with which he communicated and his obvious sincerity quickly won their confidence, so much so that they even invited him into their homes, where their dire poverty convinced Tresca that his cause was just. After several months of Tresca's persistent efforts, Sulmona's peasants overcame their inertia and joined the local *Fratellanza Agricola* in significant numbers.[23]

Tresca planned to demonstrate the peasants' strength and solidarity on May 1, 1902, the first May Day rally in Sulmona's history. A thousand or more peasants and workers from the area filled the Largo Palizze, where *Il Germe* had its office. The socialist sections of Sulmona and Pratola were also present. So, too, was a contingent of *carabinieri* (Italy's paramilitary police force) to intervene if the demonstration became aggressive. But this May Day would remain peaceful. After hearing speeches by the leaders of Sulmona's *Fratellanza Agricola* and Arnaldo Lucci, a native son and professor of law at the University of Naples, the throng marched to the grassy sheep-track on the outskirts of the city, where they listened to more speeches. However, "the honor of the last word at the country meeting was bestowed upon comrade Carlo Tresca," reported *Il Germe*. His speech "was the climax of the day: a fast-flowing stream of humor, up-to-date and fitting, which sounded a most exhilarating note of cheerfulness and generated humor in the best of taste. Lively applause paid him with interest for his special effort."[24] Tresca would always cherish the memory of his first speech:

> I didn't say much, and I didn't speak with eloquence but I heard a thunder of applause and I saw a sea of hands waving at me in praise and consent. I felt then that the people of Sulmona, my people, were christening me: I was no more a buoyant, exuberant, impertinent boy. I was a man, a man of command, of action. What a day! I will never forget it.[25]

Tresca's May Day speech confirmed his transformation from a rebellious youth to a socialist tribune. However, it was his preparatory work among Sulmona's peasants and artisans that contributed most to his development as a revolutionary. Socialism in the 19th and 20th centuries produced all too many leaders for whom the "proletariat" was an intellectual abstraction devoid of real flesh and blood, and the class struggle an ineluctable force of history to be invoked in theoretical treatises and official propaganda. Tresca was different. From these earliest days as a budding revolutionary, Tresca's empathy with the poor and oppressed was genuine and visceral. Whatever the official ideology he professed during his career—socialism, syndicalism, or anarchism—Tresca fought for the workers more than the "movement." He embraced the transcendent moral and redemptive purposes of several revolutionary ideologies, but his true place was always in the arena of daily struggle, leading and fighting as a *capo-popolo*, a "freelance of revolution," an indomitable rebel who "has a big heart, plenty of guts, and a humorous direct way of talking the plain direct language that the real people understand."[26]

The First Arrest

Another characteristic of Sulmona's young *capo-popolo* was the sheer relish and bravura with which he defied the authorities. This propensity resulted in more than thirty-six arrests during Tresca's career. The first occurred on June 1, 1902, on the occasion of a patriotic celebration organized by local monarchists to counteract the impact of the May Day rally. Tresca and Filippo Corsi, now his friend and ally, conspired to spoil the day. When local officials, dignitaries, and the special guest, the Minister of Education, rose to their feet at the playing of the national anthem, the peasant and artisan followers of Tresca and Corsi remained seated. Following this gesture of protest, the defiant peasants and artisans marched to the outskirts of town with Tresca and Corsi to savor their victory. On the way home, Tresca and some comrades encountered a procession of peasants who belonged to a conservative association faithful to the landlords. Cries of *"Viva il Socialismo!"* were raised in challenge to the marchers. A captain of the *carabinieri*, who had accompanied the conservative peasants to protect them, seized Tresca and placed him under arrest for shouting the subversive outcry. Tresca denied he had done so, but obliged the angry captain by shouting it now in his face. For this offense he was sentenced on June 11, 1902 to serve thirty days in jail.[27]

Tresca retaliated by targeting the captain in *Il Germe*, declaring that *"Il Capitano Sbirro"* (a derogatory term for policemen) was a gambler and a drunk and had arrested him "for the sole purpose of parading his imbecility and to please this city's cancerous criminal clique."[28] Such an affront might have been settled in the past by a duel. At the beginning of the 20th century, however, it had become customary in Sulmona to sue your offender for libel. Predictably, Tresca's trial before the *pretore* of Sulmona on October 4, 1902 ended with a guilty verdict and a sentence of seventy days imprisonment, which, after losing his appeal, he served from March 2 to May 12, 1903.[29]

Tresca's first incarceration was not an entirely unpleasant experience save for the lice in his cell. His friends provided an abundance of cigars and food. He emerged from jail with his reputation enhanced not only among his comrades but also among his family members:

> At home I found a remarkable change. I was received in an atmosphere of dignity and respect. I felt that for the first time my parents, my older brother and sisters took me seriously, not as a flippant, boyish, impertinent warrior of miniature battles, but as a man, a real man, a man of courage and endurance.[30]

After his homecoming dinner, with the entire family gathered around the table, Tresca's father offered him a cigar, permitting him to smoke in his presence for the first time. This gesture of acceptance and equality, marking a genuine turning point in their habitually tense father-son relationship, meant a great deal to Tresca.[31]

Union Leader and Editor

Since its founding in 1900, the *Federazione dei Sindacati e Sodalizi Ferroviari* (Federation of Railroad Workers Unions and Brotherhoods), with a membership of

12,000, had emerged as one of the largest and most militant labor organizations in Italy. One of its three affiliates, the *Sindacato dei Macchinisti, Fuochisti, ed Affini* (Firemen, Engineers, and Related Workers Union), held a conference in Milan on June 25–29, 1903. The leaders decided to establish headquarters in Sulmona because the *traslocati* from the North had played an important role in the rise of the union.[32] A few months later, the union selected Tresca to serve as its local secretary. The job provided a small stipend, but it was the only income Tresca earned during his years in Sulmona, amounting to just enough to cover his personal expenses.[33]

Save for this position as secretary, Tresca's career was not destined to include trade-union officialdom. By 1903, he had developed into a full-fledged agitator-editor in the classic tradition of Italian radicalism, much like his future enemy Benito Mussolini. Tresca's natural inclination for leadership and direct action was complemented by his considerable talents as a journalist. He had been involved with the publication of *Il Germe* from its inception, "reading proofs, writing small items and getting the paper ready for circulation."[34] Less than a year later, he was serving on the editorial staff and contributing articles; in October 1903, he became *direttore* or editor-in-chief of the newspaper.[35]

Tresca's journalistic style, ironically, was very similar to Mussolini's. The political newspaper for Tresca was not a vehicle of discourse or theorizing but an instrument of war. Replete with sarcasm, insults, contempt, irony, and dry humor, Tresca's articles blitzed his enemies ferociously and without restraint, always targeting the jugular. Yet Tresca's journalistic campaigns were driven by more than raw fury. Even as a young man he possessed acute insight into the relationship between power and corruption, and knew intimately the political terrain upon which he operated and how to obtain the ammunition needed for his campaigns. These qualities made Tresca a formidable muckraker. Thus within a month of his becoming director of *Il Germe*, Tresca attacked the richest and most powerful man in Sulmona—the Cavaliere Nicola dei Baroni Sardi De Letto, head of the *Pia Casa Santissima Annunziata*, the city's principal hospital. Tresca accused the baron of soliciting gifts from the contractors who serviced the hospital. Tresca's principal source of damaging information was none other than Don Filippo, who formerly belonged to the rival clique and knew the full extent of Sardi De Letto's transgressions.[37] The baron promptly sued Tresca for libel. Greeting the news with his characteristic indifference toward danger, Tresca responded in *Il Germe*: "Will the judge be objective or an arm of the litigant? We do not care. We are conscious of having performed our duty and we willingly accept the challenge to prove our accusations."[38] Tresca had already come to regard libel as an occupational hazard, but under Italian law libel it was a criminal offense punishable by imprisonment from one to five years and a minimum fine of 1,000 lire. Moreover, the Italian penal code, as written and interpreted, generally favored the litigant over the defendant. A libel suit, therefore, was an effective means with which to silence or intimidate an adversary. Italians of every political persuasion (except the anarchists) utilized this tactic, including Tresca.

The Baron Sardi De Letto was not Tresca's only adversary. No less than four political newspapers operated in Sulmona in 1903: the socialist *Il Germe*, the republican *La Democrazia*, the monarchist *L'Araldo*, and the clerical *Il Popolo*. Polemics between them were commonplace, but the exchanges between *Il Germe* and *La Democrazia* were more frequent because they were rivals for the same constituency. They became highly acrimonious after the death of Filippo Corsi, whose friendship with Tresca had transcended political rivalry. Elected to the Chamber of Deputies, Corsi fell off a balcony while giving his victory speech and was fatally injured. Friendship with Corsi remained a cherished memory for Tresca through his life.[39]

But no such ties existed between Tresca and the new editors of *La Democrazia*. In October 1903, they published a story claiming that Tresca had approached Corsi's widow with an offer to resurrect *La Bandiera*, the newspaper her husband had formerly published. Tresca and several railroad workers representing the local PSI section visited the widow Corsi and obtained a signed document denying that any such visit or offer had ever taken place. Eager to escalate the conflict, the republican editors responded with a flyer bearing the widow Corsi's name and reasserting the original accusation. *La Democrazia* continued to publish articles repeating the allegation. Wanting legal vindication, Tresca promptly sued the widow Corsi for libel. In exchange for dropping his suit, she substantiated Tresca's version of events, but he was not content to leave the matter at that. He now filed a libel suit against the editors of *La Democrazia*—for "phrases and affirmations offensive to my personal dignity and honor." They, in turn, counter-sued him for libel.[40]

By 1904, Tresca's record of popular agitation and outspoken advocacy of violent revolution convinced police that he was a dangerous subversive who exercised too much influence over local socialists, workers, and peasants.[41] It was only a matter of time before they moved against him. Ignoring danger signs, Tresca selected a very sensitive subject—the Italian army—to address in *L'Avvenire*, the PSI's official organ in the Abruzzo. Anti-militarism was particularly acute among Italian socialists and anarchists, and for good reason: the armed forces consumed one-quarter of government expenditures; troops were always in readiness to suppress workers and peasants; and conditions in the army were extremely brutal. Tresca's story concerned a young official who killed himself because of mistreatment. Merely publishing the story was an invitation for trouble, but Tresca recklessly provoked retaliation with his intemperate language, describing the army as "the most monstrous, immoral, degenerate organism of brutal force." Issues of *L'Avvenire* containing the offending article were confiscated and Tresca was brought up on charges.[42]

Helga

Constant involvement with labor agitation and radical journalism did not prevent Tresca from indulging in his favorite pastime—pursuit of women. Tresca's autobiography is curiously reticent about his love life, even to the extent of failing to mention that he married a young woman named Helga Guerra. Born on April 24, 1881, in the small hill town of Saludecio in the Romagna, Helga was named after the heroine in a German novel her mother had once read. Her father, Vincenzo Guerra, was the municipal clerk, a position that provided respectability and social standing, if not affluence. Helga and her five older siblings were raised as devout

Catholics, but even as a child, she experienced grave doubt about her faith and often beseeched God to prove his existence by making her believe in Him. By early adolescence she stopped asking. Helga's formal schooling also ended by this time, but she was a voracious reader and managed to educate herself—too much so, from her parents' perspective. Emotional life and interaction within the Guerra household was cold and meager, and the family values preached were inflexibly bourgeois. From this repressed environment, Helga's character retained a substantial measure of sternness and rigidity, and her emotional makeup, while volatile, lacked inner warmth and generosity. Yet she developed a spirit of rebelliousness and independence, qualities that enabled her to escape the stultifying household of a provincial bureaucrat.[43]

How and when Carlo and Helga first met is uncertain. But their attraction for each other was immediate and intense. Tresca, as young man of twenty-four, stood close to six feet in height and was still slender in body, with chestnut hair, and grey eyes from which a devilish gleam seemed to emanate. While not handsome by Hollywood standards, Tresca cut a dashing figure, possessing an abundance of charm and sexual magnetism that scores of women would find irresistible. His taste in women was ecumenical. In Helga he found an attractive but dour-looking woman with blue-grey eyes, dark blond hair worn in the "Gibson girl" fashion, and a curvaceous figure. But Helga's feisty spirit probably attracted him more than her looks.[44]

Once they decided upon marriage, Helga proved more defiant of social convention than her fiancé. She did not introduce Tresca to her family, ask their permission to marry, or invite them to the wedding, which took place in a civil ceremony of April 8, 1904. For Donna Filomena, of course, a civil marriage was no marriage at all. The newlyweds could not ignore her entreats for a "real" wedding, because they were compelled for economic reasons (Tresca's salary as union secretary could hardly support a wife) to reside within the Tresca household. Long accustomed to the emotional havoc Donna Filomena's tears could wreak, Tresca decided that domestic peace was worth a mass. A church wedding was held secretly at night so that the proud revolutionary and anti-cleric would not lose face before his comrades. A few sprinkles of holy water did not prove fatal, and the church wedding remained a carefully guarded secret.[45]

Tresca was fortunate to have married a woman who made no economic demands that would have interfered with his political activities. Despite the hardship imposed on her as a member of the Tresca household (she soon joined Anita at the sewing machine, making men's shirts), Helga did not regard Tresca's socialism as the source of her privation. She soon embraced her husband's ideas and eventually would assist his journalistic activities. Ultimately, however, the relationship proved unhappy and destructive, especially for Helga, a development attributable not only to frequent clashes of temperament, but above all to Tresca's irrepressible philandering.[46]

Within ten days of his wedding, Tresca was facing the prospect of jail. He had no illusion about the probable outcome of his court battle with Sulmona's most powerful citizen. The judiciary in Sulmona, he declared in *Il Germe*, had already given "so little evidence of independence [that] we assume the *Tribunale* will unleash all its fury against us, because—out of class interest—it wants to suffocate a rebel's voice."[47] Meanwhile, Tresca had underestimated the potential outcome of his litigation with the editors of *La Democrazia*. While his own suit against them was still pending, the *Tribunale Penale* of Sulmona, on April 18, 1904, found Tresca guilty of libeling its editors and sentenced him to serve two-and-one-half years and ten days of imprisonment and to pay a fine of 2,100 lire.[48] Less than a week later, Tresca was back in court. His acrimonious battle with the Baron Sardi De Letto had drawn the attention and support of higher echelons within the PSI, and the party dispatched a team of lawyers, including the renowned criminologist, Vittorio Lollini, to defend Tresca before the *Tribunale Penale* of Sulmona on April 25–26, 1904. What little evidence Tresca and attorneys were allowed to present in court was hopelessly outweighed by the testimony of a score of servile toadies whom the baron produced to affirm his financial honesty and moral rectitude. Tresca was therefore found guilty and sentenced to serve nineteen months and one day of imprisonment and to pay a 2,041 lire fine and court costs.[49]

At liberty pending appeal of both convictions, Tresca was compelled to make a decision that would affect the rest of his life. His standing in the local socialist movement had never been higher. On April 20, between court appearances, he was elected to the directive committee of Sulmona's PSI section.[50] The promise of a continuing career in the PSI, however, was not sufficient inducement to endure imprisonment. His legal difficulties with the editors of *La Democrazia* were settled out of court, and the criminal charges arising from that case dropped on June 18, 1904.[51] But no such accommodation was amenable to the vindictive Baron Sardi De Letto, and confirmation of Tresca's libel conviction by the Court of Appeals in L'Aquila was a foregone conclusion. Tresca decided to emigrate to America.[52]

Ettore had already established his medical practice in New York, and there were many *paesani* there and elsewhere who had been readers of *Il Germe* from its inception. When news of his dilemma reached America, a socialist group in Philadelphia invited Tresca to join them and raised money to help pay for his passage. Tresca resigned the directorship of *Il Germe* and prepared for departure. Escaping from Sulmona presented little difficulty. Local authorities had left him unmolested after his conviction, a show of leniency suggesting they knew of his decision to emigrate. For the police and Sulmona's elite, permitting Tresca to escape was preferable to sending him to jail. That way he would plague the Americans rather than return to Sulmona and resume his activities. The railroad workers, however, were unwilling to chance his safety; they secreted him on a train leaving town on June 22, 1904. Helga would rejoin him in America eleven months later. Mario and Anita followed soon thereafter, but the rest of the Tresca family remained in Sulmona. Carlo never saw them again.[53]

Meeting Mussolini

Tresca's journey north brought him to Milan, where he spent three days attending the annual conference of railroad workers. Again exercising caution, the railroad workers escorted him to the border crossing at nearby Chiasso. From there he went to Lausanne by way of Lugano, the beautiful town immortalized in the mournful song of Italian anarchist exiles, *Addio Lugano Bella*. In Lausanne, Tresca met his future nemesis, the man who would alter the destiny of the Italian people—Benito Mussolini.[54]

Lausanne was headquarters for a Swiss branch of the PSI founded a few years earlier by exiles, with strong support among the 6,000 Italians who labored in the building trades and belonged to the Italian Bricklayers' and Hodcarriers' Union. When Tresca arrived, the Italian colony was still buzzing with tales about a recent debate between the Rev. Alfredo Taglialatela, a noted Protestant evangelist, and a young socialist firebrand from the Romagna named Mussolini. Already notorious among Italians in Lausanne for his violent oratory and animal vitality, Mussolini thrilled his anti-clerical comrades by resorting to a flamboyant gesture during the debate held at the *Casa del Popolo* on March 25, 1904. The subject of the debate was "Man and Divinity." At one point in the exchange, Mussolini placed his watch on the table in front of him and exclaimed: "I will give God just five minutes to strike me dead. If he does not punish me in that time, he does not exist."

On his last night of his five-day stay in Lausanne, his curiosity peaked by all the talk about Mussolini, Tresca asked to meet this paladin of revolution. His autobiography describes the encounter:

> I was only a few years older than he and yet, taking for granted that my experience in the affairs of the Party was greater than his, I unconsciously assumed a paternalistic attitude toward his youthful impetuosity and his constant and vehement appeals to revolution. He, on the other hand, thought that I was not revolutionary enough. According to Mussolini, I was not sufficiently imbued with the spirit of revolt. Young Mussolini was a man of the barricade. I had, he contended, a too legalistic and gradualistic type of mind and a too reformistic conception of our mission. So we passed the night arguing and gesticulating.

The next morning Mussolini accompanied Tresca to the railroad station. As Tresca boarded the train for Le Havre, Mussolini bade him farewell with these words: "Well, Tresca, I am sure that America, powerful America, will make of you a true revolutionary comrade." Years later, after Mussolini became the Duce of Fascism, Tresca would send him a telegram annually, reminding him of his prediction. America would indeed make a true revolutionary out of Carlo Tresca.

2

Il Proletario

Tresca sailed from Le Havre aboard the SS *Tourraine* in August 1904. As the ship passed the Statue of Liberty, he recalled:

> There was a rush to the rail; all eyes were fixed on that beacon of light, seeking to penetrate the breast of that woman, symbolizing the most dear of human aspirations, "LIBERTY," to see if there was a heart within which beat for all the politically persecuted, for all the slaves of capital, for the disinherited of the earth.[1]

Tresca, too, got caught up in the excitement. As a socialist, he believed that capitalism was just as oppressive in America as elsewhere, but at that moment: "I thought, with a sense of relief and with a more living faith in social change, that I was setting foot upon the land plowed by Jefferson and Lincoln, the land blessed with the strongest, the sanest, the purest of bourgeois democracy."[2]

Disenchantment came quickly. Residing with Ettore at 53 Bayard Street, near Mulberry Park in Little Italy, Tresca found New York's ethnic diversity, intense commercial activity, and strange customs (chewing gum) disquieting. His ignorance of English only intensified his sense of alienation. He was greatly relieved when he departed for Philadelphia, a city with a higher percentage of familiar Abruzzese, where by pre-arrangement with the *Federazione Socialista Italiana del Nord America* (FSI), he assumed the directorship of *Il Proletario*, the federation's official organ, in October 1904.[3]

By the early 20th century, the world of Italian immigrant radicals—known generically as the *sovversivi*—had evolved into a unique subculture within the greater Italian community. Although linked through language, culture, and class, the *sovversivi* were distinct from other Italian immigrants by virtue of their ideas and values, which rejected the existing order of politics, religion, and society. In terms of class, the *sovversivi* were indistinguishable from the great majority of their compatriots, former artisans and peasants now employed as garment industry tailors, shoe makers, barbers, carpenters, cabinet makers, stonemasons, printers, waiters, miners, and mill hands. Political and social life among the *sovversivi* revolved around hundreds, if not thousands, of *circoli* and *gruppi*. The institutional nexus binding these circles and groups was the press. Over the course of a half-century (1890s to the 1940s) nearly 100 Italian radical newspapers were published across the country, most enduring for a few months or years, but some flourishing for decades. The *sovversivi* never acquired a mass following, but they wielded influence that was wholly disproportionate to their meager numbers, at least until government repression took its toll between 1917 and 1920, and Mussolini and Fascism captivated so many Italian Americans in the 1920s and 1930s. At the height of their pre-World War I influence, the *sovversivi* functioned as the militant vanguard of Italian immigrant workers against the American capitalists who exploited them at the workplace, and against the Italian elite (*prominenti*) that lorded over them within *colonie italiane*. Prior to the immigration restrictions of the early 1920s, the world of the *sovversivi* had been enriched by a steady flow of men and ideas back and forth between Italy and the United States. And although the sequential evolution of its main ideological components (anarchism, socialism, syndicalism, communism) paralleled that of Italy, the world of the *sovversivi* was no carbon copy of its counterpart in the old country. To the contrary, the prevailing environment and circumstances of life in America, factors that influenced immigrant life as a whole, ensured that the Italian immigrant Left would develop a personality and character that was unique.[4]

Tresca, *Il Proletario*, and the FSI

Looking back upon his earliest activities within the *colonie italiane*, Tresca recalled that "though living in America, my thought, my talks, my habits of life, my friends and my enemies were all Italian."[5] Initially, the workers Tresca sought to organize and lead in the class struggle were all Italian, a limitation imposed not only by his own ethnic parochialism and ignorance of English, but by the indifference and even hostility of labor unions and the American socialist parties toward "New Immigrants." Not until the Socialist Party of America (SPA) established its foreign-language federations in 1910–1912, and the Industrial Workers of the World (IWW) led the great strikes of immigrant workers in Lawrence and Paterson in 1912–1913 did the barriers begin to lift.[6]

Inside or outside the *colonie italiane*, Tresca was a very different kind of leader than the traditional socialist intellectuals and politicians. Arturo Caroti, *Il Proletario*'s administrator and the FSI's official propagandist in 1904–1905, described the comrade he came to know so well:

> Carlo Tresca, besides being a talented youth with a big heart, is a man of action, courageous to the point of recklessness, always atop the bastion, always in the front lines of the proletarian struggle, always ready to sacrifice himself for an ideal and for his brothers, the workers. He is not one of those leaders who guide the masses from the office of an organization or from the editorial board of a daily newspaper. He is a born journalist, and the newspaper serves him like a weapon. But the field of action he prefers is the speaker's platform or the head of a column of strikers, resisting the charge of the police, overcoming apathy, or thwarting the betrayal of scabs.[7]

Il Proletario immediately assumed an aggressive style that reflected Tresca's vigor and combativeness. As previously displayed in *Il Germe*, his journalistic forte was not doctrinal discourse but muckraking attacks against the Italian community leaders and institutions that exploited immigrant workers. Political developments in Italy and Europe were covered with greater frequency and depth than events in the United States, although his insights into American politics were acute. The struggles and strikes of Italian immigrant workers, as well as American labor union activities—especially concerning the United Mine Workers of America (UMWA) and the IWW—also received periodic attention. Articles about socialism, capitalism, religion—the standard fare of Italian radical newspapers—appeared weekly. Issues pertaining to the FSI received frequent and comprehensive coverage; however, he resisted devoting space to the ideological polemics and personal diatribes featured so regularly under his predecessors. Unfortunately, Tresca, too, was eventually drawn into the internecine struggles that divided and weakened the movement. He would prove himself a formidable polemicist.

Tresca stood with the revolutionary wing of the socialist movement, a position that prompted immediate attack from Teofio Petriella, the director of *Avanti!*, a reformist newspaper published in Newark, New Jersey. Tresca responded by rejecting Petriella's insistence that the socialist revolution could be won at the ballot box thanks to universal suffrage, declaring it was absurd to believe the bourgeoisie would peaceably relinquish its monopoly of power and allow itself to be expropriated by legal means. When reformists like Petriella advocated parliamentary action as the sole means by which to build a socialist society, Tresca believed they were anesthetizing the masses to the realities of the class struggle. The war between the proletariat and the bourgeoisie, he affirmed repeatedly, was a historically determined conflict that would be won through violence. Socialism would be achieved not by workers' casting votes but by forcibly seizing political power and expropriating private property.[8]

Neither dogmatic nor exclusionary about matters of doctrine, Tresca had no intention of awaiting the Armageddon of capitalism immobilized in a state of passivity and fatalistic expectation, like so many socialists and anarchists. The class struggle for Tresca was a war to be fought in the present. He demanded the full mobilization of socialist activists who were willing to march toward the conquest of the future.[9] Yet, for all his rousing calls to arms, within a few months of his arrival, he had taken accurate measure of the movement and openly expressed his disappointment:

> I arrived in America with the sweet illusion, formed in my soul by the rosy correspondence that appeared in the *Avanti!* of Rome, that here there existed a solid and well disciplined Italian socialist organization. I believed that the dormant and deprived of Italy, here before the light of socialism, had opened their hearts and minds to new social horizons. But in reality I found none of this.[10]

The vast majority of Italians, he had discovered, remained outside the orbit of the movement, and most socialists were ill equipped to remedy the situation. But some progress was achieved with Tresca at the helm of *Il Proletario*; the number of FSI sections had risen to around fifty by the summer of 1905, an increase largely due to his energizing presence and propaganda. But rising membership did not translate necessarily into greater strength. A principal cause of socialist weakness, he believed, was the FSI's lack of cohesive organization, especially at the state level. Local sections, nominally under the central authority of the executive committee, were really autonomous groups bound together only by common ideology and purpose. Zealous defenders of independent initiative, local sections usually neglected to coordinate activities state-wide, much less on a national basis. Efforts were therefore sporadic, isolated, and ineffectual. Weakness and inertia, caused by weak organizational structure, could be eliminated by creating state federations, Tresca believed, and throughout the spring and summer of 1905 he campaigned vigorously for their establishment.[11] A number of state federations were eventually formed, but they never attained the cohesion and militancy Tresca desired.[12]

The *Camorra Coloniale*

Tresca was his own instrument of class warfare. His target in 1905—and for the rest of his career—was the *Camorra Coloniale*: the term he invented to describe the triumvirate of wealthy Italian businessmen (*prominenti*), consular officials, and priests who exploited their working-class countrymen. Tresca fully expected to find Italian immigrant workers exploited by American capitalists, but he was chagrined to discover how they were victimized by their own co-nationals. From his socialist perspective, the *prominenti* were unscrupulous businessmen whose prosperity and status had been attained by fleecing immigrant workers with a multitude of ruthless practices (e.g. the *padrone* system) and duplicitous schemes. The most hated among the *prominenti* were the rich publishers of Italian-language daily newspapers: e.g., Carlo Barsotti and *Il Progresso Italo-Americano* in New York; Charles C. A. Baldi and *L'Opinione* in Philadelphia; and Mariano Cancelliere and *La Trinacria* in Pittsburgh. They were odious to Tresca not only because their newspapers fostered every manner of political, social, and intellectual conservatism. Often personal friends of American business magnates, they invariably opposed Italian workers whenever they struck for higher pay and better conditions. Moreover, their newspapers functioned as recruiting agencies for Italian strike breakers and non-union laborers. No less hated were Italian Catholic priests and the foreign-service representative of the Italian monarchy. As in the Old Country, Tresca viewed priests—he often referred to them as "*maiali neri*" (black hogs)—as purveyors of obscurantism and myth, social engineers whose pastoral function was to ensure the docility of the masses by keeping them ignorant and obedient. The royal consuls, rather than the protectors of Italians abroad, were merely extensions of Italy's parasitic bureaucracy, petty despots who devised their own techniques for exploiting immigrants.[13] In his autobiography, he described them as

> regular leeches always on the warpath for fresh blood, exacting exorbitant taxes, selling at various prices exemptions from military duty, and devouring whatever money was forthcoming to them as compensation for the death of a relative in mine explosions or industrial accidents generally. They were not unlike hyenas.[14]

In the first of many muckraking campaigns, Tresca conducted an exposé of Count Geralamo Naselli, the consul general of Philadelphia, in May 1905. Tresca's collaborator was Giovanni Di Silvestro, the editor of *Il Popolo*. Tresca accused Naselli of various deficiencies and wrongdoings: stupidity, indifference to the problems of poor immigrants, protecting the exploiters of the community, charging illegally-high fees for notary services, and selling exemptions from service in the Italian army to non-citizens.[15] Naselli filed a libel suit against Tresca, Di Silvestro, and the latter's brother, Giuseppe. Arrested twice that summer and released under $1,000 bail, Tresca was undeterred by the prospect of imprisonment or paying the $10,000 Naselli demanded in compensation. Eager to describe the "political parasitism and corruption" of the Italian consular system in an American court, Tresca dared Naselli to pursue his case so he could expose him as "inept, presumptuous, indecent and vile."[16]

The "Naselli Affair" created a sensation in Philadelphia. The Italian Foreign Ministry, hoping to dispel the doubts raised by Tresca's accusations, sent a special emissary to investigate Naselli's conduct. To nobody's surprise, Tresca's claims were deemed unfounded, and the consul was portrayed as an innocent victim of slander by subversives.[17] Not satisfied, the Italian Ambassador, Baron Mayor des Planches, wanted his pound of flesh. Expressing fear that Tresca and Di Silvestro would organize protests against the consulate, he asked Secretary of State Elihu Root to intercede with local authorities and prevent a demonstration into which "three or four disreputable individuals might drag several hundred poor deluded and ignorant Italians."[18] Scores of similar demands for repressive action against Tresca would be submitted to Washington by the Italian government over the next thirty years.

To the Mines and Mills

The anti-Naselli campaign reflected Tresca's belief in direct action to attract and assist Italian workers. Because of their ignorance, illiteracy, lack of political consciousness, and "atavistic feelings of resignation," the great majority of Italian immigrants had proven unsusceptible to "evangelical propaganda" and remained outside the ambit of the socialist movement. Tresca proposed that the socialists fulfill a guardianship role by organizing immigration offices that would provide free monetary services (handling remittances, postal savings accounts, and currency exchange), information to help immigrants acclimate to America, and most important to assist them in finding jobs. Once decent jobs were secured, the immigration offices would help immigrants organize producer and consumer cooperatives, mutual aid societies, and educational institutions. Eventually, as more immigrants came under the protective wing of the immigration offices, the FSI would be able to raise political consciousness, teach the ideals of class struggle, organize militant unions, and form chambers of labors to link local unions and other working-class organizations within a given district.[19]

Tresca still had much to learn about socialism in the United States. The formation of immigration offices, labor unions, and chambers of labor for Italian workers was completely beyond the resources and capabilities of Italian radicals in 1905 or any time thereafter. Not until 1919 was a chamber of labor established in New York, a feeble organization that bore no resemblance to the Italian originals that were about to be destroyed by the Fascists. Tresca's activity in America, therefore, was destined to remain limited to traditional means of operation: radical journalism, propaganda lectures, and labor agitation. He excelled at all three.

Tresca's responsibilities as director of *Il Proletario* required him to deliver propaganda lectures to fellow socialists and interested workers in Philadelphia and nearby cities almost on a weekly basis. For locations beyond a day's travel, Tresca would undertake a pre-organized propaganda tour (*giro di propaganda*), during which he would visit a succession of cities and towns. In 1905 and 1906, he conducted several propaganda tours that brought him to industrial and mining sites in New Jersey, Connecticut, Massachusetts, Vermont, Pennsylvania, Ohio, and Illinois.[20]

Tresca's arrival was a special event for Italian communities in the smaller mining and mill towns, and his lectures would often be followed by music, dancing, or a picnic. The Italians who attended included veteran socialists and anarchists, workers who were sympathetic to his message, and others curious to meet the new celebrity. Audience composition was generally the same in larger cities. Participants often wrote letters to *Il Proletario*, depicting him as an impassioned orator capable of stirring the emotions of the crowd and as a patient mentor who explained his ideas in language uneducated workers could understand. They also reveal how Tresca established a quick and easy rapport with audiences by means of his informal manner and hearty sense of humor. Indeed, this ready rapport was a key factor in his success and popularity with workers. As he had in Sulmona, Tresca demonstrated his unique ability to assimilate into a working-class environment, feeling entirely comfortable with rough-hewed Italian miners and mill hands, and relating to them as a friend and comrade rather than as a famous "leader." Typically, after a long day on the lecture circuit, he would enjoy himself thoroughly when invited by his hosts to share a simple meal of pasta and home-made wine and spend the evening playing cards, smoking, and telling tales. He enjoyed this conviviality without evidencing a trace of discomfort, for it was his cardinal rule never to make workers self-conscious of their poverty. Once, when his young daughter Beatrice accompanied him, she complained that the bed in which she was to sleep at a miner's home lacked sheets. He reproached her gently in private, explaining that the people were too poor to own such items.[21] Thus he never balked when obliged to share a bed with a miner during a propaganda tour: "To sleep two in a bed, in the same room is not comfortable. But it is a blow to your imagination when on entering the sleeping room, you find in it four kids. You can't refuse such hospitality. It is all the miners can offer you."[22]

These early propaganda tours profoundly influenced Tresca, as he observed first hand the oppressiveness and exploitation that defined the lives of workers in industrial America, grim realities that fortified his desire to overthrow capitalism and launch the new age of socialism. Two episodes that touched him deeply occurred in western Pennsylvania, where he was hosted by Italian miners from the Emilia who had formed a socialist enclave in Youghiogheny. After his lecture, the miners gave Tresca a quick education about coal: where the various varieties were produced, the different hours and wages that prevailed in different districts, and the miners' ongoing labor struggles with the operators. That night they brought him to a facility where bituminous coal was "cooked" into coke for factory use. The rows of furnaces spewed tongues of flame high into the night sky. Feeding them fuel with long metal shovels, which burned their hands, were exhausted men "condemned alive to a living hell." "It is necessary to see these slaves as I have seen them," he wrote in *Il Proletario*. "Then no one would repeat the lie that work ennobles; rather, as a reproach to capitalism, they would say that work brutalizes and kills."[23]

Tresca was taken next to inspect a mine at Blythedale. Standing outside the elevator as the early shift descended, Tresca wondered: "Will they all come back? This was the atrocious thought that tormented me. And in the eyes of the men, I seemed to read the same sad uncertainty—will I see my family tonight?" His mind conjured the image of Virgil guiding Dante into the depths of Hell, as he descended into the deepest recesses of the mine. Trudging for two hours through subterranean passageways too short for a man to stand erect, tensely vigilant to avoid exposed electrical wires that could dispense a lethal shock, Tresca felt exhausted, his back ached terribly, and his breathing was labored from the coal dust. The Italian miners he encountered underground were surprised that Tresca, a leader, had risked life and limb to observe them at their toil. From each he learned more about the terrors of mining. Especially feared was the *pietra della morte* (the rock of death), the sheets of slate separating the coal layers that could fall upon miners without sound or warning. With such a deadly menace always awaiting victims, why, Tresca asked, was there no first-aid station either below or above the surface? Because the coal operators considered it preferable to pay $150 in compensation to the widows of miners killed, his comrades explained. Several hours later, coughing up coal dust and unable to straighten his back, Tresca emerged from the pit head uttering a silent invocation: "Come redeeming socialism, come. Only then will the mine cease to be what it is today, a rich tomb created for men by the cruel and blind improvidence of capitalism."[24]

Propaganda tours were a vehicle to excoriate capitalism and exalt the socialist world of the future, but workers' strikes provided a natural habitat for Tresca to combat the class enemy directly and satisfy his love of the fight. The first dozen years of his career in America were the period of Tresca's greatest activity in the labor movement. During that time only a few American radicals, such as William D. ("Big Bill") Haywood, Elizabeth Gurley Flynn, and Joe Ettor, were his equal as labor agitators and strike leaders. Among Italian socialists and anarchists he had no peer.

Tresca's first strike action was against the John B. Stetson Company in Philadelphia. There, 500 Italian and 900 Jewish hat makers, representing half of the employees, walked off their job, in February 1905, to protest against the exploitative methods by which the owners generated fat profits. So-called "apprentice" workers were hired at $2 a week, with a promise that they would receive a small bonus and become permanent employees after three months. Most were discharged before the three-month "trial period." The survivors engaged in piece-work requiring them to keep their hands in near-boiling water softening felt, to stand in the overflow that covered the floor, and to breathe felt particles all day long. If the hats passed muster, workers could earn $4–5 a week; however, for every "damaged" hat—which would be repaired and sold at the regular price—50 cents would be deducted from their wages.[25]

In *Il Proletario* and at public rallies, Tresca denounced the Stetson Company owners, described their system of exploitation, and exhorted Italian strikers to continue the struggle. He and Arturo Caroti organized picket lines outside the factory; he harangued the Italian strikers while his comrade did the same in German to the Jewish strikers. Tresca also spoke on street corners in Italian neighborhoods, urging his countrymen not to replace the strikers and become scabs, a not uncommon practice for hard pressed Italians in this period. The strike also marked Tresca's first experience with the American Federation of Labor (AFL), whose affiliated hat makers' union represented the skilled workers at Stetson. Despite promises to help, the union's president never authorized his members to join the Italians and Jews, and the strike action ended in failure after five weeks.[26]

In August that year, while on a lecture tour in Barre, Vermont, Tresca was summoned by comrades in nearby Northfield to assist striking Italians employed as ditch diggers on a new water system. Each laborer had paid a $1 fee (*bossatura*) to an Italian banker in New York City to obtain this job, which required a minimum daily excavation measuring eight feet in length, seven feet in depth, and two feet in width. Deductions came out of their wages—little more than $1 a day—for inadequate food and lodgings that consisted of a windowless shanty sleeping 70 men on rotting straw. On August 21, some of the Italians threw down their shovels, demanding higher wages and better conditions.[27]

Tresca met with the socialist strike committee the next morning and proceeded to the digging site, where he urged the workers to resist. Police ordered him to stop speaking. He feigned ignorance of what they were saying and continued. When they insisted, he allegedly cited a recent Supreme Court decision about strikes, and the dumbfounded police allowed him to finish.[28] The strikers, meanwhile, were told they would have to clear out of the shanties and would not receive their pay until September 2, thereby depriving them of any means to survive. Luckily, during the next few days, local Italian socialists arranged to house and feed the strikers. Tresca gave several more speeches about socialism and visited the ditch diggers at night to convince more of them to strike. Within a month or so, many of the discharged strikers found similar work in Burlington or with the local railroad. Those who returned to the water system project received higher wages and better housing. Tresca's inspiration had contributed decisively to one of the rare victories won by unskilled Italian laborers during these years.[29]

Revolutionary Syndicalism

Tresca's earliest experiences as a strike leader paralleled the emergence of a new movement in Europe and America that would quickly win his allegiance—revolutionary syndicalism. He never described the process by which his ideological affinities shifted over the course of some nine years: from revolutionary socialism to revolutionary syndicalism in 1905, to anarcho-syndicalism by 1913. This transition resulted most likely from three related factors: ideological considerations; the need for independence demanded by his personality; and his natural propensity for direct action in labor struggles and the fight against capitalism. By 1905, Tresca had become the leading Italian proponent and practitioner of revolutionary syndicalism in the United States.

The differences between Italian revolutionary syndicalism and anarcho-syndicalism were by no means semantic. Unlike Spain, where syndicalism evolved from anarchism, or France, where it comprised anarchist, Allemanist, and Marxist elements, revolutionary syndicalism in Italy developed within the ideological context of Marxism and the institutional framework of the PSI, emerging as a fully developed movement by 1904. Although several currents of revolutionary syndicalism evolved, with varying attitudes toward political parties, parliamentarism, and electoral activity, they all stressed the primacy of proletarian action, especially the general strike conducted with revolutionary unions. The latter would become the nuclei for future social and state organization subsequent to the revolution. In contrast, anarcho-syndicalists wished to utilize unions as instruments of revolutionary struggle, but they never embraced political parties or electoral activity in any form and categorically rejected the idea that unions should constitute embryonic forms of future state and societal institutions.[30]

Given that Tresca was a voracious reader and avidly followed political and intellectual developments in Italy, it must be assumed that Italian theorists like Arturo Labriola, Enrico Leone, and Walter Mocchi influenced his espousal of revolutionary syndicalism. On a tactical level, Tresca concurred wholeheartedly with Labriola's declaration that "five minutes of direct action were worth as many years of parliamentary chatter."[31] Tresca, like other syndicalists, embraced the theory that every strike, even if lost, achieved a positive purpose by helping to develop revolutionary consciousness and militancy among the workers, objectives more important than the material gains a strike might achieve.[32]

An American development of equal importance to Tresca's evolution as a revolutionary syndicalist was undoubtedly the founding of the Industrial Workers of the World (IWW) in 1905. Until now, Tresca had considered the American trade union movement hopelessly deficient. American labor leaders, such as AFL president Samuel Gompers, who opposed socialism and sought harmony between labor and capitalism, Tresca dismissed as traitors ranking among the worst enemies of the proletariat. He condemned the craft unions affiliated with the AFL because they represented only the aristocracy of labor and discriminated against unskilled immigrants. Tresca also rejected the idea of "boring-from-within," and gradually converting the AFL to socialism. The barriers erected by conservative and corrupt union officials, he argued, were too difficult to penetrate; the only solution was for workers to create new labor organizations based on the class struggle that would fight as one body for a socialist future.[33] Only the IWW, Tresca believed, met these criteria. He hailed its formation as "an open declaration of a more effective struggle [forthcoming] between the rights of the proletariat that must be affirmed and the rights of the bourgeoisie that must fall."[34] Tresca's description of the IWW's founding convention in Chicago has led some to believe that he may have been there as an observer.[35] In fact, he had not attended, but after a six-month gestation period, Tresca publicly declared himself a revolutionary syndicalist, espousing the concept of the trade union as the principal instrument of socialist action and the nucleus around which the future society would organize itself.[36]

Since the director of *Il Proletario* wielded considerable influence, Tresca's endorsement of revolutionary syndicalism and the IWW inevitably generated profound consequences for the FSI. Since he considered both the Socialist Party of America (SPA) and the Socialist Labor Party (SLP) to be incapable of effective action, Tresca urged all FSI members to join the IWW. Although he did not recommend abandoning the SPA and SLA (the FSI had always divided its loyalties between them), Tresca reasoned that the IWW had rendered moot the question of party affiliation for Italians. As members of the new industrial union, they could fulfill their obligation as socialists, participate in the struggles of the American proletariat, and strengthen themselves for the special task of protecting the Italian immigrants. Yet Tresca himself never joined the IWW, a curious contradiction attributable to his insistence upon personal independence and free initiative. Tresca's not too subtle suggestion that the FSI look only to the IWW did not resolve internal conflict over socialist party affiliation, but the enthusiasm for revolutionary syndicalism he had generated became so infectious that the reorientation of the FSI in that direction was now inevitable. Ultimately, Tresca, more than anyone, was responsible for the FSI's ideological and tactical reorientation toward revolutionary syndicalism.[37]

Exit *Il Proletario*

Supporting the IWW and revolutionary syndicalism did not assure Tresca's position as director of *Il Proletario*, which was under attack from various quarters. Fractious squabbling, jealousy, and other manifestations of over-inflated egos, often roused for the most absurd reasons, were endemic to Italian radicals of all persuasions, and every director of *Il Proletario* had been the target of frivolous and petty attacks. Now it was Tresca's turn.[38] Ostensibly, the main cause of conflict between Tresca and the FSI executive committee was the Naselli affair. By the time Tresca and Giovanni Di Silvestro stood trial on December 20–23, 1905, the Naselli affair had become a *cause célèbre* among the Italians of Philadelphia. Radicals, progressive journalists, a significant number of prominent physicians and other professionals, as well as many workers, supported Tresca and the Di Silvestro brothers. The *prominenti*, the Catholic clergy, and the "patriotic" elements of the community sided with the consul general. The outcome of the trial, however, was a foregone conclusion. Interrogated by the prosecutor, Naselli professed ignorance of all the abuses alleged to have been practiced at the consulate. Copies of the articles written by Tresca and Giovanni Di Silvestro, translated for the court by the consul's own secretary, were woefully inaccurate; yet the most offensive portions were read into the record. Incriminating material produced by Tresca and Di Silvestro was not allowed into evidence on the grounds that the consul of a foreign country was not a public officer whose conduct could be criticized in the public press. Nor were they permitted to explain the basis of their accusations.

The prosecutor, on the other hand, was permitted to focus not only on Tresca's offending articles but also on his libel conviction in Italy and his flight from Italian justice. Defense witnesses were restricted in their testimony or dismissed because of their political sympathies. The prosecutor, in his summation, denounced the accused socialists as criminals. Then the judge gave instructions to the jury that left no doubt as to the verdict he desired. The jury took only thirty minutes to find Tresca and Di Silvestro guilty. On December 28, 1905, they were sentenced to three months imprisonment and a fine of $100. Both were released on $2,500 bail pending appeal.[39]

Rank-and-file support for Tresca was overwhelming, *Il Proletario* received thousands of small contributions for his legal expenses, totaling around $1,500. But several members of the FSI executive committee had disapproved of Tresca's campaign against Naselli from the outset and resented spending money for his defense. Chiefly, however, they feared placing *Il Proletario* at risk by attacking a formidable foe such as the consul general. Even after Naselli decided not to sue *Il Proletario*, and the Italian government recalled him to Rome, tacitly acknowledging the merits of Tresca's accusations, FSI opponents still remained bent on his ouster. Tresca offered to resign the directorship of *Il Proletario* in March 1906, but a majority of the FSI sections insisted that he remain at his post.[40]

The next crisis provided a pretext to oust him. Tension between anarchists and socialists had been high ever since the vicious polemic between Luigi Galleani and Giacinto Menotti Serrati, an earlier director of *Il Proletario*, in 1903. After anarchists broke up a socialist meeting in Boston with pistol shots on May 28, 1906, Tresca was expected to open the pages of *Il Proletario* for a new round of attacks against them. Tresca had sought to establish good relations with the anarchists and tried to broker a truce after this latest encounter, but several influential FSI leaders considered his restraint inexcusable. Under renewed pressure, Tresca resigned the directorship of *Il Proletario* on June 7, 1906.[41]

Evaluating his tenure as director of *Il Proletario*, Tresca rightly judged it a success: "I galvanized, fortified a corpse—the FSI."[42] He was not alone in this assessment. A "revolutionary faction" that broke away from the Philadelphia section, in opposition to the reformist and authoritarian tendencies quickly manifested by his successor, Giuseppe Bertelli, gave Tresca even higher marks: "...one could say that before he assumed direction, the Italian Socialist Party in America scarcely existed, whereas after he departed, he left a vast and organized party."[43] In reality, the FSI had become neither large nor well organized. But Tresca unquestionably had rendered inestimable service to Italian socialism and syndicalism in America during his twenty months as director of *Il Proletario*. The FSI's debts had been eliminated and *Il Proletario*'s circulation had risen from 4,000 to 5,600. The number of FSI sections had increased from thirty to more than eighty, and state federations had been organized in Connecticut, Illinois, Massachusetts, New Jersey, Pennsylvania, and Vermont.[44] In sum, a major resurgence of the FSI had occurred between 1904 and 1906, and the lion's share of credit belonged to Tresca.

3

Freelance of Revolution

Tresca's departure from *Il Proletario* in no way diminished his popularity among rank-and-file socialists and syndicalists, who appreciated his daring leadership far more than the FSI chieftains did.[1] But he could not capitalize on this goodwill until he found employment to provide for his family. Helga had arrived in New York on May 11, 1905; she and Tresca took up residence at 1103 Ellsworth Street in South Philadelphia, not far from his office. On March 16, 1906, Helga gave birth to a girl, named Beatrice in honor of Tresca's sister, who had died prematurely.[2] By then, Tresca had become political editor for *La Voce del Popolo*, a labor daily that Giovanni Di Silvestro started publishing after their conviction in the Naselli case. Loss of their appeal, however, sent Tresca and Di Silvestro to Moyamensing Prison for three months. Decades later, when asked where he had studied, his favorite reply was "the University of Moyamensing."[3]

Tresca's memories of Moyamensing were really anything but fond. The squalor of his cell, the solitude, and the forced idleness were "hell" to bear even for three months.[4] Tresca missed the FSI's second national congress held in Boston on November 29–December 2, 1906, which overwhelmingly endorsed the IWW and syndicalist action.[5] Although pleased with that result, Tresca was dismayed by the vicious attacks leveled against him at the congress by the Philadelphia section leaders and Giuseppe Bertelli, his successor at *Il Proletario*. Among the egregious crimes he was accused of committing were the Naselli affair, his collaboration with *Il Popolo* and *La Voce del Popolo*, and alleged lateness reading proofs and writing articles.[6] Outraged by the accusations, he responded to Bertelli and the "sect of thugs" belonging to the Philadelphia section: "I am ashamed to stay among you and I tear up my party membership card in your face."[7] Thereafter, Tresca had an on-again, off-again relationship with the FSI, usually more off than on.

Returning to his position at *La Voce del Popolo* in March 1907, Tresca discovered that Di Silvestro's real intention was not to fight the *prominenti* but to join them. The erstwhile comrades parted company and eventually became bitter enemies. Di Silvestro acquired riches as a banker, achieved notoriety as the supreme venerable of the Sons of Italy, and became one of Fascism's leading supporters among Italian Americans.[8]

Estranged from the FSI and without a job, Tresca appealed to the rank-and-file to support a syndicalist newspaper—*La Plebe* (The Populace), which he began publishing in Philadelphia on August 24, 1907. His timing could not have been worse. The economy was on the verge of a severe depression (1907–1908), yet on the basis of his reputation alone, Tresca's newspaper attracted 500 subscribers before commencing publication.[9] *La Plebe*'s office was located initially at 823 Catherine Street but moved six months later to 1029 S. 8th Street, both in the heart of South Philadelphia's Italian district. Some FSI members assumed *La Plebe* would serve as a federation organ under the direction of the local FSI section. Tresca's first issue sent a jolting message to those who coveted control: "I do not ask official recognition of any party."[10] And to leave no doubt, *La Plebe*'s masthead proclaimed itself: "Not in the service of personal cliques nor subject to the tyranny of a party, [but] in combat for the Ideal against priests, bosses, and *camorre*."[11] Liberated from FSI obligations and constraints, Tresca finally assumed the role for which his talents and temperament were best suited—Italian American radicalism's "freelance of revolution."[12]

"La Signorina"

Barely six months after launching *La Plebe*, Tresca was once more embroiled in legal trouble, but of a different sort than usual. On February 16, 1908, he was arrested for "disorderly conduct," having been caught *flagrante delicto* in a Philadelphia hotel room with Marietta Di Antonio, a girl under sixteen years of age, who had been teaching him English. Although the relationship had been consensual, Tresca was indicted on a long list of charges: assault and battery, aggravated assault and battery, assault and battery to ravish, rape, and adultery.[13] Released on $1,000 bail, Tresca claimed that one of Philadelphia's *prominenti*, Fioravante Baldi, and local priests had pressured her into giving the authorities a more damaging version of what had transpired between them.[14] Considering how intensely Tresca was hated by the local *prominenti* and clergy, his suggestion of behind-the-scenes machinations was certainly credible. More likely, the girl's father, bent on revenge and salvaging her honor, had denounced Tresca to the authorities as a violent predator.[15] Tresca's misadventure provided a juicy scandal for staid Philadelphia. The American press depicted him as a "Black Hander," child kidnapper, and worse.[16] Tresca's enemies among the *promimenti* and clergy took delight in his predicament, and even the *sovversivi*—just as conventional as non-radicals in matters of sexual conduct—were dismayed by his behavior, if not as vocal as the opposition. The incident became a permanent stain on Tresca's record.

For several months, *La Plebe* was issued with Helga's name listed as the publisher, in hope of minimizing the damage to the newspaper that might result from the scandal and the criminal proceedings facing Tresca. Subscription payments and contributions to *La Plebe* did fall off dramatically; however, the cause was the economic depression of that year, which plunged thousands of Italians immigrants into desperate straits. In August 1908, hoping to obtain new supporters, avoid harassment from postal authorities, and no doubt escape the spotlight of scandal, Tresca transferred *La Plebe* to Pittsburgh. The office was set up at 8 Tunnel Street. He and Helga resided briefly at 712 Webster Avenue, and later at 204 Robinson Street, in a home owned by an English woman.[17]

"The Republic of Priests"

Pittsburgh was an ideal base of operations for Tresca, whose labor activities now focused primarily on the coal fields of western Pennsylvania. But Pittsburgh and the nearby mining regions harbored difficulties and dangers that Philadelphia did not. The American coal, steel, and aluminum barons dominated the region like feudal lords, and the Italian *camorra colonia* wielded more power than their counterparts in Philadelphia and were much more aggressive about retaining it. The law was whatever the magnates and their satraps said it was, and those who resisted were likely to end up in jail or dead.

The *sovversivi* had acquired a substantial following among the Italian coal miners of western Pennsylvania, but the FSI section in Pittsburgh was far weaker than its Philadelphia counterpart, having been organized only in 1906 or 1907. Tresca's arrival, therefore, caused immediate alarm among local consular officials, priests, and *prominenti*. The Italian ambassador, Mayor des Planches, notified the postmaster general in Washington of Tresca's presence in Pittsburgh, hoping to suppress *La Plebe* through postal interference and financial ruin.[18] Since the 19th century, subversive newspapers were stifled through repeated confiscation of offending issues. The Postal Office Department soon found a pretext to intervene— the absence of a "legitimate list of subscribers."[19] In addition, postal authorities increased the pressure by forcing Tresca to submit "true translations" of entire issues to determine if they violated a new measure President Theodore Roosevelt signed into law on May 27, 1908, establishing political criteria by which newspapers could be barred from the mails. Tresca eventually obtained third-class mailing privileges, which slowed delivery of *La Plebe* to its 3,000 subscribers but enabled the newspaper to survive.[20]

Despite the certainty of retaliation, Tresca attacked the *camorra coloniale* with greater fervor and recklessness than he had in Philadelphia. The consul general of Philadelphia singled out Tresca and *La Plebe* from other Italian American subversive newspapers:

> *La Plebe*, an anarchistic weekly published in Pittsburgh, engages in very active subversive propaganda and is especially noteworthy for its systematic incitement to anti-militarism and draft evasion. With greater audacity than other periodicals, [*La Plebe*] is distinguished by its violence, insults, and systematic defamation of public officials and private citizens.[21]

Tresca was a staunch anti-militarist. His concern was for the young Italian-immigrant men who were not naturalized citizens. Unless they obtained deferments by bribing a consular officer (a regular practice), they were subject to conscription into the Italian army, where conditions and discipline were especially harsh. As a humanitarian, Tresca opposed the conscription of young workers and peasants to serve as cannon fodder in the interests of bourgeois capitalists, and he denounced military service as a form of slavery. As a revolutionary, Tresca understood that a primary function of armies was to suppress proletarian rebellion. Converting working-class soldiers to the cause of revolution was therefore imperative, and in his pamphlet *Non Ti Fare Soldato* (Don't Be A Soldier), published in 1909, he expressed the hope "that when the revolutionary idea has broken through the walls of the barracks, the rifles may shoot, but no longer against the strikers!"[22]

Although his anti-militarism remained constant, Tresca delighted more in attacking the *maiali neri* (black hogs) of the Catholic Church, who were so powerful in Pittsburgh that he dubbed the city the "republic of priests."[23] Conflict between Italian radicals and the priesthood in Pittsburgh had recently escalated, and the Church enlisted the support of secular authorities to assist them. The police raided several Italian bookstores that sold radical newspapers and other literature on November 30, 1907.[24] The episodes of repression in Pittsburgh were part of a larger campaign waged at this time by the Catholic Church against its ideological enemies. Typically, in February 1908, complaints from the archbishop of New York and the apostolic nuncio to Washington prompted Anthony Comstock, head of the Society for the Prevention of Vice, to arrest the owner of the S. F. Vanni bookstore in New York City—a cultural institution of the *colonia italiana*—on the grounds that the Italian anti-clerical newspapers he sold were pornographic and sacrilegious.[25] Such episodes characterized the "Red Scare" of 1908, the campaign of political and cultural repression encouraged by Theodore Roosevelt.[26]

The institution created by the *sovversivi* to counter the Church's stultifying control over the minds of immigrants was the *Università Popolare*, an informal school where qualified volunteers provided instruction in a wide range of subjects. Tresca had been instrumental in founding the *Università Popolare* in Philadelphia in January 1908 and one in Pittsburgh a year later.[27] His brother Ettore was the featured speaker at both inaugurals. The curriculum of the *Università Popolare* was not necessarily radical (Ettore, for example, lectured on the structure and function of the human body), but it was unswervingly rationalist and materialist, intellectual propensities deemed subversive by the Vatican, which still clung to the anti-modernist tenets of the "Syllabus of Errors" of 1866, and was determined to eradicate modernist tendencies within the Church itself. To achieve the latter, Pope Pius X issued the "Syllabus Lamentabili Sane" of July 1907 and the "Encyclical Pascendi Domini Gregis" of September 1907.[28] The *Università Popolare*, in contrast, could reach only a tiny segment of the Italian immigrant working class, and to undermine the Church's strength and influence by means of secular education would take generations, if not centuries.

Unwilling to wait that long, Tresca resorted to a favorite tactic employed by Italian anti-clericals: attack the Church by discrediting the priesthood, especially with revelations of sexual misconduct. On the Richter Scale of Italian moral indignation, the sexual transgressions of a priest would hardly register as an earthquake, provided they were heterosexual. Italians, for the most part, regarded male celibacy as unnatural, and the sexual peccadilloes of priests were widely regarded as inevitable and no cause for consternation. Yet, in the United States, where German and Irish Catholics controlled the Church—and considered Italians half-pagan in any case—a sex scandal involving a priest was guaranteed to outrage the hierarchy and shock the naïve among the flock. That Tresca himself was hardly a paragon of moral rectitude in matters of sexual conduct never gave him pause (after all, he had not taken a vow of celibacy), and he hastened to employ his considerable muckraking skills to unearth the dirt the *"maiali neri"* were determined to hide.

The material for his first exposé of a wayward priest, the Rev. Di Sabato of Connellsville, Pa., was allegedly furnished to him by a rival cleric who hoped to acquire his colleague's parish.[29] The incriminating evidence was a photograph of the handsome young priest reclining on a sofa with his head nestled comfortably against the breast of his lovely "housekeeper," whose left arm embraced him around the neck while her right hand upheld a perched parrot. The compromising photograph was printed in *La Plebe* and *Il Proletario*, and to ensure widespread distribution throughout the Italian community, Tresca had the photo reprinted on the back of postcards.[30] Verbal accusations could be rebutted, but a photograph defied easy denial and hit the Catholic community like a bombshell.[31]

For his act of sacrilege, Tresca was anathematized by the Pittsburgh hierarchy, arrested by the police, and sued for libel by the Rev. Di Sabato and his paramour. At his trial in Uniontown on December 18–19, 1908, Tresca established the authenticity of the photograph (taken by the priest himself) and further sullied the priest's character by identifying an unwed mother and child whom the priest had abandoned in New Kensington, PA. The Rev. Di Sabato lost his case, but the jury found Tresca guilty of libeling the priest's lady friend. The judge remanded sentencing for a month, and Tresca returned home confident that his punishment would amount to no more than a small fine.[32]

The *Camorra Coloniale* Strikes Back

That Tresca's enemies would attempt to silence him was inevitable. In December 1908, he received a visit from a leader of the local *Mano Nera* (Black Hand), a loose network of gangs engaged in racketeering and extortion, who advised him to ensure his good health by rejoining Ettore in New York City. Undeterred by this death threat, Tresca warned the gangster that he had better shoot straight. Several weeks passed without incident. Then, on January 7, 1909, after leaving his office with an acquaintance and walking toward a restaurant for lunch, Tresca was seized from behind by an assailant wielding a razor. The next split second remained fixed in his memory:

> The job would have been done perfectly but for the fact that I was able to realize what was coming as soon as I felt a strange hand over my cheek. As a defensive move I pressed my chin against my breast. The razor, instead of operating on my neck, as intended, started to work on my upper [right] lip and, coming down it, found resistance on the jaw, so much so that the blade was broken when it reached the jugular vein, which was left untouched.[33]

Bleeding profusely, Tresca grappled with his attacker until a policeman arrived on the scene and placed the culprit under arrest. He staggered into a drugstore in search of help, but another policeman, suspecting him being a "Black Hander," dragged him to the police station, where he collapsed from loss of blood. When finally brought to a hospital, twenty-six stitches—sutured aggressively by a hostile doctor—were required to close the wound.[34]

Tresca's would-be assassin was a petty gangster named Michele Giordano who had been paid $500 for his services. Several enemies hated Tresca enough to want him dead, but suspicion pointed to Mariano Cancelliere, the owner of the conservative newspaper *La Trinacria* of Pittsburgh, whom Tresca had attacked repeatedly in *Il Proletario* and *La Plebe,* and whose conviction for fraud in Italy he revealed when the latter testified as a character witness against him at his Uniontown trial.[35] Years later, Tresca attributed responsibility to a conspiracy hatched between the local clergy, Italian vice-consul Natali of Pittsburgh, whom he had accused of graft and corruption, and the Black Hand.[36]

Tresca's life remained trouble free for only two weeks after the assassination attempt. When his brother Ettore visited Pittsburgh to treat his infected wound, he brought news that Don Filippo had died in Sulmona. Tresca was haunted by thoughts that he had shortened Don Filippo's life by causing him so much worry and stress over the years. But he had no time for mourning. The next day, January 21, 1909, Tresca was scheduled for sentencing in the Di Sabato case. Instead of the $50 fine previously agreed upon by the trial judge and Tresca's lawyer, Tresca was condemned to serve six months in jail and pay a $500 fine for having libeled the priest's lady friend. "The all-powerful Catholic Church," he believed, "had dictated the heavy sentence."[37]

This latest incarceration, coming so soon after Don Filippo's death, plunged Tresca into an emotional depression all the more severe because the precarious state of his finances now threatened the well being of his family and the future of *La Plebe.* Sharing his feelings of despair with Umberto Poggi, the sympathetic new director of *Il Proletario,* Tresca wrote: "This is a grievous period I am going through, my dear Poggi. I believed I would go mad."[38] But this "grievous period" had a quick and unusual ending. Local Protestant groups and the Uniontown press had concluded that the severity of the sentence was the result of pressure from the Catholic Church. Fearing public outrage, the trial judge reconsidered the case and commuted Tresca's sentence to time already served. Thus he was back in action after only fifteen days.[39]

Pittsburgh police, meanwhile, had made no effort to pursue Giordano or discover the culprits behind the murder attempt. It was Tresca and his lawyer who traced Giordano to a small mining town in West Virginia. At Giordano's trial, his lawyer did not mount a defense of his client but focused his attack upon the victim. He asked Tresca if he believed in God, if he feared Hell, and if he was an anarchist. Then, holding an issue of *La Plebe* aloft, he accused Tresca of being an anarchist who published articles against God. The good Christians who comprised the jury found Giordano not guilty.[40] But Giordano eventually met his end at the hands of an Italian coal miner, who avenged the attack against Tresca.

Tresca's more immediate concern was his sexual misconduct trial in Philadelphia on April 14, 1909. The most serious charges against him were dropped after Marietta acknowledged that their affair had been consensual. Tresca pleaded guilty instead to adultery and was sentenced to serve nine months in the county prison. Bertelli, now publishing *La Parola dei Socialisti* in Chicago, was delighted, and attacked Tresca for his immorality. Tresca's friend Poggi counter-attacked in *Il Proletario*, alleging that Bertelli frequented brothels in Philadelphia, always leaving behind a photo-calling card that identified him as the "Leader of the Socialists."[41]

Helga

During his imprisonment from April 1909 to January 1910, Tresca was greatly concerned about the welfare of his wife and child and the survival of *La Plebe*. The burden of managing the newspaper in his absence fell entirely upon Helga. Far from being a "good Italian wife who cooked spaghetti and was a model housekeeper,"[42] the condescending portrait of her depicted by Elizabeth Gurley Flynn, Helga proved to be a woman of considerable ability and resilience. Married life with Tresca was difficult under the best of circumstances, spending days and weeks alone while he was away on propaganda tours, and never knowing whether he would land in jail or the cemetery. During his absences, besides caring for her young Beatrice and giving aid to the overburdened wives of local workers, Helga performed many functions to sustain *La Plebe*, including writing articles and giving lectures. When Tresca was arrested for his affair with young Marietta, Helga made a public demonstration of solidarity with her husband.[43]

Nevertheless, she had been emotionally wounded by Tresca's infidelity and the humiliating publicity. She probably would have left him if her family would have welcomed her back. However, after an exploratory letter to her father—perhaps the first since her elopement—Helga was coldly rebuffed and told to remain with her husband in America. Lonely and depressed, Helga found solace in the arms of Joe Ettor, executive board member and chief organizer for the IWW, who was active in the steel workers strike then in progress at nearby McKees Rocks. This was not a casual liaison. Helga's feelings for Ettor grew deep, and she might have left Tresca if a stable relationship with her lover were possible. But Ettor's career offered neither stability nor permanence, and the affair ended when Tresca was released from prison. Tresca apparently knew or learned of Helga's dalliance with Ettor and accepted it with equanimity, according to his daughter.[44] Yet it is hard to believe that his Italian male ego did not harbor resentment toward Ettor.

L'Avvenire

Helga's efforts to save *La Plebe* ultimately failed. The Postal Office Department once again had deprived *La Plebe* of discounted mailing privileges, at the behest of the apostolico nuncio in Washington, according to Tresca. The cost of mailing the newspaper plus the bills accrued from his court case placed a huge burden on Tresca and his family. *Il Proletario* helped by raising over $800 for his legal expenses, but by July 1909, *La Plebe* had ceased publishing.[45]

But soon, with the assistance of Tresca's good friend, Giuseppe Zavarella, who obtained a second-class mailing permit as the newspaper's nominal publisher, Helga transferred the newspaper to Steubenville, Ohio, where it was resurrected on July 24, 1909 under the name of *L'Avvenire* (The Future). When Tresca was released in January 1910, he transferred his family and *L'Avvenire* to New Kensington, a grimy aluminum-producing town twenty miles northeast of Pittsburgh with a sizeable FSI section led by Antonio Mariella. A new series of *L'Avvenire* was launched on August 20, 1910, and for the next three years, with Mariella fronting as publisher, Tresca continued his operations in New Kensington and opened a branch office in Pittsburgh.[46]

The Westmoreland Strike

Once out of prison, Tresca resumed his activities among Italian coal miners, many of whom had by now formed scores of radical groups and circles in Pennsylvania, Illinois, Ohio, Kansas, Oklahoma, Colorado, New Mexico, and Nevada.[47] In fact, coal miners constituted one of the largest and most militant contingents of the Italian immigrant Left, and it was among their ranks that Tresca derived his strongest support. The highest concentrations of Italian coal miners were located in the anthracite region of eastern Pennsylvania and the bituminous region of the state's western counties. By 1910, some 60,000 Italians in Pennsylvania were dependent upon the mines for their material existence, which meant living in abject poverty.[48] For Tresca, Italian coal miners represented an army of disinherited plebes for whom he might serve as revolutionary leader. His first expressions of solidarity dated from the coal miners' strike in Colorado and Utah in 1904, but his special bond with them was forged during the early propaganda tours of 1906. By 1910, Tresca was ready for more direct action at their head.

The message Tresca spread in the coal fields was one of resistance—not only against the mine owners, but against the United Mine Workers of America (UMWA). The UMWA was an industrial union dominated by conservative leaders who accepted the wage system as "a natural and necessary part of our industrial system," in the words of its first president, John B. Rae.[49] Although the union included a radical minority, the UMWA's official philosophy of class collaboration, in Tresca's view, qualified it as ally of capitalism rather than an instrument for its overthrow. Ever since the Colorado miners' strike of 1904 was squelched, Tresca harbored a special antipathy for UMWA president, John Mitchell, the quintessential labor bureaucrat and power-broker. Tresca condemned Mitchell's and his successors' practice of honoring accords and reaching settlements with coal operators in one district while miners in another were out on strike. He was appalled by Mitchell's handling of the coal strikes of April–May 1906, which saw the UMWA accept meager gains for bituminous miners in western Pennsylvania while anthracite miners in the eastern districts struggled alone and without assistance before capitulating. Why, Tresca asked, had the UMWA failed to conduct a general strike of miners instead of confronting the operators with limited and sporadic resistance? And why had strike action begun during the spring, when companies had large stock piles of coal and consumer demand was low? For Tresca such tactics smacked not of ineptitude but sell-out. Henceforth he referred to Mitchell as the "lord and master of the art of betrayal" and worse.[50]

In the wake of the 1906 strikes, Italian coal miners in western Pennsylvania offered Tresca the directorship of Il Minatore, a newspaper they planned to publish in Pittsburgh that would oppose UMWA leaders and urge miners to embrace the philosophy and tactics of class struggle. Tresca turned down the offer and recommended instead that the Italian miners organize local sections for the IWW.[51] But the IWW never conducted a serious campaign to organize coal miners in Pennsylvania.[52] So from 1906 through 1911, Tresca's activities among Italian coal miners were conducted without assistance from a sympathetic labor union or political party.

His best opportunities for revolutionary propaganda and labor agitation occurred during the great Westmoreland strike of March 1910–July 1911. Westmoreland county provided more bituminous coal than any other, but productivity never benefited local, non-union miners, who worked more hours and were paid appreciably less than their counterparts in the unionized Pittsburgh district nearby. The UMWA's success in organizing coal miners was spotty. The thirty coal operators in Westmoreland had defeated every attempt by miners to organize since 1890. To the operators and the UMWA, therefore, the primary issue of contention was unionism.[53] However, an Italian anarchist miner from Latrobe, in the heart of Westmoreland, stated the real objective of the miners: they "wanted above all to be treated like men, not beasts,"[54] a consideration largely ignored by the operators and UMWA leaders alike.

Miners of the Keystone Coal & Coke Co., around Greensburg, walked out on strike on March 10, 1910, demanding the reinstatement of a few hundred men discharged for organizing a union local, a pay increase, and a reduction of the work day. By the end of May, the strike encompassed all of Westmoreland save for the Connellsville area in the south, where the UMWA feared to antagonize the powerful Frick Coal & Coke Co., which supplied coke to U.S. Steel in Pittsburgh. During the next sixteen months, sixty-five collieries belonging to thirty coal operators of Westmoreland were struck. Company records indicated that strikers numbered 10,631 out of 15,537 miners; the president of UMWA District 5 (Pittsburgh) placed the figure at 18,000. The majority were Slavs and Italians.[55]

The owners reacted quickly and ruthlessly, evicting strikers from company houses. The UMWA provided tent camps and shanties on leased ground and weekly relief benefits; however, these measures barely prevented the strikers from freezing and starving. As was also customary, the owners hired thousands of scabs—mainly non-English speaking immigrants who frequently did not know a strike was in progress. To protect the scabs and intimidate strikers, the companies mobilized a small army comprising the state coal and iron police, deputy sheriffs, deputy constables, and the state police—all but the last paid by the owners. Company property, which included streets and roads in mining towns, was posted, and injunctions against the UMWA and strikers—readily provided by the courts—prohibited strikers from assembling near or marching past the mines lest they threaten scabs at work. Around 1,000 strikers were arrested and charged with trespass, disorderly conduct, or violent acts; most were fined or imprisoned by local justices of the peace. Deputies and constables who committed acts of violence against strikers were rarely arrested. Officially, ten deaths resulted from clashes between miners and company constabulary, but the toll was probably higher.[56]

Reports by radical Italian miners describing the strike read like the letters of soldiers under siege, defiant in the face of the enemy but sensing intuitively that help would never come. Their depictions of how the strikers suffered were especially grim. From Loyal Hanna, Guido Lanfranco wrote: "There cannot be a mining district more wretched that this. The slavery to which we are subjected is something from another world."[57] The brutality inflicted upon the miners by the constabulary was a more frequent theme than economic privation. "From the day the strike was declared the miners have been victims of the bosses' most contemptuous rage," wrote Paolo Valentini of Rillton.[58] "I cannot describe for you the outrageous and cowardly acts committed against us by the ferocious police of this state. Insults, kicks, beatings are the order of the day," noted Lanfranco in another account.[59] L. Giacometti reported that "conditions have become steadily more wretched because of the abuse and violence committed against us. We can neither walk nor stand still. As soon as they [deputy sheriffs] encounter a group of 30 strikers, they point revolvers at their throats and force them to flee."[60] At the end of January 1911, Lanfranco described the miners as still suffering terribly but unbowed: "We have had comrades wounded and our women mistreated and imprisoned, without any pity for their children; we have suffered misery and hunger, but they have not yet succeeded in breaking our fighting strength, and we will continue to hold the line until victory is complete."[61]

The plight of the miners progressively worsened in 1911. The UMWA, its coffers depleted from strikes in Ohio, Illinois, and the southwestern states, had provided little relief during the first five months of the strike and only minimal support thereafter. The reason was not only financial. UMWA president Thomas L. Lewis, who believed that "differences existing between the employer and the employee in the mining industry should be settled without resorting to strikes," had opposed the "stampede strike" in Westmoreland from the outset.[62] Local responsibility for sending union organizers into Westmoreland rested with the president of District 5, Francis Feehan, who since 1906 had resisted every request from Westmoreland miners to lead them in a strike. His motivation for supporting the strike of 1910–1911 was most likely opportunistic. By encouraging a strike in Westmoreland, Feehan was able to deny the Pittsburgh market an alternative source of coal, so when demand and prices rose, the operators in District 5 saw a chance to increase profits at the expense of Westmoreland competitors and signed news contracts with the UMWA in April 1911. By then, Feehan had been accused of collusion with local coal operators and expelled as president of District 5. He subsequently became engaged in a fierce battle with his rival Robert Gibbons to regain control of his old fiefdom.[63] For UMWA leaders, intrigue and rivalry completely superseded the interests of the striking miners.[64]

The IWW was effusive with criticism of the UMWA's handling of the strike, but failed to furnish aid in the form of strike leaders or money.[65] The syndicalists of the FSI and the social democrats who formed a rival federation in July 1910 were equally remiss. The only Italian radical leader seriously involved in the Westmoreland strike was Tresca, who performed his customary role as roving propagandist and independent agitator. Because he had no official association with the strike, the UMWA tolerated Tresca's presence but occasionally reprimanded him for his audacity and the revolutionary nature of his speeches.[66] Not that Tresca cared a jot. His already low opinion of the UMWA quickly developed into unbridled contempt. "The local officials of the UMWA," he maintained, "were all tools of the competing coal companies, and the strike was in progress not for the benefit of the miners, but as part of the game of rivalry among the mine barons… to weaken and overpower their competitors."[67] Posing as an aide to Armando Palizzari, a syndicalist and one of the few Italian organizers employed by the UMWA, Tresca visited the hangouts of the union officials who were supposedly leading the strike. "It was with disgust that I mingled with such low and repulsive creatures," he wrote. "They were all gathered every day in a saloon, where I found them all drunk and happy, with no regret for the misery, want, and disgrace that their betrayal was bringing to the miners."[68]

Tresca's first speech exhorting Italian miners to action was delivered in Greensburg, the strike's epicenter, on March 20, 1910, a few days after the walkout began. A local miner described the event: "We cannot convey the satisfaction of the comrades in again seeing the scourge of the *camorre*. He spoke to great applause before a large audience gathered to demonstrate how much affection the workers feel for him. His calm and clear words left a profound impression on the listeners."[69] Thereafter, Tresca spoke regularly to Italian miners at several Westmoreland towns and other mining communities within the Pittsburgh orbit. He also generated financial and moral support for the strikers at his lectures in Pittsburgh, New Kensington, and Chicago.[70]

Functioning as an independent strike leader required great courage. The deputy sheriffs and other hired guns, whose task was to brutalize and intimidate, might have killed or injured Tresca at any time. But Tresca confronted them face to face on many occasions. His comrade, Giulio Mazza, a miner from Irwin, recalled one encounter during which a sheriff and his deputies positioned themselves in front of a group of marchers led by Tresca and gave orders to stop. Tresca grabbed the sheriff bodily and tossed him aside, allowing the strikers to continue their march.[71] On another occasion, when Tresca harangued Italian miners at a small camp near Irwin on May 2, 1910, a group of mounted constables—referred to as "Cossacks" by the miners—approached the crowd menacingly. One of them spotted Tresca, took aim with his revolver, and fired. Tresca might have been killed if Mazza had not pushed him down, himself receiving a leg wound from the bullet intended for his friend. The "Cossacks" then charged the crowd, beating strikers with their clubs and trampling the fallen with their horses. Tresca recalled that during this encounter, "the officials of the United Mine Workers were there, in the city of Pittsburgh, in a smoky, crowded saloon, drinking."[72]

Tresca believed that the UMWA would sellout the strikers, and had been advising Italian miners for several months to leave Westmoreland. Some heeded his recommendation, going mainly to Illinois, where Tresca had spoken on several occasions and the coal miners had won a five-month strike in September 1910. But thousands of the Italian strikers remained in Westmoreland, fighting for a victory they could never achieve.[73] Tresca's suspicions were confirmed when UMWA president Lewis declared at the union's convention in January 1911 that the strike had been ill-conceived, that union funds spent on the strike had been wasted, and that the fault lay with the miners themselves for having followed poor advice and leadership.[74]

The UMWA officially called off the strike on June 27, 1911. The Westmoreland miners returned to work under the same conditions that predated the walk out. Not a single demand had been granted by the operators. The UMWA's defeat was almost as severe. The union spent $1,064,865 on the strike but had nothing to show for its effort. The twenty-three locals organized during the spring and summer of 1910 ceased to exist soon after the strike ended. Even more detrimental to the future of unionism in Westmoreland was the disillusionment with the UMWA experienced by most of the foreign-born miners, who had comprised more than seventy percent of the strikers.[75] By every measure, the Westmoreland strike was a major setback for coal miners and industrial unionism. Tresca, however, earned a rare expression of appreciation from Edmondo Rossoni, the FSI's official propagandist, who affirmed that the movement's growth in Pennsylvania and its miners had "resulted from the will and work of one man"—Tresca.[76]

Anti-Clericalism Revived

Activity during the Westmoreland strike had not deterred Tresca's campaign against the Catholic Church. This latest confrontation represented more than his personal hostility toward religion and priests. A new wave of anti-clericalism had been generated among radicals, liberals, and free thinkers in the wake of Francisco Ferrer's execution in Spain. An anarchist, Ferrer had founded the *Escuela Moderna* in 1901, a modern school where rationalist education challenged the dogmas and authority of Church and State. Determined to eradicate the threat he presented, Spanish authorities arrested Ferrer after the *Semana Tragica* (July 24–August 1, 1909), a large-scale insurrection waged in Barcelona against conscription and war in Morocco. Charged as the "author and chief" of the rebellion, Ferrer was tried by a military tribunal and executed by firing squad on October 13, 1909.[77]

For Tresca and the *sovversivi*, Ferrer's martyrdom was an atrocity comparable to the burning of Giordano Bruno in 1600, another demonstration of the Church's inquisitional spirit, blind intolerance, and inexorable determination to suffocate free thought. That Ferrer's execution had taken place in reactionary Spain made no difference. To Tresca's thinking, the Catholic Church was a single entity, a hydra-headed monster to be fought everywhere with unflagging vigor. The United States now loomed as an important field of action upon which to confront the enemy. At stake were the hearts and minds of Italian immigrants, among whom faithful Catholics still vastly outnumbered radicals and freethinkers.[78]

The anticlerical spirit of *L'Avvenire* intensified, and Tresca's methods of provoking the ire of his adversaries became more inventive. Regularly featured was a column entitled "In the Black World," which chronicled the misdeeds of the *maiali neri* throughout the world. Another column, entitled "Without Priests," periodically announced the birth of an Italian child who would not be christened or subjected "to the perverted education of the priests," but raised to become a "champion of free thought," a "rebel who is to have the kiss of the sun for his baptism, humanity for his faith, and the universe for his fatherland."[79] Tresca's efforts against baptism had implications for the *sovversivi* as well as apolitical Italians. Many *sovversivi*, despite their professed atheism and anti-clericalism, continued to baptize their children, offering various rationalizations for their contradictory behavior: to prevent their children from being stigmatized; to legitimize their legal status as Italians should they return to the Old Country; and, above all, to placate their wives, the great majority of whom were not radicals. Only the more sophisticated among the *sovversivi* understood that baptism was the first step in a process of "normalization" that resulted inevitably in the loss of a potential recruit for the movement.[80]

Tresca, meanwhile, with Ferrer's martyrdom as his point of reference, intensified his attacks against the Catholic Church not only in *L'Avvenire* but at the anti-clerical rallies that multiplied in Pittsburgh, New Kensington, and the mining towns of western Pennsylvania, where local priests served as some of the coal operators' best allies.[81] Retaliation by the Church hierarchy of Pittsburgh was inevitable. One the clerics who denounced him was the Reverend Vincenzo Marinaro of Butler, PA, where Tresca had spoken against the Church on several occasions. Tresca retaliated with a lurid story in *L'Avvenire*, charging that "The Priest of Butler, Pa." had fathered a child with one of his devotees in Italy and forced the woman to murder the fruit of their illicit union. Although the article was unsigned and did not mention Marinaro by name, the priest filed a libel suit against Tresca in July 1910. That month, Tresca was arrested and released on bail pending trial in Pittsburgh's Criminal Court on October 20–21, 1910.[82]

What transpired left no doubt that Marinaro's libel suit had been orchestrated by the Pittsburgh diocese to silence him. Before the case went to trial, the Reverend Carmelo Falconi of Sharpsburg, PA, who previously ran a church in Charleroi that Tresca threatened to destroy, had conducted an investigation of Tresca's radical activities and earlier brushes with the law in Philadelphia for use against him in court.[83] At trial, the prosecutor was hardly concerned with establishing Tresca's authorship of "The Priest of Butler, Pa." or its libelous nature. His strategy was to introduce into evidence anticlerical and other subversive articles signed by Tresca. By exposing Tresca's subversive ideas and activities, he hoped the anti-radical prejudice of the judge and jury would do the rest.[84] When Tresca took the stand in his own defense, the prosecutor objected that the accused should not be allowed to testify because he was an atheist and would not fear God's punishment if he lied. Questioned by the judge as to whether he believed in God and feared His wrath, Tresca disdainfully refused to reply. The jury returned a guilty verdict after deliberating just a few minutes. On November 5, 1910, Judge D. Carnahan sentenced Tresca to the maximum sentence allowable: nine months imprisonment, $300 fine, and the costs of the trial. A few days later, he was released from jail under $3,000 bail, pending appeal of his conviction.[85]

The verdict was no surprise to Tresca. "I have always had the full conviction," he wrote, "that the priests… of this diocese of Pittsburgh have been intriguing, praying, conjuring for months to obtain the much-desired condemnation…. The priests were seized, almost before the end of the sentence, with demoniacal hysterics, epileptic convulsions, and danced like St. Vitus whom they adore, whom they have placed upon their altars." However, he hastened to assure "the crew in cassocks" that their "sacred and furious joy" would be short lived. Even if obliged to serve nine months, "I shall return to the same post of combat and I shall empty other churches for you… as I did to that at Connellsville." [86]

Relations with the FSI

Persecution by the Catholic Church only enhanced Tresca's reputation as a *mangiaprete* (priest eater) and burnished his rising star as the revolutionary freelance of the Italian immigrant Left. Tresca's growing prestige had not been lost on the syndicalists of the FSI, who now sought to reclaim him as their own. Whether Tresca rejoined the FSI is uncertain.[87] However, reconciliation between Tresca and the FSI did not begin until after Bertelli was ousted as director of *Il Proletario* in 1907, and the syndicalists increased their domination of the FSI's executive committee. To acknowledge Tresca's outstanding achievements in Pennsylvania, the Pittsburgh members of the FSI elected him (together with Pietro Allegra, his closest friend and associate) to represent the section at the federation's national congress in Utica, New York, on April 2–4, 1911.[88]

The Utica Congress was convened primarily to formalize the schism between revolutionary syndicalists and parliamentary socialists, a process that by now was a *fait accompli*. A similar break between the two factions had already taken place within the PSI in Italy. By 1908, the revolutionary syndicalists had quit the party in disgust with the parliamentary politics of the reformists, focusing their militant efforts instead on the labor movement. Their departure left the reformist socialists—led by Turati, Claudio Treves, and Ivanoe Bonomi—as the majority and controlling faction of the PSI until 1912, when the left-wing revolutionaries captured the leadership of the party, with Mussolini as their official spokesman. In contrast, it was the reformists who had progressively defected from the FSI in the United States, leaving the revolutionary syndicalists in control of *Il Proletario* and the federation's executive committee by 1908. The exodus of reformists accelerated that same year when the IWW, which the FSI officially supported, had formally rejected alliances with all political parties, a position unacceptable to those socialists still devoted to parliamentary politics. To establish an official voice, the reformists in February 1908 launched *La Parola dei Socialisti* in Chicago under the directorship of Giuseppe Bertelli, an appointment that assured an acrimonious rivalry with the revolutionary syndicalists. The publication of *La Parola dei Socialisti* was followed by the founding of the reformists' own Federazione Socialista Italiana in New York on July 30, 1910. Claiming a membership of 1,000, the social democratic FSI affiliated itself directly with the SPA, and *La Parola dei Socialisti* became an official organ of the party. With few reformists collaborating with *Il Proletario* or concerning themselves with the affairs of the senior FSI, the Utica congress was attended primarily by revolutionary syndicalists, who adopted Edmondo Rossoni's resolution declaring revolutionary syndicalism—"the true and genuine expression of socialism"—as the official ideology of the FSI.[89]

Tresca played an important role at the Utica congress, aligning himself with the revolutionary syndicalists of the far left. His speech included a blistering critique of the state, parliamentarism, and universal suffrage. The latter was a "lie and a fraud," an "immoral swindle," based on the fiction of political equality, serving to perpetuate bourgeois interests and economic inequality. "Social revolution," he declared, "proceeds only through the economic struggle of labor unions."[90] After the congress, Tresca wrote that the Utica delegates had sought to transform the FSI from an organization "which had always been restricted within the sphere of evangelical propaganda for the masses" into "a vanguard revolutionary party" that would "create those proletarian organs that will be the guide and protection of the immigrants…, [and] spur the trade unions toward the class struggle to abolish the wage system."[91] For the revolutionary syndicalists, the opportunity to demonstrate the tactical shift from evangelical propaganda to direct action came with the textile workers strike of January 11–March 12, 1912, in Lawrence, Massachusetts, the famous labor conflict which proved to be the FSI's finest hour. But the opportunity to participate in this epic struggle was denied to Tresca. Pennsylvania's Superior Court had reversed his conviction and ordered a new trial in the Court of Common Pleas, but this second trial of June 6, 1911, Tresca recalled, "was still simpler and speedier than the first," resulting again in conviction and the same sentence.[92]

Finding himself once again "in the same crowd of cursing people, of brutalized men, of ignorant, vulgar and beastly keepers," Tresca had no one with whom he could converse intelligently or otherwise spend time, a genuine hardship for someone as gregarious and fun loving as he. As the months passed, he longed for "light for my agitated and imprisoned soul: bread for my mind that was getting lost in the fog of misery and degradation that surrounded me." The spiritual burden of incarceration was eased when news reached him of the great strike underway at Lawrence. "My cell was no longer my tomb," he recalled. "It was populated by marching strikers, speaking leaders and clubbing policemen and resounded with revolutionary songs of Labor and Faith." Tresca longed for the call that would summon him to Lawrence. It came within days of his release in March 1912, precipitating changes in his life and career he could not possibly have imagined while languishing in the Allegheny County Jail.[93]

4

Lawrence

On January 11, 1912, after mill owners cut wages in response to a state-mandated cut in the hours women and children were permitted to work, Polish, Italian, and Lithuanian mill hands—many of them women—spontaneously rebelled by shutting down their looms, slashing power belts, and exiting the mills in protest.[1] Anticipating a long strike, Angelo Rocco, secretary of Local 20's Italian branch of the National Industrial Union of Textile Workers, an IWW affiliate, requested Joe Ettor to mobilize the workers under the leadership of the IWW. Only twenty-six years old, with a shock of curly black hair and a cherubic smile, Ettor looked more like a mischievous street urchin than a fiery labor agitator and the IWW's principal organizer for its eastern branches. Born to Italian parents in Brooklyn, in 1886, Ettor grew up in Chicago and California and joined the SPA while still a teenager, laboring as an iron worker in a San Francisco shipyard. He joined the IWW in 1905 and served as an organizer among West Coast lumbermen, miners, railroad workers, and construction gangs. Elected to the IWW's general executive council in 1908, Ettor moved East the following year. His proficiency with foreign languages (he was fluent in English and Italian, and understood Polish, Yiddish, and Hungarian) proved invaluable when dealing with immigrant workers such as those in Lawrence. The strike would prove the greatest triumph of his career in the labor movement.[2]

Ettor perceived at the outset that the Italian mill workers, by virtue of their superior numbers and militancy, would constitute the backbone of the strike. To join him as co-leader of the Italians, Ettore invited Arturo Giovannitti, the director of *Il Proletario*, who arrived on January 20.[3] At twenty-eight, Giovannitti was an elegant figure, taller and thinner than his stocky comrade, with handsome features and brooding eyes. Giovannitti had an unusual background for a *sovversivo*. As a rebellious and melancholy youth from the middle class in Campobasso (Molise), Giovannitti rejected the prospect of life among the provincial bourgeois and migrated to Canada at age sixteen, supporting himself briefly as a mine worker and railroad laborer. Well educated but guided by religious and mystical tendencies, Giovannitti found work at a Presbyterian mission for Italians in Montreal and studied English and theology at McGill University. He continued his religious studies at Columbia University's Union Theological Seminary in 1904, while working at a Presbyterian mission in Brooklyn. After another stint at a mission in Pittsburgh, Giovannitti's flirtation with Protestantism ended, and he embraced syndicalism under the influence of Tresca, with whom he maintained a lifelong friendship. Back in New York and unemployed, Giovannitti spent many a winter's night on a bench in Little Italy's Mulberry Park until he found work as a bookkeeper and joined the editorial staff of *Il Proletario*. Thereafter, his rise to prominence in the Italian syndicalist movement was rapid, becoming the director of the newspaper and FSI secretary in 1911. By that time, Giovanniti had also distinguished himself as the leading poet of the Italian immigrant Left, although much of his best poetry (in English) would soon be inspired by the ordeal that awaited him in Lawrence.[4]

Giovannitti's role in the strike was that of the charismatic orator. His "Sermon on the Common" (in English), echoing Christ's "Sermon on the Mount," uplifted strikers' spirits and strengthened their resolve to fight. Ettor, while an able speaker, was the master strategist whose organizational skills and innovative tactics assured the rapid expansion of the strike. He oversaw as elected chairman the formation of a general strike committee that exercised complete authority and formulated demands: 1) 15 percent increase in wages on the fifty-four hour basis; 2) double time for overtime work; 3) the abolition of all bonus and premium systems; 4) and no discrimination against workers for strike activity. Winning these demands required enough strikers to halt or substantially decrease production. Toward that end, Ettor organized moving picket lines that regularly marched around the mills and effectively obstructed access. He also conducted giant parades through the streets of Lawrence to demonstrate the workers' strength and solidarity. By February, some 23,000—out of a labor force of 32,000—had abandoned the mills. Italians and Poles were the most numerous and militant—7,000 and 2,500, respectively—providing more picketers and marchers than other ethnic groups.[5]

But Ettor and Giovannitti would not be available to lead the strike at its height. On January 29, an Italian woman striker, Anna Lo Pizzo, had been shot and killed by a policeman; the next day a Syrian boy, John Rami, was fatally bayoneted by a militiaman. Seizing the deaths as a pretext to decapitate the strike, the authorities arrested Ettor, Giovannitti, and Joseph Caruso, a mill worker, charging them with "indirect" responsibility for Lo Pizzo's murder. But the authorities and mill owners failed in their purpose. The IWW replaced Ettor and Giovannitti with "Big Bill" Haywood, Elizabeth Gurley Flynn, William Yates, William E. Trautman, and others, who led the workers of Lawrence to victory by the middle of March 1912.[6]

Victory remained incomplete, however, so long as the strike leaders remained in prison facing possible death. The IWW therefore mounted a defense campaign that rivaled the efforts previously expended during the strike. The IWW's most important ally throughout the defense campaign, as during the strike, was the FSI, whose membership demonstrated even greater militancy and single-minded commitment to this struggle than their Wobbly comrades. The FSI's zealous determination was attributable to their political ideology as well the desire to save their Italian comrades. The FSI placed far greater emphasis on antistatism and violent tactics than the IWW, meaning that the Italian revolutionary syndicalists were more willing than the American industrial unionists to challenge state authorities in a struggle to liberate the prisoners.[7] When the accused were formally indicted on April 18, *Il Proletario* declared in its May Day issue: "It is not the time for words....It is time for action, it is time for war.... What we want is the destruction of your system of property and exploitation.... Long live the general strike!"[8]

The confrontational tactics urged by the FSI, which the IWW was loath to adopt, required a degree of unanimity and militancy that Lawrence workers no longer possessed. Little more than half of the mill operatives who had conducted the strike for material demands would prove steadfast in the agitation for Ettor and Giovannitti. The most reliable elements came from the same ethnic groups that provided the most numerous and militant strikers: Italians, Poles, Franco-Belgians, Lithuanians, and Syrians—with the Italians again performing the special role of shock troops. Although they never appealed to nationalist sentiments, FSI leaders understood that the agitation to liberate Ettor and Giovannitti was as much an ethnic conflict as a labor/political struggle. Leadership of the Italians in this bitter struggle therefore had to be entrusted to someone who commanded great respect among Italian workers, and who possessed exceptional talents as a strategist, agitator, and organizer. The man best qualified for the task, the FSI knew, was Tresca. On Giovannitti's personal recommendation, the IWW invited him to Lawrence to lead the agitation.[9]

May Day in Lawrence

Asked to address the Italians at the May Day demonstration, Tresca recalled: "I went to Lawrence like a Mohammedan to Mecca: with burning faith in my heart. When the conductor called 'Lawrence' at the station my heart began to palpitate like the engine of a great electric generator."[10] But the May Day parade attracted only 5,000 members of the IWW, mostly Italians, including many women carrying infants and pushing baby carriages. A large rally was held at the Essex County Jail on Hampshire Street, where the prisoners were held. Later than evening, Italian members of Local 20 formed their own procession.[11]

Tresca was disappointed but not surprised that the May Day celebration had attracted so few participants. Settlement of the strike had not brought industrial peace to Lawrence. The workers, he explained, "had not forgotten Ettor and Giovannitti but the epic and heroic struggle just ended victoriously had tired them and they evinced no great anxiety to start a new fight to check the unconstitutional acts of the police and openly demand freedom for the innocents facing the electric chair."[12] Rather than criticize the workers for their lethargy and demoralize them further, Tresca emphasized the gravity of the threat facing Ettor and Giovannitti. Legal defense activities should continue, he advised, but no trust should be placed in American judges and juries. Only direct action held the key to their salvation, by which he meant an operation to rescue them from prison. To prepare for such an eventuality, he declared that a general strike of all the textile workers of Massachusetts was not just a necessity but an unavoidable duty.[13]

The FSI and a reluctant IWW planned a general strike in Lawrence for May 27, the day the trial was to begin, but were spared this daunting task when the trial was postponed until September. Instead, the FSI and the IWW conducted a funeral parade on Memorial Day to honor the martyred workers Lo Pizzo and Rami. Some 15,000 workers from Lawrence, Lowell, Haverhill, and other industrial towns participated, but within a few days Lawrence lapsed back into lethargy.[14]

With agitation in Lawrence all but ceased, Tresca left town to give a series of lectures about the case to Italians in Massachusetts, New Hampshire, Pennsylvania, Connecticut, and New York before returning on August 20. By mid-September Tresca was performing the dual role of freelance organizer and agitator for Local 20. He described the different requirements and objectives of these tasks:

> The organization work prepares and thrills the army of labor, but to keep the army in the field of action you must create, through agitation, the desire and eagerness to fight, the will to go on fighting. Agitation work is different from organization work. Organization work is done methodically, slowly and quietly; agitation work aiming at mass action for an immediate and definite purpose is done in the open, noisily and spasmodically, with the intelligent and full use of individual and mass emotions stirred up by deeds and words capable of creating strong passions of hatred, sympathy, love and anger.[15]

Stirring mass emotions was precisely what the authorities had sought to prevent during the strike by denying the IWW permission to hold rallies on public property. Tresca circumvented this ruling by renting a large, privately-owned space on the corner of Short and Chestnut Streets known as "The Lots." On Saturday, September 14, around 7,000 Italians, Poles, Franco-Belgians, and others assembled there to hear Flynn and other speakers address them in 17 languages. Not satisfied with speeches, Tresca exhorted the workers to defy the police ban and march to the Lawrence Common, where Giovannitti had delivered his now famous "Sermon." Occupying the Common would constitute a moral victory for the defense campaign. With Tresca in the lead carrying a red banner, several thousand marchers singing the "Internationale" brushed past police and occupied the coveted ground without interference. "Here, on the battle ground, sacred to your birth and your victories," Tresca said, "you must renew your oath which you took when the strike was concluded. You must swear, as a man, every one of you, to fight every day, every minute of your lives, without truce or repose, for the liberation of Ettor and Giovannitti." A thousand voices, most of them Italian, roared: "We swear!"—"*Giuriamo!*"[16]

General Strike

Tresca's vacant lot demonstration was a warm-up exercise for the mass protest rally scheduled the following day at the Boston Commons. The IWW feared that Haywood, the principal speaker, might be put out of action if arrested because funds for bail were lacking. Tresca the "fixer" responded with a visit to Fabrizio Pitocchelli, a prominent Italian banker in Lawrence. Reminding Pitocchelli that many of his Italian clients were IWW members, Tresca offered him a choice: provide the bail money or face a boycott of his bank. A promise of money was immediately forthcoming. Next, he arranged railway transportation for the several thousand Lawrence workers to attend the rally, issuing red colored tickets with the imprint "I.W.W. round trip Lawrence–Boston." Sunday morning, some 3,500–4,000 workers from Lawrence arrived at North Station, and with Tresca at the head marched through the streets of Boston. They were joined at the Boston Common by workers of a dozen nationalities from Haverhill, Lynn, Lowell, New Bedford, Fall River, and other industrial towns nearby—around 20,000–35,000 in all. For several hours, Haywood and twenty-five other orators harangued the crowd, enjoining them to participate in the general strike now scheduled for September 27. Tresca, to his chagrin, remained mute that day; he had developed a bad case of laryngitis. His satisfaction derived from the large turnout and the fact that the bail money he had arranged did indeed secure Haywood's release after Boston police arrested him as expected.[17]

The IWW notables returned to Lawrence deluded in their belief that leadership of the workers was firmly in their grasp. On the evening of Wednesday, September 25, as thousands crammed into Lexington Hall and the adjacent square to await instructions regarding the industry-wide general strike, workers listened in disbelief when Flynn, Tresca, and other FSI leaders read letters sent that day from Ettor and Giovannitti, requesting a postponement of the long-awaited mass action.[18] The reason for their request, Flynn later asserted, was fear of unforeseeable repercussions:

> It was a dangerous gamble they felt, never before attempted in this country as far as we knew—a political general strike with demands directed not to the employer but to the state. They felt that the risk of failure was too great on the one hand and the temper of the workers, particularly the Italians, too explosive on the other.[19]

However, since the demand for a general strike had originated with the FSI, Tresca, and the Italian workers, rather than the IWW, it is far more likely that the decision to postpone the general strike came from Haywood, who all along had considered a confrontation with the state too dangerous.[20]

Tresca was caught in a dilemma: should he, one of the most ardent proponents of the general strike, comply with the request for a postponement, or break with the IWW leaders and urge the Italians to act on their own initiative and hopefully rally others to join them. Opting to support the wishes of his friends Ettor and Giovannitti, Tresca attempted to convince the Italian workers to acquiesce. He might have succeeded if not for the Italian anarchists who were determined to ensure that the general strike proceed as planned.[21]

New England was the stronghold of Luigi Galleani, the director of *Cronaca Sovversiva* (Lynn) and the most prominent Italian anarchist in the United States. Galleani rejected all forms of organization—trade unions as well as political parties—as harbingers of authoritarianism, a viewpoint that produced the corollary that "the anarchist movement and the labor movement travel along parallel lines… [that] do not meet and never coincide."[22] Rejecting even syndicalist unions as serious instruments of social struggle, Galleani placed his faith in all methods of revolutionary violence, including bombs and assassination.[23] His known affinity for violence and ill-concealed contempt for the IWW undoubtedly explained why his offer to assist in leading the Italian workers during the Lawrence strike was rejected by the IWW.[24] Despite the rebuff, Galleani and his followers worked diligently throughout the strike to generate support and funds through lectures, meetings, and subscriptions.[25] And it was the Italian anarchists, at a meeting with other Italian radicals in Boston in mid-January, who first suggested the idea of a children's exodus from Lawrence, the event that marked the turning point of the strike.[26] But now, with the agitation for Ettor and Giovannitti predominantly an Italian undertaking, the chance for anarchist involvement increased significantly.

This possibility had already become apparent on September 15, when Umberto Postiglione appeared as one of the main speakers at the big rally on the Boston Common. A member of *Cronaca Sovversiva*'s editorial staff, Postiglione was one of Galleani's most militant acolytes. On September 26, as Italians arrived for work, Postiglione and his comrades posted themselves outside of the Wood and Washington Mills, urging them to strike at 3:00 P.M. Tresca arrived at the Wood mill shortly afterward and was confronted by Postiglione, who demanded to know why the IWW had retreated from its original strategy. Tresca expressed regret over the decision but reaffirmed his commitment to follow the wishes of Ettor and Giovannitti. But by 3:15 P.M. the Italians began streaming out of the two mills, soon to be joined by Italians from other mills. At a large meeting at Lexington Hall that evening, the IWW and the Italian anarchists vied for leadership of the assembled crowd. Spurred by the exhortations of anarchists, the Italian workers *en masse* voiced their desire for a general strike. The following morning, September 27, several thousand angry Italians abandoned the mills. Their belligerent mood quickly proved infectious, and some 10,000–12,000 workers went on strike the next day. Facing a crisis, the IWW's general executive board in Chicago decided to compromise in hope of regaining the initiative. Instead of an industry-wide general strike of indefinite duration, the IWW board recommended that a twenty-four hour protest strike be held in Lawrence on Monday, September 30.[27]

Alternating moods of aggression and disappointment caused Tresca to worry that workers might not turn out in full force for the protest strike. To regenerate their militancy, Tresca organized another memorial parade on Sunday, September 29, to honor Anna Lo Pizzo and John Rami. His plan called for workers from Lawrence and nearby cities to convene at Lexington Hall and then march to the cemetery. Because Tresca did not follow the exact route specified in the parade permit, police intercepted the marchers and arrested him for refusing to order the workers to disperse. Flynn, who observed scene, recalled that "a tussle ensued in which he was taken away from the police by the workers who formed a flying tackle as in a football game, and pushed him through the police line."[28] Later that afternoon, in defiance of police and a torrential rain, 4,000 workers—most of them Italians—marched silently to the cemetery, with Tresca at the head standing backwards in a one-horse buggy. Tresca remembered that "one big banner, when all the others had given away to the force of the persistent downpour, remained intact. On it was a red, challenging motto, 'No God, No Master.'"[29]

Early the next morning, September 30, some 12,000 operatives amassed in the streets of Lawrence to demonstrate their solidarity with the three Italians whose trial was to begin. Sympathy strikes, attracting more than 10,000 participants, occurred elsewhere in Massachusetts, Vermont, Pennsylvania, and Ohio. The tumult originally feared by Ettor and Giovannitti did not occur. Local authorities had furtively transferred the prisoners to Salem two days earlier. The main event of the day in Lawrence was a rally held on the same vacant lot on Short and Chestnut Streets that Tresca had rented previously. Several thousand strikers listened to speeches in nine languages. Haywood, who had been expected to participate in the twenty-four hour strike, was not present at the rally and did not arrive until the following day—"whether by accident or design," Flynn cryptically remarked years later.[30] The task of recommending that the workers return to the mills and await the outcome of the trial fell to Flynn and Tresca instead. Some Italians wished to continue the strike, but the proposal failed to gain favor with other workers. The militant Italians had to content themselves with Tresca's assurance that "if Ettor, Giovannitti, and Caruso are found guilty... the Industrial Workers of the World would march to Salem, storm the jail, and rescue the prisoners, if possible."[31]

The IWW's Decline in Lawrence

Flynn would later boast that the twenty-four hour protest strike had "succeeded beyond our wildest dreams and brought order out of chaos."[32] In reality, the modest turnout in Lawrence and elsewhere demonstrated that any further attempt to mobilize local and regional workers for a general strike with political objectives would inevitably fail. The textile workers of Lawrence remained sympathetic to the plight of Ettor and Giovannitti, but they no longer possessed the will power and resources necessary for a serious struggle in the coming months. Nor was the IWW able to influence events in Lawrence to any significant degree after September 30, and the large membership the union recruited during the strike began to decline as workers came to this realization. That the IWW had become a spent force became apparent the morning after the protest strike, when some 2,000 operatives arrived at the mills only to discover that they had been locked out because of their participation in the previous day's events.[33] Besides some huffing and puffing about retaliation, Haywood and the IWW could do nothing. A week later, 500 militant strikers still remained blacklisted.[34]

The lockout and blacklisting of union militants was part of a new campaign orchestrated by leading citizens of Lawrence to defeat the IWW and radicalism once and for all. The pretext was the "No God, No Master" banner carried by Italian anarchists during the recent Lo Pizzo memorial parade. Major Michael A. Scanlon called upon all the "patriotic and law abiding citizens" to wear American flag buttons in their lapels as a rebuke to the advocates of anarchy and atheism who had invaded their God-fearing city. At a meeting in City Hall, Father James O'Reilly, the Catholic priest who was the most powerful man in Lawrence, shouted: "Those who do not want to work better take a hint and go. We will drive the demons of anarchism and socialism from our midst."[35]

Every form of violence, from the militia to the lynch rope, was recommended by Lawrence's law-abiding denizens, and vigilante activities were already well underway. More than 100 private detectives and other thugs had been recruited to intimidate workers during the twenty-four hour protest strike on September 30. Starting that day, workers wearing IWW buttons were regularly beaten. When a Polish IWW member was killed, Tresca defied Haywood's advice and organized a funeral procession to demonstrate that the IWW could not be intimidated. His only concession to the escalating danger was to select a route that avoided the Commons, where police had mobilized with guns and hoses. Arriving at the cemetery without incident, a few thousand workers strewed red carnations over the grave of their Polish comrade and listened in silence to speeches by Tresca, Flynn, and Haywood.[36]

Not surprisingly, while in Boston conferring with defense attorneys, Tresca received notification from Lawrence that his life would be in danger if he returned. Tresca never refused such challenges. To demonstrate that neither he nor the IWW could be intimidated, he planned an act of defiance when he returned on October 5. With his friend Bertrando Spada, one of the FSI's foremost leaders, armed and walking behind to cover his back, Tresca strolled conspicuously up and down Essex Street wearing an IWW button in his lapel and secreting a revolver in his pocket, almost daring the detectives he encountered along the way to start trouble. None stepped forward to challenge the "Bull of Lawrence," as he had come to be known.[37]

On Columbus Day, around 30,000 people assembled for the "God and Country" parade. A celebration of American patriotism and anti-radicalism, the parade had no place for the hated IWW, and any marcher sporting an IWW button or banner would be arrested. No manifestation of ethnic loyalty other than American was tolerated, a reflection of the Anglo-Saxon and Irish hostility to "foreigners" that had been evidenced throughout the strike and defense campaign. The display of Italian flags was expressly forbidden, the national origin of Columbus notwithstanding. Most of the marchers were children conscripted from public and parochial schools, municipal employees, members of American patriotic societies, Catholic associations, and some representatives of the AFL. Not more than 4,000 mill operatives participated in the parade, according to Haywood, although it is very likely that many more were bystanders who had turned out to observe a holiday parade and did not subscribe to the anti-IWW objectives it was intended to promote. The IWW, meanwhile, tried hard to dampen popular enthusiasm for the parade by explaining to the workers, the majority of whom were Catholics, that the IWW had never taken a position against religion, and that the issues of religion and patriotism were being exploited by city officials and mill owners in order to destroy the union. But the IWW's disclaimer did not succeed in rallying support. Only 4,000–5,000 out of an expected 10,000 showed up for the IWW's counter-celebration at the picnic grounds in Pleasant Valley.[38]

The Trial of Ettor, Giovannitti, and Caruso

The Ettor-Giovannitti Defense Committee, meanwhile, had achieved surprising success assembling an outstanding legal team, publicizing the case, raising money—around $60,000. Most of the contributions came from Italian sources, especially the coal miners among whom Tresca had been very active. *Il Proletario* raised more than $12,000, while other Italian radical newspapers raised several thousand more. The far more prosperous but conservative Order of the Sons of Italy donated only $1,500, a token of ethnic solidarity diluted by fear of being identified with radicals.[39]

Although the case against the defendants had clearly been fabricated, Tresca was unwilling to entrust the lives of Ettor, Giovannitti, and Caruso to the vagaries of capitalist justice. Thus his role in the last phase of the defense campaign was again that of the "fixer." District Attorney Harry C. Attwill's principal evidence against the accused was a statement allegedly made by Giovannitti to Italian strikers on the morning of Lo Pizzo's death: "Get up when it is dark and go out and smash the heads of these scabs, because when it is dark no one can tell who did the smashing. From now on be like wild animals looking for blood."[40] Several private detectives and reporters, despite their ignorance of Italian, testified in court that they had overheard Giovannitti utter these remarks. The defense was apprehensive about discrediting these witnesses, because Geremia Campopiano, an Italian banker and saloon keeper hostile to the strike, had vowed to corroborate their testimony in court. Tresca offered Campopiano a *quid pro quo*: the union boycott of his establishments would be lifted in exchange for his silence. Tresca's economic incentive prevailed.[41]

But Tresca wanted more insurance. He recruited dozens of Italian workers prepared to swear that Giovannitti had merely warned them to "stay away from detectives, because they are like hunting dogs craving your blood."[42] IWW lawyer Fred H. Moore, a member of the legal team, was fearful, however, that Tresca's coaching of potential witnesses might be exposed in court. All the Italian workers, it seemed, had forgotten everything Giovannitti had said in his speech except the words misunderstood by the detectives. What the defense needed was a professional or businessman, someone not a member of the IWW, who would confirm the benign nature of Giovannitti's remarks. Tresca turned to Dr. Costante Calitri, a radical sympathizer who had supported the strike. Dr. Calitri had only vague recollections of having been present when Giovannitti spoke, although the words attributed to the strike leader by Tresca did seem familiar. This was hardly surprising since the words were being repeated daily throughout the Italian section of Lawrence. Reminded by Tresca that a memory lapse on his part might endanger the lives of three countrymen, the good doctor finally remembered that he had heard the words for the first time directly from Giovannitti's lips. At the trial Dr. Calitri proved himself a star witness for the defense.[43]

Whether Tresca's "fixing" influenced the verdict cannot be determined. The defense produced dozens of witnesses, like Calitri, to establish that Ettor and Giovannitti had repeatedly urged the strikers to remain peaceful, in keeping with IWW policy. Prosecution witnesses, although equally numerous, were easily discredited because their testimony was transparently inaccurate, tainted, or fabricated. Failing to prove that Ettor and Giovannitti had exhorted the strikes to commit violence, the conspiracy theory advanced by the state collapsed. As for Joseph Caruso, the supposed accomplice of the "mysterious" gunman who killed Lo Pizzo, the defense proved conclusively that he had been home eating dinner at the time of the shooting. The deciding factor in the outcome, however, proved to be the defendants themselves. More intelligent and articulate than their interrogator, Ettor and Giovannitti outmaneuvered Attwill, answering his questions in ways favorable to themselves, and focusing attention on the social and economic causes of the strike rather than the shooting of Lo Pizzo, who was nearly forgotten during the proceedings. Their finest moment came after the District Attorney's summation. Judge Joseph F. Quinn, who exhibited his prejudice against the defendants throughout the trial, made the crucial blunder of allowing Ettor and Giovannitti to address the jury before deliberation. Their statements were so powerful and moving that any chance for a conviction was lost. That same day, Tuesday, November 23, 1912, the jury returned a verdict of not guilty.[44]

The acquittal of Ettor and Giovannitti represented a major victory for the American labor movement. The threat to workers right to strike, implicit in the conspiracy charges against them, had been defeated. To celebrate the victory Ettor and Giovannitti returned to Lawrence on Thanksgiving Day and spoke for two and a half hours before 5,000 workers gathered in "The Lots" during a snow-storm.[45] Yet the acquittal of the strike leaders did nothing to retard the IWW's irreversible decline in Lawrence. Membership virtually evaporated: from the 16,000 textile workers it claimed to have acquired by September 1912 to a mere 700 less than a year later and to 400 by 1914.[46] The FSI, which had demonstrated itself far more radical and daring than the IWW during the defense campaign, did not experience any decline in membership, but never again would Italian syndicalists play a crucial role in a major strike.[47]

Lawrence and a New Era For Tresca

For Tresca, the defense campaign for Ettor and Giovannitti represented a major success and a turning point in his career. The only negative outcome pertained to his relationship with the Galleanisti. Furious that they had lost an opportunity for a revolutionary gesture when plans for a prolonged mass general strike were scaled down to a twenty-four hour protest strike, the Galleanisti ascribed the lion's share of blame not to the IWW or the FSI but to Tresca, denouncing him for having "eviscerated the enthusiasm of the proletariat" and committing other alleged acts of apostasy.[48] That the Galleanisti singled out Tresca for blame actually had more to do with their master's previous labeling of him as an ideological adversary and their jealousy and fear that he might eclipse Galleani as a radical leader. The Galleanisti thereafter would conduct an intermittent campaign of slander and vilification against Tresca that continued until his death.[49]

But in 1912 no amount of censure and vituperation from the Galleanisti could alter the fact that Tresca had become the preeminent leader on the Italian immigrant Left, and perhaps the most important foreign-born radical active in the American labor movement. Tresca himself underscored the singular importance of the Ettor-Giovannitti campaign for the development of his career. Until Lawrence, "I was still living in Italy, both with my heart and mind. Though living in America, my thoughts, my talks, my habits of life, my friends and my enemies were all Italian." Intellectually committed to belief in the international solidarity of the working class and the universality of the class struggle, Tresca until now had nonetheless "remained indifferent to the efforts made by the American comrades to bring nearer to its realization the millennium for which I myself was fighting." Before Lawrence, Tresca's activities as a journalist and agitator had been conducted exclusively among Italian immigrants, as though "living and fighting in a world which was a slice of the mother country transplanted here by virtue of economic necessity and the spirit of adventure." Participation in previous strikes "had been for me a matter of marshalling the Italian workers as compatriots rather than as a part of the world's workers, looking forward, toward liberation." Thanks to his involvement with the Ettor-Giovannitti campaign, Tresca had outgrown the parochial mentality of the recent immigrant and entered the political and social world beyond the perimeters of the colonie italiane. "To me Lawrence was the beginning of a new era," he wrote. "With Lawrence I joined the army of revolutionary American workers for a real and greater struggle."[50]

5

On to Paterson

On New Year's Eve, 1912, several thousand hotel workers in New York walked off their jobs to protest the low wages and deplorable physical conditions that prevailed in the industry. The strike had been called by the International Hotel Workers' Union (IHWU), a newly-organized union that had broken away from the AFL; it claimed a membership of 5,000, the great majority of them foreign-born. Many of the Italian members were Wobbly sympathizers, and in response to their request for assistance, IWW headquarters sent Tresca, Flynn, and Patrick L. Quinlan to help conduct the strike. Tresca arrived directly from Little Falls, New York, where at the IWW's request he had participated at the end of December in a victorious strike of textile workers led by Matilda Rabinowitz.[1]

The hotel workers had been holding meetings at Bryant Hall, on Sixth Avenue and 42nd Street. As he walked toward the building for the first time, Tresca's imagination conjured up a vision of a thousand cheering strikers hailing him as the Messiah who would lead them to victory. His fantasy immediately faded when no one noticed him enter the building and seat himself in the back of the audience. Local representatives of the SPA were addressing the strikers that evening. Their advocacy of electoral action as the best course to pursue left Tresca and the hotel workers equally unimpressed. Introduced to the officials of the IHWU, Tresca declined their invitation to speak the next day. He wanted to gauge the mood and motives of the strikers, and determine whether there was any likelihood of success. For the next few days he did nothing more than visit union headquarters, mingle anonymously with the strikers, and attend the mass meetings at Bryant Hall.[2]

Tresca was pessimistic about the chances for victory. The disparate membership of the hotel workers' union, he observed, was not united with the spirit of solidarity he considered indispensable for an industrial union. Moreover, the strike was being waged at a time of economic depression, so there were dozens of unemployed men available to replace each striker. Therefore, Tresca approached the conflict from a revolutionary syndicalist perspective, regarding the strike primarily as an exercise in direct action that would heighten militancy and class consciousness for future struggles. The opportunity for direct action presented itself one evening when Jacob Panken, the prominent socialist attorney who was serving as legal counsel for the IHWU, urged the strikers to take their grievances to the polls and vote for the SPA. Idolized by Jewish socialist workers on the Lower East Side, Panken was famous for his foghorn voice and soapbox oratory. Not many radicals would have dared challenge him, but Tresca calmly mounted a chair in the audience and cut him short with his own booming basso. As he described the incident to his friend Max Eastman, Tresca shouted above the cheers of the strikers in his inimitable English:

> Fellow-workers, a strike, dat is not a course of lectures, but a fight!… Dis man, he talk about politic, he talk about election, while scabs betray our cause. I say we march in mass formation right away out of here and picket all hotels. I say we stop talking. I say we act. I say we win dis strike![3]

As word spread that the call for action had come from Carlo Tresca, the strikers surged out of Bryant Hall behind him and marched to the posh hotel district nearby for a demonstration. Enraged cooks and waiters hurled rocks and bottles at hotel windows and blocked traffic; the police retaliated by charging into the strikers with clubs swinging. Tresca was helping a bleeding striker outside the Hotel McAlpin when the police began making arrests. An elegant figure sporting a stylish Van Dyke beard and wearing a *pince-nez*, Tresca was gently pushed aside by a burly policeman who said: "We don't want you, doctor."[4] The clash outside the Hotel McAlpin marked the last time Tresca went unrecognized by a New York policeman.[5]

Now invigorated, the IHWU rank and file endorsed a general strike for 1:00 P.M., on January 24, while IWW leaders increased pressure on the hotel owners and scabbing workers by employing more direct action. An hour before the strike was to began, Tresca led a column of 2,000 cooks and waiters into the "Tenderloin District" (extending from Broadway to Park Avenue in the 40s) to demonstrate the militancy and strength of the insurgent hotel workers. Topping the list of targets was the Knickerbocker Hotel at Broadway and 42nd Street, whose proprietor had discharged his entire staff of waiters that afternoon. The vanguard of Tresca's column attacked the Knickerbocker, shouting "scabs" at the workers inside the hotel and smashing windows with umbrellas and rocks. A cohort of private guards hired by the Hotel Men's Association attacked the demonstrators with blackjacks and night sticks. With strikers and guards trading blow for blow, and frightened bystanders fleeing for cover, pandemonium reigned in Times Square. Tresca, in the thick of the fighting, received a powerful blow to the stomach, which would later require months of medical attention. He managed nonetheless to lead the strikers from the Knickerbocker to the Belmont Hotel on Park Avenue and 42nd Street, where they shattered the lobby windows with rocks. The ultra-deluxe Waldorf-Astoria was the next target, but a large contingent of policemen beat off the attackers.[6] The next day New York's daily newspapers lambasted the IWW and censured the "rioting waiters."[7] The socialists, too, joined the chorus of critics. The IWW's most unforgiving adversary among them was Panken. Sulking in his tent, this socialist Achilles refused to appear in court to defend arrested strikers, even though the IHWU had retained him for that purpose. Union officials who appealed to Panken for help were angrily rebuffed with the suggestion, "Go to Tresca for counsel. He will teach you how to throw stones and stay out of prison."[8]

On the afternoon of January 24, guards hired by the Hotel Men's Association were pelting Bryant Hall with rocks from the elevated train station on Sixth Avenue and 42nd Street. Hundreds of strikers poured out into the street ready to battle any adversary. Tresca and Flynn, who tried to persuade the strikers to return inside, suddenly found themselves in the path of the police reserves that had just arrived on the scene and were beating strikers and arresting anyone they could seize. Flynn was clubbed and Tresca arrested. When the strikers saw that Tresca had been taken prisoner, they attacked the police to free him. Detective David Kuhne, who had grabbed Tresca by the coat and vest, was knocked off his feet. Tresca's rescuers tried to push him to the rear of the crowd, but Kuhne and other detectives drew their revolvers to keep them at bay. Tresca found himself on the ground "with Kuhne heavily pressing his knee on my stomach, holding a pistol to my face, shouting to the strikers: 'I will kill him if you don't run away.'"[9] Fearing for Tresca's life, the strikers permitted the police to drive away with him and twelve other prisoners. Tried for disorderly conduct at the Jefferson Market Court on February 8, Tresca escaped a jail sentence when Judge Kernochan unexpectedly dismissed the charges after Tresca and several witnesses explained that what he had shouted to the strikers in Italian was only a plea to return inside the hall and avoid arrest.[10]

The melee produced a shocking revelation—Tresca and Flynn were involved in a passionate love affair that dated from their days together in Lawrence. Tresca's coat and vest had been torn from his body during his scuffle with Detective Kuhn and their contents scattered on the ground. Among the items recovered was a little volume of Browning's *Sonnets from the Portuguese* that Flynn had given to Tresca, inscribed with the words "Elizabeth to Carlo." Whoever retrieved the volume realized that the newspapers would devour this delectable morsel of gossip. As Flynn recalled in her memoirs, "What was my embarrassment the next day to see our picture, with copies of the book cover, marked sonnets, dedication and all, reproduced in the New York papers as a hidden IWW romance."[11]

Revelation of the Tresca-Flynn romance may have provided better publicity for the IWW than smashing windows and battling police, but by the fourth week of the strike, it no longer mattered. The demonstrations could not interfere with the hotel owners' ability to replace striking personnel at will, and without a complete work stoppage, there was no chance of victory. On January 31, 1913, the IHWU officially declared the strike ended. Few hotel workers in New York believed that anything positive had been accomplished. Hundreds had lost their jobs to non-union replacements, and hundreds of others were re-employed only on condition that they tear up their union cards. Conditions and wages remained the same as before the strike. The IHWU split into three factions: IWW supporters, independents, and those who wished to rejoin the AFL. By any measure, the strike was a major setback for the hotel workers of New York and a portent of worse to come for the IWW.[12]

Italians in Paterson

Despite the defeat of the hotel workers' strike, Tresca was ready for his next assignment for the IWW: to help lead the silk workers of Paterson, New Jersey, who were poised to launch a strike that would rank as one of the most bitterly- fought industrial conflicts in American history and the IWW's greatest defeat in the East.[13] As in Lawrence, Tresca was the logical choice to lead Italian strikers in a city where they represented the largest ethnic group in the industry.[14] From the perspective of the manufacturers, local officials, the police, and the English-speaking community in general, responsibility for the Paterson strike of 1913 lay primarily with the Italians and secondarily with the Jews. Testifying before the U.S. Commission on Industrial Relations (CIS) in 1914, Adolph Lessig, a local IWW leader, related that "every one blamed it on the Jews and Italians.... The year before there had been a strike and they called it a Jew strike, and last year they called it an Italian strike."[15] Unlike Lawrence, where the Italian textile workers had come primarily from the *Mezzogiorno*, the silk mills of Paterson attracted Italians from both the north and south of Italy, with the former in the majority. The northern Italians who settled in the 1880s and 1890s came primarily from Biella and Vercelli in Piedmont, Prato in Tuscany, and Como in Lombardy. Biella and Prato were textile centers that produced woolen cloth; Como specialized in the manufacture of silk; and Vercelli produced silk, cotton, and wool. As around 78 percent of the men and 50 percent of the women had previous experience in textile manufacturing, the northern Italians were easily absorbed into Paterson's industrial community, most gravitating to the broad silk mills and the dye houses. The southern Italians who began arriving in the 1890s and early-20th century were generally unskilled and found employment in the dye houses, mainly as dyers helpers, performing the lowest paid and most arduous and health destroying work in silk manufacturing. By 1913, Italians constituted the largest ethnic group in the city and in the mills, numbering around 10,000 out of a total population of 125,000, and some 7,000–8,000 out of 25,000 workers employed in silk manufacturing.[16]

Italian workers in Paterson had a tradition of militant socialism, syndicalism, and anarchism dating back more than twenty years. Italian socialists had published *Il Proletario* in Paterson in 1898–1899, and the FSI maintained a thriving section in the city after its formation in 1902.[17] Yet the socialists and syndicalists in Paterson were overshadowed by the anarchists, most of whom had migrated from Biella and Prato in the late 1880s and 1890s. The *Gruppo Diritto all'Esistenza* (Right to Exist), originally numbering 85–100 members, was the most important of several anarchist groups formed. In 1895, the visiting anarchist Pietro Gori and the multi-lingual Catalan anarchist Pedro Esteve, founded *La Questione Sociale* in Paterson, perhaps the most important voice of Italian anarchism in the United States. By 1900, thanks to the proselytizing of Errico Malatesta, who sojourned in Paterson from August 1899 to March 1900, the population of Italian anarchists increased to somewhere between 500 and 2,000, most of them weavers and dyers. Local circulation of *La Questione Sociale* reached 1,000, out of a national distribution of 3,000. That same year, Paterson became renowned as the "world capital of anarchism" after a local anarchist named Gaetano Bresci returned to Italy and assassinated King Umberto I to avenge the "May Events" of 1898—a military slaughter of workers in Milan.[18]

Following a series of natural disasters (a great fire, blizzard, ice storm, and flood), desperately poor dye workers who had been attempting to form a union launched a strike on April 23, 1902. Led by Luigi Galleani, Italian anarchism's chief apostle of violence, some 6,000–7,000 strikers laid siege to the silk mills on June 18. Wholesale violence erupted as the rampaging crowd of predominantly Italian dye workers seized control of Paterson for six hours before the state militia arrived to quell the rebellion. One policeman and eight strikers were shot in the course of the battle. Galleani, who had been shot in the mouth while leading the assault, fled to Canada to avoid arrest. Major John Hinchcliffe vowed after the strike to crush the "anarchist element" even "if every Italian in the town had to be driven out."[19]

Suppressing the anarchists was part of a broader policy to contain the threat which local authorities and English-speaking citizens believed the Italians posed to the industrial peace of Paterson. Captain John Bimson, who considered strikes and picketing tantamount to social rebellion, was promoted to chief of police. He strengthened his department by more than 50 percent, installed a telephone system of communication, and created an "Italian Division," which established a precinct in the predominantly Italian section of Riverside. During the "Red Scare" of 1908, *La Questione Sociale* was suppressed, only to be resurrected as *L'Era Nuova*. A viable group of at least 300–400 anarchists remained by 1913, many of them having become members of IWW Local 152 and advocates of syndicalist tactics. They still wielded considerable influence among other Italians employed in the mills, as Margaret H. Sanger, then an anarchist active in the Paterson strike, observed: "when the strike was called this small minority [the Italian anarchists] formed the backbone of the strike, which gave to it most of its revolutionary momentum."[20] As such, the anarchists and other Italians were considered the internal enemy by Paterson's authorities and English-speaking elements, and subjected to special vigilance and brutality by the police throughout the great strike of 1913.[21]

The Paterson Strike of 1913

The strike of 1913 largely immobilized the city's 200 broad-silk and ribbon mills, 35 silk throwing mills, and 25 dye houses for nearly 22 weeks. Physical conditions in the mills and dye houses were onerous and health threatening; ten hours or more constituted the typical workday, and wages had sunk to an average level of $11.69 a week for skilled workers and $6.00 or $7.00 a week for unskilled. But the principal issues of contention were the eight-hour day and the multiple-loom system, which required weavers to operate four looms instead of two, as had been in the custom for decades. The four-loom system, with new high-speed looms, required greater physical exertion and mental concentration; it also required a smaller labor force, creating a standing reserve of displaced weavers willing to accept the lowest wages. Thus the future for Paterson silk weavers spelled harder work for diminishing wages.[22]

After the failure of the 1911 and 1912 strikes in several silk and worsted mills in New Jersey led by the "Detroit IWW," a splinter organization formed by Daniel De Leon in 1908, local textile workers turned increasingly to Local 152, an IWW affiliate of the National Industrial Union of Textile Workers (NIUTW). Headed by Adolph Lessig and Ewald Koettgen in Paterson, Local 152 benefited significantly from the prestige generated by the IWW's victory in Lawrence. Thus when Doherty mill workers walked off their jobs on January 27, 1913, they eagerly accepted the leadership offered by the IWW.[23]

Local IWW leaders were joined by Flynn and Tresca from New York. On the morning of February 25, 1913, nearly 5,000 of Paterson's 6,000–7,000 broad-silk weavers—mostly Italians and Jews—abandoned the mills and gathered at Turn Hall to hear Tresca, Flynn, and local leaders urge them to wage a general strike. By the end of February, the striking broad-silk weavers were joined by some 6,000 dye-house workers, without whose cooperation a general shut down of the mills would not have been impossible. In early March, the predominantly English-speaking ribbon workers (English, German, and Irish), numbering around 6,000, also walked off their jobs. Only the small group of loom fixers and twisters—highly skilled and English-speaking—refused to strike, and scabbed whenever work became available. Nevertheless, by the end of March, some 25,000 silk workers had joined the strike, crippling operations for virtually all of Paterson's mills and dye houses.[24]

The IWW utilized the same methods that had proven successful in Lawrence, organizing a general strike committee invested with complete authority over the strike. Although membership in Local 152 increased from 900 to 9,000 during the strike, the composition of the strike committee remained primarily non-IWW. Specific demands included an eight-hour day, abolition of the four-loom system, a minimum wage of $12 per week for dyers' helpers, and a 25 percent increase for the other categories of silk workers. Recognition of the IWW was not one of the strike demands, nor would IWW organizers serve on any of the workers' delegations that might negotiate with the manufacturers. The official relationship of the IWW to the Paterson strike was advisory. The principal IWW advisors assigned to lead the strike were Flynn, Tresca, Haywood, and Patrick Quinlan.[25]

The intervention of "outside IWW agitators" was the pretext used by the silk manufacturers to reject any settlement short of surrender. Their intransigence derived from the huge advantages they enjoyed in conflicts with labor. Unlike Lawrence, where the woolen and worsted industry was dominated by the American Woolen Company, a single trust whose defeat would compel the smaller enterprises to accept the same settlement, the nearly 300 mills and dye houses of Paterson were individually-owned establishments. Furthermore, many of the larger companies owned annexes in various mining and industrial communities in eastern Pennsylvania—Allentown, Easton, Hazleton, Williamsport—where the labor force was 91 percent women and children (as compared to 56 percent in Paterson), worked more hours per week, and received less pay. Filling orders in their Pennsylvania mills enabled the larger establishments of Paterson to wage a war of attrition, and should any of their smaller competitors go bankrupt in the process, so much the better.[26] The manufacturers also derived strength from their virtual alliance with local authorities and police, who went to extreme lengths to break the strike. Investigators for the U.S. Commission on Industrial Relations (CIR), after studying the conduct of Paterson's police force and Inferior Courts, reported that "the police organization, coupled with the police magistrates, became tools of oppression…[and] trespassed every natural right and constitutional guarantee of the citizens."[27]

That almost 50 percent of the strikers ultimately arrested were Italians and 25 percent were Jews reflected more than the superior numbers and militancy of these two ethnic groups.[28] As Edward Zuerscher, secretary-treasurer of IWW Local 152, related to the CIR, Paterson's predominantly Irish police force "generally came with a drawn club, and sometimes with curses on their lips, especially if there were a foreign element on the picket line, and told them to get out of there, and called them Waps [sic] and Jews and such names as that which incensed the workers a great deal."[29] Such harassment reflected the "synthesis of nativist and antiradical sentiment," which had reached its peak among Paterson's English-speaking groups.[30]

When police brutality and mass arrests failed to attain their intended purpose, the manufactures employed several strategies against the IWW: using patriotism as a wedge to divide American-born and foreign-born strikers, the latter being the IWW's main supporters; and inviting the intervention of John Golden's United Textile Workers, the AFL affiliate bent on destroying the IWW. Neither strategy succeeded. What threatened the strikers' capacity to hold out was material privation—essentially no money for food, rent, and bills. Despite the generosity of local and outside sympathizers, the weekly cost of continuing the strike exceeded contributions by a wide margin.[31]

To reduce the economic strain on families and generate favorable publicity for the strike, IWW leaders organized an exodus of children, as they had done in Lawrence. The first contingent of children left Paterson on May 1, as part of a May Day celebration staged by the IWW. Altogether some 700 Paterson children were sent to stay with families in New York, Brooklyn, and Elizabeth. The children's exodus provided a small measure of economic relief, but failed to attract widespread sympathy and financial support. This was attributable to the fact that the authorities and police did not repeat the blunders of their counterparts in Lawrence, who clubbed women and children at the train station. The children of Paterson left the city unharmed and largely unnoticed.[32]

By the end of May, the plight of the strikers had become critical. Hope loomed in the form of a great pageant that would re-enact the silk workers' struggle as a theatrical production. The pageant was the brain-child of Bill Haywood, Mabel Dodge, the avant-garde hostess whose salon at 23 Fifth Avenue was New York's center of radical chic, and her new lover John Reed, a young writer and poet who belonged to a group of Greenwich Village intellectuals and bohemians drawn to the strike. Arrested on April 28, his first day in Paterson, while watching strikers picketing a mill, Reed spent several days in jail, sharing a cell with Tresca and several strikers. When the pageant was approved by the general strike committee, Reed plunged ahead with preparations, recruiting and directing a large staff of Greenwich Village artists and theatrical people who would stage the spectacle at Madison Square Garden.[33]

On June 7, 1913, more than 1,000 strikers selected to perform in the pageant crossed the Hudson River by ferry to the Christopher Street pier and marched up Fifth Avenue, carrying IWW banners and singing the "Marseillaise" and the "Internationale." That evening, 15,000 people filled Madison Square Garden, as the Paterson workers presented six episodes depicting typical scenes and dramatic high-points of the strike. As a drama, the pageant was a stirring success; as a fund raising enterprise, it was a disaster. The single performance generated a deficit of nearly $2,000.[34] Flynn, who had been skeptical from the outset, denounced the pageant for having "started the decline in the Paterson strike"[35]

Striker solidarity began to crumble by mid-June, when the socialist ribbon weavers led by Louis Magnet proposed that workers accept shop-by-shop agreements rather than continue fighting for the industry-wide settlement advocated by the IWW. When IWW leaders challenged the proposal, Magnet and his ribbon weavers declared them "outside agitators" and sought to deny them access to the general strike committee. Flynn remembered that "one day the door was virtually slammed in my face, until the Italian and Jewish workers made such an uproar, threatening to throw the others out of a three-story window, that the floor was granted [to speak]."[36] The shop-by-shop proposal was defeated by a referendum, with the highest percentage of negative votes cast by the predominantly Italian dyers' helpers, who were still faithful to the IWW. But the ribbon weavers refused to abide by the majority decision, and on July 18 they announced their withdrawal from the general strike committee and their decision to settle "their" strike themselves, shop by shop. The defection of the ribbon weavers demoralized the remaining members of the committee, who now passed a resolution endorsing shop-by-shop settlements. Flynn, Tresca, and Joe Ettor (Haywood was now too ill with ulcers to participate regularly) argued desperately in favor of continuing the strike, but by now panic was spreading among the strikers. The first to break *en masse* were the dyers' helpers, the men who had been the strike's most militant supporters. As the least skilled and most easily-replaced workers in the silk industry, they reacted out of fear that they might never regain their jobs. A week later, the broad silk weavers started returning to the mills, as did the ribbon weavers shortly thereafter. "So that," declared a bitterly angry Flynn, "was the tragedy of the Paterson strike, the tragedy of a stampede, the tragedy of an army, a solid phalanx being cut up into 300 pieces, each shop-piece trying to settle as best for themselves."[37]

When the strike ended officially on August 1, 1913, most of Paterson's silk workers had returned to the mills and dye houses under the same terms of employment against which they had rebelled twenty-two weeks earlier. About 2,500 diehard strikers left Paterson rather than accept defeat; perhaps 2,000 more were blacklisted as a result of their activities. Many others were displaced by the scabs hired during the course of the strike. The defeat of the silk workers had been crushing.[38] The IWW fared even worse. From the 9,000 silk workers enrolled at the height of the strike, the IWW's strength in Paterson declined to 1,300–1,500 dues-paying members by June 1914. Attempts to rouse demoralized workers for another strike action in the fall of 1913 and spring of 1914, failed completely. Never again would thousands of workers strike under the IWW banner in Paterson or any other city in the eastern United States. The Paterson defeat was the Waterloo of the union's eastern organization.[39]

The Italian Tribune

The Paterson strike of 1913 was the most important of Tresca's career. Bill Haywood attracted more attention from the press, but he was never active in Paterson for more than two or three days a week. His role was primarily inspirational.[40] The principal leaders of the strike were Flynn and Tresca. As in Lawrence, Flynn was enormously popular with Paterson's foreign and native-born strikers alike. She functioned as the main link between the IWW and the strikers, combining the roles of strategist, coordinator, conciliator, organizer, and agitator. Tresca performed the dual role of tribune and *condottiero* for the Italian silk workers, who constituted the backbone of the strike. Almost daily and nightly, from the speakers platform at Turn and Helvetia Halls and the window balcony of the Botto House in Haledon on Sundays, Tresca harangued the Italians countless times, explaining the need for union organization and discipline, and stirring their courage for the battles they would wage together on the picket lines against police, detectives, and scabs. Oratorical prowess on the speakers' platform and unflagging courage and combativeness in the field had become Tresca's trademark and the source of great respect from other radicals. *Il Proletario* wrote: "heedless of all persecution and danger, [Tresca] incites and electrifies the strikers to all out resistance not only with fiery words of revolutionary ardor, but with personal example and action."[41]

Without the leadership and inspiration Tresca provided to Italian broad silk weavers and dyers' helpers, the Paterson strike might never have lasted twenty-two weeks nor become renowned for its uncommon militancy. Tresca's contribution was all the more remarkable because he was essentially a one-man operation, receiving practically no assistance from the IWW or FSI. Neither organization assigned anyone to assist Tresca with Italian strikers, or serve as a substitute in the event of his imprisonment. The principal Italian leaders of the IWW and FSI, Joe Ettor and Arturo Giovannitti, were minor figures in the Paterson strike. The singularity of Tresca's role was not lost on opponents. The *Paterson Evening News* observed that "Tresca is practically the only Italian leader of the strike, and without him at the head, the great number of Italian strikers are really without a leader."[42]

Tresca became the favorite target of the police, who arrested him at least five times (eleven according to his own account), more than any other strike leader.[43] He, together with Flynn and Quinlan, was arrested for the first time on February 25, the day the strike began, after addressing strikers at Turn Hall and refusing Police Chief Bimson's invitation to leave town and never return. Charged with unlawful assembly and inciting riot, Tresca was sent to the county jail before being released on $1,000 bail provided by a local Italian. He was arrested again on March 11 for having led 400 strikers on a march the previous day to bring out the men still working at the Weidemann Silk Dyeing Co. Hauled before Recorder James Carroll, the magistrate who condemned hundreds of strikers, Tresca was sentenced the next day to sixty days for "disorderly conduct," i.e., briefly obstructing the path of a few pedestrians while leading a march. After spending several days in jail, Tresca was released on a *writ of certiorari* obtained from State Supreme Court Justice James F. Minturn, "the one bright spot on the side of the State authorities during the strike," according to Tresca's lawyer, Henry Marelli.[44] But Tresca's release failed to dispel the belief among Paterson's Italians that the special attention their leader was receiving from the police amounted to racial discrimination. Noting the mood of the Italian community, the *Paterson Evening News* commented that "there is no end of heated feeling especially in the [predominantly Italian] Sixth Ward, where Tresca was a big favorite with his fellow countrymen."[45]

Tresca also participated in the IWW's efforts to weaken the Paterson manufacturers by stopping production at their Pennsylvania annexes. After local socialists led a walk-out of the Italian dye-house workers in Allentown in mid-March, Haywood, Tresca, FSI militant Ugo Lupi, and several IWW organizers went there to convince other workers to join the strike. The Italian dye workers stayed out for several months, but efforts to broaden the strike in Allentown was unsuccessful. Another strike occurred in Hazelton, but the UTW undermined the IWW by negotiating a settlement at the beginning of April. Hopes were renewed when a minority of holdouts continued to strike and picket. Tresca, as usual, focused his attention on the Italian workers, most of whom were coal miners' children, usually girls ranging in age from fourteen to eighteen. Their efforts came to naught and the strike collapsed. The IWW's campaign to shut down the silk industry in eastern Pennsylvania failed completely.[46]

The high point of the Paterson strike for Tresca—the episode that solidified his reputation as a "dangerous revolutionary"—was the funeral of Valentino Modestino. On April 17, private detectives hired by the Weidemann Dye Co. opened fire on jeering picketers, killing a bystander named Valentino Modestino as he stood on the porch of his house. The IWW orchestrated the funeral arrangements for propaganda purposes, as it had done in Lawrence the previous year. A ten-block long funeral cortege snaked its way through the streets of Paterson en route to the cemetery, where Haywood and Tresca delivered orations honoring the deceased and condemning the mill owners, police, and detectives. Tresca's eulogy concluded with an ominous cry for vengeance, which sent chills through the onlookers: "Fellow workers, don't forget the principle of the toilers who came from Italy! For blood you must take blood!" ["*Sangue chiama sangue!*"][47] A news reporter described Tresca's exhortation:

> No finished actor could have spoken the line with more dramatic intensity, nor have sent the words home with greater force. Though the earth had not yet been cast upon the burial box the listeners loosed a volume of applause that was startlingly strange in the resting place of the dead.[48]

Then, at a signal from Tresca, thousands of silk workers filed past Modestino's grave and dropped red carnations upon the casket, flowers representing—in

Tresca's words—"a symbol of triumph in the cause for which this man was killed."[49]

As Tresca was known to disagree with the IWW's policy of passive resistance in the face of police brutality, his "blood calls for blood" speech caused a furor in Paterson, and several local newspapers urged that he be driven out of town. Daring those who voiced such demands "to do it themselves," Tresca reiterated to the press that he meant what he had said about "blood for blood."[50] A few days later, Tresca, Flynn, and Quinlan were indicted by the Grand Jury for unlawful assemblage and advocating personal injury, charges resulting from earlier demonstrations and encounters with the police. While in jail awaiting bail, Tresca had his first encounter with John Reed, who was placed in the same dirty cell. They had never met before, and Reed's incessant questioning about the strike led Tresca to believe he was a "stoolpigeon" planted by the police. Only when Bill Haywood later identified the young man as John Reed did Tresca relent and give him a warm embrace. Reed emerged from his jail house experience a devoted convert to the class struggle.[51]

Tresca, like Flynn, voiced doubt about the feasibility of the Paterson Pageant and played no role in its preparation. On the appointed day, however, Tresca led 800 strikers in a march to Union Square for a demonstration; he also participated in the performance, delivering a typical Turn Hall speech and reprising his "blood calls for blood" oration during the episode that depicted Modestino's funeral.[52] Tresca did not single out the pageant as a major cause of defeat, but his silence on the matter suggests that he may have shared Flynn's pessimism from the outset.[53]

Less than a month later, Tresca reprised his signature "blood calls for blood" speech, not on the theatrical stage, but at another funeral. During a fracas with scabs early in July, an Italian anarchist broad silk worker, Vincenzo Madonna, was shot and killed by a scab who had been given permission to carry a revolver by Mayor McBride. On the morning of July 5, under a dark and threatening sky, Haywood, Flynn, and Tresca stood at the gravesite, each overcome by emotion. Haywood, surrounded by Madonna's widow and four children, shed copious tears and managed to speak only a few words. Flynn was likewise brief. Tresca spoke last, again issuing his warning that "*Sangue Chiama Sangue!*" Voices in the crowd shouted "*Vendetta!*" in response.[54]

Belief that the silk workers would take revenge by conducting another general strike was a consoling thought for Tresca when defeat finally came in August. Like Flynn and Haywood, he believed that victory could have been won if the strike had continued for a few weeks longer. But he did not blame the strikers for capitulating. He understood how hunger, police brutality, and legalized repression by the courts had exhausted their capacity to resist. The culprits he deemed responsible were the socialists on the general strike committee, led by Magnet, who represented the English-speaking ribbon weavers. By opting for shop-by-shop settlements, the ribbon weavers and their leaders administered a *coup de grace* to the flagging strike effort. They were able to do so, Tresca believed, because the IWW had committed the "unpardonable error" of entrusting final authority over the strike—one for which it assumed moral responsibility—to a general strike committee that did not include a majority of IWW members.[55]

That the ribbon weavers had been the last to join and the first to abandon the strike in pursuit of self-interest did not surprise Tresca. Their actions confirmed his belief that the concept, much less the practice, of worker solidarity scarcely existed in the American labor movement. Contemptuous of Italians, Jews, and other "new immigrants," whom they deemed poor union material and excessively prone to strike, the English-speaking groups and those affiliated with the AFL had little compunction about breaking solidarity with "foreigners." Nor did Tresca find it paradoxical that the leaders of the conservative ribbon weavers were socialists. He had come to believe the SPA guilty of deliberately withholding financial and moral support from the Paterson strikers because it hated the IWW and feared the Wobblies' growing influence among workers.[56] Indeed, Jacob Panken attributed the failure of the Paterson strike entirely to the philosophy and tactics of the IWW. "The strike of the silk workers," he declared, "was mismanaged to the extent of amounting to a crime," because the IWW had held out for an industry-wide settlement rather than negotiations with individual employers. The root of the IWW's refusal to act like the AFL, according to Panken, lay in its philosophical commitment to direct action. Panken's implicit message was clear: Since the Paterson strike had demonstrated the ineffectiveness of direct action as practiced by the IWW, workers should place their trust in political action and support socialist politicians with their money and votes.[57]

Tresca was appalled that Panken and the socialist organ, *Call*, would exploit the defeat of the silk workers for electioneering purposes. His belief that ballot-box socialism (*socialismo schedaiulo*) amounted to little more than political opportunism was confirmed, as was his conviction that the emancipation of the proletariat could be achieved only by means of a violent revolution initiated by a general strike. And once again, Tresca saw a positive dimension to a strike that ended in material defeat, declaring that "this Paterson strike was neither the first nor the last assault by the ranks of the proletariat against the monstrous, feudal, barbarous edifice of blood draining capitalism."[58] The silk workers, he insisted, had gained valuable experience, because every strike was an episode in the class struggle, a stepping-stone on the path toward the ultimate triumph of the proletariat.[59]

6

Tresca and Flynn

Gossip among radicals suggested that when Tresca and Flynn first met in May 1912, she was involved romantically with Joe Ettor.[1] If so, with Ettor in jail, Tresca had an easy time sweeping Flynn off her feet. Subsequent activities together in 1912 and 1913 solidified the political and personal partnership that would endure until 1925. Recalling the year they met, Flynn wrote that "he was then a tall, slender, handsome man in his mid-thirties, and I was deeply in love with him." [2] Indeed, Flynn's memoirs and her many poems indicate that Tresca was the great love of her life. Tresca had expressed his romantic sentiments during the Ettor-Giovannitti agitation with several inscriptions in the copy of Gabriele D'Annunzio's *The Maidens of the Rocks*, which he gave her as a gift. The November 17 inscription, in Tresca's inimitable English, read: "Suppose at some time you read this book some flame is kindled in your heart—remember at this time *mio dolce cuore, sogno, speranza, luce dell'anima mia* [my sweet heart, dream, hope, light of my soul]—one heart has the same flame for you alone."[3] Flynn's reciprocating gift was Elizabeth Barrett Browning's *Sonnets From the Portuguese*, with poignant passages underlined. This was the little volume that Tresca lost during the hotel workers' strike.[4]

Tresca was always attracted to women who possessed keen intelligence and fiery spirit as well as good looks, and Flynn possessed all these qualities. Although not yet twenty-two years old when they met, Flynn already ranked with Emma Goldman, Mother Jones, and Kate Richards O'Hare as one of the foremost female leaders in American's radical labor movement.[5] A convinced socialist by the age of fifteen, Flynn impressed everyone with her oratorical prowess and pleasing countenance. Theodore Dreiser described the young Irish rebel girl in 1906 as "An East Side Joan of Arc," whom the capitalist world had better take seriously.[6] Flynn joined the IWW in 1906 and attended the union's convention in Chicago the following year. Impressed with her militancy and speaking ability, the IWW sent Flynn to lecture on the Mesabi Iron Ore Range in December 1907. There she became infatuated with an iron miner and sometime organizer for the IWW named Jack A. Jones. They were married within a few weeks of their meeting. Vincent St. John, the secretary-treasurer of the IWW, who became her most cherished friend, wisely perceived that "Elizabeth fell in love with the West and the miners and she married the first one she met."[7]

The marriage was destined to be unhappy and brief. Jones expected Flynn to become a housewife and mother, a prospect she dreaded. Flynn soon left for Montana and Washington, where she organized miners and lumbermen and participated in the IWW's free speech fight in Spokane. Despite the infrequency of her reunions with Jones, Flynn got pregnant and then lost the child born prematurely. She bore a second son, Fred ("Buster"), on May 19, 1910. By then, Flynn had resolved to rid herself of Jones, explaining to her father: "I don't love him any more. Besides, he *bores* me!" As for Buster, Flynn had neither the time nor inclination for parenting, and the child was deposited with her sisters, Annie Gurley and Kathie, who raised him to unhappy adulthood.[8]

In Lawrence, Flynn had distinguished herself as one of the IWW's principal strike leaders, and during the Ettor-Giovannitti defense campaign her role far exceeded that of IWW chieftain "Big Bill" Haywood. After the acquittal of Ettor, Giovannitti, and Caruso, Tresca and Flynn returned to their respective families in New Kensington and New York. Whether they had made plans to live together is not known. Given Tresca's voracious appetite for woman and past history of multiple affairs, the mere fact that Tresca had fallen in love with Flynn was no guarantee of future commitment. But once rejoined as leaders of the hotel workers strike in January 1913, their affair re-ignited and a committed relationship developed.

After the affair became public knowledge, Tresca was obliged to choose between Elizabeth and Helga. Early in March 1913, Tresca abandoned Helga and Beatrice in New Kensington and went to live with Flynn and her family at 511 East 134th Street in the South Bronx. With his handsome looks, Latin charm, good humor, and culinary talent, Tresca easily ingratiated himself with Flynn's mother and sisters, and was quickly assimilated into their bustling household. For the next twelve years, Tresca and Flynn represented the most important male/female alliance among radicals in the United States, surpassing Emma Goldman and Alexander Berkman, whose intimate relationship had ended years earlier.

In April 1914, Tresca transferred *L'Avvenire* from New Kensington to 2205 Third Avenue in the Italian section of East Harlem, and resumed publication that September with a circulation of 3,000–4,000. Home to the largest *colonia italiana* in the country and the greatest variety and number of *sovversivi*, New York provided the ideal environment in which Tresca's militant activism could impact fellow radicals and working-class Italians. Moreover, his integration into the mainstream of American radicalism would be fully realized in New York, where foreign and native-born subversives combined to form the elite of the American Left. Tresca's entrée into these circles was greatly facilitated by his partnership with Flynn, whose own network of left-wing associates and friends was very extensive. Among the radicals, progressive, and intellectuals with whom Tresca would soon associate in New York were Max Eastman, John Reed, Upton Sinclair, Scott Nearing, Lincoln Steffens, Roger Baldwin, Margaret Sanger, Mary Heaton Vorse, Mary Ganz, Alexander Berkman, Emma Goldman, and Norman Thomas. These new associations helped Tresca attain the celebrity status his ego craved.

New York also provided a social and cultural ambiance that was perfectly suited to Tresca's freewheeling and fun-loving lifestyle, qualities that defined his persona as much as radical activism. Only the depth of his commitment to the Italian coal miners and mill hands of Pennsylvania can explain how Tresca survived as long as he did living in dreary industrial towns like Pittsburgh and New Kensington. Tresca's insatiable appetite for excitement and challenge ensured that New York would remain his home, playground, and primary battlefield for the rest of his life.

Tresca had no difficulty recruiting a new staff for *L'Avvenire* among local comrades. His principal associate was his closest friend and regular collaborator Pietro Allegra. The two men shared similar backgrounds. Born to middle class parents in Palermo in 1877, Allegra had been arrested several times before his emigration to the United States in 1904 to avoid a jail term. He lived in New York for two years after his arrival, organizing a union of Italian cigar makers while working for the De Nobili Cigar Company, owned by the Marchese Prosporo De Nobili and located in Long Island City. In 1906, he moved to Pittsburgh and operated a cigar store. An active member of FSI, Allegra became Tresca's closest associate, writing articles for *L'Avvenire* and assisting with editorial functions. When Tresca transferred *L'Avvenire* to New York, Allegra followed. Because of his long association with the company, De Nobili appointed Allegra chief organizer of sales. The position required frequent traveling to Italian communities throughout the country, and Allegra utilized these opportunities to give lectures on radical themes to Italian workers. Allegra thus became the only Italian radical whose propaganda tours were financed by a capitalist. On the speakers' platform, Allegra and Tresca were studies in contrast: the one short and slight of stature, with a tenor voice that rose in pitch and sometimes cracked as his excitement mounted; the other tall and increasingly heavy-set, with a sonorous basso often compared to an organ. While Tresca almost never lost his composure in confrontational situations, Allegra's quick temper and irascibility frequently got the better of him. In *L'Avvenire* and its successor, *Il Martello*, Allegra excelled as a polemicist in dozens of the internecine rivalries that bedeviled the Italian immigrant Left.[9]

One such conflict erupted immediately after Tresca transferred *L'Avvenire* to New York. The FSI was distressed by the prospect of *L'Avvenire*'s competing in New York with *Il Proletario*, so they proposed a "fusion" of the two newspapers. Tresca spurned the proposal, declaring he would never relinquish his independence to become an employee of the FSI. Hostility intensified when Edmondo Rossoni became director of *Il Proletario* in June 1914. The future Fascist labor leader was a talented but ruthless man with authoritarian tendencies, who hated anyone who rivaled him in popularity, Tresca in particular. For more than nine months, Rossoni waged a relentless campaign to destroy Tresca's reputation and standing in the movement. Angered by Rossoni's libelous attacks and the FSI's efforts to wrest control of *L'Avvenire*, Tresca nearly severed his ties with the Italian syndicalist federation and the IWW, for which *Il Proletario* was now an official organ.[10]

On Trial in Paterson

Tresca's trial on charges of inciting riot and advocating personal injury during the strike began in Paterson on December 15, 1913. The outcome was unpredictable.

Flynn's trial on June 30 had ended with a hung jury, but fellow strike leader Pat Quinlan was sentenced to serve two to seven years by Judge Abram Klenert, who had become enraged after Flynn escaped his wrath. Tresca's earlier conviction and sixty day sentence for disorderly conduct had been overturned by the New Jersey Supreme Court, but now he faced Judge Klenert and Passaic County Prosecutor Michael Dunn. When Dunn later testified before the Senate Commission on Industrial Relations on June 17, 1914, he asserted that Tresca was "one of the worst men in the United States today," the principal leader of the "foreign element," and the man responsible for virtually every act of violence perpetrated by the "strikers." The police, of course, were entirely blameless.[11]

Tresca's "crimes" were allegedly committed when he led strikers in a protest march against scabs working at the Weideman Silk Dyeing Company on April 17, 1913. Tresca had irked the authorities by declaring: "This strike is the beginning of a great revolution."[12] But the trial focused on whether he had urged strikers to beat up scabs. The main prosecution witness was a second-generation Italian American policeman who claimed to have overheard Tresca exhort the strikers to commit violence. Under cross-examination, the detective was asked by Tresca's attorney, Henry Marelli, to write down in Italian what he claimed the accused had said. He could not do so. Marelli then asked him to conjugate the Italian verb *battere* (to beat). Again, he could not do so. Nevertheless, the jurors deliberated for twenty-one hours before announcing they were deadlocked: eight to four in favor of conviction.[13]

Dunn was irate and reactivated the charges. Tresca's second trial on June 30, 1914 was an encore of the first. Once again, the verdict hinged upon Tresca's alleged statement about "revolution" and "beatings." This time two more Italian-American policemen claimed they overheard Tresca urge violence. Their credibility was demolished anew by Marelli when they, too, failed to conjugate the verb *battere*. Dunn's depiction of Tresca as a dangerous revolutionary, who threatened national security, failed to sway the jurors imported from Hudson County. They returned a verdict of "not guilty" after deliberating only twenty minutes.[14]

Unemployment and Agitation, 1914

The United States experienced a severe depression in the winter of 1913–1914. New York was especially hard hit, as temperatures remained below freezing, snow fell incessantly, and more than 300,000 found themselves unemployed.[15] Public assistance for the unemployed was practically non-existent. Soon a broad array of radicals and liberals organized protest demonstrations and relief efforts. The IWW's plan called for the unemployed to descend upon New York's churches and request food and shelter in the name of Christian charity. This strategy has always been attributed to Frank Tannenbaum, a twenty-one-year-old waiter, anarchist, and member of the IWW who frequented the Francisco Ferrer Center and the offices of Emma Goldman's *Mother Earth*.[16] Tresca maintained that Tannenbaum was one of a number of young radicals who frequented the office of *L'Avvenire* and sought his advice about the unemployed. "So one day," Tresca claimed, "I chased them out of my office, telling them, 'Go, gather together as many unemployed as you can and lead them to the churches.'"[17]

Several of the most important Protestant churches were "invaded" by Tannenbaum and his men during February and March, with Tresca accompanying them as an observer.[18] The unemployed comported themselves peacefully, but the fact that the church invasions had been organized by the IWW caused the press to react with apoplectic fury. *The New York Times* demanded that "immediate and decisive steps should be taken by the police to suppress this I.W.W. pest, which is, in effect, nothing more than a cheap advertisement of the most abominable organization ever formed in this country."[19] The *New York World* called the church invasions "a criminal menace," and warned that "the I.W.W. leaders, who are inviting the worst elements of a great city to plunder, do not want work—they seek a social revolution!"[20]

On March 4, Tannenbaum led 300 men to the Roman Catholic church of St. Alphonsus at 312 West Broadway. Father Schneider refused to admit the men, declaring that their presence would constitute a sacrilege. "The Church of the carpenter of Jerusalem," Tresca later wrote, "refused to give aid and comfort to the hungry and unemployed carpenters, shoemakers, garment workers of New York."[21] While Tannenbaum and the priest argued, the unemployed entered the church and sat in the pews. The police were summoned, a small riot ensued, and 189 men and one woman were taken into custody, including Tannenbaum. Convicted of incitement to riot on March 27, Tannenbaum was sentenced to a year in jail on Blackwell's Island, after which he abandoned the radical movement.[22]

After receiving rave reviews from the press for their violent intervention at St. Alphonsus Church, New York's predominantly Irish police force—energized by its hatred of "foreigners," especially Italians and Jews—began to beat up the unemployed and arrest radicals at every opportunity. Tresca recalled that on one Sunday afternoon, after delivering a lecture to Italian anarchists at the Circolo Bresci at 301 East 106th Street in East Harlem, he and members of the audience were set upon by police with clubs after leaving the hall. Hearing a cry for help, "I turned back to find myself confronted by a detective who, sticking a gun in my stomach, ordered me not to move, and I had to choose between a bullet in my body and looking on without being able to interfere with the most brutal attack upon my comrades."[23] The beatings continued as long as there were victims to find.[24]

Tresca and the Anarchists

By the spring of 1914, having failed to ameliorate the conditions of the unemployed or enlist new recruits for the union, the IWW abandoned the strategy of invading churches and sharply reduced assistance for the jobless.[25] The IWW's disengagement was also hastened by the ascendance of the anarchists as leaders of the unemployed. Haywood, Flynn, and Ettor disliked collaborating with the anarchists, because their direct action approach often resulted in violent encounters with the police for which the IWW received blame. Tresca, on the other hand, who served as "a sort of connecting link between the IWW and the Anarchists,"[26] had always been a proponent of direct action and was now gravitating steadily into the anarchists' orbit. Tresca's relationship with America's two most famous anarchists, Emma Goldman and Alexander Berkman, would never become close, but he regarded them with great respect and admiration, and their collaboration during the agitation for the unemployed may well have influenced his ideological transition. For, in 1914, Tresca declared that he was now an anarcho-syndicalist in the mold of Armando Borghi, leader of the *Unione Sindacale Italiana* in Italy.[27]

Union Square and Rutgers Square, on the East Side, were the gathering places where Tresca shared the speakers' platform several times a week with anarchists and Wobblies more militant than their leaders. Tresca urged the unemployed to engage in expropriation of property in order to survive.[28] Violence, however, was the province of the police department. After a large rally in Union Square on the afternoon of March 21, Berkman, Goldman, and Tresca urged the unemployed to join them in a march to the Ferrer Center at 64 East 107th Street, where food would be dispensed and shelter provided for about 250 people that night. Behind a black silk flag emblazoned with the Italian word "*Demolizione*" (Demolition) in red letters, 2,000 men and women marched peacefully but boisterously uptown, jeering "Down with the parasites!" as they passed the Waldorf-Astoria Hotel and "Down with the Church!" as they reached St. Patrick's Cathedral.[29] *The New York Times* and other dailies reacted as if the march had sounded the tocsin for revolution, demanding use of repressive force before "the whole lawless element of gangsters and gunmen, thieves and thugs will join the I.W.W. under the banner marked '*Demolizione*'" and start looting.[30] On April 4, at a mass rally in Union Square organized by the anarchists, police attacked the crowd with exceptional brutality, injuring scores with their clubs flailing left and right. Two of Tresca's young friends, Joseph O'Carroll and Arthur Caron, were singled out and beaten so severely that they required hospitalization.[31]

The Ludlow Massacre

Agitation increased significantly after the Ludlow Massacre on April 20, 1914. The Colorado Fuel & Iron Company, of which John D. Rockefeller, Jr. was the majority share holder, conducted its mining operations like a feudal overlord, completely free from state regulation and oversight, controlling every aspect of life within the twenty-seven camps it owned. Miners and their families, primarily southern and eastern European immigrants, were ruthlessly exploited and oppressed, living in conditions aptly described as medieval. In September 1913, 250 delegates from mining camps in Colorado, encouraged by the venerable Mother Jones, met with UMWA officials in Trinidad and decided to strike for union recognition and other demands, most of which were granted by state law but ignored by Rockefeller's company. Anticipating the strike, officials expelled the miners from their company-owned shacks to face the approaching winter without food or shelter. The UMWA set up tent colonies on land rented outside the perimeter of company property at Ludlow and twelve other cites. On September 23, between 11,000 and 13,000 miners—about 90 percent of the work force—occupied the tent colonies with their families and meager possessions.

Soon they were obliged to withstand sub-zero temperatures and armed clashes with scabs, company guards, private detectives, and state militiamen.[32]

Tresca took a keen interest in the Ludlow strike. A high percentage of the striking miners were Italians, and *L'Avvenire* circulated widely within the camps. Tresca utilized the lecture circuit and his newspaper to generate moral and financial support among Italian sympathizers. His message of forceful resistance was often conveyed through graphic illustrations in *L'Avvenire*, such as one depicting a wall of flames behind a field strewn with dead women and children, through which a helmeted coal miner marching in full stride is firing a pistol in one hand and carrying a child in the other.[33]

The carnage depicted was not derived from the artist's imagination; it accurately captured the reality of the infamous Ludlow Massacre. At 9:00 A.M., on April 20, 1914, a detachment of deputies and national guardsmen began raking the tent colony at Ludlow with rifle and machine gun fire from an overlooking ridge. A thousand men, women, and children dashed about frantically trying to escape the fusillade, some running into the hills nearby, others seeking shelter in pits that had been dug under the tents. All day long the attackers shot at anything that moved. At sunset, the besiegers charged the encampment, looting, destroying, and setting fire to the tents. The next morning, thirty-two people were found dead, many of them burned and suffocated by the flames. Three strike leaders had also been deliberately murdered during the day.[34]

Infuriated by the slaughter, Tresca wanted to join the strikers at once, but the UMWA refused to invite Tresca, claiming that his presence would jeopardize the strikers' cause. Tresca finally abandoned his plan when his friend Armando Palizzari, one of the Italian organizers on the scene, advised him against visiting Ludlow because the cause was lost. Tresca devoted himself instead to the renewed agitation in New York, which now shifted focus from the unemployed to John D. Rockefeller, Jr.[35]

As one of the chieftains of the church invasions and anti-Rockefeller demonstrations, Tresca was often a magnet for reporters. He loved the attention and frequently obliged them with statements that were usually misquoted. Thus *The New York Times* declared on May 26, 1914: "TRESCA REDS GOING TO WAR: I.W.W. Leader Promises Men for Colorado Battle Ground." The next day, the prestigious daily ran a letter attributed to Tresca (actually written by a reporter), with a headline declaring: "THREAT TO ROCKEFELLER: Carlos [sic] Tresca Hints at an Eye for an Eye in Colorado War.[36]

Rockefeller, meanwhile, had concluded quite correctly that his life was in danger and took refuge at his Pocantico Hills estate near Tarrytown, some thirty miles north of New York. His tormentors followed. Between May 30 and June 22, demonstrators—most of them anarchists—tried to assemble peacefully in Fountain Square, the village's outdoor forum; however, they were attacked repeatedly by local police and outraged villagers and many arrested. Tresca participated in several of these demonstrations, but managed to escape arrest or injury. Others not so lucky began plotting revenge.[37]

Battle for the Garibaldi Memorial

In the midst of the anti-Rockefeller agitation, an event took place that demonstrated how Tresca's activities now straddled two distinct environments—one Italian and the other American—with him passing back and forth between them without breaking stride. The event was the battle for the Garibaldi Memorial of July 1914. Tresca had been contacted by General Giuseppe ("Peppino") Garibaldi, grandson of the revolutionary hero of the Risorgimento and former chief of staff to Francisco Madero during the Mexican revolution of 1910–1911. Visiting New York with his brother Ricciotti, Peppino expressed outrage that the *prominenti* of the Sons of Italy, the *Tiro a Segno* society, and other Italian nationalist organizations were planning to charge admission at the July Fourth commemoration held annually at the Garibaldi Memorial, originally the home of the Italian inventor Antonio Meucci, who gave refuge to Garibaldi from 1850 to 1853. Peppino wanted Tresca to mobilize the Italian "masses" and seize the Memorial in order to stage an anti-monarchist demonstration. Tresca did not trust Peppino Garibaldi (he and Ricciotti later became Fascist agents), and explained that the "masses" he would lead into action were revolutionary workers, not the patriotic Italians the general had in mind. But Peppino insisted and Tresca obliged.[38]

A contingent of about 600 *sovversivi* assembled at South Ferry Square, in Battery Park, on the morning of July 4. After listening to speeches by Tresca, Allegra, and other leaders, they boarded the ferry to Staten Island, disembarked at St. George, and marched to the Garibaldi Memorial at Rosebank, where they found the gates locked and guarded by members of the *Tiro a Segno* and other patriotic societies, who refused admission even to Garibaldi's grandson. Peppino was befuddled by the situation. He lamented to Tresca that it would be "a disgrace to the Italian race" if rival factions were to battle. Tresca countered that he was not there to protect the good name of the Italians but to fight. With Tresca leading the charge, the *sovversivi* routed the *prominenti*, tore down the Italian flag flying over the Garibaldi Memorial, replacing it with the red flag of revolution. They spent the rest of the day celebrating and listening to more speeches. On the return trip, Tresca's jubilant mood turned to dismay when he noticed the headlines of the evening newspapers. A big explosion on Lexington Avenue in East Harlem had claimed the lives of several young anarchists he knew.[39]

Lexington Avenue Bomb

To avenge the repeated beatings and arrests suffered by anti-Rockefeller protesters, Alexander Berkman and a number of young anarchists associated with the Ferrer Center had plotted to assassinate Rockefeller. Berkman, whose botched attempt to assassinate industrialist Henry Clay Frick in 1892 had resulted in his spending fourteen years in prison, was one of anarchism's most unabashed advocates of retaliatory violence. His plan called for bombing Rockefeller's mansion at Pocantico Hills. His fellow conspirators included Arthur Caron, Carl Hanson, Charles Berg, Charles Plunkett, Louise Berger, Becky Edelson, and perhaps a few others associated with the Ferrer Center and the Circolo Bresci.[40] After a meeting at the Ferrer Center on the night of July 3, Caron, Hanson, and Berg went to Tarrytown to commit the deed (they did not know Rockefeller was vacationing in Maine), but either they failed to gain access to the heavily-guarded estate or the bomb failed to detonate. They returned to New York that night, bringing their bomb with them to Louise Berger's apartment at 1626 Lexington Avenue, between 103rd and 104th Streets, where they had been storing dynamite. Shortly after 9:00 A.M., on July 4, the explosives somehow ignited, devastating the upper three floors of the six-story tenement. Caron, Hanson, and Berg were killed, as was Marie Chavez, a young woman who rented a room in the apartment but was not involved in the conspiracy. Another occupant, a young Wobblie named Michael Murphy, escaped injury when his bed fell through the floor to what was left of the apartment below.[41]

The next day, the office of L'Avvenire was crowded with news reporters hoping for a scoop. Tresca acknowledged his friendship with Caron and the fact that the young man had told him he wanted to assassinate Rockefeller. Asked why he had not notified the authorities, he replied: "I am not an agent of the Police Department."[42] Queried next about his association with Emma Goldman and Alexander Berkman, Tresca remained candid about his working relationship with the famous anarchists, but when asked whether Berkman was "in the bomb-throwing business," he refused to answer any more questions.[43] Tresca was subpoenaed to appear at the District Attorney's office the following day but was not interrogated.[44] Berkman, Berger, Ganz, and other members of the Ferrer Center were questioned by the police, and the Circolo Bresci was raided and several of its members manhandled. But the police were unable to identify other conspirators or prove that a bomb plot had really existed.[45]

Flynn, meanwhile, had become very concerned about Tresca's physical health and emotional state, and hoped that they and her sickly son Buster could get away from New York and spend some time relaxing at the Provincetown summer home of her friend Mary Heaton Vorse. "Carlo is suffering very much lately with stomach trouble [the lingering effect of the blow he had received during the hotel workers' strike] and I am anxious to get him away for a change," she wrote to Vorse after the explosion. "But I don't like to leave him in the city alone just yet; you know he is *hot headed* and requires ballast just now. He is almost a nervous wreck over this tragedy. He knew them all [the dead anarchists], whereas I don't remember one."[46]

Tresca did not take a vacation. Through his friend Lincoln Steffens, head of the Free Speech League and a personal friend of the police commissioner, Tresca obtain permission for a funeral demonstration in Union Square to honor the comrades who died in the Lexington Avenue explosion.[47] IWW leaders Bill Haywood and Joe Ettor, desperate to disassociate the IWW from Rockefeller's would-be assassins, vigorously opposed the plan. Ettor publicly repudiated Caron, stating that he had been rejected for membership in the union because he was unemployed, and that "the I.W.W. does not approve dynamiting or setting off bombs."[48] Tresca was outraged by Ettor's craven declaration, denouncing his remarks as "false, entirely uncalled for, and cowardly."[49]

Tresca soon crossed swords with Haywood over IWW participation in the Union Square demonstration. Tresca recalled: "Haywood wanted the IWW to withdraw from this funeral demonstration and leave it to the Anarchists alone. I was at that time identified with the IWW and refused this proposal."[50] A meeting was held at the home of Mary Heaton Vorse in Greenwich Village to decide a course of action. "The room was packed," Tresca recounted, "but everyone kept still while Bill and I fought it out." Haywood disagreed with Tresca's contention that the IWW had initiated the unemployment agitation and should cooperate with the anarchists. Confident that the young Wobblies present would support him, Haywood was shocked and silent, as if struck by a blow, when they sided with Tresca. "For the first time in our relationship," Tresca recalled, "I was no longer his lieutenant but his equal. Then in a voice I'll never forget, he said, 'It's settled, boys.'"[51] Haywood acquiesced to Tresca's demand for IWW participation in the memorial service but later reneged. Several Wobblies, such as Flynn and Charles Plunkett, agreed to speak in an individual capacity, rather than as representatives of the IWW.

Some 20,000 people assembled in Union Square on Saturday, July 11, 1914, surrounded by several hundred policemen ready to attack at the first sign of disorder. Located in the center of Union Square was a small brown cement cenotaph, with a clenched fist rising from the top, containing the ashes of Caron, Hanson, and Berg. The speakers' platform was decorated with red banners and surrounded by floral wreaths. Berkman, acting as chairman, opened the ceremonies. All of speakers eulogized the dead anarchists, attributing their tragic end to the tyranny of capitalism; some of them also sang the praises of violence and dynamite. But for all the violent rhetoric of the speakers, the memorial demonstration passed without disorder.[52]

Political Differences and Personal Life

Tresca and Flynn reacted very differently to the memorial ceremonies in Union Square. Essentially a believer in non-violence, Flynn was utterly dismayed when one anarchist speaker after the other lauded the victims and heartily endorsed the use of dynamite. She even expressed disgust over exhibiting the victims' ashes. So upset was Flynn with their behavior, that she vowed "never to speak [publicly] with the anarchists again."[53] Tresca, although never an advocate of bombs or assassinations, fervently believed in the necessity of revolutionary violence. After the IWW distanced itself from Caron and his comrades, he wrote in Goldman's *Mother Earth*: "When people get 'cold feet' and rush into print at the least sign of danger and repudiate violence, like Ettor, then I want to go on record—like my comrade Alexander Berkman—that under certain circumstances I favor violence."[54]

The contrasting positions Tresca and Flynn had taken with respect to the anarchists and the Union Square demonstration reflected a basic pattern in their partnership. They had already fought side by side in several important struggles, and would continue to do so until their separation in 1925, but Tresca and Flynn were by no means of a single mind on all issues. "My life with Carlo," she wrote, "was tempestuous, undoubtedly because we were both strong personalities with separate and often divided interests."[55] Their political differences were subtle yet substantive: Tresca was now an anarcho-syndicalist; Flynn remained a socialist, despite having "wandered afield into the path of syndicalism."[56] Their ability to overcome their political and personal differences, at least during the prime of their relationship, was attributable to the strength of their romantic bond—or, as Tresca's daughter bluntly put it, "they resolved their differences in bed."[57]

Cultural differences were as much a source of division between them as ideology and tactics. Flynn later portrayed Tresca as a parochial Italian: "He wrote and spoke only in Italian and made little or no effort to learn English or to participate in American affairs. His preoccupation was with Italian affairs, his friends were predominantly Italian anarchists."[58] Flynn's contention that Tresca was indifferent to "American affairs" was patently false. Even a casual perusal of Tresca's writings in *L'Avvenire* and its successor *Il Martello* confirm the depths of his interest in American affairs. Moreover, Tresca's association with an inherently American organization like the IWW rendered Flynn's distinction between "Italian" and "American" affairs too arbitrary and rigid. After Lawrence, the parameters of Tresca's activities and associations extended far beyond their Italian epicenter.

As for Tresca's English, Max Eastman said of his friend: "He does not talk English with an Italian accent; he talks Italian with English words."[59] Tresca's command of English was certainly limited when they first met, but his usage and proficiency increased steadily even though he would never master correct syntax, spelling, or pronunciation. Although most of his speeches were in Italian, Tresca communicated quite effectively with workers of other ethnic groups, whose English was often more limited than his. Similarly, Tresca had little difficulty conversing on a casual or intellectual level with the newspaper reporters who sometimes flocked to his office or the American radicals and intellectuals with whom he became politically associated. In fact, "Tresca had a wonderful and unique way of speaking which was really an asset," recalled his friend Norman Thomas.[60] Tresca's idiosyncratic English complimented his warm personality, humor, and *joie de vivre*, endearing him to nearly everyone he met.[61]

Tresca had no difficulty functioning in Flynn's American world, making friends and comrades of so many of her associates. The same cannot be said for Flynn in Tresca's world of Italian *sovversivi*, an alien subculture in which she, an Irish American, never felt really comfortable. Flynn patronizingly characterized the Italian anarchists as "a strange yet simple and earnest people who could be both exasperating and amusing."[62] She was critical of their movement because it was predominantly male:

> There were practically no women in the Italian movement—anarchists or socialist. Whatever homes I went in to with Carlo the women were always in the background, cooking in the kitchen, and seldom even sitting down to eat with the men. Some were strong Catholics and resented me very much; they were very disapproving of my way of life.[63]

Yet Flynn's offended feminist sensibilities never prevented her from enjoying the sumptuous meals prepared and served by these same Catholic women whenever Tresca brought her into the homes of his Italian comrades. Nor, according to Tresca's daughter, who frequently accompanied them on such visits, did Flynn "ever get off her fat behind" to help.[64]

Material life for Tresca and Flynn was always modest, with intermittent bouts of hardship. Throughout much of their relationship, they lived in the Flynn family's cold-water flat in the Bronx. Their only luxury was a rented bungalow in the hills overlooking South Beach on Staten Island, where they vacationed during the summer months beginning in 1917. By this time, however, a serious problem was already affecting their relationship, as Flynn's poem "Thoughts of Tresca at S. Beach, 1917–1925," later revealed: "Many a secret tryst was safely kept by his glib alibi 'I go to Pittsburgh.'"[65] Tresca's love for Flynn did not prevent his incessant womanizing, and for many years, she would endure the pain his infidelities caused her.

7

From Union Square to Mesabi Range

The Lexington Avenue explosion prompted the police department to form a special anti-radical unit known officially as the Bomb Squad in August 1914.[1] Commanded by Captain Thomas J. Tunney, an eighteen-year veteran who detested radicals but never learned to distinguish one from another, the Bomb Squad was stirred into action when a bomb exploded in the nave of St. Patrick's Cathedral on the afternoon of October 13, 1914, and another device exploded the following morning in front of St. Alphonsus' rectory. The bombs were most likely planted to commemorate the death of Francisco Ferrer. These *attentats* were followed by the bombing of the Bronx Courthouse on November 11, the anniversary of the Haymarket executions in 1886, and the planting of a bomb three days later in the Tombs police court, under the seat of the magistrate who had sentenced Tannenbaum and others.[2]

The chief suspects were the Italian anarchists of the *Circolo Bresci*. The Bomb Squad assigned the task of infiltrating the Bresci Circle to Amedeo Polignani, a twenty-five-year-old Italian American only recently recruited to the force. Under the alias of "Frank Baldo," Polignani began frequenting the club house and was quickly befriended by its members, particularly Frank Abarno, a twenty-two-year-old electrotyper, and Carmine Carbone, an eighteen-year-old shoemaker.[3] The two young anarchists never suspected that their new "comrade" was an *agent provocateur*, who would play the key role in a classic case of police entrapment.

The target of the bomb plot hatched by Polignani and his accomplices was St. Patrick's Cathedral. At 6:30 A.M., March 3, 1915, Polignani and Abarno began walking along 51st Street, heading toward the cathedral. Slowly trailing behind them in a limousine was Captain Tunney. Inside the Cathedral, several detectives disguised as scrubwomen and parishioners had positioned themselves in readiness. At this point, one of the church invaders—which one became a matter of dispute—withdrew a bomb from under his coat, planted the device near a pillar, and lit the fuse with a cigar he had been smoking. Immediately, the disguised detectives pounced on the pair, extinguished the fuse, and placed Polignani (still posing as "Baldo") and Abarno under arrest. Carbone, who had failed to meet his comrades that morning, was arrested en route to work.[4]

Local newspapers exulted in the "brilliant" undercover work of the Bomb Squad, and discounted the claims of Abarno and Carbone that Polignani had devised the scheme and performed most of the work manufacturing the bomb. Within New York's radical community, however, belief that the Bomb Squad had orchestrated the plot was automatic. Tresca declared the case against the two anarchists a "frame-up" and the foiled *attentat* a "police farce."[5] Tresca had previously met Polignani at an open-air meeting in Greenwich Village and was subsequently visited by him at his office. Each time, Polignani denigrated the veteran anarchists for their lack of action and boasted that he and his young comrades would teach them all a lesson. Always suspicious of men who urge others to commit bombings, Tresca never doubted that Polignani was the *agent provocateur* and Abarno and Carbone his naïve dupes.[6]

Questioned by the press, Tresca explained to reporters: "I believe in violence but only in violence that advances the cause of labor.... An attack on the Cathedral would have served absolutely no purpose."[7] But whatever the motive or role of the two anarchists, the revolutionary code of the *sovversivi* required that Abarno and Carbone be defended against the class enemy. Tresca unhesitatingly performed his now customary role of the "fixer." The office of *L'Avvenire* served as temporary headquarters for the Abarno-Carbone Defense Committee, and Tresca engaged attorney Simon Pollack as the primary defense counsel.[8]

The trial of Abarno and Carbone began on March 30, 1915. The defendants insisted that Polignani had been the architect of the bomb plot, intimidated them with threats when they expressed reluctance, and lit the fuse in St. Patrick's Cathedral. They also claimed that Captain Tunney had offered to get them off "scot free," if they testified that Tresca and other anarchist leaders had put them up to the *attentat*.[9] Under cross examination, Polignani admitted that he had purchased most of the ingredients for the bomb, had taken pieces of the fuse to police headquarters before the bomb attempt, rented the room where the device was constructed, and kept the key to the room for himself.[10] These revelations influenced the jurors to recommend mercy when they found Abarno and Carbone guilty on April 12, 1915. Judge Charles C. Nott, Jr. sentenced them to serve six to twelve years in Sing Sing prison.[11]

Italy Goes To War

Abarno and Carbone faded into insignificance when the *sovversivi* learned that Italy had declared war against Austria-Hungary on May 23, 1915. Believing war to be the inevitable consequence of capitalist rivalry and imperialism, Tresca had predicted a deadly conflagration between the great powers well before its outbreak in August 1914. But Italy had been the anomaly in 1914, declaring neutrality while weighing her options. Much of the following year was spent in a state of ferocious conflict between interventionists and neutralists amounting to political civil war, one that destroyed the fragile fabric of Italian democracy and planted the seeds of Fascism.

The Italian Left was not spared by the controversy. The anarchists, with rare exceptions, sided with their spiritual leader Errico Malatesta in opposing the war and Italian intervention. Socialists, except for a minority of reformists and revolutionaries like Mussolini, were similarly opposed to the war, although the PSI adopted an official policy of "neither support nor sabotage." Most left-wing interventionists were revolutionary syndicalists, intellectuals like Arturo Labriola and Angelo Oliviero Olivetti, and labor leaders of the *Unione Sindacale Italiana*, such as Alceste De Ambris, Filippo Corridoni, and Michele Bianchi. Embracing nationalism as a necessary complement to socialism, the renamed "national syndicalists" espoused intervention for many reasons, including the belief (shared by Mussolini) that war would lead to revolution. All of them, however, were motivated by hunger for action.[12]

The intervention controversy traversed the Atlantic at the outbreak of war in 1914, with the various currents of the Italian immigrant Left assuming virtually the same positions on the war as their counterparts in Italy. The most influential interventionist was FSI leader Edmondo Rossoni. Rossoni conceived war in terms of masculine mettle and glorified violence as a redemptive force needed to strengthen and purify the proletariat class and mankind in general.[13] Tresca denounced Rossoni publicly as a "warmonger" (*guerrafondaio*) and challenged him to go fight in the war.[14] Rossoni soon broke with the FSI, published an ultra-nationalist newspaper, *L'Italia Nostra*, in Brooklyn, and returned to Italy in March 1916. He left behind an FSI crippled by internal dissension. Like most of the national syndicalists, Rossoni sided with Mussolini and Fascism after the war and was appointed secretary general of the *Conferazione dei Sindacati Fascisti*.[15] For Tresca, Rossoni ranked second only to Mussolini as a power hungry traitor to the working class.

California Propaganda Tour

While the interventionist debate raged among syndicalists, Tresca received an urgent plea from his friend Luigi Parenti to undertake a lecture tour in California. Parenti wanted Tresca to speak against the war and raise funds for *Il Proletario*, which was deeply in debt because of the FSI's internal crisis. Although reluctant to resume his association with the FSI and the IWW, Tresca could not refuse Parenti, who had supported him against Rossoni during the latter's defamation campaign. The ensuing propaganda tour was one of the longest and most successful of Tresca's career, spanning mid-March to mid-May and including stops in San Francisco, Oakland, Eureka, Sacramento, San Jose, Fort Bragg, Willits, Cloverdale, Santa Rosa, San Rafael, Santa Clara, Martinez, and a half-dozen other towns.[16]

Tresca lectured almost every day, sometimes several times, usually about the war. One comrade in Willits described Tresca's impact on his audience: "Tresca is one of those propagandists who know how to communicate to the masses the virile throbbing of revolutionary sentiment. He left our workers in a state of emotional frenzy and with the desire to hear him speak again as soon as possible."[17] The highlights of his tour were the May Day celebration in San Francisco, where he shared the speaker's platform with Alexander Berkman, and his earlier visit to the Italian Swiss Colony winery on March 13. Virtually a feudal domain, where field workers toiled twelve hours a day for $1.15, the Italian Swiss Colony winery had never been penetrated by radicals or union organizers. Company guards quickly intervened to expel Tresca when he appeared unannounced, but they were thwarted by the threats of several hundred workers who demanded to hear him speak. An ecstatic Parenti boasted that their invasion of the Italian Swiss Colony winery represented "the most audacious undertaking possible in California.... Never would I have thought that comrade Carlo Tresca's propaganda tour of California could have aroused so much enthusiasm even in localities where until today our propagandists have never visited."[18]

Mesabi Range Strike

Tresca left San Francisco for New York on May 23, stopping frequently en route to meet with Italian radical groups and to give lectures. In Franklin, Kansas, where he visited local coal miners, Tresca was contacted by Walter T. Nef, secretary-treasurer of the IWW's Agricultural Workers Organization (AWO), headquartered in Minneapolis. Nef requested that he rush to Minnesota to help lead the strike of iron miners on the Mesabi Range, already in progress. Tresca consented despite the grave dangers he knew awaited him—dangers underscored by Nef's parting words: "I hope you get out alive."[19]

The Mesabi, Vermilion, and Cuyuna Ranges of northeastern Minnesota possessed the largest iron-ore deposits in the world. By 1916, most of the underground and open-pit mines had come under the control of the Oliver Mining Company, a subsidiary of U.S. Steel. On the Mesabi Range, more than thirty-five immigrant groups were represented among the miners, with Slovenians, Croatians, and especially Finns predominating. Italians constituted around 10 percent of the company's total labor force, more than 4,000 of them located on the Mesabi Range. Northern Italians were usually employed as underground miners, whereas more recent immigrants from southern Italy worked at poorer paying jobs in the open pits. Although numerically inferior to the Finns and Slavs, Italian miners would play a militant role in the Mesabi Range strike of 1916.[20]

The on-site workday had been reduced from twelve to eight hours between 1900 and 1912, but every reduction was accompanied by "speed-up" measures devised to prevent any increase in real wages, which for miners and laborers averaged $2.40 and $2.12, respectively—the same as in 1909. Open-pit miners could barely survive on such wages because weather condition rendered outdoor operations impossible for three to five months of the year. Some took winter jobs in lumber camps, many remained unemployed. Underground miners worked year round, but did so at the mercy of a contract system that determined wages by the amount of ore shoveled rather than hours worked. Contracts were never written, and mine captains—most of them belonging to English-speaking groups—lowered wages at will. Bribes, kickbacks, gifts, and selling the best places in the mine were the other means by which mine captains, foremen, and shift bosses exploited the miners. The pittance earned each month was further reduced by the need for miners to buy their own powder, fuses, and tools, as well as pay the high cost of food, clothing, fuel, and housing in Minnesota.[21]

Strike action erupted spontaneously on June 2, 1916, when Joseph Greeni, an Italian miner, led a walkout at the St. James mine near Aurora to protest the contract system. Within days, all the Aurora miners, sometimes accompanied by their wives and children, began marching from town to town throughout the Range, urging others to strike. Several thousand miners answered the call. Responding to requests for assistance, the IWW sent Tresca, Sam Scarlett, Joe Schmidt, Frank Little, Arthur Boose, and James Gilday to assume leadership of the strike. By the third week of June, the IWW had sent 34 organizers—a record number—to direct 10,000 strikers. The Wobblies organized committees in their usual manner, with the miners themselves formulating demands: abolition of the contract system; an eight-hour work day on site, a scale of $2.75 per day for open-pit miners and $3.00 to $3.50 for underground miners, bi-monthly paydays; abolition of the Saturday night shift, and immediate payment of back pay upon termination. Union recognition was not included.[22]

The Oliver Iron Mining Co. would not accede to any demands. Instead, it increased its private police force by recruiting 1,000 special guards from the criminal elements of Duluth and St. Paul. Armed with rifles and clubs, these thugs were deputized by county sheriffs and given free license to intimidate and brutalize strikers. Local newspapers and businessmen assisted the company by demonizing the IWW and withholding credit and supplies from the strikers. Whenever strikers marched through mining towns, the deputized guards would beat everyone within reach of their fists and clubs. The violence escalated on June 22, when strikers in Virginia resisted their attackers and company guards opened fire, killing a Croatian miner. Some 3,000 strikers marched through the streets of Virginia to the local cemetery four days later. Tresca delivered yet another "eye for an eye" speech.[23] But the Mesabi miners, to the infinite relief of the IWW, adhered to the union's policy of non-violence rather than retaliate in the manner advocated by Tresca.[24]

Tresca and the Wobbly organizers now became marked men. The first IWW leader arrested in July was George Andreytchine, a Macedonian civil engineer, who was needed to communicate with Slavic miners from the Balkans. Tresca devised a plan to secure his release on bail. Always in danger from company guards, Tresca was generally escorted by several Italian miners who served as bodyguards whenever he traveled about the Range. On this July 3, however, Tresca set out on his mission to help Andreytchine accompanied only by a local lawyer named White and an Italian supporter from Virginia who owned a grocery store and a small truck. After a three-hour drive from Hibbing, Tresca and White arrived unannounced at the office of the district attorney of Grand Rapids, Minnesota, to argue that only Andreytchine's presence could calm the angry mood of the Slavic strikers. The district attorney listened to Tresca's plea, but the conversation ended abruptly when the sheriff, "in shirtsleeves with a belt of cartridges around his belly, with one gun on his hip, ferocious looking, stepped into the office with two husky deputy sheriffs at his heels." Addressing him as "you goddamn agitator," the sheriff demanded that Tresca hand over his gun; he became even more angry and abusive when a search of his person revealed none. His scheme having failed, Tresca turned to leave and courteously said goodbye to the district attorney. The young official, polite until now, responded by saying, "Get the hell out of here, you S.O.B." This was too much for Tresca: "I stopped, looked squarely into his eyes, and told him, 'Look here, you are many and I am alone. You are armed and I am unarmed.' But before I finished, I felt the muzzle of the Sheriff's gun at my back and the Sheriff shouting, 'Get out, get out!' There was nothing to do but leave."[25]

The journey back to Hibbing was harrowing. The small truck carrying Tresca and his two companions was followed by two cars, the sheriff in one and a number of armed men in the other. Soon three more cars, each filled with riflemen, joined the others to form a menacing convoy. When Tresca and his friends reached the mining town of Mishaevaka, two columns of armed guards lined the sides of the road, eyes fixed on the approaching vehicle. White said to Tresca, "This is a lynching party for you." Hoping to save his two companions, Tresca instructed his chauffeur to drive ahead very slowly while he descended from the truck and walked alone behind it. Angry shouts of "damned agitator," "sucker," "damned foreigner," and "get the hell out of here" emanated from the guards, but no one stepped forward to challenge Tresca as he walked defiantly between them. Tresca breathed more easily when he observed that behind the lines of armed men stood groups of miners prepared to intervene if necessary. The threat of retaliation and Tresca's composure in the face danger restrained the guards. After completing his walk through the gauntlet, Tresca remounted the truck and departed.[26]

Arriving in Hibbing, Tresca learned of the deadly incident that had occurred that morning in Biwabik. Guards had burst into the home of Phillip Masonovitch, a Montenegrin striker, allegedly in search of an illegal still. When they manhandled Mrs. Masonovitch, her husband and three Montenegrin boarders put up a fight that resulted in the deaths of a guard and an innocent bystander. All five Montenegrins were arrested and charged with first-degree murder.[27] Tresca knew that the incident would serve as a pretext to attack IWW leaders, and he set out immediately for Virginia, where the strike committee was headquartered, arriving at 11:00 P.M. Tresca spurned the advice of the Italian miners, who wanted to shelter him in a safe house with armed guards. He inquired instead about IWW organizer Frank Little (lynched the following year in Montana), who had foolishly rejected an offer of protection from the Italian miners and had rented a room at the local hotel instead. Accompanied by his bodyguards and IWW organizer James Gilday, Tresca went to the hotel to rouse Little from his slumber and convince him to take shelter with the Italians. Little dismissed Tresca's concerns and refused to leave the hotel. Unwilling to leave Little alone, Tresca sent his bodyguards home and rented a room with Gilday. At 3:00 A.M., police raided the hotel and arrested Tresca, Gilday, and Little. They were soon joined in the county jail by Sam Scarlett, Joseph Schmidt, Leo Stark, and Frank Russell. As dawn broke, the IWW organizers were handcuffed and herded onto a special train—one engine and one car—bound for Duluth, where they were jailed and charged as accessories to the Biwabik murders. That Tresca and the Wobbly leaders had been in Grand Rapids at the time of the shooting, nearly 100 miles away, convinced a U.S. Attorney that "the prosecution of Tresca for this assault and murder seems to be far-fetched, and I do not think that a conviction can ever be secured."[28] But "justice" on the Range was dispensed by the Steel Trust, not the federal government.

Haywood dispatched Elizabeth Gurley Flynn and Joe Ettor to replace the incarcerated strike leaders. Flynn was often accompanied by her friend Mary

Heaton Vorse, who wrote about the plight of the iron miners in several prominent magazines. Flynn traveled the length and breadth of the Range, trying to sustain the strike with her exhortations. But prospects for a reasonable settlement, much less a clear-cut victory, were fading. The terror campaign by company guards and deputies continued unabated; hundreds were beaten, arrested, and evicted from company-owned dwellings; and strike-relief dwindled to levels that could not sustain the strikers.[29] Haywood, who had not participated in the strike, began withholding vitally needed funds in August, forcing the strikers to drift back to the mines and pits. The central strike committee had no choice but to terminate the strike on September 17, 1916. Yet the strike and the threat of another the following spring induced the Steel Trust to increase wages and implement some reforms.[30]

Imprisonment in Duluth County Jail

On August 30, 1916, the Grand Jury of Duluth indicted Phillip Masonovitch, his wife Militza, Joe Cernogovich, Joe Mikich, and John Orlandich on charges of first-degree murder in the killing of James C. Myron, the deputized mine guard who had invaded their home and assaulted them. Tresca, Sam Scarlett, and Joe Schmidt were indicated as accessories "after the fact" of murder. Never before had Tresca found himself in comparable danger. The trial date was set for December 5, 1916.

Flynn was emotionally distraught over Tresca's arrest, believing him to be in grave danger. As she explained to Vorse, "they [the authorities] are concentrating the fight on Carlo—as the brains of the crowd.… It is like the Ettor-Giovannitti case, except that in this state, accessories are guilty in the first degree and are liable to life imprisonment."[31] Her visits to Tresca in the Duluth County jail were highly emotional encounters:

> I would go weekly to the County Jail; he'd hold my hand
> & sometimes kiss me on the throat if guards turned away for a moment.
> The pain and joy of those hot fleeting caresses would
> last a whole week thru.[32]

Tresca welcomed Flynn's visits but feared she might become the target of arrest or worse while traveling throughout the Mesabi Range. When Flynn left Minnesota to conduct a fund raising tour in November, Tresca wrote to Vorse, "I am very glad she is out. I feel now very much relefe. When she was here I cant sleep. My poor girl! Cheer her up, Mary dearest, please!"[33]

Pro-Tresca Defense Campaign

The defense campaign was led by Flynn and Ettor. No help was forthcoming from Haywood, whose relations with his best lieutenants were now strained. Ettor had resigned as general organizer in opposition to Haywood's bureaucratic centralism in 1916. Flynn had antagonized Haywood during the strike when she bypassed his

Chicago office and obtained relief funds directly from AWO secretary-treasurer Walter T. Nef. Once again, Flynn appealed to Nef, who ignored Haywood's protests and provided $5,000 for the defense fund.[34]

The task of defending Tresca was also assumed by Italian radicals, who conducted a nationwide defense campaign that rivaled the agitation for Ettor and Giovannitti. Additional support was provided by Italian labor unions, mutual aid societies, Masonic lodges, and various Italian societies. The *prominenti*, not surprisingly, had no sympathy for Tresca's plight. The conservative Italian immigrant press either ignored the defense campaign or published only brief and occasional accounts.[35] Such indifference aroused the ire of the *sovversivi*. On July 29, around 1,000 demonstrators assembled in Union Square to hear speeches by Giovannitti, Allegra, Girolamo Valenti, Andreytchine (who had been released), William Shatoff, and James Larkin, the Irish labor agitator. Inflamed by exhortations urging action on Tresca's behalf, around 200 Italian radicals marched from Union Square to the offices of Carlo Barsotti's *Il Progresso Italo-Americano* on 42 Elm Street downtown. When the editor refused their demand to run articles supporting Tresca, they wrecked the place. Police were summoned and a full-scale riot ensued.[36]

In Italy, meanwhile, a pro-Tresca campaign spearheaded by the socialist deputies Arturo Caroti and Arnaldo Lucci—friends and former colleagues—attained the level of a *cause célèbre*, receiving support from the PSI; the *Confederazione Generale del Lavoro*, the *Unione Sindacale Italiana*; more than a dozen chambers of labor; and scores of socialist, syndicalist, and anarchist associations and groups. Many of the most illustrious figures on the Italian Left participated in the hundreds of pro-Tresca meetings held throughout Italy from August to December, many of them in violation of wartime restrictions on public demonstrations and meetings. In the Abruzzo, the protest campaign for a native son was led by the chamber of labor of L'Aquila and the socialist newspaper *L'Avvenire*; a citizens' committee headed by the major of Sulmona was organized to agitate on his behalf, and Tresca's younger brother Lelio appealed to the parliamentary deputies of the PSI for assistance. Even Tresca's mother, Donna Filomena, demonstrated solidarity with her son by sending him a photograph of herself holding a copy of *L'Avvenire* with the inscription: "Go On, My Son.[37]

Saving Tresca from "the revenge of American capitalists" was not the sole objective of the defense campaign in Italy. Well known as a staunch opponent of the war and Italian intervention, Tresca was a perfect symbol around which to rally working-class support for the anti-militarist agenda of the Italian Left. The Italian government recognized this aspect of the campaign and sought to nullify Tresca's influence and discredit his reputation. Alarmed by the increasing number of copies of *L'Avvenire* that were being sent to Italy, the Interior Ministry prohibited the introduction, circulation, and sale of Tresca's newspaper.[38] The War Ministry declared Tresca a deserter for having failed to report for military duty the previous May.[39] The Foreign Ministry, through the Italian Ambassador, investigated Tresca's activities in America to find damaging information. Noting that Tresca was "an individual with the worst record," the Ambassador informed the Foreign Minister that the "Mesabi Range strike was financed by Germany and Austria." Moreover, the same "trustworthy person" who provided this "reliable" information had "personally" observed Tresca giving "Evelyn Flinn" a $20,000 check drawn from the German American Bank of New York.[40] The pro-Tresca agitation and the Italian Government's counter-campaign ended when the legal proceedings in Minnesota reached an unexpected anti-climax.

Rather than go to trial with a weak case, the county attorney negotiated a plea bargain with defense lawyers in December 1916, stipulating that Masonovitch, Ccrnogovich, and Mikich would plead guilty to first-degree manslaughter and each receive a sentence of three years, with the promise of release after one. Mrs. Masonovitch, Orlandich, and the IWW organizers would go free. According to Tresca, the strike leaders awaiting trial favored the offer but left the decision to the Montenegrins. He later explained: "By advising them to face trial, I would unquestionably have egged them on towards a twenty years sentence."[41] The miners accepted the plea bargain, but the judge disregarded the agreement and sentenced them to a term of five to twenty years for manslaughter. Ultimately, they spent a little more than three years in prison before their release.[42]

The outcome of the proceedings infuriated Haywood. He asserted in his memoirs that he berated Flynn, Ettor, Tresca, Scarlett, and Schmidt when they reported to him in Chicago, because the strike leaders had acceded to a deal that sent the miners to prison.[43] But Tresca's recollections contradicted Haywood's version, claiming that his real concern was not the miners but how the plea bargain might affect the IWW: "I do not give a damn about them getting twenty years. We have to go the limit [i.e., go to trial] for the sake of the organization."[44] Whatever the truth, the Mesabi Range strike and its legal aftermath ended Tresca's association with the IWW and marked a watershed in Tresca's career as a labor leader.

8

Surviving Repression

Several thousand Wobblies and anarchists assembled at the Manhattan Lyceum Theater at 66 East 4th Street on Christmas Eve, 1916, to give Tresca a hero's welcome upon his return from Minnesota.[1] Before resuming his activities, Tresca spent several days just resting and eating at the Flynn household to regain the strength he had lost during his incarceration. The happiest member of the family was Flynn's son Buster, now a sickly child going on seven, who adored Tresca as a father and rejoiced that he was back home. This rare moment of domestic communion ended abruptly around the New Year. Like Tresca, Flynn always put career before family, and despite promises to him and Buster that she would stay home for a lengthy period, she left for Seattle to aid the seventy-four Wobblies unlawfully jailed on murder charges after the Everett Massacre, the ambush of a boat load of Wobblies by a drunken sheriff and his deputies on November 5, 1916. "Carlo was shocked and amazed," Flynn recalled, "that I would even consider leaving him after he had been in jail since July.... [He] was so angry that he did not write to me for six weeks after I arrived in Seattle."[2]

His recuperation complete, Tresca resumed the directorship of *L'Avvenire*, thanking his readers for their support and assuring them that imprisonment had not diminished his faith in the class struggle and the emancipation of the proletariat.[3] Assertions of unflagging belief in the revolutionary struggle had long been automatic and formulaic responses from all *sovversivi*, including Tresca. In reality, Tresca had been seriously disillusioned by the failure of European radicals and workers to resist the war, and was now pessimistic about the future of workers in America. He readily perceived that a wave of capitalist reaction against militant labor had been gaining momentum throughout 1916. His own ordeal in Minnesota, the Everett Massacre, the frame-up of Tom Mooney and Warren Billings for the Preparedness Day parade bombing in San Francisco, and many similar episodes prompted Tresca to declare, in January 1917, that "the proletariat of America has never been attacked, assaulted, and threatened with such fury, violence, and rage by its irreconcilable enemy, capitalism, than at the present moment."[4] With United States intervention now a virtual certainty, he feared that repression of far greater magnitude was imminent unless American workers united to resist.[5]

In the Shadow of War

Prior to America's declaration of war against Germany on April 6, 1917, Tresca's anti-militarist writings, public speeches, and exhortations to workers to employ the general strike and revolution as weapons of war resistance had prompted constant surveillance of his activities by federal authorities. The agents who followed him everywhere were fixated on the notion that antiwar radicals were German agents, and routinely reported inaccurately that the audiences listening to Tresca's speeches included more Germans, German Jews, and Austrians than Italians. Their reports invariably focused as well on his most inflammatory remarks.[6] Immediately after intervention, for example, Tresca declared that President Wilson's motive was not "to make the world safe for democracy," but to make the world safe for American capitalism. For three years, the war in Europe had proved a bonanza for American industrialists, as they reaped billions of dollars in profits selling food, munitions, and other materiel to the Allied Powers. Entering the war would not only generate even more profits for American capitalists, it would ensure that the several billions in war debts owed the United States by the Allies would be repaid. A German victory would spell financial disaster for Wall Street, and that would be impermissible, Tresca argued.[7]

A toxic atmosphere of xenophobia, ultra-nationalism, intolerance, and conformity enveloped American society after war was declared, generating a frozen mindset that equated radicalism and strike action with un-Americanism and treason. Seizing the opportunity, the federal government initiated a campaign to suppress radicalism and militant labor under the guise of thwarting antiwar activities. Highest on the government's internal enemy list were the anarchists, the IWW, and the SPA. To suppress these elements, an arsenal of statutory weapons was enacted, which violated civil and political liberties on an unprecedented scale: the Immigration Act of February 5, 1917; the Espionage Act of June 15, 1917; the Trading With the Enemy Act of October 6, 1917; the Sedition Act of May 15, 1918; and the Immigration Act of October 16, 1918. Reflecting the belief that radicalism was an un-American phenomenon, imported by recent immigration from southern and eastern Europe, provisions of the anti-radical legislation were designed specifically for suppression of anarchists, Wobblies, and socialists of foreign birth. The measure most favored was deportation, an administrative procedure under Labor Department jurisdiction, which achieved the desired results far more successfully and quickly than criminal proceedings requiring a trial.[8] In Tresca's case, establishing grounds for deportation became a goal for all the government agencies involved in the suppression of radicals.

No immigrant radicals were more despised and feared by American authorities than the Italian anarchists. Federal agents invaded the office of *L'Era Nuova* in Paterson and arrested its director, Franz Widmer, on April 17, 1917. Luigi Galleani was arrested and his *Cronaca Sovversiva* raided in Lynn, Massachusetts, on June 17, 1917.[9] These and other Italian radical newspapers were already facing oblivion because of the financial burden imposed upon them by the Espionage Act, which required foreign language newspapers to provide "true translations" to the Post Office Department of all articles pertaining to the government and the war. The raids often left ransacked offices and damaged printing equipment in their wake, but their most consequential result was the discovery of newspaper subscription lists, which identified thousands of Italian anarchists throughout the country, thereby making them more vulnerable to deportation. *L'Avvenire* had not yet been raided by the summer of 1917, but was failing financially because of compliance with the "true translations" provision of the Espionage Act. Tresca himself was followed day and night by federal and local agents, and the phone in his office was tapped.[10] The New York Bomb Squad communicated its suspicion to the War Department that Tresca was a "German agent" who had received $20,000 for his services. The Military Intelligence Division investigated his bank account and found it almost empty.[11]

The absurdity of such allegations did not diminish the danger Tresca faced. He had not yet been arrested because the Justice Department intended to include him in its prosecution of IWW leaders and militants. Federal authorities still associated him with the labor union that American capitalists feared most. On September 5, 1917, Justice Department agents raided IWW headquarters in Chicago and local halls throughout the nation, confiscating tons of documents, literature, and office equipment, and ten days later, 166 IWW members were indicted on five counts of criminal conspiracy to impede the war effort. Tresca and Flynn, together with Giovannitti, Ettor, and Giovanni Baldazzi, were included in the indictment.[12]

Sensing the net tightening around him, Tresca wrote to Galleani's chief lieutenant, Raffaele Schiavina (eventually his worst enemy among the anarchists), explaining:

> We have never gone through an epoch so dark as this. I am kept under surveillance continually. I expect to be struck (in the sense of being arrested) momentarily by the Department of Justice of Washington, which has many articles of *L'Avvenire* translated or [for] conspiracy together with Haywood and others.[13]

On September 29, 1917, Justice Department agents went to the police precinct at 158th Street in the Bronx to ascertain the whereabouts of Tresca and Flynn. Detective Harry Hand, a former beat cop who knew the family, accompanied the agents to the Flynn residence. Detective Hand apologized to her mother ("I haven't got anything to do with this, Mrs. Flynn.") as the federal agents placed Elizabeth under arrest and searched the apartment. While Flynn and the agents were standing on the elevated platform at 134th Street, waiting for the downtown train, Tresca got off the train on the uptown side and spotted Flynn and the two strangers. "I tried to ignore him and to shoo him off," Flynn recalled, "but he rushed up to me and asked what was wrong."[14] The agents arrested him on the spot.[15]

After a preliminary interrogation, Tresca and Flynn were brought to the "Tombs," where they were separated and jailed. *The New York Times* applauded the local "I.W.W. Roundup," describing Tresca as "one of the most rabid of the I.W.W. troublemakers."[16] The next day, Flynn was granted an audience with Assistant U.S. Attorney Harold A. Content, who in private practice had represented Tresca when *L'Avvenire* had legal hassles with the Post Office Department. Following Content's advice, Flynn obtained the services of a non-socialist attorney, George W. Whiteside, and was able to secure bail for herself. On October 8, Tresca, Flynn, Giovannitti, and Baldazzi went before U.S. commissioner Hitchcock for arraignment, but the proceedings were postponed. Tresca and his male comrades posted bail at the end of the month.[17]

The issue of paramount concern was legal strategy. Haywood had ordered that all Wobblies named in the government's conspiracy indictment should surrender themselves and join their comrades in Chicago for a joint trial. He believed a courtroom vindication would constitute a great political victory for the IWW. Flynn considered Haywood's strategy a recipe for disaster. Her reasoning was sound: "We argued that time was our greatest asset. The war hysteria was at its height. A trial was tantamount to a lynching.... Our plan was to tie this dragnet case up in legal knots—in a dozen places—by a fight against extradition and for severance."[18] Irked by Flynn's dissension, Haywood dispatched IWW attorney George W. Vanderveer to New York to dissuade her and others from pursing an independent course. Tresca felt no allegiance to the IWW at this point, believing it had ceased to be a syndicalist union because of Haywood's centralizing tendencies.[19] Thus "despite dictatorial attempts," Tresca related, "we remained firmly committed to our defense strategy," and instructed attorney Whiteside to apply for severance from the Chicago case.[20]

Attorney General Thomas W. Gregory was apprised at the outset that prosecution of the New York defendants might encounter difficulties because they were neither members of the IWW or had they been inactive during the period covered by the indictment. His first inclination was to let a jury decide whether this evidence was significant; however, after further consideration, Gregory concluded that granting a severance to Tresca, Flynn, Giovannitti, and Ettor might strengthen the government's prosecution of the Chicago defendants.[21] An accommodation was reached, and on February 15, 1918, Judge Kenesaw Mountain Landis, the malevolent magistrate presiding over the IWW trial, granted the order of severance on behalf of Tresca and Flynn.[22]

Flynn's prediction was soon fulfilled. After a five-month trial, Haywood and the more than 100 Wobblies who obeyed his dictate were convicted on August 31, 1918. Judge Landis, relishing his opportunity to strike a blow against radicalism, meted out prison terms ranging up to twenty years and fines totaling more than $2 million. Haywood, who received a twenty-year sentence, lost his appeal in October 1920, but rather than return to Leavenworth and endure the martyrdom he had demanded of Tresca and Flynn, jumped bail and fled to the Soviet Union in March 1921.[23]

The "Red Scare"

The danger of the Justice Department reneging and bringing Tresca and Flynn to trial for conspiracy hung over their heads until charges were dropped in March 1919.[24] But Tresca was still in danger of deportation. The Bureau of Investigation (BI) had begun gathering evidence for deportation proceedings, and the War Department's Military Intelligence Division (MI) continued its own sleuthing operations, opening Tresca's mail, accumulating information about his strike activities, and following him from place to place.[25] If anything, Tresca's reputation as a revolutionary menace was growing in official circles. One MI operative informed the War Department at the end of October 1919 that "Tresca is at the bottom of all the anarchist, ultra-radical elements, stirring up trouble and revolutionary ideas in the eastern states."[26]

The threat increased throughout the "Red Scare" of 1919–1920. The Bolshevik revolution of 1917, the ongoing civil war in Russia, the Spartacist revolt in Berlin in 1918, and the short-lived "Soviet Republics" in Bavaria and Hungary in 1919 had generated great fear that Bolshevism threatened the capitalist system in America. The ideology and movement that Woodrow Wilson called a "demonic conspiracy" was also fueled by a temporary resurgence of American radicalism. Although the IWW remained moribund, the SPA increased its membership from 83,000 to almost 100,000 between August 1918 and the summer of 1919, and in September 1919 the Communist Party (CP) and the Communist Labor Party (CLP) were formed when the left wing broke away from the SPA. This reawakening of the Left was dramatically punctuated by a rash of anarchist bombings in several major cities on May 1 and June 2, 1919, retaliatory blows against government suppression of the movement. Far more threatening from the perspective of American capitalists was the unprecedented militancy that pervaded the ranks of organized and unorganized labor in 1919. Spurred by rising inflation, workers in nearly every major sector of industry struck or engaged in some form of agitation for higher pay and fewer hours. The most important labor struggles of 1919 were the Seattle general strike in February, the Boston policemen's strike in September, the steel strike of September–January, and the coal miners' strike of November–December. But all the great strikes of 1919 resulted in defeat and regression for the labor movement, and revolution remained nothing more than a capitalist's bad dream.[27]

The absence of a genuine revolutionary threat did not deter the government's campaign of preventive counter-revolution. The worst episodes of the "Red Scare" were the "Palmer Raids," the federal raids and round-ups named after A. Mitchell Palmer, the ambitious attorney general who harbored presidential aspirations. The November 7 raid targeted the Union of Russian Workers; in New York alone, 650 individuals were arrested. The January 7 raid concentrated on the CP and the CLP in 33 cities, netting around 10,000 persons, most of them aliens. Victims were arrested without warrants, held for weeks and months without bail, denied legal counsel, generally mistreated, and sometimes brutalized while in custody. The Palmer Raids and other roundups led inevitably to the "deportation delirium," the issuing of deportation warrants for several thousand aliens. Thanks to the Assistant Secretary of Labor, Louis F. Post, one of the few government officials not motivated by irrational hysteria or political opportunism, thousands of the warrants were cancelled; only 556 persons (plus 35 left over from 1919) were eventually deported as a result of the "Red Scare."[28]

Tresca's daughter Beatrice once asked her father why he had never been deported during the "Red Scare." He replied with a casual shrug: "They never came for me."[29] But not for want of trying. Sometime between his indictment and the dismissal of the charges, a warrant for Tresca's deportation was issued by the Labor Department's Bureau of Immigration. In August 1919, special assistant to the attorney general, John T. Creighton, notified the Commissioner-General of Immigration, Anthony Caminetti, that the deportation warrant had not been served because "the subject has disappeared."[30] He generously offered "to have the agents of the Department of Justice cooperate with your [Immigration Bureau] field offices in an endeavor to locate Tresca at the present time."[31] Evidently, the attorney general's office had neglected to check with agents of the Bureau of Investigation and the War Department, who kept Tresca under constant surveillance and would have confirmed his presence in New York.

Tracking down "Reds" increased in fervor and efficiency when Attorney General Palmer formed a new General Intelligence (Anti-Radical) Division of the Bureau of Investigation on August 1, 1919, appointing the ambitious zealot J. Edgar Hoover as head. Hoover and his immediate superior, Bureau Chief William J. Flynn, undoubtedly knew that of all the alien radicals still at liberty, Tresca was the most important and best known. Deporting Tresca would constitute a career coup for both anti-radical crusaders, and shortly before the first big Palmer raid, Hoover requested for his scrutiny the complete record of Tresca's arrests and convictions.[32] The Justice Department thought it had finally bagged Tresca when BI chief Flynn identified him as member of the Galleani group suspected of perpetrating the Wall Street bombing of September 16, 1920. Newspapers throughout the country ran photos of Tresca with headlines proclaiming, "Flynn's Sleuths Watch Tresca," "Range Strike Leader May Be Involved in New York Bomb Case—Tresca Watched," and "U.S. Agents Seeking Him."[33] One suspect was arrested and given the "third degree" in an attempt to link Tresca to the bombing. But a few days later, no doubt informed by more knowledgeable underlings that he was neither a Galleani disciple nor an advocate of terrorism, Flynn announced that he was not seeking Tresca.[34] That did not prevent the Bomb Squad from raiding Tresca's new office at 208 East 12th Street on September 29, 1920, prompting him to quip: "This is quite a game, and I am ready. We will see how it is going to end. We are on guard."[35]

BI regional offices continued to monitor Tresca until long after the "Red Scare" ran out of steam. Frustrated that months of surveillance and investigation had failed to result in proceedings, BI chief Burns notified the New York office in March 1922 that "it is… our intention and desire that every effort be made to bring about his [Tresca's] early deportation, and I would care personally to call his case to the attention of the Secretary of Labor."[36] Burns directed field offices in New York, Philadelphia, Boston, Pittsburgh, Chicago, and other cities to submit detailed reports on all information that could help deport Tresca.[37] BI agents studied access points to the building at 208 East 12th Street, hoping to gain illegal entry to the private room Tresca rented upstairs from Il Martello's office. They abandoned the plan because the building was occupied entirely by radical organizations, making the risk of discovery too great.[38] For the next year, Tresca's life and activities remained under constant investigation, but the evidence required for deportation still eluded the BI.

Amazingly, what stymied the BI was its inability to ascertain two basic facts: was Tresca an alien or a naturalized citizen; and was he an anarchist who espoused violent overthrow of the government? No less than sixteen regional offices were involved in the search for answers. An abundance of anecdotal evidence indicated that Tresca was indeed an alien, but legal documentation eluded the BI because of the record-keeping method employed by the Labor Department's Bureau of Naturalization. As of 1912, application papers for citizenship were filed by courts throughout the country—2,300 of them. As it was impossible to examine so many court records, BI failed to determine Tresca's alien status with legal certainty.[39]

The BI's inability to define him legally as a violent anarchist resulted entirely from Tresca's own strategy of evasion and obfuscation. He was easily alerted to the danger by the increasing frequency with which federal agents (often posing as reporters), local police, and supposed comrades began attending his lectures and posing intrusive questions about his political ideas and alien status. Survival in this threatening environment necessitated circumvention of the anti-radical measures passed by Congress since 1917 and the more Draconian "criminal anarchy" and "criminal syndicalism" laws adopted by many states. Above all, this required careful avoidance of self-incriminating admissions concerning his anarchist beliefs. The Italian-speaking agents and informants assigned to take notes on Tresca's lectures frequently expressed frustration with the diminished tone of Tresca's revolutionary rhetoric, especially his disinclination to mention or advocate violence.[40] Nevertheless, the BI observed, "while he does not openly advocate the overthrow of Government by force, his speeches and writings tend to convey that thought to any gathering of Italian radicals before whom he appears."[41]

Tresca exercised similar caution in his management of *Il Martello* (The Hammer), his postwar newspaper. He never described *Il Martello* as an anarchist newspaper, and was very careful about the articles he wrote and accepted for publication. The Justice Department's Bureau of Radical Publications, which examined every issue from the spring of 1919 to the spring of 1922, concluded: "Although *Il Martello*… affords in every issue abundant evidence of its anarchist character, there have not been many editorials or signed articles by Tresca himself of an incriminating nature in their entirety."[42] After another year of scrutinizing *Il Martello*, the BI lamented: "while the tenor of this publication is anarchistic and many of its issues declared non-mailable by the Post Office Department, there have not been any articles which were sufficiently specific upon which Tresca might be prosecuted or a deportation case predicated."[43]

Radical Critics

Fending off the Justice Department was easier than satisfying his radical critics, whose incessant demands that he proclaim his anarchist identity threatened to place him in jeopardy. To one social democrat who tried goading him to "define" his political allegiance, Tresca explained that "by describing all my political thinking to you I may fall into the net of the criminal anarchy law of New York State."[44] One federal agent reported on Tresca's explanation to an indignant "comrade," who demanded to know why *Il Martello* was not identified as an anarchist newspaper: "instead of declaring that it was an anarchist paper, he says that it is *his* paper and does not say what it is. That is the reason why he has kept himself out of trouble so long and if he can help it he is going to keep himself out for a long while, because he can do better work outside than he can in jail."[45] But some fanatical anarchists (mostly Galleanisti) could not appreciate the logic and wisdom of Tresca's strategy for self-preservation. To them, the only way Tresca could validate his credentials as an anarchist was to get himself deported. He had no intention of obliging.

Disillusionment

By 1919 Tresca had become thoroughly disillusioned with the United States. His disenchantment derived as much from America's ill treatment of immigrant Italians as from government repression of radicals.[46] Speaking in the voice of the immigrant, Tresca declared that

> From the mines of Pennsylvania to the foundries of Ohio, from the ditches of New York State to the farms of California, we wandered for months and months offering our labor to a hundred bosses.... We did not find happiness in Westmoreland, Lawrence, Calumet, Colorado, Paterson, and Minnesota; we sought only bread that was less hard, work less exhausting.... [Instead] they gave us bullets, only, bullets and handcuffs, as in Italy. Not royal bullets but republican bullets.

The only Italians who had prospered in America

> were the bankers who steal our savings, the priests who charge dearly for paradise, the newspaper owners who sell us to the bosses for thirty pieces, and all those other species of co-nationals, who, with swindles as the means and our blood as the end, ensnare our martyred bodies with a thousand different tentacles to suck the last drop of our blood."[47]

But disillusionment did not generate thoughts of returning to Italy. On the contrary, Tresca's resolve to remain in the United States and fight the enemies of the working class, both American and Italian, was only strengthened by his recent experiences, and for the next twenty years he pursued this mission with zealous determination.

9

Postwar Activities

Tresca's most notable accomplishment amidst repression and the threat of deportation was the launching of his third independent newspaper, *Il Martello*, the most important publication of his journalistic career. True testament to *Il Martello's* status as the premier Italian radical newspaper of the 1920s was provided by the enemy that knew best—the Italian Fascists. The consul general of New York informed the Italian ambassador in 1925 that "the most dangerous [of the subversive newspapers], because of the skillful manner in which it is edited, and because of its influence over certain elements of the people, is *Il Martello*, published for years by the noted Carlo Tresca, who knows the mentality of the subversives."[1]

Tresca's acquisition of *Il Martello* demonstrated his skill in the fine Italian art of *arrangiarsi*—to manipulate a situation for the best outcome. By August 1917, with issue after issue deemed "non mailable," the cost of putting out *L'Avvenire* had become so high that Tresca terminated its publication. But Tresca quickly devised a clever stratagem that enabled him to publish a newspaper despite government censorship. The key, he knew, was to obtain second class mailing privileges. A request for a new permit in his own name would have been summarily rejected by the Post Office Department, so toward the end of 1917, Tresca purchased *Il Martello: Giornale politico, letterario ed artistico* (The Hammer: Political, Artistic, and Literary Newspaper), an anticlerical weekly founded by Luigi Preziosi in New York in November 1916. "I bought *Il Martello* from Mr. Preziosi for less than a few hundred dollars," Tresca explained, "and used it as a simple means of keeping together the addresses of good comrades, and to do what was humanly possible to do."[2]

Since the old office of *L'Avvenire* was known to the authorities, Tresca set up publishing operations in a 10th floor loft at 112 East 19th Street. *Il Martello* would change locations six times during the next twenty years, but always within the district that extended from 8th to 23rd Street and Fifth to Second Avenue, with Union Square as its epicenter.[3] This was the area where, at one time or other, numerous radical organizations and labor unions had their headquarters and published newspapers: the Rand School; the Italian Chamber of Labor; the Amalgamated Clothing Workers Union; Local 48 of the International Ladies Garment Workers Union; the Communist *Il Lavoratore*; the socialist/anti-Fascist *Il Nuovo Mondo*, and many others.[4] Given Tresca's gregarious nature, the office of *Il Martello* functioned almost as much as a social club as a newspaper. Tresca and his comrades found this "radical" district all the more attractive because it abutted Italian neighborhoods in Greenwich Village and the Lower East Side, districts offering a multitude of Italian restaurants and bars which Tresca and others frequented regularly, especially John's Restaurant at Second Avenue and 12th Street.

Tresca began to publish *Il Martello* (now subtitled *Rivista popolare di lettere, scienze ed arte)* as a semi-monthly illustrated magazine on December 14, 1917, selling for ten (later five) cents at kiosks and two dollars for a year's subscription. Tresca listed himself as publisher in June 1918, which caused immediate trouble with the authorities despite his avoidance of illegal content. Overt criticism of the war still being fought would have resulted in outright suppression, but antiwar sentiment was often represented pictorially, as with a front-page illustration of the Grim Reaper carrying away scores of bodies from a battlefield over a caption reading, "The Day's Work."[5] The bulk of material *Il Martello* published during the remainder of the war, however, was devoted to non-political subjects: biology, botany, astronomy, anthropology, economics, religion, literature, and poetry. The postal authorities, nonetheless, repeatedly deemed the newspaper "non mailable." As Tresca recalled, "*Il Martello* was confiscated many times, so many that I would confound myself if I tried to count them now."[6]

Government censorship and harassment did not cease with the war's end, and *Il Martello* was saddled with mounting deficits—a perennial condition. Despite these problems, Tresca asserted his direct control more conspicuously, publishing *Il Martello* as a tri-weekly in March 1919, and as a semi-monthly in February 1920, with his own name appearing in the subtitle: *Rivista popolare diretta da Carlo Tresca*. Finally, in January 1921, Tresca converted *Il Martello* from a magazine to a weekly newspaper, bearing the subtitle it would retain until 1932: *Settimanale di battaglia diretto da Carlo Tresca*. Also for a time, Tresca followed the Italian radical tradition of commemorating important holidays such as May Day with special issues of his newspaper bearing the title *La Guardia Rossa* (The Red Guard), only five of which were ever published.

As a weekly, *Il Martello* assumed the length, size, and format typical of most Italian radical newspapers: four to eight pages (sometimes more), measuring seventeen by twenty-two inches, each with four to six columns, frequently including political drawings and cartoons by noted radical artists, such as Art Young, Robert Minor, and Fort Velona. The first graphic logo that appeared on the masthead depicted two workers wielding a battering ram against a grotesque, Goliath-like figure representing capitalism. This logo was later changed to a worker brandishing a hammer, and changed again to a worker striking a hammer against an anvil. All pages except the last carried regular columns and articles devoted to political, social, and economic themes. The last page, as was true of all Italian radial newspapers, was reserved for letters to the editor, brief communiqués called "*piccola posta*," lists of donations, subscriptions, and expenditures, periodic announcements of benefit picnics, music concerts, and theatrical performances, as well as the titles of books and pamphlets available for purchase through the bookstore that shared the office, variously named *Libreria Rossa* or *Libreria Il Martello*. Weekly circulation figures for *Il Martello* varied from year to year, depending on the financial state of its supporters: 6,500 in April 1923; a high of 10,500 in December 1924; and 8,000 in September 1929.[7] Even in the best of economic times *Il Martello* invariably operated at a deficit.

Most of the lead articles pertaining to important political issues were written by Tresca himself. These writings revealed Tresca's keen intelligence and exceptional understanding of politics and society. Besides featured articles, he wrote several columns on a regular basis—*"Botte e Risposte"* (Attacks and Answers), *"Martellate"* (Hammered), and "Fatti e Commenti" (*Facts and Comments*)—that contained polemical exchanges with other Italian newspapers, both radical and conservative. He signed these writings with pseudonyms: Ego Sum, L'Homme Qui Rit, Il Fabbro, Je M'En Fiche, Renato Morgante, and some others. Tresca's journalistic output was prodigious, writing hundreds of articles in the course of a single year. Literary finesse was not his forte. His writing style, unchanged over the years, exhibited irony, sardonic humor, sarcasm, and raw power, best symbolized by the blunt but effective instrument that adorned *Il Martello's* masthead. Rather than slice and skewer with rapier thrusts of eloquent rhetoric, Tresca delivered hammer blows that bashed and battered. When engaged in the polemics, Tresca excelled at scatological inventiveness. But most important, Tresca wrote in a language that Italian workers could readily understand, a vibrant style that appealed to the emotions as well as the intellect.

Il Martello was not a one-man operation. Tresca's closest friends and collaborators, Pietro Allegra and Luigi Quintiliano, were the key members of the original editorial board; they remained associated with the newspaper until the mid-1930s. Allegra, the Sicilian anarcho-syndicalist who had collaborated with Tresca in Pittsburgh, fled to Palermo in the spring of 1920 to avoid deportation. Upon returning to the United States later that year, Allegra resumed his work as chief organizer of sales for the De Nobili Cigar Company and re-established his ties with Tresca and *Il Martello*. He wrote his own column, *"Appunti e Spunti"* (Notes and Cues), usually signed "Pietrino," that dealt primarily with the Italian-American press and engaged in fierce polemics. Quintiliano, an anarchist who hailed from the Abruzzo and worked as a tailor in New York, had collaborated with Tresca since 1915; he wrote articles for *Il Martello* under the pseudonym "Lucifero." Allegra and Quintiliano gave their time and talent to *Il Martello* out of political conviction rather than for financial compensation, which Tresca could ill afford to pay.[8] Non-writing functions—business manager, treasurer, secretary, mail clerks, etc.—were conducted by various members of Tresca's close-knit entourage, the *Gruppo Il Martello*. Like all Italian radical newspapers, *Il Martello* also published articles written specifically for the newspaper by regular contributors (the identity of many remain unknown because they used pseudonyms), as well as reprints of articles published in other newspapers and magazines, often by world renowned figures. Even a brief list in the early 1920s reads like a "who's who" of international radicalism: Peter Kropotkin, Emma Goldman, Alexander Berkman, Errico Malatesta, Luigi Fabbri, Vladimir I. Lenin, Leon Trotsky, Karl Liebknecht, Rosa Luxemberg, Eugene V. Debs, John Reed, Upton Sinclair, and scores of others.

Although caution dictated against writing his own articles about anarchism in the early 1920s, Tresca rarely wrote about matters of pure doctrine even in less threatening times, because he did not consider himself an original thinker or an intellectual. For propaganda purposes, he preferred to reprint the writings of Errico Malatesta (often under the heading: "Words from the Teacher"), Luigi Fabbri, Pietro Gori, Rudolf Rocker, and other noted anarchist intellectuals, whom he acknowledged to possess far greater command of theoretical issues than he. Yet the inclusion of classic anarchist thinkers did not qualify *Il Martello* as a traditional Italian anarchist newspaper or a "movement" publication representing a specific current, the way that *La Questione Sociale* and *L'Era Nuova* spoke for anarcho-syndicalists, *Cronaca Sovversiva* and *L'Adunata dei Refrattari* for anti-organizationist anarchist communists, or *Eresia* and *Nihil* for individualist anarchists. *Il Martello*'s ideological identity, like Tresca's, was too eclectic and unorthodox to be classified according to standard typology. Tresca was an anarchist *sui generis* and so was his newspaper. And like Tresca, *Il Martello*'s primary mission was not to engage in evangelical propaganda for the behalf of the "Movement" or the "Idea," but to fight the battles of the working class.

"Too Radical"

But fighting for the working class became much more difficult in the postwar period. Tresca never anticipated the extent to which labor unions would now thwart revolutionary minorities in order to avoid repression and defeat. Expecting to resume his activities as a freelance agitator and strike leader when the surge of labor struggles began in 1919, he was shocked to discover that while workers still desired his participation, union officials generally did not. In February 1919, for example, the silk workers of Paterson went out on strike. Tresca met in Passaic with his old comrade Adolph Lessig to discuss his role in the new battle. Lessig informed Tresca that he would not be invited to participate in the strike because he was "too radical," too hated by the bosses and local authorities of Paterson.[9]

Fear that he was "too radical" thwarted Tresca's full participation in a major strike underway in another industrial town associated with his name—Lawrence. Conditions for the mill workers had not improved since the great strike of 1912. Wages had doubled by 1919 but so had the cost of living, and many workers were beset by unemployment and underemployment caused by the decline of textile production after the war. Facing a 12.5 percent pay cut, almost 32,000 workers abandoned the mills on February 3, 1919, demanding a 48-hour week at 55-hours pay.

The 1919 Lawrence strike was in many respects a reprise of the 1912 struggle. The Italian workers, still the most numerous (12,000) and militant, constituted the backbone of the strike. They were joined by Poles, Lithuanians, Ukrainians, Russian Jews, Syrians, and other groups. English-speaking workers, as usual, demonstrated their lack of solidarity with these "foreigners" and soon returned to the mills. They were joined by Greeks, Portuguese, and Turks. The desertion of these elements did not cause the more militant ethnic groups to break ranks, and for the duration of the strike they endured violent attacks by the Lawrence police and the stigma of "Bolshevism," as the mill owners and patriotic citizenry now more than ever equated strikes with revolution. Father O'Reilly once again stood in the forefront of these anti-labor forces.[10]

What distinguished the strike of 1919 from the 1912 struggle was the absence of the IWW and the FSI, although several former members did participate. Local strike leaders had turned instead to A.J. Muste, Cedric Long, and Harvell L. Rotzell of the Comradeship of the New World, an organization of Christian pacifists who had embraced the cause of social radicalism.[11] Muste, who became chairman of the executive strike committee and its chief spokesman, believed that the strike could be an "expression of Gandhian non-violent resistance."[12] The strikers refrained from violence throughout the strike, but the police exceeded the extremes of 1912 by a considerable measure, attacking picketers from the first day, beating up Muste and other leaders, and arresting workers by the score; they even mounted machine guns on several street corners in readiness to suppress "revolution."[13]

A major problem for the strikers was money. Muste sought financial assistance from the Amalgamated Clothing Workers Union (ACWU), an industrial union whose resources and effectiveness outclassed the crippled IWW in the postwar period. The ACWU contributed more than $100,000 to the Lawrence strike fund and sent several organizers to help lead the workers, the most important of whom was Antonio "Nino" Capraro. A former anarcho-syndicalist turned communist, Capraro stood well to the left of ACWU leaders, notably its president Sidney Hillman and its vice president, Augusto Bellanca, both reformist socialists. But Capraro was Bellanca's *paesano* from Sciacca, Sicily, and well known for his bravery and honesty. He quickly assumed a key role, serving on numerous committees. Capraro also became the popular leader of the Italian strikers upon whose tenacity the strike depended.[14]

The Italian strikers included a radical contingent led by Tina Cacici, a syndicalist and fiery orator nicknamed *la maestra* (the teacher) by comrades. Dismayed that the strike was led by ex-clergymen and reformists, Cacici and others demanded that the strike committee invite real revolutionaries to take charge, notably Tresca and Giovannitti. Capraro and other members of the strike committee initially refused, arguing that their presence would provoke the police. Undeterred, Cacici and her comrades bypassed the strike committee and sent Tresca and Giovannitti their personal invitation to intervene. Tresca was reluctant to join the strike without authorization from the strike committee; moreover, he and Giovannitti actually agreed with the strike committee that their presence in Lawrence might disrupt negotiations to end the strike. But by April, in the face of constant demands from the Cacici faction and the plummeting morale of the strikers, the strike committee finally acquiesced and invited the heroes of 1912. Giovannitti declined the invitation, citing ill health; Tresca accepted, eager as always to get into the action.[15]

Visiting Lawrence posed considerable risk. City Marshal Timothy J. O'Brien, the former police captain whom he slapped during a confrontation in 1912, had sworn that if Tresca ever set foot in Lawrence again, it would be for the last time.[16] Tresca was undeterred. Arrangements for Tresca participation, meanwhile, were handled by Capraro. No announcement of Tresca's forthcoming visit was issued. Meeting secretly in Boston on May 1, Tresca, Capraro, and a delegation from the strike committee agreed that he would enter Lawrence by automobile the next day, go directly to Lexington Hall, and depart immediately afterward. From long experience, Tresca assumed that the committee delegation included a spy who would reveal their plan to the police, so after the group departed he and Capraro decided that he should enter Lawrence that same night. Fortuitously, in the restaurant where they dined that evening, they met Costantino Calitri, the Italian physician whom Tresca had cajoled into testifying on behalf of Giovannitti in 1912. Yielded again to Tresca's blandishments, Calitri drove him to Lawrence and put him up for the night at his home.[17]

As Tresca expected, Lawrence police had been duly notified of the original plan and spent the next day, May 2, inspecting all automobiles and trains entered Lawrence in order to apprehend the feared agitator. But Tresca had already been driven to Lexington Hall and was in hiding beneath the speakers' platform. When a crowd of several hundred Italian strikers assembled at 7:00 P.M., Capraro ordered the doors to the hall locked and guards posted so that no one could leave to inform the police about the mystery speaker. Then he summoned Tresca from his hiding place. The stunned crowd remained silent for a few moments before going wild, applauding and cheering for ten minutes. For more than an hour, Tresca exhorted the strikers to continue the fight and return to the picket lines at sunrise the next morning. They all shouted their determination to fight on. His mission completed, Tresca was whisked out of Lexington Hall while the doors remained shut to prevent spies from alerting the police. He left Lawrence by car with a bodyguard of four comrades and reached Boston without incident.[18]

Tresca's brief visit and speech, according to Muste, provided a "tremendous morale builder" for the Italian strikers.[19] But local police were furious that Tresca had escaped them, and decided that Capraro would pay for his masterful deception. During the pre-dawn hours of May 6, a group of armed men wearing masks (most likely policemen) dragged Capraro and a local strike leader, Nathan Kleinman, from their hotel rooms and drove them out of town, where they left Kleinman with a rope around his neck and beat Capraro nearly to death. Rather than terrify strikers into submission, this act of vigilantism only hardened resistance, especially among the Italians. Faced with continuing resistance, the mill owners announced a 15 percent pay increase on May 20, to become effective on June 2. After 104 days, the Lawrence strike of 1919 was over; it represented one of labor's few victories that year.[20]

For Tresca, the Lawrence strike of 1919 marked a decisive turning point in his career. Despite the accolades he received for his triumphant appearance in Lawrence, Tresca continued to encounter union leaders voicing the same refrain uttered by Lessig in Paterson: "No, we are sorry, but you may not speak; you are the *bête noir* of the bosses and the police."[21] Over the next twenty years, Tresca would deliver dozens of speeches to striking workers, but Lawrence was the last major industrial battle in which he played a significant role.

Polemics

To function in the repressive environment of postwar America, the *sovversivi* might have been expected to close ranks against the common enemy. Tresca, like Malatesta in Italy, advocated a pragmatic, non-sectarian approach to the struggle against state and capital in times of reaction. He believed that radicals of every persuasion could collaborate while still retaining their ideological identities, so he urged the *sovversivi* to form a *fascio rosso*—a red group—and wage common action against political oppression.[22] Unity required a moratorium on polemics, he insisted. But Tresca might as well have asked the *sovversivi* to stop breathing. Polemics were an incurable disease afflicting all currents of Italian radicalism, and since the days when Marx and Bakunin fought for control of the First International, the *sovversivi* had been mauling each other interminably. Therefore, while most of them were absurd and inconsequential, polemics constituted an integral feature of Tresca's career and the world of the *sovversivi*.

Internecine conflicts actually intensified during the Red Scare, as if the *sovversivi* were oblivious to the maelstrom that threatened to engulf them all. And no single figure was subjected to more attacks than Tresca. The most vicious and sustained of the attacks against Tresca were waged by the syndicalist leaders of the FSI and the editors of *Il Proletario*, now the official Italian language organ of the IWW. He had first come under fire from the FSI in 1917–1918, when he obtained a severance of his case rather than stand trial with the Wobblies in Chicago, but favorable relations were re-established between August 1919 and February 1920, as a result of Tresca's vigorous participation in the defense campaign for Romolo Bobba and Pietro Piero, two Wobblies accused of conspiring to assassinate President Wilson and his Secretary of the Treasury William G. McAdoo.[23] However, conflict erupted anew in February 1920, when *Il Proletario* published articles (unsigned) by Frederick H. Blossom, the head of the IWW local in Paterson, insinuating that Tresca was a "stoolpigeon," a "weathercock," and a "secret emissary" because he had allegedly urged silk workers to join the ACWU rather than the IWW during the strike of 1919.[24] As punishment, the FSI order its member not to utilize Tresca as a propagandist and denounced him as an "anti-socialist."[25]

Tresca decried

the nauseating sight presented by our periodicals which, in this decisive hour of hopes and torments, instead of aiming at the one and only target—the common enemy who persecutes and oppresses us—turn our best efforts toward personal attacks, attacks which are vulgar, base, petty, malicious and full of venom.... These senseless controversies are doing more harm [to the radical movement] than the merciless persecutions on the part of the ruling classes.[26]

Tresca explained that he had not responded to *Il Proletario*'s accusations "because *it hurt me and still hurts me*, sincerely and not hypocritically, to polemicize against comrades whom I love, respect, and consider as fellow-soldiers of the labor cause." And in a final plea, he declared: "Enough! Let us rise above our miserable impulses of personal resentment; let us rise above our base sectarian passions and let us struggle for the ideal."[27]

Il Proletario chose instead to escalate the conflict with an unprecedented outpouring of allegations and slander, the undisguised objective of which was to destroy Tresca's reputation. His chief character assassin was Giovanni Baldazzi, the FSI propagandist who in September 1917 had been Tresca's prison mate until Flynn secured them bail. Baldazzi branded Tresca "the most corrupt individual in the workers movement of America and the world," because of three unforgivable transgressions: he had agreed to the compromise with the Minnesota authorities; he avoided trial with the Chicago IWWs; and *Il Martello* circulated through the mail "unimpeded," because Tresca either cooperated with or enjoyed the tolerance of Attorney General Palmer and Postmaster General Albert S. Burleson.[28]

Tresca addressed Baldazzi's charges in the longest and most detailed autobiographical article of his career. Regarding the Mesabi Range, Tresca affirmed that he and fellow defendants Sam Scarlett and Joe Smith never advised the miners to accept the plea bargain that the authorities later violated. More to the point, he asked: "Why is it that the Chicago crowd [the IWW] is venting its rage only upon me, though I have never been an IWW organizer?... If the organization has committed a blunder in Minnesota, most of the blame should be laid at the door of Ettor, Flynn, Smith, and Scarlett," who were IWW leaders. "Why, then, do they assail me and not the others?" Concerning his severance from the Chicago trial, Tresca recounted the numerous times that FSI leaders had attacked him and urged the movement to boycott him because he was not an official IWW organizer. "These same men," he continued,

> now had the gall to recall that I was one of them and to ask me to come along with them!... You can't treat a man the way I was treated and then expect him to answer your call when his help is needed. This is the real reason why I was not in Chicago to face the jury together with the others.

As for *Il Martello*'s enjoying privileges unavailable to other radical newspapers, the accusation really derived from the fact that FSI leaders had never forgiven Tresca for transferring *L'Avvenire* to New York in 1913, where it competed directly with *Il Proletario*. Crediting Tresca with ingenuity for the way he acquired and operated *Il Martello* was out of the question, of course. Better to ignore how many times *Il Martello* was declared "non-mailable" in 1919 and 1920, and invent the fiction that Tresca operated with the tolerance of the authorities.[29]

What, in the final analysis, was the real motivation behind the FSI attacks against Tresca? His answer cut to the core: "sheer professional jealousy."[30] Tresca, by 1920, was indisputably the most important Italian radical in the United States. Within the fractious world of the *sovversivi*, even in the best of circumstances, anyone of Tresca's stature would have accumulated enemies and generated envy. For the syndicalists, however, circumstances could not have been worse. While Tresca was still at liberty, many FSI leaders were in jail and/or awaiting deportation. *Il Martello*, despite government harassment, was gaining readership and subscribers, while *Il Proletario* was languishing, never to regain its former preeminence. The FSI itself was facing extinction, its section and members to be absorbed directly into the IWW in 1921. As for Baldazzi, the principal instrument of the anti-Tresca campaign, he was deported to Italy, where he soon threw in his lot with the Fascists.[31]

Death on the Lecture Circuit

Despite the polemics of 1919–1920, Tresca's services as a propagandist remained in high demand. Radicals of every persuasion still turned out for his lectures, not only because he was a charismatic personality and a formidable orator, but because of his great warmth and convivial nature, which had enabled him to form lasting bonds of comradeship with ordinary men and women of the working class. Even during the "Red Scare," when he might have curtailed his activities for the sake of self-preservation, Tresca spent many weeks on the lecture circuit, trying to sustain the morale of the rank-and-file, many of whom were involved in strikes and subjected to repressive measures from employers and authorities.

The most memorable of Tresca's propaganda tours during the "Red Scare," if only because of its tragic ending, was undertaken in December 1919. The scheduled itinerary called for Tresca to travel through Pennsylvania, Michigan, and Ohio, with focus on mining towns—"the oases of our propaganda."[32] Before the war, Tresca's visits to mining towns were festive occasions, but the tense atmosphere that now prevailed made this propaganda tour a different affair. In the anthracite region of eastern Pennsylvania, the conditions he encountered in mining towns were very discouraging. In Jessup, an important center of activity before the war, the sovversivi were brawling among themselves; in Old Forge, the situation was worse because of the many strikes and battles they had lost thanks to the Coal and Iron Police, the special constabulary Pennsylvania employed to keep miners in subjugation. Initially, only four or five comrades met Tresca at the meeting hall. The miners were too afraid to come, they informed him. Slowly and timidly, more than 100 miners joined the meeting, although fearful that at any moment the "Cossacks" might burst through the doors to beat and arrest them.[33]

Tresca journeyed next to Latrobe, in the heart of Westmoreland County's bituminous fields, where he had lectured on many occasions and participated in the great strike of 1910–1911. Accompanied by Dominico Ciotti, a close friend from his early days in Pennsylvania, Tresca traveled next to Cleveland, where he was hosted by a large number of comrades, some of them veterans of the Mesabi Range strike. They reminisced about the strike and Tresca's funeral oration in Virginia, recalling their oath to meet violence with violence—"tooth for tooth, eye for eye."[34]

After a stop in Detroit, Tresca headed north to the town of Sault Ste. Marie, Michigan. The train proceeded haltingly, with endless delays due to the lack of fuel caused by coal miners' strikes. That the strikes had nearly paralyzed the railway systems of the northern Midwest Tresca considered proof of the potential power of the working class. His satisfaction was dashed, however, when he learned that UMWA president John L. Lewis had capitulated to the settlement terms dictated by President Wilson.[35] His spirit was bolstered by his visit to Sault Ste. Marie, where a substantial colony of sovversivi—mostly paper and steel mill workers—had organized a Circolo di Studi Sociali with its own meeting hall and theater, an accomplishment all the more pleasing because the hall was located next to a Catholic church—"the home of all lies."[36] Then Tresca abandoned caution and accepted an invitation to lecture to comrades in Sault Ste. Marie's sister city of the same name in Ontario, Canada. Entering Canada presented no difficulty; the problem was getting back.

Tresca would not have been allowed to re-enter if American authorities at the border crossing discovered his identity. But his impulse for a daring venture overpowered his common sense, and he visited with the comrades in Canada. Returning to the border station, Tresca was interrogated by two judges and an immigration official. He nonchalantly explained that he was a teacher in Sault Ste. Marie, Ontario, planning to visit the Italian colony in Detroit over the Christmas holiday with the intent of opening a school. His professorial demeanor lent credibility to the ruse, and Tresca passed the interrogation without a hitch. He boarded the train for Detroit, taking with him the well wishes of his interrogators.[37]

Train delays had left Tresca's timetable in shambles, but fortuitously, disruption of service also upset the timing of the authorities looking for him. Tresca's visits during the first leg of his trip had not provoked interference; however, by now police all along his scheduled route (notified by informers) were alerted to his arrival and planned to prevent him from speaking, arrest him, or worse. Police and deputy sheriffs were awaiting his arrival in Beaver Falls, Pennsylvania, but luckily Tresca had fallen asleep on the train and ended up in Pittsburgh instead. Heading back to Beaver Falls, Tresca was joined by a comrade who boarded at Rochester to inform him that police were awaiting his arrival. When Tresca finally arrived at Beaver Falls, the police were waiting on the opposite side of the platform and failed to notice his exit. The hall where he was supposed to speak was occupied by police and a big crowd of Italians. Any attempt to enter the hall would have precipitated a riot. Tresca went instead to the home of a comrade named Di Cicco, where about thirty trusted comrades gathered for a private meeting and dinner.[38]

The happy reunion ended abruptly when a squad of men led by the police chief invaded the house. When Di Cicco resisted the illegal attempt to search his home, a tussle ensued during which the police chief fired his revolver. Di Cicco's wife, thinking her husband shot, uttered a terrified scream that halted the policemen in their tracks. At this point, Tresca confronted the enraged police chief, immobilized his arms with his powerful grip, and shouted, "I am the one you want. I am Tresca." Tresca was "deported" from Beaver Falls on the next train eastward bound. Before departing, he learned that the one of the guests, Giovanni Terracciano, had been wounded in the stomach by the wayward bullet. Now a successful entrepreneur and law-abiding citizen, this former member of the peasant league that Tresca had organized in Pacentro, near Sulmona, had attempted all evening to convince Tresca to abandon his radicalism, even offering to lend him money to set up a business. He died in the hospital.[39]

Staring out the window in deep depression as his train headed toward New York, Tresca saw the blackness of the night sky illuminated by tongues of fire emanating from steel furnaces in the distance, a sad reminder that the steel workers had also lost their strike. One thought gripped Tresca's mind: "Pennsylvania, the black land of the Cossacks. Here every liberty is dead."[40]

10

Sacco and Vanzetti

The "Red Scare" provided Tresca with numerous opportunities to perform his role as the "fixer" of the Italian immigrant Left. Political or personal differences never deterred him from utilizing his skills and resources to defend fellow radicals who were victims of political persecution. Tresca's best assets were his connections with American sources of financial support and publicity, such as the Workers Defense Union (WDU) and the Civil Liberties Bureau (forerunner of the ACLU). His relationship with Flynn, who founded the WDU in 1918, helped immeasurably in his establishing and strengthening these and similar connections, as did his personal friendships with ACLU co-founder Roger Baldwin and prominent defense lawyers, such as Arthur Garfield Hays, Walter R. Nelles, and Isaac Shorr. Ultimately, over the course of the next twenty years, Tresca's contribution as a defender of Italian radicals would be unparalleled. Yet all too often his services went unappreciated, even by some he had aided directly.

Tresca devoted the May Day 1920 issue of *La Guardia Rossa* to the "White Terror in America," documenting numerous cases of political persecution as well as the lynching of African Americans, which had increased ominously during this period. Tresca observed that while the European democracies were restoring the civil and political liberties suspended during the war, the United States was doing just the opposite—intensifying its repression of radicals by extension of the Espionage Act among other means. How ironic, he noted, that while German spies had drawn sentences averaging two years, dozens of radicals like Eugene V. Debs still languished in prison, and scores of new political victims, especially IWW members, were routinely being condemned to serve five, ten, and twenty years.[1] Amidst the mounting excesses of the "Red Scare," Tresca repeatedly issued appeals for worker resistance against repression:

> Victims of capitalism's iron fist, which under the guise of law and authority persecutes free thought, bravely and without impatience and weakness await our solidarity.... How can we live freely if our conscience is oppressed by the thought that we have neglected our duty toward those who are suffering in prison?[2]

Sacco and Vanzetti

Tresca's principal defense campaign of the postwar period was the Sacco-Vanzetti case. Contrary to the liberal legend that prevailed for decades, Nicola Sacco and Bartolomeo Vanzetti were not "philosophical anarchists"; they were militant revolutionaries, devoted followers of Luigi Galleani, the man the Justice Department considered "the leading anarchist in the United States."[3] Galleani and his followers were among the most vigorous and outspoken opponents of the war and paid the price for their audacity: he and eight of his closest associates were deported on June 24, 1919. Scores of other Galleanisti, meanwhile, had heeded the master's recommendation not to register for the draft, and to go underground to avoid detection.[4] Around sixty Galleanisti, including Sacco and Vanzetti, took refuge in Monterey, Mexico, biding their time until they could return to Italy to participate in the revolution they expected to erupt momentarily. When revolution in Italy failed to materialize, the Galleanisti drifted back to the United States, fearing arrest because the Justice Department had discovered their names on *Cronaca Sovversiva*'s mailing list after a raid in February 1918.[5]

Sacco found work as an edge-trimmer in a shoe factory in Stoughton, Massachusetts, and Vanzetti peddled fish in Plymouth. They rejoined the Gruppo *Autonomo* of East Boston, but may have been involved with more than just meetings and lectures. With Galleani awaiting deportation, his hardcore disciples, including some who had gone to Mexico, launched a bombing campaign that continued intermittently for the next two years. Sacco and Vanzetti may have been peripheral players in this conspiracy, although their specific activities, if any, have not been determined.[6] The most important of the Galleanisti's *attentats* occurred on May 1 and June 2, 1919. The first was a comical failure: thirty package bombs mailed for delivery on May Day never reached their targets because at New York's main post office they had been set aside for insufficient postage. The other bombings occurred on June 2, 1919, in Boston, New York, Paterson, Philadelphia, Pittsburgh, and Washington. The targets were a few prominent symbols of capitalism like John D. Rockefeller and J.P. Morgan, as well as the federal, state, and local officials who had participated in the suppression of radicals, anti-militarists, and labor leaders during and after the war.[7] Property damage was substantial, but fatalities were limited to a security guard and single perpetrator, blown to pieces together with his target, the home of A. Mitchell Palmer. By generating widespread fear and anger, the bombings played into the hands of the Justice Department, which declared them the work of a nationwide conspiracy of revolutionaries seeking to overthrow the American government. The Justice Department intensified its anti-radical crusade, making the capture of the bombers a top priority.[8]

At the bomb sites in several cities, and among the blasted remains of the bomber who tripped while placing his device on Palmer's doorstep, a leaflet was found entitled "Plain Words." Signed "the Anarchist Fighters," its message was clear and ominous: "There will have to be bloodshed; we will not dodge; there will have to be murder: we will kill, because it is necessary; there will have to be destruction; we will destroy to rid the world of your tyrannical institutions."[9] Suspicion fell heavily upon the Italian anarchists. Due to the efforts of a handful of skilled investigators (the majority of BI agents were remarkably incompetent) and Italian informants operating within the radical movement, the BI determined that the bomber of Palmer's house was Carlo Valdinoci, one of Galleani's closest associates. Penetrating the inner circle of the Galleanisti to identify other members of the bombing campaign became the next task. It was performed brilliantly by Eugenio Vico Ravarini.[10]

A shadowy figure with an elusive past, Ravarini—code name "D-5"—proved himself a master spy, infiltrating the ranks of socialists, syndicalists, and anarchists almost at will. Among the anarchists, Ravarini posed as an expropriationist, a bomb thrower, and an expert forger. Within months he penetrated the *Gruppo Autonomo* of East Boston, the *Circolo Bresci* of New York, and the *Gruppo L'Era Nuova* of Paterson. Ravarini urged his trusting comrades to commit acts of terrorism, always with the purpose of setting them up for arrest. He possessed considerable amounts of money (supplied by the BI), which he offered to help finance new anarchist publications. For that purpose, Ravarini constantly requested the names and addresses of anarchists, as well as the subscription lists of existing newspapers—the perfect way to identify as many anarchists as possible. Ravarini also frequented Italian print shops, supposedly to publish anarchist literature, but really to search for the writers of "Plain Words."[11]

Tresca had been suspicious of Ravarini since their first meeting at the Italian Chamber of Labor. His doubts increased after hearing from other comrades about Ravarini's incessant questions and bragging. Smelling a spy, Tresca declared in *Il Martello* that all comrades should be on guard against Ravarini, who "has sprouted on the thin body of our movement like a fungus."[12] Almost no one believed Tresca's allegations, so well had Ravarini ingratiated himself with other *sovversivi. Il Proletario* even granted Ravarini space to attack his accuser.[13] But Tresca went on accumulating incriminating evidence, and in *Il Martello* of May 1, 1920, he published a lengthy account of Ravarini's activities that established beyond any doubt the latter's role as a government informant. To reach a wider audience, Tresca repeated his charges the following month in the SP's official organ, the *Call*. Ravarini disappeared, never to be heard from again.[14]

But Tresca's exposure of Ravarini came too late to save the anarchists he had implicated in the bombing campaign and other activities now deemed unlawful. Ravarini's information, plus that furnished by the anarchist Ludovico Caminita, the turncoat publisher of *La Jacquerie* in Paterson, enabled the BI to learn the names of several of the bombers and to trace the pink paper on which "Plain Words" had been printed to a shop in Brooklyn.[15] The Brooklyn Art Press employed two Galleanisti of long standing—Roberto Elia, a compositor, and Andrea Salsedo, a typesetter—who had worked on the printings staffs of anarchist newspapers for many years. Elia and Salsedo in 1919 were publishing *Il Domani* and *L'Ordine*, underground journals intended to fill the gap until a successor to *Cronaca Sovversiva* could be produced. Detained on February 25, 1919, Elia and Salsedo were held incommunicado on the fourteenth floor of the Justice Department building at 15 Park Row. Their only contact was Narciso Donato, an incompetent attorney, whose own troubles with the law dissuaded him from challenging the illegal detention of his clients. Elia was interrogated frequently but not harmed; Salsedo was beaten repeatedly by BI agents until he confessed what he knew about the bombing campaign.[16]

News of the arrest of Elia and Salsedo created consternation among the Galleanisti in the Boston area, the epicenter of the bomb conspiracy. Many of the key figures fled the country; others were arrested on suspicion of complicity and later deported. Salsedo, meanwhile, managed to smuggle several letters to his friend Vanzetti, informing him of the situation and requesting financial help for a new lawyer. The *Gruppo Autonomo* held a meeting on April 25 to discuss a course of action. Vanzetti, Sacco, Aldino Felicani, and several others soon to become involved in the famous case were in attendance. Vanzetti was chosen to find out what was happening to Elia and Salsedo. Felicani, an anarcho-syndicalist who knew Tresca well, recommended that Vanzetti request his assistance. Vanzetti, who had met Tresca a few times in Boston (Sacco and Tresca had never met), left for New York on the night of April 25.[17]

That the Galleanisti would turn to Tresca for help only confirmed his primacy as the defender of Italian radicals embroiled with the authorities. Relations between the Galleanisti and Tresca had been poor for some time. Inflexible and intolerant, Galleani never forgave anyone who defied him, and in 1915 he had declared Tresca excommunicated because the latter failed to repent his error of 1912, namely, siding with the IWW against the Galleanisti over the issue of the protest general strike: "We will no longer travel on the same path: no longer can you be an anarchist…, and I will continue to be an anarchist—like no other."[18] Thereafter, the Galleanisti never considered Tresca a "true" anarchist.[19]

Tresca, in marked contrast, was a tolerant and forgiving man who rarely harbored a personal grudge against fellow *sovversivi* with whom he had clashed in polemical exchanges. Harboring no malice against the Galleanisti, Tresca and his associate Luigi Quintiliano, secretary of the *Comitato Italiano Pro Vittime Politiche*, had sought to discover the whereabouts of Elia and Salsedo as soon as they learned of their arrest. One Sunday, Elia and Salsedo were observed walking in Battery Park accompanied by four federal agents, and were followed back to the Justice Department building on Park Row. Tresca attempted to see Elia and Salsedo but was denied access. After meeting their lawyer, Donato, whose reticence aroused their suspicion, Tresca and Quintiliano conferred with Walter Nelles, who provided free legal services for the ACLU. When Vanzetti arrived at the office of *Il Martello* on April 26, Tresca told him what little he had learned, together with a warning that Donato was most likely cooperating with the Justice Department. The next day, after learning from Nelles that the Justice Department might conduct new raids, Quintiliano and Tresca warned Vanzetti to urge his comrades to dispose of any incriminating literature that could result in deportation. Vanzetti departed for Boston on April 28 and related Quintiliano's recommendation to the *Gruppo Autonomo* three days later. Vanzetti, Sacco, Riccardo Orciani, and Mario Buda, who owned a car, volunteered to undertake the gathering and disposal of the material.[20] Before this mission could be undertaken, Salsedo's pulverized body was found on the sidewalk outside the Justice Department on the morning of May 3. The anarchists assumed that Salsedo had been thrown out the window of his room by his federal tormentors; however, he most likely committed suicide out of remorse for having provided information about comrades involved on the bombings.[21]

At the news of Salsedo's death, Tresca sent two registered letters to Vanzetti, relating what little he knew about their comrade's demise; he also repeated his warning to get rid of incriminating material: "destroy this letter; don't ever keep documents."[22] Vanzetti never had time to read the letters. The Galleanisti in Boston and Massachusetts had already learned of Salsedo's death from local newspapers, as well as his having revealed the names of some the bombing campaign conspirators. Fear of arrest now accelerated the ongoing exodus of anarchists returning to Italy or going underground. Sacco and Vanzetti were among those who decided to go back to Italy. Before they took flight, however, they still had to fulfill the mission for which they had volunteered: disposal of incriminating anarchist material, including the bomb manual *La Salute è in Voi* and perhaps even dynamite.[23]

On the night of May 5, 1920, Sacco and Vanzetti, together with their comrades Mario Buda (alias Mike Boda) and Riccardo Orciani, met at the Johnson garage in West Bridgewater to pick up Buda's car, which was needed for disposing the literature and/or dynamite. Previously alerted to notify Bridgewater police chief Michael Stewart when someone returned to claim the vehicle, the garage owner advised the Italians not to drive the car that night because it lacked a license plate; his wife, meanwhile, telephoned the police. Buda and Orciani departed on the latter's motorcycle, while Sacco and Vanzetti took a streetcar at 9:40 P.M., heading for Brockton. Twenty minutes later they were arrested by Brockton police. Both men were found to be carrying pistols and an assortment of ammunition. Later that night, without informing them as to the real reason for their arrest, Chief Stewart interrogated Sacco and Vanzetti, asking whether they knew Buda and Ferruccio Coacci, another comrade, and whether they were communists or anarchists. Certain that they had been apprehended because of their radical activities, they responded to all such questions with lies. The next day, Sacco and Vanzetti were interrogated by Frederick G. Katzmann, the unscrupulous district attorney for Norfolk and Plymouth counties. Still suspecting that their arrest was politically motivated, they again provided false and evasive answers. Their lies and evasions, coupled with their possessing weapons, convinced Katzmann of their "consciousness of guilt," a legal concept that would weight heavily in determining their fate.[24]

Even before undertaking his investigation, Chief Stewart was convinced that Italian anarchists had been responsible for the botched payroll robbery of the L.Q. White Shoe Company in Bridgewater on December 24, 1919, as well as the robbery and murder of a paymaster and guard during the payroll robbery at the Slater and Morrill shoe factory in South Braintree on April 15, 1920. Stewart believed one of the perpetrators was Ferruccio Coacci, whom he had arrested during the roundup that followed the raid on *Cronaca Sovversiva* in May 1918. Coacci had seemed to be in great haste to report for deportation on April 16, 1920, one day after the South Braintree crime. Once the deportee was out of reach, Stewart's suspicion focused on Mario Buda, with whom Coacci shared a house in West Bridgewater. Meanwhile, an abandoned Buick sedan, presumed by Stewart to be the South Braintree getaway car, had been discovered in the Manley Woods, less than two miles from the Coacci/ Buda residence. Tire tracks from another vehicle, conceivably a second getaway car used by the bandits, were discovered not far from the Buick. These tracks were narrower than those of the Buick's, and were typical of the kind of tires fitted on smaller vehicles, such as an Overland. Buda owned an Overland; therefore, the second getaway car must have been Buda's. And since Sacco, Vanzetti, Orciani, and Buda all had convened at the Johnson garage to pick up Buda's car, Steward concluded that the four anarchists must have been Coacci's accomplices in the payroll crimes.[25]

That Stewart's conclusion was based on pure conjecture did not dissuade District Attorney Katzmann from adopting the police chief's theory. Moreover, he believed the crimes were linked to a broader anarchist conspiracy. At his request, the BI checked the bank accounts of Tresca and the *Comitato Italiano per la Difesa delle Vittime Politiche* he had organized in 1919, to determine whether they had received the $16,000 stolen at South Braintree.[26] Tresca, still considered an enemy despite his assistance, was the last person to whom the Galleanisti would have entrusted the proceeds of the South Braintree robbery. (If the Galleanisti did acquire the payroll money, they most likely would have sent it to Italy to finance Galleani's new series of *Cronaca Sovversiva* in Turin.) But Tresca's bank account was discovered to be almost empty of funds, and no trace of the money was ever discovered.

Unable to link the missing payroll to Tresca or anyone else, Katzmann remained determined nevertheless to prosecute local Italian anarchists for the South Braintree robbery and murders. But the district attorney's desire to entrap an entire network of anarchists was foiled. Coacci was in now Italy, Orciani had a solid alibi for the dates on which the crimes had been committed, and Buda had gone underground and could not be found. Only Sacco and Vanzetti were available for prosecution.[27]

Very little, if any, evidence linked Vanzetti to the South Braintree crime. Katzmann's solution was to try Vanzetti for the botched Bridgewater robbery, then prosecute him as a convicted felon for the South Braintree robbery and murders, together with Sacco. Poorly defended by two local attorneys, Vanzetti's trial in Plymouth (June 22–July 1, 1920) for assault with intent to rob and murder ended in conviction. The presiding judge, Webster Thayer, a Yankee bigot whose hatred for foreigners and radicals proved a decisive factor throughout the case, sentenced Vanzetti to serve twelve to fifteen years, a term greatly exceeding the usual punishment for the crime. Then, according to plan, Sacco and Vanzetti were both indicted on September 11, 1920 for capital murder in connection with the South Braintree payroll robbery. Five days later, seeking revenge, the elusive Buda exploded a bomb on the corner of Wall and Nassau Streets, directly opposite the J.P. Morgan Bank, killing thirty-three people. This cruel deed, a departure from the Galleanisti's previous pattern of targeting specific oppressors, proved counter-productive to the defense of Sacco and Vanzetti by generating even more hostility toward anarchists.[28]

Angered by the outcome of Vanzetti's trial and fearful of a double conviction for murder if the same incompetent lawyers were retained, Tresca went to Boston to express his dismay to Felicani, now the treasurer of the Sacco-Vanzetti Defense Committee.[29] To prevent another frame-up, he insisted, the anarchists had to retain competent legal counsel and generate publicity and funding, especially from Americans. When Flynn went to Boston in July 1920, on business relating to her Workers Defense Union, Tresca told her: "Elizabetta, there two Italian comrades in big trouble in Massachusetts on account of Salsedo. You investigate while you are there and maybe get the Americans to help."[30] Flynn met with Felicani and the defense committee, establishing a relationship that would become closer and more active than Tresca's. What the committee requested of Flynn and Tresca at this time was to obtain a labor lawyer and arrange protest meetings with English speakers in order to reach American workers.[31]

Tresca and Flynn secured the services of Fred H. Moore, the IWW lawyer who had served on the legal team in the Ettor-Giovannitti case. Moore became Sacco's lawyer, while the local McAnarney brothers defended Vanzetti. Moore was an indefatigable investigator and propagandist. He and Flynn mobilized a sizeable contingent of progressives and radicals through her connections with various defense organizations.[32] Tresca likewise conscripted for the defense campaign every influential American he knew, such as Mary Heaton Vorse, the labor journalist, whom he commanded: "Maria, there is a frame-up in Boston of two young Italians that's as bad as the Mooney case and it ought to have some publicity. Maria, you go to Boston and write a story."[33]

Tresca also mobilized every resource he could within the Italian radical community. Il Martello published scores of articles about the defendants and the legal proceedings, and conducted a continuous drive to raise money.[34] To ensure full-time attention, Tresca entrusted all newspaper activities relating to the case to Quintiliano.[35] Similarly, the Comitato Italiano Pro Vittime Politiche devoted its efforts almost exclusively to the Sacco-Vanzetti case, organizing protest meetings, scheduling lecture tours, and collecting funds.[36] Tresca himself, in the months following their arrest, was very active on behalf of two anarchists, presenting a dozen lectures about the case in Massachusetts, Rhode Island, Connecticut, New York, and New Jersey in October alone. He also recruited other radicals like Giovannitti, discussed strategy with Fred Moore, and offered encouragement to Felicani.[37] To obtain help from outsiders and conservative elements, Tresca demanded that Moore and Felicani provide him with as much information as possible: "I must have facts," he wrote to Moore. "You know how badly we need facts in a case like this. Please Fred, don't forget to have the boys, both of them—Sacco and Vanzetti—write to me, as soon as they can their own biography, their story.... I need all this to speed the agitation, to intres [his spelling] peoples, to create sympathy for the prisoners. Do, Fred, don't forget this. Please! please!"[38]

Cooperation between Tresca and the Sacco-Vanzetti Defense Committee was bound to end sooner or later.[39] Of the seventeen Italians who comprised the original committee, all were Galleanisti except for Felicani, an anarcho-syndicalist, and Felice Guadagni, a syndicalist and one-time member of Il Proletario's editorial staff. Felicani was a friend of Vanzetti's, and Guadagni was well respected by all currents, otherwise neither would have been included in the committee. Although, as frequently was the case, they turned to him for help when they needed him, the Galleanisti considered Tresca to be a rival rather than an ally. Trouble began toward the end of November 1920, when a friend sent Tresca a letter that had been written by a Galleani follower in New Jersey and circulated among fellow anarchists. It alleged that the Sacco-Vanzetti Defense Committee had issued a warning to comrades not to send one penny for defense to Tresca, but to send donations directly to the Boston committee instead. The implication was that Tresca might not turn over all the money to the defense committee. Outraged, Tresca wrote to Moore, demanding to know whether the Boston committee had issued such instructions.[40] Moore reported to Tresca that the Boston committee had "thrashed out...the dispute relative to their attitude about your work," and while the committee members agreed that they did not approve or endorse the letter, "the general attitude here so far as I am able to judge is that they do not appreciate what you have done and [do not] want your assistance further."[41] Exasperated and hurt, Tresca informed Moore by telegram: "Immensely disappointed. Decided to have nothing more to do except speaking when and where requested. So don't ask me for things to do please."[42]

But Tresca was too anxious to help Sacco and Vanzetti to allow wounded pride to drive him from the fray, and the Sacco-Vanzetti Defense Committee, despite its suspicion and hostility, understood that Tresca was too valuable an asset to reject completely. When necessary, Tresca bypassed hostile members of the committee, communicating directly with Felicani and Moore, and using Flynn and Quintiliano as personal emissaries. Requests for Tresca's assistance continued unabated, especially from Moore, who was his personal friend and whose relations with the defense committee would become infinitely more contentious. For as long as Moore was on the legal team, Tresca and Flynn would serve as his special liaison with the committee, usually communicating with Felicani. As Felicani related, "if for some reason Moore needed to put some pressure on me, well, all he had to do was either go to New York, or call New York, and talk to Tresca and Flynn, and I would hear very soon from them what the difficulty was."[43]

The mastermind of the defense campaign, together with Flynn, Moore frequently called upon Tresca to perform tasks that the insular Galleanisti were unqualified or unwilling to undertake. Before the trial, for example, Tresca was asked to convince the conservative Italian language dailies to publicize the case, to approach the Sons of Italy for help, and to prod the Italian consul general of New York to investigate the case. Tresca also contacted his old comrade Arturo Caroti, now a communist deputy in Italy, asking that he persuade the Chamber of Deputies to pass a resolution calling for the Italian government to instruct Ambassador Ricci in Washington to request a continuance of the trial so the defense could secure depositions.[44]

Tresca attended the opening of the trial in Dedham on May 31, 1921. Publishing his impressions, Tresca observed: "This trial has assumed the same vast and profound dimensions as the Mooney trial. The comrades are determined to tear the veil away from this terrible plot in order to end the abusive, sinister, and brutal frame-up system in America."[45] For the duration of the trial, Il Martello published a detailed chronicle of the courtroom proceedings written by Guadagni. Tresca, Flynn, Quintiliano, and the Il Martello group continued, meanwhile, to speak about the case at scores of meetings in New York and on lecture tours, rallying support and raising money. When the trial concluded on July 14, 1921, Tresca received a telegram notifying him of the guilty verdict. Tresca was stunned but not surprised: "This verdict strikes us in the heart. It is a terrible blow. There was little to hope for given the political character the trial assumed in recent days, but nevertheless the conscience rebels at the idea that class spirit can so coldly decide the fate of two men. In five hours!"[46]

Within days of the verdict, Tresca received a letter of thanks from Vanzetti, which read in part:

This letter is dictated only by the affection I feel for you and for all the good ones, for all you have done and will do for my life and liberty; and for all the comrades did and will do, and to tell you that I have been defeated but not conquered, to exhort you from inside my cell to continue the good fight for true liberty and true justice.... Do not be overwhelmed if two soldiers fall.... Be constant, implacable, decisive and active for the good, just as the enemy is for evil.[47]

Sacco wrote to Tresca the following month:

You cannot believe the joy I feel when I receive *Il Martello*. It reminds me of the glorious days of your *L'Avvenire*, the flaming periodical which I learned to love, which was the first to enlighten my mind, urging me to walk on the path toward the ideal of the human family liberated and fraternized. Those were different time. The air we breathed was better. Now, because of the war, the air is infected with poisonous insects. But our soul will not submit. No. And you, continue hammering hard.[48]

Tresca remained active in the six-year struggle to save Sacco and Vanzetti. However, in August 1924 and May 1925, respectively, Tresca lost his two closest links to the inner circle of defenders, as Moore was dismissed from the defense team and Flynn and he terminated their relationship. But even if he had not lost Moore and Flynn as contacts, or had not been subjected to vicious attacks by Galleanisti, Tresca would have ceased to be a significant figure in the defense campaign. After Mussolini rose to power in October 1922, the primary focus of Tresca's activities was the struggle against Fascism. Sacco and Vanzetti, per force, became secondary priorities for Tresca until the final months before their execution on August 23, 1927.[49]

11

New Enemies

On the eve of World War I, every major power in Europe was beset by domestic problems that proved irresolvable in the absence of far-reaching reforms. Significant changes to the status quo, however, were not on any government's agenda. Instead, as the eminent historian Felix Gilbert observed, "there originated a longing for a turn of events which would make all these intractable problems disappear. To some politicians, weary of seeing their nation divided into hostile camps, war seemed to promise the restoration of a common purpose."[1] By the end of the Great War, all the optimistic expectations entertained by the belligerents, particularly the notion that the problems of pre-1914 would disappear in a blaze of nationalist gunfire, had been shattered. Prewar problems did not disappear; they re-emerged from the ashes of trench warfare more destructive and intractable than before, providing fertile soil for extremism of the Left and the Right: Bolshevism and Fascism. Tresca devoted his life to the fight against both new enemies of freedom and human dignity with a fierce resolve equaled by very few.

The Russian Revolution and the Bolsheviks

Like all radicals of his day, Tresca was heartened by the overthrow of the Russian Czar in March 1917, and overjoyed by the apparent victory of the workers, peasants, and soldiers led by the Bolsheviks in November. But Tresca quickly parted company with the majority of radicals everywhere who offered uncritical endorsement of the new regime. He made a sharp distinction between the revolution waged by the Russian masses and the brutal dictatorship established by the Bolshevik Party in the name of the proletariat, embracing the one and condemning the other.

As early as June 1918, amidst the general euphoria that pervaded the European and American Left, Tresca warned in typical anarchist fashion that "like all dictatorships, even the dictatorship of the proletariat has its dangers.... Lenin and Trotsky with the others [Bolsheviks] may be the dominators of tomorrow."[2] By August 1920, Tresca asserted that there was no dictatorship of the proletariat in Russian, only the dictatorship of the Communist Party, which had suppressed political and civil liberties, liquidated all left-wing rivals, and still had not expropriated all private and state owned property. He rejected the defenders of Bolshevism who argued that temporary dictatorship was necessitated by existing conditions in Russia. He was particularly worried about the threat posed by the Red Army, which, like any army, was inherently dictatorial. Despite these concerns,

Tresca in 1920 still hoped that the Russian proletariat would resume the initiative and complete the revolutionary objectives of 1917.[3]

By August 1921, in the wake of the Red Army's bloody suppression of the Kronstadt sailors, former supporers who rebelled against the Bolsevik dictatorship and Lenin's launch of his New Economic Policy (NEP), Tresca concluded that the Bolshevik experiment had been a complete failure.[4] The slaughter of the Kronstadt sailors was only to be expected of a tyrannous regime preoccupied with self-preservation, as was the NEP's partial reversion to capitalism to stave off economic collapse.[5] By the summer of 1922, Tresca had lost all hope for the Russian revolution so long as the Bolsheviks remained in power. Attacked by Italian communists, who claimed he had lost his enthusiasm for revolution, Tresca answered: "My ardor still burns— in fact, it burns all the more when I am obliged to recognize that the *Bolshevik government* has stolen final victory from the Russian revolution, suffocating that generous people in the bonds of dictatorship."[6]

Nevertheless, Tresca's personal opposition to the Bolshevik dictatorship did not result in *Il Martello*'s immediate transformation into an organ of intransigent anti-Bolshevism. Because the original Bolsheviks were revolutionaries, attacked by capitalist governments seeking to restore the *ancien régime* or a more acceptable government in Russia, Tresca's newspaper generally supported the Soviet experiment during the period of foreign intervention and civil war. A profoundly different image of the Soviet Union began to emerge in Tresca's newspaper after the May Day 1921 issue of *La Guardia Rossa*, in which the great Russian anarchist Peter Kropotkin (who had died on February 8, 1921) described the oppressive party dictatorship he had observed in Russia first hand. Kropotkin's conclusion confirmed Tresca's previous assertion: "an attempt to create a communist republic based on the iron rules of a party dictatorship is bound to founder."[7] *Il Martello* thereafter became an important outlet for critical accounts of the Soviet Union, often by radicals who had directly observed the Bolshevik regime's suffocation of popular revolutionary initiative.[8] But Tresca, unlike most anarchists, still did not become an uncompromising opponent of all communists. He operated on the ancient principle that "the enemy of my enemy is my friend," or at least a temporary ally. Throughout the 1920s, he collaborated with individual communists in the cause of anti-Fascist unity. Only by the 1930s did Tresca abandon his pragmatic approach and begin to attack the communists with the same unrelenting zeal with which he attacked the Fascists.

Mussolini and Fascism

When Benito Mussolini founded the first *Fascio di Combattimento* in Milan on March 23, 1919, no account of the event appeared in *Il Martello*. Tresca, like most radicals, was slow to perceive the danger that Fascism represented for Italy and Italian immigrants abroad. He ignored Fascism at this early juncture because he shared the same assumption as other *sovversivi* that Mussolini was politically dead, an opinion colored by his profound contempt for this "Judas Iscariot," who had prostituted the ideals of socialism by joining the interventionist cause during World War I. In late November 1919, Tresca dismissed Mussolini as "a mercenary drawing on the coffers of the Italian bourgeoisie."[9] The following summer, when Mussolini—

still posturing as a man of the Left—called for "reaction" against striking railway men, Tresca declared that "in Italy this swine Mussolini has sunk so low, and groped so much in the mud, that nobody takes notice of him any longer."[10]

Underestimation of Mussolini and Fascism was understandable in light of the *Biennio Rosso,* the "red two years" of 1919 and 1920. The PSI had won huge gains in the Chamber of Deputies and in municipal governments, membership in the *Confederazione Generale di Lavoro* (CGL) and other worker associations increased ten fold, strikes by tens of thousands of industrial workers erupted throughout northern Italy, peasants seized unoccupied lands in the South, and landless agricultural laborers organized in leagues of resistance capable for the first time of negotiating favorable contractual terms with the big landowners in the Po Valley. Observing these developments from afar, Tresca expressed hope that "revolution is on the march."[11]

While believing that a "revolutionary process" was underway, Tresca nevertheless drew a distinction between revolt and revolution. Revolt was a "dynamic manifestation of hatred, desperation, and, sometimes, the reckless selfishness of the oppressed," which may ignite "the flames of individual or collective passion," yet also "allows those flames to be extinguished without changing... the factors that cause revolt." Revolution, in contrast, "is a process of social transformation that varies in time, intensity, scope, and method, but one that is initiated and pursued to an end by a class or a group of individuals for the conscious purpose of transforming the economic or political structure of society."[12] Furthermore, if a "revolutionary process" were to have any chance of success, workers and peasants must be led by a "militant minority"—men and women capable of decisive leadership and action.[13] That the Italian masses were capable of transforming economic revolt into social and political revolution aimed at destroying the foundations of bourgeois society, Tresca believed wholeheartedly. He was profoundly dubious, however, about the revolutionary capabilities of their leaders, above all the reformist socialist leaders of the CGL.[14]

Tresca's skepticism about Italy's "militant minority" was confirmed by the dismal failure of the factory occupations in Italy's industrial triangle of Genoa, Turin, and Milan in September 1920, when PSI and CGL leaders shrank from urging workers to press on toward all-out revolution. Tresca never forgave them for stifling this "revolutionary episode."[15] But in 1920, Tresca could not have foreseen the terrible consequences of that frightening specter of revolution. One of the few who recognized the potential tragedy of the factory occupations was the legendary anarchist Errico Malatesta, who warned: "If we do not carry on to the end, we will pay with tears of blood for the fear we now instill in the bourgeoisie."[16] Indeed, the occupation of the factories, even in failure, was the crucial event that accelerated the rapid ascendancy of the Fascists, whose designated role hereafter was to wage a campaign of preventive counter-revolution, a reign of terror and destruction against the Left and its working-class supporters.

By early 1921, Tresca could no longer ignore the growing mass movement of "lowly patriotic hooligans" and their self-appointed *Duce*. His first feature article devoted to the subject analyzed the connection between Fascism and Gabriele D'Annunzio's Fiume adventure of September 1919–December 1920, an undertaking considered by many to have been the "dress rehearsal" for Mussolini and his

Blackshirts. The famous poet-*condottiero* D'Annunzio, at the head of a thousand "legionnaires" (chiefly mutinous servicemen and war veterans, especially former *arditi*, Italy's elite assault troops), defied the "Big Four" peacemakers convened in Paris and seized the contested port city of Fiume on the Dalmatian coast. During his turbulent occupation of Fiume, D'Annunzio established a bizarre nationalist-syndicalist oriented "Regency of Carnaro," with himself as Duce. By the time he was expelled by Italian forces, Fascism was in ascendance on the mainland.

According to Tresca, however, those who believed Fascism was born in Fiume, as an expression of "D'Annunzian exaltation," were only partly correct. More accurately, Fascism was a "child of war," nurtured on D'Annunzio's adventure in Fiume; it was "*arditismo* that has changed its name," an observation revealing that Tresca understood from the outset that violence and action for its own sake constituted the inner dynamic of Fascism. Rather than defending Italy from "Bolshevism"—the myth propagated by the Fascists—Mussolini's Blackshirts constituted the "white guard" that had "dipped its hands in the blood of the proletariat in order to keep it an obedient slave prostrate before capitalism."[17]

Tresca's view that the Fascists were the mercenaries of capitalism was commonly held by the Left. No one in 1921 could foresee that Fascism would wrest state power away from the traditional ruling élites and attempt to create a new political and economic system that would, in theory, incorporate and reconcile the best features of capitalism and socialism. The pressing question for Tresca and other *sovversivi* in 1921 was whether the Fascist onslaught could be turned back and the "revolutionary process" revived by the working class. He already anticipated the answer: "If the proletariat awakens, it will render justice to each and all. If it continues to remain supine, Fascism will go on until it reaches bottom and we have a return of the blissful time of the Inquisition."[18]

Tresca had surprisingly little to say about the "March on Rome" of October 28–30, 1922, which accompanied Mussolini's appointment as prime minister by King Vittorio Emanuele III. Continuing to regard Mussolini and the Blackshirts as nothing more than the instruments of bourgeois reaction, Tresca focused his animus primarily upon the king and the House of Savoy. Still the fervent anti-monarchist, Tresca had declared a few weeks before Mussolini's appointment that "Italy has a purulent wound that must be resolutely excised by the knife of revolution—the monarchy."[19] He rejected the widespread belief that Vittorio Emanuele was a timid and weak king who feared that his Fascist cousin, the Duke of Aosta, would usurp his throne if he attempted to thwart the Blackshirts. "Wolves do not eat wolves," Tresca declared, "he is the Fascist, Vittorio Emanuele III." The king and his fellow Savoyards, he maintained, had willfully permitted the Fascists to attain power, hoping to use them to achieve their long sought objective—absolute monarchy. The ascendancy of the Blackshirts amounted to "a *coup d'état* by the Savoyard monarchy [that had] become Fascist."[20]

Tresca's belief that Fascism was the instrument of a reactionary bourgeoisie, and that the House of Savoy was Mussolini's willing and eager accomplice, never wavered over the next twenty years. Nor did he relinquish, even during the darkest days of the resistance, his hope that the defeat of Fascism would result in the revolutionary triumph of the Italian working class.[21]

Fascism in Little Italy

Paralleling the rise of Fascism in Italy was the emergence of an Italian American fascist movement and subculture, sometimes described as "Mussolini's Empire in the United States."[22] Italian-American Fascism arose and derived its vitality from conditions and influences that were American as well Italian. For decades, Italian immigrants had suffered the indignities of racial discrimination and the hardships of economic exploitation. Disappointment and resentment fostered among many elements—especially middle and lower-middle class Italian Americans—a "nostalgic nationalism," which was easily transmuted into an aggressive, proto-fascist form of nationalism. A number of postwar events contributed to this metamorphosis: Italy's "Mutilated Victory" in World War I; Woodrow Wilson's contemptuous treatment of Italy at the Paris Peace Conference; D'Annunzio's seizure of Fiume in 1919; and the discriminatory immigration laws of 1921 and 1924.[23] As John P. Diggins has observed: "Psychologically the Italian immigrant was conditioned to respond positively to Fascism even before Mussolini's regime dazzled the mind. Doubtless fascist propaganda provided the fertilizer, but American society had planted the seed."[24]

Italian-American Fascism was not a transplanted version or clone of Fascism in Italy, although ties between the two movements were very close until World War II. Prior to Italy's declaration of war against the United States in 1940, Rome generally called the tune in its relationship with Italian-American Fascism, with the latter providing loyal and valuable support, both propagandistic and financial. Fascism as an ideology and political movement was rarely embraced by the older generation of working-class immigrants, especially those who had been exposed to left-wing ideas and were members of labor unions. The minority of factory workers who did support Fascism tended to be younger men imbued with strong feelings of nationalism who had fought in the war.

Italian-American Fascism enjoyed much greater support from middle and lower-middle class elements: small merchants, businessmen, contractors, clerical workers, civil servants. Also well represented were second generation Italian Americans with college educations, who had seen their professional careers stymied by Anglo-Saxon prejudice against Italians. Men and women drawn from this younger, English-speaking element often found employment in the myriad agencies of the Fascist infrastructure and propaganda machine in the United States. The leading figures among Fascists and pro-Fascists, in terms of social class and political status, tended to be professionals and substantial businessmen: doctors, lawyers, judges, journalists, and newspaper owners. Very often these men were community leaders, and like their counterparts in Italy, they were imbued with the ideals and tendencies of right-wing nationalism and social conservatism, devoted to the preservation of capitalism and traditional moral and religious values. Association with the Fascist movement also facilitated their own pursuit of social, political, and economic advancement, often the most compelling motivation for their allegiance. Yet, despite drawing primary support from middle-class and educated elements, Italian-American Fascism lacked the ideological complexity and intellectual vitality of Italian Fascism, at least in its early stages. The movement in the United States was essentially devoid of serious intellectuals, save a few like Professor Giuseppe Prezzolini at Columbia University.

And as for original thinkers and theorists, there were none. Also lacking was a left-wing component of the movement comparable to the national syndicalists—notably Edmondo Rossoni—who led the Fascist trade unions in the early 1920s, before Mussolini sacrificed them to placate big industrialists in 1927–1928. Only a few important Blackshirts, such as Umberto Menicucci and Domenico Trombetta, were former radicals, but they had abandoned the Left before the advent of Fascism.[25]

Although some measure of categorization is essential, identifying individuals as Fascists, pro-Fascists, fellow travelers, sympathizers, or simple admirers of Mussolini is a challenging task, because there are no objective criteria by which to make such distinctions with a substantial degree of certitude. The noted anti-Fascist historian Gaetano Salvemini, the foremost authority on the subject, provided the following breakdown of the Italian-American community: 10 percent anti-Fascist; 5 percent "out-and-out" Fascist; 35 percent philo-Fascist; and 50 percent apolitical.[26] But Salvemini was writing in 1940, anticipating war between Italy and the United States; his inclination was to present Italian Americans in as favorable light as possible lest they suffer persecution as supporters of the enemy. In reality, among the "apolitical" mass of first generation immigrants and their children, respect, admiration, and even veneration for Mussolini (as opposed to Fascism per se) was exceptionally strong and widespread. Consequently, it scarcely mattered that an Italian American "empire" never materialized on the scale originally conceived by Mussolini. For within the *colonie italiane*, the power and influence wielded by the Duce's regime and its local adherents was great indeed and endured for nearly twenty years.[27]

Blackshirts

The most militant individuals identified by Salvemini as "out-and-out Fascists" belonged to the network of *fasci* which emerged in the early 1920s. These men were Blackshirts who fancied themselves counterparts of the *squadristi* in Italy—the gangs of Fascists organized as action squads to terrorize workers and peasants in north-central and northern Italy during the early 1920s. The first of these official branches of the fascist movement, the *Fascio* of New York, was organized without prompting from Italy in the spring of 1921, well before Mussolini's ascent to power in October 1922, a fact demonstrating the early and eager receptivity to Fascism of some Italian Americans. The principal founders of the New York *Fascio* leaders were Agostino De Biasi, the publisher of *Il Carroccio*, Umberto Menicucci, a tailor and war veteran of the elite *Arditi*, and Carlo Vinti, a businessman and former *squadrista* of the Milan *fascio*. A second *fascio* was organized in Philadelphia later that year under the leadership of Giuseppe Del Russo, who was soon replaced by Tresca's former comrade, Giovanni Di Silvestro, a "Fascist of the First Hour." The leaders of the *fasci* were predominantly middle-class professionals and substantial businessmen. Despite their often high status within the immigrant community, *fasci* leaders were generally posturing mediocrities, with egos hyper-inflated by their delusional sense of self-importance. Among the most conspicuous were the vitriolic crank and journalist De Biasi, the unbending fanatic and racist Domenico Trombetta, and the transparent opportunist Di Silvestro, whose benefit to Fascism derived from his position as the Supreme Venerable of the Order of the Sons of

Italy in America (OSIA), the largest Italian fraternal society in the United States. Rank-and-file membership cut across class lines but was primarily petty-bourgeois. The caliber of these men, according to Prince Gelasio Caetani, Italy's recently-appointed ambassador to the United States, was exceedingly low. He considered them to be uncontrollable zealots whose exuberance invariably exceeded their intelligence. Regardless of rank within the *fasci*, the great majority of all members were war veterans, divided evenly between naturalized American and resident Italian nationals. Like so many war veterans in postwar Italy, the Italian-American Blackshirts were attracted to Fascism because of its activist (violent) orientation and exaltation of nationalism and *Italianità*.[28]

The initiative demonstrated by Italian-American Fascists delighted Mussolini. He boasted in May 1921 that "before the end of the year, hundreds of *fasci* will arise in all the republics of North, Central, and South America."[29] The role of the *fasci*, he asserted, was

> to awaken, preserve, and exalt Italian identity and sentiment [*Italianità*] among the millions of Italians scattered throughout the world, to lead them to live more intimately the life of the Fatherland, to bind and strengthen ties of every kind between the colonies and the mother country, to establish true and proper "fascist consulates" for the legal and extra-legal protection of all Italians, especially those who paid by foreign employers, [and] to hold high, always and everywhere, the name of the Italian Fatherland.[30]

Mussolini wanted the *fasci* abroad to be under the control of the *Partito Nazionale Fascista* (PNF) founded in November 1921, and for that purpose the Fascist Grand Council established the *Segreteria Generale dei Fasci all'Estero* (SGFE) in 1922 under the leadership of Giuseppe Bastianini, a veteran *squadrista* who advocated a policy of aggressive expansion of the *fasci* abroad and their recruitment of extremist elements. Bastianini's policy was vigorously opposed by Ambassador Caetani, who feared that the *fasci* would inevitably attract uncontrollable elements and disturb Italy's good relationship with the United States. He warned Mussolini repeatedly that "the least worthy elements of our [immigrant] colonies are often the most active and visible," that men of "doubtful background and dubious character" were the chief promoters of the *fasci*, and that "the action of the *fasci* cannot be controlled in a reliable and absolute manner."[31] Caetani insisted that the *fasci* should be subject to consular control, if not disbanded altogether. But Bastianini continued to promote the *fasci* by circumventing the ambassador.[32]

Weighing the divergent recommendations of Bastianini and Caetani, Mussolini still clung to his belief that spreading Fascism among Italian Americans would benefit the regime financially and politically, but he was equally determined that unruly Blackshirts should not antagonize Washington and Wall Street and put good relations with the Americans at risk. The issue became more pressing by 1923, when the number of *fasci* had increased to more than forty, with a claimed membership of 700–800 in New York, and 20,000 nationwide. No doubt at Mussolini's insistence, Bastianini in September 1923 ordered the formation of a *Consiglio Centrale Fascista* (CCF) that would supersede the New York *Fascio* as the directorate of all the *fasci* in North America. The objective was to subject the *fasci* to stricter control.

Headquartered at 220 East 14th Street, the CCF appointed Sons of Italy's Supreme Venerable Giovanni Di Silvestro as president; Giuseppe Previtali, a prominent physician as vice president; and the journalist Agostino De Biasi as secretary.[33]

Worried that its true purposes might arouse objection among Americans, the CCF asserted that its activities would be directed along "humanitarian, educational and patriotic lines, with meticulous respect for the laws and established form of government under which they live."[34] As the role of an agent of a foreign government had to be disguised, the CCF claimed that it was linked with Fascists in Italy "only through the mutual objective of universal peace and a larger share of happiness for humanity.[35] And, finally, knowing precisely what the federal government and American conservatives wanted to hear, the CCF declared that its principal objective was "to combat radicalism among the Italians of this country."[36]

Prominenti

Infinitely more valuable to Mussolini were the *prominenti*, the real power brokers of the Italian-immigrant community. Traditionally conservative, nationalist, and anti-labor, the *prominenti* always had been opportunistic and sycophantic in their relations with the Italian government. Support for Mussolini and Fascism required very little adjustment in their thinking and motivation. Only a minority of the *prominenti* belonged to overt Fascist organizations, men like Di Silvestro and Luigi Barzini, Sr., renowned international news correspondent and member of the PNF Party, who served as the editor-in-chief of *Il Corriere d'America* and as unofficial advisor to Mussolini on matters pertaining to the Italian American press.[37] The majority of the *prominenti*—newspaper publishers, politicians, judges, businessmen, lawyers, doctors, and other professionals—were "philo-Fascists," because no matter how active their support for Mussolini and Fascism, they intentionally refrained from joining identifiably Fascist organizations.

Their reluctance was observed in 1923 by an interior ministry inspector commissioned by Mussolini to report on the progress of Fascism among Italian Americans: "The Italians in high social and financial positions, in the great majority, are naturalized American citizens who do not believe it convenient, for reasons of expediency or other motives or excuses, to make open declarations of Fascism, because it might signify sympathy for a [foreign] movement or a desire for Fascism in the United States."[38] The inspector reached similar conclusions about the Italian American middle classes in general: "The Italian bourgeoisie, from whom it is natural to expect the greatest help, is composed of small shop owners, modest industrialists, professionals, apolitical and not disposed to risk their small and recent fortune, not anxious even to declare themselves Italians, are afraid of anything that might bring them trouble or responsibilities they feel themselves incapable of confronting. Here they will never be openly Fascist even if they are in their soul."[39]

That the *prominenti* were disinclined to take risks came as no surprise to Mussolini, who always retained a socialist's disdain for the bourgeoisie. He understood what these parvenus coveted, and provided them with a range of incentives and rewards: private audiences with the Duce: personal letters of thanks; various business benefits and privileges that assured a profitable relationship with Italy; and awards of medals and knighthood by the score that bestowed honor and prestige. With these rewards reinforcing their nationalist and conservative inclinations, the *prominenti* utilized their status and power to control almost the entire institutional infrastructure of the Italian-American community: the daily press, radio stations, films, mutual aid societies, cultural organizations, schools, and social clubs.[40]

The most important vehicles that purveyed Fascist propaganda by the ton were the Italian-language daily newspapers. Chief among these publications in New York in the 1920s were *Il Progresso Italo-Americano,* founded by Carlo Barsotti and edited by the Fascist Italo Carlo Falbo; *Il Corriere d'America*, owned by the Crespi brothers and directed by Luigi Barzini; and the *Bolletino della Sera* directed by the philo-Fascist brothers Vincenzo and Filippo Giordano, and later by Salvatore Parisi. *Il Progresso* and *Il Corriere d'America* published, respectively, around 100,000 and 50,000 copies daily.[41] The three New York dailies were acquired by the millionaire "sand and gravel king" Generoso Pope in the late 1920s and early 1930s, making him the most powerful pro-Fascist in the Italian-American community. Among other important dailies of pro-fascist persuasion were *L'Opinione*, owned by Charles Baldi in Philadelphia (later acquired by Pope), *L'Italia* published by the Fascist Ettore Patrizi in San Francisco, *L'Italia* in Chicago, *La Voce del Popolo Italiano* in Cleveland, and *Gazzetta del Massachusetts* in Boston.

Supplementing the pro-fascist dailies were the openly-Fascist newspapers that accompanied the rise of the *fasci* and the Fascist League of North America (FLNA) founded in 1925: the FLNA's official organ, *Giovinezza*, published in Boston by Francesco Macaluso and Toto Giurato in 1923; *Il Grido della Stirpe* in New York, published by the arch-Fascist Domenico Trombetta in 1923; and *Il Carroccio* in New York, a magazine founded by Agostino De Biasi in 1915. The circulation of *Il Grido della Stirpe* reached around 30,000 in the 1920s; *Il Carroccio* published less than half that number. All told, nearly 90 percent of the Italian-American press was pro-Fascist or Fascist.[42]

Other transmission belts for Fascist propaganda included radio and film. Italian radio stations and programs, often owned or sponsored by *prominenti* like Pope and Patrizi, were more valuable than newspapers in reaching immigrants who could not read Italian or understand English, especially housewives. The airwaves carried an endless flow of news reports and stories singing the praises of *Il Duce* and Fascist Italy. Only the few stations financed by labor unions—for example, WEVD in New York—ever carried an anti-Fascist message. Italian films laden with Fascist propaganda were standard fare at Italian movie theaters such as the Roma Cina Teatro and Cine Città in New York, as were shorts, lectures, and newsreels. Some theaters were subsidized by Mussolini's government and had to register with the State Department as a foreign agency.[43]

Likewise, under Fascist and pro-Fascist control were most of the traditional social organizations, chief among them the Order of the Sons of Italy in America (OSIA) founded in 1905. Its mission openly "ultra-nationalistic," the OSIA in June 1922 established ties with the nationalist movement (the National Association) in Italy, which was now allied officially with the Fascist party. The OSIA quickly gravitated into Mussolini's camp, and after the March on Rome, Di Silvestro telegraphed the Duce pledging the allegiance of the 300,000 members of the OSIA. Thereafter, the OSIA remained a stalwart supporter of Mussolini and a crucial disseminator of

Fascist propaganda. Other Italian-American organizations that fervently embraced the Duce were the Dante Alighieri Society, the *Tiro a Segno*, the Italian Chamber of Commerce of the City of New York, the *Casa Italiana* of Columbia University, the Italy-America Society, the Institute of Italian Culture, and the Italian Historical Society, to mention only the most important.[44]

The relationship between Mussolini and the Italian-American *prominenti* functioned to their mutual benefit for the better part of twenty years. The only temporary disturbance occurred in 1938, when Mussolini's regime enacted anti-Semitic laws that the more astute *prominenti*, like Generoso Pope, realized might undermine their professional association with Jewish politicians and businessmen. Ties between the *prominenti* and Mussolini's regime began to weaken when Italy entered the war as Hitler's ally on June 6, 1940, a pact that signaled the likelihood of war between Italy and the United States. Yet up to this point, the Fascists and pro-Fascists among the *promimenti* had had little to fear from federal and local authorities, who generally considered them loyal upstanding citizens. Since they were adamantly opposed to radicalism and generally supportive of Roosevelt's administration, the *prominenti* who had been conspicuous supporters of Mussolini were never considered an internal threat by American authorities until the Duce blundered catastrophically by declaring war against the United States on December 11, 1941. As the great majority were naturalized citizens or had friends in high places, the *prominenti* escaped the government's short-lived crackdown on Italian "enemy aliens." Nevertheless, to ensure their safety, the *prominenti* of every political stamp scurried in a panic to avow their allegiance to America and democracy.[45]

The Catholic Church

The second pillar of pro-Fascist support was the Roman Catholic clergy. The Vatican regarded Mussolini as a St. George in black shirt, who had saved Christian civilization from the Bolshevik dragon. Pope Pius XI, who reigned from 1922 to 1939, was obsessively fearful of communism and almost equally distrustful of democracy. He bestowed his blessing upon the Fascists even before Mussolini assumed power, and in 1929, when the Duce and the Vatican signed the Concordat and Lateran Accords, Pius XI heralded him as the "man sent to us by Providence." By negotiating the Concordat and Lateran Accords, which sealed the rift between church and state that had existed since Italian unification, the Vatican forged a quasi-alliance with Mussolini, which ultimately served the interests of the fascist regime more than the Catholic Church, by strengthening the political power of the former and greatly enhancing its prestige among Roman Catholics worldwide, particularly in the United States.[46]

From the beginning of his rule, Mussolini had earned the enduring admiration and support of the American Catholic hierarchy for his staunch anti-communism and willingness to restore the Catholic Church to the position of privilege and influence it had enjoyed in Italy before the advent of the liberal state. Bishops and other prelates returning from their periodic visits to Rome were invariably effusive in their praise of the Duce and his achievements, judging him the greatest leader Italy had ever had. In gratitude, Mussolini showered the American hierarchy with the highest of Fascist decorations, which they accepted with eager appreciation.

The veneration of Mussolini by American Catholics reached its peak, of course, with the Concordat and Lateran Accords. The anti-Fascist Giorgio La Piana wrote, "Catholic bishops and priests in pastoral letters and sermons, Catholic newspapers and periodicals in their articles and essays, Catholic nuns and monks in their schools and confraternities and Catholic Knights of Columbus exhausted the whole dictionary of laudatory terms in celebrating the wisdom, the faith and the religious spirit of the great Duce."[47]

The linchpin of the clerical support for Mussolini and Fascism, however, was not the Church hierarchy, which included few Italian Americans in this period, but the rectors and other priests who officiated at Italian immigrant parishes throughout the *colonie italiane*. Well before the Concordat of 1929, the great majority of Italian-American clergymen were staunch supporters of Mussolini and Fascism, priests such as Alfonso Archese, Joseph A. Cafuzzi, Joseph Congedo, Francis P. Grassi, Vincent Jannuzzi, Ottavio Silvestri, and Filippo Robotti, to mention the most prominent in New York alone.[48] Priests of this ilk encouraged the establishment of *fasci*, participated as members and directors, utilized their own buildings for Fascist meetings, bestowed blessings at fascist ceremonies and celebrations, and received decorations and knighthood from Mussolini. But the principal Catholic transmission belts for fascist propaganda were parochial and Italian language schools, where children of Italian immigrants were taught all about the Duce and his wondrous works along with catechism and irregular verbs.[49]

The Consular Network

The third pillar of the Fascist infrastructure in the United States was the *longa manus* of the Italian Foreign Ministry: the Ambassador to the United States and the network of consulates General and vice Consulates located in major centers of Italian settlement. The ambassador was the most powerful figure in the Fascist infrastructure by virtue of his access to the U.S. State Department and American banking and corporate leaders. Day to day efforts to promote Mussolini's regime were the responsibility of the consuls general, all of whom were Fascists and PNF members after 1925, having displaced the conservative career diplomats previously appointed by the crown. The principal task of the consul was to organize Fascist propaganda activities on the radio, through newspapers, and in the churches, schools, social clubs, business associations, and (after 1925) the *fasci* within their jurisdiction. The more important consulates in big cities employed a "cultural agent" to control all Fascist activities in their districts. The other major function of the consuls was to ensure the loyalty and support of the Italian-American community and to stifle the anti-Fascist opposition, using methods of coercion and intimidation in the case of the former, and by threats of retaliation against relatives in Italy or repression through American and Italian-American intermediaries in the case of the latter.[50]

American Philo-Fascism

To attack those beyond immediate reach, the Italian consuls or the ambassador himself would frequently that request American authorities conduct repressive measures on behalf of the Italian government, alleging always that the culprits were dangerous "anarchists" or "communists," whose activities constituted a threat or an insult to the Italian monarchy or a danger to the public safety of the United States. Requests of this nature had routinely been submitted to American authorities long before the advent of Fascism. In the 1920s, however, with fear of radicalism still bewitching the political ruling class, American authorities proved far more cooperative. They never understood how anti-Fascism had absorbed the revolutionary zeal of Italian radicals like Tresca; nor did they comprehend that by fighting Fascism the *sovversivi* were actually serving the cause of democracy. Instead, the association between anti-Fascists and subversives remained an *idée fixe*, so American authorities often assumed the role of partner in what was construed as a mutually beneficial struggle against the "Reds," employing such repressive measures as interference with newspaper publication and circulation, denial of free speech through prohibition of meetings and demonstrations, harassment and arbitrary arrests, arranging termination of employment, and outright deportation. All of these measures were utilized or attempted against Tresca in the 1920s.[51]

Increasing collaboration between American and Italian authorities in the suppression of Italian immigrant radicals was a corollary to the larger pattern of admiration and support for Mussolini's regime that became widespread in the United States throughout the 1920s and 1930s. Politicians, financiers, corporate magnates, university presidents, journalists, social scientists, intellectuals, and a host of other prominent elements in American society were effusive with praise for Mussolini and his regime; some even considered Fascism worthy of emulation for much of the world, including the United States. No matter that Fascism was antithetical to the purported values and practices of democracy, or that Italy had lost all her political and civil liberties—racially "inferior" and anarchic people like the Italians were unsuited to democracy in any case. What counted for Anglo-Saxon America were Mussolini's alleged accomplishments: suppression of "Bolshevism," abolition of strikes and union activity, restoration of public order, respect for private property and enterprise, bureaucratic reform, and opening Italy to American investment. These accomplishments corresponded closely with the political philosophy of the Republican administrations of the 1920s and directly resulted in favorable terms for payment of war debts in 1926, and a crucial loan of $100,000,000 from the House of Morgan that same year.

The prestige Mussolini garnered from Washington, Wall Street, and much of Anglo-Saxon America provided a major stimulus to the adulation of the Duce that developed in Little Italy. So long despised by Anglo-Saxon society, Italian immigrants and their offspring—especially among the more nationalistic middle classes—derived an appreciable measure of self-respect and ethnic pride from the notion (in reality, misplaced) that Mussolini's popularity reflected positively upon them. Furthermore, the accolades showered upon Mussolini enabled Italian Americans to ignore the political and moral contradiction of supporting Mussolini and Fascism while simultaneously swearing allegiance to the United States and democracy. If Anglo-Saxons and other "respectable" ethnic groups admired Mussolini, why should not Italian Americans? In this sense, the historian Gian Giacomo Migone was on the mark: "The philo-Fascism of the [Italian] immigrant was a reflection of the philo-Fascism of the dominant [American] classes."[52]

12

Early Anti-Fascist Activities

Fighting Fascism became the great crusade of Tresca's life, the struggle in which he achieved unrivalled preeminence among Italian-American radicals and reached the pinnacle of his career. The fight against Italian-American Fascism represented a new phase in the class struggle Tresca and other *sovversivi* had waged against the consuls, *prominenti*, and Catholic Church since the turn of the 20th century. No compromise with the enemy was possible; no quarter given and none expected. Tresca's war against Fascism was a fight to the death.

Testimony to Tresca's unique status and formidable abilities as a resistance leader was provided repeatedly by the Fascists themselves. Italian ambassador Giacomo De Martino reported to Mussolini in 1926 that Tresca topped the list of "three renegades" (Vincenzo Vacirca and Arturo Giovannitti were the others) whose deportation would most benefit the Fascist regime.[1] By 1928, Tresca had distinguished himself as such a dynamic and implacable foe of Fascism that the Political Police in Rome dubbed him the "*deus ex machina* of anti-Fascism" in the United States.[2] That same year, overjoyed that Tresca was the target of a smear campaign intended to undermine his status, the consul general of New York, Emilio Axerio, notified Ambassador De Martino that "the definitive liquidation of Carlo Tresca, imposed upon his followers as well, would administer a mortal blow to anti-Fascism, which depends so much on Tresca."[3]

Had Tresca still lived in Italy, his "liquidation" would have been physical rather than figurative. His presence in the United States, however, was no guarantee of security. Since paranoia is endemic to all police states, the Fascist regime in the 1920s consistently over-estimated the strength of the anti-Fascists, worrying that their activities might undermine Mussolini's prestige and influence among Italian Americans and jeopardize his cozy relations with the American government and the Wall Street moguls. The anti-Fascist who caused Rome its greatest concern during the early years of the regime was Tresca. Directly or in collusion with American authorities, Mussolini's official representatives and local disciples caused Tresca to suffer periodic harassment, several arrests, loss of his Italian citizenship, a four-month prison term, a narrow escape from deportation, destruction of his property, and a bomb attempt on his life. But Tresca never relented.

Tresca's principal weapon against Mussolini and Fascism was *Il Martello*, described by the consul general of New York in 1925, as "the most dangerous [anti-Fascist newspaper], because of the skillful manner in which it is edited, and because of its influence over certain elements of the people."[4] A consummate political analyst, Tresca understood that propaganda and myth were the indispensable props of Mussolini's regime. Therefore, nearly every issue delivered "hammer blows" (*martellate*) to dismantle the false image of idealism and heroism with which Fascists enveloped themselves, and to dispel the notion that the Blackshirts had turned back the red tide.[5]

The voices of anti-Fascist opposition required amplification from outside sources abroad, as the free press in Italy was progressively stifled. Tresca therefore placed *Il Martello* at the disposal of many prominent radicals who lacked publication outlets. Once *Il Martello* became distinguished as an anti-Fascist organ, letters from Italy requesting the newspaper poured into Tresca's office; he responded by sending free copies to comrades throughout the country.[6] Alarmed, the Italian Postal and Telegraph Ministry banned the importation and circulation of Tresca's newspaper in May 1923, prescribing stiff penalties for violators.[7] Tresca attempted to circumvent the ban by asking Italian Americans to send copies to friends and relatives (a risky proposition for recipients) and by establishing clandestine operations to smuggle *Il Martello* into Italy. By 1928, for example, he was sending 100 copies of each issue to a former lover in Locarno, who ferried them by boat across Lake Maggiore.[8] Tresca's efforts were greatly appreciated, as indicated by the legendary anarchist Errico Malatesta: "I receive *Il Martello* very irregularly, because it gets through only when it escapes the police bloodhounds; however, I have read enough to admire the energy and fighting courage you sustain against Fascism, which torments us in Italy."[9]

Interdiction of *Il Martello* in Italy did not prevent Tresca from utilizing his newspaper to raise vitally needed funds for the anti-Fascist opposition. Channeling money to comrades in Italy was a long-standing practice of the *sovversivi*. By raising funds, Tresca helped sustain the Italian anarchist press until its complete suppression in 1926. Funds were also collected on a regular basis to help the victims of Fascist violence and persecution.[10] Over the next two decades, countless anti-Fascists in Italy, Europe, and South America would have found themselves in hopeless circumstances if not for the financial support of Italian immigrant workers in the United States, a factor of major importance invariably overlooked by Italian historians of the anti-Fascist resistance.

Tresca was not content to attack Mussolini's regime merely with "propaganda of the word" and by assisting political victims with money. The best means of subverting Mussolini was to strike where the regime was most vulnerable—the Italian economy. Rising unemployment and taxes, falling wages, the declining value of the lira, military expenditures for the re-conquest of Libya, and the unresolved dilemma of war debts all added up to one inescapable conclusion by 1923: the Fascists could not make good on their promises to improve the lives of the Italian people. Convinced that Mussolini's prestige at home and abroad would suffer if recovery failed, Tresca advocated economic sabotage and boycotting of Italian financial and state institutions that generated income for the government. He urged workers in Italy to employ obstructionist tactics on the job, abstain from state monopolies (tobacco, salt, lotteries) that generated revenue, purchase food and other provisions only from merchants friendly to the anti-Fascist cause, avoid luxuries and other non-essential expenditures, and boycott all bourgeois establishments. On his own turf, Tresca sought to deprive the Italian economy of the benefits derived from the remittances sent to family members back home by immigrants in the United States. Tresca urged immigrant workers to boycott all Italian financial institutions that operated in the United States, to deposit their savings in American banks, and to avoid utilizing Italy's *Cassa Postale* and other agencies that collected fees for transferring remittances.[11] He also exhorted immigrant workers to boycott every Italian American—doctor, lawyer, shoemaker, grocer, barber, etc.—who was a Fascist.[12] Adoption of his boycott strategy, Tresca acknowledged, would inevitably impose hardships upon Italian workers and peasants, but in his words, "war is war."[13] Mussolini's government viewed Tresca's scheme with genuine concern, and the consul general of New York was instructed to remain vigilant for any sign that the plan was gaining momentum.[14] It never did.

Given the unlikelihood of undermining Mussolini's regime from abroad, Tresca and other anti-Fascists were obliged to conduct their anti-Fascist activities mainly within the Italian-American community. The struggle, however, was never fought on terms even remotely equal. Anti-Fascists numbered not more than 10 percent of the Italian American population, if that. The majority of anti-Fascists within the political spectrum that spanned middle-class liberal to conservative were neither organized nor generally active. Only a handful of bourgeois liberal democrats, like Gaetano Salvemini and Dr. Charlo Fama, functioned as important resistance leaders prior to 1938, when a sizeable contingent of professionals, intellectuals, and former political leaders—known collectively as the *fuorusciti* (exiles)—were admitted to the United States and assumed a dominant role. The most numerous and dedicated anti-Fascists were working-class *sovversivi*, and the chieftains of the movement were generally the same radicals and labor leaders who had led Italian immigrant workers prior to the advent of Fascism: Tresca, Giovannitti, Girolamo Valenti, Vincenzo Vacirca, Luigi Antonini, the brothers Frank and Augusto Bellanca, and many others.

But a resistance movement based on workers could not possibly generate resources comparable to those available to the Fascists, assisted as they were by Mussolini's regime, the *prominenti*, and the Italian-American middle classes generally. Moreover, the radical and labor movements were significantly weaker in the 1920s than before World War I, thanks in large measure to wartime and postwar repression. Many of the most important radical leaders and hard-core militants, who would have contributed significantly to the resistance, had been deported or imprisoned. Some had returned to Italy of their own accord, hoping to participate in the revolution that beckoned, while others sought refuge in clandestine life underground or became completely inactive. Another factor that weighed against the resistance was the ongoing hostility of the American authorities, who generally regarded Fascists and pro-Fascists as good, conservative patriots, while the anti-Fascists were considered dangerous Reds. Accordingly, fear of arrest and deportation often limited the effectiveness of anti-Fascist activity, for without such dangers hanging over them, many of the *sovversivi*—anarchists and communists especially—would have been far more aggressive in their methods.

A new levy of anti-Fascists arrived in the United States between 1919 and

1924, before the new immigration quota system effectively barred Italians. Some newcomers entered the United States illegally or arrived with provisional status as political refugees. Others had previously returned to Italy or had been deported after World War I but managed to re-enter. The most important of them would play leadership roles in the resistance: the socialist Vincenzo Vacirca; the communists Giovanni Pippan and Vittorio Vidali; and the anarchists Raffaele Schiavina, Armando Borghi, and Virgilia D'Andrea. The *fuorusciti*, the last contingent of newcomers, arriving in 1938 and 1939, included some very prominent liberal and democratic anti-Fascists (Carlo Sforza, Randolfo Pacciardi, Alberto Tarchiani, Lionello Venturi, and others) who had long resided in exile in Europe or were refugees fleeing from Mussolini's recently promulgated anti-Semitic laws in Italy. Although few in number, the *fuorusciti* provided the Italian-American resistance with an important infusion of much needed energy and talent.

Despite acquiring some new blood during the interwar period, the Italian-American resistance undoubtedly lost more adherents than it gained. The primary reason was the failure of the *sovversivi* to produce a second generation large enough to replace the departed. This was a problem of long standing for Italian-American radicalism. The offspring of the *sovversivi* were generally more assimilated into American society than their parents, accepting American values and rejecting the ideas and principles of their elders. Political and cultural discontinuity between parents and children was also a function of the disproportionate number of male to female radicals, a deficiency fatal to the movement because marital unions generally occurred between a radical father and a non-radical mother, who raised the children Catholic and conservative.

Numerical weakness might not have mattered so much if anti-Fascists had been unified and equally militant. The resistance was multi-factional: anarchists of various orientation; communists of the newly-established Communist Party; revolutionary syndicalists of the moribund IWW; left-wing and right-wing socialists of the FSI (SP); social-democratic trade unionists (particularly leaders of the ILGWU and ACWA), and a small contingent of Mazzinian (i.e., democratic) republicans. All were committed to the anti-Fascist struggle. The crusade against Fascism, as Rudolf J. Vecoli correctly asserted, was the *raison d'être* of Italian-American radicalism between the wars.[15] Yet, while commitment to the cause might have been equal in the abstract, the zeal and tenacity with which the various radical elements fought against Fascism often differed from group to group. Moreover, the internecine conflicts they incessantly waged were so ferocious and divisive that an outside observer might have concluded that the anti-Fascists devoted more time and energy to fighting among themselves than they did to combating Fascism.

Tresca always pursued his anti-Fascist mission with singular commitment and intensity, excelling at more roles than any of his radical contemporaries: journalist, public spokesman, lecturer, strategist, agitation leader, and front-line fighter. Tresca's pattern of struggle was set in the early 1920s, when the resistance existed in little more than name. High on his list of targets were local Blackshirts and visiting Fascist leaders and dignitaries. As potential opponents, Tresca held the Blackshirts of the *fasci* in low regard. Having confronted every imaginable combination of policemen, private detectives, company thugs, and vigilantes during his years as a strike leader, Tresca would not so much as flinch in the face of Blackshirts, whom he considered strutting bullies and cowards afraid to battle the *sovversivi* on even terms. If the Blackshirts dared to move against them, Tresca and his "boys" would know how to deal with them. To demonstrate his contempt for the Blackshirts, Tresca in July 1923 moved the offices of *Il Martello* to 304 East 14th Street, a mere stone's throw from the headquarters of the New York *Fascio* founded in 1921.

The presence of Giuseppe Bottai between August and October 1921 provided Tresca and the anti-Fascists with their first opportunity to make life miserable for a prominent Blackshirt visiting the United States to win favor for Mussolini and Fascism. A deputy and political secretary of the Fascist parliamentary group prior to the "March on Rome," Bottai was a particularly vicious Blackshirt who later would become a major figure in the regime. Bottai's ostensible purpose of his visit was to raise funds for blind war veterans, but he admitted to the American press that his mission as a representative of Fascism was to help fight "Bolshevism" among Italian Americans—a theme repeated endlessly by visiting and indigenous Fascists to win acceptance and support from American society.[16] In every city he visited, Bottai was feted by consular officials and *prominenti*, a clear sign of Fascism's popularity within the highest circles of the Italian-American community more than a year before Mussolini assumed power. That he should receive the red carpet treatment was galling enough, but anti-Fascists were seething because a socialist deputy had recently been murdered by Fascists, a crime that prompted Bottai to boast at a local fascist meeting that he personally had killed five communists in Rome.[17]

The arrival of this despised Blackshirt represented one of the few occasions when most anti-Fascists acted in accord. A protest campaign was launched at a mass meeting in New York, at which Tresca, Pietro Allegra, Arturo Giovannitti, Nino Capraro, and Luigi Antonini, head of the ILGWU's Local 89, each denouncing Bottai in turn. A more dramatic confrontation followed in Utica, New York, where Tresca was scheduled to address an anti-Fascist rally at the same time Bottai would address local admirers. En route to their own meeting place, Tresca led a column of several hundred anti-Fascists past the theater where Bottai had just finished his speech. Shouting "*Abbasso Bottai!*," "*Morte a Bottai!*," "*Assassino!*," anti-Fascists had to be held back by police lest they attack the fascist celebrity and his hosts. During his next engagement, in New Haven, a threatening crowd of anti-Fascists so unnerved Bottai that he spoke for only ten minutes before leaving the theater under police escort. A week later Bottai was scheduled to speak in Philadelphia, home to the largest Italian immigrant populations outside of New York. On hand to greet the Fascist were the Italian vice consul; the wealthy publisher of the daily *L'Opinione*, Charles Baldi; and a host of other *prominenti*. But the audience also included some 2,000 anti-Fascists. The orchestra attempted to play the Italian "*Marcia Reale*" and the American "Star Spangled Banner" but was drowned out by cries for the musicians to play the "Internationale." Bottai spoke for ten minutes, repeatedly interrupted by shouts of "*Abbasso Bottai!*" and "*Morte a Bottai!*" before police drove the anti-Fascists from the theater with clubs. Outside, another 4,000 anti-Fascists joined the demonstration but were dispersed by mounted police who charged the crowd.[18]

Livid with rage as he fled the stage, Bottai was overheard muttering that the demonstration had been organized by "that vulgarian Tresca" and "if only we were in Italy...."[19] Tresca answered the implicit threat:

> To be sure, if we were in Italy, you would already have had the Fascist royal guards stab us in the back. But here in America, you had to reply on your own forces or those few cowards who surround you. Here we forced you to take to your heels ashen faced, as in Utica, or to protect yourself with Cossack horsemen, as in Philadelphia.

Then Tresca issued a threat of his own: "The four fascist scoundrels in New York [leaders of the local *fascio*] know it: we will never permit them to raise their heads. We will never permit the lying consuls, the thieving bankers, the exploiting bosses to raise their heads from the swamp—never, never."[20]

Harassment of visiting fascist dignitaries became standard procedure for Tresca and his comrades. Such protest demonstrations had a threefold objective: to demonstrate that the anti-Fascist resistance in America was thriving and committed to the fight; to reject the claims of Mussolini's government that Fascism was the legitimate expression of the will of the Italian people; and to alert the American public to the realities of Fascism and the danger it would ultimately pose for the United States. Unfortunately, these protest demonstrations invariably brought condemnation from the conservative American press, which regarded clashes between Fascists and anti-Fascists either as an internal fracas between histrionic Italians, or a dangerous manifestation of the lingering influence of foreign Reds. Worse, the purpose of the demonstrations was easily distorted by fascist propaganda and media, which usurped the mantle of patriotism for the Blackshirts and branded the anti-Fascists as "un-Italian" and "anti-Italian."[21]

Protest demonstrations against the likes of Bottai generated considerable drama and publicity, but such confrontations were occasional occurrences, perhaps one or two every few years. A more frequent and important target for Tresca was the Italian consular system, the direct extension of Mussolini's regime that reached into immigrant communities everywhere, disseminating Fascist propaganda and stifling opposition. Consular officials, in Tresca's eyes, were "all members of an accursed royal [institution] of blood suckers, the fungus of a ravenous bureaucracy, transplanted here, on the bent backs of immigrant workers."[22] He had attacked Italian ambassadors and consular officials on a regular basis ever since his campaign against Naselli in 1905. The issues back then mainly involved corruption and exploitation, the myriad schemes and methods by which consular officials lined their pockets at the expense of the immigrants whom they were supposed to protect. By World War I, the role of the ambassador and consular officials had expanded to include inseminating the values of nationalism, militarism, and imperialism, so that Italian immigrants would provide political and financial support for the policies of the Italian government. The advent of Mussolini and Fascism increased pressure on the diplomatic service to fulfill these objectives, and Tresca and other anti-Fascists responded with even fiercer opposition. A heightened clash commenced in November 1922, when Mussolini made his first ambassadorial appointment to the

United States, replacing Vittorio Rolandi Ricci with the far more effective Prince Gelasio Caetani di Sermoneta.

Selecting Caetani was a smart decision. As a well-educated, English-speaking aristocrat and nationalist (not a Fascist), Caetani could serve the interests of Mussolini's regime while still retaining an image of prestige and respectability derived from his social class and party affiliation. With ready access to America's political and financial elite, Caetani undertook with consummate skill his assigned task of courting American capitalists for financial loans and investments, and negotiating with the U.S. government for reduction of Italy's war debts and reconsideration of Congress's restrictive immigration laws. Another important objective was to strengthen support for Mussolini among the Italian-American *prominenti* and workers so that the Italian vote could influence decisions favorable to Italy, and to ensure a continuous flow of remittances. The final item on Caetani's agenda, acknowledged openly in moments of candor, was to eliminate the threat posed by the anti-Fascists, with Tresca at the top of his list.[23]

Tresca's efforts to obstruct Caetani's work began the moment the new ambassador disembarked in New York, where he was greeted by a throng of *prominenti* who assured him that the three million Italians living in the United States—moved by the "regenerative spirit" that animated the "re-builders of Italy"—were at his disposal. The *prominenti* who fell all over themselves licking Caetani's boots—the "failed banker" Carlo Barsotti, the "moral degenerate" Agostino De Biasi, and the "turncoat" Giovanni Di Silvestro—spoke only for themselves, Tresca assured the ambassador. The anti-Fascist demonstrations that protested his arrival were proof that the Italian immigrant workers opposed Mussolini's regime. "You do not represent Italy as a Nation, the Italy of working people, but Fascist Italy, that is, the group of men... who have put themselves at the service of the ancient baronial scoundrels to keep the working classes in submission." Mussolini, Tresca declared, had appointed Caetani as

a challenge to immigrant workers who manifest their disgust with Fascism.... Very well: WE ACCEPT THE CHALLENGE.... We declare that from now on we will not suffer coercion of any sort. Give yourself over joyously—like your predecessors in Washington—to the customary colonial banquets. Enjoy yourself. We will remain indifferent. But we will obstruct your fascist propaganda as much as possible."[24]

The principal allies of the consuls, of course, were the *prominenti*. What Tresca now feared most about the Italian community bigwigs was their ability to deliver the immigrant masses to Mussolini and Fascism. The chief means by which they could accomplish this objective was through their control of daily newspapers—the *fungaia coloniale*, as Tresca called them—90 percent of which were philo-Fascist or Fascist. To counter the lies and distortions about Fascism's accomplishments that emanated from their pages, Tresca tracked dozens of Italian-language newspapers, blasting their owners and editors with all the vitriol, sarcasm, and creative obscenity his pen could produce. Targeted almost daily by Tresca was Carlo Barzotti, a businessman whose reputation for shady dealings and unscrupulous exploitation of his countrymen had been well earned years earlier. Barzotti founded *Il Progresso*

Italo-Americano in 1880, and by the 1920s the newspaper had acquired the highest circulation of any Italian-language daily in the country. *Il Progresso* was the most important disseminator of Fascist propaganda in the New York area. Tresca had waged a war of words with *Il Progresso* and Barsotti for many years, but now the stakes were higher. Any issue of *Il Martello* might therefore include a description like the following:

> *Il Progresso,* dripping mud, spews forth the stench of the colonial carrion that Barzotti has gathered from the sewers in order to serve his thieving endeavors…. *Il Progresso* is the true black pool of the colonies, dark and deep. There, at the bottom, is the heart of Barzotti, a sponge that wipes and swallows the tears, blood, and sweat of the people from Italy.[25]

For Tresca and other anti-Fascist journalists, the goal of countering the fascist propaganda generated by the major dailies was hindered severely by limited circulation. *Il Martello*, which published 6,500 copies per week in 1923; 10,500 in 1924; and 8,000 in 1929, could not compete numerically with *Il Progresso*'s daily circulation of 100,000; or *Il Corriere d'America*'s 50,000, even though copies of radical newspapers like Tresca's were invariably shared among several comrades.[26] One of the few advantages that *Il Martello* and other radical newspapers enjoyed over the pro-Fascist dailies was their national distribution. As Mussolini's investigator discovered to his dismay in 1923: "They are very widespread and reach… even the small mining and industrial centers where no other Italian newspaper has known how to penetrate."[27] Greater geographic distribution, however, could not compensate for the fact that *Il Martello* and other radical newspapers were read primarily by workers already committed to anti-Fascism. The real challenge was reaching Italian Americans who read the daily newspapers or none at all, and who never attended political meetings of any sort—in other words, the typical apolitical Italian immigrant.

Given the limited outreach of the radical press, Tresca sought to immunize Italian Americans against the mesmerizing appeal of Mussolini by reaching his audience through the medium of speech, or what the anarchists called "propaganda of the word." Tresca delivered scores of speeches at anti-Fascist meetings held at the Rand School, Cooper Union, the Manhattan Lyceum, Bryant Hall, and other favorite gathering places of radicals in New York, with attendance varying from a few dozen to several thousand people. But the majority of those who attended these rallies were radical workers and sympathizers, so, as with the radical press, Tresca was usually preaching to the choir.

To overcome this problem, Tresca in 1922 began holding open-air rallies in Italian neighborhoods: Greenwich Village, East Harlem, 187th Street and Gamberling Avenue in the Bronx, and various sections in Brooklyn.[28] Always able to draw a crowd with his oratory, Tresca successfully delivered his message to thousands of Italian Americans who otherwise would never been exposed to anti-Fascist propaganda. The same was true when he took to the road on his propaganda tours. Between February 1922 and July 1923, Tresca spent a cumulative total of five months on the road, lecturing on Fascism, Sacco and Vanzetti, and other themes to Italian audiences in thirteen states in the East and Midwest.[29] Unfortunately, there was no way to determine how many apolitical Italian Americans were converted to anti-Fascism by Tresca's lectures, but the numbers were probably small given the quasi-cult following the Duce was acquiring in Little Italys throughout the country.

While he continued his war of words, Tresca, along with Arturo Giovannitti, and Luigi Antonini attempted in 1923 to challenge Fascist and pro-Fascist domination of the Order of the Sons of Italy of America (OSIA), the most important Italian American social organization in the country. Despite having recently sought its cooperation to defend Sacco and Vanzetti, Tresca had always been a staunch critic of the OSIA, denouncing its conservative leaders for imposing monarchist and nationalist beliefs upon a benevolent society that was supposed to be apolitical, and for stifling the opposing viewpoints expressed by the few radicals in the organization. Moreover, he regarded the OSIA as "the greatest block of opposition to the expansion of our internationalist and classist ideas" among uncommitted Italian immigrants.[30]

Tresca frequently had chided Giovannitti and Antonini for their membership in the OSIA and their delusional notion that they constituted a leftwing vanguard capable of protecting proletariat interests within the organization.[31] But with the ascendancy of the Fascist Giovanni Di Silvestro as supreme venerable, and his famous telegram to Mussolini, pledging the allegiance of the 300,000 members of the OSIA, Tresca grew increasing alarmed. The threat of a Fascist take-over prompted Tresca to join forces with Giovannitti and Antonini in order "to enter the enemy's camp, to bring the anti-Fascist struggle into the trench selected by Mussolini."[32]

The "enemy's camp" was the OSIA's national convention, held in Providence, Rhode Island, on October 28–31, 1923, the opening date marking the one-year anniversary of Mussolini's "March on Rome." To gain admission to the convention, Tresca joined the OSIA.[33] A challenge against Di Silvestro's campaign to fascistize the OSIA already had been initiated when Judge (later State Senator) Salvatore Cotillo, the grand venerable of the New York Lodge, and Congressmen Fiorello La Guardia charged Di Silvestro with violating the organization's apolitical philosophy by his pledge of OSIA loyalty to Mussolini. Although deemed "radicals" by Di Silvestro and his fascist supporters, Cotillo and La Guardia hardly represented the vanguard of anti-Fascism. Cotillo actually admired Mussolini but believed it unwise to establish *fasci* in the United States; La Guardia, whose anti-Fascism was genuine, never criticized Mussolini publicly lest he jeopardize his political career by alienating Italian-American voters. In fact, the major issue of contention between the two factions was not Fascism, but control of the New York's Lodge mortuary and education funds, which amounted to $300,000. To prevent the Grand Lodge from appropriating these funds, Cotillo and his supporters seceded from the OSIA and incorporated themselves as the Sons of Italy Grand Lodge of the State of New York.[34]

The confrontation between Fascists and anti-Fascists that took place at the OSIA convention in Providence was far more dramatic. Giovannitti, Antonini, and Allegra, initially denied access, finally gained entry to the meeting hall after Di Silvestro's latest paean to Mussolini. Tresca, too, sought entry, but his membership card was snatched from his hand and the door slammed in his face. Once inside,

Giovannitti and Antonini demanded that the OSIA telegraph an anti-Fascist message to the Duce. Nearly hysterical with rage, Di Silvestro grabbed the Italian and American flags and demanded that Giovannitti and Antonini kneel before them. The two *sovversivi* declined, of course, but the incident encouraged Fascists to invent a story that Giovannitti and Antonini had been forced to kiss the two flags. Tresca, meanwhile, sent a message to Di Silvestro, challenging him to a debate. Having no wish to tangle with Tresca, the supreme venerable swiftly departed for the train station to greet the arrival of Ambassador Caetani, who had urged Di Silvestro to purge the OSIA of its radicals and now ventured to Providence to bestow Mussolini's blessings on his faithful supporters.[35]

That evening, a protest meeting was convened at Eagle Hall; it attracted several thousand workers and a large contingent of policemen and Justice Department agents. Tresca regaled the audience with the story of how he and Di Silvestro had once been comrades in Philadelphia. "Today, after thirteen years [sic], we have met again in Providence."

> I am still at my old battle post, under the same banner, while I find Di Silvestro, now a banker, with that foul band of decorated [*prominenti*], himself made a *Cavaliere* by the same king he once denigrated, and at the service of the brigand of Predappio [Mussolini's birthplace] who governs Italy today."[37]

When the convention reconvened on October 30, Di Silvestro, the supreme executive council, and the grand venerables met privately and voted to bar Giovannitti and Antonini from further meetings and to suspend them from the OSIA, a decision that prompted the thirty-five delegates from New York to abandon the convention in protest. With the opposition purged, the remaining delegates re-elected Di Silvestro as supreme venerable and selected a supreme executive council of twelve men who were Fascists or pro-Fascists, including Di Silvestro and two others who were both members of the Fascist Central Council. The twelve "brothers" on the supreme executive council remained in power until 1929; Di Silvestro retained his position as grand venerable until 1935. OSIA remained a bastion of support for Mussolini and Fascism throughout these years and beyond.[38]

Towards a United Front

With the Fascists building a strong infrastructure within Italian communities, the pressing issue confronting the anti-Fascist camp was whether or not radical and labor elements could overcome their traditional differences to unite effectively against the common foe. Anti-Fascists, or at least the most militant among them, would often cooperate in protest demonstrations, as they had done to harass Bottai, but not until 1923 was any attempt made to forge a united front on an institutional basis.

On the initiative of the Italian Chamber of Labor, the *Alleanza Operaia Antifascista* was founded in New York in March 1923, primarily with the backing of the Italian trade unions.[39] Existing only on paper, the *Alleanza* was quickly superseded by the *Alleanza Antifascista di Nord America* (AFANA), established on April 10, 1923. Headquartered at the Chamber of Labor, the AFANA declared its primary objective to be "the extinction of all Fascist organizations in North America, the creation of popular sentiment opposed to the Fascisti regime in Italy and the relief of radical and labor institutions in Italy which have been destroyed or harmed by the Fascisti."[40] The chairman selected to direct AFANA's activities was Frank Bellanca, editor of the ACWU's weekly *Il Lavoro*.[41] But Italian union leaders were too preoccupied with internal union affairs—particularly a communist challenge within the ILGWU—and too confident of ultimate victory over Fascism to forge a genuine united front. The AFANA, characterized by Tresca as a "financial and moral disaster," lapsed into inactivity by the end of the year.[42]

The AFANA's potential as a viable anti-Fascist organization was undoubtedly diminished by the fact that Tresca and most of the radicals on the far Left had remained aloof from the enterprise because it was controlled by the social democrats of the ILGWU and ACWU. Tresca still had not forgiven the social democrats ("rabbits") for having undermined the revolutionary potential of the Italian factory occupations of 1920; moreover, for many years he had been a strong critic of the ILGWU hierarchy, Antonini in particular. Tresca's relations with Italian trade union officials had deteriorated further in 1922, when he supported the radical dissidents within the ILGWU and was drawn into a fierce polemic waged between his friends Allegra and Antonini.[43]

Possessing little faith in the militancy of social democrats and the Italian union hierarchies, Tresca in February 1923 had already established the *Comitato Generale di Difesa Contro Il Fascismo*, through which he sought to unify the far Left of the radical movement. The *Comitato*'s leaders were Tresca, Allegra, Quintiliano, Elizabeth Gurley Flynn, and Costantino Zonchello, the first director of *L'Adunata dei Refrattari*, whose brief participation represented the only occasion when some of the Galleanisti supported an undertaking initiated by Tresca. Under the aegis of the *Comitato*, and with Tresca's leadership, the anarchists constituted the vanguard of anti-Fascist activity throughout 1923 and 1924.[44]

13

Frame-Up

That Tresca's activities would prompt the Fascists to retaliate was inevitable. Mussolini more than anyone knew that propaganda was the primary instrument to create and perpetuate the myths upon which the Fascist regime rested. He was anxious, therefore, to silence those anti-Fascists who would expose the hollowness of his regime—Tresca more than anyone. Tresca received his first threat directly from Mussolini shortly before the latter's appointment as prime minister. Furious that Tresca provided a communication vehicle for anti-Fascists in Italy, Mussolini warned him that "the eye of Fascism reaches far and the hand of Fascism even farther!… No one insults Fascism with impunity, not even in New York."[1]

Tresca issued his own challenge to "that paranoic *Sparafucile* of a Benito Mussolini":

> Here in all the streets of New York, in crowded meetings and elsewhere, we have called you [and your Blackshirts] by the names you deserve: BRIGANDS, SLAVERS, AND CUTTHROATS. Here we will continue to hurl our reproach in your face, as it is the reproach of the workers of Italy. And you will continue to keep silent because you are cowards. Because here you must fight us on equal terms on neutral soil. Your HAND THAT REACHES FAR is a bluff. It will take more than that to silence us.[2]

Demands for action against anti-Fascists began in earnest with the formation in late 1922 of the *Segreteria Generale dei Fasci all'Estero*. At a meeting of the Fascist Grand Council on February 14, 1923, Bastianini, the secretary of the *Fasci all'Estero*, denounced the "pernicious" influence exercised by *sovversivi* "who misrepresent the significance of Fascism among the masses of immigrants."[3] Bastianini would have preferred to employ violence, but local Blackshirts in 1923 would never have dared to beat or kill Tresca, as such an attack would have precipitated maximum retaliation by anti-Fascists who still outnumbered them.[4] Moreover, use of violence against anti-Fascists was vehemently opposed by Ambassador Caetani, who repeatedly warned Mussolini that irresponsible action might jeopardize Italy's good relations with the United States.[5] Caetani prevailed. Retaliation against Tresca and the anti-Fascists would be undertaken through official diplomatic channels, using the State and Justice Departments as surrogates.

"The Opportunity Which Has Long Been Sought"

The four-year effort of the Justice Department's Bureau of Investigation to obtain evidence for deportation proceedings against Tresca had come to naught by the beginning of 1923, but Burns and Hoover were more determined than ever to eliminate him from the scene. Tired of waiting for him to slip up, the BI now took steps to trick Tresca into committing an actionable offense. At the beginning of 1923, the BI infiltrated the staff of *Il Martello* with one of their agents, Giuseppe Sposa, who in his capacity as shipping clerk could monitor Tresca's activities and report on the mailing of any potentially incriminating material.[6] Almost simultaneously, the BI's plan to entrap Tresca assumed a new and more promising dimension when the Italian ambassador proposed a collaborative campaign to rid America of Italian radicals.[7] The enterprising ambassador arranged to discuss his project with Hoover and the Under-Secretary of State, W. L. Hurley, on January 30, 1923. Skillfully exploiting American obsession with the Red menace, Caetani informed Hoover and Hurley that the communists would soon meet in Pittsburgh or Chicago "for the purpose of determining an outrageous program against the Fascisti in Italy and against the Government of the United States." This information, Caetani added, had been furnished to the Italian government by "officials in Moscow," and confirmed by the ambassador's agent in Boston. The Italian government, therefore, was "very desirous of establishing the closest cooperation with the United States Government in regard to radical activities," because Premier Mussolini was "determined to bring to an end the spirit of anarchism and communism in Italy." To facilitate their suppression in both countries, the Italian government was willing to furnish American authorities with the "considerable amount of information" it possessed about Italian radicals in the United States, in exchange for similar information provided by Washington. The plan called for a representative of the Italian secret police, someone thoroughly conversant with the radical movement, to be stationed in the United States and serve as liaison between the two governments. His identity would be kept strictly confidential, known only to the ambassador, the secretaries of the embassy, and Hoover.[8]

The under-secretary of state was very eager to adopt the plan, as was Hoover, who explained to Burns that "personally, it would seem to be the opportunity which has long been sought...."[9] Burns endorsed the plan, explaining to Hurley that "there is a considerable amount of radicalism among certain groups of Italians and investigations by this Bureau have disclosed that these elements are of a more or less migratory nature, being in Italy one month and in the United States the next." "I am, therefore, heartily in accord with the proposed plan if it is consistent with the policy of the Department of State."[10]

Thus did the United States enter into collusion with Fascist Italy for the suppression of the radical anti-Fascists. Hereafter, the fight against Fascism would not be conducted on "neutral soil," as Tresca had warned Mussolini; it would be fought in hostile territory, where American authorities believed that anti-Fascists constituted a danger to capitalism and democracy. That the Fascists represented an infinitely greater threat to democracy never dawned on the State and Justice Departments in 1923.

There were multiple ways by which American authorities assisted Fascists against the anti-Fascists; the most effective method, of course, was deportation or the threat of it. But in Tresca's case, Mussolini's government understood that to silence Tresca, they would have to kill him or have the American authorities deliver him handcuffed into their clutches. Preferring the latter at this juncture, the Fascists set into motion a plan to ensnare Tresca that counted upon the active complicity of the State, Justice, and Post Office Departments. The Americans did their utmost to comply.

"Abbasso la Monarchia"

Whether an Italian secret agent was ever dispatched to Washington to serve as a liaison is uncertain. However, within one day of the meeting between Caetani, Burns, and Hoover, the BI began furnishing the Italians with information regarding *sovversivi*.[11] The Italians reciprocated by providing the American ambassador with a list of subscribers in America to a communist journal in Turin.[12] A crucial bit of information the BI's General Intelligence Division (GID or Anti-Radical Division) transmitted to the Italian Embassy at the end of March was the substance of a speech Tresca had delivered at the Manhattan Lyceum Theatre on February 23, 1923. According to a GID source, Tresca declared that funds were needed to buy bullets that would be kept in readiness, because "another Breschi [sic] will be born and they would need money to put the pound of lead into the Italian King's stomach and also in Mussolini's."[13]

Threats of regicide, no matter how far fetched, had always been taken seriously by the Italian government long before Bresci's assassination of King Umberto I in 1900. But Tresca's Manhattan Lyceum speech did more than add to the House of Savoy's paranoia; it gave the State Department the opportunity to flash a green light to Mussolini's government to initiate action against Tresca. That Caetani had been encouraged to file an official complaint against Tresca is indicated by a hand-written note from the Italian Interior Ministry to the Foreign Ministry, dated April 18, 1923, requesting immediate notification of Tresca's arrival "in case the American authorities decree his expulsion...."[14]

Fascist hopes were aroused when Tresca published an article entitled "*Abbasso la Monarchia*" (Down with the Monarchy), in the May 5, 1923 issue of *Il Martello*. With some of his choicest vituperation, he expressed his vexation with the notion that King Vittorio Emanuele III was a benign figure. Tresca's ire was triggered by an article in *Il Progresso*, written by Guido Podrecca, a former socialist turned Fascist, complaining about a "vulgar insult" allegedly made by the anti-Fascist press in regard to the "innocence" of the betrothed Princess Jolanda. Tresca always became incensed when the Fascists posed as defenders of traditional values and public morality and when the Savoyards were portrayed as paragons of moral virtue. Tresca knew that the House of Savoy (except for Vittorio Emanuele III, whose favorite past time was collecting coins) had spawned a long line of libertines. Tresca's "*Abbasso la Monarchia*" therefore provided a lengthy account of the sexual debaucheries enjoyed by Vittorio Emanuele II, Umberto I, the Duke of Aosta and other members of the dynasty. Concluding with a cry of defiance against all the fascist sycophants now defending the House of Savoy, Tresca wrote:

> Raise as high as heaven, like the braying of asses, your chorus of praise for the virtues of the royal damsel. We who know that every jewel that Jolanda wears on her nuptial crown was made of the people's tears, blood, and flesh, we will cry once again and with all the strength in our soul: Down with the Monarchy![15]

Three days after the publication of "*Abbasso la Monarchia*," Ambassador Caetani complained to the State Department about the "campaign of insults, of diffimation [sic] and hatred against the Italian Monarchy and the Italian governmental institution" conducted by "social-communist elements in New York under directions from Moscow."[16] Playing the Red menace card, the ambassador claimed that "Bolshevists see in the actual Italian Government, in Premier Mussolini and in the spiritual movement that animates Italy, the greatest check to the wild dreams of spreading the communistic revolution all over the world." Quoting almost verbatim the BI report previously transmitted to Rome, Caetani referenced Tresca's Manhattan Lyceum speech and its alleged expression of hope that someone would assassinate the king and Mussolini. According to Caetani, it was in pursuance of the idea to assassinate Italy's chiefs of state that Tresca had written the article "Abbasso la Monarchia."[17]

Caetani's note to the State Department established a pattern of complaint that the Fascists would follow thereafter. The offending culprits were never identified as anti-Fascists, but as communists, anarchists, and other left-wing elements, participating in a global conspiracy engineered by Moscow. Invariably, the embassy's complaints focused on threats of violence against the king, verbal and written denigration of the monarchy, insults to the Italian flag, and harassment of visiting officials and dignitaries. Fascism and Mussolini were rarely mentioned at all. Instead, as John P. Diggins observed, "the anti-Fascist assaults were described in such a way as to threaten not the Fascist regime but the good name of Italy."[18]

While awaiting action from the State Department, Mussolini's government continued to explore other means to deal with Tresca. The Postal Ministry already had prohibited the importation and circulation of *Il Martello*, and to drive the point home, condemned the noted anarchist Paolo Schicchi to prison for an article attacking the House of Savoy, which he published in Tresca's newspaper.[19] At a meeting of the Fascist Grand Council on July 26–27, 1923, measures to crush Italian-American anti-Fascism at its source were discussed at length.[20] The newspaper *L'Impero* of Rome alerted Ambassador Caetani and the New York *Fascio* that *Il Martello*'s continuing circulation and influence in Italy presented a danger that had to be eliminated. "It is time," urged the Fascist daily, "that once and for all we break the legs of these Italians who are worse than foreigners."[21] Caetani was almost certainly pressed to accelerate action against Tresca when he had a private *tête-à-tête* with Mussolini at the end of July. After returning to the United States, Caetani addressed a banquet held in honor of Judge Elbert H. Gary (a Fascist sympathizer) at the Waldorf-Astoria Hotel in New York, declaring that "a certain paper in the United States was embarrassing the Fascist Government and should be suppressed."[22]

Prodding the Americans was unnecessary. The Post Office Department, now working hand in glove with Hoover's GID and the State Department, had already initiated measures against Tresca, holding back the July 21 issue of *Il Martello* for ten days without explanation. Action by the Post Office, Tresca concluded, could only have been instigated by someone with influence in Washington—Ambassador Caetani.[23] Then, on August 14, 1923, the office of *Il Martello* was raided by U.S. marshals and Tresca placed under arrest for having violated Section 211 of the Federal Penal Code—the so-called "obscene matter" statute—with his article "*Abbasso la Monarchia.*" Tresca was arraigned before a U.S. Commissioner the following day and released after comrades posted a $1,000 bond. Pending his trial, Tresca continued to engage in his anti-Fascist activities while anticipating more trouble. But he could not have conceived the elaborate scheme federal authorities had set in motion to ensnare him.[24]

The Post Office Department, on its own initiative, was waging a campaign of systematic harassment against *Il Martello*. The objective was to please Mussolini's government and eventually deprive Tresca's newspaper of its second-class mailing privileges or force it into bankruptcy. The August 18 issue of *Il Martello* was stopped at the New York Post Office because of an advertisement for a raffle sponsored by the IWW. Although two other newspapers that published the same notice were ignored, *Il Martello*'s staff was required to unpack sacks, packages, and single copies of the newspaper, cross out the word "raffle" with black crayon in every copy, and then re-mail the entire edition. They were obliged to repeat the same process with the September 8 issue, when a two-line advertisement for an Italian book on birth control was ordered deleted. These tactics increased *Il Martello*'s deficit to more than $3,400, but they did not stop Tresca from delivering his *martellate* against the Fascist enemy.[25]

Suppression of *Il Martello* would not have fulfilled the State and Justice Departments' ultimate goal: Tresca's deportation. Only a felony conviction would suffice. But the plan to entrap Tresca ran into an early snag. The State Department Solicitor had determined on May 17—more than two months before his arrest—that a case against Tresca for writing "*Abbasso la Monarchia*" could not be made on the basis of the "obscene matter" statute. According to another federal statute, "the article in the MARTELLO to which the Italian Ambassador objects… cannot properly be considered as dangerous to the morals of the people, since in the last analysis it merely expressed the writer's abhorrence of a monarchical form of Government, and in violent and intemperate language charges different members of the Italian Royal family with immorality. It cannot be said either that this article contains 'matter of a character tending to incite arson, murder or assassination.'" Only if Tresca committed several additional violations might he lose his second-class mailing permit for *Il Martello* or become liable for prosecution.[26]

A stratagem to ensure future violations and a court conviction on felony charges was devised by Special Agent Charles J. Scully of the BI's New York office—the same Scully whose beatings and interrogation had precipitated Salsedo's suicide three years earlier. Scully suggested having Italian-speaking operatives or their

Italian informants send orders to Tresca from outside of New York, requesting "obscene" books sold by the bookstore associated with *Il Martello*. Orders were to be submitted from addresses in small towns lest Tresca recommend that the materials be purchased in Italian bookstores located in large cities; and to allay his suspicion, the writers were instructed to request that the materials be mailed to them in plain envelopes so as not to attract attention from postal authorities. The Post Office Department, of course, was a party to the entrapment. Inspectors at Station "D" in New York, where *Il Martello* rented a post office box, were assigned to monitor the arrival of the requests and the mailing of the materials. Ultimately, the BI offices in Pittsburgh and Boston were given the assignment. Copies of back issues of *Il Martello* were provided to them, containing lists of books and pamphlets on sale. The two books ordered which the BI and postal authorities considered "obscene" were the following: Dottoressa Cecchi, *Neo-Maltusianismo Pratico: L'Arte Di Non Fare I Figli* (Pratical Neo-Malthusianism: The Art of Not Creating Children); and F. Laccasagne, *Virginità e Pudore: Le Pertubazioni Sessuale* (Virginity and Modesty: Sexual Disorders). Between September and November 1923, orders for these books were submitted by BI agents in Washington, PA, and Haverhill, MA, and after their arrival, they were sent to the New York office for translation.[27] By the time the last order was submitted from Pennsylvania on November 7, a week after his indictment, Tresca had figured out what was afoot. *Il Martello* returned the $2.35 money order with a note explaining that "it is impossible for us to fill any orders of the books you requested, because the availability is at present questioned by the U.S. Post Office Dept."[28]

"The Art of Not Creating Children"

Tresca was brought to trial at the U.S. District Court for the Southern District of New York on November 26, 1923, charged with eight counts of violating Section 211 of the Penal Code: seven for mailing and causing to be mailed two books about sex and birth control ("of such a filthy and obscene character that a description thereof would defile the records of this Court")[29] to different persons; and one for mailing a newspaper, *Il Martello*, containing an advertisement for a book on birth control, *L'Arte di Non Fare I Figli*. The article "*Abbasso la Monarchia*," which had prompted the Italian ambassador's original complaint, did not figure into any of the charges, thus masking from public view the true reason why Tresca was on trial.[30]

That radicalism and anti-Fascism, not chastity and contraception, were the real issues behind the proceedings against Tresca was indicated by the composition of the courtroom observers: agents from the BI, the Bomb Squad and other anti-radical specialists of the New York Police Department, and numerous postal inspectors. The trial prosecutor was an aggressive young federal attorney named Maxwell S. Mattuck. Helping Mattuck in an advisory capacity was Special Agent Scully of the BI. Tresca's defense counsel was Harold A. Content, the former U.S. attorney for the District of New York. The presiding magistrate was Judge Henry A. Goddard.[31]

Just prior to the trial, a strange situation arose, which caused the prosecution no small amount of anxiety. The BI's Pittsburgh office lacked an Italian-speaking agent; therefore, the special agent in charge (SAC), R. B. Spencer, relied upon an outside source, who, in turn, secured an Italian undercover informant to mail requests for incriminating materials from Washington, Pennsylvania. Post Office inspectors believed the transactions between *Il Martello* and that informant constituted the strongest evidence against Tresca. Mattuck wanted the informant to testify at the trial, but Spencer had previously assured his intermediary that the man's identity would not be revealed. Mattuck threatened to complain directly to the attorney general if the BI office in Pittsburgh failed to deliver him, but the intermediate insisted that he could not, as "a matter of honor," disclose the individual's name. (SAC) Spencer could not provide the informant's name because he did not know who he was. Hoover became infuriated when apprised of the situation, describing it to Burns as "a most exasperating incident." He feared that "now the entire case against Tresca may fail, which will bring down upon this Department considerable criticism and Tresca will become more blatant in his activities and statements than ever before."[32]

At trial, Mattuck was obliged to drop two of the counts based on the forwarding of books to Washington, PA, but he retained five counts relating to the book (Eva Laccasagne, *Le Perturbazioni Sessuali: Virginità e Pudore*) received by Boston agents, and one count based on the advertisement in *Il Martello* for the book on birth control, *L'Arte Di Non Fare I Figli*. Witnesses for the prosecution included Post Office officials and clerks, BI agents from Boston and Pittsburgh, their respective informants (minus the unidentified recipient in Washington, PA), and Giuseppe Sposa, the "special employee" of the Justice Department. The principal defense witnesses included three members of *Il Martello*'s staff: Randolfo Vella, Antonio Aloia, and Umberto Nieri.

Mattuck's interrogation of prosecution witnesses was calculated to prove that Tresca, as the owner and manager of *Il Martello*, was responsible for the mailing of the "obscene" materials. Portraying Tresca as a habitual offender, Mattuck noted that Tresca had had "previous controversies" with the Justice Department, and that *Il Martello* had been deemed "non-mailable" by postal authorities no less than seven times during the previous three years. He never mentioned, of course, that the offending content in these instances had been political.[33]

Defense attorney Content countered by arguing that Tresca never involved himself with mundane, day-to-day operations, such as mailing books or placing advertisements, and in any case, he was vacationing on Staten Island when the offending issue of September 8, 1923 was mailed. Also, the bookstore, *Libreria dell'Martello*, which shared the same office with *Il Martello*, was owned and operated by Umberto Nieri, not Tresca. Nieri, in fact, accepted full responsibility for the books and advertisement and would later pay for his honesty with a conviction and jail sentence of six months. Moreover, as Tresca and his staff members testified and postal authorities confirmed, when the September 8 issue of *Il Martello* was stopped as "non-mailable," all the copies were retrieved and the two-lined advertisement crossed out with black crayon before re-mailing. Thus no one had read it.[34]

But inevitably, since the real objective of the trial was to establish grounds for his deportation, Mattuck introduced Tresca's beliefs and activities, despite their irrelevance to the charges. The key witness called upon to help achieve this end was Giuseppe Sposa. A "special employee" (i.e., a spy) of the Justice Department for four years, Sposa had infiltrated the anarchist movement and secured a job as a mailer for *Il Martello* that lasted from November 1921 to October 1922.[35] His assignment, he explained to the court, was "to investigate the anarchistic activities of Carlo Tresca, who is an anarchist."[36] Content, in his cross-examination, tried to get Sposa to admit that he had received specific instructions to watch for non-mailable or indecent literature. Sposa denied the suggestion: "I was in there to see that he was not violating the law in any way."[37] After leaving his employment with Tresca, Sposa moved on to other spying activities: "I went in the Communist Party."[38]

Sposa's contribution to the prosecution was twofold: he established that Tresca was responsible for all aspects of *Il Martello*'s operations and introduced the crucial issue of Tresca's anarchist beliefs. Knowing the consequences of an affirmative answer, Mattuck asked Tresca no less than seven times whether or not he was an anarchist. Tresca denied that he was or ever had been an anarchist. To support his point, Mattuck provided the jury with a *curriculum vitae* of the defendant's career, specifying his participation in the Lawrence agitation of 1912, the strikes of New York hotel workers and Paterson silk workers in 1913, other subversive activities, and his editorship of several radical newspapers since his arrival in 1904.[39]

Surprisingly, Content did not object to this line of questioning, attempting to minimize the damage to his client only by eliciting a "yes" and a "no" response to two questions: "You are just interested in labor movements, is that it?" and "Do you believe in the overthrow of the Government by force and violence?"[40] Even when he clarified that Tresca's earlier encounters with postal authorities involved the political content of *Il Martello*, rather than "obscene" matter, he probably did his client more harm than good by reinforcing Mattuck's portrait of Tresca as a dangerous radical.[41]

Both sides rested on the afternoon of November 27, 1923. Judge Goddard, at the request of the prosecutor, dismissed two of the counts pertaining to the mailing of "obscene" material. But any positive impression their dismissal might have made was out-weighed by Judge Goddard's charge to the jury. Regarding the book on birth control, he argued that "this advertisement was most obscene and most objectionable," and as for Nieri's claims of full responsibility, "this may be an offer on the part of the defendant, who is on trial, to pass it [responsibility] on to someone else." Another detrimental statement was the judge's assertion, "I think you fully understand that some of the witnesses in this case may have an interest in the result,"[42] a clear suggestion that the Italians who testified on Tresca's behalf had lied.

The jury deliberated from 4:30 P.M. until 7:00 P.M. The BI was "confidentially advised" that the jury was deadlocked over the five counts pertaining to the materials sent through the mails: eleven for conviction; one for acquittal. As "a sort of compromise," the jurors unanimously found Tresca guilty of the eighth count, mailing the two-line advertisement for the book on birth control.[43] He was released on $2,500 bail (guaranteed by ILGWU Locals 48 and 89), pending sentencing by Judge Goddard on December 8, 1923.[44] The defense team assembled for his sentencing included Content, the noted penologist George Gordon Battle, and U.S. Congressman Fiorello La Guardia, the future major of New York City. The government was again represented by Mattuck.

Having won a conviction on a minor charge of violating the mails with birth control information, the prosecution now pressed for a crushing sentence based on Tresca's political activities. Mattuck began his new tack by admitting with arrogant candor that the proceedings against Tresca had originated with a complaint from the Italian ambassador. He then produced a translation of "*Abbasso la Monarchia*" for Judge Goddard's perusal. La Guardia protested that Tresca's article attacking the Italian monarchy had nothing to do with the case, and that the prosecutor's introduction of extraneous information and material was a flagrant attempt to prejudice the Court and jury against the defendant. These and other objections were brushed aside by the judge. Continuing in the same vein, Mattuck depicted Tresca as a dangerous revolutionary who had to be stopped at all costs. He read aloud a Justice Department memorandum, dating Tresca's radical activities back to 1904. And, as if the real facts were not sufficiently damaging, Mattuck introduced the Bolshevik bogy into the proceedings, claiming that *Il Martello* was financed by Moscow. Mattuck told the Court during his summation that, if Tresca voluntarily returned to Italy, he would not ask for a prison sentence. Otherwise, "I ask your Honor that a man who has caused so much trouble to our government be immediately deported or be sent to Atlanta [Federal Penitentiary] for five years to reflect on the nature of life in this country."[45]

No one had ever been imprisoned under federal law for disseminating birth control information; the customary sentence was a $25 fine. Under state laws, punishment usually ranged from a fine of $10–100 to a jail sentence of fifteen to sixty days; the longest sentence ever imposed previously was sixty days.[46] Protesting the stiff sentence demanded by the prosecutor, Content argued that because the trial resulted from Tresca's attacks against Mussolini, he should be punished only with a fine. La Guardia demanded the same, adding that "in twenty years of professional practice I have never observed a case of political dishonesty as this one.... [Mattuck] does not want justice but revenge for Mussolini." Battle, too, denounced the charges against Tresca as a pretext to serve Mussolini, noting that while he disagreed with Tresca's ideas, he admired him "for the honesty of his soul, the sincerity of his professed faith, and the devotion he brings to the cause of the workers."[47]

Speaking in his own defense, Tresca acknowledged the accuracy of everything the prosecutor had said about his activities in the labor movement. "I have sought with all my strength," he declared, "to elevate the moral and material conditions of the Italian workers residing here, and I have sought to instill in their souls the same faith in their emancipation that is alive in me. I am a soldier of the ideal." He also explained that for the last two years he had refrained from attacking the American government, concentrating his efforts instead on the struggle against Fascism. The real issue in the case was his anti-Fascism. He ended his self-defense, declaring:

The struggle is between me and the Fascist government; I know what awaits me in Italy. Death. And when my deportation is requested, it is my life that is being requested as a gift for Mussolini. Now you know what they demand of you, your Honor. Go ahead and condemn me. I do not tremble; I do not ask for mercy.[48]

None was forthcoming. Whether swayed by the prosecutor's arguments or pressured by the Justice Department, Judge Goddard pronounced the severest sentence ever handed down for dissemination of birth control information through the mails: one year and a day, to be served at Atlanta Federal Penitentiary.[49]

While Tresca remained free on bail, La Guardia attempted to secure evidence that might be used for an appeal. He demanded that Secretary of State Charles Evans Hughes confirm or deny that the case against Tresca had been prepared by the State Department at the behest of the Italian ambassador, as Mattuck had stated openly.[50] This co-conspirator in the frame-up responded with obfuscation and evasion.[51] All efforts by La Guardia and Tresca's other legal representatives ran into stone walls. Finally, on November 9, 1924, the U.S. Circuit Court of Appeals reaffirmed the conviction and sentence.[52]

Tresca faced imprisonment with his customary equanimity. Writing to the famous birth control advocate Margaret Sanger, whom he had known since the Paterson strike of 1913, when she was a militant anarchist, Tresca expressed confidence that spending a year and a day in prison would "be ease for me. Just a vacation."[53] Upon arriving at Pennsylvania Station on January 5, 1925, handcuffed to the detectives charged with delivering him to Atlanta Federal Penitentiary, Tresca appeared "carefree, as if leaving for a picnic,"[54] according to Pietro Allegra, to whom he had entrusted *Il Martello*. Others on hand to give Tresca a rousing send-off were his daughter Beatrice, Flynn, Scott Nearing, Art Shield, representatives of the ACLU, several dozen Italian comrades, and a group of newspaper reporters, clicking away with their cameras. When the train bound for Atlanta pulled out on schedule, Pennsylvania Station reverberated with shouts of "*Viva Carlo Tresca!*" and "*Abbasso il Fascismo!*"[55] Two days later, Tresca began serving his sentence as prisoner number 19,149.[56]

Backlash

Tresca's conviction and sentence, bestowing felon status, had been conceived by the Justice Department as the basis for deportation. Proceedings toward that end had been set into motion a few days after his appeal was rejected. But three weeks before Tresca set foot in prison, the Justice Department encountered another snag: immigration regulations did not provide for deportation solely on grounds of a year and a day sentence.[57] Efforts were immediately begun to uncover additional evidence for that purpose. A prison interrogation of Tresca, conducted by an immigration inspector on February 10, 1925, yielded nothing incriminating, thereby prompting the Labor Department [the agency in charge of deportations] district director to request further investigation to "bring this alien within the anarchistic class and thus enable me to bring about his deportation."[58]

What the State and Justice Departments had not calculated was an asset no other Italian radical possessed to the same extent: American allies. Roger Baldwin, director of the ACLU, filed a petition for a commutation of Tresca's sentence with Attorney General Harlan F. Stone immediately after his imprisonment.[59] Margaret Sanger, outraged by the draconian sentence, wrote to Tresca that "I cannot believe that the laws of retribution can be so unjust. Anyone who has done so much for humanity and fought so splendid a fight as you have, cannot be treated in this unjust way."[60] She, as president of the American Birth Control League, and Flynn, as head of the Workers Defense Union, organized a letter-writing campaign, targeting the attorney general and President Calvin Coolidge.[61] Friends in the world of journalism—Heywood Broun of the *New York World*, Oswald Garrison Villard and Lewis S. Gannett of *The Nation,* and Robert Morse Lovett of the *New Republic*, among others—utilized their publishing venues to embarrass the authorities with questions such as "Is the United States Government acting as the agent of Mussolini's dictatorship?," and to denounce Tresca's trial and conviction as "indecent and dishonest persecution."[62] Tresca's Italian comrades, meanwhile, organized a defense committee, conducted lecture tours, and held public rallies to raise funds for his legal expenses.[63]

The public spotlight on Tresca's case intensified when America's celebrated iconoclast and social critic, H. L. Mencken, laid bare the pertinent facts and declared with characteristic cynicism:

> The great agencies of America will let Tresca rot in prison before they lift their hands to help him, just as they are letting his fellow Italians, Sacco and Vanzetti, rot in prison. The American Legion, though it still sweats and groans for human liberty, will not protest; on the contrary, it is more likely to pass a resolution urging that the wop be kept behind bars, guilty or not. The Sons of the Revolution will maintain a magnificent silence. Kiwanis and Rotary will not be heard from.[64]

Mencken's bromide awakened the Fascists to the possibility that their intervention against Tresca might have backfired, although the consul general of Baltimore hastened to assure Ambassador Caetani that a public campaign in Tresca's favor would not ensue.[65] He was dead wrong.

By the beginning of 1925, most fair-minded Americans aware of the case had concluded—in the words of the *New Republic*—that "Tresca's real crime consisted in his bitter opposition to Mussolini."[66] Accusatory editorials, such as that published in the *Baltimore Sun*, declared that

> the case of Carlo Tresca… raises the question, and goes far to answer in a negative way, of whether our vaunted freedom of the press is in practice that inalienable right we had believed it.… If his [Mussolini's] agents in this country can be instrumental in launching similar suppressions here, the time has come for an inquiry as to whence our Federal bureaucracies derive their power—from Mussolini or from the America people.[67]

The sharp criticism still emanating from the press, and the stream of letters to the attorney general and the president from politically- and socially- prominent figures recruited by Sanger and Flynn, soon awakened Washington to the reality that framing Tresca at the behest of Mussolini's government had been a serious blunder. To stave off further embarrassment to his administration, President Coolidge commuted Tresca's sentence on February 16 to a term of four months of imprisonment. The commutation was accompanied, moreover, by a public admission that the proceedings against Tresca had originated with a complaint from the Italian government.[68] This disclosure was not intended as an admission of wrongdoing. Justice Department officials attributed the president's mercy to the "circumstances" of the case, particularly the severity of the sentence.[69] Assistant U.S. Attorney Mattuck, not surprisingly, was irked by the commutation and its implicit censure of his prosecutorial zeal. Interviewed by the New York World, Mattuck justified his courtroom offer to drop the charges if Tresca agreed to leave the country, saying that "I made him an offer because he has been a thorn in the side of organized government for years. He would be a good riddance."[70]

Coolidge's commutation did not terminate the Justice Department's quest for new evidence upon which to base deportation proceedings. A glimmer of hope was generated when an inmate at the Atlanta Penitentiary—a former Justice Department official active during the "Red Scare"—claimed to have personal knowledge that in 1919 and 1920 Tresca had belonged to the Communist Labor Party, the Communist Party of America, the Union of Russian Workers, and the "Committee of Forty Eight," a shadow organization composed of senators, congressmen, and other prominent people.[71] On March 20, 1925, the Bureau of Immigration applied for an arrest warrant pursuant to Tresca's deportation, but examination of Justice Department files revealed nothing to substantiate the ludicrous claims made by the inmate.[72] Finally, on April 21, 1925, the disappointed district director of Atlanta received notification from his Bureau of Immigration superiors that a warrant for Tresca's arrest could not be issued without further evidence.[73] None was produced.

Atlanta Federal Penitentiary

Max Eastman's famous New Yorker magazine profile of Tresca asserted that the anti-Fascist enjoyed privileged "political offender" status at the Federal Penitentiary after receiving a letter from Eugene V. Debs, who had been imprisoned in Atlanta for his antiwar activities and had won the sympathy and respect of his jailers.[74] Eastman's version was fictional. Assigned to the most dilapidated section of a three-tiered cell block, Tresca had to share a cell, soap, and towel with a syphilitic inmate. His daily assignment was to scrub the floors of all three tiers, a tiring and monotonous task mitigated only by the fact that he remained out of his cell most of the day and became acquainted with fellow inmates, most of whom were drug addicts. At first, he was fascinated by prison culture and learned all he could about the graft and drug trafficking that dominated life in the penitentiary, but inevitably he wearied of the routine. Drudgery and denigration were also coupled with anxiety about deportation, because he was never informed of the government's inability to initiate proceedings against him.[75]

News of Coolidge's commutation on February 16 must have lessened his worries but did little to accelerate the remainder of his sentence. A month after the commutation, Tresca complained to Margaret Sanger about "the monotony of the same life days after days, without change, without opportunity of any excitement. Just live. And among 'numbers.'"[76] A visit from Sanger later in March was "a day of sunshine in the darkened days of imprisonment."[77] He vowed eternal gratitude for her help in obtaining the commutation, promising to repay his debt "with a devotion to you and to the cause for wich you so valiantly devoted all your life.... I am one of your lieutenants now."[78] On May Day—"May day in chain"—with only six days of his sentence remaining, Tresca was understandably eager to be released from "the hell in wich I am living now."[79] Prison life—especially the terrible food— had taken its toll on Tresca's health but not his sense of humor. He forewarned Sanger that she would be surprised by his appearance at their next meeting: "[I] have lost 6 inch in circumference and 35 pounds of flesh.... This is a great reducing institution."[80] The doors of Atlanta Federal Penitentiary finally opened to release Tresca on May 7, 1925.

A Visit to the White House

En route from Atlanta to New York, Tresca stopped off in Washington to break the monotony of the train ride, to rest and eat a good meal, and to shake off the plain-clothes detectives assigned to follow him. After checking into the Washington Hotel, he strolled around the city, taking in the major sights like any other tourist. Coming upon the White House, Tresca yielded to a mischievous urge and entered the building. While looking at antiques in the Blue Room, Tresca found himself surrounded by a group of students from Philadelphia who were scheduled for a reception with the president. Tresca loved children and was talking with some of the students when a voice announced that the president was ready to receive the group. An attendant, thinking Tresca was a teacher accompanying the students, instructed him to lead them into the receiving room. Expecting at any moment to be set upon by Secret Service agents, Tresca nonetheless accompanied the students into the room. President Coolidge entered, said a few words, and exited after shaking hands with everyone. Tresca, beardless and thirty-five pounds lighter, went unnoticed by the agents guarding the president; so when Coolidge left in one direction, he hastily departed in another. Once outside, Tresca felt delighted with himself. Not everyday could a famous anarchist shake the hand of the president of the United States under the gaze of the Secret Service.[81]

With Tresca's status as a victim of political persecution now firmly established, the press scrambled for personal interviews after his release from Atlanta. To *The New York Times* he declared that "When Mussolini came into power several years ago, he and his agents set out to crush me.... They have failed, miserably failed."[82] To the *New York World* he related the details of his visit to the White House, saying that he had intended to tell Coolidge that he was the man whose sentence the president had recently commuted, but had time only for a quick handshake.[83] Reassuring the reporters of his innocent intent, Tresca added, "I don't carry bombs—despite the stories of the Mussolini Government. I seek only freedom, not anarchy."[84]

By now, however, Tresca's handshake with the president had been an issue of contention.[85] The incident, whether true or apocryphal, would strike most neutral observers as trivial or amusing. But Tresca's enemies on the Right and the Left seized upon the handshake as ammunition. Fascist publications like *Il Grido della Stirpa* (Cry of the Race) characterized the visit as an act of submission, and represented the failure of the Secret Service to detect him as proof of his unimportance.[86] The Galleanisti of *L'Adunata dei Refrettari* stooped even lower than the Fascists in their efforts to exploit the incident and besmirch Tresca's reputation. During the four months between Tresca's arrest and conviction, *L'Adunata* had failed to express a single word of sympathy or solidarity. When several anarchist groups demanded an explanation, *L'Adunata* skirted the issue of its silence, declaring instead that because Tresca at his trial had "denied ever having been an anarchist or a syndicalist,... his misfortunes do not concern us."[87] Quite predictably, the Galleanisti pronounced Tresca's handshake with Coolidge an act of apostasy. Not satisfied, the manager of *L'Adunata*, Osvaldo Maraviglia—conveniently forgetting the Galleanisti's bombing campaign of 1919–1920—denounced Tresca as a renegade for tarnishing the reputation of anarchists by associating them with bombs in his remarks to *New York World* reporters.[88]

L'Adunata's attacks received strong endorsement from Galleani himself, whose chagrin at the prospect of Tresca replacing him as leader of the Italian anarchists in America had now become palpable. Writing from Italy, Galleani urged his acolytes in America to prevent Tresca from obtaining the "dictatorship about which the rogue has dreamed since our departure and the end of '*C[ronaca].S[ovversiva]*. It is well that he should be disabused, and that the unmasking continue until the immutable characteristics of his muddled and Jesuitic countenance are revealed."[89] Galleani's exhortation to destroy his rival ensured that the heretical handshake with Coolidge would remain an indelible stain on Tresca's record.

Fortunately, the petty snipping of his enemies on the Right and the Left had not detracted from Tresca's prestige and popularity among most anti-Fascists. He was given a hero's welcome at the pro-*Il Martello* benefit held at Tammany Hall on May 23, 1925. When he appeared on stage, nearly 5,000 anti-Fascists broke into tumultuous applause, with shouts of "*Viva Carlo Tresca!*" and "*Abbasso il Fascismo!*" Before this jubilant mass of supporters, Tresca delivered an impassioned speech:

> I declare that I do not belong nor want to belong to any political party or group, because I will not submit to any tyranny. I declare that bourgeois society must be changed by attacking the pillars that support it. A revolution is needed to change it, not a fascist revolution that is regressive and reactionary, but a proletarian revolution, one of slaves against slavers, of civilization agains obscurantism. I declare that I feel my spirit and strength reinvigorated every time the interests of reaction attack me with their persecution. I affirm my libertarian faith.[90]

Reaching out beyond the Italian community of New York, Tresca wrote in *Il Martello*: "I continue to stand, like an oak whose leaves do not flutter in the roar of the wind, on this side of the barricades, beneath the red flag that is the immaculate flag of the anarchist idea, the flag that is mine and that I have not forsaken."[91]

14

The Resistance Awakens

When the newly-elected Chamber of Deputies assembled for the first time on May 30, 1924, Giacomo Matteotti, the leader of the reformist Unitary Socialist Party founded in 1922, spoke for nearly two hours, bucking a chorus of incessant howls, insults, and threats from Fascist deputies. He presented documentary evidence that the electoral victories of the Fascists had been achieved in April through violence and intimidation, and demanded the nullification of the election. Departing the chamber after his speech, Matteotti said to a colleague: "And now, get ready to deliver my funeral oration."[1]

Mussolini became enraged. Whether he ordered retaliation or merely vented his anger within hearing distance of his subordinates is a matter of dispute. However, on June 10, 1924, Matteotti was kidnapped and killed by a group of Blackshirts led by Amerigo Dumini, an ex-*squadrista* attached to the office of Cesare Rossi, head of Mussolini's press bureau. Matteotti's body was not discovered until August, but his disappearance and presumed murder caused an immediate uproar throughout Italy. The police and judiciary, not yet fascistized, pursued a trail of evidence that led directly to Mussolini's inner circle. The only issue in question was whether the Duce had ordered the murder.

With the nation reeling in shock and dismay, Mussolini might conceivably have been toppled if the anti-Fascists had been united and taken decisive action. Instead, the leaders of the moderate parliamentary opposition—mainly reformist socialists, liberal-democrats, and Christian Democrats—organized a boycott of the Chamber of Deputies that came to be known as the Aventine Succession. This gesture of moral and political protest depended for success on King Vittorio Emanuele III, who alone had the power to retain or dismiss Mussolini as prime minister. But the puny Savoyard was the wrong person to trust. When confronted with proof of Mussolini's complicity, the king responded: "I am not a judge"; "I should not be told such things"; "I am deaf and blind, my eyes and ears are the Senate and Chamber of Deputies."[2]

Mussolini survived, meanwhile, by sacrificing subordinates to placate public opinion, and by making deals with Italy's traditional élites. Assured of support from the latter, who feared communism would triumph if Fascism were defeated, and prodded by Fascist hierarchs in the party and militia, who threatened to unleash a "Second Wave" of violence if he failed to act, Mussolini resolved to crush the enfeebled opposition once and for all. In the Chamber of Deputies on January 3,

1925, the Duce accepted full responsibility for the environment of violence that had engulfed Italy since intervention, and promised that "when two irreconcilable elements are at war, the solution is force. You may be sure that within forty-eight hours of my speech, the situation will be clarified all along the line."[3] And so it was. A new wave of repression terminated all semblance of opposition within the country.

Repercussions in America

Immediately after Matteotti's disappearance, the pro-Fascist dailies asserted in sycophantic unison that Mussolini was innocent of complicity—his overzealous underlings were the sole culprits. Denouncing the mendacity of the *fungaia coloniale*, Tresca laid the murder at the Duce's feet months before Mussolini's defiant admission of responsibility. The actual murderers were merely the instrument of his will:

> Mussolini, the brigand, had warned: either these voices become silent or we will silence them. And the followers of the brigand understood his sibylline language.... Since Matteotti was one of his most irreconcilable adversaries, Mussolini had him eliminated. He, not the others, is the instigator of Matteotti's murder.[4]

All anti-Fascists shared Tresca's belief that Mussolini was directly responsible for Matteotti's murder, and like no previous event, not even the "March on Rome," the crime galvanized the anti-Fascist movement into action. On June 22, some 2,000–3,000 anti-Fascists assembled at the Rand School ("People's House") at 7 East 15th Street to pay homage to Matteotti and hear speeches by Tresca, Allegra, and others, denouncing Mussolini and the pro-Fascist press. Several thousand joined a protest meeting at Carnegie Hall sponsored by the Italian Chamber of Labor four days later. In addition to Tresca, Giovannitti, Frank Bellanca, and other Italians, the meeting featured notables from the American Left and labor movement: Sidney Hillman, president of the ACWA, Norman Thomas, Jacob Panken, Elizabeth Gurley Flynn, and the communist Juliet Stuart Poyntz. Several Fascists in the audience attempted to disrupt the proceedings, and fighting broke out. Policemen and agents of the Bomb Squad, on hand to keep tabs on the radicals, intervened and restored order. Another dramatic protest occurred on June 29 in Boston, where more than a thousand anti-Fascists marched through the streets in a mourning parade, stopping in front of the Fascist newspaper, *Giovinezza*, to chant "*Abbasso Mussolini!*," "*Viva Matteotti!*" and sing "*Bandiera Rossa*," before joining 4,000 comrades on the Boston Common to hear speeches by Tresca, Felice Guadagni, and others. Similar demonstrations took place in Philadelphia and other cities. The pro-Fascist press condemned them all as "anti-Italian."[5]

Locatelli

The galvanizing effect of Matteotti's murder was intensified by the despicable reactions of Fascists throughout Italy, who openly gloated over his death, even singing a sneering couplet in the streets: "*Con la carne di Matteotti, ci faremo i salciciotti*" (We will make little sausages with the meat of Matteotti).[6] One Fascist celebrity, who had besmirched the memory of Matteotti in similar fashion, was the highly-decorated aviator and deputy Antonio Locatelli. Oblivious to the possible repercussions of his crude behavior, Locatelli had made the mistake of scheduling a publicity tour of Italian immigrant communities in August and September 1924. Upon arrival at Grand Central Station, Locatelli was greeted by the consul general, Emilio Axerio, and a bevy of Blackshirts. Also on hand to welcome the Fascist were hundreds of outraged *sovversivi*. To prevent them from suffering bodily harm, a score of policemen hustled Locatelli and Axerio into an awaiting taxi, which drove them to the Ritz-Carlton Hotel, where another contingent of gendarmes provided security. Angered by the hostile reception, the director of the *Il Popolo*, Vincenzo Giordano, called upon Fascists to "enter the field of combat" against the *sovversivi*. Tresca accepted the challenge: "We await you, without panic and without boastfulness.... We cannot forget. We do not wish to forget. We wish to hate. But in hatred we will prepare our revenge."[7] Tresca's challenge went unanswered.

After a stop in Philadelphia, where 3,000 anti-Fascists disrupted a banquet in his honor with a volley of tomatoes, rocks, and bricks, Locatelli returned to New York to attend a performance of Puccini's *Tosca* at the Metropolitan Opera House. After surviving a barrage of tomatoes outside the building, Locatelli and consul general Axerio were targeted in their box by a rain of leaflets from anti-Fascists seated in the balcony above. Upon exiting, they were greeted by several thousand anti-Fascists led by Tresca. Fistfights erupted between anti-Fascists and Locatelli's admirers as the Fascist aviator and the consul general fled in an automobile under police protection.[8]

Battle for the Garibaldi Memorial (1925)

The Locatelli demonstrations were Tresca's last skirmishes against the Blackshirts prior to his imprisonment. After his release, he resumed his position in the vanguard of the anti-Fascist movement, eager for the expected confrontation with the Fascists at the Garibaldi Memorial on Independence Day. The Blackshirts, in order to legitimize Mussolini's regime in the eyes of Italian immigrants, had to propagate the myth that Fascism was the true legacy of the Risorgimento and the Duce a political descendent of revered patriots like Giuseppe Garibaldi. For the *sovversivi*, the Garibaldi Memorial was a battleground upon which to expose the Blackshirts as false usurpers of the Risorgimento tradition, and to reaffirm their own linkage with the great revolutionary leader who had prophesied that "the International [i.e. socialism] was 'the sun of the future.'"[9]

In anticipation of the July 4 clash, Blackshirts of the New York *Fascio* issued a boastful rallying cry to their comrades, warning the *sovversivi* that "we will carry our banners and standards to destiny's heights, undaunted and scornful of our enemies."[10] Unlike previous occasions, the *sovversivi* did not interfere with the ceremony conducted by various patriotic organizations. The Blackshirts were the enemy that day. While awaiting them, speeches praising Garibaldi and denouncing Mussolini were delivered by a broad spectrum of radicals and labor leaders, including Tresca. The anti-Fascists were thus primed and ready for action. When the Blackshirts finally arrived at 1:30 P.M., all the bravura they had invested in their challenge to the *sovverisivi* evaporated in the July heat. They approached the Memorial slowly and cautiously, surrounded by a protective cordon of police. A few attacked the anti-Fascist throng but were beaten back. The main group of Blackshirts was subjected to a barrage of rocks, bricks, bottles, and pieces of wood that sent them scurrying for cover. By 3:00 P.M., the Blackshirts retreated to the Rosebank station while the police finally intervened against the anti-Fascists, clubbing all within range of their night sticks and arresting seven. Back in New York, a group of Blackshirts positioned themselves near the office of *Il Martello*, waiting to attack Tresca. But Tresca was still in Staten Island, bailing out the seven anti-Fascists arrested earlier. The victim the Blackshirts pounced upon instead was Giuseppe Genovese, an eighty-two-year-old veteran of Garibaldi's campaigns, who was walking toward *Il Martello*'s office, wearing his original red shirt. That was the extent of the Fascists' "triumph" on Independence Day.[11]

The Fascist League of North America

The humiliating defeat at the Garibaldi Memorial did not thwart the continuing growth of Italian-American Fascism. As the *fasci* in New York and other cities increased in number and membership, Rome decided to place them under the watchful eye of Mussolini's new undersecretary for foreign affairs, Dino Grandi, one of the highest ranking Fascists in the party. Grandi recognized the vital importance of American goodwill and economic assistance, and opted for a policy shift that emphasized winning mass support from ordinary Italian Americans rather than producing greater numbers of Fascists. Grandi's policy, in theory, would subordinate the *fasci* to the authority of the Italian ambassador and local consuls. To effectuate the shift, the *Consiglio Centrale Fascista* was replaced by the *Lega Fascista di Nord America* (The Fascist League of North America) in July 1925.

To avoid identification as a foreign agency, the FLNA was incorporated in New York State and pledged to obey the laws of the host country, refrain from interfering in its internal politics, and avoid provoking conflict within the Italian American-community. The man Mussolini appointed president of this "American" organization was Count Ignazio Thaon di Revel, an employee of the brokerage firm of Munds & Winslow, whose connections with Wall Street banks figured prominently in his selection. But Mussolini made a bad choice. Fancying himself the independent chieftain of Italian-American Blackshirts, Thaon di Revel recruited extremist elements, including former *squadristi* who had recently emigrated, for the purpose of crushing anti-Fascist opposition throughout the *colonie italiane*. At the time he assumed command of the FLNA, the organization included forty-seven *fasci* and 6,000 members.[12]

The growing influence of the Fascist League was evidenced by the presence of Blackshirts at all the official events sponsored by the consul general and the *prominenti*. They were conspicuously present at the banquet held in the Pennsylvania Hotel on October 28, 1925 to celebrate the third anniversary of

Mussolini's "March on Rome." An anti-Fascist protest rally was scheduled for that same evening at Bryant Hall. Unable to resist the opportunity, Tresca and Allegra led about 400 anti-Fascists in a march to the Pennsylvania Hotel, where they intended to storm the banquet hall. Considering all their boasts about crushing the *sovversivi*, the Blackshirts might have been expected to assemble their cadres to battle the expected invaders. Instead, the task of defending the Fascist celebration was left to local police and the Bomb Squad. Three times Tresca and the anti-Fascists charged the police cordon only to be beaten back by clubs. They failed to gain entry, but in the process they demonstrated to the Blackshirts that it was the *sovversivi* who possessed superior courage and militancy.[13]

L'Attentato a Mussolini

The Pennsylvania Hotel demonstration and similar episodes did not deter Washington's warm embrace of new Fascist diplomats like Giacomo De Martino, who replaced Caetani as ambassador in January 1925. De Martino quickly established excellent relations with the State Department, which saw eye to eye with him on the activities of anti-Fascists like Tresca. He found the new Secretary of State Frank B. Kellogg and his associates more committed than their predecessors to the belief that anti-Fascists were dangerous Reds, and happily informed Mussolini that "whenever a legal pretext presents itself, the Department has intervened at my request, as for example last winter, when it succeeded in preventing an injurious theatrical performance in New York."[14]

The foiled performance to which De Martino referred was the premier of *L'Attentato a Mussolini ovvero il segreto di Pulcinella* (The Attempt on Mussolini or the Secret of Pulcinella), a political satire Tresca wrote toward the end of 1925.[15] The play was based on real events. On November 4, 1925, the former socialist deputy Tito Zaniboni was arrested in Rome for plotting to assassinate the Duce. From a hotel window opposite the Palazzo Chigi, Zaniboni planned to shoot Mussolini when he stepped out onto his balcony to give a speech. Minutes before the Duce emerged, Zaniboni was arrested, betrayed by a "friend" who was a double agent. Tresca and other anti-Fascists, like most historians, believed that Zaniboni had been duped from the start, that the foiled assassination attempt was engineered by the regime as a pretext to intensify the suppression of anti-Fascists, precisely the outcome that ensued.[16]

Tresca's *L'Attentato a Mussolini* is surprisingly good political satire, with accurate character depiction, humorous dialogue, and a poignant political message. The main characters are Mussolini; Rossoni, Roberto Farinacci, the Fascist Party's secretary-general, Cardinal Pietro Gasparri, the Papal secretary of state, and a Contessa Del Viminale, mistress to both Farinacci and the Cardinal, who has ensnared Zaniboni in her amorous clutches. The opening scene takes place in the Palazzo Viminale. All the protagonists are worried about the seething economic distress of the Italian masses and the political crisis caused by Matteotti's murder. Farinacci is portrayed exactly as one of the most fanatical and vicious of all Blackshirts. For this worshipper of the "*santissimo manganello*" (sacred cudgel), the solution to every problem is violence: "only with beatings can the donkey [i.e., the Italian people] remain tethered to the halter." Rossini, the ex-syndicalist hypocrite who still feigns concern for the working class, advocates a moderate approach to tranquilizing the masses: the "'sleeping pill' of class cooperation," i.e., the Fascist labor syndicates which he headed. Cardinal Gasparri, not yet privy to the plot, is fearful that mass discontent might unseat Mussolini, "whom divine providence has willed to the motherland and the church." Pondering why religion can no longer keep the masses passive and obedient, the Cardinal pines for the good old days of the Inquisition, when torture and burning at the stake maintained social order. Poor Mussolini expresses dismay that the Italian people regard him as a tyrant, but is reassured by the obsequious Cardinal that Fascist oppression, like the Inquisition, is justified if it serves a "higher moral end." The Duce then declares that "to save the situation a heroic solution is needed, and I have taken it. It is necessary to have myself murdered like Caesar." Mussolini quickly clarifies that the assassination will be faked, with Zaniboni as the dupe.

At this point, a bumbling Italian-American banker, "*Cavaliere Brisco*," is admitted to the room to report on the status of Fascism in the United States. Addressing Mussolini as "Emperor," he admits that the Blackshirts in New York are stymied by the *sovversivi*, who on every street corner are blaming Mussolini for Matteotti's murder. Farinacci recommends that the Blackshirts subject them to the castor oil treatment, to which Brisco replies, "the castor oil we have, but we lack the courage." Quaking in his shoes when Farinacci insists that anyone who dares call Mussolini a murderer should be stabbed, the *Cavaliere* swears that he would stab Tresca himself—if not for the electric chair. Farinacci mutters, "Yes, that one [Tresca] needs to be silenced," to which Rossini adds, "like Matteotti." As the emissary departs, Rossoni asks him to give his regards to "Trombetta," the ardent Italian-American Fascist Domenico Trombetta, whose name in Italian means trumpet. The uncomprehending banker responds, "No, I don't play the trumpet. I am a *Cavaliere* and a banker." An exasperated Mussolini wonders aloud whether all the Italian-American bankers he has knighted are as stupid as this one.

Mussolini's chief concern is that Zaniboni might succeed in taking a shot at him. But the "assassin" is apprehended as planned, minutes before the Duce appears on the balcony to speak before a big crowd of Blackshirts. Having stirred applause and cheers among the adoring *camerati*, Mussolini steps back into the room, muttering contemptuously, "And now, die of hunger you idiotic and imbecilic people. Let's eat." At dinner, the conspirators are startled out of their seats by the sound of a loud bang. "A bomb?" asks the quaking Cardinal. "No, champagne," answers the waiter, who had just popped the cork. A sigh of relief issues from all the diners as the curtain falls.[17]

When the premiere of Tresca's play was first announced, Ambassador De Martino hastened to request that the State Department prevent the performance.[18] Compliance was immediate. With an audience of several thousand anti-Fascists assembled at the Central Opera House on Sunday, December 13, 1925, FBI agents and Bomb Squad officials invaded the theater and stopped the opening curtain on the grounds that the performance would violate New York City's Sunday "Blue Laws."[19] To the angry audience, Tresca explained that the prohibition was but another instance of the federal government's acting at the behest of Mussolini. Then Tresca launched into an impromptu attack against America's plutocracy and Mussolini's·dictatorship, both of which, he declared, were united in the same anti-proletarian phobia and the same submission to the interests of high-finance capitalism.[20]

State Department interference with Tresca's play backfired. The normally disapproving New York press expressed a measure of sympathy for the anti-Fascists and raised questions as to why a foreign government was being placated in this manner. And by utilizing such a lame excuse as the "Blue Laws" (violated every Sunday by millions of New Yorkers), the authorities provided Tresca with an easy means to circumvent another prohibition—scheduling the next performance for any day other than the Christian Sabbath. Thus the crowd that converged on Bryant Hall on Saturday evening, January 23, 1926, was so large that hundreds could not be accommodated, and police reserves had to be called out to maintain order. Although agents of the FBI and Bomb Squad were present, they did not interfere with the performance; nor did they do so at subsequent performances in New Haven, Philadelphia, and other eastern cities. In the absence of government intervention, the American press ignored the performances and the anti-Fascists as well.[21] This observation was not lost on De Martino, who suggested a change in strategy to Mussolini: "In my opinion it is necessary to work for the gradual depreciation of the subversives, who are now isolated, rather than provoking incidents useful only to recalling the attention of public opinion to them."[22] Thus, as a vehicle of propaganda, Tresca's L'Attentato a Mussolini was a smash hit among anti-Fascists but generated only limited and brief attention from American observers.

Not surprisingly, Zaniboni's manipulated assassination attempt provided a pretext for new repressive measures, including the "Law for Expatriates" promulgated on January 31, 1926, which provided for revocation of Italian citizenship and confiscation of personal property in Italy. The principal anti-Fascists in the United States that this law targeted were Tresca, his colleague Allegra, and the socialist Vincenzo Vacirca: "the three renegades whom we have had the greatest interest in removing from this country," De Martino informed Mussolini.[23] Depriving anti-Fascists of their Italian citizenship, De Martino knew, would not constitute cause for deportation, but he did notify the State Department that the "three renegades" had been stripped of their Italian citizenship in hope of rendering them even more undesirable in American eyes. Anticipating that victims of the "Expatriate Law" might seek protection by acquiring American citizenship, De Martino informed the State Department that granting citizenship to anti-Fascists would be considered an "unfriendly act" by the Italian government. Granting citizenship to Tresca, Allegra, and Vacirca in particular would be dangerous for the United States, De Martino warned. He claimed to possess "evidence" that the three anti-Fascists had been receiving money from Soviet sources for the purpose of conducting subversive activities. Playing the "Moscow's payroll" card was just another tactic to spook American authorities into suppressing anti-Fascists.[24] But neither De Martino's mendacious warnings to the State Department nor the Italian Law of Expatriates thwarted Tresca, who never sought the safety of American citizenship.

Garibaldi Memorial Celebration: 1926

With the approach of Independence Day, 1926, Tresca anticipated another confrontation with the Fascists at the annual Garibaldi Memorial celebration, one that would exceed the previous year's encounter in size and violence. Early in the morning of July 4, anti-Fascists kept the headquarters of the *Fascio Benito Mussolini* in Manhattan and the two *fasci* in the Bronx under surveillance. Strong contingents were posted outside the offices of *Il Martello*, *Il Nuovo Mondo* (the new anti-Fascist daily), and other radical newspapers to ensure against invasion by Blackshirts while everyone was away in Staten Island. Another group guarded the statue of Garibaldi in Washington Square Park, to prevent the Fascists from conducting a rally there. Several thousand anti-Fascists from all over the New York metropolitan area had assembled at the memorial at the appointed hour. While awaiting the Blackshirts, the crowd heard speeches by Tresca, Allegra, Luigi Antonini, Girolamo Valenti, Vittorio Vidali, and others, including "Peppino" Garibaldi. But not a single Blackshirt materialized. The intrepid *fasci* leaders had evidently concluded that a major clash with the anti-Fascists would lead to bloodshed and bad publicity.[25]

Vittorio Vidali (a.k.a. Enea Sormenti)

At the Garibaldi Memorial demonstration and other rallies, Tresca's newest associate was Vittorio Vidali, known in the United States as Enea Sormenti. Of medium height and strong build, and with a brutish face that signaled danger, Vidali was an intelligent, tough, and utterly-ruthless communist. A veteran of many battles with Fascists in the Trieste area and Central Europe, Vidali fled from Italy to avoid imprisonment, making his way to Algeria in February 1923. Assisted by Italian seamen, Vidali boarded a ship bound for the United States and entered the country illegally in August or September 1923. Once established, Vidali quickly surpassed all other Italian communists in importance, including the estimable Giovanni Pippan. By 1926, Vidali was performing multiple roles for the Italian section of the CP, including the directorship of the party organ *Il Lavoratore*. During his four-year sojourn in the United States, Vidali and Tresca were the "dynamic duo" of the anti-Fascist movement, specializing in direct confrontation with the Blackshirts.[26]

Open-Air Propaganda

With the FLNA increasing its strength and Mussolini's prestige rising internationally, anti-Fascists felt more compelled than ever to project their influence beyond the parameters of their movement and reach unaligned workers potentially receptive to Fascism. Thus, in the summer of 1926, Tresca, Allegra, Vidali, and others resumed their street corner propaganda campaign, once again targeting Greenwich Village, East Harlem, the Lower East Side, and the Bronx.[27] The borough where the Blackshirts had achieved their greatest gains was the Bronx, especially the Arthur Avenue section. In previous years, the *sovversivi* had been well represented among the workers of this Italian enclave, where a high percentage of them were tailors employed in the garment industry in Manhattan. More recently, activity among many radical groups and sympathizers had declined in this neighborhood, permitting the rise of two *fasci* to go unchallenged. One of them, the *Fascio Mario Sonzini*, located at 623 East 187th Street, near Gamberling Avenue, was determined to conquer the Bronx for the Duce, and throughout July 1926 a squad of fifteen to twenty Blackshirts roamed the neighborhood, beating up known anti-Fascists whenever they encountered them singly or in groups of two or three. Growing more brazen with attack, the *Fascio Mario Sonzini* issued a public challenge to the anti-Fascists, daring them to set foot in the Bronx. Tresca and Vidali received a special warning promising death should they venture north of Manhattan.[28]

Eager to challenge Blackshirt *squadrismo*, Tresca exhorted his comrades to action: "To the Bronx to re-conquer a lost trench."[29] Prior to an anti-Fascist rally scheduled to be held at the corner of 187th Street and Gamberling Avenue on the evening of July 31, Tresca and Vidali reconnoitered the designated area several times. Once on enemy turf, accompanied by only a handful of comrades, Tresca and Vidali could not resist the urge to bait the Blackshirts by strolling past known fascist haunts, eating ice cream and singing "*Bandiera Rossa.*" The sole response of the Blackshirts was to request police intervention after observing Tresca and Vidali enter a café. To the perplexed patrolmen sent to investigate, Tresca said, "We have accounts to settle with the Fascists, but we have no need of your assistance for that."[30] Tresca and Vidali returned a few days later, conspicuously sipping coffee in a café in full view of passers-by. Soon Fascist and anti-Fascist groups gathered outside the café as word of Tresca's presence spread through the neighborhood. A melee ensued when a Fascist threatened to set fire to Tresca's beard. The Fascists were routed. To humiliate them further, Tresca, Vidali, and fellow victors conducted an impromptu march past the headquarters of the *Fascio Mario Sonzini*, chanting "*Abbasso il Fascismo!,*" "*Abbasso Mussolini!*"[31]

On Saturday evening, July 31, 1926, around 2,500 anti-Fascists, some having come from as far as New Jersey and Philadelphia, assembled at the corner of 187th Street and Gamberling Avenue. Hundreds of neighborhood Italians observed the proceedings from rooftops, windows, and fire-escapes. The crowd was harangued by Tresca, Vidali, Quintiliano, and others, who recounted all the economic and political failures of Mussolini's regime. After the speeches ended, the mass of demonstrators marched passed the *Fascio Mario Sonzini*, singing revolutionary songs and challenging the Blackshirts to come out and fight. Wisely, not a single Blackshirt showed his face, and if not for the protective cordon of policemen requested by the consul general, the anti-Fascists would have stormed the building.[32]

Harlem Bomb

After their comrades had been humiliated several times by anti-Fascists, a group of Blackshirts resolved to retaliate by killing Tresca. The date they selected for the assassination was Saturday evening, September 11; the site was the corner of First Avenue and 116th Street, in the heart of East Harlem's "Little Italy," where Tresca and others were to speak at an open-air rally. The Fascists' incentive to eliminate Tresca was heightened when news was received that Gino Lucetti, a twenty-six-year-old anarchist, attempted to assassinate Mussolini by hurling a bomb at his passing automobile. An anonymous caller phoned Tresca at his office to warn: "You people tried to kill Mussolini. We're going to get our revenge tonight."[33]

Anticipating violence, the ACLU had requested police protection for the September 11 rally. None was provided. Only Fascists merited protection. By 9:00 P.M., an uneasy crowd of more than 500 people had gathered to hear speeches by Tresca and others. His comrade Luigi Quintiliano had just begun to speak when a rooftop barrage of tomatoes narrowly missed him. Before he could resume, Quintiliano was hurled from the speaker's platform by the shock wave from a thunderous explosion that shattered windows throughout the neighborhood and brought thousands of frightened inhabitants into the streets. A hundred yards from the platform, on First Avenue, a Ford roadster that bystanders observed circling the block several times had been reduced to a smoldering wreck. Its three occupants—or what remained of them—were strewn about nearby. All were identified as members of the Fascist Aurelio Padovani Club in East Harlem.[34]

Officials of the Fascist League labeled the incident a "communist act," claiming that a bomb had been hurled by anti-Fascists who recognized the occupants of the Ford as Blackshirts.[35] Tresca dismissed the accusation as ridiculous. If by the slightest chance anti-Fascists had been responsible, he argued, "I would not be a free man at this moment, and my comrades would all be the object of arrests, interrogations, and persecution."[36] The explosion, Tresca explained to reporters, had resulted from the premature detonation of a bomb the Blackshirts had intended for the anti-Fascist speakers. The police and fire departments rejected both bomb theories, attributing the blast to sparks from the exhaust pipe that ignited the car's gas tank.[37] Tresca charged the police and fire department with a cover-up.[38]

He was not wrong. Autopsies of the bodies discovered metal fragments and powder burns produced by dynamite encased in sheet metal, and examination of the wreckage revealed that the explosion had occurred inside the automobile.[39] The police, however, did not reveal the forensic findings until more than a week later, by which time only a few New York dailies took notice.[40] The police also sent a full account to the Italian consul general, who expressed his relief in a report to Rome indicating that "the police have not publicized the results of their latest investigation and have shown themselves rather disposed to keeping everything secret. I believe, therefore, that after a little uproar in the subversive Italian newspapers no one will speak anymore about the tragic episode in Harlem."[41] Tresca and his attorney Morris L. Ernst tried for weeks to find evidence linking the assassination attempt to officials in the Fascist League and to underworld elements that may have provided the bomb. Their efforts came to nothing.[42]

Political Refugees

More worrisome than Fascist bombs was the American government, which had resumed its campaign to deport alien radicals, especially those who had entered the country illegally or those whose visas had expired. This was one objective of the immigration bill introduced in the House of Representatives on February 18, 1926. Anti-Fascists alerted Senator William H. Borah, Representatives Victor Berger, Henry T. Rainey, Hamilton Fish, and Albert Johnson, the head of the House Committee on Immigration, to the fact that many Italian aliens had fled political persecution in Fascist Italy. They requested that the government grant these exiles a safe haven, in accordance with America's long tradition of hospitality.[43] Johnson, the architect of the immigrant law of 1924 that targeted Italians for exclusion, assured the anti-Fascists that his new bill was not aimed at political refugees. He lied. Although the expulsion bill was temporarily shelved in March 1926, the *Lega Profughi d'Italia* (Italian Exile League), the Anti-Fascist Seamen's Association (most of whose members had jumped ship), and the International Labor Defense would soon be working full-time to save anti-Fascists from deportation.[44]

Of the "three renegades" whom the Fascists wished to see deported, Tresca was in the safest position so long as he exercised the same caution that had frustrated American authorities so far. Moreover, the State and Justice Departments feared another public relations fiasco should they pursue Tresca without adequate cause. When De Martino again requested action against Tresca for an article attacking the king of Italy, the head of the Division of Western European Affairs suggested that De Martino be brought "gently and politely to a realization that it is a waste of time for him to importune the Department with trivialities."[45] Allegra, too, was relatively safe from deportation, as the Labor Department had no record of his activities, and he was not likely to give them cause for compiling one.[46] Vacirca was the "renegade" most vulnerable to deportation. His visa had expired, and the State Department had refused to grant a renewal. Tresca and other defenders mobilized a legal team for a test case; however, through the intervention of Tresca's friend, ACLU attorney Isaac Schoor, and several prominent figures such as Senator William Borah and AFL president William Green, Vacirca obtained a series of extensions to his visa, despite protests from Mussolini's government. Not until 1933 was Vacirca compelled to leave the country, although after a brief sojourn in Spain, he re-entered the United States, where he remained until his final return to Italy in 1946.[47]

Less fortunate was Vittorio Vidali, arrested by Labor Department agents on October 17, 1926, after he and Tresca addressed 2,000 anti-Fascists at Tammany Hall. As the communist leader was led away, Tresca assured his friend that "It is nothing bad! Another fight, that's all!"[48] Vidali later credited Tresca with launching the campaign to defend him by obtaining the services of the eminent attorney Clarence Darrow.[49] Meeting with Vidali and Tresca after having conferred with government officials in Washington, Darrow allegedly expressed his belief that the complaint against Vidali (illegal entry) had been lodged by "an Italian labor union leader in New York," whom Tresca suspected was Antonini.[50] Given the bitter struggle between the communists and the ILGWU hierarchy then in progress, as well as the hostility each bore the other, it was certainly plausible that Antonini had denounced Vidali to federal authorities. In reality, however, Vidali's capture resulted from information furnished by the Italian consul general of New York.[51]

The Fascists were particularly fearful of Vidali because they believed—correctly— that he was the leader of communist "action squads" willing to break heads or worse.

In April 1927, while Tresca, Allegra, and Vidali were organizing a demonstration to protest the welcoming to New York of the Italian aviator Colonel Francesco de Pinedo, the consul general became worried when his agents intercepted a telegram from a leading communist in Philadelphia, which promised Vidali the arrival of "fifty comrades willing to do anything."[52] He immediately notified his superiors in Rome that "it would be of capital importance to get rid of Vidali at this time."[53] American response was immediate. Despite Darrow's efforts, the State Department was unwilling to provide safe haven for a communist alien who had entered the country illegally. Immigration officials at Ellis Island planned to deport Vidali to Italy and certain imprisonment, but at the last moment the Department of Labor permitted him to choose his own destination. He sailed for the Soviet Union on June 11, 1927, to begin his long and nefarious career as an agent of the Comintern and the Soviet secret police.[54]

Fascist Raids

While the Italian ambassador sought the deportation of vulnerable anti-Fascist leaders, the Fascist League undertook new sorties against the *sovverisivi* after Anteo Zamboni, a fifteen-year-old member of the Fascist youth group, *Il Balilla*, who came from an anarchist family, fired upon the Duce as his open car passed by during a Fascist celebration in Bologna on October 26, 1926. The lad was stabbed to death on the spot by the Fascist crowd. But rather than attempt anything as sinister as another assassination attempt against Tresca or other anti-Fascists, the Blackshirts demonstrated their Fascist machismo on November 2 by conducting a midnight raid against the office of the anti-Fascist daily *Il Nuovo Mondo* at 81 East 10th Street, in the heart of the anti-Fascist citadel. After gaining access while a single worker was on duty, the Blackshirts wrecked two compositing machines but spared the printing press out of ignorance and the need for a speedy exist. Later, at around 5:00 A.M., another Fascist group broke the windows of *Il Nuovo Mondo*'s office by throwing rocks. Another salvo damaged the windows of *Il Martello*'s office, now located nearby at 77 East 10th Street. Such "heroic gestures" merely covered the Fascists with shame, Tresca asserted. "The only thing that displeased us about visits of this nature is that they take place when we are asleep in bed." Tresca indicated the hours when he was always in his office and invited the Fascists to drop by.[55] Although the confrontations of 1926 ended with the Blackshirts' pathetic attacks against machines and windows, the guerrilla warfare waged by the anti-Fascists the following year would attain new levels of violence.

Tresca addressing Italian workers, probably in Pennsylvania, c. 1904–1905. From the author's collection.

Tresca speaking at an anarchist picnic in the 1920s. Pietro Allegra stands to his right; Luigi Quintilliano stands in the background to his right. From the author's collection.

Il sangue irrora il germe dell'Idea

Tresca at around age 60. This photocard was printed in the thousands after his murder in 1943. From the author's collection.

Tresca in his 60s addressing a crowd. From *Omaggio alla memoria imperitura di Carlo Tresca.*

Helga Guerra Tresca. From the author's collection.

Tresca with Joe Ettor, Elizabeth Gurley Flynn, Fred "Buster" Flynn, and Sabina Flynn, lower right (other two identities unknown).

Tresca c. 1908. From the author's collection.

Bust of Tresca made by Minna Harkavy in the late 1920s, located in the Piazza Tresca, Sulmona. From the author's collection.

Carlo Tresca,
a drawing by Eliena Krylenko

Drawing of Tresca by Eliena Krylenko. From Max Eastman's *Heroes I Have Known* (1st ed.).

15

The Anti-Fascist Alliance

The resurgence of anti-Fascist activity following the Matteotti assassination generated renewed impetus to forge a united front that would facilitate greater coordination and common purpose. Tresca, by 1925, had become so concerned about the consolidation of Mussolini's regime and the rapid spread of pro-Fascist sentiment among Italian immigrants that he overcame his earlier reluctance to join forces with non-revolutionary elements and became anti-Fascism's most outspoken advocate of a united front. *Sovversivi* of every school, he now argued, were morally obligated to unite against Fascism. No one need relinquish or compromise their ideals or political program, but they should stop fixating about an abstract future and address the needs of the present. Tresca pinned his hopes for a united front on the *Alleanza Anti-Fascista del Nord America* (Anti-Fascist Alliance of North America or AFANA).[1]

Revived in September 1925, the AFANA admitted in its official "Manifesto" that the organization had failed at its inception in 1923 to remedy the fragmentation of the anti-Fascist movement. Anti-Fascists had deluded themselves with the belief that Fascism would be a "transitory and short lived phenomenon of collective madness."[2] Predicting "a new era of activity," the AFANA convened a general assembly at its headquarters in the Peoples House at 7 East 15th Street in October 1925. An executive committee of eighteen members and a three-man secretariat were chosen, which reflected the entire spectrum of left-wing elements save for the syndicalists of the IWW and the Galleanisti. With Allegra serving as general-secretary, and Tresca and Quintiliano members of the executive committee, the *Il Martello* group exercised considerable influence over the AFANA's policies and activities. The only other leaders with important status were Vidali and the republican Arturo Di Pietro, both executive committee members. The official newspapers of the AFANA were *Il Martello*, the communist *Il Lavoratore,* and the social democratic/labor daily *Il Nuovo Mondo*, founded in November 1925.[3]

Tresca, in the spring of 1926, busily promoted support for a national congress of anti-Fascists intended to end the rivalries that weakened the resistance. Success of the congress and the AFANA itself, he knew, hinged upon establishing accord between communists and social democrats. Their primary concern and the key issue dividing them was control of the ILGWU. The communists were bent on a seizure of power that would topple the social democratic hierarchy led by president

Morris Sigman. Both elements contending for control were composed primarily of Russian Jews, the dominant ethnic group in the needle trades unions. Italians constituted a sizable minority within the union but never wielded influence commensurate with their numbers, a situation that had led them to organize Local 48, the Italian Cloakmakers Union, led by Salvatore Ninfo, and Local 89, the Italian Dressmakers Union, led by Luigi Antonini. Ninfo, a traditional trade unionist, and Antonini, a former communist turned social democrat, were zealous guardians of their fiefdoms and the autonomy upon which their power depended. Facing personal disaster should the communists triumph, Antonini and Ninfo ensured that the Italian delegates under their command voted *en bloc* for Sigman at the ILGWU Congress in Philadelphia in November 1925, therefore sealing his victory over the communists.[4]

But Sigman's victory did not end the communist insurgency within the ILGWU, and as the conflict raged throughout 1926, the AFANA became a secondary arena in which the rivals fought. At a general assembly of the AFANA on January 13, 1926, social democratic union leaders increased their representation on the executive committee and secretariat. Antonini and Ninfo, moreover, had defeated their communist challengers in the April elections for general-secretary of Locals 89 and 48.[5] With their position thus strengthened, the social democrats should have been able to thwart communist ascendancy in the AFANA. However, the FSI (SP), the traditional ally of the Italian needle trades unions, doubted that social democrats would remain dominant, and many of its leaders opposed collaborating with the communists under any circumstances. The FSI therefore refused official support for the AFANA, although individual sections could affiliate if they wished. The New York FSI section did so immediately, as did many others, so rather than alienate its own rank-and-file, the FSI promised to participate in the forthcoming national congress. But after a new round of attacks from the communists in August 1926, the FSI urged all social democrats to quit the AFANA because the organization was acquiring an "anarchist-communist character"—a jab directed at Tresca and the CP. Only Vacirca's plea for unity prevented a defection by the social democrats at this juncture.[6]

The fragile unity of the AFANA was almost sabotaged by Ninfo and Girolamo Valenti, who held an interview with *The New York Times* on July 31, 1926, declaring that the AFANA had split because the communists were gaining control by organizing "fictitious" branches that increased their delegate strength. Leaders of the trade union wing, they asserted, would withdraw from AFANA and reunite under socialist auspices. Following the press conference, the FSI ordered all social democrats to abandon the AFANA and boycott the national congress, now scheduled for Labor Day.[7] But the FSI's maneuver was ill-timed. Most social democrats regarded the Ninfo-Valenti interview as an embarrassment and public relations disaster. Even Antonini and Ninfo retreated rather than incur the onus of splitting the united front. They publicly reaffirmed their faith in the AFANA, hoping to placate rank-and-file union members and possibly gain an advantage over the communists before the national congress convened. The possibility of real cooperation with the communists, however, was nil.[8]

The battles between communists and social democrats for control of the ILGWU and the AFANA only confirmed Tresca's long-held conviction that political parties and labor unions were inherently incapable of transcending their rivalries and joining together in common cause. Time and again, Tresca urged communists and social democrats not to utilize AFANA as a battleground for their political rivalry and savage polemics, as they benefited only the Fascists.[9] To perform the role of neutral arbiter, however, was difficult. Tresca in the 1920s, despite his opposition to the "dictatorial ends… and suffocating character" of the CP, stood much closer to the communists on most issues than to the social democrats.[10] His willingness to collaborate with communists derived not from any true affinity with them, but the recognition that the communists were revolutionaries and the social democrats were not. Tresca believed that the communists, as revolutionaries, were far more committed and effective anti-Fascists than their reformist rivals, a belief confirmed in his view by the consistent absence of FSI and trade union leaders in demonstrations against the Blackshirts.[11] He underscored the disparity by noting that the Ninfo-Valenti interview—an "act of pusillanimity"—occurred on the same day that he and Vidali led a protest march against a *fascio* headquarters in the Bronx.[12] Tresca was also distressed by the debacle the ILGWU had experienced because of the internal war for supremacy. Morale and fighting spirit had discernibly declined among rank-and-file workers. Anti-Fascism had thereby been weakened because the labor and anti-Fascist movements were inextricably linked. Italians should understand that "nothing can help this evil beast [Fascism] and lengthen its claws than the fratricide battle that grows daily within the labor unions of America."[13] But neither communists nor social democrats seemed to care. Control of the ILGWU and other unions was more important to them than the struggle against Fascism.

Even if anti-Fascism had not been his primary concern, Tresca probably would have favored the communists to win the conflict within the ILGWU. He had been a critic of garment industry leadership, especially Antonini and Ninfo, well before the communists appeared on the scene. Tresca believed that needle workers in every category should have been organized in a single industrial union. Although union potentates often paid lip service to this concept, he knew they would never relinquish their private fiefdoms. On the other hand, Tresca was fully aware and critical of the machinations employed by the communists to conquer the ILGWU. He regretted that disaffected elements in the union were obliged to follow the leadership of communists, who invariably subordinated the interests of the workers to those of the CP. He had often expressed hope that the anarchists within the ILGWU (mainly Russian Jews) would constitute themselves as a vanguard and infuse the union with libertarian spirit and militancy, but they were far outnumbered by the communists. So, in the end, Tresca preferred to see the union bureaucracies challenged by a communist-led insurgency rather than none at all.[14]

The Anti-Fascist Congress

Fearful that the anti-Fascists might actually form a united front, Mussolini's government requested the State Department prevent the AFANA national congress from taking place, a request that was denied.[15] Therefore, on September 4, 1926, some 3,000–4,000 anti-Fascists crowded into the auditorium at Cooper Union in New York, 246 of whom were delegates chosen by 135 anti-Fascist sections, party groups, labor union locals, and other workers' societies. They claimed to represent between 200,000–500,000 Italian-American workers, a deceptive figure that reflected union membership rather than anti-Fascist strength. After introductory remarks by the presiding officers, Allega and Di Pietro, the afternoon was devoted to speeches and revolutionary songs.[16]

The roster of speakers over the next few days indicated that American as well as Italian radicals and labor leaders had come to regard the AFANA as a significant battleground. Benjamin Gitlow, representing the CP, was the first speaker on September 5. Emphasizing the counter-revolutionary nature of Fascism, Gitlow observed that none of the capitalist governments had ever protested against the brutalities of Mussolini's regime, and that the threat of Fascism existed in the United States as well as Italy. He concluded with a plea for "international [working class] unity in the fight against the Fascist monster and against world capitalism."[17] Gitlow was followed by Frank Bellanca, senior editor of *Il Nuovo Mondo*, who pleaded for anti-Fascist unity: "Let us disarm our fraternal hatreds and concentrate our blows against one enemy, against the great enemy of the proletariat, Fascism."[18] Dr. Charles Fama, one of the few non-radical leaders of the resistance, asserted that Fascism in Europe was in decline, that Fascism had not made significant inroads among Italian Americans, and that Fascism had no future in America. Fama's assessment was completely divorced from reality, but at least he had the good sense to affirm the necessity of recruiting new converts to anti-Fascism. After Fama, Tresca mounted the podium to the accompaniment of thunderous applause. Described by *Il Nuovo Mondo* as "the dean of the anti-Fascist movement," Tresca discussed the blunders and failures of Mussolini's foreign and domestic policies, especially the much heralded "battles" for wheat and other products. He denounced the Italian monarchy as Fascism's traitorous accomplice, and warned local Blackshirts to abandon any hope of duplicating in America what they had accomplished in Italy. The anti-Fascists would stop them. The last speaker of the afternoon was Giovannitti, the "poet of the proletariat" and the secretary of the Italian Chamber of Labor. Giovannitti urged the social democrats to rejoin the AFANA because all anti-Fascists had but one enemy to fight.[19]

The next morning, as delegates met at the Rand School, an unexpected announcement was made that William Green, the president of the AFL, would address the congress. Antonini and Ninfo had been trying to persuade AFL directors to take a stand against Fascism. Almost certainly, however, they arranged Green's appearance as a *coup de théâtre* to upstage Gitlow and the communists.[20] In contrast to his predecessor, Samuel Gompers, who admired Mussolini and regarded Fascism as a model of class collaboration, Green recognized Fascism as a menace to free labor movements everywhere. He was particularly concerned about recent inroads Blackshirts had made among Italian-American workers. Branding Fascism as "an enemy of society and of humanity," Green assured the anti-Fascists that "the American Federation of Labor will stand with you, work with you and lead with you until we have succeeded in driving Fascism from the face of the earth." The audience cheered and applauded wildly.[21]

The congress then heard reports on the status of the resistance. Anti-Fascists were most successful in organizing new sections and actively combating Blackshirts in those areas where the *sovversivi* had traditionally drawn working-class support: Paterson, New Haven, Philadelphia, Pittsburgh, and the anthracite coal districts around Old Forge and Jessup, Pennsylvania. Almost no gains had been achieved by the Women's Section of the AFANA, whose contribution up to this point was "more moral than material," according to Angela Bambace, a communist organizer for the ILGWU. Most distressing of all was the fate of Italian political refugees threatened with deportation. Nino Capraro, now an organizer for the ACWUA, reported that prospects were grim for anti-Fascists who had entered the country illegally or whose visas had expired. The assurances given to the AFANA by Congressman Johnson in February 1926, that political refugees would not be deported to fascist Italy, were worthless.[22]

The evening session of September 5 was devoted to the anti-Fascist press. A committee headed by Oscar Mazzitelli, an editor for the ACWUA's *Il Lavoro*, recommended adoption of a resolution requiring all newspapers affiliated with the AFANA to refrain from personal attacks, a long-standing issue of contention between social democrats and communists. The resolution was adopted despite the certainty that neither side would abide.[23] Tresca led off the afternoon session of September 6 with a speech devoted to a favorite theme—economic boycott. The economic situation in Italy was becoming ever more critical: unemployment remained high, the value of the lira had plunged, and the standard of living was generally lower. One of the reasons for the declining value of the lira, Tresca claimed, was the reduction of remittances from Italian immigrants, so he urged anti-Fascists to intensify efforts to ensure their further decline. Boycott of Italian financial institutions, merchants, businessmen, and professionals known to be Fascist or sympathetic to Mussolini should continue. "The cause of dictatorship can be greatly harmed and its disintegration accelerated" by employing economic warfare, he concluded.[24]

Tresca was followed by another unscheduled speaker invited by Antonini and Ninfo, ILGWU president Morris Sigman. Sigman compared Fascism to the "open shop" system, stating that labor in the United States had been oppressed by an America form of Fascism, the Ku Klux Klan. Mussolini's regime, he declared, wanted to be an instrument of the capitalist class even in the United States, disseminating fascist propaganda among the workers and suppressing opposition. Sigman gave assurances that conflict within the ILGWU had ended, and he pledged "to give all the help necessary to your organization to carry out your struggle against the common enemy, Mussolinian Fascism, to a victorious end"—a promise never kept.[25]

After an account of the AFANA's financial weakness by Allegra, and an equally discouraging report from Vacirca about the threat of deportation for exiles like himself, the congress turned to the business of new officers. The delegates elected an executive committee with equal representation for all the political parties and groups, labor unions, newspapers, and auxiliary associations affiliated with the AFANA. Tresca, Allegra, Vidali, Di Pietro, and Giovanni Sala of the ACWUA were elected to the secretariat, with Allegra entrusted once again with the position of general-secretary. With the elections completed, the first congress of the AFANA ended with shouts of "*Viva l'Italia!*," "*Viva la Libertà!*," and with the hope that the second congress would be held in Rome.[26]

Tresca, although doubtless less sanguine in private, wrote in *Il Martello* that he was satisfied with the results of the national congress: "THE UNITED FRONT, yesterday debated, attacked, and sabotaged, is today an accomplished fact, a reality." His immediate concern, however, was the possibility that anti-Fascists would again lapse into inactivity because of over-confidence. The second congress of the AFANA, Tresca predicted, would not be held in Rome. Mussolini would still be in power, and nobody could predict when his downfall would come about. The AFANA had merely laid the groundwork for a revolutionary process that required anti-Fascists to prepare and organize their forces in readiness for the propitious moment when the regime could be challenged.[27]

Schism

Hopes for a united front were quickly dashed. Communist unionists resumed attacking the "Social Fascists" who dominated the ILGWU and provoked a strike of 30,000 cloak-makers on July 1, 1926. They had done so reluctantly, under pressure form the CP, which was in the throes of a civil war waged between rival factions led by William "Zeke" Foster and Jay Lovestone, respectively. Neither faction believed the strike had a chance of victory. But each was so determined to out-Bolshevik the other that defeat for the ILGWU and its workers was a trifling price to pay if leadership of the CP could be won. At a cost of $3,500,000 and terrible suffering for the workers, the strike dragged on until December 14, when the ILGWU suspended the New York communist leaders and settled with the bosses. Misled by their communist leaders, the cloak-makers returned to the social democratic fold. Never again were the communists strong enough to mount an effective challenge against the old guard leaders of the ILGWU, but as a result of the debacle they had caused, the union remained severely weakened for many years.[28]

Inevitably, the fight to control the ILGWU once again spilled over into the AFANA. After the national congress, the FSI had refused to affiliate with the AFANA, despite endorsement of a united front by the most outstanding of all Italian social democrats in the United States, Vincenzo Vacirca. However, by December 1926, even Vacirca conceded the impossibility of cooperating with the communists: "It is no longer possible to witness inertly the indecent spectacle of a group [communists]... that attacks daily, with every sort of overbearing and incoherent behavior, the cohesion of the 'Antifascist United Front.'"[29] The next day, Ninfo announced that the trade unionist majority in the AFANA was determined to expel the communists.[30] Presumably, this should have been easily accomplished, because socialist democrats outnumbered communists on the executive committee and secretariat, and because out of the 70,000 adherents (a dubious figure) claimed by the AFANA, the communists numbered not more than 200–300.[31] But expulsion of the communists never took place. Instead, the social democrats, trade unionists, and other moderates seceded from the AFANA, and on February 12, 1927, representatives of the ILGWU, ACWUA, the Italian Chamber of Labor, the FSI, the New York Federation of Italian Labor Unions, and the Italian Republican Party founded the Anti-Fascist Federation of North America for the Freedom of Italy.[32] Ironically, the defection of the social democrats and the formation of a rival organization guaranteed that the communists would gain control of AFANA. By this point, however, the social democrats no longer cared.

Tresca's Assessment

Tresca was not surprised when the AFANA finally split. He had long suspected that the social democrats were insincere from the start, and that union leaders had joined the AFANA to utilize it against the communist insurgency inside the ILGWU.[33] Tresca dismissed the claim that the communists increased their delegate strength by devious means. If true, the communists were able to act with impunity only because the social democrats had never tried to stop them. Union leaders like Antonini and Ninfo were "generals without an army."[34] They claimed to represent tens of thousands of workers but rarely attended the AFANA meetings, never participated in demonstrations, and in general contributed little to the anti-Fascist struggle. As for the union "masses" that Antonini and others claimed as their following, they rarely participated in the affairs of the AFANA. Active AFANA members who belonged to the needle trade unions were communists, anarchists, and some syndicalists. Furthermore, how could the union leaders cry perfidy over the methods employed by the communists in the AFANA when the social democratic bureaucrats of the ILGWU utilized high-handed practices to suppress radical dissidents?[35] Thus when the social democrats quit the AFANA to form their own federation, Tresca did not protest the *fait accompli*. The AFANA would survive without the social democrats, but he knew the united front was dead. Sectarianism and self-interest had triumphed anew over common cause. [36]

16

A Year of Violence and Death

The year 1927 was one of the most tumultuous and wrenching in Tresca's long career. Direct action by anti-Fascists, sometimes amounting to guerrilla war, had become a more frequent method of struggle, as the Blackshirts grew bolder and more numerous in New York and the surrounding metropolitan area. Typically, Blackshirts of a newly-organized *fascio* in Port Chester planned to demonstrate their mettle by breaking up a meeting at which Tresca and Vidali were scheduled to speak on March 20. They dared not act, however, until the arrival of reinforcements from New York led by Giacomo Bonavita, the "little Duce of the squads." At the first Fascist disruption, Tresca positioned himself in the center of the Blackshirts, an act of defiance that left them befuddled. A second interruption almost precipitated a fight, but was forestalled again by Tresca, who confronted Bonavita face to face. The Blackshirt leader immediately offered a truce: "you restrain yours, and I will restrain mine." Tresca shoved the Blackshirt back into his seat with a warning: "We will see to it that they [the Blackshirts] stay quiet."[1] Thwarted, Bonavita and his followers quit the hall and phoned the police to report that the anti-Fascists in the hall were "armed to the teeth." The police arrived but found only one anti-Fascist armed with a pistol. That the police searched only anti-Fascists reflected the friendly relationship that often developed between Blackshirt organizations and local police, prompting Tresca later to boast "if the Fascists of the United States were not assured of strong assistance by the police, they would not dare take a single step on the streets populated by Italian workers."[2] When calm was restored in the hall, Tresca gave his speech and left Port Chester with Vidali to give another speech in nearby Yonkers. Their departure was the signal for the Blackshirts to attack the remaining anti-Fascists, whom they now outnumbered, but the encounter ended with the Fascists in worse condition than their enemies.[3]

From the skirmishes in New York's periphery, attention shifted to the arrival that April of the Italian aviator, Francesco De Pinedo, whose trans-oceanic flights had earned him great renown. In contrast to the anti-Locatelli protests, opposition to De Pinedo's arrival was mitigated by respect for the aviator's courage and the fact that his accomplishments reflected positively upon Italians. Only with reluctance did some anti-Fascists, like Vacirca and Frank Bellanca, conclude that De Pinedo's visit had to be opposed.[4] Tresca was incensed by such lukewarm opposition. He acknowledged that De Pinedo merited admiration as an aviator, but insisted that the aviator and the Fascist could not be separated. De Pinedo's flight had been financed by Mussolini for propaganda purposes, and his personal appearances dressed in a black shirt were indicative of his allegiance to the Fascist regime. Rejecting sentimentality, Tresca declared: "There can be no truce between us and the Blackshirts.... For us there is only one De Pinedo, De Pinedo the Fascist."[5] In the end, De Pinedo received the standard anti-Fascist treatment, especially in New York. A new touch was the flight of an airplane over Manhattan on April 30, dropping thousands of anti-Fascist leaflets (in English).[6]

Felonious Assault

With De Pinedo's departure, Tresca redirected his efforts to home-grown Fascists. He believed that Thaon di Revel had played a key role in the escalating aggression of Blackshirts in and around New York, and set out to discover incriminating evidence against the Fascist League and its president. The quest almost ended Tresca's career. On May 6, 1927, through the intercession of a friend who owned the Torino Restaurant on 183rd Street and Third Avenue in the Bronx, Tresca met Giacomo Caldora, president of the *Alleanza Fascista Il Duce*, a dissident group he organized after his expulsion from the *Fascio Mario Sonzini*. Professing a desire to retaliate against Thaon di Revel, Caldora invited Tresca to accompany him to his office on 187th Street and Arthur Avenue, where he would provide him with documents proving that the president of the Fascist League had embezzled funds from the *Fascio Mario Sonzini*. Tresca suspected a trap but could not resist the bait.

Caldora later boasted that his intention was to open a safe where he kept a pistol and shoot Tresca while he read the documents. However, after opening the safe and giving Tresca some papers to read, he excused himself to answer nature's call. Tresca and the comrade who had accompanied him, Salvatore Riccardo Linguerri, were not alarmed because Caldora had left another Blackshirt with them in the office. But moments later, when they heard cries for help, Tresca and Linguerri rushed to the door only to find it locked from the outside. Tresca's first thought was that Caldora had summoned other Blackshirts to attack them, so he and Linguerri barricaded the door with furniture. Then the significance of the open safe dawned on him—Caldora was summoning the police. Tresca and Linguerri broke down the door and ran out into the street before a squad car arrived. Caldora threw a rock at Tresca and fled. The two anti-Fascists hailed a taxi underneath the "El" train and made good their escape.[7]

Tresca was arrested a few days later on charges of "felonious assault," allegedly for threatening Caldora with a pistol while seizing documents. Released on $2,500 bail, Tresca faced a possible ten-year sentence if convicted. At preliminary hearings, Bronx Blackshirts and priests (especially Father Cafuzzi of Our Lady of Mount Carmel) did their utmost to convince the Bronx district attorney to indict the godless anarchist. But the Grand Jury found insufficient evidence to prosecute, and the charges were dropped in June 1927.[8]

Memorial Day Murders

Soon after Caldora's attempt to frame him, Tresca became involved in the legal aftermath of the most sensational act of violence perpetrated by anti-Fascists against Blackshirts. American patriotic holidays had become prime occasions for the Fascists to pose as representatives of the Italian community and to ingratiate themselves with the general public by exhibiting their "Americanism." Anti-Fascists were determined to expose this "patriotism" for the sham that it was, and when the American Legion invited the Fascist League to march in the Memorial Day parade of 1927, they warned that the participation of Blackshirts would cause trouble. Undeterred, the Fascist League vowed to march in full Fascist regalia: blackshirts, tasseled caps, military jodhpurs, and steel-tipped whips.[9]

Shortly before 8:00 A.M., on May 30, fourteen Blackshirts, representing the *Fascio Mario Sonzini* and the *Alleanza Fascista Il Duce*, gathered beneath the "El" train at 183rd Street, en route to Fascist League headquarters, where 400 Fascists were to rendezvous before marching in the parade down Riverside Drive. One of them, a thirty-nine-year-old tailor and war veteran named Giuseppe Carisi, stopped to buy a newspaper at a street-side stand. Before he could pocket his change, Carisi was set upon by two men who had been waiting outside the Torino Restaurant, a half-block away on Third Avenue. One of the assailants stabbed Carisi twenty-one times. While the first attack was in progress, another Blackshirt, a twenty-two-year-old printer and war veteran known locally as Nicola Amoroso (real name: Michele D'Ambrosoli) was walking toward the "El" from 184th Street, when a second assailant stabbed him once and shot him several times. Both Blackshirts died at the scene.[10]

The Fascists exploited the propaganda value of the Memorial Day murders for all they were worth. Mussolini himself paid tribute to the fallen Blackshirts in the Chamber of Deputies. In the Bronx, flanked day and night by an honor guard, the coffins of the slain "martyrs" were exhibited for several days at the *Fascio Mario Sonzini*. On June 4, through streets festooned with floral wreaths, some sent by Mussolini and the Italian royal family, the funeral cortege transported Carisi and Amoroso to the Church of Our Lady of Mt. Carmel at Belmont Avenue and 187th Street. As many as 10,000 Italian Americans observed the procession as it proceeded to the accompaniment of band playing the "Star Spangled Banner" and "Giovinezza," the Fascist hymn. Mourners included Ambassador De Martino, Consul General Axerio, Thaon di Revel, and officials of the American Legion. At Our Lady of Mount Carmel, hundreds crowded the church to hear a solemn requiem mass celebrated by Father Cafuzzi. After the bodies were shipped to Italy, additional ceremonies were conducted in Naples with Fascist Party chieftains, members of the royal family, other dignitaries, and some 150,000 individuals in attendance.[11]

As the "martyrs" were enshrined in the pantheon of Fascist heroes, Mussolini's *Il Popolo d'Italia* called for revenge: "It is necessary to pursue, until the end, the struggle against antifascism,… to crush these traitors as you would a viper that wants to bite at your heel.[12] Ambassador De Martino immediately sought from the American government "measures necessary to check anti-Fascist criminality."[13] The

State Department not only demurred but gently reminded De Martino of "American sensitiveness regarding public demonstrations of Blackshirts in formation."[14] Undeterred, De Martino sought to convince New York authorities that anti-Fascists bore the "moral responsibility… for the double homicide." His proof was an article by Tresca that blamed the Fascists for the atmosphere of violence that hung over the Italian community. The article, he claimed, demonstrated "the connivance between Tresca and the authors of the crime."[15] Another Fascist attempt to put Tresca behind bars had begun.

Tresca, Quintiliano, and other knowledgeable anti-Fascists believed that the assailants were members of a communist "action squad" Vidali had organized before his deportation.[16] The backbone of the Italian Bureau of the CP was composed mainly of former seamen and exiles who had entered the country after World War I, many of them illegally.[17] Among this group were some fifty seamen from Trieste, who formed Vidali's personal entourage and the "action squad" Tresca suspected of committing the murders. The authorities knew nothing of this "action squad," but rather than conduct a serious investigation of the murders, preferred to pursue the quarry designated by the Fascist League.

The Greco-Carrillo Case[18]

The leader of the campaign to entrap Tresca and other anti-Fascist leaders was Carlo Vinti, the former *squadrista* of the Milan *fascio* and secretary-general of the *Fascio Benito Mussolini* in Manhattan. His liaison in the police department was Detective Domenico Caso, a pro-Fascist assigned to the case as chief investigator.[19] At 5:00 P.M., on the evening of July 11, 1927, Caso and his men raided *Il Nuovo Mondo* and *Il Martello*. Vacirca, the editor of the anti-Fascist daily and the intended target, was absent, so Caso arrested Mario D'Amico, the only staff member at the office. At *Il Martello*, the detectives found the entire staff except Tresca, who was out of town. They roughed-up Tresca's associates and "discovered" two pistols and a knife, weapons planted either by the detectives or Umberto Simone, a Fascist League spy who had gained employment with *Il Martello*. Caso arrested Tresca's brother Mario, Quintiliano, his secretary Mario Buzzi, and six others, including De Simone, lest they expose his identity as a spy. Elsewhere that day police arrested Tresca's friend Filippo Nardone and two anti-Fascists in Brooklyn, Calogero Greco and Donato Carillo.[20]

Quintiliano and Mario were charged with illegal possession of the pistols and released after posting a $2,500 bond; the charges were later dismissed for lack of evidence.[21] Greco, Carrillo, Buzzi, Nardone, and D'Amico were held as material witnesses in the Bronx County Jail. The anti-Fascists were not made to stand in a line-up but displayed individually to several members of the *Fascio Mario Sonzini*. One over-eager Blackshirt identified Buzzi as one of the Memorial Day assailants. No matter that Buzzi had been in jail that day following a fracas in Newark. Buzzi was beaten by Caso and other detectives, who demanded that he admit to having overheard Tresca, Vacirca, and Carlo Fama plot the murders. Held incommunicado for nearly two weeks, Buzzo was finally released after the

International Defense League posted $5,000 bail. D'Amico and Nardone were held in jail for several months as "material witnesses" but eventually released. Greco and Carrillo, however, were indicted on July 26, 1927 and charged with premeditated murder. Unable to post $50,000 bail, Greco and Carrillo remained in jail pending their trial. Also indicted for the crime was Tresca's friend Salvatore Riccardo Linguerri, but with Tresca's help, he escaped to France to avoid a previous deportation order to Italy.[22]

Greco and Carrillo were typical rank-and-file anti-Fascists. The thirty-three-year-old Greco, Sicilian born, had fought in World War I and emigrated to the United States in 1920, working as a tailor and member of Local 63 of the ACWUA. He frequented the *Circolo Volontà* in Brooklyn, a predominantly Sicilian anarchist group that supported *L'Adunata dei Refrattari.* Carrillo, thirty-seven years old and a native of Puglia, had emigrated in 1913, returned to Italy in 1915, and spent the next three years in combat. He returned to the United States in 1919, and worked as a tailor and member of Local 149 of the ACWUA. He, too, was an anarchist, who frequented a mixed group in Brooklyn, some of whose members supported Tresca, others *L'Adunata.* Carrillo himself was a Treshiano.[23]

The similarities between Greco and Carrillo and Sacco and Vanzetti were close in most respects save for their military service. Each was a working-class Italian immigrant who believed in anarchism. Each was involved in activities associated with violence. Each was viewed as a threat—real or potential—by the Italian government, the Italian-American middle class, and American governmental and law enforcement authorities. However, by the summer of 1927, the cause of Greco and Carrillo was placed on hold as world attention riveted on the final days of the "good shoe maker" and the "poor fish peddler."

Execution of Sacco and Vanzetti

On April 9, 1927, Judge Webster Thayer sentenced Sacco and Vanzetti to die in the electric chair on August 23, 1927. Tresca once again became a highly-visible figure in the defense campaign. He disagreed with the Sacco-Vanzetti Defense Committee's belief that the pressure of public opinion could still save the condemned men, arguing that only a nation-wide general strike could wrest Sacco and Vanzetti from the executioner. He aligned himself with the Sacco-Vanzetti Emergency Committee, dominated by the communists, because it advocated liberating the prisoners through direct action. Tresca was the principal Italian speaker at the mass rallies held by the Emergency Committee in Union Square and other meeting places, always urging workers to take to the streets. That Tresca seriously believed a general strike would materialize on August 22, 1927 is highly doubtful, but he continued to agitate nonetheless.[24]

On July 21, 1927, the Lowell Committee, appointed by Massachusetts Governor Alvan T. Fuller to examine the case and render an "unbiased" judgment, pronounced Sacco and Vanzetti guilty and fairly tried after a farcical "investigation." Then, on August 3, 1927, having completed an equally bogus "investigation," Fuller denied clemency. Petitions for a writ of *habeas corpus* to the U.S. Supreme Court and several lower courts were all rejected. On August 19, 1927, Tresca, Aldino Felicani, Sacco's wife Rosina, playwright Dorothy Parker, and a host of other supporters met Vanzetti's sister, Luigia, when she arrived in New York aboard the *Aquitania*. Certain that Luigia's supplications would not move Fuller, Tresca remained in New York to continue agitating for a general strike. On August 20, Tresca published his final appeal to "desert the factories and abandon the mines on the day the executioner gets ready to do his work."[25] But on the day appointed for mass agitation, August 22, only a few cities experienced protest demonstrations. The American working class went about its business as though nothing of importance was happening. Tresca's daughter Beatrice, who joined her father at *Il Martello*'s office that day, recalled how the atmosphere was laden with silent tension. Tresca, exhibiting anxiety by tugging at his beard and running his fingers through his hair, was lost in private thoughts he never recorded for posterity.[26] By nightfall, after eleventh hour appeals proved futile, Tresca and thousands of other supporters of Sacco and Vanzetti knew that nothing could save them. The long Calvary of the two Italian anarchists ended at twenty-six minutes after midnight, August 23, 1927.[27]

Il Martello's first issue following the execution featured a graphic drawing of Justice crucified alongside of Sacco and Vanzetti.[28] This well-known illustration by Fort Velona captured the sentiments of the Italian immigrant Left. Many *sovversivi* had clung desperately to the hope that justice would somehow prevail, that human decency and compassion would intervene at the final hour and stay the executioner's hand. So when political necessity and revenge triumphed over justice and mercy, the *sovversivi* reeled in shock, as though a pulse from the death current had passed through the entire movement. *Il Martello*'s financial agent, Giuseppe Popolizio, described the impact of the executions: "The blow for us proletarians was so terrible that we are stunned and seem to be dreaming and going mad. We lack the strength to speak and cry out because we feel paralyzed."[29] The Sacco-Vanzetti case and its cruel dénouement inflicted a deep and incurable wound on the spirit of the Italian immigrant Left.

For Tresca, the absence of working-class response deepened his disillusionment with the American proletariat.[30]

The Trial of Greco and Carrillo

Tresca's mission after the execution of Sacco and Vanzetti was to ensure that Greco and Carrillo did not share the same fate. He believed that the Fascists' ardent desire to see Greco and Carrillo convicted represented a new strategy. After the police failed to implicate him and Vacirca in the Memorial Day murder, the Fascists may have had become fearful that direct attempts to frame well-known anti-Fascists might spur American elements to organize greater opposition to their efforts to suppress Italian American opponents. By targeting two obscure workers, the Fascist League hoped to undermine support for anti-Fascism by demonstrating the vulnerability of rank-and-file workers to Fascist retaliation. This strategy might also generate action against anti-Fascist leaders indirectly and more inconspicuously.[31]

Thaon di Revel, too, regarded the Greco-Carrillo case as a high-stakes undertaking for the Fascist League. He boasted publicly that "the massacre of our comrades will signal the end of anti-Fascism in America."[32] What Thaon di Revel did not reveal to fellow Blackshirts was his awareness that the trial outcome could cut both ways. He informed Mussolini at the end of August: "Its outcome will be a great victory or a terrible moral defeat for us."[33] Prospects for a "great victory" seemed excellent at the time of his report. The anti-Fascists were not only deeply demoralized by the execution of Sacco and Vanzetti, they were still immersed in their habitual sectarian squabbles. Greco and Carrillo expressed their desire for a defense committee that would include representatives of all radical groups, but such a body proved impossible to assemble. The Galleanisti, for example, did not want Tresca to serve on the defense committee. But Tresca—"the first to rush to the aid of the accused and to organize a strong defense for them," according to Carrillo—bypassed the contentious factions, and with the help of Norman Thomas organized a Greco-Carrillo Defense Committee, comprising cooperative Italian anti-Fascists like Giovannitti and Vacirca and many prominent Americans of liberal, socialist, and communist persuasion, including Robert Morss Lovett, the pacifist president of the League for Industrial Democracy, Upton Sinclair, Oswald Garrison Villard, Benjamin Gitlow, and the Trotskyist secretary of the International Labor Defense, James P. Cannon.[34]

Tresca feared that the dangers confronting Greco and Carrillo were worse in some ways than those Sacco and Vanzetti had faced. Many Italian Americans outside of the radical movement had identified with and supported Sacco and Vanzetti as victims of racial prejudice. But Greco and Carrillo were being prosecuted not as Italians, but as anti-Fascists. The broad mass of apolitical Italian immigrants, therefore, was unlikely to be concerned over their fate, while the Fascists and pro-Fascists were certain to utilize their resources against them. The anti-Fascists had to fight this battle alone.[35] Tresca also cautioned against complacency because Greco and Carrillo would be tried in New York rather than in a small town with provincial prejudices like Dedham, Massachusetts, where Sacco and Vanzetti had been condemned. True, he noted, New York was not Dedham, but the Bronx was not New York:

> It is a part of New York where the Fascists have concentrated their forces and with impunity traffic in fascistized judges and district attorneys of Italian original, while outside the courtroom and along the crooked paths of political meddling intrigues a priest [Father Cafuzzi] who is more Fascist than Mussolini. The Bronx may become the Dedham of New York if we delude ourselves in the hope that here, by being more vigilant than in Massachusetts, certain crimes cannot be committed in the name of the law.[36]

Tresca recommended a different legal strategy: anti-Fascists must put the Fascists on trial and demonstrate how Greco and Carrillo were being persecuted at the behest of Mussolini."[37] Yet even if the Fascist conspiracy to frame them were exposed, Tresca knew that the fate of Greco and Carrillo would ultimately be determined by impressionable jurors whom a skilled prosecutor could manipulate.

So Tresca, the "fixer," personally obtained the finest legal talent available. He enlisted his good friend Arthur Garfield Hays, the general counsel of the ACLU, who together with Isaac Shorr and Newman Levy directed the Greco-Carrillo defense until November 1927. Still concerned, Tresca insisted that the legal team include America's greatest criminal lawyer, Clarence Darrow. Tresca himself telephoned Darrow from Hays' office, convinced him to accept the case, and personally guarantied the $10,000 fee Darrow demanded as a retainer—despite not having $1.50 in his pocket to compensate Hays for the long-distance call, much less the $10,000 for Darrow's fee.[38]

The propaganda battle, meanwhile, had turned in favor of Greco and Carrillo, largely due to Tresca's strategy of taking the fight to the Fascists. In September 1927, the New York Graphic, a tabloid whose editor was an acquaintance of Tresca's, published a series of articles (probably with Tresca's input) condemning Mussolini's government, the State Department, Carlo Vinti and the Fascist League, the Bronx District Attorney, and the New York Police Department for conspiring to frame Greco and Carrillo.[39] Then, on November 2, Tresca issued a statement to The New York Times, charging the Bronx District Attorney, John E. McGeehan, with having relied upon the Fascist League for the preparation of his case.[40] Confirmation of Tresca's accusation was available in Il Progresso, which had boasted at the outset that information and assistance from the Fascist League had been crucial to the investigation and arrest of Greco and Carrillo.[41] Irregularities in the investigation, meanwhile, were becoming more apparent. McGeehan delayed the trial on the grounds that the police were still trying to locate a third suspect, but he refused to name him on the grounds that to do so would violate the law. If so, why had the Italian pro-Fascist press been able to identify the indicted suspect as Tresca's friend, Linguerri, and publish a police bulletin with his photograph and a biographical sketch?[42] Who, Tresca asked, had furnished this information? Disclosures of this kind proved that a direct pipeline existed between the NYPD and the Fascist League. Yet, exposure of this collusion only prompted McGeehan to declare that "the State hopes to have the defendants in the death house at Sing Sing before Christmas."[43]

Greco and Carrillo went on trial at Bronx County Court on December 9, 1927, charged with the murder of Giuseppe Carisi. (Their indictment for the murder of Amoroso was held in abeyance pending the outcome of this trial.) The defense team—described by Mussolini's Il Popolo d'Italia as "a true judeo-masonic representation"—included Darrow, Hays, Shorr, Levy, and Carolyn Weiss King. The prosecutor was Assistant District Attorney Albert Henderson; the trial judge was Albert Cohn, an appointee of the Democratic Party machine at Tammany Hall and the father of Roy Cohn, Senator Joseph McCarthy's top aid in the 1950s. The impartiality and integrity of the presiding magistrate was considered crucial for the defense, as everyone associated with the case remembered how Judge Thayer had done everything in his power to condemn Sacco and Vanzetti to the electric chair. Having a Jew preside over the case was welcomed as "a hope at least of justice!," Robert Morss Lovett recalled. And when four Jews were selected as jurors, "we considered the case won."[44]

Fascists in Rome experienced a similar reaction. Two days after the trial began, *Il Popolo d'Italia* expressed fear that a conviction was already in doubt:

[It] is impossible to foresee the outcome of the trial when the insidious plot of hate conducted by the small but ferocious nucleus of anti-Fascists is at work, fomented and aided by the judeo-masonic-communist gang allied with vile Italian renegades like Tresca, Dr. Fama, and Vacirca. Some unexpected turn of events may occur.[45]

In fact, a shift of opinion favoring the defendants became evident when the conservative *The New York Times* acknowledged the political nature of the case: "the trial gave indications… of being much more than the mere 'day in court' of two unknown young men charged with the murder of a man as little known as they."[46] The illustrious caliber of the defense attorneys, the presence of policemen in the courthouse, and the great number of Italian Americans seeking entry as observers all contributed to a feeling that "Fascismo and its enemies have crossed swords above the heads of the two defendants."[47]

Tresca's plan to put the Fascists on trial was implemented by Hays, whose opening statement charged that the police had connived criminally with the Fascist League to arrest and convict Greco and Carrillo solely because they were anti-Fascists. Detective Caso desired to please the Fascist League so that he and his associates would "get something in honors from the Italian Government if they could get someone."[48] Darrow conducted the cross-examination of prosecution witnesses. He handily dissected several Fascist "eye witnesses," like Alessandro Rocco, one of the founders of the Fascist League and the organizer of the *Fascio Mario Sonzini*, demonstrating that their testimony was fabricated. A potentially damaging eye-witness was a peddler named Luigi Alfano, who had no political inclinations and was presumed unbiased. To the consternation of the prosecutor, Alfano, who initially had expressed certainty that Greco was one of the assailants, now testified under cross-examination by Darrow that he was doubtful of his original identification. Alfano also revealed that it was Vinti, not the police, who first learned that he had witnessed the crime, and that he and Rocco had brought him to a private meeting with Caso. The detective showed him photographs of various anti-Fascists, including Greco, and for several days Caso, Vinti, Rocco, and Alfano went to Brooklyn, where they secretly observed Greco going to and from work. These improper methods of investigation were responsible for Alfano's original identification. Darrow thus established what anti-Fascists had asserted from the outset—the Bronx police had acted in concert with the Fascist League. The prosecution's last witness was Umberto De Simone, the spy who had infiltrated Tresca's office. Questioned by ADA Henderson, De Simone explained that he was a Fascist League member and had joined the AFANA in order to keep Tresca and other anti-Fascists under surveillance. Simone also acknowledged that it was he who provided the information that led to the arrest of Greco and Carrillo. Darrow made short work of the spy. "You mean that you are a Fascist," he queried, "and that you joined the other group to get information? That you are a Fascist spy?" "Yes," replied De Simone. After that unsavory admission, the State rested its case.[49]

The chief "eye witness" for the defense was the dissident Fascist Giacomo Caldora, whose motive for testifying probably was hostility toward Thaon di Revel and the Fascist League rather than disapproval of their criminal methods. Under Hay's questioning, Caldora explained that he had founded the *Allenza Fascista Il Duce* because Thaon di Revel and the Fascist League were "a bunch of criminals." He allegedly reached this conclusion after learning that the Fascist League planned to bomb Tresca's office and had previously been responsible for the Harlem bomb explosion intended for Tresca in September 1926. As for the Memorial Day murders, Caldora claimed to have witnessed the killing of both Carisi and Amoroso and swore adamantly that Greco and Carrillo were not among the attackers. About ten days after the crime, while examining photographs of Greco, Carrillo, Buzzi, D'Amico, Linguerri, and other anti-Fascists provided by Detective Caso, Vinti urged him to identify them as the murderers. Vinti offered Caldora $5,000 if he would accuse these anti-Fascists of having arrived on the scene in an automobile belonging to Dr. Charles Fama. Caldora further alleged that Vinti indicated to him that new orders had been issued "to take care of Tresca." But neither money nor the aspersions cast upon his fidelity to Fascism, Caldora declared, could persuade him to cooperate with the frame-up hatched by the Fascist League and the Bronx police.[50]

When Greco and Carillo took the witness stand, they were not cajoled into revealing their anarchist affiliations, as Sacco and Vanzetti had been. Identified by prosecutor and defense attorneys simply as "anti-Fascists," both swore that on the fatal morning of May 30 they were in Brooklyn, spending Sunday in their usual fashion: Carrillo at home with his wife and son; Greco in his brother's music shop, located in their home. The defense had no difficulty producing witnesses to corroborate their alibis.[51] Luckily, neither Judge Cohn nor the jurors drew the conclusion that had nullified the testimony of Italian defense witnesses for Sacco and Vanzetti, i.e., that "all Wops stick together." Darrow then scored an emotional triumph for the defense when he summoned Greco's mother as a character witness. After relating her story, "she turned to the judge and asked with motherly affection and womanly dignity, 'Please, may I embrace my son?'" Greco, who had controlled his emotions until now, burst into tears. And at that moment, Darrow recalled, "there were few eyes in that courtroom that were not equally affected."[52]

Hays in his summation expressed outrage that Greco and Carrillo had been targeted by the police to satisfy the Fascists' desire for revenge. The real villains in this sinister drama were Detective Caso, Thaon di Revel, and Carlo Vinti, "the Machiavelli of the plot." Vinti had spent every day of the trial at the district attorney's office, where "as a general he worked behind the lines, sending individuals to the judicial front to do battle for the Fascist cause." Hays insisted, therefore, that Greco and Carrillo were not only innocent but had been "framed by the Fascist League of North America, [and] that the district attorney, perhaps unwittingly, had been the tool of the Fascist organization."[53] Darrow's lengthy summation closed with an appeal to free the two men "who loved freedom and hated despotism and who therefore hate Mussolini because the name of Mussolini throughout the world today stands as another name for despotism." The jury deliberated for nearly eight hours and returned a verdict of "not guilty" on December 23, 1927.[54]

To celebrate the victory, Tresca organized a party at the Venetian Gardens restaurant, where he honored the two anti-Fascists and their defense attorneys. Asked to speak, Darrow declared that he would have defended Greco and Carrillo even if he had known them to be guilty because of the political nature of the murders. He placed responsibility for the crime at Mussolini's feet.[55] Then Darrow motioned for Tresca to come to the podium, declaring, "It is he who you must applaud, not me. It was he who saved Greco and Carillo from the electric chair. Without him my work would have been worthless."[56] In accord with Darrow's assessment, *The Nation* elected Tresca to its 1927 "Honor Roll" for his paramount role in the Greco-Carillo Case.

Fascist Reactions

Mussolini's *Il Popolo d'Italia* reacted to the acquittal with an outburst of rage, self-pity, and demands for pitiless revenge.[57] Consul General Grazzi reported to the Duce that the verdict was due entirely to "the behavior of a few Fascists and especially Mr. Carlo Vinti who prejudiced the outcome of the trial." Motivated by "stupid ambition and an irresponsible craze for notoriety," Vinti had obstructed the consulate's own efforts to assist the investigation, spending thousands of dollars of Fascist League's money to pursue suspects single-handedly. By boasting to Italian-American newspapers that the prosecution had resulted from his efforts, Vinti "irresponsibly played into the hands of the subversives who wanted to demonstrate that the charges against their comrades resulted from a fascist plot for which local police were the instrument." All this "greatly influenced the outcome of the trial, and the Prosecutor... could not remove from the jurors' minds the belief that Greco and Carrillo were innocent victims of a fascist vendetta." Consequently, while the trial

> did not avenge the two martyrs of the fascist idea barbarously murdered, it did, unfortunately, benefit the subversives, who were able not only to raise considerable funds under the usual pretext of [financing] a "defense committee," but also to intensify their propaganda in Italian American neighborhoods and to present the activities of the Fascist League in an unfavorable light.[58]

Exploiting the acquittal to enhance his own power, Consul General Grazzo urged the new secretary-general of the *Fasci all'Estero*, Piero Parini, to conduct "a purification of the Fascist League."[59]

From the perspective of Rome, instead of the "great victory" the Fascists had anticipated, the Greco-Carrillo case ended in the "terrible moral defeat" that Thaon di Revel had warned Mussolini was a possible outcome. The adverse publicity generated by the Fascist League's campaign to frame Greco and Carrillo had elevated Fascism from an issue significant only to a minority subculture among Italian-Americans to a source of concern for increasing numbers of mainstream Americans. Rome's biggest worry, of course, was whether the irresponsible and uncontrolled antics of the Fascist League might jeopardize Mussolini's advantageous relationship with the United States. Although the Duce's sterling reputation with Anglo-Saxons remained untarnished by the case, a few American officials, such as the State Department solicitor, concluded that the Fascist League's activities were "most undesirable," and warned that the United States was facing a "serious matter" if Thaon de Revel and the Fascist League were urging naturalized Italians to retain their allegiance to Italy.[60] Responding to Ambassador De Martino's promise to stop any activities disapproved of by the American government, Under-Secretary of State William R. Castle requested information about the Fascist League from J. Edgar Hoover. FBI files contained nothing about the Fascist League.[61] This was hardly surprising, since the FBI director's eyes focused in one direction only— left.

The death knell for the Fascist League was eventually sounded by the publication of Marcus Duffield's article, "Mussolini's American Empire: The Fascist Invasion of the United States," in *Harper's Magazine* of November 1929.[62] Based on information provided by Fascists and anti-Fascists alike (Tresca claimed "it was inspired in large part by us"),[63] Duffield's article created a sensation, exposing the remarkable extent to which Mussolini's regime controlled the Italian-American community, enforcing allegiance and support. Duffield's revelations and the ensuing demands for congressional investigations signaled to Rome that the Fascist League had outlived its usefulness. On December 31, 1929, on orders from Mussolini, the Fascist League was disbanded and all of its records shipped to Rome, lest any subsequent investigation conducted by the Americans reveal the true degree to which the organization had functioned as an instrument of Fascist foreign policy and propaganda.[64] The heyday of Italian-American Blackshirts had now irretrievably passed. The future lay with more "respectable" Fascists and pro-Fascists.

17

Troubled Times for Anti-Fascism

The 1920s had ended victoriously for anti-Fascism with the acquittal of Greco and Carrillo and the disbanding of the Fascist League. Yet within a few years the resistance was floundering in crisis and decline. "To deny this is for us to close our eyes," Tresca declared.[1] This decline was attributable to the weakness and disarray of the radical movement upon which anti-Fascism was based. The anarchists were divided by the conflict between *L'Adunata* and Tresca; they would never regain the key role they had played in the early days of the resistance. Social democrats were likewise in trouble. Membership of the FSI (SP) had declined to 400 in 1929 from around 800–900 in 1920; its following remained static thereafter.[2] The Italian labor unions were experiencing grave financial difficulties because of the Great Depression and terminated their subsidies to *Il Nuovo Mondo*, which ceased publication in 1931, after its purchase by conservatives secretly in league with the consul general. The anti-Fascist daily was resurrected by the social democrats as *La Stampa Libera* in 1931 but barely survived. The few remaining Italian syndicalists of the IWW still clung to a tenuous existence but did little more than publish *Il Proletario*. The communists, too, faced dire times in the early 1930s. Their major organ, *Il Lavoratore*, folded in 1931 but was replaced in 1932 with *L'Unità Operaia*. Unlike the other *sovversivi*, however, the communists would recover and increase their strength. The Italian Bureau of the CP, which had numbered around 1,000 members during the mid-1920s and then declined by the end of the decade, successfully recruited new members by the mid-1930s, chiefly among American born Italians rather than older generation immigrants, a development stimulated by the Spanish Civil War.[3]

Numerous factors accounted for the decline of the Italian immigrant Left. Certainly one of the most serious weaknesses that plagued Italian radicalism after World War I was insularity, the inability of the *sovversivi* to establish an important presence and influence outside the boundaries of their own subculture. Tresca consider the anarchists particularly derelict in this regard: "We *sovversivi*— especially the anarchists—have always remained with our heads in Italy and our feet in America." Anarchists awaited the social revolution, convinced of its inevitability, sometimes ecstatic at the thought of participating in it themselves. Nevertheless, "we anarchists have been closed within a cul de sac…paying little attention to the environment in which we live…. Without turning our backs on the universal front of class war, we must give maximum effort to the U.S. sector, where our efforts may have the most productive effect."[4] Like most of Tresca's suggestions for remedial activity, this one was ignored.

Worse than isolation and internecine conflict was the relentless march of time. The Italian immigrant Left by the 1930s was dying out, and the departed were not being replaced. Migration from Italy had virtually ceased, limiting the infusion of new blood to a handful of exiles. Also, Italian radicalism failed to produce a new generation that shared the ideals and revolutionary aspirations of its parents. But the key factor draining the vitality and resources of anti-Fascism in the 1930s was the Great Depression. A movement that derived its political following and financial support primarily from workers could not surmount the consequences of economic disaster, unemployment above all. The *sovversivi* appear to have been particularly vulnerable to job loss because—as the Fascists noted with great satisfaction—they were often the first to be laid off by employers seeking to eliminate "trouble makers" from their labor force.[5] Finally, there was no escaping the reality that the *sovversivi* steadily lost influence as Mussolini and Fascism progressively gained admiration and support. Even the gains achieved by the communists in the late 1930s did not redress the disproportion between anti-Fascists and pro-Fascists. Indeed, there can be no disputing the accuracy of Rudolph J. Vecoli's contention that the interwar years represented the progressive "Fascistization" of Italian American communities.[6]

Fascism on the March

What caused Tresca great concern in the early 1930s was not only the debilitated state of anti-Fascism but the precipitous pace at which Fascism was gaining ground, as supporters proliferated in all spheres of the Italian-American community. Admiration for Mussolini among Italian Americans would reach its pinnacle when Italy conquered Ethiopia in 1935–1936. However, the rapid ascendance of Mussolini's prestige and popularity among average, apolitical Italian Americans really gained momentum when the Duce signed the Concordat and Lateran Accord with the Vatican on February 11, 1929. How could most Italian Americans not respond with awe and approval for the Blackshirt hailed by Pope Pius XI as "the man sent to us by Providence?"[7]

Tresca regarded the alliance between Church and State as the inevitable outcome of a process long in the making, one calculated for their mutual benefit. Mussolini had courted the Catholic Church ever since he jettisoned Fascism's original anti-clerical program in 1920. The Papacy, in turn, had regarded Fascism from its inception as Europe's bulwark against Bolshevism. All Tresca and the anti-Fascists could do in the face Mussolini's masterful coup in 1929 was to underscore the sheer hypocrisy of his behavior—he, a former atheist and anti-cleric, who had once challenged God to strike him dead to prove his existence, now stooped to kiss the ring of a pope. But branding Mussolini a hypocrite and traitor for his embrace of the Church made no impression on the apolitical Italian-immigrant working class.[8]

Fascist penetration in the United States, Tresca observed, had entered a "new phase" by the late 1920s and early 1930s, one he feared would be more difficult for anti-Fascists to resist than the *squadrismo* of the Blackshirts.[9] Tresca's analysis was remarkably accurate, even prescient. In February 1928, Tresca declared that Thaon de Revel and other chieftains of the Fascist League had been reduced to second string players. "The Fascist army here must abandon the open field. Daggers, clubs, dynamite have created poor results; the insidious campaign must be given to Consul General Grazzi, with New York the chosen battlefield."[10] The "general staff" of the "Mussolinian militia" in America had passed from the Fascist League to the ambassador, the consuls, and vice consuls. "They hope to render more secure and effective the assistance of the American authorities in case of need; they believe by so doing to be able to give to Mussolini's will, which is that of subjugating the immigrant masses to fascist domination, a character of greater trustworthiness and responsibility," he explained. If they succeeded, as Tresca feared, "the anti-Fascists will have to confront a fascist state allied with American authorities."[11]

With the Italian Ambassador serving as chief propagandist and ultimate enforcer, the primary objective of this revised Fascist policy, Tresca accurately asserted, was consular control over mutual aid (Sons of Italy) and cultural societies (Dante Alighieri, Casa Italiana, Italian Historical Society) social clubs (*Tiro a Segno*), Italian schools, the Italian Hospital, orphanages, and other organizations capable of disseminating Fascist propaganda and providing financial support for Mussolini's regime. Newly established Fascist organizations, such as the Lictor Federation, would also fall under the purview of the ambassador and consul general of New York. Highest on the immediate agenda was the re-unification of the Order of the Sons of Italy and its control by trusted Fascists, a task Consul General Grazzi of New York would assign to Supreme Venerable Giovanni Di Silvestro and Judge John J. Freschi, Grand Venerable for the state of New York.[12] "This methodical work of penetration, willed by Mussolini, to which the ambassador and consuls will devote themselves, with the help of priests, must be resisted," Tresca declared.[13]

Tresca and the AFANA

Opposing Fascist penetration had become more difficult by this period, as the lack of unity among anti-Fascists worsened in the wake of the AFANA schism. Affiliation with the AFANA had become a vexing issue for Tresca. He maintained his ties for more than a year after the schism, urging anti-Fascists incessantly to cease their internecine struggles and resurrect a united front, if only on an *ad hoc* basis. But even Tresca had difficulty adhering to his own recommendations, because these years marked the beginning of the end of his collaboration with the communists, who had achieved control of the AFANA by the end of the 1920s. Ironically, Tresca was becoming increasingly critical of the communists at the very time other anarchists intensified attacks against him for associating with them.[14]

In the summer of 1929, Tresca felt obliged to reaffirm his commitment to anarchism and clarify his position vis-à-vis the AFANA. The AFANA, Tresca explained, never became the inclusive and non-party organization he had desired. One of the main reasons for this failure was the refusal of most anarchists, especially the Galleanisti, to join a united front. Now the AFANA was merely "a branch of the Communist Party."[15] But, if that were the case, why was Tresca still a member? He gave two reasons: the leaders and rank-and-file of the AFANA had asked him to remain in the organization; and he still believed that the defeat of Fascism required all anti-Fascists to act in unison.[16] This explanation, as well as his frequent assertion that "my relationship with the communists begins and ends with the AFANA,"[17] satisfied few anarchists outside the Martello group. Tresca's failure to make a clean break with the AFANA continued to give cause for serious reproach from anarchists both sympathetic and hostile to him.[18]

Eventually, Tresca's relationship with the AFANA became untenable, not only because of communist control. In January 1932, he pronounced the AFANA dead and not worthy of resurrection.[19] Tresca's break with the AFANA had been signaled six months earlier when he, Allegra, the socialist Alberto Cupelli, and the republican Mario Carrara formed the *Comitato d'Azione Anti-Fascista* to accomplish what the AFANA had failed to do.[20] But the divided and fractious nature of the anti-Fascist movement ensured that the *Comitato d'Azione* would never create a united front, or even extend its sway beyond the small number of anti-Fascists who founded it. Soon it was supplanted by the *Comitato Antifascista Italiano*, another organization like the AFANA, purporting to represent a united front.

Tresca relations with the communists, previously based on pragmatic necessity, had become increasingly strained as he gradually distanced himself from the AFANA. Even close collaboration with the communists had never deterred him from criticizing the Soviet Union and Stalinism, and during the late 1920s he frequently warned anti-Fascists to resist the dictatorship that communists would seek to impose in Italy once Mussolini was overthrown.[21] By 1930, Tresca began expressing his opposition to the communists more vehemently and openly, expressing hope that Stalin's regime would be overthrown and the march of Russian revolution resumed.[22] Finally, by the end of 1931, following repeated attempts by the communists to sabotage the initiatives of other anti-Fascists, Tresca declared: "With the Muscovites no understanding is possible."[23]

Throughout the 1920s, the attitude of the communists toward Tresca had been one of grudging respect and cynical opportunism. Vidali, the former secretary of the Italian Bureau of the CP and Tresca's close collaborator, wrote in his secret reports to the CP in 1928: "Carlo Tresca, more than an anarchist, is a romantic revolutionary and a thoroughly cunning rogue.... His influence comes from his long career as a subversive, his courage, his unrelenting activity, his politics [which are] appropriate for the colonial mentality, and his weekly [*Il Martello*]."[24] Although Tresca had been an invaluable ally in the AFANA, Vidali had anticipated a change in that relationship:

> We will never fail to make the comrades understand that the moment may come when it is necessary to fight him.... However, it is necessary that the moment matures. One of our polemics [against him] that is not understood by the masses could ruin us, and even if it would be just, it would not be "tactical." We must reorganize the movement and place Tresca in a clear position, understood by the masses. When he abandons this position our polemic will be understood.[25]

Once their *de facto* alliance began to crumble, the communists turned up the heat as Vidali had recommended. When Tresca warned that the communists would represent a new threat of oppression in Italy after Mussolini's fall, the party organ *Il Lavoratore* snidely referred to him as "the Rope-Dancer," and declared that only the communists were capable of resisting Fascism in Italy.[26] Communist attacks against Tresca, by Americans as well as Italians, become more slanderous by 1932. In a typical accusation, an American communist professor declared that "Tresca is an individualist, owner of a newspaper, rich, and in league with enemies of the working class."[27] Over the next few years the polemical exchanges between Tresca and the communists would become far more vitriolic and hateful.

L'Adunata on the Attack

Communist barbs directed against Tresca in this period were blunt and painless compared to the defamation campaign waged by *L'Adunata dei Refrattari*. Tresca had always acknowledged the right of anarchists to criticize his pro-AFANA position if they did so for ideological reasons and refrained from personal attacks. But the distinction between ideology and character assassination held no meaning for the Galleanisti of *L'Adunata*, in whom the anti-Tresca virus grew more virulent with each passing year. When Galleani, in May 1925, privately exhorted his followers to destroy Tresca, the *L'Adunatisti* assumed the mission with fanatical zeal and determination. Their hostility for Tresca had already manifested when they declared him a heretic for allegedly shaking hands with President Coolidge. At the end of 1926, their animus was stoked red hot when Tresca blamed Galleani's dictatorial influence as the primary cause for the weakness and ineffectiveness of Italian anarchists in the United States.[28] However, it was Tresca's leadership role in the AFANA, especially because it enhanced his prestige among anti-Fascists, which provided fresh ammunition for the *L'Adunatisti*'s campaign to destroy his reputation and standing. Articles and letters lambasting Tresca for his role in the anti-Fascist alliance, and his association with the communists appeared regularly in *L'Adunata*, each one replete with personal denunciation and references to the famous "handshake" and his new designations, "the guest of the White House," and "*Carlo Pagnacca*."[29]

This campaign intensified when the renowned anarcho-syndicalist Armando Borghi arrived in the United States in November 1926. Many anarchists assumed that Borghi and Tresca would collaborate and strengthen the anarchist movement. But from the outset Borghi aligned himself with *L'Adunata*—an unnatural alliance that Borghi eventually came to regret—and began to attack Tresca for his participation in the AFANA and his collaboration with communists.[30] It was transparent that Borghi's attacks were motivated by more than a difference of opinion regarding anarchist association with the AFANA and the communists. Borghi's ego and sense of entitlement were critical factors. Having ranked second only to the legendary Malatesta in Italy, Borghi presumed he would be the foremost Italian anarchist in the United States. Tresca was in his way. As one veteran anarchist put, "For Borghi, Tresca has become an obsession!"[31] Very soon Borghi's attacks shifted from the ideological to the personal, suggesting that Tresca was a "spy" for the Soviet Union and received money directly from Moscow. Tresca responded with a blistering article at the end of 1929, declaring to Borghi that "you are affected by megalomania. You think the world revolves humbly around you."[32] He recounted how Borghi, upon his arrival in the United States, had visited him at the office of *Il Martello*—before "*L'Adunata* made him a prisoner"—and embraced Tresca with a kiss on the cheeks. This was "the Kiss of Judas."[33]

Coping with Borghi's attacks was difficult enough, but soon Tresca had to contend with the hysterical accusations of Galleani's fanatical acolyte, Emilio Coda, whose personal hatred of Tresca bordered on the pathological. Coda, who as secretary of the Sacco-Vanzetti Defense Committee had excluded Tresca from its affairs, assumed the role of chief slanderer and libeler in February 1928, after Tresca dared "to attribute deficiencies to Galleani whose name he contaminates merely by pronouncing it."[34] Included among the expletives in Coda's verbal barrage was the cryptic word "*Pagnacca*," a code word for a spy.[35] Undeterred by the skepticism voiced by other anarchists, Coda concluded this latest phase of *L'Adunata*'s smear campaign by convening a "Jury of Honor" in Hartford, Connecticut, on May 13, 1928, to try Tresca *in absentia* for his "crimes." With the exception of Felice Guadagni, the respected syndicalist who had served on the Sacco-Vanzetti Defense Committee, the "Jury of Honor" consisted of six Galleanisti personally selected by Coda. Its published verdict (Guadagni refused to sign it), stated: "after the serene documentary statement delivered by Coda, the indisputable corroboration by other depositions from comrades worthy of trust, and the evaluation of Tresca's own absence,...the accusations are found to be more than verified."[36]

Tresca was greatly disappointed that most Italian anarchists failed to rally to his defense. The aura of infallibility with which Galleani had enveloped himself and his disciples still dissuaded many anarchists from dissenting with the gospel preached in the pulpit of *L'Adunata*. It was mainly non-Italian anarchists who recognized the malignant intent of the slander campaign. Emma Goldman wrote to a friend: "I feel that the accusations against Carlo Tresca are false and... prompted by personal motives. I have known Carlo Tresca for many years.... To claim that he is a spy is absurd."[37] Alexander Berkman, responding to a letter from *L'Adunata*'s administrator, Osvaldo Maraviglia, condemning Tresca as a "spy" and "worse than a communist," wrote: "I must say that the whole thing... makes me very sad. Our whole movement is eaten by an ulcer, which corrodes the best elements and almost paralyses all real work.... I refer here to charges, counter-charges, incriminations and recriminations which fill our movement with filth, in almost every country."[38] Malatesta, the greatest living anarchist, now residing in Rome under house arrest, wrote to *L'Adunata*, expressing his "pain and disgust" over the polemics tearing apart the movement in the United States. "It is painful in a moment when concord and unity are more necessary than ever that men who basically fight for the same cause waste their power attacking each other in a most indecent manner." Polemics, formerly engaged in purposes of exchanging and clarifying ideas, are now "violent and outrageous attacks inspired only by hatred, rancor, and other bad passions." "To overcome an adversary they seek not the best arguments and probative facts, but the most obscene, insulting, and bloody words." "Frankly, the situation is unbearable. I am surprised to find myself thinking that in the case of a revolution these men, thinking perhaps sincerely that they were serving the interests of the revolution, would seek to guillotine each other." Malatesta pleaded that personal polemics cease.[39] The only response to Malatesta's plea came from Galleani's chief disciple and *L'Adunata*'s director since 1928, Raffaele Schiavina (a.k.a. "Max Sartin," a.k.a. "Bruno"), who wrote: "comrade Malatesta may be uninformed about what goes on abroad."[40]

Tresca, unfortunately, never heeded the advice of Allegra and other close associates who urged him to treat *L'Adunata*'s accusations as too ridiculous to dignify with a response.[41] He continued to retaliate against his detractors with each new accusation, demanding they either prove him a spy or desist.[42] They did neither. Since *L'Adunata*'s objective was not to prove Tresca a spy but to destroy his standing in the anarchist movement, the smear campaign continued unabated.[43] Hoping to end the cycle of attack and counter-attack, Tresca announced a unilateral cessation of hostilities: "for me the personal polemic is finished."[44] But not even a truce, much less peace, could be secured from *L'Adunata*, with the newspaper now under Schiavina's control. Just as sectarian and unforgiving as his master, Schiavina would become Tresca's most implacable enemy among the Galleanisti, availing himself of every opportunity to invigorate the campaign against him.[45]

The Fascists, meanwhile, had been carefully monitoring the conflict between the Galleanisti and Tresca, recognizing that the anti-Tresca campaign not only created havoc within the anarchist movement but also weakened the anti-Fascist resistance as a whole. Mussolini's political police expressed delight when the "Jury of Honor" rendered its verdict of "guilty." They concluded that "anti-Fascism, which is headed in America by Carlo Tresca, has received a terrible blow. Its major exponent has been definitely liquidated."[46] Fascist hopes became less sanguine when confidential agents reported that the downfall of Tresca and *Il Martello* should not be anticipated any time soon, "because there are too many people who swear upon the innocence of Tresca despite all the warnings [of *L'Adunata*]."[47] Nonetheless, the Fascists remained encouraged by *L'Adunata*'s relentless campaign, hoping that "the definitive liquidation of Carlo Tresca, imposed upon his followers as well, would administer a moral blow to anti-Fascism which depends so much on Tresca."[48]

There can be no doubt that *L'Adunata*'s smear campaign succeeded in undermining Tresca's standing among the Italian-American anarchists. Outside of the anarchist camp, anti-Fascists considered *L'Adunata*'s accusations absurd and malicious. On May 27, 1928, a few days after Coda's Star Chamber Court pronounced its verdict, some 2,000 Italian anti-Fascists meeting at Cooper Union rose to their feet, applauding and shouting "*Viva Tresca!*" and "*Parli Tresca!*" (Let Tresca speak!),[49] when Giovannitti made a passing reference to him. The poet Nino Caradonna expressed the general consensus when he wrote that *L'Adunata*'s campaign "had been launched with the firm knowledge that Tresca was not a spy, but with the sole objective of depriving Tresca of some of the fame he enjoys among the subversive element in America."[50]

Targeting More Dignitaries

Tresca's role as the "*deus ex machina*" of Italian-American anti-Fascism was secure despite attacks from the Galleanisti and the communists, and although the resistance had weakened, there remained one activity at which anti-Fascists still excelled: making life miserable for visiting Fascist dignitaries. The chief targets in the late 1920s and early 1930s were two of the most prominent hierarchs in Mussolini's regime: Italo Balbo and Dino Grandi.

Balbo, a famous pilot and Mussolini's Minister of Aviation, had come to the United States to attend the Congress of Civil Aviation in Dayton, Ohio, at the end of 1929. In the early years of Fascism, Balbo had compiled a blood-stained record as the "*Ras*" (chieftain) of Ferrara. He participated in the "March on Rome" as one of the party's *Quadrumvirs*, but his career was temporarily eclipsed when he was implicated in the murder of the anti-Fascist priest, Don Giovanni Minzoni, in August 1923. By 1929, however, his star was re-ascending as Fascism's most popular personality save for Mussolini himself.[51]

Tresca denounced Balbo as a "Fascist gangster," and declared that the Aviation Congress was "getting smeared with blood" by permitting him to attend.[52] His attacks had prompted concern in Washington, a conclusion he drew when postal authorities refused to circulate two December issues of *Il Martello*, containing inflammatory accounts of Balbo's sanguinary career.[53] Tresca called for large-scale demonstration against Balbo's arrival in New York on January 3, 1929. Meanwhile, anti-Fascists placed thousands of placards in store windows and subway cars, featuring a photo of Balbo with a caption reading: "Balbo: Wanted For Murder." After waiting six hours in the cold, 500 anti-Fascists greeted Balbo's arrival at City Hall with a chorus of boos and shouts of "*Abbasso Balbo!*" and "*Abbasso il Fascismo!*" Only the heavy cordon of policemen and bomb squad detectives prevented the anti-Fascists from gaining entry to City Hall, where Mayor Jimmy Walker bestowed the usual accolades upon the visiting Fascist official. Later that day, when various Italian-American societies treated Balbo to lunch aboard the *Vulcania* at Pier 94, an airplane flew over Manhattan, trailing a smoke signal declaring: "Balbo Murderer." Another demonstration took place that evening outside the Biltmore Hotel, where Balbo was feted by Mayor Walker, Consul General Grazzi, and a coterie of local Fascist *prominenti*.[54]

Tresca's next involvement in a protest demonstration of this magnitude occurred in November 1931, when Italy's Foreign Minister, Dino Grandi, visited the United States to confer with President Hoover and other government officials. Italy, Tresca maintained, was an economic vassal of the United States, because "Mussolini had sold her to Wall Street."[55] Although typically hyperbolic, Tresca's view of Italy derived from the fact that Mussolini's regime had been buttressed economically by multi-million dollar loans, investments, and favorable terms for war debt payments from the United States. Tresca's claim that Grandi's mission was "to pay homage to the bosses; to beg for favors; and to take orders" was not a stretch.[56]

But Grandi was no errand boy. Tresca understood that his visit reflected the high esteem in which Mussolini and his Fascist regime were held in Washington and on Wall Street. This was vividly demonstrated when Girolamo Valenti's request that President Hoover not extend Grandi an official welcome was answered with a police raid of *La Stampa Libera*, which he edited.[57] Tresca insisted, therefore, that a major protest campaign against Grandi was essential if the voice of anti-Fascism was to be heard among the official paeans to the Duce and his accomplishments. Once again, he called upon rival anti-Fascists to observe a truce and protest Grandi's visit in unison. But a united front failed to materialize even for this purpose. At a meeting at Irving Plaza on November 8, 1931, Dr. Carlo Fama, president of the Defenders of the Constitution and the most prominent anti-Fascist conservative, spoke out against using force and violence on the occasion of Grandi's visit. Communists responded by trying to break up the meeting by shouting and throwing chairs. Interpreting "united front" to mean control by the CP, the communists attempted to sabotage another meeting on November 15, even going so far as to beat up Allegra when he sought to assure them that their voice would be heard. After the communists were expelled, the remaining anti-Fascists led by Tresca and Valenti organized an International Committee on Anti-Fascism, headed by A. J. Muste, whose Conference for Progressive Labor Action was cooperating with the Italians. The communist *Daily Worker* declared that "Fascist Tools" and "labor fakers" had denied the floor to "Workers" at the meeting, which broke up when "socialist and anarchist thugs" attacked M. I. Malkin, a member of the International Labor Defense. The communists also distributed leaflets attacking Tresca and Muste, and published a manifesto branding anarchists and socialists as "traitors" and "Social Fascists." They did not cooperate with any of the demonstrations organized against Grandi, notwithstanding their call for "mass agitation."[58]

Anticipating Grandi's arrival in New York on November 20, Tresca, Valenti, Mario Carrara, Fort Velona, and Alberto Cupelli conducted open air rallies in Greenwich Village and the Bronx, denouncing the fascist foreign minister in vehement language. Those anti-Fascists eager for more direct action rampaged through Italian neighborhoods, breaking store windows that exhibited photos of Grandi, while affixing thousands of placards with Grandi's photo that declared, "This man wanted for murder and arson."[59] When Grandi arrived and was feted at City Hall, the most elaborate security precautions ever organized for a foreign dignitary were in place. More than 1,500 policemen and Bomb Squad agents presented a solid phalanx facing the several hundred anti-Fascist demonstrators assembled along Broadway near City Hall. While distributing their "Wanted for Arson and Murder" leaflets and shouting "*Assassino!*" and "*Abbasso il Fascismo!*," the anti-Fascists mingled involuntarily with several thousand Italians favorable to the foreign minister and Mussolini, who were shouting "*Viva Grandi!*" and "*Viva Mussolini!*" Undisturbed by the outbursts emanating from the throng, Grandi and Mayor Walker exchanged amenities inside the safety of City Hall. Grandi's speech sounded the theme that Mussolini's government was hyping at this juncture: "I am proud that there are so many Americans of Italian descent in this great city who have become fine and loyal citizens. They make for a permanent link between Italy and the United States."[60]

Two days later, some 350 anti-Fascists assembled at Irving Plaza to serve as the "jury" for a mock trial of Grandi, who was charged with theft, arson, and murder. Roger Baldwin of the ACLU served as the judge, Valenti was the prosecutor, and Tresca the defense attorney. *The New York Times* described the proceedings: "The defendant, a crude stuffed figure in a black shirt, with a blood-stained wooden sword in one hand and a torch in the other, sat at center of the stage. Its head was a rough caricature of Signor Grandi, and its breast covered with tin ashtrays to represent medals."[61] After the prosecution rested its case, Tresca announced that he had no witnesses to speak on Grandi's behalf; however, he put in a good word for the foreign minister nonetheless: "Grandi is a good public servant. He obeys Morgan, Lamont, Stimson, and Mussolini."[62] Found guilty, Grandi's effigy was taken to Union Square, where it was burned to shouts of approval. The trial was later recreated and broadcast on an Italian radio station.[63]

For several days, while visiting cultural sights and attending banquets with his wife, Grandi was escorted by policemen to ensure his safety from the anti-Fascists shadowing his every move. Major demonstrations occurred nevertheless at the Metropolitan Opera House and the Commodore Hotel. Returning to the "safety" and "freedom" of Fascist Italy must have come as a great relief to the beleaguered foreign minister.[64] Tresca, however, was dissatisfied with the scope and intensity of the protest demonstrations. His only satisfaction derived from the fact that Grandi could not show his face in public without a protective escort.[65]

The Easton, PA Bombing

On December 30, 1931, a bomb exploded in the post office of Easton, Pennsylvania, killing three employees and injuring several others. The bomb was one of five brought to the post office for mailing. The intended targets were Generoso Pope, the millionaire publisher of three pro-Fascist newspapers; his Fascist editor of *Il Progresso*, Italo Carlo Falbo; the Italian consul general of New York, Emanuele Grazzi; and the Argentine vice consul in Baltimore. The next day similar bombs mailed from New York were intercepted by postal authorities before delivery to the Italian consul general of Chicago, the publisher of *L'Italia*, a pro-Fascist newspaper in Chicago, the Italian vice consul of Detroit, the Italian vice consul of Cleveland, and an Italian consular agent in Youngstown.[66]

The Italian government demanded immediate action from American authorities.[67] Tresca ranked high on the FBI's and New York Bomb Squad's list of suspects. His phone at *Il Martello* was tapped and his correspondence examined by local police. Particularly suspect was a cablegram Tresca sent on November 12 to his mistress Minna Harkavy, who was visiting Moscow, that read: "Best wishes loving thoughts on birthday hoping occasion birth letter from you to us Lonnie home all well love," signed "Louis/Carlo" (Louis was Louis Harvaky, Minna's husband). The geniuses in the Bomb Squad interpreted Tresca's garbled English to be a coded message containing information relative to the Easton bombing. Transmitted by the FBI to the Intelligence Service of the War Department for "decoding," the military experts concluded that the message was precisely what it appeared to be—a birthday greeting.[68]

While Tresca's "coded message" was being deciphered, the Bomb Squad paid a visit to his office. Accustomed to such visitations whenever a bomb exploded, Tresca employed his charm and good humor to neutralize the zeal and hostility of the Bomb Squad agents. On this occasion, he observed a name tag indicating that one of the officers was of Italian descent. Asking the young fellow his surname, Tresca exclaimed that the officer's father was a friend and subscriber to *Il Martello*. Then he withdrew a bottle of whiskey from his desk drawer and proposed they drink a toast to the policeman's father. The officers all partook of the prohibited libation, shook hands with Tresca, and departed quite content.[69]

Although questioning Tresca about bombings had become routine, the FBI really suspected that this latest bombing campaign was the work of the *L'Adunata* group, with its director Schiavina functioning as the mastermind.[70] This theory was compelling because it was based on information furnished to the FBI by Umberto Caradossi, a member of the Italian secret police whose official cover was that of vice consul in New York. He had learned of the plot from a spy operating within the group. The motive for targeting consular officials was revenge for the execution of one of their own, Michele Schirru, the would-be assassin of Mussolini who was executed on May 29, 1931.[71] What neither Caradossi nor the FBI ever discovered was why a bomb had been sent to the Argentine vice consul. Most likely, he was targeted in revenge for the execution on March 28, 1931 of Severino Di Giovanni, an Italian anarchist terrorist in Argentina who was in frequent correspondence with Schiavina.[72] The FBI never found sufficient evidence to charge the *L'Adunata* group, and the case remained unsolved.

Battle for the Garibaldi Memorial, 1932

June 2, 1932 marked the fiftieth anniversary of Garibaldi's death. A major confrontation at the Garibaldi Memorial on Independence Day was a certainty. Shortly before 2:00 P.M., Tresca and some 350 anti-Fascists disembarked from the Staten Island ferry at St. George and marched the three miles to the Garibaldi Memorial at Rosebank. They immediately sought entry but were physically barred by the police. Augmented by 150 new arrivals, the anti-Fascists again surged forward around 6:00 P.M., when the gates to the grounds swung open to receive the 3,500 members of the Sons of Italy and many Blackshirts dressed in full regalia. A melee ensued and the anti-Fascists were beaten back by police swinging clubs. But the din they raised prevented honored speakers like Consul General Grazzi and Generoso Pope from being heard. After the ceremonies concluded, all factions boarded the same train to St. George. A scuffle broke out in one of the crowded cars and a pistol shot was fired, killing Salvatore Arena, a member of Giuseppe Caldora's Il Duce Fascist Alliance. His Fascist comrades accused Clemente Lista, a thirty-five-year-old painter and Treschiano from New Jersey, and police took him into custody.[73]

Arena's funeral was held at the Dominican Church on Lexington Avenue and 66th Street in Manhattan, with Italian Ambassador de Martino, Consul General Grazzi, a host of *prominenti*, and Blackshirts from the Lictor Federation and the Il Duce Fascist Alliance in attendance. Arena's coffin was welcomed aboard the ocean liner *Saturnia* by an honor guard of Fascist militia who stood guard throughout the entire voyage. The burial, with military honors, was held in Arena's hometown in Sicily. But Arena's quasi-canonization was soon marred by news that he was wanted by police in Montreal for bank robbery and murder.[74]

Tresca's first act in Lista's defense was to provide to the district attorney of Staten Island the name of the man who really killed Arena, explaining that the shot had been fired by a Fascist and intended for Lista. Speaking at the Rand School, Tresca and Valenti blamed Mayor Walker and Tammany Hall for the fracas at the Garibaldi Memorial, because the mayor had ordered the police to prevent the anti-Fascists from laying a wreath at the shrine. Before Tresca could assemble a defense team, however, the case against Lista collapsed. Several eye-witnesses testified to the Staten Island district attorney that they had observed Arena arguing with Domenico Trombetta, the fanatical Blackshirt publisher of *Il Grido della Stirpe* (Cry of the Race) and the president of the Lictor Federation. As the Fascists and anti-Fascists were leaving the train, Trombetta allegedly drew a pistol and shot Arena. Trombetta's main accuser was Giacomo Caldora, the chief rival of the Lictor Federation, whom Tresca had persuaded to testify, evidently without much difficulty. Charges against Lista were dropped and Trombetta brought to trial for Arena's murder. Since internecine struggle was ubiquitous among Blackshirts as well as *sovversivi*, the conflicting testimony provided by rival Fascist organizations resulted in Trombetta's acquittal. A few months later, Caldora was shot and severely wounded by a rival Fascist in revenge for having testified against Trombetta. Detectives investigating the case were not the least bit concerned about the identity of the assailant. Instead, they hounded Caldora relentlessly to extract an admission that Tresca and the anti-Fascists had convinced him to give false testimony against Trombetta. Putting Tresca in jail was still a higher priority for the police than convicting a Fascist murderer.[75]

The Terzani Case

Fascism in the United States was not confined to Italians and Germans. The early 1930s saw the emergence of the Khaki Shirts of America, commanded by "General" Arthur J. Smith. The political agenda of the Khaki Shirts included the abolition of Congress and its substitution with a board of dictators; immediate payment of the bonus promised to soldiers after WWI; large-scale federal unemployment relief; revaluation of silver at a rate of sixteen to one; and the largest army and navy in the world. The Khaki Shirts planned a "March on Washington" with several million armed men on Columbus Day 1933. The coup would overthrow the government and establish a Fascist dictatorship.[76]

Headquartered in Philadelphia, Smith and the Khaki Shirts sought to expand their ranks in New York, scheduling a rally at Columbus Hall in the "Little Italy" section of Astoria, Queens, on July 14, 1933. Informed on short notice of the impending rally, anti-Fascists had no time for a preparatory meeting and sought Tresca's advice instead. On the morning of July 14, the headline of *La Stampa Libera* sounded Tresca's exhortation: "*MOBILITAZIONE ANTIFASCISTA*," with the subtitle: "This evening everyone to Columbus Hall in Astoria against the Khaki Shirts."[77] Some 150–200 Khaki Shirts (many of them second generation Italian Americans) and Italian Blackshirts gathered in the hall to hear speeches by Smith and other Fascists. The anti-Fascist contingent that assembled to challenge them was composed primarily of Tresca's young followers. Rather than enter the hall, Tresca advised the anti-Fascists to wait outside and attack the Khaki Shirts and their Blackshirt allies when they left. But a small group went inside to disrupt the Fascist speakers. One of them, the noted illustrator Fort Velona, shouted "*Morte a Mussolini!*" when he heard the Duce's name praised. He was immediately set upon by a group of Khaki Shirts and clubbed unconscious. When Volona's comrades came to his assistance, a general melee erupted. One of the anti-Fascists was a twenty-two-year-old student at City College named Antonio Fierro. Smith himself attacked the young man, striking him repeatedly over the head with his riding crop. Then a shot was fired, killing Fierro instantly. When the police and two assistant district attorneys arrived, Fierro's friend, Athos Terzani, a thirty-one-year-old taxi driver and Treschiano, was identified by one of Smith's bodyguards, Frank Moffer (real name Moddifori), as the shooter. Smith, too, identified Terzani as the killer, claiming that the shot had been intended for him. Queens District Attorney Charles S. Colden immediately ordered Terzani's arrest, charging him with murder in the second degree. He was released from custody on $15,000 bail pending trial. Smith and Moffer returned the next day to Philadelphia, where the "General" boasted that the Khaki Shirts had killed a "communist" and beaten up many others.[78]

After organizing an elaborate funeral for Fierro in the Bronx, Tresca recruited a broad-based Terzani Defense Committee that included himself, Roger Baldwin, and Norman Thomas as chairman. Leader of the legal team was Arthur Garfield Hays. The biggest obstacle confronting the defense was the absolute refusal of the Queens district attorney to investigate leads pointing to suspects other than Terzani. Colden, it seems, was coveting electoral support from elements that desired a conviction. To prevent a blatant frame-up, the defense conducted its own investigation to contest the Fascists' version of the shooting.[79]

The Khaki Shirts' "March on Washington" never materialized. Philadelphia police raided their headquarters on October 12 and discovered a cache of weapons but not Smith, who disappeared after absconding with the organization's funds. Smith surrendered himself to the police a few days later and was charged with fraud. Smith's betrayal destroyed the Khaki Shirts and encouraged some former members to furnish information about the Terzani case. Chief among these was Samuel Wein, a Jewish member of the "general staff," who confessed to Norman Thomas and Rabbi Louis I. Newman that he had lied to the Bronx Grand Jury about Terzani because Smith had threatened to kill him as an example to all Jews. At Terzani's trial on December 11–13, 1933, Wein and several other ex-Khaki Shirts identified Frank Moffer as the shooter who killed Fierro. The jury required only thirty-two minutes to reach a verdict of "not guilty." Shortly afterward, Terzani and his fiancé were married at a victory celebration hosted at Irving Plaza, with Norman Thomas as best man and Tresca's companion, Margaret De Silver, as matron of honor. As for Smith and Moffer, it was only after Thomas brought considerable pressure to bear that Colden prosecuted the real culprits. Convicted in April 1934, Smith was sentenced to three to six years for perjury and Moffer received a five to ten year term on a reduced charge of first degree manslaughter, having confessed his guilt. Terzani's acquittal and the disintegration of the Khaki Shirts represented anti-Fascism's most significant victory of the 1930s.[80]

18

The Depression and the New Deal

The travails suffered by working class people during the Great Depression evoked a visceral reaction within Tresca, which increased his already profound hatred for capitalism and government. Gone was the self-imposed "moderation" Tresca had exercised in the 1920s, when, for example, he had refrained from criticizing the American president as a precautionary measure. Now Tresca was attacking every important political figure, policy, and institution associated with American capitalism, while hoping that the dreadful conditions produced by the Depression would generate radical action by the working class.[1]

Tresca denounced Wall Street as "the most vile, fetid, and deadly cave in America," which "serves to enrich ten and impoverish ten thousand."[2] He rejected conventional explanations attributing the Depression to objective market forces. The Wall Street Crash of October 1929 had resulted from "human imbecility" and greed. When the economy worsened in 1930, Tresca assailed President Hoover's "myopic" view of the Depression, rejecting his claim that the return of prosperity was just "around the corner." He was not surprised that Hoover's "remedy" was to give assistance to ailing corporations and banks and nothing to the poor and unemployed. The greed of capitalists rendered them incapable of seeing beyond the short term. Why else, in a crisis generated by over-production and under-consumption, would they cut workers' wages, when such action only depressed consumption still further? Indifference to the suffering of the poor and class cupidity were the inevitable consequence of a political system controlled by and operated for the benefit of corporate capitalists.[3]

Yet for all his empathy with their suffering, Tresca expressed more disdain for American workers during the Depression than at any previous time in his career. He was dismayed and disillusioned by their failure to respond to the economic crisis with anything resembling a revolutionary threat to capitalism. He stated repeatedly that "the most tragic thing about this present historical moment is the supine resignation of the masses."[4] American workers, he believed, thought with their stomachs, not their brains. They would tolerate exploitation and corruption so long as they could eat. They deluded themselves that a cosmetic change in the political order would solve their problems and fill their stomachs. Americans had lost their survival instincts because they had been domesticated with the deception of patriotism and religion:

In the name of patriotism they yield to misery, because the nation must not be disturbed with uprisings and agitation. In the name religion they are resigned, because, if hunger squeezes their insides, it is God who has sent it, and they must bow down before the will of God.[5]

On the Labor Front

The state of the labor movement in the early 1930s was worse than lamentable from Tresca's perspective. The principal culprits were the leaders of the AFL, the UMWA, and the ACWUA. The AFL's traditional policy of cooperation rather than conflict with capitalism reached new heights during the Depression, as President William Green and the craft union hierarchies remained docile and even reactionary in the face of massive unemployment and industry pressure for wage cuts, and as they continued to oppose organizing millions of non-union workers along industrial lines. Tresca's characterization of the AFL as a "bulwark of capitalism" was hard to dispute.[6]

His other enemy of long-standing, the UMWA, was now a mere "shadow of its former self." Although aware that production surpluses and mechanization were affecting coal miners adversely, Tresca laid most of the blame at the feet of John L. Lewis, the president of the UMWA since 1919. Lewis personified everything Tresca hated about powerful union leaders: he was conservative in political outlook, despite supporting the Democratic Party, dictatorial and corrupt in his running of the union, intolerant of radicals and "unauthorized" strikes, negotiated weak contracts detrimental to miners, and always hesitated to confront the coal company operators. He was committed above all else to crushing internal opposition to his rule. The UMWA under Lewis' leadership, therefore, had become "a strait jacket," experiencing "disaster after disaster."[7]

Tresca was even more critical of the needle trades unions. While coal miners frequently resisted the dictates of the UMWA, the garment workers of the ACWUA remained inert, allowing themselves to remain under the "fascist tyranny of the union bureaucracy."[8] Tresca had been supportive of the ACWA during its early years, attending its first conference in 1916 and participating in the Lawrence strike which the union led in 1919. By the late 1920s and early 1930s, however, Tresca had become an unrelenting critic of the ACWU, focusing his animus against union president Sidney Hillman, who now ranked with Lewis as Tresca's most despised labor potentates. Hillman, he maintained, was guilty of collaboration with management, a betrayal that resulted in lower wages, longer hours, Sunday work, increased use of the "check-off system," countenance of scab labor, abandonment of efforts to organize non-union shops, abolition of union local autonomy, and use of gangsters to suppress dissidents within the union. Hillman's Italian lieutenants—Augusto Bellanca, Giovanni Sala, and Giuseppe Catalalotti—were equally tarred by Tresca's brush. To describe them, Tresca coined the term "*Bellanchismo*," by which he meant union despotism and corruption.[9]

Strike of the Rockmen

Although renowned in radical circles as an astute and unrelenting critic of union potentates and bureaucracies, Tresca would have much preferred to re-join the fray, utilizing his skills as agitator and strike leader rather than censure from the sidelines. He explained to his friend Margaret Sanger: "A strike, a battle is for me a dream. I forget the world when I am in the action."[10] The Depression presented the ideal environment in which to resume his labor activities; however, the obstacles facing Tresca were the union leaders he had antagonized and the indelible stigma of still being "too radical."

The prospect of agitation and strike leadership loomed in the coal fields of Pennsylvania. Agitation and wildcat strikes had erupted in the anthracite region during the winter of 1929–1930, especially in Lansford, Tamaqua, Coaldale, Summit Hill, and Nesquehoning. Here the rockmen—the miners who dug and cleared tunnels—were in conflict with the contractors who employed them in the service of the Lehigh Consolidated Coal Company. Both the rockmen and the contractors were overwhelmingly Italian, with the latter exploiting their co-nationals by paying lower wages, demanding more hours and days of labor, using fewer men, and engaging in other corrupt practices in blatant violation of existing contracts with the UMWA. But the union did nothing to help its members.[11]

The syndicalist Felice Guadagni and the socialist Giuseppe Popolizio, a new associate of the Martello group, were the first Italian radicals from outside the region to arrive, attending a number of meetings of rockmen in Lansford to assess the situation. Representatives of the communist National Miners Union (NMU) also attended, but when it became clear that their primary purpose was to recruit new members for the NMU and the CP, the rockmen rejected their appeals. Instead, they called upon Tresca for leadership. He arrived on January 26, 1930 and urged the rockmen to force the UMWA to help them defeat the contractors. In response, the sub-district president of the UMWA, Thomas Kelly, put in an appearance at a meeting of 600–700 rockmen in Lansford. At first, Kelly refused to participate because Tresca was present. The clamorous response of the rockmen in favor of Tresca's right to speak compelled him to acquiesce. A debate (in English) between Tresca and Kelly resulted in the latter's expressing agreement with Tresca, adding that "if this intelligent and powerful orator will help us, we will get rid of the contractors."[12] He assured the rockmen that the UMWA would help them fight the contractors.[13]

Tresca's plan of action, approved by Kelly, called for the formation of an agitation committee of rockmen, and for meetings between the committee and UMWA to formulate demands obligating the contractors to honor existing agreements. Tresca returned to New York only to be summoned back after no progress was achieved. At a meeting of 800 rockmen in Lansdale on February 9, Kelly refused to share the platform with Tresca because he was a "New York man" and not a member of the UMWA. When the Italians demanded that Tresca speak, Kelly and his underlings tried to quit the hall but were stopped and roughed up by angry rockmen. After escaping, Kelly returned with the police chief and a contingent of mounted officers armed with rifles and tear gas bombs. A melee erupted. Tresca was arrested and charged with inciting riot and held on $10,000 bail. Not a single rockman or miner went to work the next day. Released by a local magistrate, Tresca concluded that his continuing presence would hinder the rockmen's cause. After Tresca returned to New York, Kelly ordered the rockmen back to work because the UMWA and the contractors had declared the strike "illegal." As Tresca had witnessed so many times, the coal miners were betrayed by their own union.[14]

Eager for more action, Tresca turned his attention to the "unauthorized" strikes that coal miners in Pennsylvania, Ohio, West Virginia, and Kentucky were conducting in 1931, often in the face of violence from the authorities and mine owners. He noted that strikes were much more common among non-union miners. Wherever the UMWA held sway, the miners were repeatedly betrayed. He was particularly impressed by the tenacious resistance of the miners in Kentucky, a state which the UMWA had failed to unionize, and where the IWW was achieving a small measure of success.[15] On June 27, Tresca wrote to Herbert Mahler, secretary-treasurer of the IWW, offering his services for the Kentucky strikes or any others he could help.[16] He never received a reply. Tresca's hope of resuming his former place in the labor movement remained unfulfilled.

The Depression Strikes Home

Before the stock market crash, *Il Martello*'s deficit had already reached around $5,300.[17] Tresca told Margaret Sanger that the months of November and December 1929 were "crushing," because "the unemployment crisis is hurting me more than any one could imagine." As frequently happened when confronted by financial adversity, Tresca lapsed into an emotional depression. He lamented to Sanger:

> I did spend, as a human being, the most miserable and demoralizing Xmas I ever have spended in my life. No money, no peace. Litterally no money to live and forced to send the workers home without pay…. I am tired. Tired not because I find to hard the fights for the triumph of my ideal, but tired of this petty, discouraging, humiliating search for money to keep the candle burning…. I am here on the cros, a pauper, a regular beggar, asking my followers for the penny to go on battling for them, the friends for loan that are hard and almost impossible to repaid.[18]

Publishing the newspaper became more problematic as the economy continued its downward spiral. Hundreds of readers who had lost their jobs could no longer afford to pay subscription fees or contribute donations. Brother Ettore, to whom he usually turned when the coffers were empty, could not provide the necessary funds. In desperation, Tresca obtained a substantial loan from a friend of Margaret Sanger's. But this loan, like most he secured, would never be repaid.

During the best years of the 1920s, Tresca paid himself a handsome stipend out of operating expenses—$50 a week. From January 1930 to July 1931, however, he took no salary in order to pay *Il Martello*'s mounting debt. But this personal sacrifice scarcely helped bring his newspaper to press. To raise funds to save *Il Martello*, Tresca's comrades organized a banquet to honor his "25 [actually 27] years of struggles in the United States."[19] Held at the Irving Plaza on May 24, 1931, the banquet attracted more than 500 people, including many of American's most celebrated radicals and liberals: Joe Ettor, Roger Baldwin, Arthur Garfield Hays, Benjamin Gitlow, Mike Gold, A.J. Muste, Heywood Broun, Vito Marcantonio, and many others. The banquet represented a great tribute to Tresca's popularity and prestige, but did little to erase *Il Martello*'s deficit. As a result, only thirty-nine issues of *Il Martello* were published in 1931, instead of the customary fifty-two.[20]

The Italian consulate, not surprisingly, had been observing Tresca's travails with great satisfaction. One of their spies—someone "on excellent terms of friendship with the noted Carlo Tresca"—reported that "Tresca for some time has been in poor health and appears very depressed, also because the contributions of his 'comrades of the faith' are becoming ever more scarce. He complains continually and says 'I have never gone through such a dark period in my life.'"[21] A few weeks later, lacking money even for stamps, Tresca suspended publication of *Il Martello* after the issue of May 7, 1932. He had no idea if his hammer would ever strike again.

Il Martello ultimately did resume publication as a biweekly on January 27, 1934, with a new office at 94 Fifth Avenue. The largest infusion of cash needed to resurrect the newspaper undoubtedly came from Margaret De Silver, the new woman in his life. But all was not well within the *Il Martello* group. Several of the comrades were discontent with Tresca's management, and proposed replacing him as director with Domenico Zavattero, a veteran anarchist and regular contributor, or Luigi Fabbri, the renowned disciple of Malatesta, who resided in Montevideo. Nothing came of these proposals. What emerged was an arrangement that designated the *Il Martello* group as the new owner and publisher of the newspaper, with Tresca continuing as director. A "control commission" was formed to determine editorial policy and administration. In reality, the bureaucratic transformation proved merely cosmetic—the "new" *Il Martello* was virtually indistinguishable from the "old." Tresca was still the boss.[22]

Roosevelt

The revival of *Il Martello* occurred in a political atmosphere substantially different from that which had permeated American society when the newspaper suspended publication. The transformation was attributable to Franklin Delano Roosevelt and the "New Deal." Tresca had erred when he previously argued that a transfer of power from Republicans to Democrats would change nothing. Roosevelt, he quickly recognized, was a new species of political animal, a man of infinitely greater finesse and acuity than Hoover. And unlike most Americans, who appreciated the modicum of redress the "New Deal" reforms would bring, Tresca did not appreciate them.

Tresca asserted that Roosevelt's conservative critics were fools to regard him as a "revolutionary," whose policies and methods would destroy capitalism and hasten the advent of socialism. Roosevelt, in Tresca's view, was a "constitutional dictator," whose "New Deal" represented novel forms of state intervention designed to correct the inherent instability of traditional *laissez-faire* capitalism.

Far from being a threat, the "New Deal" was a "salvaging operation for capitalism." Roosevelt was a "demagogue" and quintessential counter-revolutionary, whose inaugural rhetoric had duped the "blind and patient American people."[23] Tresca's perception of Roosevelt as the "savior of capitalism," dispensing palliatives to undermine the potential militancy of the American working class, explained the inordinate hostility he demonstrated toward the president and his "New Deal" policies until 1940.

San Francisco General Strike

While the Roosevelt administration churned out measures to ameliorate the effects of the Depression, hundreds of thousands of workers and the unemployed were agitating, striking, and organizing new unions at a feverish pace, invariably outside the ambit of the AFL, which still adhered to its philosophy of cooperation with management and its reluctance to organize unskilled workers in mass-production industries, such as steel and automobiles. Of the many strikes that raged in 1934, none riveted Tresca's attention as much as the San Francisco general strike of July 17–19, which involved some 150,000 longshoremen, teamsters, and maritime workers. For three days the strikers brought San Francisco to a virtual standstill, only to succumb to massive retaliation by police, vigilantes, and some 4,500 National Guardsmen.[24]

Despite its defeat, Tresca was greatly encouraged by the general strike, which suggested American workers might be awakening from their coma. He applauded the action as "the beginning of a new era of the labor movement in the United States."[25] Because of the violent behavior of local officials and police, as well as the efforts of the Roosevelt administration, first to delay the longshoremen's strike and then to appoint conservative officials and citizens to mediate—efforts he interpreted as purposefully intended to help the shipping companies break the strike—Tresca maintained that the general strike had "shattered the myth that the U.S. government is by the people and for the people." Capitalist democracy had been attacked by the force of the strike, class consciousness had arisen among the mass of California workers, the class struggle had been clarified, and the demarcation line drawn.[26]

America Leaning Toward Fascism

Tresca believed that the American environment of 1934 revealed ominous portents of future suppression of strikes, the undermining of free unionism, and the emergence of Fascism. San Francisco had demonstrated that when the interests of capitalism were in dire jeopardy, the police, judiciary, and military powers of the state stood in readiness to suppress rebellious workers in the event that vigilantes and hired thugs proved unequal to the task. To justify legal and extra-legal repression, the myth of a communist menace had been resurrected and exploited to the fullest by the government and the bourgeoisie. The parallels between Italy in the early 1920s and the United States in the 1930s were unmistakable in Tresca's view, leading him to believe that "Fascism in the United States is no longer a tendency or a theory, but a fact."[27] Signs were everywhere: suppression of the San Francisco strike, the Khaki Shirts, the Silver Shirts, the American Legion, the Daughters of the American Revolution, the Ku Klux Klan, Huey Long, Father Coughlin, even Roosevelt himself. "The dictator, the demagogue Roosevelt vacillates. Tomorrow the dictator will remove his mask," Tresca predicted. "Meanwhile, we head toward obligatory arbitration; toward government control of unions; toward the reduction of the workers' standard of living; toward laws increasingly restrictive of liberty; toward Fascism."[28]

The CIO and Worker Militancy

As Roosevelt's second term approached, Tresca continued to warn that America was galloping steadily toward a "totalitarian state."[29] He was disgusted, therefore, when William Green and other leaders of the AFL supported Roosevelt's re-election at their Madison Square Garden rally in May 1935. The big mistake of AFL leaders, Tresca maintained, was to think that Roosevelt was "a friend of labor" (their term) because the backward and orthodox forces of capitalism opposed him. It had become all the more imperative, therefore, that American workers liberate themselves from the yoke of the AFL and form new militant unions.[30]

Given his inveterate hostility to the AFL and his advocacy of industrial unionism, Tresca might have been expected to bestow his blessings upon the Congress for Industrial Organization (CIO), the confederation of industrial unions that broke away from the AFL in November 1935. He did not. Although the CIO espoused industrial unionism and attracted many bona fide radicals (communists, socialists, and Trotskyists), some of whom became excellent organizers and second-echelon leaders, Tresca would not invest his revolutionary faith in a labor organization controlled by the likes of John L. Lewis, Sidney Hillman, and Charles Howard, men whom he considered power hungry despots and pro-capitalist traitors to the working class. Signs of betrayal, he believed, were evidenced by Lewis' role in compelling the UMWA, a CIO affiliate, to support Roosevelt's re-election.[31] Rather than support Roosevelt or any other party politicians, Tresca argued, "labor unions should pursue only one political objective—whatever leads directly to the abolition of the state and capitalism."[32]

"Where is this growing conflict between capital and labor...heading?," Tresca asked in the summer of 1937. "Toward a ferocious reaction that will rout and defeat the forces of labor? Toward Fascism? Or toward a new, auspicious era of proletarian conquests, toward greater class consciousness, and toward greater political and economic maturity of the American proletariat?"[33] What prompted Tresca's question was the wave of strikes and sit-downs led by the CIO throughout much of the Midwest in 1936 and 1937, in rubber, steel, and automotive plants in Akron, Flint, Cleveland, Chicago, Youngstown, Johnstown, and other centers in the American heartland. Never before in the 20th century had tens of thousands of largely-unorganized American workers demonstrated such a degree of militancy and resolve. Equally unprecedented was the scale on which workers struck against such giants of industry as Good Year, U.S. Steel, and General Motors, utilizing a tactic rarely employed by American labor: the sit-down strike, an illegal occupation of factories by its workers.[34]

Having been disillusioned with the American working class for so many years, Tresca did not respond with jubilation and naïve expectations when the strike wave erupted, but he was pleased that the objective of so many strikes was union recognition, the right to organize and join unions without employer interference, an achievement Tresca considered more important than wage increases. Moreover, the workers were fighting to join, not the AFL-type craft unions, which had shunned the unskilled workers in mass-producing industries for decades, but industrial unions such as Tresca had long favored because they engendered class unity and solidarity. The sit-down strikes were also encouraging because they demonstrated defiance of America's quasi-religious belief in the sanctity of private property, and opened workers to the realization that the means of production rightfully belonged to them. Tresca also applauded the spontaneity of the workers, the fact that they frequently initiated sit-downs on their own accord, without awaiting orders from CIO officials. Nevertheless, while the new strike tactics exhibited a degree of "instinctive revolutionary spirit," he explained, it was still a "superficial instinct." The "criterion of revolutionary organization" had not yet developed.[35]

Tresca also believed the angry reaction the sit-down strikes had produced among industrialists and much of America's anti-labor middle class was symptomatic of incipient Fascism. Industrialists, he believed, were hoping that the strikes would prompt the government to suppress the workers and form a Fascist state like Italy. Conservatives groups such as the American Legion, the Daughters of the American Revolution, the Catholic Church, and a multitude of citizens groups who wanted the strikes declared illegal were conducting a violent campaign in the press, pulpit, and speaker's platform against "Communism." The reactionary propaganda emanating from these quarters was intended "to create the psychological moment for a frontal attack, for the fascist 'push.'" Equally threatening were the retaliatory measures already in motion, as police, vigilantes, and company thugs disrupted union meetings, beat up picketers, and even killed striking workers throughout the Midwest. Such reactions confirmed "one indisputable fact: to the legitimate demands of workers the ruling class responds with violence."[36]

But the possibility of a nationwide clash between capital and labor was soon precluded by Lewis and other supporters of capitalism within the CIO. Unauthorized strikes were prohibited, effectively putting an end to sit-downs. And with the sit-downs went the militancy of 1937. CIO radicals, especially the communists, who had been instrumental in the success of the sit-downs and organizing drives, were increasingly subordinated to the union's power barons, like Lewis.[37] Once the union was tamed, Tresca considered the CIO as much an auxiliary of capitalism as the AFL. American capitalism, with the aid of union despots, had won the struggle against labor without the need for Fascism.

19

Fascism on the March

During the twenty-one months that *Il Martello* remained in limbo, Tresca ventured a second time into the realm of play writing with *Il Vendicatore* (The Avenger). As a literary undertaking, this three-act drama falls short of *L'Attentato à Mussolini*. The clever banter and sardonic humor that distinguished the former are missing, and the dialogue is replete with lengthy passages that sound like a political speech. Nevertheless, *Il Vendicatore* contains raw passion reminiscent of a *verismo* opera by Mascagni or Leoncavallo.

Signora Nardi fears that a deadly fate awaits her son Remo, a revolutionary involved in a conspiracy against the Fascist regime. His sister Luisa, a gullible young woman who believes the myths manufactured by Mussolini's propaganda machine, cannot understand her brother's political motivation and values. Moved by her mother's entreaties, Luisa discloses Remo's revolutionary intent to her fiancé, a Fascist commandant named Emanuele, believing that he can steer her brother back to a safe path. Emanuele has Remo arrested but convinces Luisa (shades of Puccini's *Tosca*) that he will arrange safe passage for him to France if she yields to his lust. The Fascist's promise is worthless, and Remo is tortured to death without exposing his comrades. Luisa flees when she learns of Emanuele's betrayal and Remo's death. Many years later, now elevated to the rank of Fascist *podestà*, Emanuele has arranged to dine with a proletarian family as a pubic relations ploy to demonstrate concern for suffering workers. The "Riva" family was selected for this honor because the son, Vittorio, is the head of the local Fascist university militia. Unknown to Emanuele, the family members are all anti-Fascists. The mother, whom he does not recognize, is really Luisa, and Vittorio is the product of Emanuele's seduction. The boy has been raised to be the avenger—*Il Vendicatore*. The target, of course, is Emanuele. Luisa reveals her true identity and that of their son just as Vittorio plunges a dagger into Emanuele's chest, declaring: "Yes, I am the son that Fascism has taught to kill, and I kill you."[1]

Il Vendicatore premiered in Ukrainian Hall at 217 East 6th Street on April 3, 1934, performed by the Filodrammatica Moderno and directed by Salvatore Pernicone. Successive performances were given in New York, Philadelphia, and other cities, but the play never achieved the popularity of *L'Attentato à Mussolini*. Perhaps that was just as well. Play writing was not the best utilization of Tresca's time and energy.

Pope: "Gangster and Fascist"

Tresca was able to revive *Il Martello* in January 1934. Having lost none of his audacity and zeal, Tresca targeted the most powerful of all the *prominenti*—Generoso Pope—for attack. Born in a small village not far from Naples, Pope arrived in New York in 1906 at the age of fifteen, unable to read or write English, with ten dollars in his pocket. By the late 1920s, Pope was the richest Italian American in New York, having amassed millions as the owner of the Colonial Sand and Gravel Company, the largest supplier of building materials in the country. By the early 1930s, Pope had acquired ownership of *Il Progresso Italo-Americano, Il Corriere d'America*, and *Bolletino della Sera* in New York, and *L'Opinione* in Philadelphia. As the grand mogul of the Italian-language press, Pope was able to influence the majority of Italian American voters to support Tammany Hall candidates in New York and the Roosevelt administration in Washington. His role as the premier Italian-American vote-getter earned Pope direct access to the White House and Roosevelt himself. He capitalized on this connection to serve as Mussolini's unofficial emissary to the American government.[2]

That Pope would rise to the top of Tresca's list of most hated *prominenti* was inevitable once he acquired his newspaper chain, which functioned as the most pervasive and influential purveyor of Fascist propaganda. What made Pope all the more reprehensible in Tresca's eyes was the hypocrisy inherent in his political stance: pro-Mussolini and Fascism in Italy; pro-Roosevelt and democracy in the United States. Tresca perceived that Pope, unlike Luigi Barzini, the former director of *Il Corriere d'America*, harbored no real devotion to Fascism per se. His primary motive for supporting Mussolini was rank opportunism and an insatiable desire for glory and self-aggrandizement, needs that the Duce satisfied with medals, honors, and special privileges. Attuned to Pope's vanity and need to play the "*grand'uomo*," Tresca delighted in denigrating him as an ignorant, vulgar peasant, favoring insulting terms like "king of the *cafoni*," "illiterate quadruped," and "golden ass."[3]

Tresca's attacks against Pope had begun with the latter's acquisition of *Il Progresso* from the estate of the late Carlo Barzotti in 1928. They escalated to an unprecedented level of ferocity in October 1934, when on the front page of *Il Martello* (in Italian and English), he accused Pope of being "a gangster and racketeer."[4] For Pope, "journalism is not a mission but a racket," a charge Tresca substantiated with information, garnered from his own sources, describing how Pope employed underworld strong-arm men to intimidate rival Italian newspaper publishers, other business associates, and his own workers when they attempted to unionize. Addressing all the American dailies of New York (again in English), Tresca charged:

> In the city of New York today, the editor of a newspaper is in constant danger of physical attack, perhaps of death, at the hands of underworld elements who disapprove, or represent others who disapprove, of this editor's political view! An attempt is being made by Generoso Pope in this city to exercise censorship over the Italian-language press by means of gangsters. An attempt is being made to inaugurate in the Italian colony in the United States the same political regime in the press as prevails today in Mussolini's Italy.[5]

No one had ever dared attack Pope in this manner, and anti-Fascists awaited his reaction with tense anticipation. A week or so after the offending article was published, Tresca received a "courtesy call" from two of Pope's henchmen. One of emissaries, according to Tresca, was ceremoniously polite, requesting only the issue of *Il Martello* in which Tresca's attack against Pope had appeared, but the intent was clear.[6] A later version, provided by Girolamo Valenti, portrayed the encounter as more threatening and more typically Treschian. Threatened with death if he persisted in attacking Pope, Tresca allegedly told his potential killer to "get out, and if Generoso Pope wants to know how to kill people, tell him to come to me instead of sending cheap hoodlums like you."[7] The gangster who delivered the threat was allegedly Frank Garofalo, Pope's chief henchman and second in command of the Castellamare gang of *Mafiosi* headed by Giuseppe Bonanno.[8]

An article soon appeared in *Il Progresso* entitled: "For the Peace of Our Community," calling upon all Italian-American elements not to fan the flames of political division, not to divide immigrants between Fascists and anti-Fascists.[9] But neither the threat of violence nor this olive branch deterred Tresca from his campaign against Pope. With a headline declaring "The Fascist Gene Pope Is A Man of Straw," Tresca challenged Pope to do his worst, even urging him to sue for libel so could prove his accusations in court. He also warned that any attempt at violence would be answered in kind: "Keep your men in check. This is not a game you will settle the way you did with Giordano, Sisca, and Bernabei [people threatened by Pope]. If I fall, you will follow me, inevitably." Nor could there be peace between them: "You with your newspapers represent everything we *sovversivi* hate: you are the state, religion, and capital." As for peace in the Italian community,

the anti-Fascists will never give you peace so long as you continue to favor Fascism with your newspapers. Only when the tyrants of Italy are hanging from the highest lampposts of Rome and the liberation of the proletariat is an accomplished fact. Who knows? Perhaps then we can discuss peace. Until then, no.[10]

Italo-Ethiopian War

An astute observer of international relations, Tresca in the 1930s predicted repeatedly that a military clash among the great powers of Europe was virtually inevitable and would lead ultimately to world war. The precipitating cause would be Fascist aggression. Mussolini, Tresca insisted, wanted to conquer Ethiopia by military force even though he could absorb most of the East African country by the peaceful means that Great Britain and France sought to arrange. The Duce needed war to divert attention from the serious failure of all his economic programs, to re-energize the Fascists grown complacent with power, and to satisfy his insatiable lust for glory and prestige. In the last analysis, Mussolini would go to war because war was inherent to Fascism and essential to the survival of his regime. As Tresca put it, Fascism is "violence erected into a system," requiring "war for its own sake" as a "self-sustaining mechanism."[11]

Mussolini's armies invaded Ethiopia from Italy's colonies in Eritrea and Somaliland on October 3, 1935. Tresca pondered the Duce's folly: "Where Mussolini's madness reaches its height is not in this stupid and absurd war against Abyssinia, but in his remaining indifferent to the possibility of world conflagration that he will initiate by his African adventure."[12] Great Britain could have brought Italy's war machine to a halt in Ethiopia simply by refusing passage of fuel tankers through the Suez Canal. Tresca knew, however, that Great Britain's conservative leaders were great admirers of Mussolini. They would make a great show of moral outrage but do nothing to stop Mussolini so long as Britain's interests in Europe and Africa were not threatened. British unwillingness to impede Mussolini was motivated primarily by fear that an Italian defeat in Ethiopia might cause the downfall of the Fascist regime and spur a communist revolution, a concern shared also by many American capitalists who had invested in Italy. "It is the vision of a red tomorrow that terrifies the gentlemen of gold," Tresca declared.[13]

Tresca also understood Hitler's attitude toward Mussolini's Ethiopian adventure. The Duce, at this juncture, still viewed the Fuhrer as a rival rather than ally. But Hitler would not protest Italy's conquest of Ethiopia because he hoped the Italians would become bogged down in Africa, thereby facilitating Germany's annexation of Austria, which Mussolini had helped thwart in 1934.[14] The needs of *realpolitik* also explained the Soviet Union's cooperation with Mussolini. Italy and Stalin's regime enjoyed excellent diplomatic and economic relations in 1935, with the latter providing the Fascist war machine with large supplies of wheat, barley, and oil. Naturally, in Tresca's view, Soviet support for a Fascist war of aggression against an innocent people was disgraceful. "The international proletariat is with Abyssinia. Will Russia scab against international solidarity?" Tresca asked rhetorically, already knowing the answer.[15]

Italian Americans and the Ethiopian War

What could anti-Fascists do in the face of Mussolini's aggression? Opposition of any kind would inevitably be considered "un-Italian" and "anti-Italian" by their co-nationals, the great majority of whom supported Mussolini's quest for empire in East Africa. Tresca declared nonetheless that "our duty...is to sabotage the war."[16] Only three means of opposition were possible: explode the myths utilized by the regime to justify the war; undermine the Fascists' pursuit of financial aid from Italian Americans; and thwart the political influence of *prominenti* like Pope who were working to ensure American neutrality.[17]

Scarcely a week passed during the entire war that did not see Tresca denouncing Fascist aggression before Italian audiences in New York, Connecticut, Massachusetts, New Jersey, and Pennsylvania. In *Il Martello*, Tresca conducted a spirited counter-propaganda campaign aimed specifically against Generoso Pope's newspaper empire, the principal source of misinformation regarding Mussolini's objective in Ethiopia and the success of Italy's military campaigns.[18] Tresca demolished several myths propagated by the Fascist regime during the war: that

Mussolini was conducting a "civilizing mission" to liberate the Ethiopians from slavery and savagery; that Ethiopia was an El Dorado of natural resources and rich soil that would provide prosperity for the Motherland and for millions of Italian settlers; and that the rule of the Duce and the King [e.g., as proclaimed in the Fascist song "*Facetta Nera*" (Little Blackface) would be kind and benevolent. Tresca also reported regularly on the progress (or the lack of same) of Italy's invasion, contradicting the exaggerated claims and outright lies that filled *Il Progresso* and *Il Corriere d'America*. The primary military consideration that the pro-Fascist press chose to ignore, and that Tresca constantly underscored, was the vast disparity between the Italian forces, equipped with artillery, tanks, airplanes, and mustard gas, and the Ethiopian infantry and cavalry, fighting only with light artillery, small arms, spears, and swords.[19]

But Tresca's counter-propaganda, like that disseminated by other anti-Fascists, had virtually no impact. "Because we like to look at reality in the eyes and take refuge from all forms of infantile illusion," he wrote, "we wish to say frankly that this supremely insane African enterprise has not only the consent but the adherence of the great majority of Italian Americans."[20] The Italian-American community had responded almost *en masse* to the Ethiopian war, exhibiting a frenzy of nationalistic pride that embarrassed and demoralized the anti-Fascists. To do so, Tresca pointed out, was cost free. While Italians had to face the realities of war and its consequences, Italian Americans had nothing to lose by their chauvinist embrace of Mussolini's imperialist venture. Certainly they were not willing to risk their own lives. Despite Mussolini's call for volunteers, fewer than 800 Italian Americans returned to Italy to join the fighting.[21] Most were content to follow the lead of the *Camorra Coloniale* and engage in fanatical exaltation of the Duce and his great conquest. Actual sacrifices entailed little more than a few dollars or a gold wedding band donated to the war effort.[22]

That most Italian Americans responded positively and callously to Mussolini's rape of Ethiopia was inevitable, according to Tresca. In a classic blend of Treschian sympathy and disdain, Tresca provided an analysis of the phenomenon that anticipated by several decades the interpretation of modern historians. The visceral appeal of Mussolini and his imperialist venture was fundamentally "the product of asinine ignorance and childish ingenuousness more than anything."

This Italian, when he is not completely unlettered, is politically illiterate and subject to the pull that love of his far-away country exercises on his feelings. Conscious of his immense ignorance and his social inferiority, he is happy when someone excites his self love and elevates him in an unreal and chimerical world where he finds compensation for the humiliations he has suffered. This man, who often in his immigrant life has experienced only poorly concealed contempt from other people with whom he has come into contact, and whose vague sense of the injustice he has suffered, conceals an intuitive pride knowing that he is a part of a great historic race and the product of an ancient civilization. He is prompted to rise up when someone shouts to him: "you are great, you belong to the greatest nation in the world" that was humble yesterday and very proud today, and is ready to rebel against all the injustices and defeats. Still poor today it [Italy] will be rich tomorrow by right of conquest. And you poor immigrant, lost amidst the confusion of a frightening, mechanical civilization that does not even assure your bread, you, if you wish, may leave the land that gave you miserly hospitality and transfer to a new land of conquest, under the protection of your own flag…. These tales that the merchants of patriotism have repeated and go on repeating have overheated the heads of our *cafone*, touched the most sensitive chords of his heart, and created a complete fantasy…. Everything has been turned upside down, revolutionized, adulterated, distorted, to be transformed into a simple intellectual meal that nourishes the weak brain and naïve faith of our *cafone*.[23]

Yet Tresca urged his fellow anti-Fascists not to be discouraged by this unfortunate spectacle. For now it was futile to attempt to enlighten those immigrants whose heads were filled with pseudo-patriotic lies. "Have a little patience, my friends, and you will see that the *cafone* will return to his senses."[24]

Meanwhile, as ordinary Italian Americans flocked to pro-war rallies, the pro-Fascist infrastructure rapidly and effectively pursued the political and financial objectives that would assist Mussolini's campaign, with instructions and direction provided by the Italian embassy and the consular network.[25] The greatest danger for the Fascists was the possibility that Roosevelt, who disapproved of Italy's aggression, might revise the Neutrality Act in ways that would adversely affect Mussolini's war effort—for example, an embargo on oil. On instructions from the embassy, therefore, *prominenti* like Pope and organizations such as the Sons of Italy and the new Fascist *Unione Italiana d'America* orchestrated a letter-writing campaign to Roosevelt and key members of Congress. Pope even visited Roosevelt at the White House and conferred with New York Senator Robert Wagner and Interior Secretary Harold Ickes. Faced with the likelihood that Italian American voters would desert the Democrats in the 1936 election if Mussolini were opposed, Roosevelt abandoned his plan to seek discretionary power under a revised Neutrality Act to ban certain exports needed by Mussolini's war machine. Thus the Neutrality Act of 1935 was renewed unchanged, despite the opposition of most Americans to Mussolini's war.[26]

While Pope helped neutralize the threat of an embargo, the pro-war campaign undertaken by Fascist emissaries and local *prominenti* successfully collected money, wedding rings, and other gold and brass objects by the bushel, ostensibly to help the Italian Red Cross. This fund-raising drive had been launched on December 14, 1935, with a mass rally held at Madison Square Garden and attended by some 20,000 Italian Americans. Among the featured speakers were Ambassador Augusto Rosso, Consul General Gaetano Vecchiotti, Generoso Pope, Judges Ferdinand Pecora, Salvatore Cotillo, and John Freschi, representatives of the Fascist *Unione Italiana d'America*, the War Veterans Association, and even Mayor Fiorella La Guardia. Outside Madison Square Garden, some 500 policemen prevented a large contingent of anti-Fascists from entering the arena. Beaten back by nightsticks, the anti-Fascists withdrew singing the "Internationale" and distributing leaflets to passersby that read: "The Italian People Are Not Responsible for Mussolini's Aggression Against Ethiopia," and "Fascist Civilization: Bombing Defenseless Houses and Hospitals and Killing Thousands of the Helpless."[27]

Tresca denounced the illustrious assemblage of Fascist dignitaries and *prominenti* in a headline: "The overflow from the sewers of the *cafoni* invades Madison Square Garden."[28] He revealed how political opportunism accounted for the presence of so many Italian-American public officials at the function, and how powerful was the influence that Pope wielded over such individuals. Judge Cotillo needed Pope and Tammany Hall to get re-elected. Judge Pecora, having criticized the banking establishment, needed Pope's influence with the House of Morgan to prevent its opposition to his bid for re-election. Even La Guardia, a silent anti-Fascist who detested Pope, was blackmailed into cooperating lest Pope oppose him in his newspapers.[29] (Dependent upon Jewish and Italian voters, La Guardia always attacked Hitler but never condemned Mussolini in public.) Tresca's revelations may have caused these politicians some embarrassment, but they did not alter their behavior or support for the war effort.

Tresca caused a moment of fear among the Fascists when he exposed the fund- raising campaign overseen by Pope as a big swindle to exploit the patriotic sentiments of Italian-American workers. The American Red Cross had offered its services to both sides at the outbreak of hostilities. The Ethiopians accepted, but Mussolini refused, declaring that Italy did not require assistance. If Italy did not need help, why then was the Italian Red Cross soliciting funds in the United States, Tresca asked. Money raised ostensibly to aid wounded Italian soldiers was really to be used for Mussolini's war machine, he maintained. Tresca also demonstrated that the fund-raising campaign conducted by the Italian Red Cross violated international regulations because only the American Red Cross had the right to solicit funds in the United States.[30]

That the Italian-American *prominenti*, in league with the ambassador and consuls general, were conducting an illegal fund-raising campaign to aid Mussolini's war effort did not prompt Washington to halt the drive. Moreover, the Fascists made it easy for American officials to ignore the scam by masking their activities under a new name, the *Pro Opere Assistenziale* (Assistance Agencies). The final sums raised probably approached $1,000,000, and the money, as Tresca had predicted, did not go to the Italian Red Cross. In a telegram sent to Pope and published in *Il Progresso*, Mussolini thanked him for "the conspicuous contributions you sent to the Royal Treasury. The very efficient initiative taken by *Il Progresso Italo-Americano* and *Il Corriere d'America* has offered to the Italians in America a way of showing their glowing and patriotic devotion."[31]

Meanwhile, the advances of the Italian army in Ethiopia continued to be encumbered by the enemy's fierce resistance, torrential rains, floods, the high altitude, and the forbidding terrain, especially the lack of roads. Tresca still persisted, therefore, in expressing the hope that once the Italian people learned of the terrible conditions facing their sons in Ethiopia and experienced the hardships of war, they would rebel. Some American and British experts also believed that if the war continued for another year or more, the burden placed on Italy's economy would force Mussolini to negotiate a settlement. What neither Tresca nor the experts anticipated was the depth of brutality to which Mussolini would go to achieve victory. Although the Italian army had utilized poison gas from the outset, during the last phase of the war, airplanes were rigged with devices that sprayed mustard gas over vast areas. Tresca attributed moral responsibility for this atrocity not only to Mussolini but to King Vittorio Emanuele III, who was officially the commander-in-chief of the Italian army.[32] But with the Ethiopian army literally dissolving from this horrific blistering agent, Emperor Haile Selassie realized the war was lost and fled into exile. Mussolini, luxuriating in the oceanic applause of assembled Blackshirts in Rome on May 9, 1936, announced that "Italy finally has its empire!"[33]

The Ethiopian War represented the apogee of Mussolini's popularity among Italian Americans and the nadir of anti-Fascism. The fervor and cooperation with which so many Italian Americans responded to Fascist aggression demonstrated how thoroughly Fascist and pro-Fascist leaders dominated their community and how effectively they could manipulate ordinarily apolitical individuals for their own ends. Nevertheless, even allowing for the irrationality of nationalist passion and human susceptibility to political propaganda, the surge of pro-Mussolini support that accompanied the Ethiopian war marked the most shameful hour in the history of Italian Americans.

The Spanish Civil War

Reason and logic dictated that Mussolini should have refrained from further military aggression after the Ethiopian war. Italy's economy, already faltering before the conflict, had been weakened by the military effort and the sanctions leveled against her by the League of Nations. But Mussolini's megalomania, his insatiable desire for glory and prestige, and his belief that war would vitalize and spread Fascism outweighed every other consideration and virtually guaranteed Italy's involvement in the Spanish Civil War of 1936–1939. Besides satisfying his gargantuan ego, Mussolini supplied the rebel forces of General Francisco Franco with troops, aircraft, weapons, and supplies in hopes of acquiring a naval base in Spain's Balearic Islands, from where he could contest British domination of the Mediterranean. Following Italian intervention, all the great powers of Europe became involved in the Spanish Civil War, directly in the case of Germany and the Soviet Union, or indirectly in the case of Great Britain, France, the United States, whether through action or inaction.[34]

Regarding Fascist aggression as inevitable, Tresca focused his analysis first on Great Britain and France, whose motives and objectives were less obvious but no less opportunistic. From Tresca's perspective, the Fascist dictatorships and the Western democracies—all of them capitalist despite their political dissimilarities—were *de-facto* allies when it came to Spain. The policy of "neutrality" pursued by Great Britain and France (and by extension, the United States as well) was purely hypocritical, constituting a flagrant betrayal of Spain's Republican government and the Spanish people. The Spanish Republic, Tresca noted, was a legitimate, democratically-elected government, which should have been afforded the right to buy arms under international law, but was refused such assistance by the Western democracies. While Italy and German furnished military aid to the insurgents, "the bourgeois world remains deaf to the torment of the Spanish people. They all admit the ferocious injustice of which they are victims but do not lift a finger to stop this injustice."[35] His point of reference was the so-called Non-Intervention Committee, organized in August 1936 and based in London, which bound twenty-seven signatory nations—including all of the major powers—to an accord promising their "neutrality" *vis-à-vis* the Spanish conflict. However, as Tresca quickly asserted, the

Non-Intervention Committee's purported mission was an obscene farce, as four of the signatory powers—Italy, Germany, Portugal, and the Soviet Union—rendered military assistance to their chosen side, while Britain and France embargoed arms to the Republic and turned a blind eye to Fascist intervention.[36]

The duplicitous policy of "non-intervention," Tresca argued, reflected the desire of capitalists and political conservatives for a victory of the insurgent forces. He rejected the argument that British and French assistance to the Republic would lead to a European war. Italy and Germany would not have risked war in 1936. Non-intervention was adopted by Britain and France because it provided a suitable cover for their special interests and fears. Great Britain was the greater culprit in this regard, already appeasing Hitler and Mussolini, and threatening to leave France to Hitler's mercy if she intervened unilaterally on the Republican side. British and French conservatives wanted to exploit rather than liberate Spain, an objective the Spanish reactionaries would not oppose if they received their share of the profits. In short, "the politics of neutrality serves the rapacious and thieving capitalists of France, England, Germany, and Italy in their violation of international pacts which harm the legitimate government in Madrid and help fascistize Spain."[37]

Throughout the Civil War *Il Martello* provided thorough accounts of political and military developments in Spain, information usually at variance with the propaganda and outright distortion published by the most widely-read organ of the American Left, the communist *Daily Worker*.[38] Tresca also lectured about the Civil War throughout the New York area, New England, Pennsylvania, and the Midwest. On these lecture tours, he raised desperately-needed funds to purchase weapons, food, and medical supplies for the anarchist militias fighting in Catalonia and Aragon, which were deliberately starved of these necessities by the Republican government in Madrid from the outset.[39] One military endeavor Tresca supported with his fund raising was the formation of the *Colonna Italiana*, a unit of around 130 men, mostly anarchists, organized by the anarchist Camillo Berneri, the republican Mario Angeloni, and Carlo Rosselli, the radical democrat and founder of *Giustizia e Libertà*, an independent anti-Fascist organization of major importance. Assigned to the anarcho-syndicalist *Columna Francisco Ascaso*, the *Colonna Italiana* first saw action on August 28, 1936 at Monte Pelato near Huesca, in Aragon, defeating a force of insurgents several times its size.[40]

Once the Huesca front became static, Tresca's attention turned to the siege of Madrid, the primary target of Franco's forces. He rejoiced when Madrid, with the help of the first contingents of the International Brigades recruited by the Comintern, withstood rebel attacks in November and December 1936. Despite his fierce opposition to Soviet objectives and methods in Spain, Tresca had nothing but admiration for the rank-and-file communists who comprised the majority of the volunteers in the International Brigades. But other than Madrid's survival, the situation in Spain was bleak. In February 1937, the important coastal city of Málaga fell to the insurgents and the Americans of the Lincoln Battalion were decimated on the Jarama front. Málaga had special significance for Tresca and the Italian anti-Fascists because the military units chiefly responsible for its capture were army troops and Fascist militia of Mussolini's

Corpo Truppe Volontarie (CTV).[41] Responding to the fall of Málaga, Tresca denounced the CTV as a gang of "professional assassins" recruited from among "born criminals," characterizations guaranteed to outrage Mussolini's Italian-American supporters.[42] Tresca also understood the international implications of Málaga. The British dominated Non-Intervention Committee ignored the participation of Italian troops in the capture of the port city, as it ignored public events organized by Mussolini to celebrate the victory of his "volunteers." There was no greater proof for Tresca that "the Non-Intervention Committee serves the interests of Fascism."[43]

The discouragement generated by the Italian victory at Málaga was dispelled briefly by the battle of Guadalajara. Four mechanized and well-equipped divisions of Italian legionnaires (40,000 strong) were soundly defeated by elements of the International Brigades and the Republican army in mid-March 1937. The victory provided a great boost to the morale and hopes of Italian anti-Fascists because the men fighting in the Republican vanguard were members the Garibaldi Battalion of the 12th International Brigade. Never before had Italian anti-Fascists confronted Mussolini's forces in armed conflict on this scale. Count Galeazzo Ciano, Mussolini's foreign minister and son-in-law, remembered March 19, the day he received news of the humiliating defeat, as the "worst day" of his life. He and other Fascist officials "nearly turned each other's hair white" discussing the debacle.[44] For Mussolini, avenging the humiliation at Guadalajara became an obsession, and he ordered that not a single Italian legionnaire would leave Spain until the humiliation had been expunged.[45]

The anti-Fascists' victory at Guadalajara did not diminish Tresca's personal distress over Italian intervention in Spain. He rejected any notion that Italians should lament the defeat on patriotic grounds. On the contrary, Tresca angrily denounced Mussolini's troops as "the savage beast in a black shirt,…brigands in the pay of international capitalism." He felt shame that Italian troops were fighting on behalf of Franco—"Ashamed to be Italian."[46] Although nothing then or later would have mitigated his condemnation of Italy's role, Tresca did not know at the time that compared to the savageries perpetrated by the Spaniards, foreign legionnaires, and Moroccans under Franco's command, Italian troops in Spain conducted themselves like Boy Scouts.

Perhaps inspired by Guadalajara, Tresca resolved to go to Catalonia to observe or participate in the revolutionary experiment being conducted by the anarchists in Aragon and Catalonia. Since he did not possess proper papers, Tresca went to Washington several times to obtain an American passport, but each time his request was denied.[47] Going to Spain without a passport was out of the question. American authorities would never have allowed him to re-enter the country. Ironically, on this occasion, Tresca unknowingly owed his life to the American government. His arrival in Spain would have coincided with the "May Days" of Barcelona, the murderous counter-revolutionary offensive the Stalinists launched against anarchists and dissident Marxists in Catalonia. Tresca would have been a prime candidate for liquidation by the OGPU, the Soviet secret police.

20

Taking on the Stalinists

The era of the Popular Front saw Tresca emerge as one of the most aggressive critics of Stalinism and the Soviet Union. The communist parties of Europe and the United States, together with numerous front and auxiliary organizations under their influence, had come to dominate the Left by the mid-1930s. Tresca, who had been in a minority position by virtue of his cooperation with communists in the 1920s, would once again find himself again in a minority as an anti-Stalinist leftist in the mid-1930s. Although relatively few in number compared to the communists, their broad array of sympathizers, and their socialist allies in the Popular Front, leftists in America who shared Tresca's anti-Stalinist views constituted an impressive group of intellectuals and political activists, such as Edmund Wilson, James T. Farrell, Sidney Hook, Irving Howe, Dwight MacDonald, Hebert Solow, Philip Rahv, Max Eastman, James Rorty, Eliot Cohen, and others.[1] Operating with few allies did not deter Tresca from attacking the Stalinists as fiercely as he did the Fascists. For in his mind, the time when there was any significant difference between them had long since passed.

Tresca was suspicious of the Popular Front from its inception. Rooted in leftwing and trade-unionist agitation in Spain and France in 1934, the Popular Front policy was officially promulgated by the Comintern in August 1935. An electoral alliance of communist, socialist, and bourgeois democratic parties joined in opposition to rightwing and Fascist candidates, the Popular Front policy was a strategy intended by Stalin to induce the Western democracies to form a collective security pact with the Soviet Union and stand firm together against Nazi-Fascist aggression. As an anarchist, Tresca rejected electoral alliances of any kind, but he might not have opposed the Popular Front if it were a true "united front" of anti-Fascists functioning as equals, that is, "a sincere and spontaneous accord between the workers of the world." But a united front dominated by a partnership between communist and socialist parties essentially serving the foreign policy interests of the Soviet Union was unacceptable to him.[2]

The Spanish Revolution

The policy and tactics of the Popular Front acquired far more ominous meaning for Tresca with the outbreak of civil war in Spain. Spain had captured Tresca's attention since the formation of the Second Spanish Republic in 1931. Conditions of political instability and social unrest gave portent of a seismic showdown between the forces of revolution and reaction. Spain was the only country in Europe where social revolution was a genuine possibility. The anarcho-syndicalist labor union, the *Confederación Nacional del Trabajo* (CNT), together with the secret anarchist organization, the *Federación Anarquista Ibérica* (FAI) constituted a militant mass movement that began collectivizing agriculture and industry in Catalonia and parts of Aragon and the Levant after rebel forces in these areas were initially defeated.[3] But once the anarchists' drive to liberate Aragon was stopped at Huesca and a stalemate ensued on this front, CNT-FAI leaders, especially those who reluctantly accepted ministerial positions, adhered to the Madrid government's formula: "the war first, the revolution after."[4]

Tresca believed "the war first, the revolution after" policy was suicidal. He recognized that Stalin's policy toward Spain was strictly counter-revolutionary, predicting as early as August 1936 that the Stalinists were preparing "another betrayal of the proletariat, as it invites them to fight for democracy against Hitler."[5] "Spain will be saved only by a revolutionary alliance between anarchist and socialist workers, not by a Popular Front government."[6] The Bolsheviks had liquidated anarchists in Russia after the 1917 revolution; the Stalinists would try to eliminate the anarchists and other dissenters once they acquired control of the Republican government. It was imperative, Tresca insisted, that the Spanish anarchists remain vigilant against Stalinist subterfuge and pursue the defeat of Fascism by means of social revolution.[7]

Tresca's warnings were justified. Juan Hernandez, the editor of the communist *Mundo Obrero* and a member of the Spanish parliament, indicated in August 1936 what lay in store for the anarchists and other revolutionaries: "You need not pay much attention to them.... the Spanish people and their official bodies will rise against them.... We don't want to hear any more about libertarian communism. Immediately after victory, they [the anarchists] will be settled with as they must."[8] Stalin's personal organ, *Pravda,* declared on December 17, 1936: "So far as Catalonia is concerned, the cleaning up of the Trotskyist and Anarcho-Syndicalist elements has already begun; it will be carried out with the same energy with which it was conducted in the U.S.S.R."[9] Behind the scenes, in his oft-quoted letter of December 21, 1936, Stalin made clear to Prime Minister Francisco Largo Caballero that Soviet policy called for support of the democratic republic and defense of bourgeois property, not revolution.[10] "This is necessary," he indicated, "in order to prevent the enemies of Spain from considering her a Communist republic, and to forestall thus their open intervention, which constitutes the greatest danger for republican Spain."[11]

Tresca argued that what Stalin really feared was the formation of an anti-communist alliance between Germany, Italy, Great Britain, and France, designed to wage war against the Soviet Union and overthrow Stalin's regime.[12] Consequently, Stalin's cynical policy vis-à-vis the Spanish revolution derived from the Soviet Union's need for self-preservation. Victory by the insurgents might lead to a Fascist state in Spain and compel greater British and French accommodation with Hitler. A republican victory, on the other hand, might accomplish the same undesired end by increasing French and especially British paranoia about communism achieving state power in a Western European nation. Soviet intervention in Spain, therefore, was calculated to forestall victory by either side, and prolong the Civil War until the Western democracies came to their senses and aligned with the Soviet Union against Nazi Germany.[13]

The May Days of Barcelona

The commanding influence the Stalinists quickly established over the Spanish Republican government derived from Soviet military and economic aid. To ensure adherence to Soviet policy, a host of Comintern officials and secret police (NKVD) agents[14] were sent to guide the war effort and liquidate left-wing elements bent on revolution. Tresca's former comrade Vittorio Vidali (now known as "Carlos Contreras") became one of the Comintern's premier operatives in Spain, winning notoriety and inspiring fear as the commander of the communist Fifth Regiment and one of the NKVD's top executioners.[15]

Stalin's counter-revolutionary policy was ruthlessly carried out during the "May Days of Barcelona" (May 3–6, 1937), when elements of the communist *Partido Obrero Unificat de Catalunya* and Catalonian government police battled and defeated workers of the CNT, the Friends of Durutti (anarchists), and the *Partido Obrero de Unificación Marxista* (POUM: a dissident Marxist party), leaving some 500 dead and 1,500 wounded. Among those deliberately selected for liquidation was the Italian anarchist Camillo Berneri, publisher of *Guerra di Classe* in Barcelona and one of the most outspoken advocates of defeating Fascism by means of social revolution. Like Tresca, Berneri had predicted Stalinist suppression of the revolution as early as December 16, 1936: "already today, Spain is between two fires: Burgos [the insurgents' capital] and Moscow."[16]

Berneri's murder cast a pall over the entire anarchist movement. *Il Martello* bristled with angry articles by Italian anarchist eyewitnesses, describing the May events and condemning the Stalinists for the crimes they committed in Barcelona and other parts of Spain.[17] Tresca attributed Berneri's murder to the counter-revolutionary campaign of suppression and liquidation the Stalinists had waged for many months preceding the May Days. He rejected communist claims that the POUM and the CNT had been infiltrated by Fascists, who were responsible for the violence that occurred. The clash in Barcelona had been deliberately provoked by the Soviet consul general, Vladimir Antonov-Ovseenko, for the purpose of crushing the POUM and the anarchists of the CNT-FAI. Tresca denounced communist accusations that Berneri was a "counter-revolutionary" as outrageous. He lambasted not only the Stalinists in Spain but their brethren in New York, who published *Unità Operaio*. They had described the May Days as a "Hitlerian revolt," executed by "other forces" under Fascist control, and dared to imply that Berneri had received the punishment he deserved.[18] A few months later, Tresca identified the architect of Berneri's murder as George Mink, the former head of the American CP's seamen's organization on the New York waterfront, who served as the chief of Soviet secret police in Barcelona, overseeing the liquidation of scores of anti-Stalinists held captive in republican jails.[19]

The murders of Berneri, POUM leader Andrés Nin, and hundreds of other anti-Stalinists convinced Tresca that any anarchist or dissident communist who ventured to Spain risked ending up with a bullet in the back of his head. That was the fate he predicted to the many radicals who sought his advice about going to Spain.[20] The Stalinist executioner whom Tresca detested most by now was his former associate Vidali. Ernest Hemingway told *The New York Times* reporter Herbert L. Matthews that the skin between the thumb and forefinger of Vidali's right hand had become badly burned from the number of times he had shot someone with his revolver.[21] Confirmation of Vidali's murderous capabilities came directly to Tresca from a more immediate source—Tony Ribarich, a member of the *Il Martello* group. Ribarich and Vidali had been communist activists and close friends in Trieste in the early 1920s, and their friendship and political association as CP members continued after their arrival in the United States in 1923. After Vidali's deportation, they continued to correspond until 1929, when Ribarch was expelled from the CP as a "counter-revolutionary" for speaking his mind. Misinformed that his former comrade intended to fight for the Spanish Republic, Vidali wrote a letter to Ribarich's mother in Trieste, warning that he had a gun, bullets, and a grave all picked out for her son, and that if Ribarich went to Spain he would personally kill him.[22]

After the May Days, Tresca warned some of his famous friends against going to Spain lest they be deceived and exploited by the communists. The writer John Dos Passos believed that a documentary movie about the Spanish Civil War would capture the attention of the American public and bring pressure to bear on the government to allow Republican Spain to purchase arms. Tresca invited Dos Passos to dinner shortly before his departure for Spain. After Dos Passos described his project, Tresca told him: "John… they goin' make a monkey outa you… a big monkey." When Dos Passos insisted that he had complete control over the production, Tresca laughed in his face, explaining:

> How can you? When your director is a Communist Party member, when everywhere you go, you will be supervised by Party members. Everybody you see will be chosen by the Party. Everything you do will be in the interests of the Communist Party. If the Communists don't like a man in Spain right away they shoot him.

"It didn't turn out quite that way," Dos Passos later wrote, "but almost." "I'd hardly been in Valencia a day before I realized that we were licked before we started." Little wonder that Dos Passos' account of this story also described Tresca as possessing "the shrewdest kind of knowledge of men and their motives with profound information on the realities of politics he'd acquired in a lifetime of partisan warfare in the anarchist cause."[23]

The John Dewey Committee

Tresca's fight against Stalinists and Soviet dictatorship received national attention when he embraced the defense of Leon Trotsky in 1937. During the Moscow show trials of 1935–1938, which purged and liquidated most of the old Bolshevik party leaders and the highest echelons of the Red Army, Trotsky was portrayed as the ex-Marxist Anti-Christ, masterminding Machiavellian conspiracies against communism and the Soviet Union. Tresca again and again mocked the spectacle of CP leaders dutifully parroting Stalin's fantastical ravings about Trotsky. To combat this campaign of nauseating lies and distortion, he joined the American Committee for the Defense of Leon Trotsky, organized in October 1936 and chaired by the eminent educator and philosopher John Dewey.[24] Tresca's importance to the Trotsky defense committee derived mainly from his reputation as a labor leader, the only member possessing such credentials. His activities included speaking at all five of the mass meetings convened by the committee and serving on the smaller investigative sub-committee of ten headed by Dewey. The rest of the committee included more than thirty prominent figures, including Suzanne LaFollette, John F. Finerty, Benjamin Stolberg, John R. Chamberlain, Edward A. Ross, Wendelin Thomas, Otto Ruehle, Albert Goldman, and Francisco Zamora. Herbert Solow, a good friend of Tresca and Margaret De Silver, was a key behind-the-scenes figure.[25]

That Tresca should have become involved in Trotsky's defense was characteristic of his non-sectarian approach to fighting tyranny. Trotsky was universally hated by the anarchists. Not only had Trotsky, Lenin, and other Bolsheviks transformed a popular revolution into a party dictatorship, as commander of the Red Army, Trotsky had destroyed the anarchist forces of Nestor Makhno in the Ukraine and crushed the Kronstadt Rebellion of March 1921, the revolt of Baltic fleet sailors who had helped the Bolsheviks seize power in 1917 but came to oppose Lenin's repressive regime. But Tresca's opposition to Trotsky was mitigated by his habitual sympathy for the underdog, a tendency that extended to other Trotskyists in the 1930s. They merited assistance because they were revolutionaries and opposed Stalin. But, in the final analysis, serving on the Dewey Committee was a means to not only defend Trotsky but to strike a blow against Stalinism and its sycophantic acolytes in the United States.[26]

Tresca's decision to join the Dewey Committee must also have been influenced by his new companion Margaret De Silver. Although a civil libertarian and self-professed "bourgeois liberal,"[27] Margaret admired Trotsky for his intellectual brilliance and courage. Assisting the Dewey Committee was typical of the political causes she regularly embraced. Her role, although hidden from the public, was actually more important than Tresca's. She contributed $5,000 to the defense campaign and went to Mexico to meet with Trotsky personally. Tresca did not accompany her because American authorities would not have allowed him to re-enter the country. Trotsky, in a letter to Margaret, expressed his disappointment at Tresca's absence: "I should be very glad to meet comrade Tresca some time. Naturally not with the naïve aim of converting him (we old revolutionaries are stubborn people) but with the aim of discussing the possibilities for common measures against the Stalinist gangrene."[28]

Meanwhile, the CP, the Friends of the Soviet Union, various communist agencies, and party publications were all attacking the Dewey Committee and its members with as much vitriol as they could produce. The *Daily Worker* denounced the visit to Trotsky in Mexico as "a whitewash expedition" intended "to provide a new forum to enable this agent of fascism to pour forth his streams of poisonous abuses of the Soviet Union, the labor movement, and the democratic forces of the world."[29] Committee members such as Stolberg, Goldman, Ruehle, and LaFollette were labeled "gangsters of the pen." John Dewey's integrity was besmirched and Tresca branded an agent of Mussolini.[30] No amount of "whitewashing" could mask Trotsky's nefarious activities, the *Daily Worker* professed, because "the courts of the Soviet Union finally and irrefutably exposed the nature of Trotsky's plotting with German Fascism and Japanese militarism for war against the U.S.S.R."[31] Ignoring this barrage of slander, Dewey, Goldman, Finerty, and others conducted thirteen lengthy interrogations of Trotsky in his home in Mexico City on April 10–17, 1937. Trotsky employed his extraordinary knowledge of Soviet and world affairs, his awesome intellectual power, and his trenchant logic to demonstrate that the Moscow trials of old Bolsheviks were nothing more than elaborate frame-ups ordered by Stalin. The Dewey Committee pronounced Trotsky "Not Guilty" of all charges on September 21, 1937.

Juliet Stuart Poyntz

Committed now to exposing the crimes of Stalin and his Comintern agents, Tresca became one the first anti-communist radicals to reveal how the *longa manus* of the NKVD extended even to American soil. The disappearance of Juliet Stuart Poyntz in 1937 provided the opportunity to draw national attention to these nefarious activities, and to earn Tresca the inextinguishable enmity of the communists. Theodore Draper, the preeminent historian of the American CP, described Poyntz as a "strong female personality and the only one ever considered a threat to the male monopoly in the top leadership."[32] An all-American type from the Midwest, Poyntz was highly educated and already a professional when she joined the CP in 1921. An excellent speaker and propagandist, she served on several important CP committees, attended CP conventions as a party delegate, and ran unsuccessfully for public office several times between 1924 and 1931. Poyntz disappeared from public sight in 1934, when she was recruited by the OGPU (later the NKVD). Recalled to Moscow, Poyntz observed first hand some of Stalin's purge trials, and may even have participated in interrogations with the infamous George Mink.[33]

Poyntz had become thoroughly disillusioned with the Soviet Union and the American CP by the time she re-surfaced in the United States in 1936. She confided these sentiments to Tresca. Although they differed politically, Tresca and Poyntz had been personal friends for more than twenty years, and he became fearful for her safety. Tresca never saw Poyntz again. She disappeared without a trace after leaving her room at the Women's Association Clubhouse in Manhattan on June 5, 1937, a fact her attorney failed to report to the police until six months later.[34]

Tresca concluded that Poyntz had been "lured or kidnapped" back to the Soviet Union because she had broken with the communists and "knew too much."[35] Interviewed by *The New York Times* on February 7, 1938, Tresca announced that he would present his theory to Assistant U.S. Attorney Lester C. Dunigan and the name of the man he believed was the only person who could have lured Poyntz to her death. The man Tresca identified was Sachno Epstein, a former assistant editor of the communist *Freiheit*, an NKVD agent, and her one-time lover, whom he had met several times. Epstein, who also disappeared sometime later, had been seen together with Poyntz around the time she went missing.[36]

Tresca also suggested a possible link between Poyntz and the Reubens/Robinson case, under investigation by a federal grand jury. Arnold Reuben and his wife, traveling under the names of "Mr. and Mrs. Robinson," were Comintern agents whose job was to obtain phony passports for use by American communists traveling to the Soviet Union. The Soviet press had charged that Reubens and his wife were American Trotskyists involved in anti-Soviet plots, and that the West Coast of the United States was teeming with Japanese and German spies. The purpose of the Reubens frame-up, Tresca explained to *The New York Times*, was to create a spy scare in the United States that would achieve two objectives: hasten a war between Japan and the United States, and thereby deflect Japanese aggression away from Soviet territory (there were already Russo-Japanese clashes along the Siberian-Manchurian border); and to smear opponents of Stalin's regime, especially Trotskyists and other anti-Soviet radicals like himself. Tresca concluded his interview with a warning:

> The time has come when radicals in the United States who dare to speak against the Stalin regime should take some measures of self-defense against the terrorism of the Soviet G.P.U. If Miss Poyntz could be kidnapped, taken aboard a Soviet vessel in New York or some other American port and hustled off to Russia, there is no guarantee that others may not suffer the same fate."[37]

Tresca's interview with *The New York Times* and his subsequent meeting with Francis A. Mahoney, acting chief of the Criminal Division of the United States Attorney's office, resulted in his being subpoenaed to appear before a federal grand jury on February 21, 1938. He testified for two hours about Poyntz, providing his own theory about her disappearance and naming fifteen witnesses who could shed light on her and the Reubens case. Among the names he provided was that of George Mink.[38] But the federal grand jury and New York police investigations failed to discover any concrete evidence about her presumed murder. The Poyntz case was never solved.

What Tresca's press interview and federal grand jury appearance did accomplish was to provoke an avalanche of hateful attacks and threats against him, the likes of which he had never experienced. The *Daily Worker* declared that Tresca was vying with Herbert Solow and Benjamin Stolberg (both critics of Stalinism under CP attack) for "stool-pigeon honors."[39] Consigning him to membership in the "'left-wing plus line-up," the *Daily Worker* dismissed Tresca's accusations as "an anti-Soviet cock and bull story,... and a tissue of lies."[40] Attacks come next from the CP's Italian National Commission and fellow travelers—notably Pietro Allegra, Girolamo Valenti, and Vito Marcantonio, identified in the *Daily Worker* as noted anti-Fascists who "ridiculed the rantings of Carlo Tresca as the actions of a 'discredited' and 'disgruntled' man."[41]

Allegra was a prized acquisition for the communists, as he had been Tresca's closest associate and friend for so many years. Relations between the two had become strained, both for personal and political reasons, after *Il Martello* was resurrected in 1934. They both had joined the *Comitato d'Azione Contro il Fascismo e la Guerra* (Action Committee Against Fascism and War) formed in July 1935, as anti-Fascists attempted once again to forge a united front. The Action Committee soon fell under communist control. Tresca quit in February 1936, but Allegra did not. By then, Allegra had become a strong advocate of a united front under communist control and a fervent supporter of the Soviet Union. He ended his association with *Il Martello* and went on to become the general organizer for the Italian Anti-Fascist Committee, another communist front organization. After Tresca's interview with *The New York Times*, Allegra accused him of having "enlisted on the side of the Trotskyists in the fight against the united anti-Fascist front of the people against fascism in the United States, Spain, and Italy."[42]

Valenti, the director of *La Stampa Libera*, was now working hand in glove with the communists as mandated by the Popular Front pact between the Italian Communist and Socialist parties. He described Tresca as "disgruntled" and "devoting his time to the fight against other sections of the labor movement, particularly against Soviet Russia and Loyalist Spain." Marcantonio, the communist sympathizer who was now out of political office and serving as president of the International Labor Defense, declared that Tresca was "completely discredited in the eyes of the population of New York.....Therefore it is no wonder that the reactionary forces use him for their dirty jobs against the people. Pick out a stooge anywhere and you will find he has been discredited."[43] The Italian National Commission was not only critical but threatening, declaring that

> Tresca's isolation is a measure of elementary defense for all anti-Fascism. Without any other preoccupation except that of protecting and safe-guarding anti-Fascism, we therefore launch a fraternal appeal to the militants of all groups or political parties... that in the common interest they make Tresca understand that police informers will no longer be tolerated in the political and labor movement.[44]

For Tresca the message the communists intended to deliver was clear:

> Tresca continues to present himself in anti-Fascist circles. Horrors! If he is alive, healthy and not disposed to die—either physically or politically to please the melancholy Pietrino [Allegra]—to prevent him from presenting himself, it is necessary to make an end of him, definitively. In a word: what is needed is a George Mink, member of the Communist Party of America and the assassin of comrades Berneri and Barbieri.

Demands to "impose the isolation of Tresca," and affirmations that "it would be a betrayal of antifascism and their conscience" if they tolerated him any longer, were reminiscent of the words Mussolini used to spur the assassins of Matteotti to action, Tresca noted. Defiant as always in the face of threats, he declared: "I await unwaveringly for the four swine of the bombastic National Commission of the Communist Party of America to take action."[45]

Tresca continued to defend his actions and decry the hypocrisy of his critics. He affirmed that he had never been, consciously or otherwise, a tool of the government or in its service, as the communists charged. Moreover, in the past, when he had provided district attorneys with incriminating evidence against the Fascists—after the Harlem bombing in 1926 and to save Clemente Lista in

1932—anti-Fascists, including the communists, had approved his actions. Why was providing evidence to solve the disappearance of Poyntz now considered an act of apostasy? Because the communists feared what he would reveal about OGPU [NKVD] operations on American soil, he answered. By giving an interview to *The New York Times* and testifying before a federal grand jury, he had reached millions: "I 'used' the Federal Jury as a platform to speak to the public. I 'used' the Federal Jury to denounce to the world the monstrous crimes of the police system organized by Stalin. I fulfilled a duty. My conscience is clear."[46]

Attacks on his integrity continued unrelentingly. The most savage came from Pietro Allegra in October 1938, a vengeful venting of bile in a pamphlet entitled *Il Suicidio Morale di Carlo Tresca*. Allegra claimed that he was attacking Tresca for "reasons of public welfare and the interests of antifascism." Tresca's anti-communism,

> is suicide for himself, is a true betrayal against the anti-Fascist movement because he has created confusion, dissent, sabotage, and nausea in the ranks of antifascism and given hope to the fascist camp.... [If] he—Carlo Tresca—has completely lost his sense of reason and decency, then... for reasons of public welfare and antifascism, it is a duty to put a STOP to his deleterious, disgusting work as an enemy of antifascism.

By attacking Tresca, Allegra was performing "a civil and social act..., a work of protection, of elimination from society, of beings who are hateful to themselves and to the society that gives them hospitality."[47]

Despite their past disagreements, such an attack coming from Allegra must have hurt Tresca deeply. But convinced that Allegra had now become a communist puppet (evidenced not only by his writings, but by his complete silence when the communists murdered Berneri), Tresca dismissed him contemptuously as a hired pen: "When [the communists] can't utilize George Mink, the professional butcher, they use someone like Pietro Allegra, who on command hurls himself against the target indicated by Moscow, with a pen for a knife, a pen bathed in poison." However, "if Moscow wants to make an end of me, it had better use George Mink rather than Allegra."[48]

Was Tresca's life truly in jeopardy? Writing to Margaret De Silver on March 31, 1938, Trotsky warned: "The Kremlin beast is wounded but not dead. Its last convulsions can be terrible. I believe, for example, that Comrade Tresca is now one of the targets for the hatred and revenge of the G.P.U."[49] Tresca's entire career had been punctuated with threats upon his life, but he had never allowed them to interfere with his activities. He always believed that publicity afforded some measure of security, which is why he was so public in his accusations against Pope in 1934, and now when he charged the Soviet secret police with responsibility for Poyntz's abduction. After the Poyntz case, Tresca did not take any extraordinary precautions, even though he believed Mink had returned to New York.[50] However, at the insistence of De Silver, they moved from her brownstone in Brooklyn Heights to an apartment at 130 West 12th Street, near St. Vincent's Hospital, so he could be close to his office.[51]

L'Adunata Attacks

As if slander and threats from the communists were not trouble enough, Tresca had to contend once again with the *L'Adunatisti*, who seized upon the Poyntz case to reactivate their campaign to bring him down. Tresca attempted to stem their criticism by publishing a sympathetic letter Emma Goldman had written to him about the Poyntz case: "It's a rather disagreeable job to have to apply to a Capitalist court to expose the Stalinist gangsters. All in all I do not envy your job though I think you should go ahead and expose the disappearance of Miss Poyntz."[52] But the wrath of *L'Adunata*'s high priest Raffaele Schiavina, alias "Max Sartin," was not assuaged by Goldman's empathy for Tresca. He denounced "*Pagnacca*" for his "act of collaboration with the police, an act of informing and of spying."[53] "Collaborating with the police," Schiavina insisted, "is the foulest form of collaboration with the State."[54] Tresca's good intentions were irrelevant: "Whoever, out of hatred for the communists, resorts to the office of the bourgeois police, puts himself on a level with the most perverse communists, and... does the work of a spy." [55]

Tresca counter-attacked by accusing "Pope Sartin" of never fighting the communists with anything but words. He belittled him as "a mole, traveling underground," who possessed "the courage of a rabbit."[56] (It is worth noting that Tresca always referred to him by his pen name "Sartin" rather than his real name Schiavina, which would have alerted the FBI to his clandestine presence in the United States.) *Il Martello* then published a second letter from Goldman (who had been rebuked by Schiavina for supporting Tresca), which underscored the danger Tresca had courted by exposing Stalinist crimes. "It was not your appeal to the authorities that I approved of," she wrote, "but your courage in concerning yourself with [such] matters, knowing that by lifting the veil from the activities of the GPU you run the risk of losing your life."[57]

As Schiavina's attacks continued, Tresca became more infuriated and his bromides more denigrating. He typically described "Pope Sartin of the non-libertarian Apostolic Catholic Church" as "vile down to his marrow," and "the most repugnant professional slanderer."[58] What Tresca wanted, above all, was a showdown with his adversary. He challenged Schiavina to debate him in public, but "the rabbit still hides."[59] An exasperated Tresca wrote to Alberto Meschi at the end of 1938: "Now I await the comrades to afford me the opportunity—insistently requested—to find myself... face to face with Sartin. But the fine man flees. I have never succeeded in seeing him in front of me. Evidently he crosses the street whenever we might encounter each other by chance."[60] A year later, when anarchist groups in Chicago invited Tresca and Schiavina to meet and put an end to the polemic that had proved so divisive for the movement, Tresca responded: "Any time; any day of the week; anywhere in the United States."[61] Schiavina ignored the invitation.

Nothing could deter the *L'Adunatisti* from waging their campaign against Tresca, and he would remain their *bête noir* until long after his death. But even Italian anarchists who rejected *L'Adunata*'s portrayal of Tresca as a "spy" were dismayed by his action in the Poyntz case, for by providing information to the government he had violated a sacred tenet of anarchism. Many old comrades severed relations with him. Thus, in the end, the Poyntz case, rather than enhance his reputation as an anti-Stalinist, accelerated the decline of his career.[62]

21

The Town Anarchist

Tresca, by the 1930s, had acquired celebrity status in New York City as the "Town Anarchist."[1] Major newspapers and prestigious magazines now portrayed him as a revolutionary icon, a flamboyant and larger-than-life character, a die-hard rebel of the old school who no longer posed a menace to society. Always amenable to public notoriety, Tresca willingly provided vivid accounts of his tumultuous career, stimulating the pens of noted columnists Joseph Mitchell of the *New York World-Telegram*, Archer Winston of the *New York Post*, and the radical intellectual Max Eastman, who described his friend in a two-part "Portrait" for *The New Yorker*.[2] Tresca relished his title of "Town Anarchist," and was delighted to remind America that he had been "at the violent center of more labor trouble over a period of thirty years than any other known agitator."[3]

Journalistic accounts of the "Town Anarchist" were usually accompanied by a description or photograph which captured the flamboyance and dash of this defiant rebel, with his signature goatee hiding the scar on his cheek, the glowing eyes beneath his steel rimmed glasses, his five-and-a half gallon black felt hat, and the pipe or cigar habitually clutched in his teeth. But the photographs and exciting stories reflected only the "Town Anarchist." Tresca, the private man—his personality, lifestyle, family, and friends—generally eluded published portrayals.

"Carlo was always *lovable*," recalled Lewis S. Gannet.

> That was the quality that surprised many people, meeting him for the first time, when they had heard only of his fighting quality. Perhaps they heard him labeled "anarchist" or "revolutionary," and they came prepared to see a man of hate. That Carlo, at his fiercest, was not... He loved people, and people of all kinds responded to his world-embracing smile, to his caressing smile, to his caressing voice, to the obvious enjoyment of life and love of mankind that bubbled out of his whole big personality.[4]

Many friends and associates, in fact, considered the "soft side" of Tresca to be more representative of the man than his political activism. Roger Baldwin related that his closest ties with Tresca were established not in the sphere of social activism but in their personal interaction: "Carlo with his explosive humor, his hearty laughter, his bantering comment... His gusto was contagious. We were always cheered up by a session with him, however badly the world was going.... Unless one knew him well it was hard to guess that underneath his joy in living lay such profound convictions as to human freedom and progress."⁵

Added to these qualities was a child-like playfulness and mischievousness that belied his image as the fierce revolutionary. His daughter Beatrice remembered with fondness an incident involving her and Edna Ferber at a speakeasy on Bedford Street in Greenwich Village in 1929. Beatrice had just been hired at her first teaching position, and Ferber had just published her novel *Cimarron*. Happily discussing their achievements over dinner, the two women were suddenly thrown into a panic as two policemen burst into the speakeasy announcing a raid. A scandal, they feared, would envelop them both if they were hauled off to jail. Then they noticed Tresca laughing so hard that he nearly fell off his chair. He had paid the beat cops to raid the speakeasy as a prank.⁶

Tresca was no saint, however. His behavior was often contradictory and worthy of censure, as he was the first to admit. But Tresca's mantra for his personal and political life was unequivocal: "I have to be who I am."⁷ This lifestyle credo produced an independent firebrand who devoted his entire life to the cause of social justice, as well as a self-indulgent egoist who placed his own desires and needs above those of family, friends, and lovers. Yet Tresca's frequent neglect of those closest to him did not arise from indifference; he loved his daughter and siblings deeply, as he did—at least temporarily—several of the many women in his life. Nevertheless, he proved unwilling or incapable of making the compromises in his career and lifestyle that would have made for more harmonious and considerate relationships.

The Tresca Family

Tresca had demonstrated his cavalier attitude toward marital and family commitment by conducting numerous affairs with women other than his wife. This tendency would have manifested even if he and Helga interacted splendidly. But their relationship had been strained long before he became involved with Flynn. His philandering, to be sure, accounted for much of their marital discord; nonetheless, as his daughter Beatrice candidly acknowledged, Helga was a very difficult person with whom to live. If anything, given his self-indulgent nature and lust for women, it is a wonder that Tresca remained with Helga for as long as he did. As he explained to Max Eastman in 1934:

> I no like married life.... I like one woman an' then time pass an' I like another. I make many good friend'ship with women because I always say ver' frank: "Don' trus'me. My character ver' emotional.
> I have gran' an' real passion now, but when dat gone, I gone too!"⁸

Beatrice believed that Tresca's love for Flynn had been genuine, but she always clung to the belief that his break-up with Helga might not have been permanent. She frequently recounted a conversation she had with her father years later, in which he indicated that he had never understood Helga's reaction to his affair with Flynn, implying that, if she had been patient, he would have returned to her eventually because she was his wife. This might have been true, or he might have made these remarks for her benefit. She herself admitted this was the only occasion she ever heard her father say anything that smacked of a double standard about marriage and infidelity.[9] But the fact remains that Tresca did not return to Helga—he abandoned his wife and child alone and penniless in a foreign country. As a grown woman, Beatrice came to accept his unorthodox lifestyle and frequently irresponsible behavior, chiefly because (unlike Helga) he was always open and honest about his personal deficiencies.

Helga, at the time, was emotionally devastated by feelings of rejection and full of resentful over her abandonment, for which she blamed Flynn more than her husband. But she might not have welcomed him back in any case. Flynn was the proverbial last straw. Helga filed suit for a divorce on May 23, 1913, claiming desertion and non-support. The following year, Tresca filed his own suit for divorce and custody of Beatrice on the ground that Helga was not a fit mother, a charge without basis. While the case languished in court for the next few years, relations between Tresca and Helga remained acrimonious. Whenever he visited his daughter a battle would invariably ensue, usually over the $4.00 a week of child support that he rarely provided.

In 1915, Beatrice was sent to live with a French-Swiss couple in St. James, Long Island, from whom she learned to speak French. When she returned a year later, Helga was living with Tullio Bellotti, a waiter (later *maitre d'*), whom Tresca had met during the hotel workers' strike of 1913 and of whose relationship with Helga he approved. After both divorce suits were denied by the courts the same year they were filed, Beatrice continued to reside with Helga and Bellotti in their apartment at 686 Third Avenue near 43rd Street. Helga and Bellotti lived together happily in common-law marriage, but in the late 1920s, she had another fling with Joe Ettor, who had returned briefly to New York from California after his long retirement from the labor movement. The relationship between Helga and Tullio survived, and the three eventually settled in better accommodations in Queens.[10]

Tresca always retained respect and affection for the woman who officially remained his wife until 1942, when a divorce decree was finally granted. Helga, whose anger subsided but never resolved completely, retained contact with Tresca because they shared a daughter. Eventually, she, Beatrice, Bellotti, Carlo, and the rest of the Tresca family would spend Christmas holidays together at brother Ettore's home. The chief source of contention between Tresca and Helga over the years—aside from his perennial failure to provide adequate child support—was how Beatrice should be raised. Beatrice depicted Helga as an inflexible and self-righteous person, determined to raise her daughter as a proper bourgeois. Tresca's approach was genuinely libertarian, believing that Beatrice should be allowed to grow up as a free spirit and lead whatever kind of life she chose for herself. He never attempted to constrain her development within the narrow boundaries of conventional morality and family values. Helga was always worried about Tresca's "bad influence," and was very jealous that Beatrice felt much closer to her father. As Beatrice put it, Helga provided material support, but "I received my spiritual sustenance from my father." Helga remained a stern and resentful person until her death in her nineties. Yet her influence ultimately prevailed, as Beatrice became "a bourgeois mamma," experiencing a fulfilling life as a wife, mother, and teacher, living until her late eighties.

Little is known about Tresca's relationship with his siblings in America other than that they were close and often stormy, a balance typical of most Italian families. The every-friendly, cigar-smoking Mario had little education and was severely handicapped by nearsightedness; he lived with his brother Ettore and worked at getting out the mail in the *Martello* office and sometimes in drugstores around Chatham Square in lower Manhattan. He doted on Beatrice, adored Helga, and played cards with Tullio. Ettore, a highly-respected physician in the Italian immigrant community, was the family's anchor. He supported Mario and rescued Carlo from financial trouble on countless occasions. Tresca's abuse of Ettore's generosity eventually caused a rupture in their relationship. Tresca's sister Anita was married to Ernesto De Pamphilis, who owned a print shop that printed *Il Martello* in its early days. She never forgave Tresca for deserting Helga.[11] As for extended family, Tresca was very close to Giuseppe Canzanelli, Beatrice's father-in-law and an old friend from Sulmona.

The Martello Group

Giuseppe Popolizio, a close associate for thirty years, related to the author that "those who loved Carlo Tresca did not know him; those who were close to him, hated him."[12] This characterization stands in jarring contrast to the accolades Popolizio heaped upon Tresca in his other letters and writings and was probably influenced by old wounds: "Carlo... even though he praised and cared for me, betrayed me many times."[13] Popolizio's assertion is contradicted, moreover, by the accounts of numerous comrades who were equally close.[14] Yet, however exaggerated his claim, there is no doubt that Tresca did alienate—even to the point of hatred—some of his closest friends, although not necessarily for the reasons they professed.

Between the wars, Tresca's political associates or "my boys" comprised a disparate bunch that included anarchists, syndicalists, socialists, republicans, and even a former communist. At one time or another, this entourage included Pietro Allegra, Luigi Quintiliano, Umberto Nieri, Mario Cafiso, Alberto Cupelli, Fort Velona, Vincenzo Alvano, Pasquale Scipione, Domenico Rosati, Giuseppe Popolizio, Mario Buzzo, Giuseppe Marascia, Frank ("Ciccio") Cancellieri, Tony Ribarich, Vincenzo Leonetti, brother Mario, and others too numerous to list. Attracted to Tresca's genial personality as well as his politics, these comrades formed a group of devoted friends as well as political associates. During the 1930s, Tresca's "boys" were augmented by a dozen or more comrades who populated the *Il Martello* office on a daily basis. To outsiders it appeared that Tresca had a small army at his disposal; in reality, many of these men hung around the office because they were unemployed. But this misperception often dissuaded political enemies from entertaining thought of violence against Tresca.[15]

Trouble within the Martello group developed in the mid-1930s and was thickest at its center, involving Tresca, Allegra, and Quintiliano. The latter once described the trio as the "three musketeers."[16] That was never the case. Tresca was the "boss" and Allegra and Quintiliano were his lieutenants. Fourteen years Tresca's junior and a tailor by trade, Quintiliano was *Il Martello*'s administrator in the 1920s; he wrote regularly for the newspaper, but never had his own column, as did Allegra. Quintiliano was always entrusted with important tasks, such as fund-raising tours, service on important committees, and as *Il Martello*'s contact with the Sacco-Vanzetti Defense Committee. Nevertheless, Tresca could hardly have bolstered Quintiliano's sense of importance and equality by routinely obliging him to take Beatrice home by taxi to Queens after she visited her father at his office. The frequency of Quintiliano's escort service led to false rumors that he and Beatrice were having an affair.[17] More important, when *Il Martello* resumed publication in 1934, Quintiliano was replaced as administrator by Pasquale Scipione, although he remained an editorial associate. Eventually, the friendship between Quintiliano and Tresca became strained, and he ceased to collaborate with the newspaper. But Quintiliano never expressed ill will toward Tresca publicly, and he certainly did not hate him. Not so Allegra.[18]

Allegra had been Tresca's closest comrade since their prewar days in Western Pennsylvania. Allegra's commitment to *Il Martello* was total; he wrote a weekly column, never took a salary, and contributed thousands of his own money to keep the newspaper afloat. For many years they had marched in tandem whatever the cause, with Allegra often serving as Tresca's surrogate. Nevertheless, though well respected for his honesty and commitment, Allegra probably would not have been chosen for key positions, such as general-secretary of the AFANA, if not for Tresca's influence. Thus Allegra had always stood in Tresca's shadow. His first open conflict with Tresca occurred after *Il Martello* was resurrected in 1934, but his permanent break with the newspaper and Tresca came in 1938, with Tresca's attacks against the communists in Spain and after the disappearance of Poyntz.[19] Allegra insisted that the motive for his attack against Tresca was political; nonetheless, his pamphlet *Il suicidio morale di Carlo Tresca* reeks of personal vendetta. His charge that Tresca was an "enemy of antifascism" was outrageous and ludicrous. Most of Allegra's other accusations amount to a grievance list of petty incidents and minor transgressions. Yet some of Allegra's assertions struck a resonant chord, underscoring tendencies that even Tresca's admirers lamented.[20]

A major sore point for the *Martello* group was Tresca's administration of the newspaper. They had taken him at his word, after *Il Martello* resumed publication in 1934, that the group would assume ownership and administration while he functioned solely as director. The change was intended as a means to lift the weight of financial responsibility from Tresca's shoulders while he still ran the operation. But the big issue of contention remained financing the newspaper and how Tresca contributed to its financial woes.

Financing his newspapers and maintaining his lifestyle at the same time constituted a major problem for Tresca. Publishing operations as well as his personal income were dependent upon subscriptions, contributions, speaking engagements, and funding events like plays and picnics. These sources were rarely sufficient to keep his newspaper afloat, so Tresca regularly borrowed from friends and relatives, money he knew he could not repay. For years Allegra, Ettore, and others tolerated this drain on their own resources, rationalizing the losses as their contribution to the newspaper's survival. Not infrequently, however, Tresca took advantage of their generosity in ways that were unethical and even illegal. Poor Ettore not only sustained the loss of money he lent to his brother, but he sometimes had to cover the checks Tresca wrote under his name.[21] Creditors of every kind were always demanding repayment. Giuseppe Popolizio related a scene he observed personally: a woman with three children in tow visited Tresca at his Il Martello office, withdrew a revolver from her purse, and threatened to blow his brains out if he did not repay the $150 he owed her. Another debtor sent a gangster to threaten to shoot Tresca if he failed to pay up. Finding Tresca absent from the office, the gangster fired several shots around the office, wounding Popolizio in the leg.[22]

Tresca was also suspected of sometimes retaining for himself a portion of the contributions intended for his newspaper or for political defense campaigns. The Sacco-Vanzetti Defense Committee, ill disposed toward Tresca in any case, more than a few times expressed such concern.[23] The possibility that Tresca withheld some funds as a "commission" cannot be dismissed. Easier to substantiate was Tresca's personal use of funds intended for Il Martello. Major Italian radical newspapers were generally the property of a political party or labor union. The directors, editors, and staff of these newspapers received a stipend or worked on a voluntary basis. Anarchist newspapers did not have such formal affiliations; they belonged to the "movement," but the men who published them received compensation or worked gratis as with other radical newspapers. Tresca's situation differed in that the newspapers he published were legally his, despite lip service to the "movement." And in Tresca's mind, nothing differentiated his own needs from those of his newspaper.

In the "good times" of the late 1920s, Tresca paid himself a handsome weekly salary of $50, but his spending habits were uncontrollable. Popolizio related that Il Martello once had $40,000 in its treasury thanks to the careful administration of Umberto Nieri, but after Nieri left in 1924, Tresca supposedly squandered the money. Popolizio also described how brother Mario, who possessed the only other key, would rush to the post office to collect the checks and cash that had accumulated in Il Martello's postal box. If Tresca arrived first, the money would disappear, to be spent primarily on women. Such tales of Tresca's financial profligacy were so commonplace among his comrades that, even if exaggerated, they cannot be dismissed as false.[24]

But Tresca could not indulge in irresponsible spending on women or anything else during the early years of the Depression. To sustain Il Martello, he took no salary for himself from January 1930 to July 1931 and mired himself deeper and deeper in personal debt.[25] Although he lived in a pleasant house with his lady friend of the moment (discussed below), Tresca at times had so little spending money that the line separating funds for Il Martello or himself was obliterated by sheer necessity. One time, when he received a windfall donation of $26 for Il Martello, Tresca used the money to buy himself a new pair of shoes and get his beard trimmed. He had neglected his beard because he was too embarrassed to go to the barbershop lest anyone see the holes in the soles of his shoes. Tresca at this juncture in his life was actually poor.[26]

The contradictory nature of his personality and behavior was such that while Tresca could be utterly irresponsible with his spending habits, he was always extraordinarily generous, a trait considered one of his finest attributes by everyone who knew him. On one occasion during the Depression, an unemployed friend of Popolizio's implored him to arrange a visit with Tresca so the latter might help him. After conversing for a half-hour, Popolizio's friend left the office, happily relating that Tresca he had given him $5. When Tresca emerged a few minutes later, he asked Mario if he knew the identity of the man who had just left. Mario was flabbergasted that his brother had given $5 to someone unknown to him. Tresca responded that it did not matter whether he knew him or not: "I had five dollars and I gave it to him; if I had had more, I would have given him more."[27] Sam and Ester Dolgoff, Jewish anarchists of the Vanguard Group that briefly published an English page in *Il Martello*, remembered one evening dining with Tresca when they saw a veteran of the Spanish Civil War who had been tortured and still looked in poor condition. Tresca walked over to the man and inconspicuously put $25 dollars in his pocket without saying a word.[28] Whenever he provided direct monetary assistance, in fact, Tresca would always proffer the bills in a discreet handshake so as to avoid embarrassment to the recipient.[29] Dolgoff called Tresca "a one-man social agency." People in need of assistance with all kinds of problems depended on him for help. "Tresca was a 'soft touch.' He just could not turn anyone down."[30]

Tresca's Women

Tresca's reputation as "Don Juan" was widespread throughout the Italian and American circles he frequented. What distressed so many friends and comrades, however, was not only his inveterate womanizing but his inability to observe boundaries that should not be crossed. He first demonstrated this tendency by having an affair with a teenage girl in Philadelphia. But later, Tresca surpassed even that level of irresponsible sexual indulgence, causing incredible pain to someone he had once loved.

When Tresca was released from Atlanta Federal Penitentiary in May 1925, his thirteen-year relationship with Flynn had come to an end. She described their life together as having been "tempestuous, undoubtedly because we were both strong personalities with separate and divided interests."[31] But the real cancer devouring their relationship for many years had been Tresca's endless infidelities. In their early years together, as she related in a poem written years later, Flynn deluded herself that Tresca was faithful: "Many a secret tryst was safely kept by his glib alibi 'I go to Pittsburgh!' Eagerly I believed, glad for the task well done." But reality inevitably dawned, and the pain she so vividly remembered commenced: "Gone are the nights of lonely waiting and of tears of anxious worry and a comrade's fears."[32] Flynn maintained that they would have separated sooner than 1925, if not for their mutual interest in the Sacco-Vanzetti case and Tresca's own legal battle in 1923–1924. After his sentencing for violating Federal Obscenity laws, "we walked out on the street together and stood outside in front of the Woolworth Building. I felt badly because Carlo had just been taken to the Tombs [jail] and I knew we were parting our ways when this ordeal was finished. A man had come to my office with a package of love letters Carlo had written to the man's wife, of such a nature that I had no choice."[33] Little did she suspect at the time how much more grief Tresca would cause her.

It was typical of Tresca that he could walk away from his relationship with Flynn without experiencing any discernible regret yet still remain very concerned about her welfare. In 1926, after returning to New York after a frenzied round of activity and the end of an unhappy affair with the Passaic strike leader, Albert Weisbord, Flynn was exhausted and despondent. Learning of her predicament, Tresca invited Flynn to get away from New York and take a vacation with him. Flynn had made her peace with Tresca by now and was sorely tempted by his offer, explaining to her friend Mary Heaton Vorse that "he's an old dear and to tell him my troubles and weep on his shoulder doesn't seem to bother him and helps me a lot."[34]

Around this time, however, Flynn learned that Tresca and her sister Sabina ("Bina") had conducted a love affair behind her back while the three shared an apartment in Greenwich Village. Bina was not involved with the radical movement, inclined instead to run in bohemian circles in Greenwich Village, where she pursued her interest in literature and the theater. Eight years younger than Elizabeth, who by now had gained considerable weight and looked older than her years, Bina was thin, attractive, vivacious, and readily susceptible to Tresca's romantic appeal. She got pregnant in May 1922. To keep her pregnancy a secret from Elizabeth and the Flynn family, Tresca sent Bina to stay with his family in Italy, but fearful of what might happen after Mussolini took power in October 1922, she returned to New York, where she gave birth to a son named Peter on January 6, 1923. The boy's surname, Martin, was that of Bina's estranged husband, James J. ("Slim") Martin, to whom she was still legally married.[35]

Tresca and Bina did not resume their affair after his release. Bina, by this time, was working as an editor for *Ranch Romances* magazine and faced difficulties raising a young child alone. Peter was sent to a boarding home for infants in Alfred, New York, and then entrusted to the foster care of a German couple in Queens. Every other Friday, the woman would bring Peter to visit his father in Manhattan, where Tresca would take him to the speakeasy above John's Restaurant to play with Danny, the son of the owner, John Pucciatti. Despite their infrequent and superficial interaction, Peter loved Tresca very much and retained fond memories of him as a warm and kindly man who brought him presents, the best of which was a roll-top desk, which made him feel grown up.[36] In 1927, Bina married Romolo Bobba, an ex-Wobbly and successful businessmen whose legal defense Tresca had assisted in 1919, and who demonstrated his appreciation by slandering him as a "police informer."[37] Peter's visits with his father became rare. Bobba hated Tresca because of his affair with Bina, and detested Peter, whose physical resemblance to his father was a constant reminder. In 1931, having lost all his money in the stock market crash, Bobba found work in Arizona before bringing his family with him for a fresh start. On the day Bina and Peter left New York, Tresca accompanied them to the train station. Peter remembered them saying goodbye to each other with a stream of tears, hugs, and passionate kisses, their feelings of mutual affection not yet expunged. Tresca and Peter never saw each other again.[38]

Although it was only after his release from prison that she learned of Bina's affair with Tresca, Flynn did not discover that he was the father of her sister's child until a year or so later. Flynn was emotionally devastated by this revelation, and became ill and more depressed than ever. To recover, she placed herself under the care of her friend Dr. Marie Equi in Portland, a lesbian and noted radical on the West Coast. What developed was an unhealthy relationship that lasted—with only a brief hiatus—for ten years. Trapped by inertia and a sense of obligation, Flynn ended up nursing Equi, who became an invalid after 1930 and expected Flynn to become her lifetime caretaker. When Flynn finally extricated herself from Equi's grip in the summer of 1936, she returned to New York to pursue a new political career in the CP. She continued to serve the party until her death in 1964.[39]

By the time Peter and Bina exited his life, Tresca was in the final throes of a relationship that was bizarre even by his own standards of unorthodoxy. In the fall of 1927, Tresca had become involved romantically with Minna Harkavy, an Estonian-born communist and sculptress of minor repute whose works have been displayed in museums in New York and Moscow. She "immortalized" Tresca in a bronze bust, one copy of which stands in Sulmona's Piazza Tresca, the other in the Botto House in Haledon, New Jersey. What made the relationship with Harkavy so strange was that it included the Stalinist Moissaye Olgin, an important figure in the CP who edited the party's Yiddish-language newspaper *Freiheit*. With the bills paid by her rich husband Louis Harkavy, Tresca, Olgin, and Minna lived in a *menage à trois* at 5 St. Luke's Place, a pleasant house in the southwestern part of Greenwich Village, just a few doors down the street from the residence of Mayor Jimmy Walker, with whom Tresca chatted from time to time.[40]

Tresca and Olgin were a study in contrasts. Olgin was a vitriolic little Stalinist who adhered slavishly to every aspect of Soviet policy, the kind of fanatic Tresca loved to torment. The ex-communist Benjamin Gitlow, a frequent visitor, described the turbulent ambiance at 5 St. Luke's Place:

> The sculptress poured the coffee, Olgin stuck his nose into a *Daily Worker* or a *Freiheit*, Carlo gave the sculptress a squeeze and a compliment, shot a glance at Olgin and opened up with a remark: "When will the [party] line change and the American Fuehrer [Earl] Browder get the hook?" An argument generally started, in which Tresca blasted away at the Communists, while Olgin, livid with rage, attempted to answer back. The sculptress tried to maintain a semblance of peace in the family.[41]

When he was not driving Olgin to the brink of apoplexy, Tresca participated in discussions with the numerous communists who frequented the Harvaky household, including agents of the Soviet secret police. These encounters considerably enhanced Tresca's knowledge of communist affairs in the United States and the Soviet Union, information he would later utilize in his attacks against the Stalinists. But political discussions were not enough to sustain his waning interest in Harvaky, and in 1931 he ended the relationship. The writer James Farrell remembered a story circulating at the time—perhaps apocryphal—which related that after Tresca's departure, Harkavy picketed the *Martello* office.[42]

Tresca's breakup with Harkavy may have been accelerated by his involvement with Margaret De Silver, the woman who would remain his devoted companion until his death. Margaret came from a wealthy family of Quakers living in Philadelphia's elite "Main Line." Her father was an executive for the Baldwin Locomotive Works. After graduating from Vassar College, she married Albert De Silver, a lawyer and co-founder, with Roger Baldwin, of the Civil Liberties Union (later the ACLU). Basically a liberal with a penchant for socialistic causes, Margaret served for many years as a member of the ACLU board of directors. She and her husband had met Tresca and Flynn (the two women later became implacable enemies) in 1923, when the ACLU assisted Tresca with his obscenity case. Margaret was widowed in 1924, when Albert accidentally fell off a moving train. Several years of loneliness and depression followed. She met Tresca again in 1931. Knowing that Margaret frequently used her inherited wealth to subsidize artists, writers, and political causes, Tresca asked her to contribute some money to help him revive *Il Martello*. A relationship quickly developed, and Tresca moved into her house at 98 Joralemon Street in fashionable Brooklyn Heights. Uncertain of how her three children—Harrison, Burnham, and Anne—would react to his presence, she gently informed Harrison that "an old radical friend has come back into my life."[43]

Many Italians who had no knowledge of Margaret, other than the fact that she was wealthy, made cynical assumptions about the basis of their relationship. The labor leader Vanni Montana maintained that with Margaret "Carlo had cured the chronic anemia of his purse."[44] While it is true that Margaret occasionally assisted *Il Martello*, Tresca always sought to keep the newspaper afloat by his own efforts, as she herself attested. Her wealth was certainly no disincentive, but the relationship between them was by all accounts one marked by love, warmth, friendship, great fun, and intellectual and physical compatibility. Tresca was always demonstrably affectionate toward Margaret, addressing her with unusual terms of endearment like "my little *scamorza*," a pear-shaped cheese. On one occasion before World War II, when Margaret was visiting Europe, Tresca sent her a postcard of a cow, saying that it had reminded him of her. For most women, being compared with a cow would hardly qualify as a compliment; however, coming from Tresca, it was—cows were his favorite animal. Since Margaret was quite fat and Tresca, too, had acquired considerable girth by the late 1930s, Beatrice wondered how "the two whales" could possibly have functioned in bed. But evidently their sex life was excellent, as Margaret confided to a friend. This did not prevent Tresca from continuing his philandering ways, a tendency Margaret tolerated and even found "amusing," according to Peter Martin, with whom she became very close after Tresca's death.[45]

Tresca provided Margaret with the kind of happiness she had not experienced for years and made vital contributions to the emotional well-being and development of her children. Margaret, her sons attested, was "not a good mother" in any conventional sense, as she lacked maternal feeling and never really wanted the responsibility of three children. She abdicated control of the household to her maid Josie, who qualified as a member of the family. Harrison and Burnham attributed their adolescent insecurity, loneliness, and lack of direction to Margaret's inability to cope with family problems or to nurture her children in a manner essential for healthy maturation. Ann, the youngest, was a fragile and dysfunctional child with whom Margaret could not cope; she eventually manifested schizophrenic symptoms in adulthood. All three children were delighted when Tresca entered Margaret's life and filled the emotional void within the De Silver family. "He was extraordinary," Harrison recalled. "He put me at ease, and at the same time made me feel important."[46] His role was not that of a stepfather but rather that of a friend to whom the boys could always go for comfort and advice. Tresca also made a special effort to reach Ann. He hired someone to give Ann lessons in Italian and would take her to restaurants, where they spoke only in Italian to each other and to the waiters. These were rare moments of happiness for her.[47]

Together with a loving companion and her adoring children came a degree of material comfort that Tresca had never before experienced. With Margaret he lived in a stately three-story brownstone in Brooklyn Heights and then an elegant apartment at 130 West 12th Street in Greenwich Village, having moved in 1939 or 1940 at the insistence of Margaret, who feared for his safety traveling back and forth to Brooklyn. Their favorite leisure spots were Martha's Vineyard and Cape Cod, frequented during summer by upper-middle class and cosmopolitan Anglo-Saxons. Recalling the social ambiance at Martha's Vineyard and Cape Cod, Nancy MacDonald indicated that "Carlo was an exotic flower to the WASPS. He made them feel wicked."[48] Even in a center of nonconformity such as Provincetown, Tresca stood out, walking about as he often did wearing pajamas and a *carabiniere's* cape. Cooking, skinny-dipping in the ocean, hosting parties, and playing poker were Tresca's and Margaret's usual activities. Among the habitués with whom they associated at these vacation haunts were Roger Baldwin and Max Eastman, whom Tresca had known and worked with for years. But most were Margaret's friends, including the writer John Dos Passos, the journalist Herbert Solow, the novelist Dawn Powell, the political activists Nancy and Dwight McDonald, Eastman's wife Eliena Krylenko, who painted a portrait of Tresca, and many other figures such as James Thurber, Thomas Hart Benton, and Canby Chambers. Margaret's circle of friends in New York included among others James T. Farrell, Edmund Wilson, philosopher Sidney Hook, John Dewey, journalist Heywood Broun, and Norman Thomas.

The lifestyle changes resulting from Tresca's relationship with Margaret, therefore, were not just material. Associating with individuals of prominence and high caliber from the world of American politics, art, literature, journalism, and education was a source of great enrichment and satisfaction for Tresca, so different from the sectarian acrimony and back-stabbing he had experienced for so long in the world of the *sovversivi*. As an integral member of Margaret's circle of friends and associates, Tresca found the admiration, respect, and appreciation he justly deserved but was now losing among Italian radicals. All factors considered, Margaret was an ideal mate for Tresca, and the twelve years he spent with her were in many ways the happiest and most fulfilling of his life.[49]

22

Tresca and World War II

War Clouds on the Horizon

War was an ineluctable function of capitalism, Tresca had always insisted. As early as 1934, he predicted that Europe and Asia would soon plunge into the abyss of bloody conflagration. The capitalist nations, understanding the reciprocal relationship between war and revolution, were trying to postpone war lest it unleash a revolt of t he masses that was their uppermost fear. Postpone but not eliminate, because the Great War had demonstrated how the workers could be manipulated into fighting for the material interests of capitalists so long as they were provided with an "ideological dimension" to arouse their ardor. The ideological dimension destined to be exploited was the notion, representing the accepted wisdom of the European and American Left, that the next war would be fought—in the parlance of the Popular Front—between "democracy" and "Fascist dictatorship." For Tresca the assumed polarity between democracy and Fascism was a myth. Plutocratic democracy and totalitarian Fascism were both capitalist systems under the skin, and Soviet communism was just state capitalism masquerading as socialism. The inevitable war that was simmering to boil by the late 1930s would be caused not by antithetical ideologies but by rival imperialism: democratic, Fascist, and communist.[1]

With the Rome-Berlin Axis of November 1936 now transformed into a *de-facto* alliance, Germany's absorption (*Anschluss*) of Austria a *fait accompli*, Japan's invasion of China a rape in progress, and Franco's victory in Spain an imminent certainty, Tresca's May Day message of 1938 warned of the dangers threatening to engulf Europe and Asia. "There on the horizon," he wrote, "burns not the flame of revolt but the sinister flame of war, a war of conquest in Spain and China that tends to spread, devouring and destroying that which until now was called 'civilization.'" "To deny the gravity of the moment would be hypocrisy."[2]

Tresca saw disillusionment everywhere around him, especially in regard to the staying power of Fascism in Italy. During the early 1920s, anti-Fascists had believed that Mussolini's regime would not endure because of its economic failings, the irresolvable conflict between Church and State, and the acute rivalry between the army and the Fascist militia. But, by 1938, those who still waited "in messianic expectation for the contradictions of the regime and the rivalries among the rulers to create the motor of demolition of Fascism are deluded." Tresca certainly was not one of them. He concluded his May Day message with a typical exhortation: "Tomorrow still belongs to those who, laden with chains, look to the future and prepare and resist. In heroic resistance still can be found the force of will to challenge the bourgeois world in the name of the working class…. We who still and always have faith declare that resistance is the sure guarantee of victory."[3]

Although still expressing unbreakable faith in the working class and the viability of direct action, Tresca could find nothing on the international scene that encouraged hope that war might be avoided by means of popular resistance. He was particularly disturbed by the extent to which Mussolini had come under Hitler's spell, a development that was progressively reducing Italy to a state of vassalage under Germany and exposing the Italian people more directly to the inevitable disasters of war. A glaring example of this insidious trend was the anti-Semitism that became Fascist Italy's official policy after the publication of the *Manifesto of Fascist Racism* in July 1938. Enactment of anti-Semitic laws surprised most Italians and even many Fascists, although there was no dearth of anti-Semites among fanatical PNF members like Roberto Farinacci. Tresca denounced the new policy, asserting that "whoever knows the Italian people knows indeed that nothing is more contrary to its nature than this absurd pseudo-scientific doctrine that comes from Germany, and that is a sure sign of human civilization's regression and barbarization." Mussolini had embraced anti-Semitism, Tresca maintained, because absorbing Nazism into Italian Fascist ideology and its governmental system was a function of the Duce's commitment to Hitler—the "abnormal maniac."[4]

That a few months later the Western Democracies would sell out Czechoslovakia to Hitler at the Munich Conference was no surprise to Tresca. The only ones surprised and dismayed by Munich were Stalin, the communists, and the Popular Frontists, who for three years had preached "collective security" and "defense of democracy" while the social revolution was crushed in Spain. Like Spain and Ethiopia, Czechoslovakia was an expendable pawn in the imperialist game. According to Tresca, Neville Chamberlain, the British prime minister and chief architect of appeasement, had not been deceived by Hitler at Munich. Chamberlain's objective had been to give a clear message to Hitler that Britain would not oppose the dismemberment of Czechoslovakia. What motivated Chamberlain and the British conservatives to make concessions to Hitler was the "specter of revolution" and the desire to protect the British Empire. They did not object to the Fascistization of Europe so long as the Empire was not threatened. Tossing the Czechoslovakian lamb to the German wolf was a means to deflect Hitler toward the Soviet Union, where with British blessings he could conquer *Lebensraum*, exploit the resources of Russia, Ukraine, and the Caucasus, and destroy Bolshevism in the process. Only when Hitler directly threatened British imperial interests would Perfidious Albion draw the line and go to war. Meanwhile, it was necessary to extinguish the flame of social revolution wherever it existed—a job Britain would leave to Stalin and the Popular Frontists.[5]

Munich, Tresca argued, was merely a link in the chain of events reflecting the imperatives of British imperialism. In 1938 and 1939, as from its inception, Tresca underscored the direct connection between British imperialism and the Spanish Civil War. British conservatives from the outset had worked for a Franco victory. The worker's revolt in Barcelona had accelerated the heartbeats of workers everywhere; therefore, the flame of social revolution had to be extinguished. The fall of Barcelona to insurgent forces in January 1939 was as much the fault of British imperialism as Soviet duplicity and counter-revolutionary policies. France, now a vassal state of Great Britain, was almost equally culpable. Leon Blum, the man most responsible for the Popular Front in France, had betrayed the Spanish people in 1936 by holding back assistance; Edouard Daladier, who won the April 1938 election with the aid of communists and socialists, betrayed the Czechs at Munich. Hence the Popular Front was as responsible as the French imperialists: "They are all betrayers."[6]

World War II

A nine-month hiatus in the publication of *Il Martello* (May 1939–February 1940) prevented Tresca from giving his first impressions of the Nazi-Soviet Non-Aggression Pact (August 22, 1939) and Hitler's invasion of Poland on September 1, 1939. His earliest observations of the military progress of the war proved remarkably prescient. Despite Hitler's early successes in Poland and Western Europe, Tresca predicted that the Allies, with their greater industrial resources and manpower, would ultimately win, albeit by means of a protracted conflict that would cost millions of lives, even more than were lost during World War I.

Not surprisingly, Tresca and the *Il Martello* group declared themselves "irreconcilable opponents of the war." They maintained that "the war between capitalist nations is the natural and logical consequence of the bourgeois regime"; therefore, to put an end to wars, it is necessary to destroy the system that generates them.[7] However, Tresca would reject the traditional anarchist view that all governments are alike, an abstract notion he knew was a denial of reality. And he soon parted company with most anarchists by declaring openly his desire for the triumph of the Allies, because a victory for Hitler would mean disaster for the entire world. This departure from anarchist orthodoxy did not prevent Tresca from suggesting "would it not be better if the decision were removed from the blood drenched battlefields and be decided by all the people by means of a liberating revolutionary uprising?"[8] Indeed, Tresca avowed that, as an anarchist, he would do whatever he could "to transform the war of international imperialism into an international civil war for social revolution—the only solution to world problems."[9]

Early Commentary on the War

After its revival in February 1940, *Il Martello*'s collaborators provided very thorough coverage of the military aspects of the war, while Tresca focused more on specific issues and personalities. As he had done since the mid-1930s, Tresca wrote more about Stalin and the Soviet Union than Hitler and Germany. For Tresca, Hitler and Nazism were more easily explainable—they were degenerate products of capitalism. Stalin and the communists, no less tyrannous than the Nazis, bore the additional stigma of having betrayed the 1917 revolution and oppressed the Soviet peoples thereafter. Hitler's personality and motivation were less perplexing to Tresca than Stalin's—the Fuhrer was an "abnormal maniac" who lusted for the conquest of all Europe.[10] Stalin was more complex and elusive, his crimes prior to the war more egregious, and his duplicity unmatched even by the Fuhrer.[11] Insisting on the inherent evil of the communist Czar and his brutal regime, Tresca wrote that "no other party has served the cause of reaction as much as Stalin's party. No other state during the last twenty years has contributed more to destroy ethics, character, and every form of morality than the government of Stalin."[12]

Tresca's hatred for Stalin and the Soviet system, and his instinct to always favor the underdog, prompted him to focus considerable attention on the Russo-Finnish War of December 1939–March 1940. Certainly no admirer of Karl Gustav Mannerheim and the Finnish authoritarians, Tresca was nevertheless repelled by the spectacle of the Soviet colossus attacking its small neighbor, and incensed by the servility of communists everywhere ("Stalin's Foreign Legion"), who justified Stalin's every move with outright lies and hypocritical rationalizations. Thus he ridiculed the contortions of the *Daily Worker*, which initially identified Finland as the aggressor, and then flip-flopped with the lame justification that the Russians had invaded their neighbor to "liberate" the Finns from their capitalist masters.[13]

Mussolini's Debacles

Once the *Sitzkrieg* on the Western front finally turned into *Blitzkrieg* in the spring of 1940, Tresca had the pleasure of delivering his *martellate* against Mussolini and his "Parallel War." The Duce had waited until Germany brought France to her knees before invading his Latin neighbor on June 10, 1940—six days before the French capitulated to the Nazis. To the distress of many Italian-Americans, President Roosevelt aptly characterized this act of treachery as a "stab in the back." Tresca was even more scathing in his condemnation, declaring that "Mussolini has waited, cat-like, until France had its back forced against the wall by Hitler's legions. Now that he is convinced he can demand, like a hyena, a share of the spoils, now that there are only bodies over which to pass, he orders his men to march."[14] Actually, to Mussolini's chagrin, there were few bodies over which to tread. After advancing only a few miles into French territory in the Maritime Alps, thirty-two Italian divisions were stopped in their tracks by a mere five French divisions, a humiliating defeat that would be duplicated many times during the next three years.

Mussolini was not Tresca's only target. He did not exempt the Italian people from blame. Fascist Italy had dishonored itself before the civilized world, but so had the Italian people who demonstrated "the collective cowardice of a brutalized people." They had failed to break the chains that bound them; they attacked at the whim of the Duce, committing the cowardly deed of attempting to kill a wounded and already defeated enemy.[15]

Although still hoping that Mussolini would go down in defeat, Tresca softened his criticism of the Italians when the Duce's ill-timed and ill-equipped invasion of Greece ended in disaster in November 1940. Besides the winter weather, poor equipment, incompetent leadership, and inferior numbers that contributed to defeat, Tresca observed that the Italian army lacked the human factor indispensable for victory: they did not believe in the cause for which they were fighting. Italian soldiers, even under Fascism, retained the distinguishing feature of the "Italian soul": a sense of independence and individuality. The Italian remained a "man" under his uniform, unlike the Germans, who were "automatons" blindly following orders.[16]

The Italian army's defeat in Greece, a portent of Mussolini's future demise, was followed by a succession of defeats at British hands in the Mediterranean and North Africa. Once again, Tresca ascribed Italy's military reverses, in part, to the same lack of morale and commitment that contributed to her debacle in Greece. Tresca further observed that with each defeat, Mussolini drew closer to Hitler, staking his regime and life on the belief that ultimate victory would go to the Germans. But the more Mussolini tied his fate to Hitler's, the more he transformed Italy into a German satellite that would ultimately suffer the consequences of subjugation. Manifesting his love and fear for Italy, Tresca declared: "If we were patriots, we would ask for the head of Mussolini for high treason."[17]

Although confident that the combined industrial might of the Allies would ultimately defeat the Axis powers, Tresca was not optimistic about Allied intentions for postwar Italy, particularly those of Winston Churchill. Tresca remembered that Churchill had once counted himself among Mussolini's great admirers, writing to the Duce in January 1927: "If I had been an Italian I am sure I should have been entirely with you from the beginning to the end of your victorious struggle against the bestial appetites and passions of Leninism."[18] Tresca's suspicions about Churchill's intentions toward Italy were justified even before Italian forces in Libya advanced into Egypt to attack the British in June 1940. On a BBC broadcast addressed to the Italian people in May 1940, the British prime minister declared that "one man and one man alone" was leading Italy to war against the wishes of the Savoy Monarchy and the Papacy.[19] Anyone familiar with Italy knew that Churchill's "one man alone" characterization was a blatant distortion of history. For Tresca, however, Churchill's assertion was not simply a misstatement of the facts—its nefarious purpose was patently obvious. By blaming Mussolini alone for all the suffering Italy would endure, Churchill's intent was to fool the Italian masses into forgetting that the real cause of Fascism was capitalism. Also clear to Tresca was Churchill's ultimate objective: the preservation of Italy's monarchical and ecclesiastic institutions by fostering a new clerico-Fascist regime without Mussolini and men in monochromatic shirts, one that would prevent communist domination of the country after the war.[20] Looking to Great Britain or even the United States to establish a "new order" in Italy would therefore constitute a grave error. Anti-Fascists had to remain vigilant against the machinations of Churchill and all others who would betray the Italian people yearning for liberty.[21] "Liberty," he declared, "must be conquered."[22] To the very end of his life, Tresca clung to the dream of the Italian people liberating themselves from Fascists and Allies alike, and marching to victory under the red flag of revolution—a dream he would not live to see shattered.

Operation Barbarossa

The Nazi invasion of the Soviet Union ("Operation Barbarossa") on June 22, 1941 was a crucial turning point in the war, pitting Germany against the world's second greatest industrial power, whose military potential would eventually spell doom for the Teutonic aggressors. But unlike so many critics of Soviet communism, who suppressed their opposition for the duration of the war, Tresca remained unrelenting in his attacks against Stalin and the Soviet regime. He hastened to point out that for Stalin to strengthen the resolve of his people, he had needed to characterize the conflict as the "Great Patriotic War" to defend "Mother Russia." Stalin's appeal to Russian nationalism was for Tresca incontrovertible proof of the moral and political bankruptcy of Soviet communism. Yet he hoped that Stalin's "Patriotic War" would not end in a Pyrrhic victory for the Soviet working class. Distinguishing between states and peoples, Tresca expressed sympathy for the plight of the Soviet masses caught in the path of the Nazi onslaught, but he hoped that the Nazi-Soviet war would result in more than military victory for Stalin and his oppressive regime. "The Russian people are in need of help," he wrote, "but they must be helped to liberate themselves not only from the grip of the German invader, but also from the equally suffocating grip of the bureaucracy and the GPU, that is, from the sinister and ferocious police force of Stalin, the new and more terrible Nero…. We are not interested in saving Stalin's Russia as it is. We are strongly interested in seeing Russia saved by the Revolution." [23]

The tergiversation that characterized Soviet policy, first with the Nazi-Soviet Pact, and then with the Nazi invasion, inevitably became a target for Tresca, who delighted in underscoring the hypocrisy of Stalin's worshippers. At the time of the Nazi-Soviet Pact, communists everywhere—in accordance with Moscow's latest dictates—had ceased to condemn Hitler and Nazism as the fomenters of war, attributing blame instead to British imperialism. But now, as German panzers thrust relentlessly into Soviet territory, the British suddenly metamorphosed into Russia's heroic ally in the crusade for "liberation" and "democracy." Roosevelt, previously denounced by post-Pact Stalinists as a "war monger" for his support of Britain, was now beseeched to aid the beleaguered peoples of the Soviet Union. Tresca noted, moreover, that the 180-degree shifts in party line executed by the Stalinists in 1939 and 1941 did not cause them the slightest embarrassment: "They are habituated to doing so; they are hardened to lies and hypocrisy." [24] Nor did Tresca exclude the possibility of yet another *volte face*, namely, Stalin's concluding a separate peace with Hitler: "Everything is possible… among gangsters. In that case, they [Stalinists] will take off the republican cockade and don again the livery of the abject servants of one of the bloodiest despots history has ever recorded." [25]

The War and the United States

As early as 1938, Tresca had predicted that Roosevelt would bring the United States into the coming war. [26] Like Woodrow Wilson before him, Roosevelt would maintain an official antiwar policy prior to the election of 1940, but intervene subsequently when American economic interests became seriously threatened, most likely by Japan. As war between the United States and Japan became imminent, Tresca revealed a surprisingly new attitude toward Roosevelt, demonstrating once again how in matters of great importance he was not bound by ideological orthodoxy.

The differences between the Democratic and Republican parties, Tresca believed, were more cosmetic than real—they both shared the same political lineage as descendents of capitalism. Their party platforms were practically the same beneath the rhetoric, and although Republicans advocated orthodox economic liberalism, the reforms of the New Deal had left too deep a mark to be dismantled. Accordingly, the Republican candidate, Wendell Willkie, promised to continue and improve the New Deal reforms. Even their foreign policies were not that different. Both parties spoke the language of non-intervention, but Tresca believed either one would go to war if American interests demanded. Yet despite the similarities between the parties and their platforms, Tresca hoped for a Roosevelt victory—not that Tresca had suddenly come to support or like Roosevelt. He gave the president his due as "the most politically astute man in the American political world," but still believed the "New Deal, with its social and economic reforms, has chloroformed the proletariat and further enriched the wealthy." [27] Nor did he harbor any special antipathy for Willkie, whom he considered just another tool of Wall Street. What aroused Tresca's concern was the nature and objectives of Willkie's supporters, particularly the America First Committee and other isolationist contingents, which included many conservatives, anti-Semites, and Nazi sympathizers like Charles Lindbergh, Henry Ford, Herbert Hoover, General Motors Vice President James D. Mooney, Thomas Watson of IBM, and Ernest Weir of "Little Steel." Tresca believed that for these reactionaries, isolationism was a guise for Fascism. They wanted Europe under German talons and full cooperation between Hitler and the United States, objectives that could be realized completely only if the United States were Fascistized. These Fascist Americans were the real "Fifth Column" in America. [28]

Roosevelt's victory in November 1940 brought Tresca "great pleasure."

> Willkie's election would have frozen my blood; Roosevelt's re-election warmed it up. And I say this in all frankness and sincerity, because to keep one's emotions hidden in these times is hypocritical. I am not a hypocrite. When I saw all the Fascist and Nazi legions and the followers of Father Coughlin… looming behind Willkie, my reaction was spontaneous: I hoped for Roosevelt's victory." [29]

Representing a moral and material defeat for the Axis, Roosevelt's victory could not be regarded as a matter of indifference even to those who believed one capitalist president was as bad as the next. "As a matter of fact," Tresca insisted, "even those who foolishly repeat those phrases know in their hearts that there is a difference." There was a difference between Roosevelt and Willkie, just as there was between Britain and Germany. And so, Tresca declared: "as the foremost task of humanity in this tragic hour… is to strike Fascism and Nazism dead, I, who am part of humanity…, live day by day hoping for the most of sensational defeat of Hitler, Mussolini, and Stalin." [30]

Endorsement of Roosevelt's victory and hope for a British triumph represented unorthodox views that Tresca admitted he had embraced only after an inner struggle between the conflicting imperatives of reason and sentiment. Reason told him that the war was the result of imperialist rivalries, but sentiment caused him to prefer one of the fighting camps rather than the other. Tresca urged others to consider that "it is not necessary in this hour so bestial, gloomy, and threatening to place our emotions in a straightjacket of dogma, doctrine, and immutable principles. Let them free to express themselves. Who knows? In this dark hour that passes, sentiment will enlighten us more than reason. Who today, forced to live in this great madhouse, considers himself so sane as to affirm—I stand for reason, I am infallible?"[31]

Turning his attention to the Far East, Tresca maintained for years that conflicting economic interests in Asia would produce a *causus belli* between Japan and the Europeans and Americans, and he accurately predicted that once Japan set its sights on French Indo-China and the Dutch East Indies, the United States would intervene against her, as she did with embargoes on exports to Japan of oil, aviation fuel, iron, and scrap steel in July 1940 and July 1941, action amounting to economic warfare. Tresca considered it one of the ironies and contradictions of capitalism that during the years preceding Pearl Harbor, the United States had exported these essential elements of war-making to her Asiatic enemy. Although he could not have known that Pearl Harbor would be the initial target, Tresca mocked the notion than Japan's attack against American territory had come as a "surprise" to the American government. Japan's previous aggression against Manchuria, China, South East Asia, and her Tripartite Pact with Germany and Italy had left no doubt as to the warlike intentions of the Empire of the Rising Sun. He also predicted from the outset that "time is the ally of the United States, whose formidable resources will be utilized for one end: the defeat of the Axis."[32]

The events of 1939–1941 did not require revision of anarchist principles, Tresca argued, but his support for the Allied cause was now strong and unwavering:

> We hate Nazism, Fascism, totalitarianism; we hate them all with the force of insuppressible passion. We hope, in the depths of our conscience, that victory smiles on the enemies of Italy, Germany, and Japan.... Yesterday we said: on British bayonets rests the hope of conserving what past revolutions have given us, of resuming the march until the bastions of suffocating totalitarianism will fall. Today we say: on American bayonets rests, for all of us whose backs are against the wall in this difficult hour, the hope that one day we will again see the light.[33]

Despite his sincere desire for an Allied victory, Tresca continually expressed the hope for a transformative war, namely, the post-war eruption of a class war that would destroy bourgeois hegemony and create a free libertarian society. Did Tresca not see the contradiction between these two objectives? Did he seriously believe in the possibility of a social revolution emerging from the war, or was he merely engaging in formulaic anarchist rhetoric? As a realist, Tresca feared that the fate of Europe would be determined by the occupying armies of the victors, an outcome that surely would preclude social revolution along libertarian lines. On the other hand, dreams of liberty and equality died hard for anarchist revolutionaries, and for Tresca, the dream may still have been a source of spiritual sustenance.

23

The Last Years

All was not well with Tresca as he approached his sixtieth birthday on March 9, 1939. His health was generally poor. He was forty or fifty pounds overweight, his teeth were bad, his lungs weakened from emphysema due to more than forty years of smoking, and his face and chest occasionally hurt from injuries sustained in an automobile accident six years earlier.[1] More pressing than his physical ailments, however, was the burden of *Il Martello*, which he described to his friend Alberto Meschi in France as a "real and very heavy cross…, a sponge that dries me out."[2] The newspaper had operated continuously in the red since its revival in 1934. Subscriptions and circulation were both declining, in part because of the Poyntz affair, and in part because of the now indelible misperception that Margaret was bearing the cost of publication. Tresca had drawn no salary since 1934, and had even contributed more than $2,000 from his own savings. In July 1938, he filed a petition for bankruptcy, claiming assets of $98.24 in cash and liabilities of $4,420.24 in unpaid debts, some of which dated from 1918.[3] Tresca's only recourse was publishing irregularly (only thirty-six issues in 1938) and to revert to a bi-weekly publication.[4]

The Tresca Jubilee

To raise funds for *Il Martello* and bolster Tresca's spirit, a number of his Italian friends and Herbert Solow organized a banquet to commemorate his sixtieth birthday and his forty years of activity. The "Tresca Jubilee" was held on April 14, 1939, at the Irving Plaza on 15th Street and Irving Place. The hall, which normally accommodated 500 people, had to be renovated to make room for the more than 800 guests expected. The walls were festooned with placards listing the prisons where Tresca had served time, the strikes he had led, and the defense campaigns he had organized. Sixteen union locals were represented by more than a hundred labor officials. The famous individuals who attended came from every walk of American cultural and political life: John F. Finerty, Isaac Schorr, Edmond Wilson, Dawn Powell, James Farrell, Anita Brenner, Paul Berlin, Benjamin Stollberg, Lewis Gannet, Ludwig Lore, Eugene Lyons, Susanne LaFollette, Sidney Hook, Benjamin Gitlow, Max Eastman, and Harry Kelly. Scores of other well-known figures, unable to attend, telegraphed their congratulations to Tresca, including John Dewey, John

Dos Passos, Norman Thomas, Oswald Garrison Villard, Ernest Hemingway, Roger Baldwin, David Dubinsky, Margaret Sanger, Emma Goldman, and Leon Trotsky.[5] Trotsky, grateful for Tresca's efforts on the Dewey Committee, wrote: "Dear Comrade Tresca: In spite of all the profound differences which neither you nor I have the habitude to deny or attenuate, I hope you will permit me to express the deepest esteem for you, as for a man who is in every way a fighter. Your sixtieth birthday is being celebrated by your friends and I take the liberty of counting myself among them. I hope that your moral vigor and revolutionary ardor will be conserved for a long time to come."[6] Tresca's thank-you note to Trotsky read: "You are right: 'in spite of all the profound divergences,' we do respect each other."[7]

Conspicuously absent at the Jubilee were important Italian radicals like Valenti, Quintiliano, Allegra, all of the communists, the syndicalists, the L'Adunatatisti, and most other anarchists. There was no better indication that at this stage of his career, Americans were more appreciative of Tresca than the *sovversivi*, and he of them. As Tresca indicated to Meschi: "I live here closer to American elements than to our Italian elements; and, without exaggeration, close to the best American elements."[8] Nevertheless, while his estrangement from many old comrades was irreversible, Tresca was drawing closer to Italian trade union leaders than ever before, particularly Luigi Antonini.

Certainly, by the late 1930s, Tresca had "mellowed" to some degree, and his past feuds with figures like Antonini seemed less important in light of the terrible events taking place throughout the world. But Tresca's rapprochement with Antonini and other labor leaders had tangible causes as well. Antonini had recently impressed Tresca by expressing his anti-Fascism more publicly than in the past. And thanks to Antonini, the Fascists' monopoly on Italian radio broadcasting was finally broken. On November 23, 1940, at Antonini's invitation, Tresca spoke for the first and only time on WEVD. Tresca often had sought opportunities to speak on radio in the past, but had always been refused access. The explanation for denying him air-time echoed a familiar refrain: "You are too radical."[9] There was also another, more practical and self-serving aspect to Tresca's increasingly cordial relations with labor leaders he had previously scorned. Antonini, Giovanni Sala, Serafino Romualdi, and Louis Nelson were among of the few sources of revenue he could now tap to sustain *Il Martello*. The union leaders, in turn, welcomed Tresca as a valuable ally.[10]

Recourse to union leaders for financial assistance was not intended solely for his own needs. Tresca was still an important benefactor for political refugees who needed money, visas, and other lifesaving aid. Tresca, for example, was serving as an advisor and fund-raiser for the New World Resettlement Fund for Spanish Refugees. As he wrote to Trotsky in August 1939, "the necessity of taking *personal* charge of the life of so many of my personal friends and comrades, refugees after the Spanish defeat, has put me at the point of exhaustion."[11] On his own initiative, Tresca badgered Antonini and other union leaders with requests—more like demands—to aid several Italian anti-Fascists who had fought in the *Colonna Italiana* and the Garibaldi Brigade, but who were now isolated and poverty stricken as exiles in France and Switzerland. Similarly, Tresca sought financial aid for destitute anti-Fascists in the United States and legal aid for those facing deportation to Italy.[12] Not surprisingly, Tresca's humanitarian activities on behalf of anti-Fascist refugees were considered suspect by J. Edgar Hoover, but the FBI took no action.[13]

The Anarchist Conference of April 1–2, 1939

While continuing his activities on behalf of refugees, Tresca was soon caught up in another spate of internecine conflict. Italian anarchists from seven states convened in New York on April 1–2, 1939 for one of the movement's rarest events—a conference. The purported objective was to establish "harmony" within the movement, invigorate its militancy, and publish a newspaper in Philadelphia, *L'Intesa Libertaria* (Libertarian Understanding) that would represent all anarchists—a utopian dream if ever there was one.[14]

Tresca welcomed the project and challenged Schiavina and his crowd to attend. They ignored the conference, but their participation was not required for the movement's cannibalistic tendencies to manifest. Some delegates demanded that Tresca be barred from attending. For others, particularly the *Gruppo Berneri* of New York, the objective was to wrest *Il Martello* from Tresca or destroy the newspaper altogether. Tresca expressed his willingness to step down from the directorship (a clear reflection of his frustration) if that was the wish of the Martello Group. It was not. Yet Tresca and the Martello Group promised to support *L'Intesa Libertaria*, and suspended publication of *Il Martello* after the May 14th issue. But *L'Intesa Libertaria* folded after publishing only four issues published between April and June 1939.[15]

Il Martello resumed publication on February 28, 1940, with Tresca back at the helm as director and sole owner. Energized by the war in Europe, Tresca increased his share of writing editorials, feature articles, and a new column, "*Appunti a Lapis*" (Pencil Notes). But within a year *Il Martello* was facing another crisis. Returning to work too soon after a severe bout of influenza, Tresca suffered four nasal hemorrhages that required blood transfusions, a lengthy hospital stay, and several months of recuperation. A photo of Tresca, his nostrils packed with gauze, appeared in the *New York Post*, together with a typical quip: "I don't theenk I die. I must be strong to fight. Mussolini is on his last leg."[16] Against the advice of his doctors, Tresca resumed his publishing activities at the end of April 1941, only to encounter even greater financial difficulties, as donations and subscriptions continued to decline and circulation reached a low of 2,100 copies by 1942.[17]

Resurgence of Anti-Fascism

At the outbreak of the war, Italian-American Fascists and pro-Fascists were still ardently committed to Mussolini and campaigned for non-intervention among the ranks of the isolationists. Within a year, however, the mutually beneficial relationship between Mussolini's regime and the Italian-American *Camorra Coloniale* began to waver, as fear of potential retaliation by American authorities began to spread. Typical was the Sons of Italy, which officially condemned Nazism,

Fascism, and Communism in 1941. For Tresca, such eleventh-hour conversions to anti-Fascism were hypocritical and opportunistic.[18] The Italian ambassador reached the same conclusion, as he observed the growing disloyalty and the craven behavior of the *prominenti*. In his reports to Rome, Ascanio Colonna revived the doubts that Fascists in Italy had always harbored about the sincerity of the Italian-American bourgeoisie: "It will be necessary, once the war is over, to re-examine in light of recent events the many problems relating to the Italian-American community, those pertaining especially to the '*prominenti*,' who, noisy in easy times, exploit the Italian-American masses for their personal ends, [and] have been the first to defect and turn against their country of origin when put to the test."[19] Five months after Colonna's report, in an act of monumental folly, the Duce declared war against the United States, thereby sealing the doom of Italian-American Fascism and hastening the political metamorphosis of its feint-hearted supporters.

Even before Mussolini's Italian-American "empire" began to crumble, the war had generated more vitality and determination among anti-Fascists than at any time since the mid-1920s. The movement had changed in vital aspects, however. Anti-Fascism in the 1920s and early 1930s was primarily an immigrant working-class movement led by radicals associated with the labor unions or subversive political parties and ideologies. But, by the time the war began, the sun was setting on this movement. Except for Antonini and a few other union leaders who still wielded power in the Italian-American community, old-guard leaders like Tresca, Valenti, and Vacirca had largely been superseded by a group known collectively as the *fuorusciti*: political refugees who were well-educated bourgeois professionals, politicians, and intellectuals, mainly of liberal-democratic persuasion, who had arrived in the United States only a few years earlier. Some were Jews who had left Italy after passage of the Anti-Semitic decrees of 1938; others were exiles of long standing in France who fled to the United States when the country fell to the Nazis in 1940. On September 24, 1939, a group of *fuorusciti* founded the Mazzini Society, the most important anti-Fascist organization to arise in the United States during the war.[20]

The principal leaders of the Mazzini Society were the historian Gaetano Salvemini, the former diplomat Count Carlo Sforza, the liberal journalists Alberto Cianca and Alberto Tarchiani, and the academics Giuseppe A. Borgese, Lionello Venturi, and Max Ascoli, who replaced Salevemini as president in June 1940. Several newspapers were published consecutively as official voices: *Mazzini News*, *Il Mondo*, and *Nazioni Unite*. Headquartered at 1775 Broadway in New York, the Mazzini Society established groups in 50 cities but remained an elite organization, with not more than 900 members. It survived financially with the support of Italian labor unions and Ascoli's rich wife. The Mazzini Society's primary objective was to mobilize the American public and its political leaders against totalitarianism, monarchism, and clericalism, with a view toward establishing a secular, democratic government in postwar Italy. Its interest in the Italian-American community was limited to the elimination of Fascist influence over its people and institutions and marshalling support for democracy in Italy. However, the *fuorusciti* possessed few links to immigrant workers or their American-born children save through the few union leaders who were members.[21] As Ascoli acknowledged, "We were *quattro gatti* ["four cats," i.e., a handful]. In no way did we represent anything really substantial in the Italian-American community."[22]

Tresca and the "Pearl Harbor Anti-Fascists"

Ascoli and others among the *fuorusciti* considered Tresca "the grand-father of the Mazzini Society," but for several years, Tresca refrained from joining in order to retain his freedom of action. "Tresca was above all a fearlessly independent man," Ascoli explained. "He was very close to the *'quattro gatti'* of the Mazzini Society, but he was essentially his own man."[23] Tresca was ambivalent about the organization because it was too moderate and bourgeois for his taste, striving to create a republican and democratic Italy, while he still yearned for the revolutionary control of workers who would overthrow the old order. He valued the high-profile leadership the Mazzini Society brought to the anti-Fascist cause, and he greatly respected men like Salvemini, even though they were not revolutionaries. But he questioned the anti-Fascist credentials of some members, and was outraged by the posturing of others who acted as though anti-Fascism had never existed in America until the Mazzini Society. He contrasted the militancy they exhibited now, in a safe and favorable environment, with his own activities in the 1920s, when Anti-Fascists had to contend with American authorities as well as Fascists. Most of all Tresca faulted the Mazzini Society for its claim to speak for the Italian-American community, despite its having almost no connection with the immigrant working class. All of Tresca's criticisms were correct to some degree. Nevertheless, his writings about the Mazzini Society clearly reflected the resentment of an old warrior who believed his contribution to American anti-Fascism was unappreciated and his leadership role usurped by newcomers.[24]

Accordingly, while a *de facto* ally, Tresca fought his own "parallel war" against Fascism from 1940 to 1942. His primary objective remained what it had been from the outset: eradicate the cancer of Fascism within the Italian-American community. Excising the disease, Tresca affirmed, required exposing the activities in the "Fascist Fifth Column" in the United States and Canada. Tresca's writings during this renewed offensive revealed the extraordinary depth and breadth of his knowledge about Italian-American Fascism. Not even Salvemini, who amassed 6,000 index cards with information about Fascist individuals and organizations, possessed Tresca's intimate familiarity with the enemy. Tresca shared this information not only with his usual audience but with FBI agents investigating potential subversion and sabotage by Mussolini's followers.[25] As Tresca related to his friend Canby Chambers,

The Secret Service are funny. Before the war, they put me in prison. Now they are in my office every day. "Good old Carlo," they say. "Tell us who are the leading Fascists in this country." "So I tell them." "Good old Carlo! Now tell us where is Mussolini's short-wave sending station." "You are the FBI, and you do not know?" I ask. "I am Carlo Tresca. I know it is in New Jersey—off Cape May." "They laugh. They think I am keeding.... But they get the radio; pretty soon they get the men."[26]

Tresca demonstrated anew that the nerve center of the Fascist "Fifth Column" was "the Nest"—the New York consulate. Tresca exposed the consulate's more nefarious activities, those hidden from public view, including the disruption of anti-Fascist group activities and the intimidation of individual anti-Fascists and non-compliant immigrants. These nastier tasks, Tresca revealed for the first time, were the special province of *Cavaliere* Caradossi, an agent of the Fascist Secret Police (the OVRA), attached to the consulate since 1926. Tresca exposed Caradossi's possession of a list of Italian Americans working in war materials production, whom he would seek to recruit for sabotage in the event the United States went to war against Italy. Tresca assured his readers, however, that "we will keep on eye on him, we who do not fear his ire and his intrigues."[27] "The Nest" officially closed when Mussolini declared war against the United States and withdrew all diplomatic personnel.

Well before that day, as Ambassador Colonna had observed, Fascist and pro-Fascist organizations and individuals began scurrying for safety. In reality, most of them had little to fear, especially if they were American citizens and politically well connected. Prior to the war, the American government paid scant attention to Italian-American Fascists, much less the more cautious pro-Fascist *prominenti*. Investigations conducted in the late 1930s by the House Un-American Activities Committee and the Dickstein-McCormick Committee of New York discounted the possibility that Italian-American Fascists might represent a subversive threat.[28] Some degree of danger threatened in 1942, when 600,000 non-citizen Italian Americans were classified as "enemy aliens." Not more than 4,000, however, were detained, and only 210—mostly diehard fanatics like Domenico Trombetta—were interned for the duration of the war.[39] No matter if they had sung *"Giovinezza"* for twenty years, the majority of Italian-American Fascists and pro-Fascists had only to hum a few bars of the "Star Spangled Banner" to qualify for forgiveness.

Tresca did everything he could to thwart the "rehabilitation" of these elements, mainly by exposing the identity of individuals and organizations unknown to American authorities and the clever methods by which they obscured their true nature in order to survive the crisis unscathed. A prime example was the Morgantini Club in the Bronx, which had been intimidating anti-Fascists on Vecchiotti's orders. Like many Fascist organizations, the Morgantini Club possessed direct ties with the criminal underworld. The club's president, Renzo Abbondandolo, was the former private secretary and accountant of mobster Vito Genovese, alias "Don Vitone." The latter, in fact, had direct ties to the consulate in New York. Genovese had contributed generously to the *Opere Assistenziali* during the Ethiopian War, and in gratitude (plus some monetary compensation), when Genovese fled to Italy in 1936, one step ahead of New York's Special Prosecutor, Thomas E. Dewey, Vecchiotti furnished him a passport containing false information that facilitated his escape. For his financial contributions to the Fascist cause in America and later in Italy, Genovese was made a *Cavaliere* of the Crown in 1938. His old factotum, Abbondandolo, an American citizen, had no wish to rejoin "Don Vitone" in Italy. Instead, he ensured his own security and the "Americanization" of the Morgantini Club by stepping down as president and recruiting new, untainted officers.[30]

The biggest target of Tresca's latest campaign, predictably, was Generoso Pope. By 1940, Pope was under attack by nearly all important anti-Fascists except

Antonini, who played a key role in white-washing the publisher's pro-Fascist past and accommodating his rehabilitation as a "democrat." Having established a truce in 1935 (Antonini stopped attacking Pope in exchange for Pope's favorable press coverage of Local 89), Antonini hoped to utilize Pope for his own ends.[31]The publisher's newest adversary was the Mazzini Society, which sought to wrest editorial control of *Il Progresso* away from its Fascist editors and transform it into an anti-Fascist organ.[32] Tresca, on the other hand, was bent on utterly destroying Pope's reputation within the Italian-American community and preventing his re-ascent to power and respectability. Pope had been "the link conjoining the 'Nest' with the mass of Italians," the man most responsible for spreading the Fascist bacillus. That Tresca might forgive him was out of the question.[33]

Tresca demonstrated how Pope had still supported the Fascist regime and Axis policies when Mussolini entered the war as Hitler's partner, justifying Italian intervention and depicting Great Britain as Italy's enemy and the instigator of conflict. Once again, he deplored Pope's hypocritical advocacy of democracy for the United States and Fascism for Italy, an old argument based on the premise that Italy was still too backward for democracy. "I, who have never professed *Italianità* every hour of the day," Tresca wrote, "think that Pope is a defamer of the Italian people when he maintains that they must be governed by castor oil."[34] Pope's commitment to democracy was a sham, amounting to nothing more than his commitment to Tammany Hall and the political and economic benefits derived therefrom. Tresca also renewed his long-standing charge that this phony democrat relied on the *malavita* to do his dirty work. And, as usual, his exposé of Pope was laced with his choicest vituperative and characterizations of the millionaire publisher as the "illiterate quadruped," whose editorials were always written by Falbo or other Fascists on his staff.[35]

Tresca's campaign against Pope included embarrassing revelations about the roles played by important political figures, including Mayor La Guardia, in sanitizing his past and assuring his future. Tresca did not hesitate to put out that La Guardia, for the sake of political expedience, had never criticized Mussolini publicly prior to the war. In 1941, when the State Department finally began to scrutinize the activities of Italian Fascists, Tresca chided La Guardia for putting Pope on the committee sponsoring "I Am An American Day": "Pope has made the most of it. He has used the invitation as evidence of the fact that he is an American. He is not. He is, and he is proud of it, a Fascist to the core and La Guardia knows it."[36] Tresca also revealed how La Guardia came to Pope's assistance a year earlier, expunging his name from an official memorandum describing Fascist activities in New York.[37]

Tresca may have been unaware that while political necessity compelled the mayor to court Pope publicly, La Guardia had previously urged Roosevelt to have the FBI investigate Pope, warning that "in the event of war it would be necessary to take some extraordinary means of changing the editorial and news policy of Pope's newspapers."[38] La Guardia's request had followed repeated complaints to the Justice and State Departments from the Mazzini Society, denouncing Pope as a Fascist agent whose newspapers still supported Mussolini. This potential firestorm must have been discomforting for Roosevelt as he contemplated the loss of Italian-American votes were he to deal aggressively with Pope. Meeting at the White House in April 1941, Roosevelt advised Pope to get off the "mistaken path" he had been traveling, and warned him of the Mazzini Society's recommendation that Pope's Fascist editors be discharged and replaced by anti-Fascists, with Tarchiani serving as editor-in-chief. Pope heeded the warning only to the extent of eliminating pro-Fascist articles from *Il Progresso*'s English-language section, replacing them with obsequious pledges of loyalty to Roosevelt. The Italian-language section continued its praise of the Duce.[39] Roosevelt's warning did not deter Pope from trying to silence his critics. First, he asked Antonini and Bellanca to intercede on his behalf and request that Giuseppe Lupis, the editor of the Mazzini Society's organ, *Il Mondo*, cease attacking him. The request was categorically rejected. Pope turned next to the NYPD's Alien Squad, one of whose detectives, Mario Fochi, was a personal friend and former employee. The Alien Squad sent Detective Stanley Gwazdo, an anti-Semite, to visit Mazzini Society headquarters and intimidate its leaders with the threat of an "official investigation." A similar attempt at intimidation was conducted by Richard Rollins, a former investigator for HUAC and for the Anti-Nazi League, who was now employed as the confidential secretary of Congressman Samuel Dickstein, a local politician comfortably nestled in Pope's pocket. Rollins delegated the mission to one Frank Lee and Casimir Palmer, the latter a sometime undercover agent for the FBI, but their "friendly" conversation with the Mazzini Society's office manager, Alfredo Coen, failed to achieve the intended results.[40]

While his minions were attempting to intimidate his critics behind the scenes, Pope arranged a public defense in the U.S. House of Representatives, with Dickstein serving as his foil. A Tammany Hall hack, Dickstein had been a co-founder, with John W. McCormack, of the House Un-American Activities Committee in 1934, which investigated "un-American" subversion but ignored Italian-Fascist activities. Now on the Immigration Committee, Dickstein championed Pope before the House on March 25, 1941, describing him as "an upright, honest, law-abiding American citizen whose honesty and integrity cannot be questioned by anyone who knows him."[41] Pope "has always condemned Fascism and the Mussolini movement," and is "loyal to the American philosophy of life and to American principles."[42] He reiterated on June 17 that Pope was not a Fascist; his attackers in the Mazzini Society were. Heaping lie upon lie, in distorted profusion, Dickstein added a little Red baiting to the mix, claiming that Max Ascoli, in particular, was busy "conducting communistic propaganda … amongst Americans of Italian origin."[43] Dickstein also targeted Tresca, introducing into the Congressional Record a purported copy of Tresca's New York Police file, and denouncing him for "anarchism and subversive activities."[44]

Dickstein's performance provoked Tresca to respond with an English-language editorial entitled: "Mr. Dickstein, You Are a Jackass." Tresca admonished the congressmen, stating that "whatever the motive of your action might be, the fact remains that in making ridiculous, idiotic, and asinine speeches in the U.S. Congress in behalf of a man like Pope—a Fascist—at this very moment…when legislators ought to devote their minds to solving hard-pressing problems of social and economic nature, you have debased the standard of the House of Representatives and yourself." Tresca mocked Dickstein's description of him as an anarchist: "Hurray for Mr. Dickstein! Columbus discovered America, and you discovered me. Anarchist!!!

So what!!! Mr. Dickstein! There are several asses in Congress, but you are the most ridiculous one."[45]

Further revelations about Pope's duplicitous editorial policy placed him in renewed jeopardy. He was about to cede control of editorial policy to a committee composed of Mazzini Society leaders when Roosevelt cut the ground out from under them. After another powwow in July 1941, the president furnished Pope with one of his "Dear Gene" letters, expressing full confidence in him, and requesting only that he dismiss the most blatant Fascists on his staff. Thus assured of Roosevelt's continuing support, Pope made no concessions to the Mazzini Society, never transformed *Il Progresso* into an anti-Fascist organ, and continued to receive preferential treatment from politicians in Washington and New York eager to sanitize his past.[46]

Tresca and the Mazzini Society

Tresca finally joined the Mazzini Society in May 1942. This caught the interest of the Foreign Nationalities Branch of the Office of Strategic Services (OSS), the forerunner of the CIA. An OSS profile described him as follows:

Tresca was one of the "elder Statesmen" of the Italian-American radical movement and fancied his role. He was the leader of an insignificant number of Anarchists who were, for the most part, politically ineffectual. However, because of the violence of his publication, he personally could not be dismissed as powerless and had often to be reckoned with as a decided force. His attacks have been in wholesale lots, and against members of organizations often known for violent deeds. Persevering in his assaults, he was fearless and unswerving and most pointed in his expression, not given to co-operation or appeasement, not to compromise. A great individualist, he held tenaciously to his hatreds.[47]

The OSS profile further indicated: "It is possible that Tresca was brought into the Mazzini Society not so much for the love the Mazzini membership bore him as for the venom which he bore in his heart for the Communists."[48] The OSS was correct. With Pope and other "ex-Fascists" having no chance of gaining admission, Tresca's goal of excluding totalitarian elements from the Mazzini Society was directed primarily against the Stalinists, whom he was still attacking fiercely despite the Soviet Union's status as an ally of the United States and Britain.[49]

Tresca was particularly unsparing of Vittorio Vidali, whom he reviled as one of Stalin's most villainous praetorians. After escaping from Spain in 1939, Vidali had taken refuge in Mexico, where he become a key figure in the local communist movement. Given his reputation as an OGPU murderer, Vidali was automatically suspected of complicity in the assassination of Trotsky in August 1940, a crime for which he professed his innocence.[50] Vidali was later suspected of murdering his own lover, the photographer Tina Modotti, at the order of the OGPU, because she had become disillusioned with communism and might reveal damaging information about party activities in Europe, Spain, and Mexico.[51] Tresca repeated the charges with little doubt as to their veracity.[52]

Vidali's new objective in the spring of 1942 was penetration of the Mazzini Society. From Hitler's invasion of Poland to the Nazi Soviet Pact, the communists showed no interest in the Mazzini Society other than to condemn it as an instrument of British imperialism. Their main focus during this period was Generoso Pope, whom they courted unctuously in order to gain control of *Il Progresso*.[53] After Germany invaded the Soviet Union, the communist party line reversed itself one more time, calling for a new "united front" of all anti-Fascists. Vidali, together with Francesco Frola, created the *Alleanza Internazionale Anti-Fascista Giuseppe Garibaldi* in Mexico for the purpose of organizing Italian anti-Fascist refugees in Latin America. The next coveted prize was the Mazzini Society, which promised even greater possibility of influencing postwar Italian politics. Preliminary feelers for a rapprochement were extended by surrogates like Marcantonio and Bellanca, but their efforts quickly encountered opposition, especially from Tresca.[54]

Informed of communist intentions by his contacts in Mexico, Tresca wrote an editorial, "The Praetorians of Stalin Move Against the Mazzini Society," warning that Vidali's orders were "either conquer or destroy the Mazzini Society." The professed objective of the communists, once again, was a "united front." But "the method is the same," Tresca reminded, "you don't want unity with us? Then you are agents of Hitler and Mussolini." Opposing the Stalinists was dangerous: "You don't fool around with the GPU.... In the name of unity too many crimes have been committed by Stalin's agents throughout the world." Nevertheless, to Vidali he issued a challenge: "Don Carlos—shameless Sormenti—we know you well. We will not let you pass."[55]

Communist admission to the Mazzini Society was vigorously debated at its national congress held at the New York School for Social Research on June 13–14, 1942, with more than 600 delegates attending.[56] A "declaration of principles," placed on the agenda by Salvemini, advocated a Wilsonian peace, punishment of leading Fascists after the war, and the barring of monarchists and communists from the Mazzini Society.[57] When discussion turn to the issue of admitting the communists, Tresca generated a stir by producing a letter written by Vidali to Allegra, now a writer for communist *L'Unità del Popolo*. Purloined by someone friendly with Tresca, the letter urged that Randolfo Pacciardi, the republican and former commander of the Garibaldi Brigade in Spain, be persuaded to support unity with the communists. Tresca continued: "Unity is spoken of here as it was spoken of during the time of the Spanish Civil War. But we have seen in practice how the communists interpret unity. If the communists were sincere I would extend my hand for common action. But if they were, they would demonstrate it by not seeking to enter the Mazzini Society."[58]

Salvemini's proposal to bar the communists passed by a margin of nearly three to one. Tresca took sole credit for the victory in a letter to Marceau Pivert in Mexico City: "The Stalinists tried to get the control of the 'Mazzini Society' here in the U.S. I blocked them."[59] Tresca's bragging was typical of his unfortunate tendency to self-aggrandize, but at this stage of his career, it revealed his almost desperate need to prove that he was still a major figure in the anti-Fascist movement. Exaggeration aside, Tresca had indeed played a significant role in keeping the communists out of the Mazzini Society, even if he had to share credit with others.

The Manhattan Club Incident

The white-washing of Pope, meanwhile, continued unabated. One means of demonstrating his "conversion" was to include him in patriotic endeavors and ceremonies. Such an event took place on September 10, 1942 at the Italian American War Bond banquet organized by Paolino Gerli at the Manhattan Club in New York. Attending that evening were numerous *prominenti* and public officials who had supported Mussolini in the "old days": Edward Corsi, chairman of the N.Y. State Industrial Commission; City Treasurer Almerindo Portfolio; Paolo Rao, a U.S. Customs Judge; Monsignor Joseph Cafuzzi; Pope; and others. A handful of genuine anti-Fascists were also present. According to his friend Alberto Cupelli, Tresca was invited to this gathering by Gerli, an importer who had towed the Fascist line out of business necessity but who had regularly contributed $50–$100 to *Il Martello* as "insurance." Gerli hoped that Tresca's presence would bestow a "blessing" on his own rehabilitation.[60] The invitation also might have been a scheme to create the false impression that his presence at the gathering meant that Tresca had sanctioned Pope's rehabilitation.[61]

Tresca went to the banquet out of a sense of gratitude to Gerli, but was wary of attending a function that might include Pope. Assured beforehand that Pope was not among the invited guests, Tresca arrived at the Manhattan Club—a half-hour late, as usual—accompanied by Cupelli. They seated themselves at a table with their backs to the dais. Tresca asked Cupelli to turn around inconspicuously and tell him who was present. Cupelli identified the guests one by one. When he mentioned Caffuzzi, the Fascist priest, Tresca made an Italian hand gesture that signified warding off the "evil eye." Seated next to Caffuzzi was Pope, whose name prompted Tresca to mutter to his comrade: "Where have I fallen tonight, into a nest of Fascists? This is no place for me, I'm leaving." Cupelli managed to calm Tresca and persuade him to stay. Some minutes later, a well-dressed man entered the dining room and sat next to his girlfriend, Assistant U.S. Attorney Dolores C. Faconti. The man was Pope's gangster henchman Frank Garofalo. Now furious, Tresca declared in a loud voice, "Not only the Fascist Pope, but even his gangster is here!" He then stormed dramatically out the room, but not before instructing Cupelli to remain and to report later about the repercussions. Contrary to some accounts, Tresca's insult did not result in an angry exchange of words with Garofalo in the foyer. But rumors buzzing in Italian circles after the banquet suggested that when Garofalo overheard the table gossip about Tresca's outburst, he said to Faconti, "Within a week I'll show Carlo Tresca who I am."[62]

Frank Garofalo ("Don Ciccio") was no ordinary thug. Born in 1891, the son of a leather worker in the Mafia-ridden town of Castellammare, Sicily, Garofalo by now had become the "right-hand man" of Mafia chieftain Joseph Bonanno. Standing 5'7" and weighing 160 pounds, with rugged but not displeasing features, Garofalo cut a dapper figure, "dressed as well as Cary Grant," according to his mob boss. Bonnano also described Garofalo as "a self-educated man [who] could talk about literature and history.... His manners were impeccable. What I especially admired about him was his self-taught facility in English.... He was an urbane and sophisticated man with a fondness for good opera, good food and good conversation."[63]

But Garofalo did not become Bonanno's "right hand man" because of his expensive suits and ability to select French wines. An associate of Charles "Lucky" Luciano, Garofalo had been involved in criminal activities (bootlegging among others) for many years, although he never came under police scrutiny. In fact, his clean record enabled him to obtain a license to carry a gun. And like most intelligent Mafiosi, Garofalo engaged in several legal enterprises that enabled him to pose as a legitimate businessman. Thus he had been a part owner of several clothing factories in Brooklyn and now operated the Colorado Cheese Co. at 176 Avenue A in Manhattan.[64] FBI reports refer to Garofalo as "a sort of bodyguard for Pope and the latter's contact with the underworld element."[65] But how and when Garofalo's relationship with Pope was established is unknown. Among anti-Fascists, Garofalo had gained notoriety in 1934, when at Pope's behest he visited *La Stampa Libera*, *Il Martello*, and other newspapers to threaten violence should they persist in attacking his boss. Among his other responsibilities was "settling" labor disputes with Pope's employees.[66]

Garofalo's affair with Faconti pre-dated the Manhattan Club incident by a year or more. A graduate of Fordham Law School, Faconti was appointed Assistant U.S. Attorney, Southern District of New York, during the early 1940s.[67] Her relationship with Garofalo began to raise eyebrows in February1942, when she brought him into the Greater New York Lodge of the Sons of Italy as a new recruit. Garofalo's admission to the lodge was not desired by its members, but his reputation as a dangerous criminal dissuaded objection. The Sons of Italy episode and Faconti's relationship with Garofalo became known to the FBI that November, and Hoover, who disapproved, alerted the Attorney General about Faconti's conduct.[68] Although warned about Garofalo repeatedly by friends such as Edward Corsi, her Fordham classmate, Faconti staunchly defended him against allegations that he was a gangster, which qualified her as a master of self-deception or a liar misguided by love.[69] In either case, Faconti's role in the events following the Manhattan Club incident was critical.

That Tresca had committed a dangerous blunder by insulting Garofalo was recognized by many who attended the banquet, if not by Tresca himself. The next morning Tresca received a phone call from the city treasurer, Almerindo Portfolio, asking him to remain silent about what had transpired at the Manhattan Club. A half-hour later, Tresca received a phone call from Faconti, imploring him not to publicize the events of the previous evening or her presence there with Garofalo. Tresca agreed. Not satisfied, Faconti visited him later that day to discuss the matter further. Again she pleaded with him not to write anything about the banquet. Tresca reassured Faconti that he would not expose her affair with Garofalo, but warned her against associating with him, explaining that he was a criminal who did "dirty work" for employers like Pope. When she protested that Garofalo was an importer of Italian cheese and olive oil, with an establishment on Avenue A, Tresca insisted that the store was merely a front. Faconti wept and then kissed Tresca goodbye. Then Faconti foolishly told Garofalo about her meeting with Tresca; he beat her black and blue for humbling herself before Tresca. She later described Garofalo's violent reaction to her friend Corsi, who was the son of Tresca's old comrade in Sulmona, and whom Tresca had befriended despite his sympathies for Mussolini. Seriously alarmed, Corsi told Cupelli to warn Tresca about possible retaliation from the gangster. Tresca paid no heed.[70]

OWI and the Italian-American Victory Council

While the white-washing and rehabilitation of Pope and other former supporters of Mussolini continued apace, the attention of anti-Fascists shifted in late 1942 to a government project designed to rally "trustworthy" Italian Americans behind the war against the Axis and garner support for American policies toward postwar Italy.[71] The direction of this undertaking was dictated by the political and strategic policy embraced by the State, Justice, and Treasury Departments. An internal memorandum circulated within the government's Office of War Information (OWI) explained the policy:

> The government and for the present, the Communist party, each for its own reasons, wants the broadest possible unity of Italians in America and of Italian Americans. This unity can better be reached on an anti Mussolini than on an anti-Fascist basis. Therefore the tendency is strong to support the position which Churchill has twice stated, namely, that one man, Mussolini, and he alone is responsible for Italy's plight. Therefore, for the present at least, nothing ought to be said against the monarchy which so easily capitulated to Mussolini in Italy or even against fascism.[72]

Long before this policy became official, even before Italy entered the war, Tresca suspected the intentions of Britain and the United States toward postwar Italy. His suspicions were confirmed when Churchill, in a BBC broadcast to the Italian people in May 1940, declaring that "one man and one man alone" was leading Italy to war against the wishes of the Savoy Monarchy and the Papacy.[73] Tresca and anyone else familiar with Italian history knew that Churchill's assertion was a blatant lie. By blaming Mussolini for all the evils that had befallen Italy, Tresca argued, Churchill's intent was to fool the Italian people into forgetting that the real cause of Fascism was war and capitalism. Churchill's ultimate objective was the preservation of Italy's monarchical and ecclesiastic institutions by fostering a new Fascist regime without Mussolini that would prevent communist domination of the country after the war. Looking to Great Britain or even the United States to establish a "new order" in Italy after the war would constitute a grave error. Anti-Fascists had to remain vigilant against the machinations of Churchill and all others who would betray the Italian people yearning for liberty.[74] But opposition from anti-Fascists like Tresca and the leaders of the Mazzini Society did not deter Washington from embracing Churchill's strategy for gaining Italian popular support.

To rally Italian American support for America's postwar policies toward Italy, the Office of War Information devised a plan to organize Victory Councils that would serve as vehicles for news releases, educational programs, and Americanization efforts—propaganda, in a word. The project was entrusted to the OWI's Foreign Language Branch (FLB), headed by Alan Cranston. Cranston's initial hope was to deal only with Italian Americans untainted by Fascism. But, as he explained to OWI head, Elmer Davis, the more powerful departments of government sabotaged this possibility from the outset. He lamented that the Justice Department had interned only a handful of Fascist leaders when the war began, and that it had permitted Italian newspapers to continue publishing pro-Fascist propaganda. The Treasury Department appointed Italian War Bond committees dominated by Fascists. When anti-Fascists in New York refused to serve on a committee that included Pope, "the Treasury appointed Pope and a dozen other Italians with Fascist records to a committee containing not one anti-fascist."[75] Cranston had no choice, therefore, but to include "Pear Harbor Patriots" still entrenched in positions of influence. This meant, of course, that Tresca and the other anti-Fascists whom Cranston asked to assist with the Victory Councils project would not cooperate. In the end, Cranston and the OWI discovered that achieving unanimity of mind and purpose among Italian Americans on matters concerning anti-Fascism and postwar Italy was an impossibility.[76]

Far more controversy and public exposure occurred in December 1942 and early January 1943, when Cranston and his assistant Lee Falk, held several meetings with anti-Fascist leaders to recommend that the Italian-American Victory Councils include communists. The most vocal opponents to the idea were Antonini and his factotum Vanni Montana. Hoping for a different response from Tresca, Lee Falk invited him to a preparatory meeting on January 14. Tresca asked his friend Umberto Gualtieri, vice-president of the Mazzini Society's New York chapter, to accompany him and observe the proceedings. He insisted to Guartieri that if communists and ex-Fascists were present, they would leave the assembly. Tresca never wrote about the Victory Council project in *Il Martello*; however, his opposition to the inclusion of both "ex-Fascist" Pope and the communists was well known to all anti-Fascists, a position later misrepresented by Falk, who claimed that Tresca went on record in opposition to the inclusion of communists but agreed not to make an issue of it. Ultimately, suspicion and disenchantment on the part of most anti-Fascists ensured that an IAVC chapter was never organized in New York.[77]

The Final Days

On New Year Eve, 1942, Tresca phoned his daughter Beatrice at her home in Arlington, Massachusetts. Ordinarily, on such an occasion, Tresca would have been bursting with good cheer often eating a substantial Italian meal and plenty of wine. On this evening he was somber and sober. "*L'ho scampato*," (I escaped it), he muttered as much to himself as to Beatrice.[78] The cryptic remark required no explanation. The "it" Tresca believed he had escaped was death.

In January 1942, Tresca's brother Ettore, the much-beloved physician, died of cancer. Nine months later, his brother Mario succumbed to the same disease. Ettore's death had hit Tresca particularly hard because the two brothers had been on the verge of re-establishing their relationship after a long estrangement. To Antonini he confided: "I am going trough a very serious spiritual crises since the death of my brother. I have a crushing feeling. I feel like a wandering whom have lost his way."[79] Tresca never emerged from this depression. To people long accustomed to his radiant warm and ebullience, Tresca seemed transformed into a brooding man oppressed with thoughts of imminent tragedy. Beatrice knew that her father was harboring an almost suspicious premonition that, somehow, with Ettore and Mario gone, he would not survive to see the dawn of 1943.[80] Others had become aware of Tresca's depression as well. On January 8, when he visited the Cocce Press on Barrow Street, where *Il Martello* was printed, the proprietor observed that Tresca was distracted and grim, leaving without his customary jests, saying to the Italian linotype operators in a gloomy tone, "Well, I'm going. I guess this is goodbye."[81]

Added to Tresca's woes was the perennial problem of *Il Martello*'s deficits. Hoping to raise funds, Tresca and his Martello group hosted a lunch at John's Restaurant on Saturday afternoon, January 9, for a group of knitgoods workers headed by Louis Nelson of Local 155. The gathering turned into a tribute to Tresca. Nelson declared: "To us, Carlo Tresca is not just an Italian anti-fascist. He belongs to all of us, to the entire labor movement. He has spent his life fighting for the workers regardless of race or creed." Tresca smiled yet appeared sad at hearing his past glories praised. "Was he thinking of the many struggles he had engaged in and whether he might yet march with is flock into the Promised Land?" pondered Arturo Giovannitti. Sensing his friend's somber mood, the poet interrupted the tributes that focused on Tresca's past, declaring "We are not making a eulogy. Our friend, Carlo, he is with us today and will be with us for many years." Perhaps doubtful of his friend's prediction, Tresca pronounced what was to be his last public statement: "When I see young people who carry on the struggle against Fascism and totalitarianism, then I am glad. For I know that my life work has not been lost; that the seeds I have sown are bearing fruit."[82]

24

Murder in the Dimout

The Assassination

Tresca awoke on Monday, January 11, 1943, fully expecting to divide his day between the two disparate worlds he inhabited: the upper-middle class and cosmopolitan elite of American writers, artists, intellectuals, and political activists; and the Italian anti-Fascist subculture, where old-guard fighters like him had been relegated to secondary roles by the *fuorusciti* who dominated the Mazzini Society. That afternoon Tresca enjoyed a leisurely lunch with Margaret De Silver, her son Harrison, and John Dos Passos at John's Restaurant at 612 Eighth Avenue near 40th Street. The proprietor and several other diners observed that Tresca was in a good mood, even joking with the chef about the spaghetti. After lunch, Tresca went to his *Il Martello* office at Fifth Avenue and 15th Street, where he planned to meet that evening with several members of the Mazzini Society and form a committee to undertake cultural, educational, and propaganda activities among Italian Americans. His expected guests included Vanni Montana, Antonini's factotum and the educational and publicity director of Local 89; Giovanni Sala, an ACWU official; Giovanni Profenna; Gian Mario Lanzilotti; and Giuseppe Calabi, a Jewish lawyer and refugee from Milan.[1]

The timing of the meeting was unusual for Tresca, who rarely stayed at his office past 6:00 P.M. because of Margaret's concern for his safety. On such occasions, he was usually accompanied by Vincenzo Leonetti, the genial iceman and sometime longshoreman, or Tony Ribarich, the tough Triestine tailor, who served as his unofficial bodyguard. That evening neither Lionetti nor Ribarich went to the office, probably because Tresca had informed them that he was expecting the committee members. The only other person present at the office was Luigi Ciccone, a member of *Il Martello*'s staff, whom Tresca told to go home at around 8:00 P.M., believing his guests would arrive momentarily.

The only person who showed up was Calabi. They had waited for an hour, as Tresca attempted unsuccessfully to reach the others by telephone. By 8:30 P.M., the four members had neither arrived nor telephoned to explain their absence. Fed up with waiting, Tresca and Calabi left the office at 8:38 P.M., intending to have dinner at a nearby tavern. They exited on the 15th Street side of the building, as was Tresca's habit, walked about seventy-five feet to Fifth Avenue, and crossed to the northwest corner of the intersection. The time was 8:40 P.M. The streets of New York were dark because of the wartime dimout. As Tresca and his companion waited for the light to turn green, a short, heavy-set man emerged from the shadows and fired four shots, disrupting the rhythm of the street sounds. One bullet hit Tresca in the left side of his back, penetrating the lung; a second struck him under the right eye and entered his brain as he turned toward his assailant. He died instantly. The gunman jumped into a waiting automobile that sped westward on 15th Street, disappearing in the night.

A score of policemen and onlookers quickly converged on the grisly scene. Although unharmed, Calabi was too shocked to relate what had happened. Rumors spread that the slain man was the poet Arturo Giovannitti, whose office was only a half-block away. Like his good friend, Giovannitti was a familiar figure in this neighborhood of radical and labor organizations. He, too, sported a goatee and stood a portly six feet. A waiter who worked at the tavern which had been Tresca's destination informed the police that, if the slain man was Giovannitti, they were certain to find the ornate cane that he carried everywhere. Instead of a cane, they found a clay pipe within arm's reach of the body—the pipe that was as much a part of Tresca as his broad-brimmed hat. Soon two patrolmen arrived who identified the slain man as Tresca. The next morning every New York daily newspaper featured headlines reporting that the venerable old anarchist, Carlo Tresca, had been murdered in the dimout.[2]

Tresca's funeral became an issue of contention among the Italian groups who wished to take charge of the arrangements, prompting his infuriated daughter Beatrice to demand that they decide upon a site or face exclusion from a private family ceremony she would arrange in Boston if they persisted in squabbling.[3] Finally, after Tresca's body lay in state at the Campbell Funeral Parlor on Madison Avenue, the *Il Martello* group and the Italian-American Labor Council selected the Manhattan Center on 34th Street and 8th Avenue for the tributary ceremonies. Its huge auditorium could scarcely accommodate the 5,000 people who turned out to pay their respects. Tresca's gray metal casket rested on the ballroom platform. Unlike the funerals of so many Italian radicals, whose ideals were defiled in death by conventional Catholic relatives, there was no religious paraphernalia on display, the proximity of which would doubtless have caused Tresca to rise from the dead in protest. Instead, his casket was enveloped with red carnations, the floral symbol of revolutionaries. The lapel of his black suit was similarly adorned. Seated on the platform with Margaret, Beatrice, and family friends was a large contingent of notables representing the non-communist Left and the labor movement. Luigi Antonini described Tresca as "one of the greatest anti-Fascists and a man with a sole purpose, which was to rid the world of Fascism." He urged that everyone continue the fight Tresca had represented. David Dubinsky, president of the ILGWU, expressed the hope that Tresca's murder would not become "another Krivitsky case," a reference to the "suicide," in a Washington hotel two years earlier, of the disaffected former chief of Soviet Military Intelligence in Western Europe, a deed generally attributed to the NKVD. The level of emotional intensity increased when Tresca's old revolutionary comrades rose to speak. Harry Kelly, the American anarchist and labor organizer, declared that "if Carlo knew I would be speaking to you today, he would say, 'Harry, say to them that I stood for a free society where men and women for the first time, perhaps for ages, will be able to say and have what they please.'

When that society comes, we will remember and appreciate the work of Carlo Tresca." Angelica Balabanoff, the grand old lady of European Socialism, who had known both Tresca and Mussolini as exiles in Switzerland, described him in Italian as one of Italy's great martyrs, "slain by those who are afraid of enlightenment, truth and reason." Norman Thomas, who soon headed a Tresca Memorial Committee that would press the DA's office for years to solve the crime, declared: "Here lies Carlo, the victim of a hired assassin, the victim of some political group.... Tresca was a man of great courage; he was a fighter who despised cruelty... [who] more than any other man was responsible for checking the Blackshirt groups from treading the streets of New York." Vincenzo Vacirca, comparing him to the great heroes of literature, said "he was always ready to fight; he loved to live dangerously." Arturo Giovannitti, the bard of Italian-American radicalism, was the last speaker. Through a flood of tears Giovannitti declared in Italian: "Carlo Tresca made a religion out of the fight for freedom. [He] will never die in the minds of the lovers of liberty.... Carlo Tresca, in this solemn moment, we swear to destroy the totalitarian concepts against which you so courageously and nobly fought." A thousand voices responded to Giovannitti's exhortation: "*Giuriamo!*" (We Swear!) [4]

After the eulogies ended with a battle cry, the mourners filed passed the coffin, bidding farewell to the fallen tribune of the Italian immigrant working class, many of them genuflecting and making the sign of the cross. [5] Although an atheist and inveterate priest hater, Tresca would have understood the sincerity of these religious gestures. After the final viewing, a funeral cortege of fifteen floral cars and seventy-five passenger cars drove from the Manhattan Center to the northwest corner of 15th Street and Fifth Avenue. The spot where his slain body had lain was blanketed with red carnations. The cortege proceeded next to Tresca's apartment, and then to his favorite eating place, John's Restaurant. The final destination was the Fresh Pond Cemetery in Queens where his body was cremated.

Tresca's eulogists had failed to mention that the flamboyant rebel undoubtedly would have preferred such a dramatic death to a quiet, peaceful, and unheralded departure. Tresca always had believed and predicted that his enemies would kill him sooner or later. His dire prediction reflected the life of a man who, during his tempestuous career, had narrowly escaped an assassin's razor, a sheriff's bullet, a lynch-mob's rope, and a Fascist bomb. Ironically, at a time when his political career was in decline, the violent manner of his death propelled Tresca back into the public eye, generating more notoriety and sympathy than he had enjoyed in many years. To Italian Americans, in particular, Tresca's murder was a poignant reminder, not only of the tempestuous career he had had, but of his heroic efforts—absolutely unequalled among his co-nationals—to win social justice and liberty for the working class, endeavors unappreciated more often than not during his lifetime.

Recollections and Tributes

Tresca's murder generated a voluminous outpouring of recollections and tributes from old friends and colleagues, many of them published in a special edition of *Il Martello* entitled "*Omaggio alla memoria imperitura di Carlo Tresca*" (Homage to the Imperishable Memory of Carlo Tresca). Defining Tresca politically, even as an anarchist, presented a challenge to those who had worked with him closely for years. All agreed that Tresca dealt with real-life situations pragmatically rather than in accordance with preconceived and abstract doctrines, a tendency that precluded his being a theorist or an ideologue. Roger Baldwin, president of the ACLU, wrote that "he was far from any traditional picture of an anarchist. Indeed, I always thought the world 'libertarian'... fitted him much better. For he always reacted at once to any challenge to liberty."[6] The American philosopher Sidney Hook maintained that "despite his ideological professions of class war, he was primarily a humanitarian..., [and] essential decency, not dogma nor doctrine, guided his political actions."[7] Norman Thomas also understood the relationship between Tresca's humanitarianism and lack of dogmatism: "He loved men better than the abstraction, mankind. He loved life too much to be forced into any Procrustean of dogma. He had a great faith without bitter intolerance."[8] Angelica Balabanoff maintained that "the 'dominant thinking' of Carlo Tresca... was protest against social injustices, rebellion against oppression of the weak, and an ardent hope for the triumph of liberty and human brotherhood."[9]

None of Tresca's former associates perceived him as an "intellectual," in the conventional sense of the term, but they all agreed that his intelligence and political acumen were outstanding. The writer John Dos Passos, who came to know Tresca in the 1930s, wrote that "[he] had the best Italian type of brains, the Machiavellian type, cool, clear, always ready to move... in the light of reason. His comments on men and politics were the shrewdest I heard anywhere."[10] Oswald Garrison Villard wrote that Tresca possessed "an astonishing knowledge of men and affairs. Upon them his comments were always as illuminating as they were deep and searching, and they gained no end of the quaintness of his English and the twinkle in his eyes."[11] Edmund Wilson observed how Tresca "would calculate political problems with a logic of trenchant intellect and an insight of intimate experience which made him one of the most interesting and profitable of all the commentators to consult."[12]

Some of the signature aspects of Tresca's career as a revolutionary, his friends and colleagues agreed, were his absolute fearlessness and courage in a struggle. Matteo Siragusa, a socialist who had known him since 1906, described Tresca as "an indomitable fighter, always in the front ranks, courageous to the point of foolhardiness, he filled out the many gaps in our movement with his exuberant nature so many times, always leaving, wherever he saw action, an indelible impression of his complex, unique, and powerful personality."[13] Action for Tresca, they recognized, was indispensable for his spiritual well being. His pursuit of action as an independent, without official affiliation or support, evoked for some an image of Tresca as a revolutionary "artist." This image was captured by Lionello Venturi, one of the founders of the Mazzini Society: "Rebellion, insurrection, revolution had not only a social objective for him, but also a beauty in and of itself.... Tresca, in his fashion, in his deeds, was a poet. It was poetry that enabled him to elevate his action above the level of mere politics; and it was his 'amateur status' that enable him to hear the poetry of action."[14]

Carmine Galante

Investigation of Tresca's murder was the responsibility of the New York Police Department and the Manhattan District Attorney's office headed by Frank S. Hogan. Assistant DA Jacob Grumet, head of the Homicide Bureau, was entrusted with the general supervision of the case. Working directly under Grumet were ADAs Eleazar Lipsky, Louis A. Pagnucco, Vincent J. Dermody, and three others. Attached to the DA's office were six special investigators. Thirteen police officials and detectives from various squads were assigned to the case under the direction of Deputy Chief Inspector Conrad Rothengast, as were ten detectives from the Grand Jury Squad. Other elements involved included the Alien Squad, the Police Technical Research unit, the Manhattan and State Departments of Correction, the State Parole Commission, the U.S. Bureau of Narcotics, and the Special Investigation Bureau of the U.S. Alcohol Tax Unit.[15]

With this small army of law enforcement officials mobilized for the investigation, expectations for a speedy resolution of the crime were high. The police investigation began promisingly enough. The autopsy and an empty cartridge case found at the scene revealed that the fatal bullets had been fired from a .32 caliber automatic, which was never recovered. Detectives also discovered a loaded .38 caliber revolver behind an ashcan less than 100 feet from the Fifth Avenue entrance to Tresca's office building. The weapon bore no fingerprints, and efforts to trace its ownership failed. However, its presence suggested that a second gunman was waiting for Tresca, in the event that he exited from the Fifth Avenue side of the building.

A few hours later, police found a dark 1938 Ford sedan abandoned on 18th Street, just east of 7th Avenue, five blocks from the murder site. The Ford matched the description given of the getaway car by Calabi and two Norwegian attachés who had witnessed the escape. The automobile, with all four doors open and the keys still hanging in the ignition, had been abandoned in haste just a few paces from the entrance to the 7th Avenue subway, a convenient escape route. Suspicions were heightened when Tony Ribarich identified the Ford as the vehicle that had nearly run him and Tresca down two days earlier as they walked passed the New School for Social Research on West 12th Street near Sixth Avenue. No fingerprints were discernible, but police traced to vehicle to the Con-Field Motors Co. in Manhattan that had sold it on December 24, 1942 to one "Charles Pappas" of Brooklyn, who paid $300 in cash and brought his own license plates so he could drive the vehicle immediately. But "Charles Pappas" of Brooklyn proved to be non-existent.[16]

The method of obtaining a getaway car and the likely presence of a second gunman near the scene led police to conclude that Tresca's murder had been the well-planned work of professional criminals. This conclusion was reinforced when the District Attorney's office announced the apprehension of a "prime suspect" just two days after the murder. Recently out of prison, Carmine Galante had made his weekly report to parole officer Sidney H. Gross at 7:30 P.M. on the evening of January 11. Suspecting Galante of new criminal activities, Gross had arranged for his colleague Fred Berson to follow him after his next visit to the Parole Board at 80 Center Street. At 8:10 P.M., Galante rushed from the building after meeting with Gross; Berson trailed behind unnoticed. When Galante reached Lafayette Street, he entered a dark-colored sedan which sped away north. Berson was unable to follow because the wartime shortage of gas and rubber obliged parole officers to relinquish their official vehicles, but he managed to copy down the license plate number of the speeding vehicle. The next morning, David Dressler, Executive Director of the State Division of Parole, was reading about the Tresca murder when he realized that the license of the suspected getaway car matched the one submitted to him by Berson in his report on Galante. Dressler telephoned DA Hogan, and the search for Galante was on.[17] Galante's hangouts in "Little Italy" were known to the NYPD, so he and his friend Joseph Di Palermo were easily apprehended on Elizabeth Street at 10:30 P.M., Tuesday night. Later suspected of being Galante's accomplice, Di Palermo gave a statement and was released. Galante was held in custody for parole violation. Police did not inform him that he was a suspect in Tresca's murder.[18]

Born in East Harlem in 1910, Galante was a brutal young thug in the Castellammarese gang in New York, which had roots in the Mafia-ridden town of Castellammare del Golfo in Sicily, birthplace of gang leader Giuseppe Bonanno, his *consigliere* Frank Garofalo, and Galante's parents. Growing up in Brooklyn, Galante had become a seasoned criminal by age fourteen, and after many arrests, he was convicted of armed robbery in 1926 and sentenced to serve two-and-one-half to five years at Sing Sing Prison, where he was diagnosed as "Neuropathic, with a pathological personality."[19] Nicknamed "Lilo" and "The Cigar," Galante was known even among his criminal associates as "a vicious killer without emotions."[20] Paroled in 1928, Galante was charged with complicity in the murder of a patrolman killed during a payroll robbery in 1930, but the charge was dropped for lack of evidence. Immediately re-arrested, this time for a holdup of a Prudential Life Insurance branch in East New York, Galante was again set free. Finally, on Christmas Eve, 1930, Galante fought a gun battle with two policemen in Brooklyn who had sought to question him. Captured after a wild chase, he was identified as one of the gunmen who had robbed the Lieberman Brewery in Brooklyn. Pleading guilty to a lesser charge of unarmed attempted robbery, Galante was sentenced to twelve-and-one-half years, plus the two years and five months for violating parole on his 1926 conviction. He spent the next eight years at Sing Sing and Clinton Prisons and was paroled in May 1939. At the time of his arrest in connection with Tresca's murder, Galante was working occasionally for the United Sportswear company owned by his gangster friend, Giovanni Dioguardi ("Johnny Dio"); he supposedly held another job as a driver's helper for the Knickerbocker Trucking Company, although he never did any actual work.[21]

After his arrest on January 12, Galante was brought to the office of the Homicide Bureau for questioning. Galante realized that the assemblage of top brass present for his interrogation could not possibly be interested in his parole violation. Former ADA Eleazar Lipsky recalled that the scene was "like something out of the movies."[22] Inspector Rothengast bore down on the suspect with questions and admonitions. Galante merely looked up at his adversary and said: "What do you think I am, a child?"[23] At a later interrogation, when ADA Pagnucco caught him in a contradiction, Galante lost his temper, shouting "Don't you put words in my mouth." He refused to answer any more questions.[24] Coercing a confession out of Galante was out of the question, as he was well accustomed to police brutality and had never broken. In underworld parlance, Galante proved he was a "stand-up guy," one who remained true to the Italian underworld's code of silence—*omertà*. ADA Lipsky concluded that Galante would have gone to the electric chair rather than provide information.[25]

Galante insisted that after leaving the parole office, he took the Lexington Avenue subway uptown to Times Square, shuttled over to the 7th Avenue line, and went a few stops uptown to the Hollywood Theatre on Broadway, where he saw the movie *Casablanca* by himself. He soon changed his story, indicating he saw the film in the company of his girlfriend and future wife, Helen Marulli, whose reputation he sought to protect because they had spent the rest of the night in a hotel room. He asserted that they entered the theater just as the credits appeared on the screen, i.e., a few minutes after curtain time, 8:30 P.M. Interrogators noted the impossibility of reaching the Hollywood Theatre in time for the opening credits if he had taken the subway route he indicated. But even a late arrival could not explain Galante's vagueness about the details of the film, particularly one as memorable as *Casablanca*. Although Galante's girlfriend corroborated his story, her roommate told the DA's office that she, not Carmine, had spent the evening of January 11 with Marulli. That Galante obviously had instructed Marulli in advance to verify his presence at the movie around 8:30 P.M. impressed his interrogators as highly damaging. Nevertheless, when challenged with all the inconsistencies in his alibi, Galante merely shrugged his shoulders and professed his innocence anew.[26] When nothing more could be extracted from Galante, a weary DA Hogan announced to the press: "This fellow has spent years in prisons. He's prison wise and a tough nut to crack."[27]

Without a confession, the case against Galante would depend upon eye-witness testimony. A dark complexioned man, 5'4" and 142 pounds, Galante definitely fit the general description of Tresca's murderer. But the Norwegian attachés who had seen the murderer dash across the street could not identify Galante in a line-up. The automobile salesman who sold the getaway car to the mysterious "Pappas" indicated that Galante was not the same man. The key eye-witness, Calabi, neither identified nor excluded him as the shooter. Lipsky and the other ADAs were perplexed by Calabi's failure to make a positive identification given that he had been standing under a street lamp, just a few feet from Tresca's killer. The reason for his equivocation was never revealed to the public. Identifying Galante had posed a moral dilemma for Calabi, especially because murder was a capital offense. A practicing lawyer for thirty years in Italy, Calabi knew how easily ideas and impressions can be suggested to a witness. Because he had seen a photo of Galante in the newspapers before the line-up, Calabi would not exclude the possibility that his judgment might have been compromised. Had it not been for the newspaper photos and the severity of the sentence, Calabi admitted he would have identified Galante as the killer, according to Lipsky. Unable to proceed without a confession or eye-witness identification, the DA's office announced that pending further investigation Galante would be held in the Tombs Prison as a parole violator.[28]

In cases involving a tight-lipped suspect, it had become standard procedure for the DA's office to employ the services of Emilio "Nick" Funicello, a professional stool pigeon. A not unsympathetic figure, who Lipsky incorporated into his crime novel, *The Kiss of Death*, Funicello in 1932 had been sentenced to life imprisonment as a fourth-time offender for a robbery that had netted him $1.50.

After his wife died and his two children were placed in an orphanage, Funicelli turned jail-house informer in November 1937, in order to get out of prison. He served thereafter as a direct pipeline between the Tombs and the DA's office, and the information he obtained won many a conviction in court. In fact, Funicello became so skilled at his craft that law enforcement officials came to regard him a part of the establishment.[29]

Placed in the same cell with Galante, Funicello slowly won Galante's confidence and eventually heard four versions of the murder. Galante admitted shooting Tresca, and identified his two accomplices as "Buster" and "Pap," one of whom pointed out the intended victim. But Galante's jail-house "confession" did not reveal the motive for the murder nor the identity of its instigator. True to form, when confronted with Funicelli's allegations by the DA's office, Galante reaffirmed his original story and then clammed up. No further attempts to trick Galante into making a confession were undertaken.[30]

The police, meanwhile, had arrested one of Galante's friends, a twenty-three-year-old bootlegger named Frank Nuccio. A key found in the glove compartment of the getaway Ford was traced to an eight-car garage leased by Nuccio near Elizabeth Street, where police suspected the vehicle had been hidden prior to Tresca's murder. Nuccio conceded that the Ford had been kept in his garage prior to the crime, and that he had changed the lock after its departure, suspecting some criminal purpose. But the police never revealed whether Nuccio identified the person to whom he rented the garage space. Nuccio was held in jail as a material witness until November 1943, when the Court of General Sessions ordered his release. Nothing more was heard about Nuccio.[31]

By now, with little to show for its eight-month investigation, the DA's office, as a half-way measure, charged Galante with parole violation and transferred him to Clinton Prison at Dannemora. The decision to indict Galante for Tresca's murder or to await new revelations still had to be made. The DA's case was weak. Unless a stronger statement was forthcoming from Calabi, the only evidence that could be presented at trial consisted of Galante's presence in the getaway car less than two hours before the murder, the discrepancies in his alibi, and the alleged admission of guilt provided by Funicello. But on April 13, 1944, the Court of Appeals rejected the testimony of Funicello in another case, describing him as "a seasoned reporter of oral admissions of high criminal guilt" who could boast of "no less than a thousand felonies [sic] of his own."[32] The impeachment of Funicello by the Court of Appeals precluded the DA's using him against Galante. At this critical juncture, as former ADA William J. Keating wrote, "Hogan and Jack Grumet and Lee Lipsky and Louis Pagnucco and all the others…were trying to decide whether it would be worse to prosecute Galante and risk an acquittal or not prosecute him and have their ears burned interminably."[33] According to Lipsky, he, Pagnucco, and Grumet wanted to seek an indictment but Hogan did not.[34] Without the testimony of this jail-house informer, Hogan preferred to retain the option of prosecuting Galante at a later date, as there was no statute of limitations for first-degree murder. Thus began the long and futile wait for new developments to arise. Meanwhile, on December 22, 1944, Galante was released from Dannemora after the New York Supreme Court Justice Andrew W. Ryan ruled that the Parole Board lacked the authority to detain him any longer.[35]

25

Theories and Investigations

No one who knew Tresca believed for a second that Galante was anything other than a professional criminal who had been paid to assassinate the old anarchist. The District Attorney's Office and the NYPD held the same opinion.[1] The key issue in the case was the identity of the person or persons who had hired Galante to commit the crime. What was so remarkable about the investigation, however, was the degree to which the DA's office and the NYPD focused primarily on Galante and undertook only feeble attempts to determine the real culprits behind the murder. The abject neglect of this crucial dimension of the case led to widespread belief that political motives had ensured that the true instigators of the murder would never be revealed or prosecuted. Careful study of the investigation confirms this conclusion.

From the outset the investigation was disadvantaged by almost total ignorance of Tresca's political world. Astonished at the plethora of enemies Tresca had accumulated, Hogan announced after two weeks: "It seems at one time or other, in politics and personalities, that Tresca was 'agin everything.'"[2] Virtually all the information relevant to Tresca's activities as well as the theories purporting to identify the instigators of his murder were provided to the DA's office by the victim's friends and associates, and for years thereafter, investigators uncovered little of importance to augment the input of these accusers.

Theories

The majority of Tresca's friends and comrades believed the murder was politically motivated, although opinion split as to the originators of the deed, some believing the communists responsible, others attributing blame to "ex-Fascists." Specific accusations pointed to Vittorio Vidali among the communists and Generoso Pope and Frank Garofalo among "ex-Fascists" and their gangster henchmen. The most vociferous and persistent accusers of Vidali and the communists were Luigi Antonini and Vanni Montana. Their belief may have been sincere, but there was no doubt that their accusations fostered a political agenda, having become the leading anti-communists in the Italian-American community by 1943. Their efforts were part of a broader campaign to prevent communist hegemony in Italy after the war. The OSS, keenly interested in the postwar politics of Italy, easily recognized the additional motivation behind Antonini's and Montana's accusations, concluding that they "seized on the assassination immediately with a plan for making maximum capital out of it."[3]

Montana spent several hours at the DA's office immediately following the murder, recounting Tresca's opposition to communist infiltration of the Mazzini Society, the Italian-American Victory Councils, and their long range plans to control Italy. Hogan was more confused than enlightened by Montana's account, as an OSS report revealed, "because it was difficult to get something definite to support certain statements which Mr. Montana had been willing to make."[4] Antonini, meanwhile, went to the press to level his charges: "If I had to choose between the Fascists and the Communists, I will give the Communists 95 per cent that they did it, and the Fascists 5 per cent."[5] The Fascists, Antonini explained, "at this time are running and it is not a good time to do anything of the kind."[6] The communists, in contrast, "are in a better position to do it in revenge on this man."[7]

Antonini's accusation prompted outrage and counter-attack from Italian communists and American leaders of the CP.[8] Antonini seized upon their reaction to escalate his anti-communist campaign by accusing Vidali outright of instigating Tresca's murder. Vidali's motives were the violent attacks Tresca had directed against him since the Spanish Civil War, his incessant denunciations of Stalinists and the Soviet Union, and his exposés of NKVD crimes such as the Poyntz kidnapping.[9] Most telling, Antonini insisted that Tresca himself had identified Vidali as his likely assassin during a lunch a few weeks before the murder. Tresca allegedly told him:

> Luigi, the "friend" is here.
> What "friend"?
> Enea. [Enea Sormenti, Vidali's pseudonym in the United States.]
> Are you sure?
> Very sure. He is here, and I smell the stink of death in the air.[10]

Antonini supported his claim by noting that Tresca had expressed similar remarks about Vidali's presence in New York to several other friends, which was apparently the case.[11]

While Antonini and Montana continued to accuse the communists, Tresca's former colleague Ezio Taddei and the noted socialist Girolamo Valenti emerged as the principal proponents of the competing theory that attributed responsibility to Pope and Garofalo. Taddei was a problematic figure. An anarchist writer who had spent seventeen years in fascist prisons, Taddei arrived in the United States in 1939 as a stow-away, and like so many penniless refugees, sought out and received help from Tresca. After a few years of wandering from place to place, Taddei secured a position on *Il Martello*'s editorial staff.[12] Ironically, when first interviewed by the DA's office, Taddei accused the communists of the murder because Tresca had attacked them for years and prevented their infiltration of the Mazzini Society.[13] Yet three weeks later Taddei joined forces with the Italian communist newspaper *L'Unità del Popolo* and its editor Ambrogio Donini, allegedly because he believed the DA was trying to frame the communists for Tresca's murder.[14] The more likely explanation was opportunism—the communists were the only group that would accept him. Antonini and Montana, who dubbed him the "little serpent," reported that Tresca had become disenchanted with Taddei shortly before his death and had dismissed him from *Il Martello*.[15]

Taddei gave a speech at the Rand School on February 14, 1943, later published as a pamphlet entitled *The Tresca Case*, charging that Tresca's assassination had been orchestrated by Pope and Garofalo. He recounted Tresca's long campaign against Pope, especially his 1934 exposé of Pope's intimidation of rival newspaper editors, and he identified Garofalo as Pope's gangster emissary. Taddei reminded his listeners of Tresca's own words in regard to the Pope/Garofalo death threats: "if I am murdered, look for Generoso Pope." Taddei also described Tresca's efforts to prevent Pope's political rehabilitation and his insulting remark directed at Garofalo during the Manhattan Club banquet in September 1942. Taddei claimed to have been in the office of *Il Martello* when City Treasurer Almerindo Portfolio phoned to request that Tresca not mention the Manhattan Club incident, and when Faconti visited to beg Tresca to remain silent about her relationship with Garofalo. He claimed that after Portfoglio's phone call Tresca became concerned and telephoned Agent Joseph Genco at the FBI.[16] Taddei further revealed the little known fact that Galante's alleged employer, the Knickerbocker Trucking Co., retained Samuel De Falco, a city councilman and chairman of the Democratic Club (whose membership included many gangsters), as its legal counsel. Di Falco, it just so happened, was Pope's nephew and godson.[17]

Shortly after Taddei's Rand House speech, an unpublished "Memorandum Re: Assassination of Carlo Tresca" was circulated among Italian anti-Fascists and other friends of the deceased. Unsigned but written by Girolamo Valenti, the editor of *La Parola*, the "Memorandum" covered much the same ground as Taddei's indictment of Pope and Garofalo, albeit in more accusatory language and with greater emphasis on the conflict between Tresca and Garofalo. Valenti advanced three conclusions: Galante participated in the murder and could identify his accomplices; Tresca's murder could not have been committed if not sanctioned or ordered by Garofalo; and Pope was either directly implicated, in that he expressed a wish for Tresca's death, or tacitly approved of the plan to murder him by offering no objection to the plan.[18]

A third theory regarding Tresca's murder was posited by a Brooklyn gangster named Ernst "The Hawk" Rupolo more than a year after the crime. Facing a lengthy prison term, Rupolo obtained a reduced sentence in exchange for giving the Brooklyn DA information about underworld crimes, one of which was Tresca's murder. Rupolo asserted that Mussolini and his son-in-law and Foreign Minister Count Galeazzo Ciano had ordered the murder, and that the intermediary who arranged the shooting was the notorious Mafia leader Vito Genovese. Rupolo indicated that Tresca was killed because of new attacks against the Duce and Fascism in *Il Martello*, noting also that Tresca had been on the Mussolini's "death list" since 1931.[19]

Hogan and the Investigation

Investigating Tresca's murder posed a major dilemma for Manhattan DA Frank Hogan. The crime was indisputably one of the most famous in New York City history, and the clamor for justice transformed the case into an instant *cause célèbre*. Yet the very prominence of the case became a disincentive to prosecute Galante. FBI agents who conferred with Hogan and his ADAs were very unimpressed with the quality of the DA's investigation. So much so, that the Bureau concluded that DA Hogan's decision to postpone indefinitely any prosecution of Galante was not based on the evidence or its lack. To FBI field agents the Tresca case appeared to have "many political ramifications"; therefore, "it is within the realm of possibility that due to these political ramifications the New York State authorities have considered it advisable to 'soft pedal' the instant investigation." This view was supported by an FBI informant's opinion that "the District Attorney's Office is not anxious to prosecute anyone for the Tresca murder." The FBI ultimately concluded that "the New York State authorities are inclined, for reasons presently unknown to the Bureau, to give this matter the 'brush-off,' even though they undoubtedly have in their possession sufficient information to present the facts on Galante to a Grand Jury."[20]

William J. Keating, a former ADA in Hogan's office, wrote that "rarely have politics and the fear of criticism been more rampantly disadvantageous to the operation of a prosecutor's office...."[21] Hogan's primary concern was not justice for Tresca but fear of the political consequences should a trial of Galante end in acquittal. Elected to replace Thomas E. Dewey in 1941, Hogan was unwilling so early in his career to risk losing such a high profile murder case. The safer course, as Keating explained, was to have his "ears burned interminably." Keating's assessment was later confirmed by former ADA Lipsky.[22]

That Hogan would have much preferred the Tresca case to go away was evidenced by his shocking unfamiliarity with the details of the investigation.[23] Such detachment might have been customary in a run-of-the-mill murder case assigned to ADAs, but a high-profile assassination like Tresca's presumably should have merited a more hands-on approach from the DA. Virtually all aspects of the investigation were delegated to subordinates with no apparent input from Hogan—or none evident in the DA files. According to procedure, Eleazar Lipsky was in charge of the investigation because he had been the first ADA to arrive at the crime scene. In reality, the investigation was headed by ADA Louis Pagnucco, who was far more experienced than Lipsky, having become an ADA in 1938, and because he was the only ADA who spoke Italian. Pagnucco's role would become one of the most controversial aspects of the case.[24]

Whether a conviction could have been won if Hogan had risked prosecuting Galante cannot be determined. The investigators attached to the DA's office, the detectives of the Grand Jury Squad who reported to the DA's office, and other NYPD detectives assigned to the case amassed a great deal of information about Galante and his mob associates from "confidential sources," direct surveillance, interviews, phone taps, and mail interception. The detectives of the Grand Jury Squad in particular operated like vacuum cleaners, sweeping up gangster gossip by the pound. However, no attempts were made to distinguish between the plausible and the preposterous. Valuable information pertaining to "Little Italy" mobsters and their activities was mixed indiscriminately with numerous assertions that can only be described as ludicrous.[25] But hearsay evidence of this nature might not have played well in court in any case.

Investigating the Communists

Efforts to determine communist culpability never proceeded very far. The theory that Vidali was the agent of Tresca's assassination was weakened at the outset when it became known that he had an air-tight alibi. On the night of Tresca's assassination, Vidali, along with 300 other guests, was attending a banquet at the El Lido Restaurant in Mexico City to honor Mexico's ambassador to Russia, Luis Quintanilla.[26] Vidali's alibi was secretly confirmed by the FBI, but Antonini's vigorous assertions that Tresca himself had asserted Vidali's presence in the area compelled Hogan to regard the possibility of his involvement nevertheless. Pressure to explore the Vidali connection emanated also from the conservative press. The *Journal American* (a Hearst publication), announced: "LINK TRESCA'S SLAYING TO OGPU AGENT." This headline was followed a few days later with a photo of Vidali's brutish face and the caption: "Do You Know Him?"[27]

Asked by reporters if he wished to question the "OGPU agent," Hogan answered with words reflecting his indecisiveness: "If Contreras [Vidali's pseudonym during the Spanish Civil War] is around, he certainly will be questioned."[28] Hogan knew full well by now that Vidali had been in Mexico City at the time of the murder. Nevertheless, if only to exclude the possibility of communist involvement, the DA's office might have sought to question Vidali in Mexico City. Instead, Hogan declined to send anyone to interview the Soviet agent, much to the relief of ADA Lipsky, who was frightened at the prospect of venturing into such "dangerous" territory. Nor did Hogan do so much as wire Mexican authorities for confirmation of Vidali's whereabouts and activities.[29]

Hogan's "hunt" for Vidali extended no farther than a farm in Landisville, New Jersey, where Vidali was alleged to have been seen prior to Tresca's murder. The source of this information was Antonini and Montana. But from the Italian owner of the farm, detectives learned only that Vidali had been there in 1927, while hiding prior to his deportation; no one in the area had seen him since.[30] Pursuit of evidence linking Vidali to Tresca's murder stopped at this point. According to Lipsky, the DA's office quickly gave up on the communist angle because of their unshakable belief that Galante was the trigger-man. The possibility that the communists might have hired Galante through intermediaries was rejected on the grounds that they would not have trusted a common criminal to kill Tresca. The communists had their own assassins to perpetrate political murders.[31]

Renewed consideration of the communist theory flickered briefly at the beginning of 1944, when the DA's office awoke to the possibility that another NKVD gunman, George Mink, may have been involved in Tresca's murder. The FBI was thinking along the same lines, and Bureau agents conferred with the DA's office to ascertain what evidence, if any, might connect Mink to the murder. Pagnucco informed the FBI that the NYPD was not pursuing Mink, and that "he was convinced that Mink was not the murderer and that the Communist Party had nothing to do with it."[32] Always desirous of incriminating communists, the FBI came away from the meeting highly dissatisfied. After an interview with Lipsky, who had explored the Mink theory, the FBI concluded: "From the nature of the conversation with Mr. Lipsky it appeared to Special Agent [name censored] that the Assistant District Attorney had only made casual inquires concerning the whereabouts of Mink and that he had not made a detailed investigation to determine if Mink was actually connected with the Tresca case."[33] Lipsky acknowledged that he derived his information about Mink only from books written by ex-communists, such as Benjamin Gitlow's *I Confess*.[34]

The publication in 1949 of Gitlow's second book, *The Whole of Their Lives*, prompted demand from Tresca's friends that Hogan once more explore the veracity of his accusations.[35] The former secretary general of the Communist Party charged that Tresca was murdered by the communists because of his long-standing feud with Vidali, his revelations concerning the disappearance of Poyntz, and his opposition to their admission into the Italian-American Victory Council.[36] The only new information he provided was speculation that the "Charles Pappas" who purchased the getaway car might have been "the strong-arm man of the Communist Furrier's Union goon squad."[37] When questioned by Pagnucco on December 8, 1948, Gitlow admitted that he had no definite information regarding Tresca's murder. Nor did Gitlow have anything new to add when Pagnucco questioned him before the Grand Jury two months later.[38] The DA's investigation of the communist theory was suspended permanently.

Investigating Pope and Garofalo

With little evidence to suggest communist complicity, the information marshaled by Taddei and Valenti regarding Pope and Garofalo cried out for serious consideration. But the DA's office never explored this theory with even minimum conviction, giving credence to suspicions that powerful political forces were obstructing the logical course of investigation. All evidence available suggests that Pope was never regarded as a possible suspect. He was never questioned by the DA's office or the police.[39] The only time Pope set foot in the DA's office (perhaps accompanied by Garofalo) was to inquire about suing Taddei for libel. Hogan decided not to pursue a libel charge against Taddei prior to prosecuting someone for Tresca's murder.[40] Nor was a flicker of suspicion raised when Pope's nephew and godson, Samuel S. Di Falco, went to the DA's office to represent Galante's alleged employer, the Knickerbocker Trucking Company.[41]

The NYPD was no more inclined to investigate Pope than was the DA's office. Pope possessed his own supporters within the police force, such as the two detectives from the Alien Squad assigned to the Tresca case, Stanley Gwazdo and Mario Fochi. In 1941, Gwazdo, a Nazi sympathizer who believed that Jews could not be true Americans, had been the detective recruited by Congressman Dickstein to threaten the Mazzini Society with investigation unless its attacks against Pope ceased. Detective Fochi was a friend and former employee of Pope. This information was obtained directly from Gwazdo by Casimir Palmer, a former Scotland Yard investigator turned undercover informant for the FBI, who furnished it to DA Hogan in February 1943. Hogan never acknowledged Palmer's letter.[42]

The DA's office and NYPD were only slightly more disposed to consider Garofalo a suspect. Lipsky later asserted that Garofalo was the most likely instigator of Tresca's murder, avenging himself for Tresca's insult at the Manhattan Club.[43] He maintained, however, that the authorities could not tie Garofalo and Galante together as criminal associates.[44] Did Lipsky and Pagnucco fail to read the numerous reports of their own investigators, which left no doubt as to the connection between the two mobsters? One detective wrote that "Carmine Galante at one time use [sic] to help [Giuseppe] Bonanno deliver liquor while working for Garofalo."[45] Another reported (erroneously) that Garofalo and Galante were cousins.[46]

Even more elusive for the DA's office than Garofalo's ties with Galante was his relationship with Pope.[47] Lipsky later maintained that while the DA's office knew that Garofalo and Pope were linked, the precise connection could not be determined.[48] The entire anti-Fascist movement knew that Pope and Garofalo were joined at the hip, and that the mobster did Pope's dirty work as an intimidator of business rivals and dissatisfied employees. Likewise, they knew all about the long-standing enmity between Tresca and Pope and the inflammatory incident involving Tresca and Garofalo at the Manhattan Club. The DA's office had been apprised of these facts at the outset, yet collusion between Pope and Garofalo in the murder of Tresca was apparently never considered a possibility. When Garofalo was brought in for questioning, Dolores Faconti allegedly insisted that she be present at the interrogation because she did not trust the DA's office and feared that her lover might be framed. It is not known whether the DA granted her request.[49] Only some fragmentary notes remain of Garofalo's interrogation at the DA's office on January 14, 1943 (Faconti was also questioned that day), and no mention of Pope is evident.[50] A single report on Garofalo's chat with the NYPD indicates that his interrogators learned only that he was involved in several legitimate business enterprises and had a permit to carry a gun. No mention of a Garofalo-Pope link was made.[51] The same is true of the reports filed by the detectives assisting the DA's office. They seemed incapable of connecting the dots. They discovered, for example, that both Galante and Garofalo were friends of the Fascist gangster Vincenzo Martinez, who had worked for *Il Progresso*. Yet detectives refrained from concluding that if Garofalo knew Martinez, he undoubtedly knew Pope as well.[52] And had they casually perused the pages of *Il Progresso*, they would have discovered numerous photos of Garofalo and Pope attending social and political functions together. Did these lapses in the investigation result from incompetence and ignorance of Garofalo's criminal activities? Or was there a tacit understanding among ADAs and the NYPD to ensure that any criminal connection between Garofalo and Pope the Untouchable was never to be revealed or investigated?

Preventing public disclosure of the Pope-Garofalo connection proved impossible. The famous news columnist Walter Winchell wrote in the *Daily Mirror*: "The story that won't be hushed, despite police and others arguing 'it isn't true,' is the one naming the real murderer and instigator of Tresca's slaying… Men on other newspapers are telling it… They add that their editors won't even hint at it. The legend says that Tresca's murder was instigated by another publisher (who runs a foreign-language sheet) and that the killer was his bodyguard."[53] Although Winchell refrained from naming Garofalo and Pope directly, no one knowledgeable about the case could mistake the identity of the men to whom Winchell alluded. The DA's office, however, did not see fit to question Winchell as to how he came by this information.

With important people now insinuating the involvement of Pope and Garofalo in Tresca's murder, the DA's office placed Garofalo under surveillance for more than a year, recorded his correspondence in New York and Florida, where he visited that summer, and perhaps tapped his phone. Pagnucco at one time contemplated a subterfuge that would enable investigators to enter Garofalo's apartment and search through his effects.[54] But beyond tailing him and tracing his mail, little seems to have been done to confirm Garofalo's link to Galante and Tresca's murder. Suspicions of a cover-up mounted, and faith in the integrity of the DA's office plummeted. These sentiments were particularly rife among Italian anti-Fascists. Giuseppe Lupis, the former editor of Il Mondo, who, like Tresca, furnished the FBI with information about Fascist activities, went directly to Mayor La Guardia to tell what he suspected regarding Pope and Garofalo rather than talk to the police. He feared the information would get back to Garofalo if provided to the NYPD.[55] Even if such suspicions were unfounded, the inability or unwillingness of New York authorities at every level to investigate the Tresca case with necessary zeal and objectivity was affirmed by the FBI, whose informants indicated by the spring of 1944 that the NYPD no longer considered Garofalo a suspect.[56]

The Genovese theory was investigated with even less enthusiasm. It was 1944 when Ernest "The Hawk" Rupolo claimed that Genovese had Tresca murdered at the behest of Mussolini and Ciano. Perhaps the unlikelihood of this scenario factored into the inaction of the DA's office, but ADA Pagnucco waited two years before interviewing "The Hawk." On this occasion, Rupolo altered his story somewhat, claiming that his friends Gus Frasca and George Smurra had told him that they had been Galante's accomplices in Tresca's murder, and that Frasca on another occasion had identified Genovese as the instigator, supposedly because he feared Tresca would expose his activities. Questioned again in 1953 by ADA Vincent Dermody, Rupolo admittedly that the story he had told to Pagnucco in 1946 was false. He still maintained that Galante was the assassin, but admitted that his earlier statements, accusing Genovese of ordering the murder, were based solely on underworld hearsay.[57]

A variation of Rupolo's story, proved by Genovese's sometime chauffeur Nino Mirabini in 1946, held that Tresca and Genovese had crossed swords as early as 1936, when Genovese approved a plan by two Fascist associates to open a maritime club for Italian sailors. When Tresca allegedly sent word that he would oppose the opening of a Fascist club, Genovese retreated, stating that he did not want trouble with Tresca. By 1940, according to Mirabini, Tresca had earned Genovese's enmity anew by writing letters to Fascist officials, informing them of his criminal activities in the United States. Thus Genovese ordered Tresca killed in 1943 to prevent further revelations concerning his operations.[58] Remarkably, in light of these allegations, the possibility that Genovese might have had his own motives for wanting Tresca dead never seems to have dawned on the DA's office. When Genovese was returned to the United States by military authorities in 1946,[59] to stand trial in Brooklyn for the murder of Ferdinand Boccia in 1934, the New York DA's office evidently made no effort to interrogate him in connection with Tresca's murder.

Finally, another gangster-inspired lead ignored by Hogan's office was the claim made to the Brooklyn DA by John Sorlucco, ex-head of the liquidated "Black Hawk" gang, that he and his accomplice, Joseph Di Somma, had pointed out Tresca to the gunman, and received $2,000 for his service.[60] While an admission of this nature may have amounted to nothing more a gangster's attempt to reduce his jail time, Tresca supporters believed that Hogan's failure to comment publicly on the Sorlucco/Di Somma and Rupolo allegations was proof that by 1946 the Tresca case had been relegated to a scarcely-simmering back burner.

The FBI and the Tresca Murder

One day after Tresca's assassination, J. Edgar Hoover received a memorandum from the director of the Alien Enemy Control Unit, Edward J. Ennis, requesting that he authorize the FBI to investigate the crime because of possible Fascist involvement. Hoover denied the request. Investigation of the case, he explained, lay within the jurisdiction of local law-enforcement agencies rather than the FBI.[61] In report after report, Hoover emphatically denied that the FBI was investigating Tresca's murder, a dictate dutifully repeated by his obedient agents. Nevertheless, orders were repeatedly issued to collect as much information as possible about the case, orders diligently carried out. Moreover, meetings and information exchanged between the FBI's New York office and DA Hogan's office occurred frequently over the years. That the FBI conducted an unofficial but unpublicized investigation of the Tresca murder cannot be doubted.[62]

The power and the prestige of J. Edgar Hoover in 1943 were so enormous that FBI intervention in the Tresca case would never have been challenged, jurisdictional considerations notwithstanding. The FBI's contradictory approach to investigating Tresca's murder case thus raises questions as to Hoover's motives. Hoover's entire career pivoted around the enhancement and perpetuation of his power and the independence of his fiefdom. The difference between "investigation" and "information gathering" may have reflected Hoover's desire to avoid exposing certain individuals and criminal enterprises.[63] Hoover informed the Alien Enemy Control Unit that "to date nothing has come to the attention of this Bureau which would indicate that Fascist elements are responsible for the murder of Carlo Tresca."[64] Hoover's assertion was false. The FBI Director had been notified by Assistant Director Percy L. Foxworth on January 12 that Frank Garofalo had motive to assassinate Tresca, and Hoover knew from previous reports about the Manhattan Club incident that Garofalo and his lover Dolores Faconti were both linked to Generoso Pope.[65]

FBI files also indicate that the Bureau was fully aware of Pope's history as Mussolini's most important supporter among Italian Americans prior to Pearl Harbor. The FBI was equally knowledgeable about Tresca's long campaign against Pope and his more recent efforts to prevent the political rehabilitation of the millionaire publisher. Yet Hoover and the FBI never considered Pope a suspect. One factor accounting for this disinclination was transparent. Since he was one of New York's most important and high-profile supporters of Roosevelt, Pope's exposure as a murder suspect would have proven embarrassing for the president. FBI revelation of Pope's activities and associations might also have proven costly for Hoover himself. A public probe would have revealed Pope's connections to criminal elements, such as Garofalo, Martinez, and Frank Costello, the noted mobster who was godfather to Pope's son Generoso Jr. Turning up these stones might have exposed Hoover's egregious failure to investigate the Mafia, which he denied even existed as a national crime syndicate. Furthermore, exposure of the Pope-Costello connection might have revealed Hoover's own friendship with Costello, a fellow gambler who sometimes accompanied the FBI chief to the racetrack and advised him on betting. Thus Hoover's veto of an official FBI investigation may have been motivated by the desire to protect himself as well as Pope.[66]

Garofalo had appeared on the FBI's radar screen in 1942 because of his affair with Faconti, a relationship that perturbed the puritanical Hoover. Hoover also knew about the Manhattan Club incident involving Tresca and Garofalo.[67] Yet despite information indicating that Garofalo had "good motive" to assassinate Tresca, the FBI deemed Garofalo "to be politically harmless but to be criminally dangerous."[68] However, when another FBI informant (probably the anti-Fascist Giuseppe Lupis) asserted that Tresca's murder had been "directly instigated by Frank Garofalo and that Generoso Pope…was one of the beneficiaries of the act,"[69] Hoover ordered the Special Agent in Charge of the New York office "to endeavor to discreetly determine the up-to-date status of this case," noting that the Bureau was "particularly interested in determining whether Frank Garofalo… is still considered a suspect in this case by the investigating authorities in New York City."[70] Whether Hoover's purpose was to determine Garofalo's possible guilt, or to have advanced warning of any embarrassing information that might be uncovered by his agents, cannot be determined. But even if Hoover's motives were well intentioned, the fact remains that the FBI never conducted a serious investigation to determine whether Garofalo was responsible for Tresca's murder.

Not so Vittorio Vidali and the communists. FBI documents reveal that the possibility of communist responsibility for Tresca's murder whetted Hoover's appetite for a Red hunt. Within a fortnight of the crime, the FBI director instructed the American Embassy in Mexico City to collection information about Vidali, his whereabouts, and his activities.[71] The FBI's investigation quickly ascertained that on the night of Tresca's murder Vidali had attended a banquet at the Lido Restaurant in Mexico City, as he had claimed. Nor was any record of his entrance into the United States found at border crossing points along the American-Mexican border.[72] But Hoover's interest in Vidali did not wane. His marginal comments on FBI reports typically read: "I think we ought to get all we can on Sormenti [Vidali]," and "Keep after this."[73] Hoover considered Vidali "the most important suspect," and he explained to the embassy in Mexico City that the Bureau was "presently conducting an expeditious and intensive investigation of Contreras' [Vidali's] activities in both the United States and in Mexico."[74] The investigation uncovered nothing incriminating about Vidali, and by October 1945 the FBI's New York Field Division considered the Tresca murder case closed.[75]

Receptivity to the communist theory was rekindled in 1950, well after the Bureau had received a memorandum from Norman Thomas, calling attention to Gitlow's allegations concerning George Mink. The FBI had previously interviewed Gitlow on several occasions but concluded after further interrogation that Gitlow's latest book contributed nothing new to the information already in the FBI's possession on Vidali and the communists.[76] But failure to discover a convincing link between the communists and Tresca's assassination did not terminate the FBI's accumulation of information. Its last substantive report on the crime was filed in April 1950. Nor did FBI interest in Vidali end with the Tresca case. The Cold War prompted the FBI to continue gathering information about Vidali's activities until 1956, by which time the communist gunman has become a deputy and senator representing Trieste in the Italian Parliament.[77] In this instance, the FBI's lack of jurisdiction failed to deter Hoover's hunt for communist culprits.

The Tresca Memorial Committee and Ernst Group

Tresca's friends and associates suspected from the outset that the DA's office was reluctant to pursue Galante's conviction and expose the instigators of the crime. After two months of frustrated waiting, the Tresca Memorial Committee (TMC) was formed in March 1943, under the chairmanship of Norman Thomas. Mainly Tresca's and Margaret's American friends, the members of the TMC were prominent individuals whose voices reached high places, and who could not be easily ignored by the DA's office. Among the better known individuals affiliated with the TMC were John Dewey, Sidney Hook, Sidney Hertzberg, A. Philip Randolph, Oswald Garrison Villard, Edmund Wilson, and Bertram D. Wolfe. Margaret was involved in every aspect of TMC's work and its principal financial supporter. Serving behind the scenes, John Nicholas Beffel handled all the publicity out of the TMC office at 119 East 19th Street. Beffel also conducted most of the investigative legwork and wrote the TMC's pamphlet *Who Killed Carlo Tresca?* published in October 1945. Another important contributor to TMC's independent inquires was Margaret's good friend Herbert Solow.

A second group that worked in tandem with the TMC included Tresca's lawyer Morris L. Ernst; John N. Finerty, an attorney renowned for his successful campaign to free the famous labor leaders Tom Mooney and Warren Billings; Roger Baldwin, executive director of the ACLU; Dorothy Kenyon, attorney and former Municipal Court Judge; and Eduard Lindeman, faculty member of the New York School of Social Work.[78] Further assistance was provided by the Workers Defense League's national secretary, Morris Milgram, and its chairman, C. Dickerman Williams.

The TMC, Ernst group, and WDL pursued common objectives: to prod the DA's office, generate publicity, and uncover evidence relevant to the crime. Much of the TMC's and Ernst group's dissatisfaction focused on ADA Louis Pagnucco. Although ADA Lipsky was nominally in charge, the lead investigator from the outset was the far more experienced and talented Pagnucco, and after Lipsky was transferred to the Court of General Sessions several months after the crime, Pagnucco took over the case officially and continued in this role for the next two years. In August 1944, the Ernst Group presented Hogan with incontrovertible evidence that Pagnucco had been closely associated with Fascists and Fascist sympathizers in the past, especially Pope. Pagnucco had graduated from the City College of New York in 1929, where he wrote a senior thesis that heaped glowing praise on Mussolini and the Fascist regime, and for which he was awarded a gold medal from the Italian Government. He graduated from Fordham Law School in 1932, attended the Royal Technical Institute of Novara in Italy in 1933, received a DJS degree from New York University in 1933, as well as an M.A. from Columbia University in 1936. That year he received an academic scholarship from Pope. After serving for seven years as an interpreter in the Court of General Sessions, Pagnucco was appointed ADA by the then District Attorney of New York County, Thomas E. Dewey, in 1938. As court interpreter and later as ADA, Pagnucco participated with Consul General Vecchiotti, Pope, and other pro-Fascist *prominenti* at various celebrations and political functions that lauded Mussolini and the Fascist regime. Naturally, his association with Pope disqualified Pagnucco as an objective investigator in the minds of Tresca's friends.[79]

Demands from the Ernst group and TMC that Pagnucco be removed from the case were stonewalled for months with assurances from Hogan that he was supervising the "larger aspects" of the Tresca case himself, while day-to-day efforts were directed by Jacob Grumet, the head of the Homicide Division.[80] Assuring critics that Pagnucco was "a man of the highest integrity,"[81] Hogan continued to defend his ADA and affirm the diligence of the investigation. He convinced nobody. Margaret De Silver, dismayed by Hogan's attitude and lack of progress, advised her associates to go over his head to Governor Thomas E. Dewey.[82] The Ernst group and 117 prominent individuals prepared a petition requesting that Dewey appoint a special prosecutor to oversee the case.[83] Facing public humiliation should Dewey take such action, Hogan finally relented in October 1944, reassigning the case to Lipsky, with Pagnucco assisting to maintain continuity. Two months passed and Lipsky was still busy with other trial work. He began examining witnesses only after 1,200 persons gathered at Webster Hall on January 11, 1945 to demand action. By this juncture, however, Hogan and Grumet were convinced that no breakthrough would be achieved unless somebody squealed. Margaret posted a $5,000 reward for information leading to a conviction.[84]

Operations at the DA's office did not significantly change. Lipsky by March 1945 was preoccupied with the murder of a coat manufacturer named Salvatore Bianco. "From that time until last month," declared Norman Thomas at a Tresca memorial meeting in January 1946, "a deep fog of official silence settled down over the Tresca slaying."[85] The only news forthcoming was that of Lipsky's resignation from the DA's office in December 1945. He preferred private practice and writing crime novels like *The Kiss of Death*. Throughout this period, Pagnucco had been the principal investigator.[86]

Whether Pagnucco allowed his old political sentiments and ties with Pope to influence his investigation will never be known. Norman Thomas remembered Pagnucco actually weeping as he tried to convince him that he was free of Fascist sympathies and how desirous he was to achieve results.[87] Lipsky, years later, maintained that Pagnucco had been completely unbiased and devoted to solving the case.[88] In all likelihood, Pagnucco was no more disinclined to investigate Pope than Hogan or others might have been. Yet Pagnucco remained reticent about the case. In 1974, now a judge in Family Court, Pagnucco refused a request by the author for an interview regarding the Tresca case, claiming "I am forbidden by the Canons of Ethics and the law to disclose any facts or information" because the case remained unsolved.[89] Neither Lipsky nor Grumet had any such compunction.[90] A follow-up request to discuss only Pagnucco's political associations prior to the Tresca case went unanswered.

Frustrated by the DA's lack of cooperation and success, Tresca's friends sought redress among higher political authorities, such as Mayor La Guardia. In January 1943, La Guardia had advised the FBI to interview Dolores Faconti for possible information about the murder, but proved surprisingly unwilling thereafter to apply pressure on Hogan's office or to provide other assistance, despite having known Tresca personally for more than twenty years.[91] Three times La Guardia denied requests from Margaret De Silver for an interview.[92] When Aldino Felicani questioned whether the "dark forces" that murdered Tresca (a clear allusion to Pope) were obstructing the investigation, La Guardia responded only with quotes from a report by Police Commissioner Valentine, affirming the fairness and thoroughness of the investigation.[93] An FBI informant suspected that La Guardia was cool to any prosecution because he may have received political support from Garofalo's gang.[94] Such suspicions could not be confirmed, but La Guardia's lack of interest in the Tresca case prompted Ernst to write to Valentine: "If the Mayor paid as much attention to a political crime in his great City as he does to old women who play pinochle for nickels, we would have a safer City in which to live in and you would have far more ease in running an effective Police Department."[95]

Ernst, who was on a first name basis with J. Edgar Hoover, had also written to "Dear Edgar" in April 1943, explaining that "I knew Carlo for 20 years, loaned him money, loved him, and at times represented him." The crime, he assured the FBI director, was "the most important political murder of this period." Ernst reminded Hoover that Tresca had provided valuable information to the FBI concerning Fascist activities; he even sought to entice the old Red hunter by intimating that Tresca's murder probably had been the work of the communists.[96] Hoover denied his request. Margaret De Silver, the TMC, and the Ernst group attempted to involve the FBI at a later date, arguing that Tresca's murder might have international ramifications. They asked Hogan to request FBI intervention; he refused, contending that his men were just as competent as those of the FBI. They repeated the same request in 1947 to Mayor William O'Dwyer, but were rebuffed once more.[97] The Ernst group then prevailed upon Congressman Will Rogers, Jr. of California to introduce a resolution "to authorize the FBI to assist local police authorities in apprehending perpetrators of acts of violence for political reasons."[98] Opposed by the FBI, the resolution failed to pass in the House of Representatives. Appeals to Attorney General Thomas A. Clark were similarly rebuffed.[99]

The DA's annual reports for 1946–1948, meanwhile, had omitted any mention of the Tresca case, prompting Thomas to ask, "Why is the District Attorney officially silent about the Tresca case? Would he and his staff prefer to forget that killing?"[100] The answer was obvious. After Pagnucco left the DA's office in January 1951, no ADA knew much about the case or showed any inclination to learn. The NYPD's investigation remained officially open throughout the 1950s and even into the 1960s, but amounted to nothing more than assigning a new detective to the case every few years, a bureaucratic formality that resulted in no action.

The TMC continued its efforts to keep the case alive. Every year until 1954, they organized anniversary meetings to pay tribute to Tresca's memory and to publicize the DA's lack of action. If new information was uncovered or a different avenue of inquiry appeared promising, the TMC investigated, issued press releases, rallied influential people, and demanded action. This level of commitment inevitably declined after Margaret De Silver's death in 1960, and other individuals involved with the TMC and Ernst Group finally abandoned hope that the murderers would ever be brought to justice.

Their assumption was correct.

26

Who Ordered Tresca's Murder?

Part I: The Literature

The question of who ordered the murder of Carlo Tresca has never been answered with absolute certainty and probably never will. Since the first flurry of accusations leveled by Antonini/Montana and Taddei/Valenti, few inquiries into the crime have followed the example of the Tresca Memorial Committee's *Who Killed Carlo Tresca?*, published in 1945. Ghost written by John Nicholas Beffel, the pamphlet provided an objective and balanced exposition of competing theories without offering one of its own, either because of insufficient evidence or fear of interfering with the official investigation. Most interpreters since then have directly espoused the communist or Fascist-gangster theory, often with political partisanship clearly evident or without insufficient knowledge of Tresca's career and its historical context. Only one writer, Dorothy Gallagher, has written a comprehensive, thoroughly-researched, and well-reasoned treatment of Tresca's murder, and readers would benefit from consulting her account. The discussion that follows examines some of interpretations previously advanced and provides the author's own conclusion as to the most likely culprits.

Vidali and the Communists

It has already been suggested that Antonini and Montana, the first individuals to accuse Vittorio Vidali and the communists, were motivated as much by their anti-communist agenda as by genuine belief, if not more so. The same was true of the ex-communists, Trotskyists, and professional anti-communists who wrote about Tresca's murder in the early years of the Cold War: e.g., Julian Gorkin, the former leader of the POUM in Spain, and the ex-communist leader Benjamin Gitlow.[1] This genre of anti-communist historiography included Tresca among other victims of the OGPU/NKVD, such as Camillo Berneri, Andrés Nin, Juliet Stuart Poyntz, the Polish socialists Henryk Ehrlich and Victor Alter, Ignatz Reiss, Rudolph Klement, Leon Trotsky, and Walter Krivitsky. Further assertions of communist guilt, not surprisingly, were advanced during the Cold War. In 1964, Francis Russell, an amateur historian, whose claim to fame rested on his writings about Sacco and Vanzetti, declared on the basis of *a priori* assumptions and no research: "Vidali took his revenge. He was the type who liked to take his revenge personally. Possibly he was the gunman waiting near the Fifth Avenue entrance to Tresca's office building. Almost certainly he was in the getaway car."[2]

But primacy of place among professional anti-communists was held by Guenther Reinhardt. A Walter Winchell protégé, whose resumé boasted spying activities for the House Committee on Immigration and Naturalization (forerunner of HUAC) and the FBI, Reinhardt wrote a potboiler in 1952 entitled *Crime Without Punishment*. Combining sycophantic adulation of J. Edgar Hoover with "never-before-told" revelations about communist crimes, Reinhardt alleged he learned all about Tresca's murder while working undercover at CP social gatherings in Mexico City. On the basis of such "firsthand" information, Reinhardt asserted that Tresca was targeted for death because he represented a major obstacle to the "united front" the communists sought to create in 1942, and to their infiltration of the OWI Victory Councils. Rather than utilize their own gunmen, the communists contracted Tresca's assassination out to the Mafia, with Vidali negotiating the arrangements. Reinhardt claimed Tresca as a friend and purported to have worked with him on anti-communist assignments since 1939. Yet, after supposedly having learned about the assassination plans a few days before the deed was committed, Reinhardt somehow failed to "put the picture together" and neglected to notify the intended victim.[3] In short, giving Reinhardt's account any credence requires an act of anti-communist faith that few, save the converted, should be willing to make.

The last writer to ascribe Tresca's murder to Vidali and the communists was Vanni Montana. In his memoir, *Amarostico*, published in Italian in 1975, Montana essentially re-hashed the accusations that he and Antonini had made in 1943: Tresca opposed admitting communists into the Italian-American Victory Councils; the OWI was staffed largely by communist fellow travelers like Lee Falk; Tresca had indicated Vidali's presence in New York prior to his murder; the communists, assisted by Antonini's rival Augusto Bellanca of the ACWUA, waged a campaign to deflect suspicion away from the communists and onto Pope and Garofalo. Montana circumvented one of the principal factors that argued against communist responsibility—the Garofalo-Galante connection—by resurrecting a rumor that attracted scant attention in 1943, namely, that Galante was not only in Garofalo's service but also in the pay of the communist Furriers Union. Thus, like Reinhardt, Montana validated the "communists-did-it theory" by connected them to the Mafia.[4] While Montana lacked Reinhardt's creative imagination, his account nevertheless must be classified under the rubric of professional anti-communism.

Pope-Garofalo

Since Taddei and Valenti wrote their indictments in 1943, proponents of the Pope-Garofalo theory have been few compared to the accusers of the communists. They include Alan A. and Marcia J. Block, Furio Morroni, and Dorothy Gallagher. The Blocks placed their synoptic account of Tresca's murder within the larger context of Fascism, organized crime, and foreign policy. They emphatically rejected the notion of communist involvement, attributing this interpretation to Cold War attitudes: "The murder of Carlo Tresca reveals just how malevolent a force militant anti-communism has been."[5] The Blocks focused their spotlight instead on Pope, his pro-Fascist activities prior to World War II, and his relationships with numerous professional criminals, including Galante, Garofalo, and others they believed likely to have been involved in Tresca's murder. The Blocks attributed great significance to Tresca's opposition to Pope's admission to the Italian-American Victory Councils and the latter's ties to numerous criminals capable of eliminating the obstacle Tresca represented. They spotlighted not only Garofalo but Vincenzo Martinez, a former leader of the Fascist League and a staff writer for *Il Progresso*, whose business enterprises were located at 225 Lafayette Street, headquarters for many other racketeers and Fascist associations. Convinced of a Pope-Garofalo-Galante connection, the Blocks concluded:

> ... it appears that the murder of Carlo Tresca was the malign result of the merger of organized crime and fascism and that the killer was Carmine Galante; although it is not certain whether he murdered Tresca solely to please Garofalo, or to satisfy the mutual interests of Garofalo-Pope, or those more complex ones of Pope-Antonini, or most expansively the shared concerns of a considerably larger network of fascists and professional criminals.[6]

Of similar persuasion, the Italian journalist Furio Morroni wrote an study (unpublished) of Tresca's murder based mainly on documents in the FBI and DA files. Morroni rejected the possibility of communist involvement on the grounds that no evidence supported the theory. Instead, Morroni argued along the same lines discussed in the previous chapter, namely, that J. Edgar Hoover's contradictory orders regarding the Tresca case indicated that he knew the identity of the instigators (Pope and Garofalo), and prevented his agents from conducting an official investigation in order to protect President Roosevelt and himself from scandal. Utilizing sources unavailable to earlier writers, Morroni described Antonini's campaign to rehabilitate Pope, the controversy surrounding Pagnucco, the myriad bits of underworld gossip provided by the DA's investigators but never pursued by Pagnucco, and Casimir Palmer's revelations regarding Pope. Curiously, after presenting material that supports no other conclusion, Morroni refrained from directly affirming the responsibility of Pope and Garofalo, thus ending with a whimper a study that begins with a bang.[7]

Vito Genovese

The first writer to advance the Genovese theory of Tresca's murder was reporter Ed Reid, whose original articles in the *Brooklyn Eagle* and the *New York Post* were rehashed in his book entitled *Mafia*, published in 1952. Taking his cue from Rupolo's earlier allegations, Reid claimed that Mussolini paid the Mafia $500,000 to assassinate Tresca, who had been on the Duce's "death list" since 1931. The engineer of Tresca's murder was the Mafia kingpin Vito Genovese, then residing in Naples, who had close ties with Fascist officials. Genovese's contact man in New York, according to Reid, was probably Frank Garofalo.[8] After Reid's book, the "Genovese-did-it" version of Tresca's murder was frequently repeated and embellished by various mobsters claiming to be "in the know." The infamous Mafia chieftain Charles "Lucky" Luciano asserted:

> When the war was still going pretty good for Mussolini, Vito was always trying to prove what a good friend he was to that fascist son-of-a-bitch. There was a newspaper publisher in New York by the name of Carlo Tresca. He was strictly Anti-Mussolini and he was knockin' the shit out of him in every edition of his paper.... So what does that prick Genovese do? He tells Mussolini not to worry about it, that he, Don Vitone, would take care of it. And godamm it if Vito don't put out a contract from Italy on Tresca, with Tony Bender to do the job.[9]

There was no love lost between Luciano and Genovese, and Tresca's murder irked "Lucky" because it had been unauthorized: "I made up my mind that someday I was gonna have a little talk with either or both of them guys—Vito and Bender. They knew the Union rule that nobody on the outside gets hit under no circumstances without a vote of the Council."[10] By the time Luciano's "testament" was published in 1981, the Mussolini-Genovese version of Tresca's murder had long since became part of Mafia folklore, and has been cited as gospel by innumerable "experts" on the Mafia. Probably for this reason a recent (2004) History Channel documentary on the Mafia, entitled *Godfathers*, repeated the same story without a hint of tentativeness or doubt.

A similar version, claiming the authority of archival research, albeit without accompanying notes, was posited by the prolific Italian historian Mauro Canali, who gained notoriety by advancing a much-challenged claim that the great writer Ignazio Silone was once a spy for the Fascists. In an article modestly entitled "All the Truth about Carlo Tresca," Canali traverses familiar ground, arguing that Genovese, thanks to his donations to Fascist building projects like the *Casa del Fascio* in Nola (Sicily), enjoyed good relations with several Fascist officials, including Carmine Senise, the Fascist Chief of Police, a tie also attributable to his friendship with Senise's nephew, Renato Carmine Senise, in the United States. Without establishing a motive, Canali concludes that Tresca's murder was arranged by Genovese at the behest of, or to please (he does not clarify which), "Fascist hierarchs."[11]

Only one writer who has studied Tresca's murder provides an account that explores every theory with equal consideration: Dorothy Gallagher. Limited only by the author's inability to read sources in Italian, Gallagher's treatment of Tresca's murder and its background, accounting for one-third of her biography, provides the best researched, most comprehensive, and thoroughly detailed examination of the competing theories, one that is also well reasoned and free of preconceptions. With proper deference to all the uncertainties surrounding the case, Gallagher concluded: "If by now there is no doubt that Galante was the *de facto* murderer, the identity of the person on whose order he acted is still not clear. My own conviction is that the simplest explanation is the correct one in this case, and that Frank Garofalo fills the role of instigator.[12]

Part II: Author's Assessment

The Communists

Proponents of "the-communists-did-it" theory uniformly have argued that the motivation for killing Tresca derived from a combination of settling old scores, like the Poyntz affair, and the need to eliminate his opposition to communist penetration of the Mazzini Society and the OWI Victory Councils. This proposition rests on a false premise. Although the old rebel remained unbending in his opposition and was still capable of making his angry voice heard, the Tresca of 1943 was not the Tresca of 1927. It is simply incorrect to believe that Tresca represented a solitary and insurmountable obstacle to communist objectives during the early 1940s. Tresca's desire to keep the communists out of the Mazzini Society and the Victory Councils was shared by the great majority of anti-Fascists, some of them more influential at this time than Tresca. If their primary concern in 1943 was to eliminate opposition to their infiltration efforts, the communists would have been far better advised to assassinate Antonini than Tresca. Nor can it be argued that by murdering Tresca the communists were eliminating a symbol of opposition and thereby giving warning to other enemies to desist. The communists did not require a crystal ball to foresee that murdering Tresca would inevitably generate the kind of negative publicity and opposition that would thwart their intended objectives—precisely what happened in the wake of Tresca's slaying. And for the same reason, murdering Tresca just to settle old scores dating back several years would have been counterproductive. The communists may have been unscrupulous in pursuit of their political ends, but they were not stupid. Thus, without excluding them with absolute certainty, the communists must be considered to have had insufficient motive to want Tresca eliminated in 1943.

Fascists

The same holds true for Italian Fascists. The theory advanced by underworld elements and hack journalists that Mussolini and Ciano paid a huge sum of money to Vito Genovese to have Tresca murdered is preposterous. By the end of 1942, with his armies defeated in Greece, North Africa, and Russia, and with members of his own party already plotting his overthrow, Mussolini's world was collapsing all around him. What earthly reason could account for the Duce's ordering such a meaningless deed? The same holds true for the "Fascist hierarchs" to whom Canali alluded. Nor is it credible that Genovese issued orders on his own to have Tresca killed in order to ingratiate himself with Mussolini or Fascist officials in high places, like Senise, who by this time was himself plotting against Mussolini. Surely Genovese would have known that eliminating an ancient but powerless enemy in America like Tresca would hardly have enhanced his standing with the Fascists in Rome.

That Genovese may have wanted Tresca eliminated for his own reasons is a much more plausible thesis, although not for the reasons suggested in 1943–1944. The notion that Tresca, by means of anonymous letters, was "making trouble" for Genovese by revealing details of his criminal enterprises (e.g. drug smuggling) to the Fascists in Rome flies in the face of everything known about Tresca. If he had accusations to make regarding Genovese's drug smuggling operations, he would have done so openly and in print. In this regard, the idea of a preemptive strike by Genovese against Tresca must be considered a possibility. Support for this hypothesis lies in the pages of *Il Martello*. It may be assumed that "Don Vitone" was displeased when Tresca in 1940 revealed his former ties to the Fascist Morgantini Club in the Bronx and to Consul General Vecchiotti in New York. In that first mention of Genovese, moreover, Tresca made a cryptic reference to "Genovese's moral sense," adding "that [his moral sense], if ever, is something to be discussed."[13] Was that a hint of future revelations about Genovese's criminal activities, perhaps the murder of the man whose wife he desired for himself? Tresca never commented further about Genovese, but it is certainly possible that his revelations of 1940–1941 alarmed Genovese enough to take preventive measures. The obvious factor that weakens this hypothesis is the considerable time lapse between Tresca's revelations in 1940–1941 and his murder in 1943.

Pope

Much the same reasoning that minimizes the likelihood of communist culpability applies as well to Generoso Pope. The long duration and the intensity of the enmity between them cannot be denied, nor the fact that Pope probably rejoiced when his most vociferous enemy departed this world. But did Pope have sufficient motive to order Tresca's murder in 1943? Writers who considered Pope the prime mover in Tresca's murder generally have misinterpreted the context within which the act was perpetrated, and exaggerated the danger Tresca represented. Pope was most vulnerable to attack in 1940–1941, when leaders of the Mazzini Society were on the verge of forcing Pope's divestiture of *Il Progresso* because of his pro-Fascist activities. At this juncture, Tresca was an enemy of secondary importance for Pope compared to Salvemini, Ascoli, and Tarchiani; his opposition to Pope's admission to the Mazzini Society only reinforced an outcome already determined by the anti-Fascists at the helm. Nor was membership in the Mazzini Society as essential for Pope's rehabilitation as commonly thought. Once Pope complied with Roosevelt's advice of April 1941, to change his tune about Fascism and Mussolini, the publisher's rehabilitation was virtually assured. With sanction from the White House, and with the power of Tammany Hall and Antonini behind him, Pope's road to respectability would be traversed with relatively few bumps along the way, such as rejection from the Mazzini Society.

Tresca's opposition to Pope's membership in the OWI's Italian-American Victory Council must be considered from the same perspective. Credible sources indicated that prior to his death Tresca attended preparatory meetings and opposed the admission of Pope and the communists to the IAVC. Yet Tresca never discussed the future IAVC in *Il Martello*, a rather curious omission if he attributed any importance to this new organization. Other information about Tresca and the IAVC is based on hearsay. An FBI informant (probably Lupis) reported that "it was the consensus of opinion that Tresca was holding off an attack on Pope until the time when it would be announced that Pope was being placed on the Office of War Information Victory Council."[14] Even if the FBI informant's information was accurate, and even if Pope had received advanced warning of Tresca's intentions, it was unlikely that Tresca would have attacked Pope with charges other than those he had leveled a dozen times before. Another story based on hearsay was related by the communist Ambrogio Donini, editor of *L'Unità del Popolo* in 1943, who suggested that a few weeks before the murder, Pope sent Garofalo as his emissary to Ezio Taddei with a peace offering for Tresca. In response, Tresca supposedly threw Taddei out of his office in anger. Failure to obtain a truce with Tresca would thus have been interpreted by Pope as a guarantee that Tresca would continue to obstruct his admission to the IAVC.[15] But there are several problems with this scenario, not least of which is the questionable veracity of Taddei and the fact that Donini never mentioned it in his memoirs, despite his account of Taddei's joining the communists in the wake of Tresca's murder.[16] Would Pope have been so naïve as to think that extending an olive branch to an implacable enemy like Tresca might have established peace between them? And would Pope have considered Tresca influential enough to preclude his admission even before the Italian-American Victory Council was organized? Membership in the IAVC, although coveted, was hardly a *sine qua non* for rehabilitation and power retention. And if not the New York IAVC, which died in embryo after Tresca's murder, other important organizations were readily open to him (compliments of Antonini), such as the American Committee for Democracy created in the fall of 1943, for which he served as treasurer.[17] Nor were there any lack of high-profile public functions that enhanced his prestige within the Italian-American community. Pope was the Grand Marshall and principal sponsor of the Columbus Day celebrations in New York in 1943. The following year, Pope was appointed to the board of directors of American Relief for Italy, Inc. and received from the Navy Department an award for meritorious service as president of the Colonial Sand and Stone Co. "for achievements in construction of wartime installations."[18] Tresca, in short, might have represented an annoyance but hardly an insurmountable obstacle for Pope and his accommodating allies. Adequate motive for Pope to order Tresca's murder in January 1943 was lacking.

Garofalo

The same cannot be said for Garofalo. That there was long-standing enmity between Tresca and Garofalo is indisputable, although not as open as some contemporaries suggested. Tresca never identified Garofalo by name when he denounced the efforts of Pope and his henchmen to stifle criticism and rival publishers in his famous article of 1934. Nor did he attack Garofalo in print any time thereafter, not even after the Manhattan Club incident. But the absence of public attacks preceding and following the Manhattan Club incident would not have detracted from the seriousness with which Garofalo regarded Tresca's insult that night, or his anger over Faconti's pleading with Tresca on his and her behalf. For a mobster of Garofalo's stature, the "right-hand man" of Joseph Bonnano, maintaining his "honor" and prestige in the face of a blatant insult was essential, and exacting revenge by means of blood-letting was standard practice according to the underworld code by which he lived and was judged. Furthermore, Garofalo's relationship with Galante both before and after Tresca's murder suggests a connection that is hard to dismiss as coincidence. In the opinion of former·ADA Lipsky, Tresca's Manhattan Club insult and his criticism of Faconti for associating with a gunman represented sufficient motive for Garofalo to have paid Galante to murder Tresca.[19] This viewpoint became more widespread with Galante's ascendance in the underworld, and was publicly affirmed by John T. Cusack, district supervisor of the Federal Narcotics Bureau, in 1958.[20]

While the Genovese theory, as qualified above, remains plausible, the weight of evidence points to Frank Garofalo as the instigator of Tresca's murder. The tantalizing but unanswerable question is whether Pope was complicit in any way, despite not having a compelling need to have Tresca eliminated. Such was the closeness of their relationship that it would not be unreasonable to assume that Pope knew about Garofalo's intentions and had given his sanction, but this is by no means certain. If Garofalo had been a low-echelon thug employed solely for strong-arm purposes, it is hard to believe he would have had Galante murder Tresca without Pope's approval. Given his standing in the Mafia, however, Garofalo would not have required Pope's permission to do anything. Thus we can only conjecture that Pope may have known that Garofalo wanted Tresca dead and gave his blessings, or that he was not privy to his henchman's intentions and therefore free of complicity. We may never know for sure.

Tresca and the Sacco-Vanzetti Case: Innocence or Guilt?

The issue of Tresca's relationship with the Sacco-Vanzetti Defense Committee is germane not only to his career but to the question of whether Sacco and Vanzetti were truly innocent or one or both guilty. In 1962, the author Francis Russell (now deceased), in his widely read book *Tragedy In Dedham*, posited a split-guilt theory, i.e., that Sacco was involved in the South Braintree crime, but not Vanzetti.[1] Russell based his conclusion primarily on statements made by Tresca to his friend Max Eastman in 1942, to the effect that Sacco was guilty and Vanzetti innocent. The credence Russell placed in Tresca's remarks was based on the following suppositions: Tresca had succeeded Galleani as the "acknowledged and admired leader" of the Italian anarchists in the United States; he was the person most likely to know their "innermost secrets"; he had "played the part of guardian angel or great-uncle" for the defense; and that "if anyone should have had inside knowledge of the affair, Tresca was the man."[2]

Tresca himself left no written record that would suggest he ever doubted Sacco's innocence. Several individuals who were on the closest terms with him during the period of the case have attested that Tresca always asserted the innocence of both Sacco and Vanzetti. Tresca's daughter Beatrice asserted that neither during the period of the case nor any time thereafter did her father every say anything that would cast doubt upon Sacco's innocence.[3] Luigi Quintiliano, as secretary of the Italian Committee for Political Victims, conducted extensive fund-raising tours during the early years of the case, occasionally encountering comrades and readers of *Il Martello* who asked his personal opinion in regard to a rumor casting doubt on Sacco's innocence. Quintiliano spent many nights discussing with Tresca what he had heard on his travels. Tresca dismissed the rumor and repeatedly assured Quintiliano of Sacco's innocence.[4] Giuseppe Popolizio, a personal friend and member of *Il Martello*'s staff during the period of the case, insisted that if Tresca had suspected Sacco, "I would have been the first to know about it."[5]

Suspicion concerning Sacco resurfaced after the execution in 1927, with Fred Moore as the root source. Moore had begun to entertain doubts while still working on the case, suspecting that some of Sacco's alibi witnesses were unreliable.[6] He expressed these doubts to Roger Baldwin and Elizabeth Glendower Evans during the trial; Evans became outraged at the suggestion, and Baldwin believed that witnesses inevitably tailor their testimony.[7] Moore's suspicions undoubtedly deepened after his dismissal from the legal team in August 1924. Relations between Moore and the

Italian anarchists on the defense committee had been difficult from the beginning. Moore considered them to be incompetent and obstructionist; the defense committee was always displeased with Moore because of his erratic behavior and huge expenditures, particularly on investigations to discover the real perpetrators of the South Braintree crime, a task the committee and the defendants deemed fitting only for the police, not anarchists.[8] (Emilio Coda threatened to kill him if he persisted with his investigations.) The final act that precipitated Moore's dismissal was his attempt to bypass the Italians on the defense committee by creating another organization, the New Trial League, that would accommodate his needs.[9] The person selected by the defendants and defense committee to convey the bad news to Moore was Flynn, who remembered that "it was a devastating blow" to him.[10]

Now a broken man, harboring feelings of resentment and disillusionment, Moore conveyed his suspicions shortly after the execution to Upton Sinclair, who was completing research for *Boston*, his historical novel about Sacco and Vanzetti. Sinclair's own doubts had been raised after a brief introduction to Sacco's wife Rosina, who appeared suspicious and uncooperative: "there was some dark secret" in the Sacco household.[11] (In fact, Rosina never discussed the case with any outsiders after the execution.) When Sinclair visited Sacco's former counsel for more information, Moore indicated that "he had come reluctantly to the conclusion that Sacco was guilty of the crime for which he had died and that possibly Vanzetti also was guilty."[12] Moore admitted that he had no proof to substantiate his suspicions, nor had he ever heard the defendants or members of the defense committee admit or intimate their complicity in the South Braintree crime. He justified his suspicions on the grounds that some anarchists did engage in expropriation for the benefit of the movement.[13] Alarmed by Moore's allegations, Sinclair conferred with ACLU leader Roger Baldwin to ask what he knew. To reassure himself, Baldwin discussed the matter with Tresca and Flynn, both of whom dismissed Moore's suspicions as unfounded.[14]

Further confirmation that Tresca harbored no suspicions at this time was provided by Michael A. Musmanno, an attorney who joined the defense team at the end of the struggle and who later became a Supreme Court Justice in Pennsylvania. Musmanno saw Tresca regularly during the months preceding the execution and later wrote: "[Tresca] was always consistently and enthusiastically voluble in his assertion of the innocence of Sacco and Vanzetti."[15] Moreover, as late as 1939, while writing his own book about the case, *After Twelve Years*, Musmanno again conferred with Tresca, "who was just as devoted to the innocence of Sacco and Vanzetti then as when they were living."[16]

Nevertheless, several Americans—Norman Thomas, John Roche, and Max Eastman among others—have attested that in the early 1940s, Tresca told them that Sacco was guilty and Vanzetti innocent.[17] Norman Thomas, the old socialist leader, acknowledged in a 1963 interview with the author that Tresca had made these remarks to him, although he, Thomas, was unable to elaborate.[18] A letter from Norman Thomas to John Nicholas Beffel, on the occasion of an anniversary celebration of the Sacco Vanzetti case in 1967, provided further confirmation: "How do you expect to handle the charges that at least one of them, Sacco, was guilty—as Carlo Tresca told some of us shortly before his own assassination?"[19]

John Roche and Max Eastman have provided brief accounts of the circumstance in which they heard Tresca make his claim regarding Sacco. Roche, later the dean of the Fletcher School of Diplomacy at Tufts University, related that at a gathering of the Youth Committee Against War, held at the home of Norman Thomas sometime in 1941, "Tresca came bounding in enraged about something or other and took over the show." The subject of Sacco and Vanzetti came up, and Roche asked Tresca about it: "the gist of his vigorous remarks was that Sacco had murdered a good comrade (Vanzetti) because he thought he could beat the rap. Vanzetti was innocent, but Sacco was involved and refused to plead guilty and save Vanzetti." Roche, who considered Tresca "a great eccentric, not above improving on the truth," did not believe him. Neither Thomas nor anyone else present at the meeting challenged or questioned Tresca ("arguing with Tresca was a volcanic experience"), and the conversation moved on to other matters.[20] Since Roche placed no credence in Tresca's allegations, he did not raise the issue again until 1972, when Russell contacted him in preparation for a second book about the case.[21]

Eastman related that after learning about Sinclair's doubts some fifteen years after the execution, he decided to ask his friend Tresca the truth about Sacco and Vanzetti. Tresca allegedly replied: "Sacco was guilty, but Vanzetti was not." Before Eastman could ask Tresca to elaborate, people came into the room and the conversation ended. Eastman claimed he had no opportunity to see Tresca alone again before he was murdered a few weeks later.[22] Eastman made these revelations in 1961, long after he had completed his ideological transformation from Marxism to right-wing conservatism.[23]

Some of Tresca's intimates, notably his daughter Beatrice and his friend Luigi Quintiliano, steadfastly maintained that Tresca never held such an opinion of Sacco, or would have told them if he did.[24] Nevertheless, the evidence leaves virtually no doubt that Tresca, by the early 1940s, told several individuals (curiously, no Italians) that Sacco had been guilty, but Vanzetti innocent. The principal questions that must be asked are when and how did Tresca come to hold this view, and what weight does his opinion carry *vis-à-vis* the greater historical issue of Sacco and Vanzetti's innocence or guilt.

We have demonstrated in our narrative that Tresca was not greatly admired or particularly trusted by the Galleanisti in general, although they were perfectly willing to accept his assistance whenever they needed it. He did not know the defendants and did not have close ties with members of the original defense committee, except for Felicani and Guadagni. Thus any contention that Tresca was necessarily privy to all information concerning Sacco and Vanzetti, and "must" have known the truth about their innocence or guilt, as argued by Eastman and Russell, is untenable. On the other hand, the possibility that Tresca, on the basis of information received second hand, believed Sacco guilty from the outset but decided to defend him as a fellow anarchist, cannot be excluded. But the preponderance of evidence suggests that in the 1920s and 1930s, Tresca sincerely believed both men to be innocent. We must conclude, therefore, that something happened in the late 1930s to change his mind.

In a previous study, the author proposed a theory that attributed Tresca's new opinion about Sacco to his hostile relationship with the Galleanisti. As previously noted, between 1925 and 1938, a vicious campaign of slander and denigration—motivated by political rivalry and jealously—was waged against Tresca by the directors of *L'Adunata dei Refrattari*—first Emilio Coda, then Raffaele Schiavina (alias Max Sartin) for the purpose of destroying Tresca's reputation and standing in the anarchist movement.[25] Tresca was very hurt and demoralized by *L'Adunata's* attacks; for forty years he had struggled on behalf of the working class only to have his efforts and his person insulted, scorned, and unappreciated by anarchists who should have been his comrades.[26]

Is it mere coincidence, therefore, that every known instance of Tresca's declaring Sacco guilty occurred a few years after the climax of *L'Adunata's* campaign against him in 1938? Is it possible that Tresca had always believed Sacco guilty but convincingly feigned belief in his innocence, and that the miserable treatment he endured from the Galleanisti caused him to disregard the anarchists' code of silence and finally speak his mind? Or, more credibly, did Tresca originally believe Sacco innocent but eventually concluded that the Galleanisti had deceived him from the beginning in order to use him, and that the rumors he had heard over the years concerning Sacco might, in fact, have been based on the truth? Believing that he had been led down the garden path by the Galleanisti might also explain the anger that usually accompanied his new assertions of Sacco guilt. There is no way, of course, to prove this theory in the absence of more concrete evidence, but it warrants consideration as a possible explanation for Tresca's behavior.

Francis Russell, in a letter to the author in 1977, rejected the hypothesis outlined above, arguing instead that some "unknown person" had to be responsible for changing Tresca's mind. He further elaborated: "... I do feel that the unknown person must have had compelling knowledge of the facts to have convinced Tresca. I do not know him as you do, but he seems to me a man of great integrity who would not have accepted such a reversal of a cause he believed in unless the evidence he received was overwhelming."[27] Then, in 1982, Russell discovered his "unknown person." In the winter of that year, Russell received a letter from Ideale Gambera, whose recently-deceased father, Giovanni Gambera, had been an anarchist member of the original Sacco-Vanzetti Defense Committee. Repeating what his father allegedly told him, Ideale informed Russell that "Everyone [in the Boston anarchist circle] knew that Sacco was guilty and that Vanzetti was innocent as far as the actual participation in the killing. But no one would ever break the code of silence even if it cost Vanzetti's life."[28] Russell subsequently visited Ideale in California in hope of obtaining additional information. All he found was a dozen pages of a "memoir," which said nothing about Sacco's guilt—an omission attributed to his unwillingness to commit such incriminating information to paper, according to his son, and a tape recording of Gambera's old voice, saying "Sacco was guilty! Sacco was guilty!"[29] Russell's knowledge of Giovanni Gambera was based entirely on the glowing portrait provided by his son Ideale, whose filial admiration is understandable. According to Ideale, Giovanni Gambera "commanded great respect and loyalty amongst the anarchists combined with an aura of deadly intent." Of the Galleanisti who served on the defense committee, "my father was always the most astute and intelligent thinker of them all."[30] From what source, other than his own father, did Ideale acquire the information upon which to base such a positive characterization? Certainly not from the Italian anarchists in and around Boston who knew Giovanni Gambera personally: "Gambera was an eccentric in every way" (Jenny Salemme); "Giovanni was one of the original members [of the Sacco-Vanzetti Defense Committee], but he was never important" (Joseph Moro, who served as the last secretary of the Defense Committee); "Johnny Gambera was on the Defense Committee at the beginning, but he didn't do anything and was not much to talk about" (Sebastiano Magliocca); "Gambera was a windbag, who liked to talk" (Harry Richal, born Evaristo Ricciardelli); "The worst of the lot was Giovanni Gambera. He was absolutely insufferable. He agreed with no one and argued with everybody. He believed that only he knew what was right. He was very contentious and was always arguing with Felicani" (Oreste Fabrizi).[31]

This was the man whose "voice from beyond the grave" represented for Russell "the last word" on the case, and constituted "irrefutable proof" of Sacco's guilt.[32] He was also the *deus ex machina* whom Russell believed was responsible for changing Tresca's opinion about Sacco:

> In 1941 Gambera was preparing to leave Boston for California, and in leaving his past behind him he must have felt free in meeting Tresca to tell him the bedrock truth about Sacco and Vanzetti.[33]

There is not a shred of evidence to substantiate that Tresca and Gambera were even friends, much less that Gambera made a special trip to New York to tell Tresca the truth about Sacco before departing for California. Russell's hypothesis amounts to more than conjecture and theory; it is a venture into the realm of creative fantasy, conceived for the purpose of reinforcing a guilty verdict for Sacco that Russell had already rendered many years earlier.

In the final analysis, all that can be stated with certitude is that on several occasions in the early 1940s, Carlo Tresca declared that Sacco, but not Vanzetti, was guilty of the crime of robbery and murder for which they were condemned.[34] By the rules of evidence, however, anecdotal information of this nature must be considered hearsay and, by definition, too problematic to be attributed great importance. Consequently, in the absence of further elucidation, Tresca's statements, while suggestive and plausible, do not qualify as concrete evidence for judging Nicola Sacco guilty.[35]

Notes

Introduction

1. Felice Guadagni and Renato Vidal, eds. *Omaggio alla memoria imperitura di Carlo Tresca* (New York: Il Martello, 1943), 43. [Cited hereafter as *Omaggio*]
2. Ibid., 46.
3. David Montgomery, *Workers' Control in America: Studies in the history of work, technology, and labor struggles* (Cambridge: Cambridge University Press, 1979), 105.
4. Arturo Giovannitti's foreword to *Who Killed Carlo Tresca?* (New York: Tresca Memorial Committee, 1945), 3.
5. Nomad wrote an unpublished biography of Tresca bearing that title. Copies in the author's collection and the Tresca Memorial Committee papers at the New York Public Library.
6. *Omaggio*, 46.

1. Revolutionary Apprenticeship

1. See Italia Gualtieri, ed., *Carlo Tresca: Vita e morte di un anarchico italiano in America* (Chieti: Casa Editrice Tinari, 1994).
2. For Tresca's parents, see *The Autobiography of Carlo Tresca*, ed. by Nunzio Pernicone (New York: The John D. Calandra Italian American Institute, 2003), 1–7; *Omaggio*, 6–7. Also, the author's interview with Tresca's daughter, Beatrice Tresca Rapport, Arlington, Mass., November 12–14, 1973. After the initial interview, Mrs. Rapport provided the author with additional information in several lengthy letters and more than a dozen long-distance telephone calls. For the sake of brevity, only the interview will be cited hereafter.
3. Tresca, *Autobiography*, 11–15; Interview with Beatrice Tresca Rapport, November 12–14, 1973; Cenno Biografico, in the Archivio Centrale dello Stato, Ministero dell'Interno, Direzione Generale di Pubblica Sicurezza, Casellario Politico Centrale, Tresca, Ettore. [In the past, CPC dossiers were cited with "busta" numbers; however, as more dossiers were frequently added, the busta numbers changed. Therefore they will be omitted in the notes.] See also the commemorative issue of *Il Martello* (February 17, 1942), honoring Ettore after his death on January 15, 1942.
4. *Cenno Biografico*, ACS, Min. Int., CPC, Tresca, Carlo.
5. Tresca, *Autobiography*, 21.

6.   Ibid.

7.   Giovanni Giolitti, *Discorsi parlamentari*, 2 vols. (Rome, Camera dei Deputati, 1953–1956), 2:633.

8.   See Rinaldo *Rigola, Storia del movimento operaio italiano* (Milan: Editoriale Domus, 1947), 158–159, 214–223, 282–283; Daniel Horowitz, *The Italian Labor Movement* (Cambridge: Harvard University Press, 1963), 48–78; Maurice Neufeld, *Italy: School For Awakening Countries* (Ithaca: New York State School of Industrial and Labor Relations, 1961), 227–232; Nunzio Pernicone, "The Italian Labor Movement," in Edward R. Tannenbaum and Emiliana Noether, eds. *Modern Italy: A Topical History Since 1861* (New York: New York University Press, 1974), 201–203.

9.   Alfredo Angiolini and Eugenio Ciacchi, *Socialismo e socialisti in Italia* (Florence: Casa Editrice Nerbini, 1919), 367, 381; Roberto Michels, *Il Proletariato e la borghesia nel movimento socialista italiano* (Turin: Fratelli Bocca Editore, 1908), 137–138, 174–175.

10. *Decreto di scioglimento del circolo socialista di Sulmona*, May 13, 1898, with attached list of members, dated June 4, 1898, and *Decreto di scioglimento della sezione della lega di resistenza tra i ferrovieri*, May 24, 1898, in Archivio di Stato dell'Aquila, Sezione di Sulmona, Tribunale di Sulmona, b. 255, fs. 214.

11. Ibid.; Angiolini, *Socialismo e socialisti in Italia*, 559–563; Christopher Seton-Watson, *Italy from Liberalism to Fascism* (London: Methuan, 1967), 255–256; *Il Germe* (Sulmona), March 2, 1902.

12. Issue N. 14 of *L'Araldo*, quoted in *Il Germe*, December 15, 1901.

13. *Il Germe*, December 15, 1901.

14. Tresca, *Autobiography*, 25.

15. Ibid., 39.

16. Tresca, *Autobiography*, 24–25; *Elenco degli affiliati ad circolo socialista di Sulmona*, June 4, 1898, in ASA, SS, Tribunale di Sulmona, b. 255, fs. 214.

17. Tresca, *Autobiography*, 26.

18. L'Aquila prefect's reports of April 21 and August 22, 1888, and March 23, 1889, in ACS, Min. Int., Gabinetto, Rapporti dei Prefetti, b. 2, fs. 3, L'Aquila.

19. *Il Germe*, January 5, March 2, March 13, April 6, 13, and 20, 1902, *et seq.*

20. *Il Germe*, January 5, April 3, 13, 1902; Tresca, *Autobiography*, 25–28.

21. *Il Germe*, January 5, April 6 and 13, 1902.

22. Tresca, *Autobiography*, 26.

23. Ibid., 27–28; *Il Germe*, May 11, 1902. In a memory lapse, Tresca mistakenly referred to the *Società dei Contadini di Sulmona* in his autobiography instead of the *Fratellanza Agricola*.

24. *Il Germe*, May 11, 1902.

25. Tresca, *Autobiography*, 32.

26. This description was given by the anti-Fascist leader Max Ascoli in *Nazioni Unite* (New York), January 21, 1943.

27. Tresca, *Autobiography*, 43–46; ASA, Sezione Sulmona, Fondo Giudiziario, Pretura di Sulmona, Sentenze: n. 237/1902. Archival documents do not indicate whether Tresca served this sentence.

28. *Il Germe*, June 8, 1902.

29. ASA, SS, Fondo Giudiziario, Pretura di Sulmona, Sentenze: n. 308/1902; also the Cenno biografico in ASA, Questura, Cat. 8, b. 5, fs. 10: Tresca, Carlo; Tresca, *Autobiography*, 46–50.

30. Tresca, *Autobiography*, 50–51.

31. Ibid., 51.

32. *Il Germe*, July 26, 1903; Libertario Guerrini, *Organizzazioni e lotte dei ferrovieri italiani, vol. I: 1862–1907* (Florence, 1957), 237.

33. Tresca, *Autobiography*, 42.

34. Ibid., 34.

35. Cenno biografico, in ASA, Questura, Cat. A8, b. 5, fs. 10: Tresca, Carlo.

36. *Il Germe*, October 18, November 7, 15, 22, 1903.

37. Tresca, *Autobiography*, 58.

38. *Il Germe*, November 15, 1903.

39. Interview with Vincenzo Alvano, Brooklyn, NY, September 20, 1974. Alvano was a close comrade of Tresca.

40. See the court documents in ASA, SS, Fondo Giudiziario, Tribunale Penale di Sulmona, b. 312, fs. 16. Also *Il Germe*, November 7, 22, December 25, 1903, January 10, 1904. The quote is from Tresca's written complaint of January 8, 1904.

41. Commisario di Pubblica Sicurezza to Giudice Istruttore di L'Aquila, May 5, 1904, ASA, Questura, Cat. A8, b. 5, fs. 10: Tresca, Carlo.

42. Cenno biografico, ASA, Questura, Cat. A8, b. 5, fs. 10: Tresca, Carlo. The documents do not specify the exact charges nor indicate whether the case went to trial.

43. Ibid.

44. Ibid.

45. Ibid.

46. Ibid.

47. *Il Germe*, November 22, 1903.

48. Cenno biografico, ASA, Questura, Cat. A8, b. 5, fs. 10: Tresca, Carlo.

49. For the Tribunal's decision and Tresca's appeal, see ASA, SS, Fondo Giudiziario, Tribunale Penale di Sulmona, b. 314, fs. 69.

50. Cenno biografico, ASA, Questura, Cat. 8A, b. 5, fs. 10: Tresca, Carlo.

51. Ibid.

52. Tresca, *Autobiography*, 63.

53. Cenno biografico, ASA, Questura, Cat. 8A, b. 5, fs. 10: Tresca, Carlo; *Omaggio*, 8.

54. Tresca, *Autobiography*, 64, 67–68.

55. Ibid., *67–68*; Renzo De Felice, *Mussolini il rivoluzionario, 1883–1920* (Turin: Giulio Einaudi Editore, 1965), 35.

56. Tresca, *Autobiography*, 68.

57. Ibid.

58. Interview with Vincenzo Alvano.

2. Il Proletario

1. *La Guardia Rossa* (New York), May 1, 1920.

2. Ibid.

3. Tresca, *Autobiography*, 67–73; *Omaggio*, 8; *Il Martello* (New York), December 1, 1920; Mario De Ciampis, "Storia del movimento socialista rivoluzionario italiano," *La Parola del Popolo: Cinquantesimo Anniversario (1908–1958)* 9 (December 1958–January 1959): 144.

4. For an overview of Italian-Amercian radicalism and labor, see Rudolph·J. Vecoli, "Italian American Workers, 1880–1920: Padrone Slaves or Primitive Rebels," in Silvio M. Tomasi, ed., *Perspectives in Italian Immigration and Ethnicity* (New York: Center for Migration Studies, 1977), 25–49; *idem.*, "The Italian Immigrants in the United States Labor Movement From 1880 To 1929," in Bruno Bezza, ed., *Gli Italiani fuori d'Italia: Gli emigrati italiani nei movimenti operai dei paesi d'adozione 1880–1940* (Milan: Franco Angeli, 1983), 257–306; Edwin Fenton, *Immigrants and Unions, A Case Study: Italians and American Labor, 1870–1920* (New York: Arno Press, 1975), 136–196; Adriana Dadà, "I radicali italo-americani e la società italiana," *Italia Contemporanea* 34, nos. 146–147 (June 1982): 131–140; Bruno Ramirez, "Immigration, Ethnicity, and Political Militance: Patterns of Radicalism in the Italian-American Left, 1880–1930," in Valeria Gennaro Lerda, ed., *From "Melting Pot" To Multiculturalism: The Evolution of Ethnic Relations in the United States and Canada* (Rome: Bulzoni Editore, 1990), 115–141; Nunzio Pernicone, "Italian Immigrant Radicalism in New York," in Philip V. Cannistraro, ed., *The Italians of New York* (New York: New York Historical Society, 2000), 77–90.

5. Tresca, *Autobiography*, 75.

6. Charles Leinenweber, "The American Socialist Party and 'New Immigrants,'" *Science & Society* 32, no. 1 (Winter 1968): 1–25; Vecoli, "The Italian Immigrants in the United States Labor Movement," 262–267; Ramirez, "Immigration, Ethnicity, and Political Militance," 116–117.

7. Arturo Caroti, *Per Carlo Tresca* (Milan: Libreria Editrice "Avanti!," 1916), 28–29.

8. *Il Proletario*, December 18, 1904; January 1, February 12, 1905.

9. Ibid., April 9, 1905.

10. Ibid., February 12, 1905.

11. Ibid., April 9, May 7, June 11, September 10, 1905.

12. Information about state federations is scattered through *Il Proletario*.

13. *Il Proletario*, January 14, February 5, April 9, May 28, 1905.

14. Tresca, *Autobiography*, 79–80.

15. *Il Popolo*, May 27, June 3, 17, 1905; *Il Proletario*, August 6, 13, September 3, 4, 1905. The issues of *Il Popolo* have not survived. See the translations provided by the Italian Ambassador to the Secretary of State, in National Archives, Record Group 59, General Records of the State Department, Notes from the Italian Legation in the United States to the State Department, 1861–1906, M-202, Roll 18 [hereafter cited as Italian Legation Notes.]

16. *Il Proletario*, June 25, August 6, 1905.

17. Ibid., August 6, 1905.

18. Italian Ambassador to U.S. Secretary of State, August 2, 1905, in Italian Legation Notes.

19. *Il Proletario*, April 9, June 11, September 10, 1905.

20. *Il Proletario* carried notices and letters to the editor regarding all these visits.

21. Interview with Beatrice Tresca Rapport.

22. Tresca, *Autobiography*, 84. Tresca's special rapport with workers was described by several of his closest comrades: Arturo Giovannitti, "Ecco Carlo Tresca," *L'Avvenire* (New York), August 25, 1916; Giuseppe Popolizio, "Carlo Tresca-dimenticato?," *Controcorrente* 20, No. 2 (Winter 1966): 17–18; Interview with Sam Dolgoff, December 8, 1973.

23. *Il Proletario*, Numero Straordinario, May 1, 1906.

24. Ibid., April 15, 1906.

25. Ibid., September 3, 1905.

26. Ibid., February 26, March 5, 12, 1905; *Omaggio*, 8.

27. *Il Proletario*, September 3, 1905.

28. This description sounds apocryphal, considering that Tresca barely spoke any English at the time.

29. *Il Proletario*, October 1, 1905.

30. Alceo Riosa, *Il sindacalismo rivoluzionario in Italia e la lotta politica nel Partito socialista dell'èta giolittiana* (Bari: De Donato, 1976), 173–216; David D. Roberts, *The Syndicalist Tradition and Italian Fascism* (Chapel Hill: University of North Carolina Press, 1979), 49–82. For Italian-American syndicalism, see Michael Miller Topp, *Those Without A Country: The Political Culture of Italian American Syndicalists* (Minneapolis: University of Minnesota Press, 2001).

31. Quoted in A. William Salomone, *Italy in the Giolittian Era* (Philadelphia: University of Pennsylvania Press, 1960), 51.

32. *Il Proletario*, May 14, 1905.

33. Ibid., June 25, July 23, 1905.

34. Ibid., July 23, 1905.

35. Fenton, *Immigrants and Unions*, 174.

36. *Il Proletario*, January 28, 1905.

37. Ibid., February 4, 26, April 8, 1906.

38. Ibid., December 10, 1905; April 8, 22, 1906.

39. *Il Proletario*, January 7, 1906.

40. Ibid., March 18, December 9, 23, 1906; De Ciampis, "Storia del movimento socialista," 144–146; idem., *"Il Proletario"* (unpublished manuscript on deposit at the Immigration History Research Center, University of Minnesota), 566.

41. *Il Proletario*, June 3, 24, July 16, 1905; De Ciampis, *"Il Proletario,"* 566.

42. *Il Proletario*, June 24, 1906.

43. Ibid., June 24, 1906.

44. Ibid., June 14, 1906.

3. Freelance of Revolution

1. Expressions of support for Tresca appeared in *Il Proletario* for months following his resignation.

2. *Il Proletario*, February 4, March 25, 1906.

3. Interview with Peter Martin, New York City, December 11, 1973. Martin was Tresca's illegitimate son.

4. Tresca, *Autobiography*, 81.

5. *Il Proletario*, December 9, 16, 1906. See also Fenton, *Immigrants and Unions*, 176–177; Anna Maria Martellone, "Per una storia della sinistra italiana negli Stati Uniti: Riformismo e sindacalismo, 1880–1911" in Franca Assante, ed., *Il movimento migratorio italiano dall'unità ai gioni nostril* (Geneva: Librairie Broz, 1948), 193.

6. *Il Proletario*, December 9, 1906.

7. *La Voce del Popolo* (date not given), as quoted in *La Questione Sociale*, October 13, 1906.

8. Tresca, *Autobiography*, 82–83; Philip V. Cannistraro, *Blackshirts in Little Italy: Italian Americans and Fascism 1921–1929* (West Lafayette, IN: Bordighera Press, 1999), 18–20.

9. Only fifteen issues of *La Plebe* have survived.

10. *La Plebe*, August 24, 1907.

11. Ibid.

12. "Freelance of revolution" is one of the terms most commonly used by Italian radicals to describe Tresca. See Felice Guadagni, "Un profilo di Carlo Tresca," in *Omaggio*, 4; Max Ascoli, "In Commemoration of Carlo Tresca," *NazioniUnite*, January 21, 1943; De Ciampis, *Il Proletario*, 567.

13. True Bill of Indictment, February 20, 1908, Court of Quarter Sessions, February Session, Commonwealth of Pennsylvania vs. Carlo Tresca, in the Municipal Archives of Philadelphia; Interview with Beatrice Tresca Rapport; De Ciampis, *Il Proletario*, 566.

14. *La Plebe*, February 22, 1908.

15. Interview with Beatrice Tresca Rapport. For additional details of this incident, see Dorothy Gallagher, *All the Right Enemies: The Life and Murder of Carlo Tresca* (New Brunswick: Rutgers University Press, 1988), 27–29.

16. *La Plebe*, February 22, 1908.

17. Ibid., February 22, May 1, September 5, 1908; *Il Proletario*, November 6, 1908.

18. Italian Ambassador to U.S. Postmaster General, October 24, 1908, in National Archives, Washington, D.C., RG 59, General Records of the State Department, Decimal File, 1910–1929, Doc. No. 811.918/3 [hereafter cited as NA, RG 59, SD, DF.].

19. Third Assistant Postmaster General to Assistant Attorney General for the Post Office Department, October 29, 1908, in NA, RG 28, Records Relating to the Espionage Act, WWI, 1917–1921, File No. 23483.

20. Ibid; *Il Proletario*, November 6, 1908; Report from U.S. Immigration Inspector in Charge at Pittsburgh to Commissioner of Immigration, Boston, December 7, 1908, quoted in report of Bureau of Investigation, Boston Office, May 5, 1922, in U.S. Department of Justice, Federal Bureau of Investigation, Carlo Tresca File [Hereafter cited as Tresca FBI File.]

21. Quoted in a report from the Ministry of the Interior to the Prefect of L'Aquila, April 13, 1909, in ACS, Min. Int., CPC, Carlo Tresca.

22. Carlo Tresca, *Non Ti Fare Soldato* (Pittsburgh: Tipografia Editrice La Plebe, 1909).

23. *La Plebe*, December 16, 1907.

24. *Il Proletario*, December 8, 1907.

25. *La Plebe*, February 22, May 1, 1908.

26. See Robert J. Goldstein, "The Anarchist Scare of 1908: A Sign of Tensions in the Progressive Era," *American Studies* 15 (1974): 55–78.

27. *La Plebe*, January 18, 1908; *Il Proletario*, January 19, 1908; January 29, 1909; *La Questione Sociale*, February 8, 1908.

28. See Anne Fremantle, ed., *The Papal Encyclicals In Their Historical Context* (New York: The New American Library, 1956), 197–207.

29. Tresca, *Autobiography*, 85.

30. Ibid. The issue of *La Plebe* containing the photograph has not survived; however, it was feature prominently in *Il Proletario* of January 1, 1909.

31. Tresca,, *Autobiography*, 86.

32. Ibid., 86–87; *Il Proletario*, January 1, February 9, 1909.

33. Tresca, *Autobiography*, 89.

34. Ibid.; *Il Proletario*, January 15, 1909.

35. *Il Proletario*, January 21, 25, 1905; April 2, 1909.

36. Tresca, *Autobiography*, 87; *Il Martello*, August 13, 1921.

37. Tresca, *Autobiography*, 90–91; *Il Proletario*, January 29, February 5, 12, 1909.

38. Letter of February 5, 1909, in *Il Proletario*, February 12. 1909.

39. *Il Proletario*, February 19, 1909.

40. Ibid., April 2, 23, 1909; J. Joseph Murphy, Motion to Quash Indictments, April 1909, Court of Quarter Sessions, Commonwealth of Pennsylvania vs Carlo Tresca, attached to True Bill of Indictment cited above.

41. The verdict and punishment rendered on April 14 were recorded on the original True Bill of Indictment, cited above. See also *Il Proletario*, May 28, August 6, 1909.

42. Elizabeth Gurley Flynn, *The Rebel Girl: An Autobiography, My First Life (1906–1926)* (New York: International Publishers, 1973), 333–334.

43. *La Plebe*, February 22, 1908.

44. Interview with Beatrice Tresca Rapport.

45. Tresca, *Autobiography*, 97; *Il Proletario*, July 9, August 6, 1909.

46. Tresca, *Autobiography*, 97; *Il Proletario*, September 24, 1909; January 14, February 11, 1910.

47. The geographic distribution of radical coal miners is readily ascertained from the correspondence published in the socialist and anarchist press.

48. Foerster, *The Italian Emigration of Our Times*, 350.

49. Quoted in Craig Phelan, *Divided Loyalties: The Public and Private Life of Labor Leader John Mitchell* (Albany: State University of New York Press, 1994), 16–17.

50. *Il Proletario*, May 20, 1906.

51. Ibid., August 5, 1906.

52. Phelan, *Divided Loyalties*, 256; John H. M. Laslett, *Labor and the Left: A Study of Socialist and Radical Influences in the American Labor Movement, 1881–1924* (New York: Basic Books, 1970), 209–211.

53. For the strike, see U.S. Congress, House of Representatives, *Report on Miners' Strike in Bituminous Coal Field in Westmoreland County, PA. in 1910–1911*, by Walter B. Palmer, House Document 847, 62nd Cong., 2nd session, June 22, 1912 (Washington, D.C.: U.S. Government Printing Office, 1912), 6, 21–22, 43–44 [hereafter cited as *Report on the Westmoreland Strike*]; U.S. Congress, Senate, *Reports of the Immigration Commission* 41 vols., Senate Doc. 747, 61st Cong., 3rd session (Washington, D.C.: U.S. Government Printing Office, 1911), 6: 100–103 [hereafter] cited as *Reports of the Immigration Commission*]; Robert R. Kollar, "Divided They Fell: Unionization and the Westmoreland County Coal Strike of 1910," *Westmoreland History Magazine* 1. No. 1 (Summer 1995): 15–25; Judith McDonough, "Worker Solidarity, Judicial Oppression, and Police Repression in the Westmoreland County, Pennsylvania Coal Miner's Strike, 1910–1911," *Pennsylvania History* 64 (Summer 1997): 384–406.

54. *L'Era Nuova* (Paterson), July 23, 1910.

55. *Report on the Westmoreland Strike*, 9–10, 14, 24–26, 47–52.

56. Ibid., 14–15, 63–64, 77–93, 228–230.

57. *Il Proletario*, July 8, 1910.

58. Ibid.
59. Ibid., May 27, 1910.
60. Ibid., August 19, 1910.
61. Ibid., January 27, 1911.
62. *Proceedings of the Twenty-Second Convention of the United Mine Workers of America, Held in the City of Columbus, Ohio, January 17 to February 1, 1911* (Indianapolis: The Cheltenham Press, 1911), 1:46–47 [hereafter cited as *UMWA Convention Proceedings, 1911*].
63. *UMWA Convention Proceedings, 1911*, 46–47; Kollar, "Divided They Fell," 15–25.
64. See the *United Mine Workers Journal* for its minimal attention to the miners manifested by UMWA leaders.
65. *Il Proletario*, October 7, 1910.
66. Tresca, *Autobiography*, 108.
67. Ibid.
68. Ibid.
69. *Il Proletario*, April 1, 1910.
70. Ibid., March 25, April 1, May 6, June 10, September 23, 30, October 14, November 28, December 2, 9, 16, 30, 1910; January 20, 1911.
71. *Il Martello*, September 15, 1923.
72. Tresca, *Autobiography*, 109–110; *Il Proletario*, July 22, 1910.
73. Tresca, *Autobiography*, 110; *L'Avvenire*, September 17, 1910 (FBI).
74. *Il Proletario*, March 10, 1911.
75. *Report on the Westmoreland Strike*, 103–110.
76. *Il Proletario*, March 24, 1911.
77. See Gerald Brenan, *The Spanish Labyrinth* (London: Cambridge University Press, 1974), 34–35, 165, 174.
78. *L'Avvenire*, September 10, 1910 (FBI).
79. Ibid., October 29, September 24, 1910 (FBI).
80. For an insightful commentary on this issue, see the letter by "Freeman" from Monongehela in *L'Era Nuova*, September 4, 1909.
81. *L'Avvenire*, August 20, October 29, 1910 (FBI); *Il Proletario*, March 25, June 10, July 9, 22, October 14, 21, December 30, 1910.
82. *L'Avvenire*, September 10, October 29, 1910 (FBI); Tresca, *Autobiography*, 98.
83. Bureau of Investigation report, Pittsburgh, May 15, 1922, Tresca FBI File.
84. Ibid.; *L'Avvenire*, October 29, November 19, 1910 (FBI).
85. *L'Avvenire*, October 29, November 19, 1910 (FBI).
86. Ibid., November 19, 1910 (FBI).
87. Rossoni (March 24, 1911) indicated that Tresca did not belong to the FSI; De Ciampis ("Storia del movimento socialista rivoluzionario italiano," 152) claimed that he had rejoined around 1909. Tresca's *Autobiography* and other writings do not provide an answer.
88. *Il Proletario*, April 14, 21, 1911.
89. Ibid., April 14, 1911. Also De Ciampis, "Storia del movimento socialista rivoluzionario italiano," 147–155; Fenton, *Immigrants and Unions*, 176–185; Martellone, "Per una storia della sinistra italiana negli Stati Uniti," 193–195; Vezzosi, *Il socialismo indifferente*, 53–110; Topp, *Those Without A Country*, 43–57.

90. *Il Proletario*, April 21, 1911.

91. Ibid., April 14, 1911.

92. Tresca, *Autobiography*, 99; FBI report, Pittsburgh, May 15, 1922, Tresca FBI File.

93. Tresca, *Autobiography*, 101–106; Consul General of New York to Minister of the Interior, November 20, 1911, in ACS, Min. Int., CPC: Carlo Tresca

4. Lawrence

1. For the Lawrence strike, see Justus Ebert, *The Trial of a New Society* (Cleveland: I.W.W. Publishing Bureau, 1913); Donald B. Cole, *Immigrant City: Lawrence, Massachusetts, 1845-1921* (Chapel Hill: University of North Carolina Press, 1963), 177–197; Melvin Dubofsky, *We Shall Be All: A History of the Industrial Workers of the World* (New York: Quadrangle, 1969), 227–258; Philip S. Foner, *A History of the Labor Movement in the United States, 1896-1932*, vol. 4: *The Industrial Workers of the World 1905-1917* (New York: International Publishers, 1965), 306–350; Patrick Renshaw, *The Wobblies: The Story of Syndicalism in the United States* (New York: Anchor Books, 1968), 97–112; Ardis Cameron, *Radicals of the Worst Sort: Laboring Women in Lawrence, Massachusetts, 1860-1912* (Urbana and Chicago: University of Illinois Press, 1993), 117–186; David J. Goldberg, *A Tale of Three Cities: Labor Organization and Protest in Paterson, Passaic, and Lawrence, 1916-1921* (New Brunswick and London: Rutgers University Press, 1989), 83–96.

2. *Ettor and Giovanniitti before the Jury at Salem, Massachusetts, November 23, 1912* (Chicago, n.d.), 8–17; William D. Haywood, *The Autobiography of Big Bill Haywood* (New York, 1929), 239; Justus Ebert, *The Trial of a New Society*, 68–71; Fenton, *Immigrants and Unions*, 181, n. 142.

3. Ebert, *The Trial of a New Society*, 83; *Solidarity* (New Castle, Pa), July 6, 1912.

4. For Giovannitti's career, see Mario De Ciampis, "Un poeta ribelle: Arturo M. Giovannitti," Parts 1, 2 *Controcorrente* 16 and 17 (February, April 1960): 18–21, 20–22; Nunzio Pernicone, "Arturo Giovannitti 'Son of the Abyss' and the Westmoreland Strike of 1910–1911," *Italian Americana* 17, No. 2 (Summer 1999): 178–192; *La Parola del Popolo* 24, No. 124 (July–August 1974): G1–32.

5. *Senate Report on the Strike of Textile Workers in Lawrence*, 9, 13, 31–36; Flynn, *The Rebel Girl*, 128

6. Flynn, *Rebel Girl*, 128–143; Foner, *The Industrial Workers of the World*, 325–343; Dubofsky, *We Shall Be All*, 250–254.

7. Topp, *Those Without a Country*, 111–113.

8. *Il Proletario*, May 1, 1912.

9. *Il Proletario*, May 1, 11, 1912; Flynn, *Rebel Girl*, 147; Topp, *Those Without a Country*, 111–114.

10. Tresca, *Autobiography*, 111.

11. *Solidarity*, May 11, 1912.

12. Tresca, *Autobiography*, 148.

13. *Il Proletario*, May 18, 1912.

14. *Solidarity*, June 8, 1912.

15. Tresca, *Autobiography*, 121.

16. Ibid., 119. Also *L'Era Nuova*, September 21, 1912; *Solidarity*, September 21, 1912.

17. Tresca, *Autobiography*, 121–129; *Boston Evening Transcript*, September 16, 1912; *L'Era Nuova*, September 21, 1912; *Il Proletario*, September 21, 1912; *Solidarity*, September 21, 1912.

18. Letters reprinted in *Solidarity*, October 5, 1912.

19. Flynn, *Rebel Girl*, 148.

20. Topp, *Those Without a Country*, 111.

21. Ibid.; *L'Era Nuova*, October 12, 1912; *Cronaca Sovversiva* (Lynn), October 19, 1912.

22. Luigi Galleani, *La fine dell'anarchismo?* (Newark, NJ: Edizione Curata da Vecchi Lettori di Cronaca Sovversiva, 1925), 83.

23. Nunzio Pernicone, "Luigi Galleani and Italian Anarchist Terrorism in the United States," *Studi Emigrazione* 30, No. 111 (1993): 469–488.

24. *Cronaca Sovversiva*, June 29, 1912; March 3, October 2, 1915.

25. These efforts are amply documented in *Cronaca Sovversiva* and *L'Era Nuova*.

26. *Cronaca Sovversiva*, January 27, 1912.

27. *Cronaca Sovversiva*, October 19, 1912; *L'Era Nuova*, October 12, 1912; *Il Proletario*, October 19, 1912; *Boston Evening Transcript*, September 27, 1912; *Lawrence Daily American*, September 27, 1912.

28. Flynn, *Rebel Girl*, 147. Phillips Russell, another eye-witness, confirms Flynn's account in his "The Second Battle of Lawrence," 418–420.

29. Tresca, "Autobiography," 171–172. See also *Lawrence Telegram*, September 30, 1912, and *The New York Times*, September 30, 1912.

30. Flynn, *Rebel Girl*, 149.

31. Ibid.; *The Lawrence Daily American*, October 1, 1912; Tresca's statement quoted in *Boston Evening Transcript*, October 1, 1912, and *The New York Times*, October 1, 1912.

32. Flynn, *Rebel Girl*, 149.

33. *The Lawrence Daily American*, October 2, 1912; *Boston Evening Transcript*, October 1, 1912.

34. Ebert, *The Trial of a New Society*, 98; *Boston Evening Transcript*, October 7, 1912.

35. Russell, "The Second Battle of Lawrence," 421.

36. Tresca, *Autobiography*, 140; Flynn, *Rebel Girl*, 151.

37. Tresca, *Autobiography*, 141–142; *Il Proletario*, October 19, 1912.

38. *Solidarity*, October 19, 1912; *Boston Evening Transcript*, October 14, 1912; Ebert, *Trial of a New Society*, 99–100.

39. Ebert, *Trial of a New Society*, 87–90; *Solidarity*, October 19, 1912; *Il Proletario*, September 21, November 30, 1912; Baldo Aquilano, *L'Ordine Figli d'Italia in America* (New York: Società Tipografica Italiana, 1925), 90.

40. *Boston Evening Transcript*, October 17, 1912.

41. Tresca, *Autobiography*, 145–146.

42. Ibid., 147.

43. Ibid., 147–148.

44. The fullest account of the trial is given in Ebert, *The Trial of a New Society*, 102–150. For the complete text of their statements, see *Ettor and Giovannitti Before the Jury at Salem, Massachusetts, November 23, 1912* (Chicago, I.W.W. n.d.).

45. Ebert, *The Trial of a New Society*, 150.

46. For a discussion of the IWW's decline in Lawrence, see Foner, *The Industrial Workers of the World*, 348–349; Dubovsky, *We Shall Be All*, 255–258; Brissenden, *The I.W.W.*, 292–293;

Goldberg, *A Tale of Three Cities*, 91–93.

47. For an excellent discussion of the significance of the strike and agitation for the FSI, see Topp, *Those Without a Country*, 99–134.

48. *Cronaca Sovversiva*, October 19, 1912; *L'Era Nuova*, October 12, 1912. For Tresca's response to such accusations, see *Il Proletario*, October 19, 26, 1912.

49. See Nunzio Pernicone, "War Among the Italian Anarchists: The Galleanisti's Campaign Against Carlo Tresca," in Philip V. Cannistraro and Gerald Meyer, eds., *The Lost World of Italian-American Radicalism* (Westport, CN: Praeger, 2003), 77–97.

50. Tresca, *Autobiography*, 75, 106, 111.

5. On to Paterson

1. Flynn, *Rebel Girl*, 152; Frank Bohn, "The Strike of the New York Hotel and Restaurant Workers," *International Socialist Review* 13 (February 1913): 620–621; *The New York Times*, January 1, 1913.

2. Tresca, *Autobiography*, 165–166.

3. Max Eastman, "Profile of Carlo Tresca: Troublemaker-I," *New Yorker* 10, no. 31 (September 15, 1934): 32–33.

4. Tresca, *Autobiography*, 167.

5. Ibid.

6. *The New York Times*, January 13, 14, 16, 17, 24, 1913; *New York Tribune*, January 24, 1913; Tresca, *Autobiography*, 168–169.

7. *The New York Times*, January 24, 25, 1913; *New York Tribune*, January 24, 25, 1913.

8. Tresca, *Autobiography*, 170.

9. Ibid., 171.

10. Ibid., 172; Flynn, *Rebel Girl*, 153; *New York Tribune*, January 25, 1913; *The New York Times*, February 9, 1913.

11. Flynn, *Rebel Girl*, 153.

12. *The New York Times*, January 26–28, February 1, 1913; *New York Tribune*, January 26–28, 1913.

13. For the Paterson strike of 1913, see Steve Golin, *The Fragile Bridge: Paterson Silk Strike, 1913* (Philadelphia: Temple University Press, 1988); Anne Huber Tripp, *The I.W.W. and the Paterson Silk Strike of 1913* (Urbana and Chicago: University of Illinois Press, 1987); James E. Wood, "History of Labor in the Broad-Silk Industry of Paterson, New Jersey, 1879–1940" (Unpublished Ph.D. dissertation: University of California, 1942), 244–265. An indispensable primary source is U.S. Congress, *Senate Commission on Industrial Relations: Final Report and Testimony*, 64th Cong., 1st session, doc. No. 415 (Washington: Government Printing Office, 1916), vol. 3: 2411–2645 (hereafter cited as *C.I.R.*). For accounts by direct participants, see Tresca, *Autobiography*, 175–178; Flynn, *Rebel Girl*, 154–173, *idem*, "The Truth About the Paterson Silk Strike [a speech delivered to the New York Civic Club Forum, January 31, 1914])," in Joyce L. Kornbluh, ed., *Rebel Voices: An I.W.W. Anthology* (Ann Arbor: University of Michigan Press, 1964), 215–226; Patrick L. Quinlan, "The Paterson Strike and After," *The New Review* 2 (January 1914): 26–32. See also Gregory Mason, "Industrial War in Paterson," *Outlook* 104 (June 7, 1914): 283–287; Howard Levin, "The Paterson Silkworkers' Strike of 1913," *King's Crown Essays* 9 (Winter

1961–1962): 45–64); Dubofsky, *We Shall Be All*, 263–285; Foner, *The Industrial Workers of the World*, 351–372; Renshaw, *The Wobblies*, 112–118.

14. For the Italian dimension, see Fenton, *Immigrants and Unions*, 366–376; Golin, *The Fragile Bridge*, 25–32, 55–58 et passim; James D. Osborne, "Italian Immigrants and the Working Class in Paterson: The Strike of 1913," in Paul A. Stellhorn, *New Jersey's Ethnic Heritage* (Trenton: New Jersey Historical Commission, 1978), 11–34, and his "Paterson: Immigrant Strikers and the War of 1913," in Joseph A. Conlin, ed., *At the Point of Production: The Local History of the I.W.W.* (Westport: Greenwood Press, 1981), 61–78. One of the few studies of the Italians in Paterson prior to the 1913 strike is Carlo C. Altarelli, "History and Present Conditions of the Italian Colony of Paterson, N.J." (Unpublished M.A. thesis: Columbia University, 1911).

15. *C.I.R.*, 3: 2467.

16. Altarelli, "The Italian Colony of Paterson," 2–3; Golin, *The Fragile Bridge*, 25, 29; Luigi Vittorio Ferraris, "L'Assassinio di Umberto I e gli anarchici di Pateson," *Rassegna Storico del Risorgimento* 55, No. 1 (January–March 1968): 51; Arrigo Petacco, *L'Anarchico che venne dall'America* (Verona: Mondadori, 1969), 51.

17. De Ciampis, "Storia del movimento socialista rivoluzionario italiano," 136.

18. De Ciampis, "Storia del movimento socialista rivoluzionario italiano," 138, 148; *La Questione Sociale*, September 2, 9, December 23, 1899, January 6, April 7, 1900; *L'Aurora* (West Hoboken), September 16, 1899; *L'Era Nuova*, July 17, 1915; *L'Adunata dei Refrattari*, October 15,, 1932; Max Nettlau, *Errico Malatesta: Vita e pensieri* (New York: Casa Editrice "Il Martello," 1922), 255–256; Ferraris, "Assassinio di Umberti I," 51–54; George Carey, "'La Questione Sociale,' an Anarchist Newspaper in Paterson, N.J. (1895–1908)," in Lydio F. Tomasi, ed., *Italian Americans: New Perspectives in Italian Immigration and Ethnicity* (Staten Island, N.Y.: Center for Migration Studies, 1985), 289–297; Salvatore Salerno, "No God, No Master: Italian Anarchists and the Industrial Workers of the World," in *Lost World of Italian-American Radicalism*, 171–187. For a definitive study of Bresci and his attentat, see Giuseppe Galzerano, *Gaetano Bresci: Vita, attentato, processo, carcere e morte dell anarchico che "giustiziò Umberto I* (Casalvelino: Galzerano Editore, 2001).

19. *The New York Times*, June 23, 1902.

20. Margaret H. Sanger, "The Paterson Strike," in Hippolyte Havel, ed., *Revolutionary Almanac, 1914* (New York: The Rabelais Press, 1914), 47.

21. Altarelli, "The Italian Colony of Paterson," 11; Osborne, "Immigrant Strikers and the War of 1913," 69; Carey, "Anarchists in Paterson," 56–57; Golin, *The Fragile Bridge*, 27; Salerno, ""No God No Master," 176–177, 179–181; oral account by William Gallo, in Paul Avrich, *Anarchist Voices: An Oral History of Anarchism in America* (Princeton, NJ.: Princeton University Press, 1995), 153–157; *L'Era Nuova*, February 22, 1913; Gallo's father, Firmino Gallo, was a silk weaver and one of the most prominent anarchists in Paterson.

22. Quinlan, "The Paterson Strike and After," 27–28; William D. Haywood, "The Rip in the Silk Industry," *International Socialist Review* 13 (May 1913): 783–785; testimony of Adolph Lessig, in *C.I.R.*, 3: 2453–2454.

23. Testimony of Rudolph Katz in *C.I.R.*, 3: 2472–2474; Quinlan, "The Paterson Strike and After," 27–28; Mason, "Industrial War in Paterson," 284–285; Golin, *The Fragile Bridge*, 33–36; Tripp, *The I.W.W. and the Paterson Silk Strike of 1913*, 44–64; Wood, "History of

Labor in the Broad-Silk Industry of Paterson," 232–245.

24. Flynn, "The Truth About the Paterson Strike," 215–216; Quinlan, "The Paterson Strike and After," 27–28; Golin, *The Fragile Bridge*, 36–41; Tripp, *The I.W.W. and the Paterson Silk Strike of 1913*, 65–71; Wood, "History of Labor in the Broad-Silk Industry of Paterson," 244–248.

25. Flynn, "The Truth About the Paterson Strike," 216; testimony of Edward F. L. Lotte, a silk company manager, and Adolph Lessig in *C.I.R.*, 3: 2448–2449, 2452–2457; *Paterson Evening News*, March 11, 1913; Mason, "Industrial War in Paterson," 285; Wood, "History of Labor in the Broad-Silk Industry of Paterson," 248–250.

26. Flynn, "The Truth About the Paterson Strike," 216; Haywood, "The Rip in the Silk Industry," 785–786.

27. Patrick F. Gill and Redmond S. Brennan, "Report on the Inferior Courts and Police of Paterson, N.J., October 1914," 3, in the National Archives, RG 183, General Records of the Department of Labor, Reports of the Commission on Industrial Relations, Misc. 14 (hereafter cited as Gill and Brennan, "Report on the Inferior Courts and Police of Paterson.")

28. Osborne, "Paterson: Immigrant Strikers and the War of 1913," 70.

29. *C.I.R.*, 2594.

30. *Osborne*, "Italian Immigrants and the Working Class in Paterson," 27.

31. *Paterson Evening News*, March 15, 17, 1913; Golin, *The Fragile Bridge*, 48, 81–82; Mason, "Industrial War in Paterson," 287; Tripp, *The I.W.W. and the Paterson Strike of 1913*, 90; Wood, "History of Labor in the Broad-Silk Industry of Paterson," 259–261.

32. Golin, *The Fragile Bridge*, 133–135; Tripp, *The I.W.W. and the Paterson Silk Strike of 1913*, 117–119.

33. Mabel Dodge Luhan, *Intimate Memoirs*, vol. 3: *Movers and Shakers* (New York: Harcourt Brace & Co., 1936), 187–189; John Reed, "War in Paterson," *International Socialist Review* 14 (July 1913): 43–48; Granville Hicks, *John Reed: The Making of a Revolutionary* (New York: The MacMillan Co., 1937), 98–100.

34. The most sympathetic account of the Paterson Pageant and its antecedents is Golin, *The Fragile Bridge*, 109–179. See also Martin Green, *New York 1913: The Armory Show and the Paterson Strike Pageant* (New York: Charles Scribner's Sons, 1988).

35. Flynn, "The Truth About the Paterson Strike," 221.

36. Ibid., 223.

37. Ibid., 223–224; *Paterson Evening News*, June 23, 24, July 7, 15, 16, 17, 21,24, 1913; *Il Proletario*, August 2, 1913; Quinlan, "The Paterson Strike and After," 29–30.

38. Quinlan, "The Paterson Strike and After," 30–31; "End of the Paterson Strike," *Outlook* 104 (August 9, 1913): 780.

39. Testimony of Edward Zuersher, *C.I.R.*, 3: 2598; Dubofsky, *We Shall Be All*, 283–285; Foner, *The Industrial Workers of the World*, 371–372.

40. Testimony of Adolph Lessig, *C.I.R.*, 3: 2455; Tripp, *The I.W.W. and the Paterson Silk Strike of 1913*, 80.

41. *Il Proletario*, May 3, 1913.

42. *Paterson Evening News*, March 15, 1913.

43. *Paterson Evening News*, February 25, March 11, April 21, 26, May 21, 1913; *Il Martello*, December 1, 1920.

44. Testimony of Henry Marelli, *C.I.R.*, 3: 2530; *Paterson Evening News*, February 25, 26,

March 11, 12, 13, 15, 1913.

45. *Paterson Evening News*, March 15, 1913.

46. Ibid., March 5, 10, 21, April 1, 1913; Robert J. Wheeler, "The Allentown Silk Dyers' Strike," *International Socialist Review* 13 (May 1913): 820–821; Haywood, *Autobiography*, 268; Golin, *The Fragile Bridge*, 43–45.

47. Quoted in the *New York World*, April 23, 1913.

48. *New York World*, April 23, 1913.

49. Ibid.

50. *Paterson Evening News*, April 24, 1913.

51. Hicks, *John Reed*, 97–98; John Reed, "War in Paterson," *International Socialist Review* 14 (July 1913): 43–46.

52. *Paterson Evening News*, June 7, 1913; Flynn, *The Rebel Girl*, 169; Kornbluh, *Rebel Voices*, 210–211.

53. *Il Prolertario*, August 2, 1913.

54. *L'Era Nuova*, July 12, 1913.

55. *Il Proletario*, August 2, 1913.

56. Ibid.

57. New York *Call*, July 26, 1913.

58. *Il Proletario*, August 2, 1913.

59. Ibid.

6. Tresca and Flynn

1. "The Reminiscences of Aldino Felicani," (1954): 69, Oral History Collection, Columbia University.

2. Flynn, *Rebel Girl*, 152.

3. The book with Tresca's inscription is part of the microfilm collection of the Elizabeth Gurley Flynn Papers, Reel 4201, on deposit at the Tamiment Institute Library, New York University, New York City. Many years later, under Tresca's inscription, Flynn wrote: "I always remember. And you, Carlo? How soon you forgot."

4. Ibid.

5. Flynn's *Rebel Girl* is the best source of information about her early life and career. See also Helen C. Camp, *Iron In Her Soul: Elizabeth Gurley Flynn and the American Left* (Pullman, WA: Washington State University Press, 1995); Gallagher, *All the Right Enemies*, 41–43 et passim; Rosalyn Fraad Baxandall, introduction to her *Words on Fire: The Life and Writing of Elizabeth Gurley Flynn* (New Brunswick: Rutgers University Press, 1987); Stephen C. Cole, *Elizabeth Gurley Flynn: A Portrait* (Ann Arbor: University Microfilms International, 1991).

6. Quoted in Flynn, *Rebel Girl*, 65.

7. Quoted in Ibid., 85.

8. Ibid., 113–114, 118–119. For Flynn's relationship with Buster, see Gallagher, *All the Right Enemies*, 118, 120, 122, 163; Camp, *Iron In Her Soul*, 25, 42–43, 60, 117, 126–127, 191–192.

9. Interview with Allegra's friend Matteo Renna, Brooklyn, NY, May 29, 1974. The Marchese Propero De Nobili was an enlightened employer who organized a mutual aid society for his workers that provided for pensions and medical assistance. He tolerated Allegra's

political activities largely because he feared he could organize retaliatory strikes against the company, but was ultimately compelled by Mussolini's government to discharge him in 1927.

10. *Il Proletario*, November 1, 15, 26, December 13, 1913; September 26, October 10, November 28, December 19, 1914; January 16, February 6, May 15, 1915. Also *Il Martello*, December 1, 1920.

11. For Dunn's comments on Tresca, see *C.I.R.*, 3: 2551.

12. *Paterson Evening News*, December 15, 1913.

13. Ibid., December 15, 16, 1913; *L'Era Nuova*, December 20, 1913.

14. *L'Avvenire*, July 4, 1914; *L'Era Nuova*, July 4, 1914; *Paterson Evening News*, July 1, 1914; Flynn to Vorse, July 5, 1914, in the Mary Heaton Vorse Collection, The Archives of Labor and Urban Affairs, Wayne State University, Box 54. [Hereafter cited as Vorse Papers].

15. Foner, *The Industrial Workers of the World*, 442–450.

16. Avrich, *Anarchist Voices*, 507.

17. Tresca, *Autobiography*, 209–210.

18. Ibid., 210–211.

19. *The New York Times*, March 4, 1914.

20. *New York World*, March 3, 1914.

21. Tresca, *Autobiography*, 213–214.

22. Flynn, *The Rebel Girl*, 182–183; Paul Avrich, *The Modern School Movement: Anarchism and Education in the United States* (Princeton: Princeton University Press, 1980), 187; Foner, *The Industrial Workers of the World*, 446–448.

23. Tresca, *Autobiography*, 216.

24. Ibid.; Foner, *The Industrial Workers of the World*.

25. Foner, *The Industrial Workers of the World*, 448–449.

26. Tresca, *Autobiography*, 233.

27. *Il Martello*, September 30, 1922; June 8, 1929.

28. Tresca, *Autobiography*, 217–218.

29. *New York Herald*, March 22, 1914; *The New York Times*, March 22, 1914.

30. *The New York Times*, March 23, 1914.

31. Avrich, *The Modern School Movement*, 190–191.

32. Ibid., 196–204.

33. *L'Avvenire*, July 4, 1914.

34. Philip S. Foner, *History of the Labor Movement in the United* States, vol. 5: *The AFL in the Progressive Era, 1910–1915* (New York: International Publishers, 1980), 206–207.

35. Tresca, *Autobiography*, 234–235. See also Vincenzo Massari, "Il Massacro di Ludlow davanti alla storia," *La Parola del Popolo* 9, no. 37 (December 1958–January 1959): 97–115.

36. *The New York Times*, May 26, 27, 1914; Tresca, *Autobiography*, 238–240.

37. Tresca, *Autobiography*," 240–241; Avrich, *The Modern School Movement*, 195–196.

38. Tresca, *Autobiography*, 242–243.

39. Ibid., 242–244; *L'Avvenire*, July 11, 1914; Consul General of New York to Ministry of the Interior, July 6, 1914, in Min., Int., CPC: Tresca, Carlo.

40. Avrich, *The Modern School Movement*, 183–216.

41. Ibid.

42. Tresca, *Autobiography*, 245–246.

43. Ibid., 246.
44. Ibid.
45. Avrich, *The Modern School Movement*, 202.
46. Flynn to Vorse, July 5, 1914, in Vorse Papers, Box 54.
47. Tresca, *Autobiography*, 248.
48. Quoted in *Mother Earth* (New York), July 1914.
49. *Mother Earth*, July 1914.
50. Tresca, *Autobiography*, 248–249.
51. Ibid., 249.
52. Ibid., 249–250; *Mother Earth*, July 1914.
53. Flynn to Vorse, July 17, 1914, Vorse Papers, Box 54.
54. *Mother Earth*, July 1914.
55. Flynn, *The Rebel Girl*, 333.
56. Ibid.
57. Interview with Beatrice Tresca Rapport.
58. Flynn, *The Rebel Girl*, 333.
59. Eastman, "Profile, I," 31.
60. Interview with Norman Thomas, New York, March 28, 1963.
61. Interview with Roger Baldwin, New York, June 6, 1973.
62. Flynn, *The Rebel Girl*, 333.
63. Ibid.
64. Interview with Beatrice Tresca Rapport.
65. Poem in Flynn Papers, R. 4201, Tamiment Institute Library.

7. From Union Square to Mesabi Range

1. Thomas J. Tunney (as told to Paul Merrick Hollister), *Throttled!: The Detection of the German and Anarchist Bomb Plotters* (Boston: Small, Maynard & Co., 1919), 3–4.
2. Ibid., 44; *The New York Times*, October 14, 1914; Paul Avrich, *Sacco and Vanzetti: The Anarchist Background* (Princeton, NJ: Princeton University Press, 1991), 100.
3. Tunney. *Throttled!*, 47–61.
4. Ibid., 62–66; *The New York Times*, March 3, 1915.
5. Quoted in *The New York Times*, March 3, 1915.
6. Tresca, *Autobiography*, 254–255.
7. Quoted in the *New York World*, April 3, 1915.
8. Tresca, *Autobiography*," 257–259; *L'Era Nuova*, March 13, 1915; *The New York Times*, April 3, 1915.
9. *The New York Times*, April 3, 1915.
10. Ibid., March 31, 1915.
11. Ibid., April 13, 1915.
12. See Roberts, *The Syndicalist Tradition and Italian Fascism*, 104–128; Seton-Watson, *Italy from Liberalism to Fascism*, 413–450.
13. For Rossoni and the FSI schism over interventionism, see Topp, *Those Without a Country*, 128–138, 146–173; Rudolf J. Vecoli, "The War and Italian American Syndicalists," (unpublished paper presented at the Organization of American Historians, 1978): 1–24;

De Ciampis, "Storia del movimento socialista rivoluzionaro italiano," 154, 159–162; Tinghino, *Edmondo Rossoni*, 33–74.

14. *Il Proletario*, October 31, 1914.

15. Topp, *Those Without a Country*, 148–168; Vecoli, "The War and Italian American Syndicalists," 10–21; De Ciampis, "Storia del movimento socialista rivoluzionario italiano," 160–161; Tinghino, *Edmondo Rossoni*, 64–73.

16. *Il Proletario*, March 11, 25; April 8, 15, 29; May 6, 13, 27; June 24, 1916; *Il Martello*, December 1, 1920.

17. *Il Proletario*, April 15, 1916.

18. Ibid., May 6, 1916.

19. *Il Martello*, December 1, 1920.

20. For general accounts of the strike, see Foner, *The Industrial Workers of the World*, 486–517, and Dubofsky, *We Shall Be All*, 319–333. For the Italians on the Mesabi Range, see Rudolph J. Vecoli, "Italians on Minnesota's Iron Range," in Rudolph J. Vecoli, ed., *Italian Immigrants in Rural and Small Town America* (Staten Island, NY: American Italian Historical Association, 1987), 179–189. See also Donald G. Sofchalk, "Organized Labor and the Iron Ore Miners of Northern Minnesota, 1907–1936," *Labor History* 12 (Spring 1971): 214–242, and Neil Betten, "Riot, Revolution, Repression in the Iron Range Strike of 1916," *Minnesota History* 41 (Summer 1968): 82–93.

21. Foner, *The Industrial Workers of the World*, 486–489; Dubofsky, *We Shall Be All*, 319–321.

22. *Il Martello*, December 1, 1920; Foner, *The Industrial Workers of the World*, 493–497; Dubofsky, *We Shall Be All*, 322–325.

23. U.S. Attorney Alfred Jacques to the Attorney General, October 18, 1916, in NA, RG 59, Department of Justice, Mail and Files Division, file no. 182749.

24. *Industrial Worker*, July 1, 1916.

25. Tresca, *Autobiography*, 179–182.

26. Ibid., 182–183.

27. Foner, *The Industrial Workers of the World*, 500–501.

28. U.S. Attorney Jacques to Attorney General, October 18, 1916, NA, RG, DS, MFD, fn. 182749.

29. Foner, *The Industrial Workers of the World*, 506–511.

30. Ibid., 511–512; Flynn, *The Rebel Girl*, 213.

31. Flynn to Vorse, Duluth, July 24, 1916, in Vorse Papers, Box 55. Also quoted in Vorse, *Footnote to Folly*, 135.

32. Flynn Papers, Tamiment Institute Library, R. 4201; also quoted in Gallagher, *All the Right Enemies*, 59.

33. Tresca to Vorse (undated), in Vorse Papers, Box 55.

34. Flynn, *The Rebel Girl*, 214–215; Foner, *The Industrial Workers of the World*, 514–515.

35. Foner, *The Industrial Workers of the World*, 514–515.

36. *The New York Times*, July 30, 1916; *L'Era Nuova*, August 26, 1916.

37. Tresca's Italian police dossier contains around 100 telegrams and reports from prefects and government ministers devoted to the pro-Tresca agitation in Italy. See also *Il Proletario*, September 30, 1916; Caroti, *Per Carlo Tresca*, 3–5, 31–32; Gino Cerrito, *L'Antimilitarismo anarchico in Italia nel primo ventennio del secolo* (Pistoia: Edizioni RL, 1968), 57–58, fn. 121; Adriana Dadà, "I radicali italo-Americani e la società italiana,"

Italia Contemporanea 34, N. 146–147 (June 1982): 133–135. The photograph of Donna Filomena is reproduced in *Omaggio*, 7.

38. Department of Military Censorship of Foreign Mail (Bologna) to Ministry of the Interior, October 14, 1916, and Decree of November 1916 by Secretary of State for Internal Affairs, in ACS, Min., Int., CPC: Tresca, Carlo.

39. Minister of Foreign Affairs to the Minister of the Interior, September 20, 1916, in ACS, Min., Int., CPC: Carlo Tresca.

40. Italian Ambassador in Washington to the Foreign Minister, reports of September 12, 20, and October 1, 1916, in ACS, Min., Int., CPC: Carlo Tresca.

41. *Il Martello*, December 1, 120.

42. Flynn, *The Rebel Girl*, 214–216; Foner, *The Industrial Workers of the World*, 515–516; Dubofsky, *We Shall Be All*, 331–332; Gallagher, *All the Right Enemies*, 61–62.

43. Haywood, *Autobiography*, 292.

44. *Il Martello*, December 1, 1920.

8. Surviving Repression

1. "In Re: Carlo Tresca. Resume of Activities," New York, May 7, 1920, Tresca FBI File.

2. Flynn, *The Rebel Girl*, 220–221.

3. *L'Avvenire*, January 19, 1917.

4. Ibid., January 26, 1917.

5. Ibid., February 2, 1917.

6. "In Re: Carlo Tresca. Resume of Activities," New York, May 7, 1920." Tresca FBI File.

7. *L'Avvenire*, April 6, 1917.

8. For the persecution of radicals prior, during, and after the war, see William Preston, Jr., *Aliens and Dissenters: Federal Suppression of Radicals, 1903–1933* (New York: Harper & Row, Publishers, 1963), passim; and Robert Justin Goldstein, *Political Repression in Modern America, 1870 to the Present* (Cambridge/New York: Schenkman, 1978), 105–191.

9. Avrich, *Sacco and Vanzetti*, 94–95.

10. Report: "In Re: Carlo Tresca. Resume of Activities," New York, May 7, 1920, Tresca FBI File.

11. New York Police Department to the Bomb Squad, September 20, 1917, in NA, RG 165, War Department General Staff, Military Intelligence Division, 1917–1941, box 3010, file series 10110-308. [Hereafter cited as NA, RG 165, MID]

12. Preston, *Aliens and Dissenters*, 118–122; Goldstein, *Political Repression in Modern America*, 115–118.

13. Translated letter quoted in "In Re: Carlo Tresca. Resume of Activities," New York, May 7, 1920, Tresca FBI File.

14. Flynn, *The Rebel Girl*, 233.

15. Report of agent William W. Blatchford, New York, October 1, 1917, in NA, RG 165, MID, box 3021, file series 10110-308.

16. *The New York Times*, October 1, 1917.

17. Flynn, *The Rebel Girl*, 235–236; *Omaggio*, 30; Camp, *Iron In Her Soul*, 80; *The New York Times*, October 9, 1917.

18. Flynn, *The Rebel Girl*, 236.
19. *L'Avvenire*, June 4, 1917.
20. *Il Martello*, September 1, 1918; Flynn, *The Rebel Girl*, 236–237; Vorse, *Footnote to Folly*, 156–157.
21. Attorney General Thomas W. Gregory to U.S. Attorney Charles F. Clyne, October 29, 1917, in NA, RG 60, DJCF, file no. 188032-51; Attorney General Gregory to Assistant Attorneys General Claude R. Porter and Frank K. Nebeker, and U.S. Attorney Clyne, December 14, 1917, in Ibid., file no. 188032-88.
22. Assistant Attorneys General Nebeker and Porter to Attorney General Gregory, February 15, 1918, in NA, RG 60, DJCF, file no. 188032-161.
23. For the Chicago trial and Haywood's flight, see Dubosky, *We Shall Be All*, 428–437, 459–460.
24. Assistant Attorney General Porter to U.S. Attorney Clyne, March 15, 1919, in NA, RG 60, DJCF, file no. 188032-396.
25. Various Lawrence newspaper articles contained in NA, RG 165, MID, box 3042.
26. Operative's report, "Anarchists and Ultra-Radical Socialists' Convention, New York City, October 12–15, 1919," Chicago, October 29, 1919, in NA, RG 165, MID, box 3056, file no. 10110-1398.
27. Goldstein, *Political Repression in Modern America*, 139–154.
28. For the Palmer Raids and the Deportation Delirium, see Ibid., 144–163; Preston, *Aliens and Dissenters*, 181–276; Robert K. Murray, *Red Scare: A Study in National Hysteria, 1919–1920* (New York and Toronto: McGraw Hill, 1955), 166–262; Philip S. Foner, *History of the Labor Movement in the United States*, vol. 8: *Postwar Struggles, 1918–1920* (New York; International Publishers, 1988).
29. Interview with Beatrice Tresca Rapport.
30. John T. Creighton, Special Assistant to the Attorney General, to Anthony Caminetti, Commissioner-General of Immigration, Washington, D.C., August 25, 1919, in NA, RG 68, DJCF, file no. 204106-1.
31. Ibid.
32. Summary report on Tresca [date and place censored], in Tresca FBI File.
33. Some were reprinted on the front page of *Il Martello*, October 1, 1920, and in *Omaggio*, 32.
34. *Omaggio*, 32–33; *The New York Times*, September 19 and 20, 1920.
35. *Il Martello*, October 1, 1920.
36. Burns to SAC Brennan, Washington, D.C., March 24, 1922, Tresca FBI File.
37. Burns to SACs in New York, etc., May 2, 1922, Tresca FBI File.
38. New York Office report to Burns, May 6, 1922, Tresca FBI File.
39. Report, Washington, D.C. office, April 19, 1922.
40. Report, "Carlo Tresca—Radical I.W.W.," St. Paul, December 4, 1922, Tresci FBI File.
41. "Memorandum In Re: Carlo Tresca," March 6, 1923, Tresca FBI File.
42. Bureau of Radical Publications (R.A.B.), "Report on Carlo Tresca Articles in Il Martello, April 25, 1919–May 5, 1922, Tresca FBI File.
43. "Memorandum In Re: Carlo Tresca," May 6, 1923, in Tresca FBI File.
44. *Il Martello*, June 11, 1922.
45. Report, "Re: Carlo Tresca," New York, May 7, 1922, Tresca FBI File.
46. *Il Martello*, June 20, 1919.
47. Ibid.

9. Postwar Activities

1. Report of October 19, 1925, in ACS, Min. Int., Divisione Affari Generale Riservati, Anno 1925, b. 130.
2. *Il Martello*, December 1, 1920.
3. The locations were as follows: 112 E. 19th St. (Jan. 1918–Feb. 1920); 208 E. 12th St. (Feb. 1920–July 1923); 304 East 14th St. (July 1923–Dec. 1925); 77 E. 10th St. (Dec. 1925–June 1928); 82 E. 10th St. (June 1928–May 1932); 94 Fifth Avenue (Jan. 1934–Sept. 1936); and 96 Fifth Avenue (Sept. 1936–March 1946).
4. For a good account of the ambiance of this radical district, see Vanni B. Montana, *Amarostico: Testimoniance euro-americane* (Livorno: U. Bastogi Editore, 1975), 96–108.
5. *Il Martello*, July 1, 1918. The illustration was drawn by Rollin Kirby.
6. Ibid., December 1, 1920.
7. A circular of April 18, 1923, written by Elizabeth Gurley Flynn, appealing for financial support for *Il Martello,* in the Peter Martin Papers in the author's collection. See also *Il Martello*, December 27, 1924 and September 3, 1929.
8. Interview with Matteo Renna, Brooklyn, May 29, 1974; interview with Luigi Quintiliano, New York, May 7, 1963.
9. *Il Martello*, April 1, 1920.
10. Goldberg, *A Tale of Three Cities*, 83–100, 107–110; Rudolf J. Vecoli, "Anthony Capraro and the Lawrence Strike of 1919," in George E. Pozzetta, ed., *Pane e Lavoro: The Italian American Working* Class (Toronto: The Multicultural History Society of Ontario, 1980), 3–7.
11. Goldberg, *A Tale of Three Cities*, 103–104; Vecoli, "Anthony Capraro and the Lawrence Strike," 9.
12. "The Reminiscences of A.J. Muste" (Columbia University Oral History Collection, 1965), 364. [Hereafter cited as Muste, "Reminiscences."
13. Ibid., 368–374.
14. Goldberg, *A Tale of Three Cities*, 101–103; Vecoli, "Anthony Capraro and the Lawrence Strike of 1919," 10–13; Vittorio Buttis, *Memorie di vita di tempeste sociali* (Chicago: Comitato "Vittorio Buttis," 1940), 104–105.
15. Vecoli, "Anthony Capraro and the Lawrence Strike of 1919," 15; Buttis, *Memorie di vita di tempeste*, 15; Tresca, *Autobiography*, 152–154.
16. *Il Martello*, June 15, 1920.
17. Tresca, *Autobiography*, 155.
18. Ibid., 156–157; *Il Martello*, May 20, 1919 and June 15, 1920; Goldberg, *A Tale of Three Cities*, 121; Vecoli, "Anthony Capraro and the Lawrence Strike of 1919," 15–16; *Lawrence Telegram*, May 3, 1919; *Lawrence Eagle*, May 3, 1919.
19. Muste, "Reminiscences," 399.
20. Ibid., 399–406; Goldberg, *A Tale of Three Cities*, 121–122; Vecoli, "Anthony Capraro and the Lawrence Strike of 1919," 17–18.
21. *Il Martello*, May 1, 1920.
22. Ibid., February 16, 1919.
23. Ibid., December 1, 1920.
24. Ibid., April 1, 1920; *Il Proletario*, February 28, March 27, 1920.
25. An FSI circular ordering a boycott of Tresca is reproduced in *Il Martello*, May 1, 1920.

26. *Il Martello*, March 15, 1920.
27. Ibid.
28. *Il Proletario*, November 13, 1920.
29. *Il Martello*, December 1, 1920.
30. Ibid.
31. Ibid.
32. Tresca provided a detailed account of this propaganda tour in *Il Martello* of January 15, 1920; he also described the same events in his *Autobiography* (189–199), but for some inexplicable reason he misdated them to December 1917. The *Autobiography* also describes the detour to Canada, which was not included in his original newspaper account, perhaps for reasons of security.
33. *Il Martello*, January 15, 1919.
34. Ibid.
35. Ibid.
36. Ibid.
37. Tresca, *Autobiography*, 191–194.
38. Ibid., 194–195; *Il Martello*, January 15, 1920.
39. Tresca, *Autobiography*, 194–199; *Il Martello*, January 15, 1920.
40. *Il Martello*, January 15, 1920.

10. Sacco and Vanzetti

1. *La Guardia Rossa*, May 1, 1919.
2. *Il Martello*, March 23, 1919.
3. Quoted in Paul Avrich, *Sacco and Vanzetti: The Anarchist Background* (Princeton: Princeton University Press), 95; William Young and David E. Kaiser, *Postmortem: New Evidence in the Case of Sacco and Vanzetti* (Amherst: University of Massachusetts Press, 1985), 15.
4. *Cronaca Sovversiva*, May 28, 1917.
5. Avrich, *Sacco and Vanzetti*, 58–72; Robert D'Attilio, "La Salute è in Voi: the Anarchist Dimension," *Sacco-Vanzetti: Developments and Reconsiderations—1979* (Boston: Trustees of the Public Library of the City of Boston, 1982), 79–80.
6. Avrich, *Sacco and Vanzetti*, 102–103, 157–158.
7. Ibid., 137–148.
8. Ibid., 166–168; Goldstein, *Political Repression in Modern America*, 149–150.
9. Quoted in Avrich, *Sacco and Vanzetti*, 149.
10. Ibid., 165–177.
11. Ibid., 178–179; *Il Martello*, February 15, May 1, October 15, 1920; New York *Call*, June 14, 1920.
12. *Il Martello*, February 15, 1920.
13. Ibid., October 15, December 1, 1920; *Il Proletario*, April 3, 1920.
14. *Il Martello*, May 1, 1920; New York *Call*, June 14, 1920; Avrich, *Sacco and Vanzetti*, 180.
15. Avrich, *Sacco and Vanzetti*, 180–181.
16. Ibid., 180–187.
17. Ibid., 188–189.

18. *Cronaca Sovversiva*, December 4, 1915.

19. Raffaele Schiavina, interview with the author, Brooklyn, January 10, 1974; and letter to the author, January 15, 1974.

20. Avrich, *Sacco and Vanzetti*, 188–191; Luigi Quintiliano, "Preludii alla tragedia di Dedham," *Controcorrent* No. 7 (August 1958): 19–21.

21. Avrich, *Sacco and Vanzetti*, 191–193; Louis F. Post, *The Deportations Delirium of Nineteen-Twenty* (Chicago: Charles H. Kerr & Co.,1923), 281.

22. D'Attilio, "La Salute è in Voi," 86.

23. Ibid., 88; Avrich, *Sacco and Vanzetti*, 196–197.

24. Avrich, *Sacco and Vanzetti*, 201–202.

25. Ibid., 199–202.

26. Summary of Files of Bureau of Investigation, United States Department of Justice: Relating to Nicola Ferdinando Sacco and Bartolomeo Vanzetti, no date but compiled in fall of 1927, in FBI file of Nicola Sacco and Bartolomeo Vanzetti [hereafter cited as Sacco-Vanzetti FBI File).

27. Avrich, *Sacco and Vanzetti*, 204.

28. Ibid., 205.

29. "The Reminiscences of Aldino Felicani," (1954): 70.

30. Flynn, *The Rebel Girl*, 299–300.

31. Ibid., 302.

32. Ibid., 299, 303–307, 311–314.

33. Vorse, *Footnote to Folly*, 330.

34. The first issue of *Il Martello* that dealt with Sacco and Vanzetti was that of June 15, 1920.

35. Interview with Luigi Quintiliano, New York, March 28, 1963.

36. *Il Martello*, June 15, 1920ff.

37. Tresca to Felicani, New York, October 7, 1920, in Felicani Sacco-Vanzetti Collection (Ms. 2030), Boston Public Library, Category .7A—Tresca-Felicani correspondence. [Hereafter cited as Felicani Collection.] Also, *Il Martello*, November 1, 1920.

38. Tresca to Fred Moore, New York, August 31, 1920, in Fred Moore Correspondence, Category .4A, Felicani Collection.

39. Nunzio Pernicone, "Carlo Tresca and the Sacco-Vanzetti Case," *The Journal of American History* 66, No. 1 (December 1979): 535–547. For the names of the original committee, see *Il Martello*, June 15, 1920.

40. Tresca to Fred Moore, New York, [n.d., but late November 1920] in Report, Re Carlo Tresca, Boston, May 5, 1922, Tresca FBI File. The name of the recipient is blacked out in the FBI document, but it was undoubtedly Moore.

41. Moore to Tresca, Boston, November 29, 1920, Cat. .4A, Felicani Collection.

42. Tresca to Moore, New York, December 9, 1920, Cat. .4A, Felicani Collection.

43. Felicani, "Reminiscences," 87. Also, Pernicone, "Carlo Tresca and the Sacco-Vanzetti Case," 541.

44. Moore to Tresca, Boston, September 10, 1920; Tresca to Moore, New York, November 9, 1920; Tresca to Arturo Caroti, February 16, 1921, Cat. .4A, Felicani Collection. Also, *Il Martello*, April 9, 1921; New York *Call*, June 10, 11, 12, 13, 1920.

45. *Il Martello*, June 11, 1921.

46. Ibid., July 16, 1921.

47. Ibid., September 3, 1921.

48. Ibid., October 22, 1921.
49. Regarding the controversy that resulted from Tresca's comments in the 1940s, suggesting Sacco's guilt, see Pernicone, "Carlo Tresca and the Sacco-Vanzetti case" and the Addendum to the present volume.

11. New Enemies

1. Felix Gilbert and David Clay Large, *The End of the European Era: 1890 to the Present*, 5th ed. (New York: W.W. Norton, 2002), 112.
2. *Il Martello*, June 1, 1918.
3. Ibid.
4. Ibid., August 6, 13, 1921.
5. Ibid., August 6, 1921.
6. Ibid., August 13, 1921.
7. *La Guardia Rossa*, May 1, 1921.
8. *Il Martello*, August 13, 1921; August 2, 1924.
9. Ibid., November 15, 1919.
10. Ibid., June 15, 1920.
11. Ibid., February 16, 1919.
12. Ibid., September 15, 1920.
13. Ibid., July 10, 20, 31, 1919; September 15, 1920.
14. Ibid., July 10, 1919.
15. Ibid., September 15, 1920.
16. Quoted in Angelo Tasca, *Nascita e avvento dal fascismo* (Bari: Laterza, 1965), vol. 1, 82.
17. *Il Martello*, February 12, 1921.
18. Ibid., February 12, 1921.
19. Ibid., August 12, 1922.
20. Ibid., October 28, 1922.
21. Ibid., April 28, 1941.
22. Gaetano Salvemini, "Mussolini's American Empire in the United States," in Frances Keene, ed., *Neither Liberty Nor Bread: The Meaning and Tragedy of Fascism* (New York: Harper, 1940), 336–349.
23. Salvemini, *Italian Fascist Activities in the United States*, ed. Philip V. Cannistraro (New York: Center for Migration Studies, 1977), 4; John P. Diggins, *Mussolini and Fascism: The View From America* (Princeton, NJ: Princeton University Press, 1972), 78–81; Massimo Salvadori, *Resistenza ed azione: Ricordi di un Liberale* (Bari: Laterza, 1951), 162–163; Louis L. Gerson, *The Hyphenate in Recent American Politics and Diplomacy* (Lawrence, KN: University of Kansas Press, 1954), 5–10; John Higham, *Strangers in the Land: Pattens of American Nativism 1860–1925*, 2nd ed. (New York: Atheneum, 1975), 66, 90–91, 160, 169, 254–255; Aquilano, *L'Ordine figli d'Italia in America*, 16–22.
24. Diggins, *Mussolini and Fascism*, 78.
25. For general accounts of Italian-American Fascism see ibid., 78–110; Salvemini, *Italian Fascist Activities in the United States*, ed. Philip V. Cannistraro (New York: Center for Migration Studies, 1977); Philip V. Cannistraro, *Blackshirts in Little Italy: Italian Americans and Fascism, 1921–1929* (West Lafayette, IN; Bordighera, 1999); Marcus

Duffield, "Mussolini's American Empire: The Fascist Invasion of the United States," *Harper Magazine* 159 (November 1929): 661–672.

26. Salvemini, "Mussolini's Empire in the United States," 345–346.

27. Ibid., 336–349.

28. Report from the Segreteria Generale dei Fasci all'Estero [hereafter cited as SGFR] to Ministero degli Affari Esteri [undated; received July 29, 1923]; also Ambassador Caetani to Mussolini, January 28, 1923, in ACS, Ministero della Cultura Popolare, b. 163, f. 18, sf. 71–71A [hereafter cited as MCP]. Also Salvemini, *Italian Fascist Activities in the United States*, 11–14; E. Ruperto [pseudonym of Giorgio La Piana], "Italian Fascism in America-II," *Il Mondo*, July 1940; Philip V. Cannistraro, *Blackshirts in Little Italy: Italian Americans and Fascism, 1921–1929* (West Lafayette, Ind,: Bordighera, 1999), 8–18.

29. *Il Popolo d'Italia*, May 3, 1921, in *Opera Omnia di Benito Mussolini*, Edoardo and Duilio Susmel, eds. 35 vols. (Florence: La Fenice, 1951–1963), vol. 16, 297 [cited hereafter as Mussolini, *Opera Omnia*].

30. Ibid.

31. Caetani to Mussolini, two telegrams dated January 28, 1923, ACS, *MCP*, b. 163, f. 18, sf. 71–71A.

32. Cannistraro, *Blackshirts in Little Italy*, 8–35; Alan Cassels, "Fascism for Export: Italy and the United States in the Twenties," *American Historical Review* 69, No. 3 (April 1964): 707–709.

33. Salvemini, *Italian Fascist Activities in the United States*, 14–15; Cannistraro, *Blackshirts in Little Italy*, 24–36; Ruperto, "Italian Fascism in America-II," *Il Mondo* (July 1940): 11–12.

34. *New York Herald*, March 20, 1923.

35. Ibid.

36. *The New York Times*, March 21, 1923.

37. Salvemini, *Italian Fascist Activities in the United States*, 11–16; Cannistraro, *Blackshirts in Little Italy*, 18–19, 46–47; Barzini to Mussolini, New York, Novembere 28, 1930, in National Archives, Washington, D.C., "Personal Papers of Benito Mussolini, Together with Some Official Records of the Italian Foreign Office and Ministry of Culture," [hereafter cited as *Captured Italian Documents*] National Archives, Washington, D.C., "Personal Papers of Benito Mussolini, Together with Some Official Records of the Italian Foreign Office and Ministry of Culture," [hereafter cited as *Captured Italian Documents*] T586, doc. no. 015112/1.

38. Report, "Fasci e fascismo agli Stati Uniti, from Umberto Colossi to Mussolini, June 6, 1923, in ACS, *MPC*, b. 163, f. 18, sf. 71–71A.

39. Ibid.

40. Salvemini, *Italian Fascist Activities in the United States*, passim; idem, "Mussolini's Empire in the United States," 338–345, 349; Diggins, *Mussolini and Fascism*, 81–86, 94–95.

41. N. W. Ayer and Sons, *American Newspaper Annual and Directory: A Catalogue of Newspapers* (Philadelphia: Ayel, 1926), 725, 747.

42. Diggins, *Mussolini and Fascism*, 81–86, 107; Salvemini, "Mussolini's Empire in the United States," 339–341; Cannistraro, *Blackshirts in Little Italy*, 52.

43. Diggins, *Mussolimi and Fascism*, 97; Salvemini, "Mussolini's Empire in the United States," 342.

44. Salvemini, *Italian Fascist Activities in the United States*, 5–9, 91–93; Cannistraro,

Blackshirts in Little Italy, 18–19; Diggins, *Mussolini and Fascism*, 94–95.

45. Investigations conducted in the late 1930s by the House Un-American Activities Committee and the Dickstein-McCormick Committee of New York virtually discounted any threat from Italian-American Fascists. See Salvemini, *Italian Fascist Activities in the United States*, 189–197; Diggins, *Mussolini and Fascism*, 102–104, 344n38

46. Salvemini, *Italian Fascist Activities in the United States*, 145–148; and especially Gaetano Salvemini and George La Piana, *What To Do With Italy* (New York: Duell, Sloan and Pearce, 1943), 80–99.

47. Giorgio La Piana, "Italian Fascism in America," *Il Mondo*, February 1941.

48. Anti-Fascists priests were as rare as white flies. Perhaps the most prominent was Monsignor Joseph Giarocchi, editor of the Catholic *La Voce del Popolo* in Detroit.

49. Salvemini, *Italian Fascist Activities in the United States*, 145–164.

50. Salvemini, "Mussolini's Empire in the United States," 337; Diggins, *Mussolini and Fascism*, 102.

51. The Italian-American radical press abounds with accounts of such repressive activities.

52. See Gian Giacomo Migone, "Il regime fascista e le comunità italo-americane: la missione di Gelasio Caetani (1922–1925)," in his *Problemi di storia nei rapporti tra Italia e Stati Uniti* (Turin: Rosenberg & Sellier, 1971), 27–29. Also John B. Duff, "The Italians," in Joseph O'Grady, ed., *The Immigrants' Influence on Wilson's Peace Policies* (Lexington, Ky: Univesity of Kentucky Press, 1967), 115–117, 123, 127–133; Alexander De Conde, *Half Bitter, Half Sweet: An Excursion into Italian-American History* (New York: Schribner's & Sons, 1971), 158, 174, 179; Higham, *Stranges in the Land*, 177–178, 234–263, 309–310, 313–319; Monte S. Finkelstein, "The Johnson Act, Mussolini and Fascist Emigration Policy: 1921–1930," *Journal of American Ethnic History* 8, No.1 (Fall 1988): 774–775; Constantine Pannunzio, "Italian Americans, Fascism and the War," *Yale Review* 31 (Summer 1942): 774–775; Ruperto, "Italian Fascism in America," *Il Mondo*, February 1940; Max Ascoli, "On the Italian Americans," *Common Ground* 3, No. 1 (Autumn 1942): 46; Diggins, *Mussolini and Fascism*, passim.

12. Early Anti-Fascist Activities

1. Report of July 3, 1926, ACS, Min., Int., DGPS, DAGR, Anno 1926, b. 102.

2. Report of November 6, 1928, ACS, Min., Int., Divisione Polizia Politica, cat. C-10/7, b. 13, f. 5: "Stati Uniti – Anarchici dal 1928 al 1935."

3. Direttore, Capo Divisione Polizia Politica, to Divisione Affari Generali Riservati, October 22, 1928, in ACS, Min. Int., CPC: Carlo Tresca.

4. Consul General Axerio to Ambassador De Martino, October 10, 1925, in ACS, Min., Int., DGPS, DAGR, Anno 1925, b. 130.

5. *Il Martello*, October 31, 1919; February 12, March 12, 1921; October 21, 1922.

6. Ibid., October 21, 1922; February 17, July 21, 1923.

7. Ibid., June 2, 1923.

8. Minister of the Interior to Minister of Foreign Affairs and to the Prefect of Como, June 12, 1928, in ACS, Min. Int., CPC, Carlo Tresca.

9. Malatesta to Tresca, Rome, October 15, 1923, in *Il Martello*, November 10, 1923.

10. *Il Martello*, February 17, March 3, April 28, May 5, 1923.

11. Ibid., February 17, July 21, 1923.

12. Ibid., December 5, 1926; *The New York Times*, December 3, 1925.

13. *Il Martello*, February 17, July 21, 1923.

14. Consul General of New York to Interior Minister, September 7, 1926, in ACS, *Min., Int.*, DGPS, DAGR, a. 1926, Cat. C-2, b. 102.

15. Vecoli, "The Italian Immigrants in the United States Labor Movement," 304.

16. *New York Evening Journal*, August 18, 1921.

17. *Il Martello*, October 1, 1921.

18. Ibid., September 3, October 1, 8, 1921.

19. Ibid., October 8, 1921.

20. Ibid.

21. Diggins, *Mussolini and America*, 116–117, 122–124, 128; Pellegrino Nazzaro, "Fascist and Anti-Fascist Reaction in the United States to the Matteotti Affair," in Francesco Cordasco, ed., *Studies in Italian American Social History: Essays in Honor of Leonard Covello* (Totowa, NJ: Rowman and Littlefield, 1975), 59–60, 63–64.

22. *Il Martello*, July 23, 1921.

23. On Caetani, see Gian Giacomo Migone, "Il regime fascista e le comunità italo-americane: la missione di Gelasio Caetani (1922–1925), 25–41; Philip V. Cannistraro, "Caetani, Gelasio," in Cannistraro, ed., *Historical Dictionary of Fascist Italy* (Westport, Conn.; Greenwood Press, 1982), 96.

24. *Il Martello*, January 7, 1923.

25. Ibid., December 1, 1919.

26. Nunzio Pernicone, "Carlo Tresca's *Il Martello*," in *The Italian American Review*, 8, No. 1 (Spring/Summer 2001): 13, 27–28, 45, n. 29.

27. Investigator on Assignment to Mussolini, June 6, 1923, in ACS, MCP, b. 163, f. 18, sf. 71/71a.

28. *Il Martello*, September 10, 1921; June 10, October 7, 1922; June 12, 1926.

29. For the cities and towns visited and the letters describing his lectures, see *Il Martello* from October 1922 through April 1923.

30. Ibid., September 24, 1921.

31. Ibid., September 24, 1921; February 10, 1923.

32. Ibid., November 17, 1923.

33. Ibid., November 17, 1923; January 5, 1924.

34. Domenico Saudino, "Il Fascismo alla conquista dell'Ordine Figli d'Italia," *La Parola del Popolo* 11. No. 37 (December 1958–January 1959): 247–254; Salvemini, *Italian Fascist Activities in the United States*, 92–93; Baldo Aquilano, *L'Ordine Figli d'Italia in America* (New York: Società Tipografica Italiana, 1925), 134.

35. *Il Martello*, November 17, 1923.

36. Saudino, "Il Fascismo alla conquista dell'Ordine Figli d'Italia," 247–248; Aquilino, *L'Ordine Figli d'Italia in America*, 135–136; Cannistraro, *Blackshirts in Little* Italy, 19; *Il Martello*, November 17, 1923; *Providence News*, October 29, 1923.

37. Ibid.; Saudino, "Il Fascismo alla conquista dell'Ordine Figli d'Italia," 247–248; Aquilano, *L'Ordine Figli d'Italia in America*, 135–138; Report, Providence office, October 29, Tresca FBI File.

38. Aquilano, *L'Ordine Figli d'Italia in* America, 138–140; Salvemini, *Italian Fascist Activities in the United States*, 93, 97.

39. Italian Ambassador to Ministry of Foreign Affairs, March 25, 1924, ACS, Min., Int. Div. AGR, anno 1924, b. 88.

40. *The New York Times*, April 9, 1923.

41. Ibid., April 9, 11, 1923; Serafino Romualdi, "Storia della Locale 89," in *Local LXXXIX: XV Anniversary* (New York: ILGWU, 1934), 48.

42. *Il Martello*, August 7, 28, 1926; Report of the Questore in Missione to Mussolini, June 6, 1923, ACS, MCP, b. 163, f. 18, sf. 71–71A.

43. Romualdi, "Storia della Locale 89," 47–48; *Il Martello*, April 21, June 9, October 23, 1923.

44. *Il Martello*, April 21, June 9, October 23, 1923.

13. Frame-Up

1. *Il Popolo d'Italia*, October 4, 1922.

2. *Il Martello*, October 21, 1922. Sparafucile is the assassin in Verdi's opera *Rigoletto*.

3. Quoted in *Il Martello*, March 1, 1923. See Benito Mussolini, *Opera omnia*, eds. Edoardo and Duilio Susmel (Florence, 1956), 19: 140–142.

4. Bastianini to Mussolini, March 24, 1924, in ACS, *MCP*, b. 163, f. 18, sf. 71–71A. This and other MCP documents cited below are reproduced among the "Personal Papers of Benito Mussolini, Together with Some Official Records of the Italian Foreign Office and the Ministry of Popular Culture, 1922–1944," in NA, RG 242, T-586, Roll 429.

5. Caetano to Mussolini, January 28–November 26, 1923, in ACS, *MCP*, b. 163, f. 18, sf. 71–71A.

6. *Il Martello*, December 22, 1923, May 23, 1925.

7. Caetani to Mussolini, January 28, 1923, ACS, *Min. Int.*, DGPS, DAGR, a. 1924, cat. J4, b. 88.

8. Hoover to Burns, January 31, 1923, in NA, RG 59, General Records of the Department of State, Office of the Counselor, File no. 865-192. [Hereafter cited as NA, RG 59, DS, OC.]

9. Ibid.

10. Burns to Hurley, February 14, 1923, NA, RG 59mDS, OC, File no. 865-191.

11. Caetani to Foreign Ministry, January 31, 1923, quoted in Foreign Ministry report to Interior Ministry, February 9, ACS, *Min. Int.*, DGPS, AGR, a. 1924, cat. J4, b. 88.

12. Thank you letter from American Ambassador to General Emilio De Bono, Director General of Public Safety, March 3, 1923, ACS, *Min. Int.*, DGPS, AGR, a. 1924, cat. J4, b. 88.

13. "Memorandum in Re: Carlo Tresca," March 6, 1912, Tresca FBI File; Burns to Hurley, March 19, 1923, and Hurley to Andrea Geisser Celesia, Secretary of the Italian Embassy, March 30, 1923, NA, RG 59, DS, OC, File no. 865-172.

14. Interior Ministry to Foreign Ministry, April 18, 1923, ACS, *Min. Int.*, DGPS, CPC: Tresca, Carlo.

15. *Il Martello*, May 5, 1923.

16. Italian Ambassador to U.S. State Department, May 8, 1923, NA, DS, Decimal File [hereafter DF], RG 59, File no. 811.918/175.

17. Ibid.

18. Diggins, *Mussolini and Fascism*, 119, fn. 11.

19. *Il Martello*, September 15, November 17, December 8,1923.

20. So reported the pro-Fascist dailies *Il Progresso Italo-Americano* and *Il Corriere d'America*, as cited in *Il Martello*, December 22, 1923. Official accounts of the meeting described only the progress of Fascism abroad, not its difficulties. See Mussolini, *Opera omnia* 19, 337–338.

21. Quoted in *Il Martello*, August 4, 1923.

22. Quoted in American Civil Liberties pamphlet, *Foreign Dictators of American Rights: The Tresca and Karolyi Cases* (New York: ACLU, June 1925), 3. See also the *New Repuiblic* 37 (January 16, 1924): 188.

23. *Il Martello*, August 4, 1923. Tresca may have known more about Caetani's activities than he acknowledged publicly. As the BI and Italian Embassy would learn to their horror the following year, Tresca had a lawyer friend, Pietro Mancini, who held a clerical position at the Italian Consulate in New York. Somewhat eccentric in nature, Mancini had no radical inclinations and strongly disapproved of Tresca's ideas and associations. Nevertheless, this consular employee, as far back as August 1922, often visited Tresca's office and furnished him with information pertaining to Italians arrested or designated for deportation. Burns to Norman Armour, State Department, April 1, 1924; Report, New York office, April 23, 1924, Tresca FBI File.

24. *Il Martello*, August 18, 1923; Postmaster General to Secretary of State, August 18, 1923, NA, RG 59, DS, DF, File no. 811.918/179; Report, New York office, August 21, 1923, Tresca FBI File.

25. *Il Martello*, September 8, November 10, 14, December 22, 1923; ACLU, *Tresca Case*, 4–5.

26. Solicitor, Department of State, to Mr. Hyde, May 17, 1923, NA, DS, DF, RG 59, File no. 811.918/177.

27. Post Office Inspector C. A. Keen to Inspector in Charge, New York, August 23, 1923; Chief Inspector, Post Office Department, to Burns, August 30, 1923; SPC Edward J. Brennan, New York, to Burns, September 19 and September 21, 1923; Burns to SAC Lawrence Letherman, Boston, September 28, 1923; Burns to SAC R. B. Spencer, Pittsburgh, September 28, 1923; Burns to SAC Edward J. Brennan, New York, September 28, 1923; report, SA Charles M. Hoyt, Boston, October 5, 1923; report, SP Mortimer J. Davis, New York, October 6, 1923; report, SP H. J. Lenon, Pittsburgh, October 12, 1923; report, [name censored], Pittsburgh, November 19, 1923: Tresca FBI File.

28. Report, Pittsburgh, November 19, 1923, Tresca FBI File.

29. Indictment, U.S. Circuit Court of Appeals for the Second Circuit, Carlo Tresca, Plaintiff-in Error against United States of America, Defendant-in-Error: Record on Appeal, Error to the U.S. District Court for the Southern District of New York, No. 8311, p. 10, in National Archives and Records Administration, Northeast Region, New York. [Hereafter NARA]. The Record on Appeal contains the indictment, trial transcript, and other legal documents relating to the case. [The latter will be cited hereafter as NARA, Record on Appeal]. The Appeal decision is also found in NA, Department of Justice, Mail and Files Division, RG 60, File no. 48-51-3-5.

30. Ibid., 7–15; SAC Edward J. Brennan, New York, to Burns, November 1923, Tresca FBI File.

31. *Il Martello*, December 22, 1923; ACLU, *Tresca Case*, 4.

32. Hoover, "Memorandum for Mr. Burns," November 20, 1923; SAC R. B. Spencer, Pittsburgh, to Burns, November 22, 1923; Burns to SAC R. B. Spencer, November 21, 1923; SAC R.B. Spencer, Pittsburgh, to Burns, November 12 and 16, 1923; SAC Edward J. Brennan, New York, to SAC Spencer, November 9, 1923: Tresca FBI File.

33. Trial Transcript, Record on Appeal, 29–62, 90–95.

34. Ibid., 77–83, 97–124.

35. Ibid., 63–65.

36. Ibid., 71.

37. Ibid.

38. Ibid., 65.

39. Ibid., 88–90.

40. Ibid., 95–96.

41. Ibid., 96.

42. Ibid., 136–138.

43. SAC Edward J. Brennan, New York, to Burns, November 28, 1923, Tresca FBI File.

44. Trial Transcript, Record on Appeal, 1.

45. Il Martello, December 22, 1923; ACLU, Tresca Case, 4; SPC Edward J. Brenan, New York, to Burns, November 28, 1923, Tresca FBI File.

46. "Previous Sentences of Birth Control Advocates," U.S. Library of Congress, The Margaret Sanger Papers, reel 10, frame 804. [Hereafter cited as Margaret Sanger Papers.]

47. Il Martello, Deember 22, 1923.

48. Ibid., December 22, 1923.

49. ACLU, Tresca Case, 3; New York World, February 17, 1925. Umberto Nieri, who pleased guilty to violating the mail, was sentenced to six months in the Westchester County Penitentiary and served four.

50. La Guardia to Hughes, January 31, 1924, NA, DS, DF, RG 59, File no. 811.918/191.

51. Hughes to La Guardia, February 29, 1924, NA, DS, DF, RG 59, File no. 811.918/191.

52. U.S. Circuit Court of Appeals for the Second Circuit, Carlo Tresca, Plaintiff-in-error, against the United States of America, Plaintiff-in-error [November 9, 1924], No. 8311, in NARA; also in NA, JD, MFD, RG 60, File no. 48-51-3-5.

53. Tresca to Sanger, New York, January [?] 1925, Margaret Sanger Papers, 10:0825.

54. Il Martello, January 10, 1925.

55. Ibid., January 10, 1925.

56. Ibid., January 10, 24, 1925.

57. SAC Edward J. Brennan, New York, to Director Burns, December 14, 1924, Tresca FBI Papers.

58. Report, Immigration Inspector Charles L. Masek, Immigration Service, District 13, February 10, 1925; District Director, Immigration Service, District 13, to Commissioner of Immigration, Ellis Island [n.d. but attached to previous document], in U.S. Department of Justice, Immigration and Naturalization Service, Tresca File. [Hereafter cited as INS Tresca File.]

59. The New York Times, January 6, 10, 1925.

60. Sanger to Tresca, New York, January 7, 1925, Margaret Sanger Papers, 10:0824.

61. ACLU, Tresca Case, 6; Flynn, The Rebel Girl, 334–335; Margaret Sanger Papers, 10:804-823.

62. The Nation 117 (August 29, 1923): 207; and Ibid., 117 (December 12, 1923): 676.

63. *Il Martello*, January 5, 1924 et seq.

64. *Baltimore Evening Sun*, January 12, 1925.

65. Consul General of Baltimore to Italian Ambassador, January 13, 1925, Archivio del Ministero degli Affari Esteri, Rome, Ambasciata di Washington, 1925–1940, b. 16, fs. 122: "Il Martello."

66. *New Republic* 37 (January 16, 1924): 188.

67. *Baltimore Evening Sun*, January 29, 1925.

68. *New York World*, February 17, 1925.

69. Ibid. .

70. Ibid.

71. District Director of Immigration Service, Atlanta, to Commissioner General of Bureau of Immigration, March 20, 1925, INS Tresca File.

72. Ibid.; Acting Commissioner General, Labor Department, to Attorney General, Department of Justice, April 1, 1925; Chief Attorney, Department of Justice, to Assistant Secretary of Labor, April 8, 1925, in INS Tresca File.

73. Assistant Commissioner General, Department of Labor, Washington, to District Director of Immigration, Atlanta, April 21, 1925, in INS Tresca File.

74. Eastman, "Profile: Trouble Maker – I," 36.

75. Esther Lowell, "Carlo Tresca Home From Jail," *New Leader*, 2, N. 20 (May 16, 1925). Tresca also described his prison experience in a selection from a rare publication that may have been intended to be included in his autobiography. See *I'll Never Forget* (New York: Vanguard Press, 1929), 263–270.

76. Tresca to Sanger, March 17, 1925, Margaret Sanger Papers, 10:0826.

77. Ibid.

78. Ibid.

79. Tresca to Sanger, Atlanta, May 1, 1925, Margaret Sanger Papers, 10:0827.

80. Ibid.

81. Tresca related this episode in *Il Martello*, May 23, 1925. He provided a more detailed account, taken down almost verbatim by a Fascist spy, at a meeting in Cleveland in 1929. See the unsigned spy report, Cleveland, June 30, 1929, ACS, Min., Int., DGPS, DAGR, 1927–1933, Sezione I, Cat. J-4, a. 1929, b. 188.

82. *The New York Times*, May 7, 1925.

83. *New York World*, May 11, 1925.

84. Ibid.

85. Almost a decade later, Tresca indicated that a handshake with Coolidge had occurred but no words were exchanged. See *New York World-Telegram*, December 1, 1933.

86. *Il Martello*, May 23, 1925.

87. *L'Adunata dei Refrattari*, January 5, 1924.

88. Ibid., May 30, 1925.

89. Galleani's letter of May 30, 1925 was not published until thirteen years later, during another phase of the anti-Tresca campaign. See Ibid., May 20, 1938.

90. *Il Martello*, May 30, 1925.

91. Ibid., May 23, 1925.

14. The Resistance Awakens

1. Quoted in Salvemini, *The Fascist Dictatorship in Italy* (New York: Holt, Rinehart and Winston, 1927), 246.

2. Quoted in Seton-Watson, *Italy from Liberalism to Fascism*, 654.

3. Quoted in Giorgio Pini and Duilio Susmel, eds, *Mussolini: l'uomo e l'opera*, 4 vols. (Florence: La Fenice, 1954): vol. 2: *Dal fascismo alla dittatura (1919–1925)*, 409–410.

4. *Il Martello*, June 21, 1924.

5. Ibid., June 21, 28, July 5, 1924; *The New York Times*, June 27, 1924.

6. *Il Martello*, August 30, 1924.

7. Ibid., September 6, 1924.

8. Ibid., September 13, 1924; *The New York Times*, September 16, 17, 1924; Pellegrino Nazzaro, "Fascist and Anti-Fascist Reaction in the United States to the Matteotti Murder," in *Studies in Italian American Social History: Essays in Honor of Leonard Covello*, ed. Francesco Cordasco (Totowa, NJ: Rowman and Little Field, 1975), 50–65.

9. Quoted in Nello Rosselli, *Mazzini e Bakounine: 12 anni di movimento operaio, 1860–1872* (Turin: Fratelli Bocca), 1927), 387.

10. Quoted in *Il Martello*, July 11, 1925.

11. Ibid.

12. Salvemini, *Italian Fascist Activities in the United States*, 14–21,75; Ruperto, "Italian Fascism in America-II," 11–14; Cannistraro, *Blackshirts in Little Italy*, 34–36, 52, 56–109 passim.

13. *Il Martello*, October 24, November 7, 1925; *The New York Times*, October 29, 1925.

14. De Martino to Mussolini, July 3, 1926, ACS, Min. Int., DAGR, anno 1926, cat. C-2, b. 102.

15. Published in 1925 by the Casa Editrice "Il Martello" of New York. Pulcinella was a character in popular Neapolitan comedy.

16. *Il Martello*, November 14, 1925; Charles F. Delzell, *Mussolini's Enemies: The Italian Anti-Fascist Resistance* (Princeton, NJ: Princeton University Press, 1961), 33–34; Adrian Lyttelton, *The Seizure of Power: Fascism in Italy, 1919–1929* (New York: Charles Scribner's Sons, 1973), 267.

17. Tresca, *L'Attentato a Mussolini*, 6–32 passim.

18. De Martino to Mussolini, July 3, 1926, in ACS, Min. Int., DAGR, anno 1926, cat. C-2, b. 102.

19. *Il Martello*, December 26, 1925; *The New York Times*, December 24, 1925. The author was provided with a first-hand account of the episode by his father, Salvatore Pernicone, who produced and directed Tresca's play and performed the role of Farinacci.

20. *Il Martello*, December 26, 1925.

21. Ibid., January 16, 23, 1926; *Il Nuovo Mondo*, January 26, 1926; *The New York Times*, January 26, 1926.

22. De Martino to Mussolini, July 3, 1926, in ACS, Min. Int., DAGR, anno 1926, cat.C-2, b. 102.

23. Ibid.

24. *Il Martello*, March 20, 27, 1926; *Il Nuovo Mondo*, January 29, 1926; *New York World*, March 16, 1926; *The New York Times*, March 16, 1926.

25. *Il Martello*, July 10, 1926; *Il Nuovo Mondo*, July 5, 1926; *The New York Times*, July 5, 1926;

Consul General of New York, Emilio Axerio, to Ministry of the Interior, July 5, 1926, in ACS, Min. Int., DAGR, anno 1926, cat. C-2, b. 102.

26.   Enzo Collotti, "Vittorio Vidali," in Franco Andreucci and Tommaso Detti, eds., *Il movimento operaio italiano: Dizionario biografico* (Rome: Editori Riuniti, 1978), 5, 229–232; Gallagher, *All the Right Enemies*, 137–138; idem, "Revolutionary Requirement, Etc.," *Green Street* 4, No. 2 (Winter 1985): 226–234.

27.   *Il Martello*, June 12, 1926.

28.   Ibid., July 24, 1926; *Il Nuovo Mondo*, July 28, 1926.

29.   *Il Martello*, July 24, 1926.

30.   Ibid.

31.   *Il Nuovo Mondo*, July 28, 1926.

32.   Ibid., August 2, 1926; *Il Martello*, August 7, 1926.

33.   Quoted in *The New York Times*, September 13, 1926 and the *New York Journal*, September 13, 1926. For his failed attempt, Lucetti was sentenced to thirty years of imprisonment.

34.   *The New York Times*, September 13, 1926; *New York Journal*, September 13, 1926, *New York World*, September 13, 1926; *Il Martello*, September 18, 1926; *Il Nuovo Mondo*, September 13, 1926; Consul General of New York to Foreign Ministry, September 17, 1926, in ACS, Min. Int., DAGR, anno 1926, cat. C-2, b. 102.

35.   *New York World*, September 13, 1926.

36.   *Il Martello*, September 18, 1926.

37.   *The New York Times*, September 13, 1926; *New York World*, September 13, 1926; *New York Journal*, September 13, 1926.

38.   *Il Martello*, October 2, 1926.

39.   Findings of the Assistant Medical Examiner included in "Memorandum Re: Tresca," Morris L. Ernst Papers, Humanities Research Center, University of Texas. Also, Consul General of New York to Foreign Ministry, September 17, 1926, in ACS, Min. Int., DAGR, anno 1926, b. 102.

40.   *New York Mirror*, September 22, 1926.

41.   Consul General of New York to Foreign Ministry, September 17, 1926, in ACS, Min. Int., DAGR, anno 1926, Cat. C-2, b. 102.

42.   See the various memoranda and notes relating to the Harlem bombing in the Morris L. Ernst Papers.

43.   *Il Nuovo Mondo*, February 24, 1926; *The New York Times*, February 19, 1926.

44.   *Il Martello*, April 17, May 8, 15, 1926; *Il Nuovo Mondo*, July 4, 9, 1926.

45.   Report of July 25, 1927, NA, RG 59, DS, Decimal File, doc. no. 811.918/204.

46.   Second Assistant Secretary of Labor W.W. Husband to A. Kirk, June 3, 1926, in NA, U.S. Department of Justice, Department of Immigration and Naturalization Service: Carlo Tresca file.

47.   Cenno biografico of Vacirca, in ACS, Min. Int., CPC: Vincenzo Vacirca; *Il Nuovo Mondo*, September 29, 1926; John F. *Romanucci*, "The Italian Labor Press in America," *La Parola del Popolo* 26 (September–October 1976): 226–229; Giuseppe Miccichè, "Vincenzo Vacirca, " *Il movimento operaio italiano: Dizionario biografico*, 5: 160–163.

48.   *Il Martello*, October 23, 1926; *Il Nuovo Mondo*, October 19, 1926. Tresca's remarks quoted in Vidali's letter to *Il Nuovo Mondo*, October 21, 1926.

49.   "Storia di una persecuzione politica," *L'Unità del Popolo* (New York), May 21, 1943; reproduced in Vidali's *Dal Messico a Murmansk* (Milan: Vangelista editore, 1975), 91.

50. Ibid.
51. Consul General of New York to Italian Ambassador, October 20, 1926, in ACS, Min. Int., CPC: Vittorio Vidali; *Il Martello*, November 16, 1926.
52. Consul General of New York to Foreign Ministry, April 2, 1927, in ACS, Min. Int., CPC: Vittorio Vidali.
53. Ibid.
54. Ibid.
55. *Il Martello*, November 6, 1926; *Il Nuovo Mondo*, November 3, 1926.

15. The Anti-Fascist Alliance

1. *Il Martello*, August 7, 1926.
2. *Il Nuovo Mondo*, August 26, 1926. Also reproduced in Nazzaro, "Il manifesro dell'alleanza anti-Fascista del Nord America," 171.
3. *Il Martello*, October 31, November 14, 1925; February 13, April 10, 24, May 29, November 14, 1926.
4. Romualdi, "Storia della Locale 89," 49–50; Benjamin Stolberg, *Tailor's Progress: The Story of a Famous Union and the Men Who Made It* (Garden City, NY: Doubleday, Doran & co., 1944), 108–155; Theodore Draper, *American Communism and Soviet Russia: The Formative Period* (New York: The Viking Press, 1960), 221–233; Irving Howe and Lewis Coser, *The American Communist Party: A Critical History*, 1919–1957 (Boston: Beacon Press, 1957), 245–251; Charles A. Zappia, "Unionism and the Italian American Worker: The Politics of Anti-Communism in the International Ladies' Garment Workers' Union in New York City, 1900–1925," in *The Italian Americans Through the Generations*, ed. Rocco Caporale (New York: The American Italian Historical Association, 1986): 77–91.
5. *Il Martello*, February 13, 1926.
6. Ibid., August 7, 1926; *Il Nuovo Mondo*, September 11, 1926.
7. *The New York Times*, August 1, 1926; *Il Nuovo Mondo*, September 2, 3, 1926.
8. Consul General of New York to Minister of the Interior, August 25, 1926, in ACS, Min. Int., AGR, anno 1926, b. 102.
9. *Il Martello*, November 20, 1926; January 1, 8, 22, 1927.
10. Ibid., January 1, 1927.
11. Ibid.
12. Ibid., August 7, 1926.
13. Ibid., November 20, 1926.
14. Ibid., August 7, November 20, 27, 1926; January 1, 1927.
15. Italian Ambassador to Minister of Foreign Affairs, September 5, 1926, in ACS, Min. Int., AGR, anno 1926, b. 102; *Il Nuovo Mondo*, September 7, 1926.
16. Ibid., September 5, 8, 1926. *Il Nuovo Mondo* provided the most extensive accounts of the congress. See also Vanni Montana, "Il primo congresso della Alleanza Antifascista del Nord America," *La Parola del Popolo* 24 (May–June 1974): 41–42.
17. *Il Nuovo Mondo*, September 5, 1926; *The New York Times*, September 5, 1926.
18. *Il Nuovo Mondo*, September 5, 1926.
19. Ibid.
20. Ibid. September 6, 1926; Consul General of New York to Minister of the Interior,

September 7, 1926, in ACS, Min. Int., AGR, anno 1926, b. 102.

21. Diggins, *Mussolini and Fascism*, 170–173; *Il Nuovo Mondo*, September 6, 1926; New York *World*, September 6, 1926; *The New York Times*, September 6, 1926.

22. *Il Nuovo Mondo*, September 6, 1926.

23. Ibid.; Consul General of New York to Minister of the Interior, September 7, 1926, in ACS, Min., Int., AGR, anno 1926, b. 102.

24. *Il Nuovo Mondo*, September 7, 1926.

25. Ibid.

26. Ibid. September 9, 1926; *Il Martello*, September 11, 1926.

27. *Il Martello*, September 11, 1926.

28. Stolberg, *Tailor's Progress*, 137–142; Romualdi, "Storiale della Locale 89," 51–53; Howe and Coser, *The American Commmunist Party*, 248–251; Irving Howe, *World of Our Fathers* (New York: Simon and Schuster, 1976), 334–335.

29. *Il Nuovo Mondo*, December 23, 1926.

30. *The New York Times*, December 24, 1926.

31. Ibid.

32. Ibid., February 13, 1927; *Il Nuovo Mondo*, February 14, 1927.

33. *Il Martello*, August 7, 1926; January 1, 1927.

34. Ibid., January 1, 1927.

35. Ibid., August 7, 1926; January 1, 1927.

36. Ibid., November 20, 27, 1926; January 1, 8, 1927.

16. A Year of Violence and Death

1. *Il Martello*, March 26, 1927. *Il Nuovo Mondo*, March 22, 1927.

2. Ibid., May 28, 1927.

3. Ibid., March 26, 1927; *Il Nuovo Mondo*, March 22, 1927.

4. *Il Nuovo Mondo*, February 17, March 27, April 10, 1927.

5. Ibid., April 29, 1927; a similar article in *Il Martello*, April 9, 1927.

6. *Il Martello*, May 7, 28, 1927; *Il Nuovo Mondo*, April 16, 27, 30, May 1, 1927. The text is reproduced in *Il Nuovo Mondo*.

7. *Il Martello*, May 14, 21, 1927; *Il Nuovo Mondo*, May 10, 1927; Consul General of New York to Italian Ambassador, May 14, 1927, in ACS, Min. Int., CPC: Tresca; Sworn affidavits of Battista Cazzitarti, Luigi Bloise, and Antonio Barrelli, May 26, 1927, in Morris L. Ernst Paper, Humanities Research Center, University of Texas.

8. *Il Martello*, May 21, 1927; *Il Nuovo Mondo*, May 14, 15, 16, 1927; *The New York Times*, May 15, June 8, 1927; Consul General of New York to Italian Ambassador, May 14, 1927, in ACS, Min. Int., CPC: Tresca.

9. *The New York Times*, May 27, 31, 1927; *New York World*, May 31, 1927; *Il Progresso Italo-Americano*, May 31, 1927; *Il Nuovo Mondo*, 30, 1927; Charles Harrison, *Next Please!: The Story of Greco and Carrillo* (New York: International Labor Defense, 1927), 9.

10. *The New York Times*, May 31, 1927; *New York World*, May 31, 1927; *Il Progresso Italo-Americano* (May 31, 1927.

11. *The New York Times*, June 1, 2, 5, 25, 1927; *Il Progresso Italo-Americano*, June 2, 3, 4, 5, 15, 19, 26, 27, 1927; Fasci Italiani all'Estero, *Trentacinque morti, duecento feriti* (Rome:

n.p, 1930), 34–38.

12. *Il Popolo d'Italia*, May 31, 1927.

13. Mussolini to De Martino, June 1, 1927, in *Archivio Storico dell'Ministero degli Affari Esteri* [hereafter: ASMAE], Fondo Ambasciata di Washington, 1925–1940, b. 61, f. 619: "Incartamento riguardante i Fasci negli Stati Uniti tenute presso S. E. De Martino per le pratiche riservate. [hereafter] IRFSU]"

14. De Martino to Mussolini, June 1, 1927, in ASMAE, Fondo Ambasciata di Washington, 1925–1940, b. 61, f. 619: IRFSU.

15. Ibid.

16. Interview with Luigi Quintiliano, May 7, 1963. The existence of a communist "action group" was confirmed by the Consul General of New York, in his report to Interior Minister of May 14, 1928. See ACS, Min. Int., DAGR, 1927–1933, sez. I, cat. J-4, anno 1929, b. 188. The group went into decline after Vidali's expulsion.

17. Report from Vittorio Vidali, secretary of the Italian Bureau, Mexico City, January 14, 1928 to the Communist Party of America for the party convention of February 1928; also Vidali, "Il movimento communista italiano negli Stati Uniti: Alcune note necessarie," n.d (but late 1928), in Archivio Fondazione Istituto Gramsci [hereafter IG], Roma, Fondo Partito Comunista d'America [hereafter APC], 1917–1940, f. 695/1 and f. 695/41-45.

18. For a more detailed treatment of the Greco-Carrillo case, see Nunzio Pernicone, "Murder Under the 'El'": The Greco Carrillo Case, *The Italian American Review*, 6, No. 2 (Autumn/Winter 1997–1998): 20–44.

19. Emanuele Grazzi to Mussolini, December 24, 1927 and January 14, 1928; Grazzi to Piero Parini, secretary general of the Fasci all'Estero, March 30, 1928, in ACS, Min. Int., DGPS, AGR (1927–1933), a. 1928, sez. III, cat. J-4, b. 206. Also *Il Martello*, August 6, September 3, October 22, November 12, 26, December 24, 1927; *Il Nuovo Mondo*, December 16, 1927; Arthur Garfield Hays, "A Second Sacco-Vanzetti Tragedy Averted," *The Lantern* 1, No. 3 (January 1928): 5–6. Carlo Vinti was often identified mistakenly (even by the pro-Fascist press) as the secretary-general of the Fascist League.

20. *Il Nuovo Mondo*, July 12, 1927; *Il Martelllo*, July 16, 1927; *Il Progresso Italo-Americano*, July 14, 1927.

21. The collaboration between the New York Police Department and the Fascists is proven by the set of Mario Tresca's fingerprints, which the former provided to the latter. They were included in Mario's Italian police dossier. See ACS, Min. Int., CPC: Mario Tresca.

22. Consul General to Mussolini, January 28, 1928, in ibid; *Il Martello*, July 16, 23, October 22, 1927; *Il Nuovo Mondo*, July 13, 1927; *The New York Times*, July 1, 13, 21, 27, 1927; *Il Progresso Italo-Americano*, July 27, 1927; *Evening Graphic* (New York), September 27, 28, 30, 1927; Harrison, *Next Please!*, 19–21; Arthur Garfield Hays, *City Lawyer: The Autobiography of a Law Practice* (New York, 1942), 211–212. For legal documents pertaining to the case, I have consulted the case file of the Bronx District Attorney's office made available to me by Philip V. Cannistraro.

23. Biographical information provided by Valerio Isca. Also *The New York Times*, May 23, December 13, 1927; Consul General of New York to Minister of the Interior, July 24, 1931, and Carrillo's "cenno biografico," in ACS, Mind. Int., DGPS, CPC: Calogero Greco; and CPC: Donato Carrillo.

24. *Il Martello*, April 16, 23, May 28, July 30, August 13, 20, 1927.

25. Ibid., August 20, 1927.

26. Interview with Beatrice Tresca Rapport.

27. Russell, *Tragedy in Dedham*, 410–450.

28. *Il Martello*, August 27, 1927.

29. Ibid., September 3, 1927.

30. Interview with Beatrice Tresca Rapport.

31. *Il Martello*, September 27, 1927; Ettore Frisina, "Why Greco and Carrillo?" *The Labor Defender* 2 (December 1927): 183. This author, although favorable to Greco and Carrillo, was later exposed as a spy.

32. Thaon di Revel to Mussolini, n.d. [end of August], in ASMAE, Serie politica (1919–1930), Stati Uniti, 1927, f. "Walker, Sindaco."

33. Ibid.

34. Thomas, "Reminiscences of Norman Thomas," 84–85; *Il Nuovo Mondo*, December 11, 1927; *Il Martello*, December 10, 1927; Robert Morss Lovett, *All Our Years* (New York: Viking Press, 1948), 191.

35. *Il Martello*, September 3, 1927.

36. Ibid.

37. Ibid.

38. Interview with Peter Martin, New York, December 11, 1973; Harry Fleischman, *Norman Thomas* (New York: Norton & Co., 1964), 110. Another version has Thomas making the phone call and hesitating when Darrow asked for the enormous fee. Tresca then shoved him in the back and ordered him to say yes. See Kevin Tierney, *Darrow: A Biography* (New York: Thomas Y. Crowell, 1979), 388.

39. *Evening Graphic*, September 23, 24, 26, 27, 29, 1927.

40. *The New York Times*, November 3, 1927.

41. *Il Progresso Italo-Americano*, July 14, 1927.

42. *Il Martello*, November 12, 1927. For Linguerri and his photograph, see *Il Progresso Italo-Americano*, July 27, 28, 30, 1927. An original copy of the New York Police Department's bulletin for Linguerri is contained in his CPC file, proving another instance of the police having furnished restricted material to the Fascists.

43. *New York Telegram*, November 15, 1927.

44. Lovett, *All Our Years*, 191.

45. *Il Popolo d'Italia*, December 11, 1927.

46. *The New York Times*, December 19, 1927.

47. Ibid.

48. Ibid., December 13, 1927; *New York World*, December 13, 1927; *Il Nuovo Mondo*, December 13, 1927.

49. *The New York Times*, December 16, 17, 1927; *Il Nuovo Mondo*, December 16, 1927.

50. *The New York Times*, December 17, 20, 1927; *Il Nuovo Mondo*, December 17, 29, 1927.

51. Lovett, *All Our Years*, 191.

52. Clarence Darrow, *The Story of My Life* (New York: Charles Scribner's Sons, 1932), 312.

53. Hays, "A Second Sacco-Vanzetti Tragedy Averted," 5–6.

54. *The New York Times*, December 23, 1927.

55. *Il Martello*, January 7, 1928.

56. Unpublished article (no date) by Giuseppe Popolizio, Tresca's friend and collaborator for thirty years, who was present at the celebration and recorded Darrow's remarks. Article in the author's collection.

57. *Il Popoli d'Italia*, December 25, 1927.
58. Grazzi to Mussolini, January 14, 1928, in ACS, Min. Int., DGPS, AGR, 1927–1933, sez. III, a. 1928, cat. C-2, b. 192.
59. Grazzi to Parini, March 30, 1928, in Ibid.
60. Soliciter's memoranda of May 22 and June 12, 1929, quoted in Cannistraro, *Blackshirts in Little Italy*, 103.
61. Cannistraro, *Blackshirts in Little Italy*, 103–104.
62. *Harper's Magazine* 159 (November 1929): 661–762.
63. *Il Martello*, December 29, 1929.
64. Cannistraro, *Blackshirts in Little Italy*, 102–109.

17. Troubled Times for Anti-Fascism

1. *Il Martello*, December 5, 1931.
2. Egidio Clemente, "Radicalismo italiano negli Stati Uniti," unpublished essay written in September 1978, in the author's possession. Clemente was the FSI's national secretary from 1929–1941, and the director of the post-World War II journal *La Parola del Popolo*.
3. Montana, *Amarostico*, 129–130; Bénédicte Deschamps, "Il Lavoro: The Italian Voice of the Amalgamated, 1915–1932," *Italian American Review* 8, No. 1 (Spring/Summer 2001): 109–110; Gerald Meyer, "L'Unità del Popolo: The Voice of Italian American Communism, 1939–1951," in Ibid., 121 et passim; Fraser M. Ottanelli, "'If Fascism Comes to America We Will Push It Back into the Ocean': Italian American Antifascism in the 1920s and 1930s," in Donna R. Gabaccia and Fraser M. Ottanelli, eds. *Italian World of the World: Labor Migration and the Formation of Multiethnic States* (Urbana and Chicago: University of Illinois Press, 2001), 186.
4. *Il Martello*, August 28, 1934.
5. Ministry of Foreign Affairs to Ministry of the Interior, March 1931, in ACS, Min. Int., DAGR, anno 1930–1931, sez. I, b. 384.
6. Rudolph J. Vecoli, "The Making and the Un-Making of the Italian American Working Class," in Cannistraro and Meyers," eds., *The Lost World of Italian American Radicalism*, 53–55, et passim. See also Salvemini, *Italian Fascist Activities in the United States,* 91ff; Montana, *Amarostico*, 116–117, 157.
7. Denis Mack Smith, *Italy: A Modern History*, Rev. ed. (Ann Arbor: The University of Michigan Press, 1969), 440–443.
8. *Il Martello*, March 23, 1929.
9. Ibid., February 25, September 22, 1928.
10. Ibid., March 10, 1928.
11. Ibid., February 25, 1928.
12. Ibid., February 25, March 3, 10, 1928.
13. Ibid., March 3, 1928.
14. Consul General of New York to Italian Ambassador, November 22, 1928, in ACS, Min. Int., Div. AGR, 1927–1933, Sez. III, Anno 1928, b. 192.
15. *Il Martello*, June 8, 1929.
16. Ibid.

17. Ibid., December 7, 1929.
18. Ibid., September 22, 1928; December 7, 1929.
19. Ibid., January 16, 1932.
20. Consul General of New York to Italian Ambassador, July 21, 1931, in ACS, Min. Int. Div. AGR, anno 1930–1931, Sez. I, Cat. J-4-1, b. 398.
21. *Il Martello*, June 8, 1929.
22. Ibid., February 1, 1930.
23. Ibid., December 12, 1931.
24. Vittorio Vidali, "Il movimento comunista italiano degli Stati Uniti: Alcune note necessario," n.d. [but late 1928], in IG, APC, 1917–1940, f. 695/41-42.
25. Report from Vittorio Vidali, secretary of the Italian Bureau, to the Communist Party of America for the party convention of February 1928: "Attività svolte dal marzo 1926 al giugno 1927," Mexico City, January 14, 1928, in IG, APC, f. 695/1.
26. *Il Lavoratore*, March 3, September 22, 1928, as cited in Luciano J. Iorizzo and Salvatore Mondello, *The Italian-Americans* (New York: Twayne Pubs., 1971), 201, 249.
27. *Il Martello*, March 19, 1932.
28. Ibid., November 13, 1926.
29. *L'Adunata dei Refrattari*, November 6, 13, 20, 27, 1926; January 8, 22; February 10; March 12, 1927.
30. After World War II, the *L'Adunatisti* ostracized Borghi because they disapproved of politics and his private life, namely, the woman he had chosen for his companion. Interview with Valerio Isca, June 5, 1975; Sam Dolgoff, *Fragments: A Memoir* (Cambridge, MA: Refract Publications, 1986), 33.
31. Ralph Piesco, in *Il Martello*, August 31, 1929.
32. Ibid., December 7, 1929.
33. Ibid., December 11, 1926; September 22, 1928; December 7, 1929.
34. *L'Adunata*, February 25, 1928.
35. Ibid., March 31, 1928.
36. Ibid., May 19, 1928. The *Galleanisti* who signed the declaration were Girolamo Grasso (Hartford), Giovanni Scussel (Needham, M.A.), Tony Mascioli (Old Forge, P.A.), Domenico Rosati (New York), Frank Guida (New York), Ilario Bettolo (Chicago). Also *L'Adunata dei Refrattari*, June 2, 16, 1928.
37. Letter quoted in *Il Martello*, August 11, 1928.
38. Osvaldo Maraviglia to Alexander Berkman, Newark, N.J., July 6, 1928, and Berkman to Maraviglia, New York, November 19, 1928, in the Berkman Archive, International Institute of Social History, Amsterdam. Information provided to author by Paul Avrich.
39. *L'Adunata dei Refrattari*, January 11, 1930.
40. Ibid.
41. *Il Martello*, March 3, 17, 31, 1928.
42. Ibid., May 23, 1925; October 23, 30, 1926; February 11, 18; March 3, 17, 31; April 14; May 26; June 2, 9, 16, 23, 30; July 7, 1928.
43. *L'Adunata dei Refrattari*, June 2, 16, 23; July 7, 21, 28; August 11; September 1; October 6, 1928.
44. *Il Martello*, February 8, 1930.
45. *L'Adunata*, June 14, July 5, 1930, September 2, 1933.
46. Divisione Polizia Politica, note of June 28, 1928, in ACS, Min.Int., DGPS, CPC, Carlo

Tresca, b. 5208.

47. Direttore, Capo Divisione Polizia Politica to Divisione Affari Generali Riservati, October 22, 1928, in ibid.

48. Ibid.

49. *Il Martello*, June 2, 1928.

50. Ibid., June 30, 1928.

51. Saudino, *Sotto il segno del Littorio*, vol. 2: *Le attivita del fascismo negli Stati Uniti* (unpublished manuscript), 27–38.

52. *Il Martello*, December 29, 1928.

53. Ibid.

54. Ibid., January 12, 26, February 9, 1929; Saudini, *Sotto il segno del Littorio*, vol. 2, 27–28; *The New York Times*, January 6, 1929.

55. *Il Martello*, November 14, 1931.

56. Ibid.

57. Saudino, *Sotto il segno del Littorio*, 38; *The New York Times*, November 16, 1931.

58. *Il Martello*, November 21, December 5, 1931; *The New York Times*, November 16, 1931; *Daily Worker*, November 16, 1931.

59. *Il Martello*, November 21, 1931.

60. *The New York Times*, November 21, 1931.

61. Ibid., November 23, 1931.

62. Ibid.

63. Ibid., November 23, 1931; *Il Martello*, December 5, 1931.

64. *Il Martello*, December 5, 1931; Saudino, *Sotto il segno del Littorio*, 41.

65. *Il Martello*, December 5, 1931; *The New York Times*, November 16, 1931.

66. *The New York Times*, December 31, 1931; January 1, 1932; Philadelphia *Evening Bulletin*, December 30, 1931; and scores of documents in the FBI's file on Raffaele Schiavina.

67. Memo by E. Nathan, Bureau of Investigation, for Director J. Edgar Hoover, December 31, 1931.

68. Assistant Director FBI to Chief, Division of Eastern European Affairs, State Department, January 8, 1932; FBI Memorandum for the Director, January 9, 1932; Memo marked N.Y. 60-3013, n.d., in FBI File: Schiavina.

69. Mentana, *Amorostico*, 118–119. Montana observed the exchange from a window in the office of *La Stampa Libera* across the street, and heard the details from comrades who were in the office. For the interview, see *New York World-Telegram*, December 1, 1933.

70. In response to a request for Schiavina's FBI file, the author received instead several hundreds documents pertaining to the bombing. That the FBI connected the bombing with *L'Adunata* was obvious.

71. Reports of Special Agent L. G. Turrou, New York, for Director Hoover, January 18 and 29, 1932, in Schiavina FBI File.

72. The Ugo Fedeli Papers at the Internationaal Instituut voor Sociale Geschiedenis in Amsterdam contains a three-way correspondence between Fedeli, Di Giovanni, and Schiavina, discussing the use of terrorism.

73. *Omaggio*, 36; *The New York Times*, July 6, 1932.

74. *The New York Times*, July 8, 15, 1932.

75. Ibid., July 12, 18, 20, 21, 27, 30; September 8; October 6, 12, 15, 18, 20, 21, 22, 26, 27, 29, 1932; *Omaggio*, 36; Montana, *Amorostico*, 122–123; Saudino, *Sotto il segno del Littorio,*

2: 86.

76. *The New York Times*, July 15, 1933. For a succinct account of the case, see Diggins, *Mussolini and Fascism*, 131–132.

77. Montana, *Amorostico*, 124–125.

78. Ibid., 125–126; *Omaggio*, 3; *The New York Times*, July 15, 16, 1932; John Herling and Morris Shapiro, *The Terzani Case: An Account of a Labor Battle Against a Fascist Frame-Up* (New York: League for Industrial Democracy [1934]), 3–5; John Nicolas Beffel, "Memorandum for Dr. John P. Diggins about Carlo Tresca," [hereafter Beffel, "Memo to Diggins] New York University, Tamiment Institute Library, John Nicholas Beffel Papers, box 2.

79. Ibid; Herling and Shapiro, *The Terzani Case*, 4–7.

80. *The New York Times*, August 29, 31; October 13, November 5; December 12, 13, 14, 19, 1933; January 3, February 7, 8, 9, 14; March 22, 24, 31; April 12, 13, 14, 28, 1934; Herling and Shapiro, *The Terzani Case*, 6–12; Beffel, "Memo to Diggins"; Diggins, *Mussolini and Fascism*, 132.

18. The Depression and the New Deal

1. Many of Tresca's articles on these themes were written under the pseudonym of "Renato Morganti."

2. *Il Martello*, November 10, 1929.

3. Ibid., January 30, February 15, November 8, 16, 29, December 6, 1930; March 19, April 23, 1932.

4. Ibid., October 3, 1931.

5. Ibid., November 29, 1930.

6. Ibid., March 19, 1929; December 6, 1930; April 4, May 16, 1931. See also Sidney Lens, *The Labor Wars: From the Molly Maguires to the Sitdowns* (Garden City, NY: Anchor Books, 1974), 281–282.

7. *Il Martello*, March 17, 1928; February 1, 1930; July 11, August 1, 1931; Lens, *The Labor Wars*, 263–275.

8. *Il Martello*, December 12, 1931.

9. Ibid., August 2, 1930.

10. Tresca to Marget Sanger [n.d. but mid- or late 1930], in the Margaret Sanger Papers, 10:0872.

11. *Il Martello*, February 15, 1930.

12. Ibid.

13. Ibid.

14. Ibid., February 15, March 1, 1930. In Tresca's letter to Sanger, cited above, he claimed that the strike had been victorious. This was an idle boast, expressing wishful thinking, not reality.

15. *Il Martello*, July 4, 11, August 1, 1931

16. Ibid., August 1, 1931.

17. Ibid., September 14, 1929.

18. Tresca to Sanger, [n.d. but early 1930], in Sanger Papers, 10:0870.

19. For a copy of the invitation, see Margaret Sanger Papers, 10:834.

20. *Il Martello*, August 2, 1930; June 6, September 19, 1931; January 2,9, 1932.

21. Consul General of New York to Minister of the Interior, April 30, 1932, in ACS, Min. Int., DGPS, CPC: Tresca, Carlo.

22. Pasquale Scipione, *La conquista della felicità: Intorno al revisionismo anarchico* (n.p.: n.p., n.d. [but after 1934], 86–91; Interview with Beatrice Tresca Rapport; *Il Martello*, January 27, February 10, March 31, 1934. From July to November 1934, the newspaper included a page in English edited by the Vanguard Group, most of whom were young Jewish anarchist friends of Tresca's, such as Sam Dolgoff.

23. *Il Martello*, January 27, February 24, June 14, 1934.

24. See Samuel Yellen, *American Labor Struggles: 1877–1934* (New York: Monad Press, 1974), 327–353; Sidney Lens, *The Labor Wars; From the Molly Maguires to the Sitdowns* (Garden City, NY: Doubleday Anchor, 1974), 283–304.

25. *Il Martello*, August 28, 1934.

26. Ibid.

27. Ibid., February 28, 1935.

28. Ibid., August 28, 1934; February 28, March 28, 1935.

29. Ibid., May 28, 1935.

30. Ibid.

31. Ibid., February 28, 1936.

32. Ibid., July 14, 1936.

33. Ibid., June 28, 1937.

34. See Lens, *The Labor Wars*, 332–375; Rayback, *A History of American Labor*, 351–355.

35. *Il Martello*, June 28, 1937.

36. Ibid.

37. Ibid., March 7, 14, May 9, 1938; Lens, *The Labor Wars*, 380–381.

19. Fascism on the March

1. *Il Vendicatore: Dramma Antifascista* (New York: Il Martello, 1934).

2. For Pope, see Diggins, *Mussolini and Fascism*, 84–86; Philip Cannistraro, "Generoso Pope and the Rise of Italian American Politics, 1925–1936," in Lydio F. Tomasi, ed., *Italian Americans: New Perspectives in Italian Immigration and Ethnicity* (Staten Island, NY: Center for Migration Studies, 1985), 264–288.

3. *Il Martello*, November 14, 1934.

4. Ibid., October 28, 1934.

5. Ibid.

6. Ibid., November 14, 1934.

7. Unpublished "Memorandum Re: Assassination of Carlo Tresca," 1943. Unsigned, the memorandum was written by Girolamo Valenti, the former director of *La Stampa Libera*, who himself was a target of Pope's emissaries. A copy was furnished to the author by Luigi Quintiliano. Other copies are available in the Tresca Memorial Committee Papers at the New York Public Library, and in the John D. Nicholas Papers at the Tamiment Library at New York University.

8. Ibid.

9. Quoted in *Il Martello*, November 14, 1934.

10. Ibid.

11. Ibid., March 28, August 31, September 14, 1935.

12. Ibid., August 31, 1935.

13. Ibid., July 16, August 31, September 14, 28, 1935.

14. Ibid., August 31, September 14, 28, 1935.

15. Ibid., September 14, 1935.

16. Ibid., July 16, 1935.

17. See Salvemini, *Italian Fascist Activities in the United States*, 199–208; Fiorello Ventresco, "Italian-Americans and the Ethiopian Crisis," *Italian Americana* 6, No. 1 (Fall/Winter 1980): 4–27, 1–13; Salvatore J. LaGumina, "African-American and Italian-American Relations in the Light of the Harlem Riots of 1935," in Dan Ashyk, Fred L. Guardaphé, and Anthony Julian Tamburri, eds. *Shades of Black and White: Conflict and Collaboration Between Two Communities* (Staten Island, NY: Italian American Historical Association, 1999), 122–133.

18. On the distortions and outright lies that appeared in Pope's publications, see Eleanor Clark, "The Press Goes to War," *The New Republic* 84, No. 1092 (November 6, 1935): 356–357.

19. *Il Martello*, May 14, July 16, September 14, 28, October 14, 28, 1935, November 14, 29, 1935; January 14, 28, February 28, March 14, April 14, 1936.

20. Ibid., October 28, 1935.

21. Ventresco, "Italian-Americans and the Ethiopian Crisis," 14.

22. *Il Martello*, April 14, 1936.

23. Ibid., October 28, 1935.

24. Ibid.

25. Salvemini, *Italian Fascist Activities in the United States*, 199–208; Diggins, *Mussoloni and Fascism*, 305.

26. Diggins, *Mussolini and Fascism*, 302–306.

27. Salvemini, *Italian Fascist Activities in the United States*, 205; Diggins, *Mussolini and Fascism*, 302–303.

28. *Il Martello*, December 14, 1935.

29. Ibid.

30. Ibid., December 14, 1935; January 14, 1936.

31. Salvemini, *Italian Fascist Activities in the United States*, 207–208.

32. *Il Martello*, May 14, 1936.

33. Philip V. Cannistraro and Brian R. Sullivan, *Il Duce's Other Woman* (New York: William Morrow, 1993), 482–483. Mussolini's victory speech was widely distributed on recordings still available today.

34. See Robert Preston, *The Spanish Civil War, 1936–1939* (Chicago: Dorsey Press, 1986, 73–76; Dante A. Puzzo, *Spain and the Great Powers 1936–1941* (New York: Columbia University Press, 1962), 65–67.

35. *Il Martello*, October 14, 1936.

36. Ibid., January 14, 1937.

37. Ibid.

38. The degree to which the *Daily Worker* was a repository of Soviet propaganda and false information about the Spanish Civil War was remarkable. Fascist forces were depicted as having been "routed" so many times, one wonders how the Republic lost the war.

39. *Il Martello*, September 14, 1936; June 14, 1937.

40. Camillo Berneri, *Pensieri e battaglie* (Paris: Comitato Camillo Berneri, 1938), 236–238; Umberto Calosso, "La battaglia di Monte Pelato," in Ernesto Rossi, ed., *No al Fascismo* (Venice: Einaudi editore,1956), 239–253; *Il Martello*, September 14, October 14, 1936.

41. For Italy's participation, see John F. Coverdale, *Italian Intervention in the Spanish Civil War* (Princeton: Princeton University Press, 1975).

42. *Il Martello*, January 28, 1937.

43. Ibid. Despite the date, this issue was published after the fall of Malaga on February 8, 1937. Most issues of *Il Martello* in this period were published after the date indicated in the newspaper because of production problems.

44. Malcolm Muggeridge, ed., *Ciano's Hidden Diary* (New York: E.P. Dutton, 1953), 4, 91.

45. *Documents on German Foreign Policy 1918–1945*, Series D (1937–1945), 3 vols, "Germany and the Spanish Civil War 1936–1939" (Washington, D.C.: U.S. Government Printing Office, 1954): 2, 261, et passim. For the Garibaldi Battalion (later a Brigade), see Randolfo Pacciardi, *Il Battaglione Garibaldi: volontari italiani nella Spagna Repubblicana* (Lugano: Edizioni di Capolago, 1938).

46. *Il Martello*, March 14, 1937.

47. Tresca to Alberto Meschi, n.d, in Internationaal Instituut voor Sociale Geschiedenis, Amsterdam, Meschi Papers. Meschi's handwritten notation indicates that he replied to Tresca from France on May 19, 1937.

20. Taking on the Stalinists

1. Alan M. Wald, *The New York Intellectuals: The Rise and Decline of the Anti-Stalinist Left from the 1930s to the 1960s* (Chapel Hill: North Carolina University Press, 1987).

2. *Il Martello*, September 14, 1934.

3. Sam Dolgoff, ed., *The Anarchist Collectives* (New York: Free Life Editions, 1974).

4. Vernon Richard, *Lessons of the Spanish Revolution (1936–1939)* (London: Freedom Press, 1953), 22–30.

5. *Il Martello*, August 14, 1936.

6. Ibid., August 28, 1936.

7. Ibid., August 28, October 28, 1936.

8. Stated in his interview with the *Paris-Midi*, quoted in *Il Martello*, September 28, 1936.

9. Quoted in Brenan, *The Spanish Labyrinth* (London: Cambridge University Press, 1974), 328; and Felix Morrow, *Revolution and Counter-Revolution in Spain* (New York: Pioneer Publshers, 1938), 67.

10. Reproduced in full in Dante A. Puzzo, *The Spanish Civil War* (New York: Van Nostrand, 1969), 139–141.

11. Ibid., 141.

12. *Il Martello*, August 14, 28, 1936.

13. Puzzo, *Spain and the Great Powers*, 141–148.

14. The name of the Soviet secret police was changed from OGPU to NKVD in 1934, but most activists still used the term OGPU.

15. Bolletin, *The Spanish Civil War* (Chapel Hill, University of North Carolina Press, 1991), 133–134, 219–221, et passim; Broué and Témine, *The Revolution and the Civil*

War in Spain (Cambridge: MIT Press, 1970), 229; Thomas, *The Spanish Civil War,* rev. ed. (New York: Harper & Row, 1977), 323, 340, 434, 705; Isaac Deutscher, *Stalin: A Political Biography* (New York: Oxford University Press, 1967), 423–425. For Berneri, see also *Memoria antologica saggi scritti e appunti biografici in ricordo di Camillo Berneri nel cinquantesimo della morte* (Pistoia: Archivio Famiglia Berneri, 1986); Antonio Zambonelli, "Camillo Berneri," in *Il movimento operaio italiano italiano: dizionario biografico* (Rome: Editori Riuniti, 1975): 1, 254–258.

16. *Guerra di Classe* (Barcelona), December 16, 1936. For Berneri's murder, see Supplemento al N. 15, *Guerra di Classe,* May 9, 1937; *Il Martello,* May 28, 1937. Also, Augustin Souchy, *The Tragic Week in May* (Barcelona: Edición de la Oficina de Información Exterior de la CNT y FAI, 1937), 18–19; Felix Morrow, *Revolution and Counter-Revolution in Spain* (New York: Pioneer Publishers, 1938), 78–102. Interview with Frank Brand (Enrico Arrigoni), New York, May 15, 1974, who identified Berneri's body at the city morgue. An alternate theory posited by Carlos Rama suggests that Berneri's murder was perpetrated by Franco fifth columnists, disguised as PSUC agents, on orders from the OVRA, the Italian secret police. See Bolletin, *The Spanish Civil War,* 876.

17. *Il Martello,* May 28, June 14, 28, July 14, 1937.

18. Ibid., May 28, June 14, August 14, 1937.

19. Ibid., March 7, 14, 1938. For Mink, see also Benjamin Gitlow, *The Whole of Their Lives* (New York: Scribners, 1948), 343; Whittaker Chambers, *Witness* (New York: Random House, 1952), 302–303.

20. Interview with Jack Frager, New York, November 24, 1974. Frager, a Russian Jewish anarchist, repeated numerous times at meetings of the Libertarian Book Club in the early 1970s that Tresca had saved his life by dissuading him from going to Spain, as he had others.

21. Herbert L. Matthews, *Half of Spain Died: A Reappraisal of the Spanish Civil War* (New York: Schribner's, 1973), 120–121.

22. Quoted in an FBI interview with Ribarich regarding Vidali, June 21, 1956. See Vidali FBI File.

23. John Dos Passos, *The Theme is Freedom* (New York: Dodd, Mead & Co., 1956), 116–118.

24. The Committee was also known as the Commission of Inquiry into the Charges against Leon Trotsky in the Moscow Trials.

25. See *Not Guilty: Report of the Commission of Inquiry Into The Charges Made Against Leon Trotsky In The Moscow Trials* (New York: 1938); Isaac Deutscher, *The Prophet Outcast: Trotsky: 1929–1940* (New York: Vintage Books, 1963), 371–382; "Report on the Work of the American Committee for the Defense of Leon Trotsky, submitted by the Secretary (n.d.), Executive Committee "Report to the Members on the Work of the American Committee for the Defense of Leon Trotsky (c. April 1938), and John Dewey, *Truth Is On The March: Reports and Remarks on the Trotsky Hearings in Mexico* (New York: ACDLT, 1936). The last three items are among the Margaret De Silver Papers held by Burnham and Claire De Silver. See also Alan Wald, "Herbert Solow: Portrait of a New York Intellectual," *Prospects: An Annual of American Cultural Studies,* No. 3 (1977): 440–443.

26. Max Shachtman, "Radicalism in the Thirties: The Trotskyist View," in Rita James Simon, ed., *As We Saw the Thirties: Essays on Social and Political Movements of a Decade* (Urbana,

Il: University of Illinois Press, 1967), 40; interview with Nancy MacDonald, New York, May 12, 1974.

27. Margaret De Silver to Leon Trotsky, October 13, 1937, in Leon Trotsky Papers, Houghton Library, Harvard University, bms Russ 13.1 (n. 759). Margaret's self-description was confirmed by her daughter-in-law Claire De Silver in a letter of July 13, 1996.

28. Trotsky to De Silver, Mexico City, October 23, 1937, in Margaret De Silver Papers cited above.

29. *Daily Worker*, April 3, 1937.

30. Ibid., April 10, 1937; Report from the American Committee For The Defense of Leon Trotsky, March 12, 1938, in the Margaret De Silver Papers cited above.

31. *Daily Worker*, April 19, 1937.

32. Theodore Draper, *The Roots of American Communism* (New York: Viking Press, 1957), 193.

33. Ibid.; Gitlow, *The Whole of Their Lives*, 331–334; Carlo Tresca, "Where Is Juliet Stuart Poyntz?" *The Modern Monthly* (March 1938): 12; Herbert Solow, "Missing A Year: Where is Julia Poyntz?," *New Leader*, June 30, 1938; Alan Weinstein, *Perjury: The Hiss-Chamber Case* (New York: Knopf, 1978), 310; Harvey Klehr, "Juliet Stuart Poyntz," in Bernard K. Johnpoll and Harvey Klehr, eds. *The Biographical Dictionary of the American Left* (Westport, CN: Greenwood Press, 1986), 317–318.

34. *The New York Times*, December 18, 19, 1937.

35. Ibid., February 8, 1938.

36. Ibid., February 8, 9, 1938; Herbert Solow, "Missing A Year: Where is Julia Poyntz?"

37. *The New York Times*, February 8, 1938.

38. Ibid., February 9, 15, 22; March 7, 1938.

39. *Daily Worker*, February 10, 1938.

40. Ibid.

41. Ibid., February 14, 1938.

42. Ibid.

43. Quoted in Ibid.

44. *L'Unità Operaia*, February 28, 1938, as quoted in *Who Killed Carlo Tresca?* (New York: Tresca Memorial Committee, 1945), 12–13.

45. *Il Martello*, March 7, 1938.

46. Ibid., April 11, 1938.

47. Pietro Allegra, *Il suicidio morale di Carlo Tresca* (New York: n.p., 1938), 3.

48. *Il Martello*, October 17, 1938.

49. Trotsky to De Silver, March 31, 1938, the Margaret De Silver Papers (Burnham and Claire De Silver).

50. *Il Martello*, August 29, 1938.

51. Interviews with Burnham and Claire De Silver, July 15, 1975, and Beatrice Tresca Rapport; Eastman, "Profile: Trouble Maker-I," 34.

52. *Il Martello*, April 11, 1938. For the English original, see Gallagher, *All the Right Enemies*, 173–174.

53. *L'Adunata dei Refrattari*, May 7, 1938.

54. Ibid.

55. Ibid., October 22, 1938.

56. *Il Martello*, May 9, 1938.

57. Ibid., July 11, 1938.
58. Ibid., September 12, 1938.
59. Ibid., October 17, 1938.
60. Tresca to Meschi, n.d. but December 1938, in Albert Meschi Papers, IISG.
61. *Il Martello*, December 28, 1939.
62. Interviews with the anarchists Sam Dolgoff (December 8, 1973) and Valerio Isca (June 5, 1975).

21. The Town Anarchist

1. *New York World-Telegram*, December 1, 1933.
2. Ibid.; *New York Post*, October 12, 1934; *The New Yorker* 10, Nos. 31 and 32 (September 15 and 29, 1934).
3. *New York Post*, October 12, 1934.
4. *Omaggio*, 44.
5. Ibid., 42.
6. Interview with Beatrice Tresca Rapport.
7. Interview with Beatrice Tresca Rapport.
8. Max Eastman, "Profile [Carlo Tresca]: Troublemaker II," *New Yorker* 10, No. 32 (September 22, 1934): 26–27.
9. Interview with Beatrice Tresca Rapport. Beatrice also related this exchange to Dorothy Gallager (*All the Right Enemies*, 40).
10. Interview with Beatrice Tresca Rapport; FBI report, Pittsburgh, May 15, 1923, and FBI summary report, January 30, 1946, in Tresca FBI File.
11. Interview with Beatrice Tresca Rapport; Giuseppe Popolizio to the author, November 10, 1978.
12. Giuseppe Popolizio to the author, November 10, 1978. Also, a copy of his article "Commenti ad una ribalderia: Testimonianze sull'opera di Tresca, in *Controcorrente*, March 1950.
13. Popolizio to the author, May 6, 1978.
14. Interview with Luigi Quintiliano; Interview with Alberto Cupelli, New York, February 28, 1974; Interview with Sam and Esther Dolgoff, December 8, 1973.
15. These names were culled from numerous articles in *Il Martello* and from dozens of Fascist police reports. See especially Consul General of New York to Ministry of the Interior, July 24, 1931, in ACS, Min. Int., DGPS, CPC: Tresca, Carlo.
16. Interview with Quintiliano.
17. Interview with Quintiliano; Interview with Beatrice Tresca Rapport.
18. Interview with Vincenzo Alvano; Interview with Alberto Cupelli.
19. Allegra, *Il suicidio morale di Carlo Tresca*, 3.
20. Ibid., 3–6.
21. Interview with Beatrice Tresca Rapport; Popolizio to the author, November 10, 1978.
22. Popolizio to the author, May 6 and November 10, 1978.
23. For example, Defense Committee to Tresca, Boston, June 30, 1927, in BPL, Felicani Collection, ms. 2030.2A.
24. Popolizio to the author, May 6, 1978; Interview with Luigi Quintiliano.

25. *Il Martello*, August 2, 1930; June 6, September 19, 1931; January 2, 9, May 7, 1932.

26. Untitled typewritten article, no date, perhaps published originally in *Controcorrente*.

27. Popolizio, "Commenti ad una ribalderia."

28. Interview with Sam and Esther Dolgoff.

29. The author's father, Salvatore Pernicone, observed Tresca do this on many occasions.

30. Dolgoff, *Fragments*, 34.

31. Flynn, *The Rebel Girl*, 333.

32. "Thoughts of Tresca at S. Beach, 1917 to 1925," and "South Beach (after 14 years) 1925–1939." These and other poems by Flynn were provided to the author by a former student at Barnard, Masie Smith, who in turn obtained them from Rosalind Baxindall. At the time they were on deposit with Flynn's other papers at the American Institute of Marxist Studies, where scholars gained access only with extreme difficulty. They are now on deposit at the Tamiment Institute Library.

33. Flynn, *The Rebel Girl*, 335.

34. Flynn to Vorse, September 11, 1926, as quoted in Camp, *Iron In Her Soul*, 119, and in Gallagher, *All The Right Enemies*, 117.

35. Interview with Tresca's son, Peter Martin, New York, December 11, 1973. Also, Camp, *Iron in the Soul*, 113.

36. Interview with Peter Martin.

37. *Il Proletario*, November 3, 1920.

38. Interview with Peter Martin.

39. Camp, *Iron In Her Soul*, 111–137; Gallagher, *All the Right Enemies*, 113–121, 123–125.

40. Interview with Beatrice Tresca Rapport; Gitlow, *The Whole of Their Lives*, 338.

41. Gitlow, *The Whole of Their Lives.*, 339.

42. Gallagher, *All the Right Enemies*, 122.

43. Interviews with Carll Harrison De Silver, New York, November 30, 1973; Burnham De Silver and his wife Claire, New Canann, CT, July 15, 1975; Beatrice Tresca Rapport.

44. Montana, *Amorostico*, 221.

45. Interviews with Beatrice Tresca Rapport and Peter Martin; Gallagher, *All the Right Enemies*, 148.

46. Interview with Harrison De Silver.

47. Interview with Harrison De Silver.

48. Interview with Nancy MacDonald, New York, May 24, 1974.

49. For additional details on this phrase of Tresca's private life, see Gallagher, *All the Right Enemies*, 148–149, 179–180.

22. Tresca and World War II

1. *Il Martello*, May 28, 1934; January 28, 1935; August 29, 1938; April 28, May 28, 1939.

2. Ibid., April 25, 1938.

3. Ibid.

4. Ibid., September 5, 12, 1938.

5. Ibid., September 12, 19, 1938.

6. Ibid., January 28, February 14, 1939.

7. Ibid., February 28, 1940.

8.   Ibid., May 14, 1940.

9.   Ibid., July 28, 1942.

10. Ibid., September 12, 1938.

11. Ibid., March 14, 1937; February 28, September 14, 1940; April 28, June 14, 28, October 14, 1941.

12. Ibid., June 14, 1941.

13. Ibid., February 28, March 14, April 14, 1940. See *Daily Worker*, December 1, 1939.

14. Ibid., June 14, 1940.

15. Ibid.

16. Ibid., November 1940.

17. Ibid., January 14, 1941.

18. Quoted in Gaetano Salvemini, *The Fascist Dictatorship in Italy* (New York: Holt, Rinehart and Winston, 1927), 9.

19. Charles Killinger, *Gaetano Salvemini: A Biography* (Westport, CN: Praeger, 2002), 288.

20. Ibid., January 14, 1943.

21. *Il Martello*, January 14, February 28, 1941.

22. Ibid., January 14, February 28, 1941.

23. Ibid., June 14, 1941.

24. Ibid.

25. Ibid., December 14, 1941.

26. Ibid., February 14, 1938.

27. Ibid., March 14, 1940.

28. Ibid., August 28, November 14, 1940.

29. Ibid., November 14, 1940.

30. Ibid.

31. Ibid.

32. Ibid., May 14, August 14, 1940; November 28, 1941.

33. Ibid., November 28, 1941.

23. The Last Years

1.   Autopsy report, New York Municipal Bureau of Records; Consul General of New York to Ministry of the Interior, December 6, 1933, in ACS, CPC: Tresca.

2.   Tresca to Meschi, n.d. but end of 1938, in Meschi Papers, IISG.

3.   *The New York Times*, July 2, 1938; *Il Martello*, December 14, 1938.

4.   Ibid.; Tresca to Luigi Antonini, n.d. but March or April 1939, in Luigi Antonini Paper, box 45, file folder 10, ILGWU Archives; *The New York Times*, July 2, 1938; *Il Martello*, December 14, 1938. The author consulted the Antonini Papers at the ILGWU Archive. The papers and the ILGWU archives have since been transferred to the N.Y. State School of Industrial and Labor Relations at Cornell University.

5.   *Il Martello*, April 28, 1939.

6.   Trotsky to Tresca, April 19, 1939, in Tresca Memorial Committee scrapbook, quoted in Gallagher, *All the Right Enemies*, 178.

7.   Tresca to Trotsky, August 12, 1939, in Leon Trotsky Papers, Houghton Library, Harvard University, bms Russ 13.1 (5534).

8. Tresca to Meschi, n.d. but 1937 or 1938, in Alberto Meschi Papers, IISG.

9. *Il Martello*, November 28, 1940.

10. Antonini to Tresca, July 17, 1939, Antonini Papers, box 11, folder 2, in ILGWU Archives.

11. Tresca to Trotsky, August 12, 1939, Leon Trotsky Papers, bms Russ 13.1 (n. 5534).

12. Tresca to Louis Nelson, April 17, 1940, in MDS Papers; Tresca to Antonini, January 4, 1939, and December 19, 1940; Tresca to Giovanni Sala, June 27, 1940, all in the Antonini Papers; Tresca to Baruch Vladeck, n.d., in Addendum to Vladeck Papers, Tamiment Library.

13. FBI Report, October 13, 1941; Hoover to SAC, New York, October 30, 1941. Tresca FBI File.

14. *Il Martello*, March 28, 1939.

15. *Il Martello*, May 14, 1939; February 28, April 28, 1940.

16. *New York Post*, February 26, 1941.

17. *Il Martello*, January 28, February 14, 28, March 28, April 28, May 14, 1940; June 28, October 14, 1941. A bill from the Cocce Press, indicating the number of copies printed, was found among Tresca's papers by Herbert Solow and is included in the MDS Papers (PM). Because of publishing irregularity, issues of *Il Martello* in this period predated the events covered in its pages.

18. *Il Martello*, August 28, 1941.

19. Italian Ambassador, Washington, to Ministry of Foreign Affairs, July 26, 1941, NA, *Captured Italian Documents*, doc. no. 015347.

20. Michele Cantarella to the author, Leeds MA, September 24, 1975,

21. For the *fuorusciti* and the Mazzini Society, see Diggins, *Mussolini and Fascism*, 139–143, 344–345; Killinger, *Gaetano Salvemini*, 281–282; Garosci, *Storia dei fuorusciti*, 219–224; Maddalena Titabassi, "La Mazzini Society (1940–1946): Un'associazione degli anti-Fascisti italiani negli Stati Uniti," in *Italia e America dalla Grande Guerra a oggi*, eds. Giorgio Spini, Gian Giacomo Migone, and Massimo Teodori (Venice: Marsilio, 1976): 141–158; Max Salvadori, "Antifascisti italiani negli Stati Uniti," in *Atti del I Congresso Internazionale di Storia Americana: Italia e Stati Uniti dall'Indipedenza Americana ad Oggi* (Genoa: Tilgher, 1978): 269–280; Consul General Vecchiotti to Ambassador Colonna, August 17, 1941, ACS, *Min. Int.*, DGPS, PCP, Mario Tresca.

22. Interview with Max Ascoli, March 27, 1974.

23. Letter from Ascoli to the author, April 16, 1974.

24. *Il Martello*, August 28, September 15, October 28, 1941; May 28, June 14, 1942; January 14, 1943.

25. FBI Memo Re: Carlo Tresca, January 13, 1943. He was last contacted by a Bureau Agent on January 6, 1943. Tresca FBI File.

26. Quoted from a testimonial written by Canby Chambers for the *Omaggio* that was omitted because of space considerations. Original in MDS Papers, author's possession; also *Il Martello*, April 14, 1943. That Tresca provided information to the FBI about the Fascists is confirmed by several documents in his FBI file.

27. *Il Martello*, January 14, 1941.

28. Salvemini, *Italian Fascist Activities in the United States*, 189–197; Diggins, *Mussolini and Fascism*, 102–104, 344n38

29. Rudolf J. Vecoli, "The Making and Un-Making of the Italian American Working Class,"

in *The Lost World of Italian-American Radicalism*, 63.

30. *Il Martello*, September 28, 1940; January 14, 1941.

31. Montana, *Amorostico*, 159–160; Philip V. Cannistraro, "Luigi Antonini and the Italian Anti-Fascist Movement in the United States, 1940–1943," *Journal of American Ethnic History* 5, No. 1 (Fall 1985): 26.

32. See Philip V. Cannistraro and Elena Aga Rossi, "La politica etnica e il dilemma dell'antifascismo italiano negli Stati Uniti: il caso di Generoso Pope," *Storia Contemporanea* 17, No. 2 (April 1986): 217–243.

33. *Il Martello*, June 28, 1940.

34. *Il Martello*, September 28, 1940.

35. *Il Martello*, June 28, July 14, August 14, September 28, 1940; January 14, 1941.

36. *Il Martello*, May 14, 1941.

37. *Il Martello*, May 14, 1941. *The New York Times* (June 14, 1940) reported on the memorandum and cited details about Vecchiotti and various Fascists organizations. But no mention was made of Pope, suggesting that Tresca's allegation was correct.

38. FBI report, October 3, 1944, quoted in Cannistraro and Aga Rossi, "Il caso di Generoso Pope," 232.

39. Cannistraro and Aga Rossi, "Il caso di Generoso Pope," 231–234.

40. Casimir P. Palmer to George Walker, State Department, October 28, 1942 and accompanying memo, furnished to the author by Philip V. Cannistraro. Also Cannistraro and Aga Rossi, "Il caso di Generoso Pope," 235–237.

41. *Congressional Record*, vol. 87, Part 3 (Washington, D.C.: Government Printing Office, 1941), 2568.

42. Ibid., 2569–2570.

43. Ibid.

44. Ibid., 5279–5280.

45. *Il Martello*, June 14, 1941.

46. Cannistraro and Aga Rossi, "Il caso di Generoso Pope," 234–243.

47. OSS profile on Carlo Tresca, prepared by G. M. Proctor, January 29, 1943, in U.S. National Archives, Suitland, Maryland, R.G. 226, Records of the Office of Strategic Services, Foreign Nationalities Branch, Entry 100, Box 63, It-557.

48. OSS profile of Tresca, January 29, 1943, NA, RG226, OSS, FNB, Entry 100, Box 63, It-557.

49. *Il Martello*, March 14, April 14, August 14, 28, 1940; April 28, June 28, July 28, August6 28, October 14, 1941.

50. Vidali, *Dal Messico a Murmansk*, 84–85.

51. Robert D'Attilio, "Glittering Traces of Tina Modotti," *Views* (Summer 1985): 8–9. Vidali declared these charges baseless slander originating from his detractors. See *Dal Messico a Murmansk*, 85.

52. *Il Martello*, May 14, 1942.

53. OSS memo on Mazzini Society, June 7, 1942, NA, RG 226, OSS, FNB, Entry 100, Box 60, It-216.

54. *Who Killed Carlo Tresca?*, 11–12; *Il Martello*, May 28, 1942; Salvadori, "Anti-Fascisti Italiani negli Stati Uniti," 276.

55. *Il Martello*, May 14, 1942.

56. *Il Martello*, May 28, 1942; Killinger, *Gaetano Salvemini*, 290–291.

57. Killinger, *Gaetano Salvemini*, 291.

58. *Nazioni Unite*, June 18, 1942.

59. Censor intercept, November 23, 1942, Tresca FBI File.

60. The author's description of the Manhattan Club incident is based on an account provided by Cupelli in an interview of February 28, 1974.

61. FBI Memo Re: Carlo Tresca, February 17, 1943, Tresca FBI File. Most of the information in this memo is based on the account by Ezio Taddei, *The Tresca Case* (New York: n.p., 1943).

62. This account of the Gerli banquet is derived primarily from the author's interview with an eye-witness, Alberto Cupelli, February 28, 1974. Similar accounts, with slight variations amounting to errors, are also given in *Who Killed Carlo Tresca?*, 24; Taddei, *The Tresca Case*, 4–5; PM, January 13, 1943; and FBI Memo, February 17, 1943. Garofalo's purported comment is quoted in a memorandum of November 6, 1944, from John Nicholas Beffel to Morris Ernst, Dorothy Kenyon, Roger Baldwin, John F. Finnerty, Eduard C. Linderman, and Margaret De Silver, in Margaret De Silver Papers (Peter Mertin).

63. Joseph Bonnano with Sergio Lalli, *A Man of Honor: The Autobiography of Joseph Bonnano* (New York: Simon and Schuster, 1983), 190.

64. Supplementary Complaint Report, 10th Precinct, 3rd Detective District, Homicide Squad, SCR, No. 18, January 14, 1943, in New York Police Department, Homicide Division, Legal Bureau, 1 Police Plaza, New York. [All the police reports on the Tresca case provide the same source information and will be abbreviated as NYPD, SCR, No. 18, date.]

65. Confidential Report, New York Office, April 7, 1943, Tresca FBI File.

66. Taddei, *The Tresca Case*, 4; Valenti, "Memorandum Re: Assassination of Carlo Tresca," 1.

67. Biographical information about Faconti is scarce. See *Il Progresso*, October 13, 1949. By then, she had resigned as Assistant Federal Attorney and had married a conductor named William Scotti.

68. Hoover, Memorandum for the Attorney General, November 27, 1943; J.C. Strickland, Memorandum for D. E. Ladd, February 9, 1943, Tresca FBI File.

69. Interview with Alberto Cupelli.

70. Interview with Alberto Cupelli; *Who Killed Carlo Tresca?*, 24; Taddei, *The Tresca Case*, 5.

71. Statement by Augusto Bellanca, Vice-President of the Italian-American Victory Council. January 29, 1943, NA. RG208, OWI, Records of the Bureau of Field Operations, Arts Section, Italian Radio Scripts, "Carlo Tresca," box 1114.

72. Memorandum on Assassination of Carlo Tresca and the Italian Situation [n.d. but after Tresca's death and before Mussolini's overthrow in July 1943], NA, RG208, Records of the OWI and the Director, E. Davis, "Propaganda-1943," box 8.

73. Killinger, *Gaetano Salvemini*, 288.

74. *Il Martello*, January 14, February 28, 1941.

75. Cranston Memorandum to Davis, January 21, 1943, NA, RG208, RCDS of the OWI and Director, "Propaganda-1943," box 8.

76. Ibid.

77. *New York Post*, January 18, 1943; Memorandum from K.R. McIntire to F. L. Welch, January 27, 1943, Tresca FBI File; Norman Thomas to Elmer Davis, January 19 and 25, 1943; David to Thomas, January 23, 1943; Augusto Bellanca to Antonini, January 23,

1943; Antonini to Bellanca, January 25, 1943, NA, RG208, OWI, Entry 221, Box 1070. Also OWI Memo, Cranson to Davis, January 21, 1943, Box 8; *The New York Times*, January 22, 1943.

78. Interview with Beatrice Tresca Rapport.
79. Tresca to Antonini, n.d., in Antonini Papers, I.L.G.W. U. Archives. Later published (in corrected English) in *Giustizia*, February 1943.   .
80. Interview with Beatrice Tresca Rapport.
81. PM, January 13, 1943.
82. Quotes in *Justice*, February 1, 1943.

24. Murder in the Dimout

1.   *Who Killed Carlo Tresca?*, 7; PM, January 13, 1943.
2.   *Who Killed Carlo Tresca?*, 7–8; *La Controcorrente*, January 1943; *Daily News*, January 1, 1943; *World-Telegram*, January 12, 1943; *Sun*, January 12, 1943; *Daily Mirror*, January 12, 1943. Also NYPD, SCR. No.18, January 12, 1943 and Autopsy Report, January 12, 1943.
3.   Interview with Beatrice Tresca Rapport.
4.   Quotes from Alien Squad report, January 20, 1943, NYPD; also *Herald Tribune*, January 17, 1943.
5.   Alien Squad report, January 20, 1943; *The New York Times*, January 16, 1943; *Herald Tribune*, January 16, 1943; *World-Telegram*, January 16, 1943.
6.   *Omaggio*, 42.
7.   Ibid., 44.
8.   Ibid., 46.
9.   Ibid., 40.
10. Dos Passos to John Diggins, July 24, 1966, in Beffel Papers, box. 2.
11. *Omaggio*, 43.
12. Ibid., 46.
13. Ibid., 41.
14. Ibid., 40.
15. "Persons Who Worked in the Investigation of the Death of Carlo Tresca," Files of the Manhattan District Attorney, Series 3, Folder 2, Municipal Archives of the City of New York [hereafter cited as DA Files.] The files on deposit at the Municipal Archives represent only a small fraction of the materials the DA's office must have accumulated. According to former ADA Lipsky, the DA's office held many filing cabinets overflowing with material on Tresca's murder. An inquiry by the author as to the missing documents supposedly lead to a search for additional material but nothing further was found. Director of Public Information, Manhattan DA's Office, to the author, May 16, 1986. Also, Interview with Eleazar Lipsy, March 6 and April 24, 1974; William J. Keating, with Richard Carter, *The Man Who Rocked the Boat* (New York: Harper, 1956), 37–38.
16. See the numerous Supplementary Complaint Reports, NYPD, describing the crime scene, getaway car, and initial investigation. Copy of sale certificate in DA Files, S2, F3. Also *Who Killed Carlo Tresca?*, 15; *Journal American*, January 12, 1943; PM, January 12, 1943; *Herald Tribune*, January 13, 1943.

17. Documents entitled "Sidney H. Gross" and "Fred Berson" (n.d.), in DA Files, S1, F2 and F7.

18. SCRs, January 11, 14, 1943, March 20, 1943; *Who Killed Carlo Tresca?*, 15–16; *World-Telegram*, January 14, 1943; *The New York Times*, January 13, 1943.

19. Details and quotes in Summary Reports of March 7 and April 30, 1958, in Galante's FBI File; NYPD, SCRs, January 12, 13, 18, 1943; also *New York Post*, January 13, 1943.

20. Quoted in Summary Report, April 30, 1958, Galante FBI File.

21. Summary Report, March 7, 1958, Galante FBI File. Also, Galante's Prisoner's Criminal Record, NYPD, DA Files, S5, F2.

22. Interview with Eleazar Lipsky.

23. Ibid.

24. Notes on Galante interrogation, February 9, 1943, DA Files, S3, F2.

25. Interview with Eleazar Lipsky.

26. Ibid.

27. Quoted in *The New York Times*, January 13, 1943; Interview with Eleazar Lipsky; Keating, *The Man Who Rocked the Boat*, 37–38.

28. Interview with Eleazar Lipsky.

29. Notes of Emilio Funicello in "Re: Carlo Tresca," S5, F1, DA Files; Interview with Eleazar Lipsky.

30. Interview with Eleazar Lipsky.

31. *Who Killed Carlo Tresca?*, 17; Fred Berson, *After the Big House: The Adventures of a Parole Officer* (New York: Crown Publishers, 1952), ix, 11. Berson described his encounter with Galante at the Parole Office, but changed his name to "Charles Carletti" in order "to continue the habit of breathing."

32. *Reports of Cases Decided in the Court of Appeals of the State of New York* (Albany: Williams Press, 1944), 292: 300.

33. Keating, *The Man Who Rocked the Boat*, 42.

34. Interview with Eleazar Lipsky.

35. Ibid.; Keating, *The Man Who Rocked the Boat*, 42–44; FBI Summary Reports, March 4 and April 40, 1958, Galante FBI File.

25. Theories and Investigations

1. Interview with Eleazar Lipsky.

2. *Time Magazine*, January 25, 1943, 1.

3. Albion Ross, Report on Montana-Antonini campaign, January 14, 1943, in National Archives, RG 226, Records of the Office of Strategic Services, Foreign Nationalities Branch, Entry 100, Box 63, IT-525.

4. Ibid.

5. *The New York Times*, January 12, 1943.

6. Ibid.

7. Ibid.

8. *Daily Worker*, January 14, 19, 1943; *L'Unità del Popolo*, February 13, March 6, 1943.

9. *Giustizia*, March 1943. Also *Il Martello*, July 28, 1942.

10. *Giustizia*, March 1943.

11. Ibid.; Interview with Beatrice Tresca Rapport.

12. For Taddei's activities in America, see Domenico Javarone, *Vita di scrittore (Ezio Taddei)* (Rome: Macchia, 1958), 59–101.

13. Supplementary Complaint Report, 18, January 18, 1943, NYPD.

14. Javarone, *Vita di scrittore*, 82–88.

15. *Giustizia*, March, June 1943.

16. In a telephone-interview with the author on March 14, 1975, Genco, then a professor at Pace University, denied that Tresca had ever phoned him. "If he had, I might have been able to save him."

17. Taddei's Rand School speech was reprinted as *The Tresca Case* (New York: Trades Union Label Council, 1943.

18. An original, typewritten copy was provided to the author by Luigi Quintiliano.

19. *Brooklyn Eagle*, August 9, 1944; *New York Post*, October 9, 1944; Memorandum for Mr. Ladd Re: Carlo Tresca, November 4, 1944, in Tresca FBI File. Journalist Ed Reid, who wrote the article that appeared in the *Brooklyn Eagle*, repeated Rupolo's story in his book *Mafia* (New York: Random House, 1952), 70–77.

20. FBI memo, March 28, 1944, Tresca FBI file.

21. Keating, *The Man Who Rocked the Boat*," 35.

22. Ibid.; interview with Eleazar Lipsky.

23. DA Files, S3, F2.

24. Interview with Eleazar Lipsky

25. See throughout DA Files.

26. *L'Unita del Popolo*, June 12, 1943.

27. *Journal American*, January 14, 18, 1943.

28. Ibid., January 14, 1943.

29. Interview with Eleazar Lipsky.

30. "Factual Analysis of Chapter 4—'Killing for Cash'" [in Gunther Reinhardt's *Crime Without* Punishment], DA Files, S5, F6; *Journal-American*, January 28, 1943.

31. Interview with Eleazar Lipsky.

32. Memo from SAC E.E. Conroy to Hoover, January 18, 1944, in Tresca FBI File.

33. SAC E. E. Conroy, New York office, to Hoover, January 18, 1944, Tresca FBI File.

34. Ibid.

35. Thomas to Hogan, December 1, 1948, in Tresca FBI File; *World Telegram*, December 7, 1948.

36. Gitlow, *The Whole of Their Lives*, 337–341.

37. "'The Whole of Their Lives,' by Benjamin Gitlow. Digest of Chapter XI—'Liquidation,'" DA Files, S5, F6.

38. Ibid.

39. The files of the DA's office and NYPD have no record of any interrogation of Pope. Moreover, the late Professor Philip V. Cannistraro, who had conducted research for a biography of Pope, was certain that the publisher was never summoned for questioning.

40. TMC, Confidential Memorandum, September 28, 1944; Nicholas Beffel to Oswald Garrison Villard, June 23, 1945, Beffel Papers (WS), box 16 and 17.

41. *Who Killed Carlo Tresca?*, 16–17.

42. Casimir Palmer to George Walker, State Department, February 27, 1943; Palmer to

Hogan, January 16, 1943, in NA, RG59, Records of the Department of State, doc. no. 865.20211. This material on Pope was provided to the author by Professor Cannistraro.

43. Interview with Eleazar Lipsky.

44. Ibid.

45. Det. James P. Petrosino Memorandum, May 6, 1943, DA Files, S3, F1.

46. Dets. Anthony Mancuso and Philip Abbate, March 12, 1943, DA Files, S3, F1.

47. Interview with Eleazar Lipsky.

48. Interview with Eleazar Lipsky.

49. Valenti, "Memorandum Re: Assassination of Carlo Tresca."

50. FBI report, January 14, 1943, Tresca FBI File.

51. Notes on Garofalo interview, NYPD Files, SCR, No. 18, January 14, 1943.

52. Memorandum from Petrosino and Laghezza, April 16, 1943, DA Files, S3, F1.

53. *Daily Mirror*, March 8, 1943.

54. Memorandum from Philip Abbate and Modesto Laghezza, July 30, 1943, DA Files, S3, F1.

55. Memorandum Re: Carlo Tresca, January 13, 1943, Tresca FBI File.

56. Memorandum for Mr. Ladd, March 22, 1944, Tresca FBI File.

57. Pagnucco Memorandum on Rupolo, March 26, 1946, and Rupolo's hand-written statement, January 9, 1953, DA Files, S5, F4.

58. Pagnucco's notes of interrogation of Nino Mirabini, March 26, 1946, DA Files, S3, F2.

59. Genovese had been active during the war in Italy as a translator and intermediary for various military government officials and a black-market kingpin, trafficking in merchandise stolen from the U.S. Army.

60. TMC press release, June 4, 1946, in Beffel Papers (PM).

61. Hoover, memorandum for Mr. Edward J. Ennis, Director, Alien Enemy Control Unit, January 25, 1943, Tresca FBI File.

62. Numerous documents in the FBI Tresca and Galante files.

63. The journalist Furio Morrini considered this possibility indisputable. See his "Il 'Caso Tresca': Anatomia di un omicidio politico" (unpublished manuscript, c. 1985), 49–55. Copy in the author's collection.

64. Ibid.

65. Foxworth to Hoover, January 12, 1943; Foxworth to Hoover, November 9, 1942; Asst. Dir. D. M. Ladd, memorandum for the Director, November 19, 1943; Hoover memorandum for the Attorney General, November 27, 1942, in Tresca FBI File. Information regarding the Manhattan Club incident was furnished to the FBI by another anti-Fascist informant, Giuseppe Lupis. Morroni maintains that Pope and Antonini were the individuals Hoover wished to protect from suspicion.

66. For Hoover's inactivity regarding organized crime and his personal association with Frank Costello, see Richard Gid Powers, *Secrecy and Power: The Life of J. Edgar Hoover* (New York: The Free Press, 1987), 332–336; Anthony Summers, *Official and Confidential: The Secret Life of J. Edgar Hoover* (New York: G. P. Putnam's Sons, 1993), 12–13, 237–240.

67. Hoover Memorandum for the Attorney General, November 27, 1942, Tresca FBI File.

68. Memorandum Re: Carlo Tresca, January 13, 1943, Tresca FBI File.

69. Memorandum for the Attorney General Re: Carlo Tresca, February 20, 1943, Tresca FBI File.

70. Hoover to SAC of New York, July 7, 1943, Tresca FBI File.

71. J. Edgar Hoover to the American Embassy, Mexico City, January 26, 1943, in Tresca FBI File.

72. Clippings from Mexican newspaper *El Popular*, January 12, 1943; Report on Vidali, July 12, 1943;

73. Summary report on Carlo Tresca, January 30, 1946, in Vidali FBI File. Memorandum Re: Carlo Tresca, Victim; Murder, April 2, 1943; Memorandum for the Director Re: Carlo Tresca, April 12, 1943, in Vidali FBI File.

74. Hoover to America Embassy, Mexico City, May 13, 1943, in Tresca FBI File.

75. SAC, New York, to Hoover, October 2, 1045.

76. Memorandum from D. M. Ladd to Hoover, April 26, 1950, in Tresca FBI File.

77. Vidali FBI File.

78. Tresca-related materials are in the Finerty Papers on deposit at the University of Oregon Library.

79. Ibid., 19–21. Beffel to Ernst, July 7, 1944, Beffell Papers (WS), box 14; Statement by Norman Thomas to Tresca Memorial Meeting, Cooper Union, January 10, 1946, in Beffel Papers (WS), box 15.

80. Hogan to Morris L. Ernst, August 6, 1944, in Beffel Papers (PM) and WS, box 14.

81. Hogan to Morris Ernst, August 8, 1944, in Beffel Papers (PM).

82. Margaret De Silver to Beffel, June 16, 1944, in Beffel Papers (PM). A copy of the proposed letter from the Finerty group to Governor Dewey is in Beffel Papers (PM).

83. For various drafts of the group's letter to Dewey, see Beffel Papers (WS), box. 15.

84. Finerty group to Friends [all who signed the proposal for Dewey), November 10, 1944; Beffel to Finerty group, November 1, 1944, in Beffel Papers (PM); Thomas statement of January 10, 1946, Beffel Papers (WS).

85. Thomas statement, January 10, 1946, Beffel Papers (WS), box 16.

86. Interview with Eleazar Lipsky.

87. Norman Thomas to Luigi Criscuoli, September 19, 1955, in Beffel Papers (PM).

88. Interview with Eleazar Lipsky, March 6, 1974.

89. Pagnucco to the author.

90. Dorothy Gallagher interviewed Grumet.

91. SAC T.J. Donegan, New York, to Hoover, February 1, 1943, Tresca FBI File.

92. *Who Killed Carlo Tresca?*, 26.

93. La Guardia to Felicani, July 8, 1944, Beffel Papers (PM).

94. Internal Security Memo Re: Carlo Tresca to Hoover, July 14, 1943, Tresca FBI File.

95. Ernst to Valentine, February 2, 1945, in Finerty Papers.

96. Morris L. Ernst to J. Edgar Hoover, April 9, 1943, in Tresca FBI File.

97. Norman Thomas to William O'Dwyer, June 3, 1947, Beffel Papers (PM).

98. House of Representative Resolution, No. 71, March 6, 1944, in Beffel Papers (WS), box 18.

99. Norman Thomas to Tom A. Clark, July 16, 1947; Beffel to Margaret De Silver, August 19, 1947, in Beffel Papers (PM).

100. Norman Thomas, letter to friends, announcing a commemorative meeting, January 1, 1950, Beffel Papers (WS), box 16.

26. Who Ordered Tresca's Murder?

1. General Leandro A. Sanchez and Julian Gorkin, *Murder in Mexico: The Assassination of Leon Trotsky* (London: Secker & Warburg, 1950), 214; Gitlow, *The Whole of Their Lives*, 337–341.
2. Francis Russell, "The Last Anarchist," in his *The Great Prelude* (New York: McGraw Hill, 1964), 141.
3. Gunther Reinhardt, *Crime Without Punishment: The Secret Soviet Terror Against America* (New York: Hermitage House, 1952), 71–83.
4. Montana, *Amarostico*, 214–228, 240–241.
5. Alan A. Block and Marcia J. Block, "Fascism, Organized Crime and Foreign Policy: An Inquire Based on the Assassination of Carlo Tresca," *Research in Law, Deviance and Social Control*, 4 (1982): 53–84. The essay was first presented at the annual conference of the American Society of Criminology in 1980.
6. Ibid., 75. A few FBI documents, taking noting of Antonini's "alliance" with Pope, have inadvertently cast suspicion on the labor leader.
7. Morroni, "Il 'Caso Tresca.'"
8. Ed Reid, *Mafia* (New York: The New American Library, 1952), 70–74.
9. Martin A. Gosh and Richard Hammer, *The Last Testament of Lucky Luciano* (New York: 1981), 285.
10. Ibid.
11. Mauri Canali, "Tutta la verità sul case Tresca," *Liberal* No. 4 (2001): 147–153.
12. Gallagher, *All the Right Enemies*, 270.
13. *Il Martello*, September 28, 1940.
14. Hoover, Memorandum for the Attorney General, February 20, 1943, Tresca FBI File.
15. This story was related by Donini to Furio Morroni, who in turn told it to Gallagher. See *All the Right Enemies*, 271–273. Gallagher considers the story plausible but not certain.
16. Ambrogio Donini, *Sessant'anni di militanza comunista* (Milan: Nicola Teti Editore, 1988), 93–95.
17. Cannistraro, "Luigi Antonini and the Italian Anti-Fascist Movement in the United States," 33.
18. *PM*, October 5, 1944.
19. Interview with Eleazar Lipsky.
20. *The New York Times*, January 10, 1958.

Addendum. Tresca and the Sacco-Vanzetti Case

1. Russell, *Tragedy in Dedham*, xi–xxiii, 461–467.
2. Ibid., 40, 463.
3. Interview with Beatrice Tresca Rapport.
4. Quintiliano to Oliver Jensen, New York, undated but 1962, in the author's possession.
5. Giuseppe Popolizio, letter to Nunzio Pernicone, Rivesville, WV, August 1, 1977; idem, letter to editor, *La Parola del Popolo*, 28, N. 141 (November–December 1977): 2.
6. Interview with Roger Baldwin, New York, June 6, 1973, conducted together with Robert D'Attilio.

7.   Ibid.; Report, Pittsburgh office to Director, April 26, 1922, Sacco-Vanzetti FBI File.

8.   Flynn, *The Rebel Girl*, 325–330; Report, Pittsburgh office to Director, April 26, 1922, FBI Sacco-Vanzetti File.

9.   Russell, *Tragedy in Dedham*, 252–253.

10. Flynn, *The Rebel Girl*, 330; "The Reminiscences of Aldino Felicani," 111.

11. Upton Sinclair, "The Fishpeddler and the Shoemaker," *Institute of Social Studies Bulletin* 2, No. 2 (Summer 1953): 23–24.

12. Ibid.

13. Ibid.

14. Interview with Roger Baldwin, New York, June 6, 1973. Gardner Jackson, one of the key members of the Boston defense committee, accused Baldwin of having been one of the first persons to spread doubts about Sacco's innocence in the 1920s. Jackson believed both men innocent, and attributed the suspicions concerning Sacco to the negative impression he evoked in some with his volatile personality. See "Reminiscences of Gardner Jackson" (1955), 209–210, Oral History Collection, Columbia University Michael A. Musmanno, "The Sacco-Vanzetti Case: With Critical Analysis of the Book 'Tragedy in Dedham' by Francis Russell," *Kansas Law Review* 11 (1962–1963): 519.

15. Ibid.

16. Others who indicated that Tresca told them Sacco was guilty include Isaac Don Levine, James Rorty, Sidney Hook, and James Farrell; however, it more likely that several of them heard it secondhand from Eastman.

17. See Russell to Pernicone, Sandwich, MA, November 29, 1976; Gallagher, *All the Right Enemies*, 284.

18. Norman Thomas, interview with the author, New York, March 28, 1963.

19. Norman Thomas to John Nicolas Beffel, New York, August 11, 1967, Beffel Papers, Tamiment Institute, New York University. A socialist journalist previously associated with the IWW, Beffel handed publicity for the Sacco-Vanzetti Defense Committee; he also knew Tresca very well. Unfortunately, no comments from Beffel regarding this issue have survived.

20. John P. Roche to Francis Russell, Waltham, MA, September 25, 1972.

21. *Sacco and Vanzetti: The Case Resolved* (New York: Harper & Row, 1986). Russell read Roche's letter at the conference on Sacco and Vanzetti, sponsored by the Boston Public Library, on October 26, 1979.

22. Max Eastman, "Is This the Truth About Sacco and Vanzetti?" *National Review* 11, No. 15 (October 14, 1961): 262–264.

23. Indicative of his right-wing orientation, Eastman's well-known *New Yorker* "Portrait" of Tresca, which was included in the 1942 edition of his book, *Heroes I Have Known*, was dropped from a later edition.

24. Interview with Beatrice Tresca Rapport; Interview with Luigi Quintiliano.

25. *L'Adunata dei Refrattari*, May 30, July 4, 1925; February 25, March 31, May 19, October 22, 1928; June 14, October 22, July 5, 1930; September 2, 1933; May 7, 1938.

26. Interview with Beatrice Tresca Rapport. See also Nunzio Pernicone, "War Among the Italian Anarchists: The Galleanisti's Campaign Against Carlo Tresca," in *The Lost Word of Italian American Radicalism*, ed. Philip V. Cannistraro & Gerald Meyer (Praeger, 2003).

27. Russell to Pernicone, Sandwich, MA, January 14, 1977.

28. The letter is reprinted in Francis Russell, "Clinching the Case," *The New York Review of Books* 33, No. 4 (March 13, 1986): 32; and idem, *Sacco and Vanzetti: The Case Resolved*, 12–13.
29. Russell, *Sacco and Vanzetti: The Case Resolved*, 217–220.
30. Ibid., 12–13.
31. Avrich, *Anarchist Voices*, 110, 114, 121, 130, 140.
32. Russell, *Sacco and Vanzetti: The Case Resolved*, 13.
33. Ibid., 31.
34. The most recent study of the case, *Sacco & Vanzetti: The Men, the Murders, and the Judgment of Mankind* (New York: Viking, 2007) by Bruce Watson, briefly mention's Tresca's comments about Sacco but offers no assessment.
35. For the original version of this essay, see Nunzio Pernicone, "Carlo Tresca and the Sacco-Vanzetti Case," *The Journal of American History* 60 (December 1979): 535–547.

Bibliographical Essay

Rather than a standard bibliography, which would add too many pages to an already lengthy book, the following is a bibliography essay that indicates the most important sources pertaining directly to Tresca's life and career.

The most important sources utilized for this biography were Tresca's own newspapers and other Italian immigrant radical publications, without which no scholar can study Tresca's political career in depth or understand the Italian radical movement. Unfortunately, with the passing of old radicals, a great wealth of periodical material was discarded by surviving relatives who were ignorant of or indifferent to its historical value. Accordingly, there is not a single collection of Tresca's newspapers extant today that is complete. Only about fifteen issues of *La Plebe* have survived. The files of *L'Avvenire*, although more extensive that those of *La Plebe*, have wide gaps, especially during the World War I years. Scattered issues of *La Plebe* and *L'Avvenire* are available at the Immigration History Research Center, University of Minnesota; the International Institute for Social History in Amsterdam; and the U.S. Post Office Department, which confiscated and copied many. Incomplete collections of *Il Germe* are available at the Archivio Diocesano in Sulmona and the Biblioteca Nazionale Centrale of Florence. The files of *Il Martello* on microfilm at the NYPL are the most complete. Several issues from 1918 and 1919 that are not included in this microfilm collection were given to the author by one of Tresca's former comrades. In addition to Tresca's own newspapers, the official organ of the Italian Socialist Federation, *Il Proletario*, is indispensable for the pre-World War I period of his career.

The unfortunate propensity of indifferent relatives to discard the private holdings of departed radicals also accounts for the paucity of surviving letters from Tresca, who must have written many hundreds, if not thousands, in the course of his career. Of the surviving letters, many are scattered throughout various collections of private papers on deposit at the Internationaal Instituut voor Sociale Geschiedenis in Amsterdam; the Immigration History Research Center at the University of Minnesota; the Labadie Collection at the University of Michigan; the Archives of Labor and Urban Affairs at Wayne State University; the New York State School of Industrial and Labor Relations at Cornell University; and a few other repositories cited in the notes. Less than a score, however, are particularly revealing about his personal and political life. Some letters regarding his political activities are so specific in detail that they are of little value for a comprehensive study. And more often than not, Tresca's letters are undated, making it difficult to place their contents in proper chronology and historical context.

The scholar can only wish that Tresca's autobiography had made up for the scarcity of surviving correspondence. He began writing his memoirs sometime in the 1920s, but made little progress until the late 1930s and early 1940s. Even by that date, however, he never finished the project. Aside from a few pages dealing with the Lawrence strike of 1919, and Mussolini and Fascism in the 1920s, the autobiography essentially stops at 1917. Its contents are devoted entirely to Tresca's political career. Except for a discussion of his childhood and youth in Sulmona, the autobiography says nothing about his personal life. But even with it deficiencies, Tresca's autobiography is an indispensable source. After his death in 1943, several copies of the unpublished autobiography were held in private possession, namely, by Beatrice Tresca Rapport and Peter Martin. Peter Martin provided the author with an earlier draft and the final version of the autobiography. Another copy of the autobiography was deposited with the Tresca Memorial Committee papers at the NYPL. Still another copy is held by the library of the Facoltà di Magistero of the University of Florence. It should be noted, however, that Tresca's own manuscript version, written in English, has been lost. The existing autobiography was ghost-written by Max Nomad. This version was recently published as *The Autobiography of Carlo Tresca,* edited with introduction and notes by Nunzio Pernicone (New York: The John D. Calandra Italian American Institute, CUNY, 2003).

For information about Tresca's private life and political activities not included in his *Autobiography,* I conducted numerous interviews and corresponded with those close relatives, former comrades, and other individuals who were still living when this biography was initiated. The following individuals—almost all deceased—provided essential information about Tresca's personal life, his activities, and Italian-immigrant radicalism in general, although not all are cited directly in the notes: Tresca's daughter Beatrice Tresca Rapport; his son Peter Martin; Margaret De Silver's sons and daughter-in-law Harrison, Burnham, and Claire De Silver; Luigi Quintiliano; Giuseppe Popolizio; Vincenzo Alvano; Alberto Cupelli; Giuseppe Ienuso; Hugo Rolland; Mario De Ciampis; Egidio Clemente; Raffaele Schiavina; Valerio Isca; Michele Cantarella; Norman Thomas; Roger Baldwin; Morris L. Ernst; James T. Farrell; Nancy MacDonald; Eleazar Lipsky; Max Ascoli; and Morris Milgram. Several of these individuals, in addition to interviews and letters, provided vivid portraits of Tresca in the invaluable special issue of *Il Martello* entitled: *Omaggio alla memoria imperitura di Carlo Tresca,* eds. Felice Guadagni and Renato Vidal (New York: Il Martello, 1943).

Supplementary memoir material by former associates of Tresca is surprisingly limited. Most important is the partial autobiography written by Elizabeth Gurley Flynn, *The Rebel Girl: An Autobiography: My First Life, 1906–1926* (New York: International Publishers, 1973). Essential for the Italian radical ambiance in New York is the memoir of Vanni Montana, *Amarostico: Testimonianze euro-americane* (Livorno: U. Bastogni Editore, 1975). As much a memoir as a secondary source, given the author's personal involvement with the (syndicalist) Italian Socialist Federation and *Il Proletario,* the article by Mario De Ciampis, "Storia del movimento socialista rivoluzionario italiano," in *La Parola del Popolo* 9, No. 37 (December 1958–January

1959): 136–163, is a fundamental source for the historical context of Tresca's early activities.

Other than Tresca's newspapers and the personal recollections of relatives and former associates, the most important primary sources utilized for this biography were the hundreds of documents amassed by the Italian government, both Fascist and pre-Fascist. Indispensable are the ambassadorial, consular, and prefecture reports to the Direzione Generale di Pubblica Sicurezza of the Italian Ministry of the Interior, especially the individual dossier on Tresca in the Casellario Politico Centrale, a collection of dossiers on thousands of Italian radicals compiled by the authorities. Other essential categories of Interior Ministry documents include the Divisione Affari Generali e Riservati and the Divisione Polizia Politica. These collections are on deposit at the Archivio Centrale dello Stato in Rome. Similar documents relating to Tresca are also available at the Archivio di Stato di L'Aquila, in the regional capital of the Abruzzi region.

Of the American government documents relating to Tresca, the most important are in the files of the Justice and State Departments. The former include the dossier compiled by the Bureau of Investigation and its successor, the FBI. Heavily censored, the file was obtained directly (and piecemeal) from the FBI under the Freedom of Information Act. The file is presently available on the FBI's website. Other relevant State and Justice Department records are found in various categories within Record Group 59 and 60, respectively. Post Office Department files contain translations of some of Tresca's offending articles from *La Plebe* and *L'Avvenire*. All of the above, and other U.S. government documents, such as the War Department, the Office of Strategy Services, and the Office of War Information, are on deposit at the National Archives, formerly in Washington, D.C., but since transferred to Suitland, Maryland. The last category of official documents utilized for this biography include the New York District Attorney's Office and New York Police Department records pertaining to Tresca's murder, on deposit at the N.Y. Municipal Archive and NYPD Headquarters, respectively. Former Assistant District Attorney Eleazar Lipsky indicated to the author that his office possessed "several filing cabinets" full of documents pertaining to the Tresca case. If that were true, then the available files are frustratingly incomplete. Furthermore, Tresca's comrades affirmed that after the murder, the police removed a treasure trove of newspaper collections, books, pamphlets, correspondence, and other documents from the office of *Il Martello*. This material was never returned to the new publishers of the newspaper or to Tresca's family. They must be presumed lost.

Unpublished material in collections of private papers is also quite voluminous, especially in regard to Tresca's murder. For the latter, see the files of the Tresca Memorial Committee on deposit at the NYPL, and the papers of John Nicholas Beffel (the chief investigator and publicist for the TMC) at the Tamiment Institute Library, New York University, and the Archives of Labor History & Urban Affairs, Wayne State University. Another collection of Beffel papers was given to the author by Peter Martin, who in turn had received them from Margaret De Silver. Additional unpublished material relating to Tresca's murder was given to the author by Alberto Cupelli and Mrs. John Ciaccio, niece of Luigi Quintiliano. Other private papers that provided valuable information about Tresca's career include: the Elizabeth Gurley

Flynn papers, Tamiment Institute Library (NYY); the Girolamo Valenti papers, Tamiment Institute Library; the Margaret Sanger papers, Library of Congress; Mary Heaton Vorse papers, Wayne State University; Morris L. Ernst papers, University of Texas at Austin; John Finerty papers, University of Oregon; Luigi Antonini papers, Archives of the ILGWU, NY State School of Industrial and Labor Relations, Cornell University. Of a related nature are the recollections of several important figures that knew and worked with Tresca, which are part of the Columbia University Oral History Collection: Aldino Felicani, Max Shachtman, Norman Thomas, Roger Baldwin, and A.J. Muste.

Biographical works devoted to Tresca have been few. Max Nomad, at the request of Margaret De Silver, wrote a biography entitled "Rebel Without Uniform" that was never published. Based almost entirely on Tresca's autobiography, some articles from *Il Martello* and American newspapers, as well as the author's considerable knowledge of the radical movement, Nomad's account does not approach the standards of a scholarly biography. A very colorful profile of Tresca was written by Max Eastman for the *New Yorker* (Vol. X, September 15, 1934, pp. 31–36, and September 22, 1934, pp. 26–29), however, it contains more than a small amount of invention, some of it provided no doubt by Tresca himself. Francis Russell devoted a chapter to Tresca, "The Last Anarchist," in his book *Neglected Events and Persons from the First World War to the Depression* (New York: McGraw Hill, 1964). Superficial, poorly researched, and marred by factual errors, Russell's essay added nothing to our knowledge of Tresca. Several specific aspects of Tresca's career were previously treated by the present author: "Carlo Tresca and the Sacco-Vanzetti Case," *The Journal of American History*, 60 (November–December 1979): 132–140; "Murder Under the 'El': The Greco-Carrillo Case," *The Italian American Review* 6, No. 2 (Autumn/Winter 1997–1998): 20–44; "War Among the Anarchists: The Galleanisti's Campaign Against Carlo Tresca," in Philip V. Cannistraro and Gerald Meyer, eds., *The Lost World of Italian-American Radicalism* (Westport, CN: Praeger, 2003), 77–97. The only full-length biography of Tresca published prior to the present account was that written by Dorothy Gallagher, *All the Right Enemies: The Life and Murder of Carlo Tresca* (New Brunswick: Rutgers University Press, 1988). Gallagher's book is divided into two parts: the first focusing on Tresca's life and related people and events; the second on his murder. Gallagher provides skillfully-drawn portraits of the individuals in Tresca's life, such as Helga Guerra, Elizabeth Gurley Flynn, and Vittorio Vidali, but her account of his ideas and activities is relatively brief, a limitation attributable to her inability to read crucial sources in Italian, especially Tresca's newspapers. Her treatment of the murder and investigation, on the other hand, is well researched, thorough, and critically accurate.

Index

H

Q

R

T

Support AK Press!

AK Press is one of the world's largest and most productive

anarchist publishing houses. We're entirely worker-run and democratically managed. We operate without a corporate structure—no boss, no managers, no bullshit. We publish close to twenty books every year, and distribute thousands of other titles published by other like-minded independent presses from around the globe.

The Friends of AK program is a way that you can directly contribute to the continued existence of AK Press, and ensure that we're able to keep publishing great books just like this one! Friends pay a minimum of $25 per month, for a minimum three month period, into our publishing account. In return, Friends automatically receive (for the duration of their membership), as they appear, one free copy of every new AK Press title. They're also entitled to a 20% discount on everything featured in the AK Press Distribution catalog and on the website, on any and every order. You or your organization can even sponsor an entire book if you should so choose!

There's great stuff in the works—so sign up now to become a Friend of AK Press, and let the presses roll!

Won't you be our friend? Email friendsofak@akpress.org for more info, or visit the Friends of AK Press website: http://www.akpress.org/programs/friendsofak